THE CONQUEROR'S GIFT

The Conqueror's Gift

ROMAN ETHNOGRAPHY
AND THE END OF ANTIQUITY

Michael Maas

PRINCETON UNIVERSITY PRESS
PRINCETON & OXFORD

Copyright © 2025 by Princeton University Press

Princeton University Press is committed to the protection of copyright and the intellectual property our authors entrust to us. Copyright promotes the progress and integrity of knowledge. Thank you for supporting free speech and the global exchange of ideas by purchasing an authorized edition of this book. If you wish to reproduce or distribute any part of it in any form, please obtain permission.

Requests for permission to reproduce material from this work should be sent to permissions@press.princeton.edu

Published by Princeton University Press
41 William Street, Princeton, New Jersey 08540
99 Banbury Road, Oxford OX2 6JX

press.princeton.edu

All Rights Reserved

ISBN 9780691259024
ISBN (e-book) 9780691259048

British Library Cataloging-in-Publication Data is available

Editorial: Rob Tempio and Chloe Coy
Production Editorial: Theresa Liu
Jacket / Cover Design: Katie Osborne
Production: Danielle Amatucci
Publicity: William Pagdatoon
Copyeditors: Anne Cherry and Amanda Gillette

Jacket image: © Dumbarton Oaks, Coins and Seals Collection, Washington, DC

This book has been composed in Classic Miller

Printed in the United States of America

10 9 8 7 6 5 4 3 2 1

For Paula
and the rest of my family, past and present

CONTENTS

List of Figures and Maps · ix
Acknowledgments · xi
A Note on Translations and Abbreviations · xv

INTRODUCTION	Empires Need Ethnography	1
CHAPTER 1	Conquest and Curiosity: Creating a Roman Imperial Ethnography	21
CHAPTER 2	"Hostiles and Friendlies": Diplomacy and Patterns of Subordination to Rome	53
CHAPTER 3	"Include Me Out": Ethnography, Settlement, and Law at the Edges of Empire	99
CHAPTER 4	Divine Providence and the Power of the Stars	123
CHAPTER 5	The Controlling Hand of the Environment	157
CHAPTER 6	Christianity and the Descendants of Noah	185
CHAPTER 7	Babel and the Languages of Faith	219
CHAPTER 8	The New Ethnography of Christian Heresy	236
CONCLUSION	The Conqueror's Gift	261

List of Abbreviations · 271
Notes · 273
Bibliography · 361
Index · 407
Index Locorum · 423

[vii]

LIST OF FIGURES AND MAPS

Figures

1. Gold medallion of Constantine I (326–27 CE)   58
2. Barberini Diptych, bottom panel (ca. 527–65 CE)   59
3. Obelisk base of Theodosius I, Constantinople, west face (392–95 CE)   61
4. King Shapur I at Naqsh-E Rostam (ca. 241–72 CE)   66
5. Gold medallion of Constantine I (327 CE)   67
6. Solidus of Justinian, obverse and reverse (538–45 CE)   154

Maps

1. The Roman Empire at Its Greatest Extent (ca. 211 CE)   xvi
2. Kingdoms of the Mediterranean World (ca. 530 CE)   xvii
3. The Roman Empire at Justinian's Death (565 CE)   xviii

ACKNOWLEDGMENTS

THIS BOOK WAS written over a long period, with frequent pauses taken for other projects. It is a pleasure to thank the individuals and institutions who helped it reach completion. I am most grateful to Brigitta van Rheinberg at Princeton University Press for initially supporting the project and to Rob Tempio, Chloe Coy, and Theresa Liu for seeing it through. Copyeditors Anne Cherry and Amanda Gillette and proofreader Lachlan Brooks prepared the final version of the manuscript for publication with accuracy, patience, and good humor.

I am deeply grateful to several scholars who read the entire manuscript and made invaluable suggestions for its improvement. Chief among them is Peter Brown, friend and mentor since Berkeley days. His cheerful encouragement has been a sustaining force in this book as in much else, and his presence is felt on every page. A more recent friend, Elena Boeck, most generously shared invaluable insights that have given the book tighter focus and clarity. It has been a great pleasure discussing the material in the book with her. Caroline Humfress and Michael Kulikowski, the outside readers of the manuscript for PUP, made their names available to me. Their acute comments have been enormously helpful, and I very much appreciate their kind willingness to share their expertise with me.

A number of distinguished experts read individual chapters. I owe special thanks to Audrey Becker, Susanna Elm, Scott Johnson, Ekaterina Nechaeva, Helmut Reimitz, Jonathan Shepard, and the late Joseph Solodow for their friendship, wisdom, and warm collegiality. Jonathan Shea, the Curator of Coins and Seals at Dumbarton Oaks, gave invaluable advice on the numismatic images in the book and kindly arranged for me to use them. Other figures were obtained through the good services of Sherri Jackson and Casey Schweiger at Bridgeman Images.

I want to express my sincere thanks to other friends who answered questions, exchanged ideas in many pleasant conversations, and shared their work, sometimes before publication. These are Stuart Airlie, Emily Albu, Joseph Alchermes, Patrick Amory, Peter Bell, Tolly Boatwright, Alan C. Bowen, Tom Brown, Leslie Brubaker, Marie-Pierre Bussières, Averil Cameron, Jean-Michel Carrié, Jonathan Conant, Robert Connor, Brian Croke, April DeConick, Michael Decker, Aitor Fernández Delgado, Nicola Denzey Lewis, Nicola Di Cosmo, Christophe Erismann, Stefan Esders, Eloi Ficquet, Andrew Gillett, Margerita Vellejo Girvés, Patrick T. R. Gray, Geoffrey Greatrex, Tim Greenwood, Ira Gruber, Erich Gruen, Randal Hall, Guy Halsall, Matthias Henze, the late Kenneth Holum, John Howe, Sergey Ivanov, Aaron Johnson,

[xi]

Danielle Joyner, Young Richard Kim, Christine Kondoleon, Shira Lander, Louise Loehndorff, Natalia Lozovsky, Hilary Mackie, Lucas MacMahon, Yuliya Minets, Donald Morrison, Yannis Papadogiannakis, Richard Payne, Charles Pazdernik, Andrea Piras, Walter Pohl, Charles Radding, Kent Rigsby, Filippo Ronconi, Alexander Sarantis, Peter Sarris, Sebastian Schmidt-Hofner, Brent Shaw, Teresa Shawcross, Rustam Shukurov, Kocku von Stuckrad, Richard Talbert, Gary Urton, Susan Wessel, and Christian Wildberg.

Some of the material developed in this book was first presented as invited lectures or as talks at different conferences and colloquia. I am grateful for the invitations to speak and for the stimulating discussions that followed at the following places: The American Academy in Rome; Brown University; Dumbarton Oaks; The Institute for the Study of the Ancient World (ISAW); The University of New Mexico; The Five College Lecture, Northampton, MA; The École des Hautes Études en Sciences Sociales (EHESS); The Itinerant Paleographic School (IIPS), Rome; The Collegium Helveticum, Zurich; The Deutsches Archaeologisches Institut, Berlin (DAI); The University of Maryland; The University of Alcalá de Henares; The Institute for Advanced Study (IAS), Princeton; The Institute for Medieval Research, Vienna; Trinity College, Oxford; and Mount Holyoke College.

Editorial assistance was essential to complete this book. I owe special gratitude to Ilia Calogero Curto Pelle for performing the Herculean labor of checking the notes and kindly helping with many other tasks. Peggy Polydoros was a peerless research assistant who began putting the bibliography on Zotero, and Isabella Impalli ably completed that task. Jane Zhang, Director of the Digital Media Commons at Rice University, gave welcome advice on digital matters. Meg Olsen expertly compiled the finished chapters for submission to PUP, and Jennifer Ottman produced the indices with skill and precision.

Some undergraduate and graduate students formerly at Rice and other institutions assisted with various research tasks before going on to other careers. I wish to thank Glenn McDorman, Maya Maskarinec, Jonathan Parts, Joseph Ricci, Hannah Thalenberg, Anthony Tohme, Kara van Schilfgaarde, and Anne Truetzel for their diligence and interest in the project.

The resources of many libraries were invaluable: I thank the staff at Rice University's Fondren Library for their assistance. The members of the Interlibrary Loan Department found often obscure materials with amazing speed. The book would not have been completed without their assistance. Anna Shparberg, Humanities Librarian for History, was an indispensable source of assistance and expertise. Marsha Tucker, Librarian for Historical Studies— Social Science Library at the Institute for Advanced Study, Princeton, NJ, provided a matchless place to work; the Librarians at the Dumbarton Oaks Byzantine Research Center, Deb Stewart and then Daniel Boomhower and their staffs, always showed exceptional courtesy and professionalism. The

ACKNOWLEDGMENTS   [xiii]

same may be said of Sebastian Hierl and his library staff at the American Academy in Rome.

My research was made possible by fellowships from the following institutions, to which I am extremely grateful: the American Council of Learned Societies; the American Philosophical Society; the Dumbarton Oaks Research Library and Collection; the Institute for Advanced Study, Princeton; the National Endowment for the Humanities; the National Humanities Center; and Trinity College, Cambridge. I thank the Rice University History Department, Humanities Research Center, and School of Humanities for additional funding.

The greatest pleasure lies in thanking my family for their affectionate support and interest in this project. My brother and sister and their spouses, Peter Maas and Lesley Carson, and Sue and Mel Melnick, have been a constant source of encouragement. My late parents, Dorothy and J. J. Maas, were with me in spirit every day. Conversations with my late uncle Joseph Natterson were always enjoyable and thought provoking. Most of all, I wish to acknowledge Paula Sanders, my companion throughout the writing of this book. She has been a learned interlocutor, insightful editor, unfailing source of support and good humor, and a wealth of computer savvy at critical moments. This book is for her and the rest of my family, with my love and gratitude.

A NOTE ON TRANSLATIONS AND ABBREVIATIONS

FOR THE SAKE of convenience, I have for the most part used the Loeb Classical Library, though I have occasionally made small changes in the translations to bring them up to date or for consistency in the spelling of names. Ancient names of people and places appear in their Latinized forms. The spelling of the names of Sasanian monarchs follows the *Cambridge Ancient History.* A list of commonly used abbreviations of journals, encyclopedias, and series is given before the bibliography. The first time a work is cited in a chapter it receives a full citation in the notes. The bibliography has full citations except for certain series of texts. Legal texts given in abbreviated form in the notes (e.g., *Nov. Just.* and *Cod. Th.*) have complete citations of the text and translation in the bibliography under Primary Sources. The Patrologia Latina and Patrologia Graeca series appear in the notes as PL and PG, with text citation and date of publication. Clarity for the reader has always been preferred to absolute consistency.

[xv]

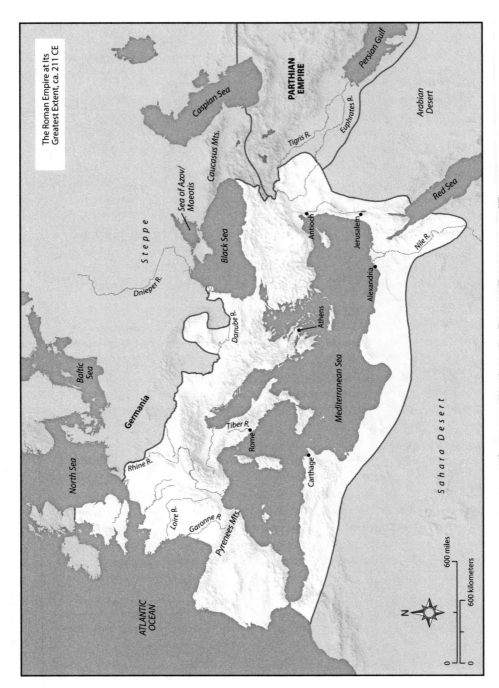

MAP 1. The Roman Empire at Its Greatest Extent, ca. 211 CE

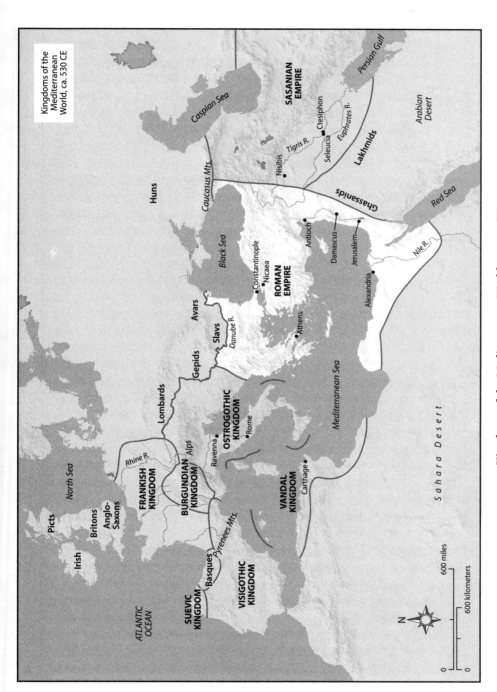

MAP 2. Kingdoms of the Mediterranean World, ca. 530 CE

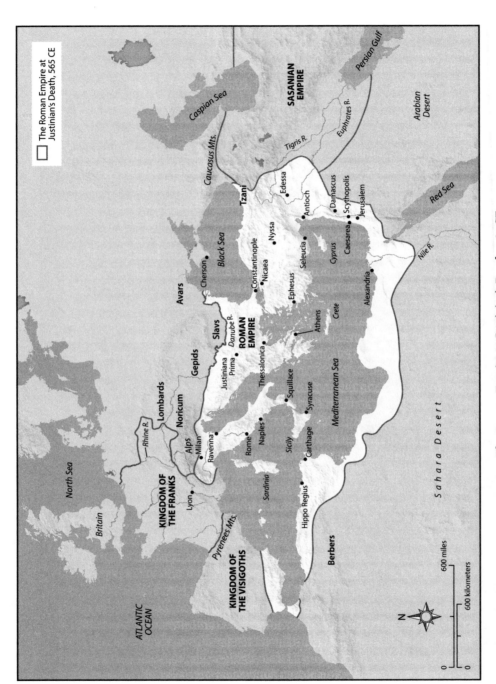

MAP 3. The Roman Empire at Justinian's Death, 565 CE

THE CONQUEROR'S GIFT

INTRODUCTION

Empires Need Ethnography

Ethnography is actively situated between powerful systems of meaning.
It poses its questions at the boundaries of civilizations, cultures, classes,
races, and genders. Ethnography decodes and recodes, telling the grounds
of collective order and diversity, inclusion and exclusion.

—JAMES CLIFFORD, "INTRODUCTION: PARTIAL TRUTHS"[1]

Ethnography in the Imperial Toolkit

The elites who control empires require ethnography. They are driven not simply by curiosity about the various peoples they keep under their thumb or glare at across imperial borders. Rather, they need ethnography to help them rule, in fact to survive in the business of control and exploitation, expansion and defense. Ethnography is as important as soldiers and bureaucrats because it lets rulers put a face on outsiders, drawing them into imperial history and moral vision. It provides a structured way to find a place for foreigners in the imperial worldview and helps justify action regarding them, thus relating perceptions to imperial practice. It provides terms and concepts with which to make sense of challenging new circumstances and imposes a measure of order on them. It has the capacity to adjust and respond. At the same time, in articulating cultural contrasts and similarities with outsiders, ethnography voices the underlying attitudes of those who guide an empire's course. Some sort of ethnographic vision comes into play every day while conducting the business of empire, whether making grand decisions about war and peace or simple ones about buying foreign goods in the marketplace. Always hurrying to keep up in a world of constant change, ethnography may be seen as "a discourse in anxious flux."[2]

This book operates from a broad and inclusive definition of ethnographic thought as it was expressed by a wide range of Roman authors. The evidence embraces far more than the familiar and well-studied passages about the habits of particular groups, such as Julius Caesar's picture of Gauls found in his war commentaries or Tacitus's presentation of peoples beyond the Rhine found in the *Germania*, a self-standing essay. These works exemplify classical literary ethnography, a genre that was, as Patrick Amory put it, "only a small part of the story."[3]

To tell more of the story, this book takes a wider view because in the Roman Empire ethnography appeared in a variety of guises and written formats. By

[1]

the term *ethnography* I mean any consideration of a foreign community that dealt at length or in passing with some aspect of its appearance or character, regardless of the genre in which the discussion is found. An organized set of ideas always lay behind the ethnographic texts, which displayed many interests. Roman authors, including Christian ones, dealt with such topics as social organization, religious practice, battlefield tactics, physical appearance, or geographical setting in which the foreigners lived. Rome was always the implicit or explicit reference point. As a descriptive medium, therefore, ethnography was more than a single genre and less than a complete, monolithic view of society. The communities under scrutiny often lay beyond imperial borders, yet an imperial presence always pervaded the description. Appraisal of outsiders was not random, though it was often highly tendentious or critical. Value judgments were never absent, and tempers often ran high.

In the epigraph at the head of this chapter, James Clifford describes modern ethnography's function as decoding and recoding critical information, turning it into knowledge with a working role in the worldview of the observer. The same may be said for ethnography in imperial Rome. From this perspective, the Roman ethnographer was a dragoman, a translator, interpreter, and guide, who explained "who's in and who's out" of the dominant Roman community. The voices encountered in this book express a wide range of opinion about what those distinctions signified. They bring to life a changing empire of diverse and discordant parts.

Rome's ethnographic infrastructure was a bundle of roughly integrated ideas regarding the significant differences separating Romans and non-Romans. It consisted of discrete and ethnographic discourses, each of which represented an ethnographic tradition serving a particular purpose. The discourses supported the imperial Romans' views of themselves regarding the many peoples of the world, shaping and reflecting interactions with them. The discourses did not always dovetail neatly, and the ideas expressed within them were not always congruent. Collectively, however, they constitute a coherent body of study. This book suggests that to understand how the Roman Empire changed and what it became, the evolution of its ethnographic underpinnings deserves to be examined. Over many centuries, Romans created a far-flung empire unified in part by an evolving ethnographic vision that renewed itself in Late Antiquity. I call this profoundly influential vision "the conqueror's gift." Roman imperial ethnography has a rich history and a fascinating story to tell.

Why Is This Book Called The Conqueror's Gift?

Books need titles that indicate their content, fit on the cover, and catch the reader's eye. *The Conqueror's Gift* meets those requirements. *Roman Ethnography and the End of Antiquity*, which follows the colon, tells the subject matter and suggests a chronological development. Calling Rome's ethnographic infrastructure "the conqueror's gift," however, requires some explanation. Since the appearance of Marcel Mauss's pathbreaking essay *The Gift* (*Essay sur le don*) in 1923, social scientists have recognized how gift exchange reveals complex, interactive social networks and hierarchies in different societies.[4] The gift in the title of my book alludes to these insights and finds analogous networks and hierarchies of difference in Rome's ethnographic infrastructure, suggesting that it was a gift in several figurative ways. Imperial Roman ethnography was a gift the Romans made for themselves, because it embraced concepts with which they could address the great cultural diversity of their world. It was a gift that came from the conquerors, reflecting their supposition of preeminence. At the same time, Roman ethnography was a somewhat less welcome present for the many peoples who found themselves trapped in Rome's vision, needing to find a place within it that made sense to Roman demands. For moderns, Rome's ethnography has proven to be a mixed legacy, not always welcome, but greatly influential all the same. The different parts of Rome's ethnographic infrastructure are discussed in the pages that follow and are summarized, with further comments about the conqueror's gift, in chapter 9.

The Historical Frame

How the rich matrix of classical antiquity in the Roman Mediterranean developed into what we label the medieval world has remained one of the most intriguing questions of historical investigation since the Renaissance, one that has been explored in a host of different ways. In recent years, many historians have hunted for answers in Late Antiquity (roughly ca. 250–ca. 650 CE), an epoch of critical transition and transformation, during which time new societies coalesced and older cultural and political formations either adjusted to new circumstances or fell by the wayside. Remarkable changes throughout western Eurasia can be traced that were local as well as long-range and interconnected through time and space. The path across these centuries was not a straight line, however, and no single cause lay behind all that happened. No timely asteroid struck to finish off the dinosaurs of the classical world. Instead, a diverse array of percussive events—plagues, invasions, civil wars, dynastic collapses as well as sudden turns of heart and mind—helped jump-start changes at different levels of society that had long been percolating. The stakes in exploring this material have always seemed very high because so many of the great narratives of modernity rightly or wrongly find origins in the crucial late antique centuries.[5] For good reason, exploration of this period has generated a vast literature, popular as well as academic. For those readers unfamiliar with the late antique era, a brief overview of key developments is warranted. I identify three great areas of change.

[4] INTRODUCTION

(1) First, Late Antiquity witnessed the dissolution of the Roman Empire in Western Europe in the course of the fifth century, accompanied by the development of new successor states basic to the formation of medieval Latin Christendom. The empire continued in the eastern Mediterranean, guided from the palace in Constantinople, the New Rome, where a new and distinctly Christian imperial culture emerged that we call Byzantine.[6] At the same time, in northern Europe, in the lands that Romans called *barbaricum*—territories packed with menacing peoples whom they had never ruled—new political communities and cultures took shape.[7] Farther to the east, nomadic peoples of the Eurasian Steppe, which reached from central Asia to the Great Hungarian Plain, asserted themselves as a lasting threat in European affairs, notably during the terrifying ascendancy of Attila the Hun (r. 434–53). Iran, under the direction of the Sasanian dynasty, reasserted its ancient role as a strategically important player in geopolitics, located as it was between Central Asia, Middle Eastern, and Mediterranean lands. It fell to Muslim armies in the seventh century, part of the same movement that displaced Roman rule from North Africa and the Middle East. With the rise of Islam and the establishment of the Umayyad Caliphate, Late Antiquity came to an end. As a result of these changes, the geopolitical map of western Eurasia was utterly transformed and the old Roman Mediterranean core lost its centripetal force. In Peter Brown's words, "The problem that urgently preoccupied men of Late Antiquity themselves was . . . the painful modification of the ancient boundaries."[8]

(2) In addition to the political changes and the social and economic refiguring that accompanied them, Christianity in its different forms caused a revolution in perspective across the board. Formation of Christian communities of faith began with Paul in the first century. By the end of the fourth century, the new religion in various forms had become dominant in Roman lands and extended its fingers beyond Rome's borders as well. The Christian writer Prosper of Aquitaine observed in the first half of the fifth century, as the empire collapsed around him in western Europe, "The grace of Christianity is not content to have the boundaries of Rome as its limits; for it has submitted to the sceptre of Christ's cross many peoples whom Rome could not subject with its arms."[9] The expansion of Christianity produced new reasons and new ways for communities to unite—and disagree.

With its text-based understanding of universal mission transcending both the pull of local divinities and the unifying imperial cult, as well as its own internal organization, Christianity created meta-communities not dependent on imperial government that could reach lands beyond Rome's reach. Because it offered novel, integrated views of all aspects of human society and experience to its followers, Christianity placed great strain on the age-old determinants of community and identity that had shaped life in the Roman world. Within the religion lay the elements of a new ethnography. Determining the particular authoritative texts that invigorated communities of Christian faith was a complicated process that had begun in the first century and that matured and found fiercely agonistic expression in Late Antiquity. The easy-going imperial approach to most forms of worship seen in the Augustan age vanished entirely.[10] Just as Romans had written themselves into a vision of the inhabited world (what Greeks called the *oikoumene*) when their empire was getting under way in the second century BCE, Christian Romans in Late Antiquity produced a revised vision of the *oikoumene* defined by consider-ations of faith and doctrine as well as long-standing imperial goals. Elements of received classical traditions of history, geography, and other knowledge also played a major part in shaping this worldview. Christian writers claimed absolute moral authority and a new centrality for their beliefs in a varied and complex world. Zoroastrian Iranians, and later, Muslims, expressed simi-larly religion-based perspectives. "Empires of faith," to borrow Peter Sarris's term, confronted one another at the end of our period in a way unimaginable to Romans in the days of Augustus or even Constantine, the first Christian emperor.[11]

Within the Roman state, Christians suppressed polytheism, and much of the associated intellectual legacy of classical antiquity drew suspicion and hostility from the new establishment. Christians also devised definitions of community that could stand independently of the Roman Empire. To be Christian, one did not have to be a Roman, though by the end of Late Antiq-uity within the empire it was necessary to be Christian (and, as ever, rich) to enjoy the full benefits of Roman life. No single interpretation of the Chris-tian faith won absolute ascendancy, however. Bishops inside and outside the empire quarreled fiercely, hurling charges of heresy at one another as they pursued doctrinal correctness, which became a defining basis of their author-ity. Christian communities of various sorts established themselves inside the empire and beyond imperial borders as well, from the Atlantic to the Red Sea, to Iran and Tang China. Different doctrines and sacred texts, languages and cultural backgrounds, kept them distinct and defiantly self-aware ethno-religious groups. Heaven, not Rome and its gods, became the new center of attention with its own attendant social and moral peripheries.

(3) Against this backdrop of geopolitical and religious developments came a third general body of changes that are central to this book. A major eth-nographic shift occurred in western Eurasia. From a Roman vantage point, this was a reworking of paradigms of perception, judgment, and inclusion of foreigners. In Late Antiquity, many new identities were ascribed to foreign groups, and some were even accepted by them. Such ascription or imposi-tion of identities is the act of the ethnographer as well as the imperial admin-istrator. New names for political and ethnic groups came into play, and old ones were repurposed. This process of identifying communities differently responded to political, religious, and social changes of many kinds, and it pro-vided categories and language with which those changes could be interpreted

[6] INTRODUCTION

and explained. The scale of these shifts in perception and interpretation of cultural difference must be emphasized. Because new categories of identification spread over great distances, we must be on the lookout not simply for migrating people but for migrating terms of identification carried in different ways, probably the most significant movement across space in our period. From a geneticist's perspective, the populations of western Eurasia might seem remarkably stable.[12] From an imperial, political vantage point, however, the *oikoumene* might seem to have been largely repopulated. Rome's ethnography responded to the movement of terms that identified self and community, both foreign and domestic.

The ethnographic shift, so palpable in Roman contexts, came at a considerable cost. It brought change more pervasive than any damage caused by Huns, Goths, or Vandals. Greg Woolf, in his study of developments in Gaul after Roman conquest in the first century BCE, calls such disruption "epistemic violence," meaning the severing or rearticulation of ties with previous identities and previous pasts that accompanied them.[13] During the period of expansion in the late Republic and early Empire that he examines, the Romans generated new knowledge about their history, community, and identity and especially about the rest of the world's populations. Other peoples reinvented themselves and their pasts as well, deeply responsive to the Roman presence. This book will show similar developments in Late Antiquity.

Since new kinds of religious self-identification became a more significant marker of identity of communities and polities than ever before, and since conflict among groups increasingly was justified in religious terms, I suggest that a major consequence of the ethnographic shift was the beginning of a sectarian age.[14] Especially when wed to the state, communities of faith became aggressive communities of power, reflecting a major shift of perception and justification for action.

One dramatic manifestation of this shift still resonates today. At the beginning of the first century CE, Jews alone understood themselves to be the children of Abraham, with their remotest history narrated in the Bible. By the end of the late antique centuries, many millions of Christians, and then followers of Islam, believed Abraham to be the distant father of their communities as well, which connected them to biblical historical narrative through the medium of new and vigorous faiths. Communities from Ireland to Yemen, from the Atlas range to the Caucasus and beyond, acknowledged common biblical foundations. This was a true transformation in self-understanding for the peoples of western Eurasia, an imaginative leap about personal and community identity. As mentioned above, the shift was not based simply on the movement of peoples. It was based on the fact that some new, vital categories of identification and principles of evaluating collective difference had come to the fore and were being disseminated over great distances. In other words, Romans gained a fresh way of looking at the peoples of the world. Theirs had

EMPIRES NEED ETHNOGRAPHY   [7]

become a sectarian world to the extent that primary markers of identity for individuals, communities, and larger polities rested on religious affiliation, though older ethnic identities were scarcely forgotten.

In the midst of all these transformations, many peoples familiar to us but new to antiquity climbed onto the stage of western Eurasian history, often grabbing the spotlight and stealing the best lines—Huns, Goths, and others whom we will encounter in the pages ahead. Yet, if barbarians sometimes chewed the scenery, Romans still owned the theater, and focus throughout this book remains on the Roman imperial impresarios. The Roman Empire and the ethnographic writing produced by its elites are the center of attention. This is partly because most of the written sources from the period were composed by Romans. More important, however, is the fact that Roman civilization had dominated the greater Mediterranean world and the westernmost reaches of Eurasia for more than half a millennium before our period came to an end. Its institutions, ideas, and vocabularies of description and analysis provided the starting point of subsequent developments in the medieval period, in eastern as well as western arenas. In Late Antiquity, the Roman Empire's ethnographic infrastructure supported reworkings of the social imagination of peoples over an enormous area.

Ethnography Ancient and Modern

Because of its Greek roots (*ethnos* means "a people" and *graphein* means "to write"), the word *ethnography* looks ancient, but it is not. Never uttered or written in antiquity by any Greek or Roman, it is a modern coinage that emerged only in the second half of the eighteenth century, the creation of German scholars who explored Siberia at the behest of Russian authorities[15] and who believed that scientific terms should be rendered in Greek.[16] One of these intrepid scientists, Gerhard Friedrich Müller (1705–83), developed a research program for the orderly "description of the world's peoples" (*Völker-Beschreibung*) for the purpose of systematic comparison.[17] The term first appeared in German as *Ethnographie* by 1767, in English for the first time in 1811, and again in an English encyclopedia in 1834.[18] Ethnography became a recognized academic discipline in the course of the nineteenth century, deeply enmeshed in the exploration and colonization of the globe by imperial European powers. It often reflected the biological racism then in vogue. Understanding of ethnography has evolved significantly since then. There are many schools of ethnographic theory and practice today, some of which contest the legitimacy or even the possibility of ethnographic description of other peoples because of its place in modern colonial activity.[19] As this book shows, its roots ran far deeper.

Ethnographic *interest*, by which I mean displaying curiosity moreover about foreign peoples and developing shared ideas about their differences,

[8]   INTRODUCTION

must be a habit as old as humanity. Emma Dench calls it the ethnographic gaze.[20] We can be sure that there existed, as Joseph Skinner points out, "ethnography before ethnography," meaning ethnography even before it began to be written down by Herodotus, considered the first historian in the Western tradition, and others in the ancient Greek world.[21] When Greeks started to record their observations and elaborate their thoughts about foreigners in the fifth century BCE in historical, geographical, dramatic, and other narrative genres, they did so with no particular word matching our modern *ethnography* to mean the specialized examination of a foreign group. In his great historical work, which he simply called "investigations,"[22] Herodotus included many long descriptions of foreign peoples. Following his lead, later writers sometimes referred to the locations, customs, laws, or origins of peoples in their titles, such as Tacitus's *De situ et origine Germanorum* (*On the Location and Origin of the Germans*). Similar formulations continued to be employed for descriptive literature through the Middle Ages into the modern period. Ethnography was off to a running start.

In the modern world ethnographic interest started to come into focus in the sixteenth century as European conquerors, settlers, merchants, missionaries, and other travelers encountered peoples new to them around the globe, with the Americas providing an especially rich field of interest. When their observations found their way into print, they were generally labeled accounts of "laws, customs, and beliefs." For example, an influential compendium by Johannes Boemus, first published in Latin in Augsburg 1520 and translated into Spanish in 1556, had the title *The Customs, Laws, and Rites of All Peoples*,[23] following Latin models. Everyone composing such works was an amateur, because the formal discipline of ethnography did not yet exist. Like Romans before them, the ethnographers of the early modern age came from many backgrounds and wrote for many purposes.

Tacitus, or indeed any of the Roman writers considered in this book, would have been bemused at the disdain of modern scholarship that sees ethnography in negative terms as a creature of imperialism, colonialism, and oppression of all sorts. Though he may have disagreed with specific military policies or noted wryly how Rome's recently conquered subjects could be seduced by Roman culture for which they innocently sacrificed their own freedom, Tacitus thought Rome's expansion to be glorious and worthwhile,[24] and from his own military experience, he knew a barbarian when he saw one. Our job is not to dismiss his enterprise because he espoused values out of fashion in our postcolonial age, but to try to understand his descriptive concerns within the context of his own times. It is also important that we not be bound by modern assumptions about what constitutes ethnography. There is room for a broader understanding of the phenomenon of writing about foreign peoples without anachronistically imposing the strictures of genres developed only in the last two hundred years or agreeing with ancient attitudes.[25] Writers today in many academic fields other than anthropology unapologetically use the word *ethnography* to refer to the practice of describing the habits and customs of peoples in other historical periods without involving themselves directly in the current debates of anthropologists and other social scientists.[26]

What Was Roman about Roman Ethnography? Three Basic Functions

Romans knew they lived in a world of great cultural diversity. Pliny the Elder, the scholar and military commander who died in Vesuvius's blast at Pompeii in the first century, marveled that the "manners and customs [of humanity] are beyond counting, almost as numerous as the groups of mankind."[27] Members of the ruling elite like Pliny believed that their empire brought civilized order to a world of constant movement and instability. Images of defeated barbarians filled public spaces throughout the empire as reassuring reminders of Roman control. Writers likewise filled their pages with descriptions of foreigners in a wide variety of genres. In response to the grand variety of the inhabited world, ethnographic writing served three general functions. First, it described foreign peoples, placing them in established and accessible systems of knowledge. Second, it judged them on various registers of distance from Roman norms, with "most like us" the best possible evaluation. Third, ethnography indicated explicitly or implicitly what the possibilities of participation within the imperial community might be. In other words, writers could imagine transformation of societies through imperial agency.[28] All three had in common an aspect of self-representation. We will look at each of these three functions briefly. Together they indicate how notions of Romanness changed over time.

FUNCTION 1: DESCRIPTION

When Romans contrasted their civilization to barbarism,[29] they invoked broad assumptions about their innate superiority and dominant place in the world. Informed by writers of previous generations as well as by their own experience, authors focused on different aspects of foreignness, such as physical characteristics, cultural habits, or forms of government. Most obviously, Romans wrote in a world in which the blight of biological racism did not yet exist, and where—for the Roman governing class, at least—imperialism brought great rewards. Their default observations were not ours.

The act of describing foreigners in words (or depicting them in paint, metal, or stone) made them intelligible and lent a measure of coherence and order to the rush of information that would otherwise seem chaotic and unmanageable. Thus, Roman ethnographic description stood between the

[10] INTRODUCTION

Roman world and foreign lands, a protective barrier as formidable as any barricade or fortress. Yet it was a defensive wall with many gateways. Foreigners might enter Roman lands and even become Romans, as long as they did so on Roman terms.

For the purposes of this book, I am not concerned with the ethnographic representation as a truth-telling enterprise (that is, not with whether the Huns were ugly or the Persians lazy) but with what the representation may tell us about the Roman on the flip side of the ethnographic coin. More often than not, ethnography somehow linked perception of non-Roman communities to Roman political dominion. It infused what the empire's leaders considered to be normative into a vision of the world, enabling judgment of others and justification for imperial action. Thus, ethnographic descriptions were as much a statement of Roman values and assumptions about society as a description of a non-Roman people. As Guy Halsall has remarked, "In constructing the barbarian world the Roman Empire defined itself."[30]

FUNCTION 2: JUDGMENT

Descriptions, no matter how finely tuned, were never value blind. Ethnographers of all stripes were confident that imperial Rome established and embodied the norms of civilization. (Many Christian writers would take exception to such claims, as we will see). These norms, stated and unstated, were the starting point for judgment of foreign groups. They anchored registers of difference that radiated outward to the edges of the inhabited world. For example, closest to the Roman ideal of normative life were people like the Greeks, who enjoyed the benefits of civilization. At the farthest point along the continuum of distance from Rome were beings with feet on backward who wrapped themselves in their ears every night to sleep. These were creatures of fantasy.[31] By marking degrees of difference from Rome, ethnographic material indicates the possibilities of inclusion within Roman society. These registers of distance indicate degrees of belonging. Taking a place within a greater Roman community could be imagined.

FUNCTION 3: INCLUSION

Romans understood that the many peoples of the *oikoumene* constantly moved about and were susceptible to changes caused by all the forces, earthbound and celestial, that affect human affairs. Furthermore, Romans understood themselves and their empire to be one of the possible agents of change. This transformative role must be emphasized. Turning barbarians into Romans always was a possibility and sometimes even an expectation of imperial rule.[32] At other times, keeping them at arm's length was preferable.[33] Imperial Rome offered entry into a cosmopolitan world of stability and peace (as they understood their civilization) to all the outside "barbarians" not yet part of their community. Roman notions of what some might call a civilizing mission were based on the capacity to bring about change.

From an early stage in the development of the empire, Romans took an interest in how cultural contact or political control could alter a foreign culture. Strabo, for example, the great geographer of Augustan Rome, illustrates this idea in his description of the transformation of the Iberians (in Spain) under Roman rule: "for both the Cantabrians . . . and their neighbours have been subdued by Augustus Caesar; and instead of plundering the allies of the Romans . . . now take the field for the Romans. Further, Tiberius, his successor, has set over these regions an army of three legions . . . and it so happens that he already has rendered some of the peoples not only peaceable but civilised as well."[34] By the end of the period discussed in this book, the emperor positioned himself not only as the greatest agent of change but also as the agent of Christ in making the changes.[35] Procopius, who wrote in the sixth century in Constantinople, described how the emperor Justinian caused the Tzani, a remote people in the Caucasus region, to adopt Christianity. He built new roads to connect them to a cosmopolitan outside world, built churches for them, and enabled them to discover their full humanity.[36]

The Shape of the Book

THE CHRONOLOGICAL FRAME IN RECENT STUDIES

The story told in this book has a beginning and an end. Two most helpful recent works of scholarship provide rough chronological bookends and raise important methodological concerns. Greg Woolf's *Tales of the Barbarians: Ethnography and Empire in the Roman West* deals with Roman territories in western Europe from their initial conquest until the end of the first century CE,[37] offering a number of key ideas that underlie the pages ahead. Woolf's concern is to examine how new knowledge was created about recently subjugated peoples. He describes an ethnography of the lived experience of conquest and assimilation built on the shoulders of literary convention, noting how "barbarian *érudits* and Greek grammarians rubbed shoulders with Roman conquerors across a vast and variegated contact zone."[38] Woolf treats ethnography as an "artefact of Roman power"[39] that involved the erasure of the pasts of conquered people and the slow emergence of new mythic histories and traditions through interaction with Roman patterns of thought and explanation.

Woolf uses the powerful term *epistemic violence* to indicate the severing of ties between the knowledge worlds of local societies before and after Roman conquest. In doing so, he brings attention to the cultural consequences of ethnographic description for both the describers and the described. We will see the same thing happening with imperial describers of the world around them in Late Antiquity. These disruptions provoked profound reassessment for all concerned.

Next, Woolf emphasizes that "authors and readers inhabited the world their texts describe."[40] This is a wise cautionary reminder. We must not forget that even though many of the tropes of Roman ethnographic discussion had become hoary with age by Late Antiquity (and some of them were already venerable in Greek contexts when Rome first began to expand its empire), it was through those conventions that contemporary circumstances and the evident differences between Romans and other peoples were interpreted and through which change could be imagined and managed to some degree. This leads to two important insights. The first is that while ethnographic writing can have a long shelf life and appear to be constant, its traditional elements may become inadequate in the face of new realities. This is important because the repertoire of classical ethnographic genres lost initial vigor by the end of antiquity to be supplanted or augmented by new categories of analysis energized by Christianity. The second insight to which Woolf leads us is that while the readers of the late empire may have recognized that some of their analytical models were outmoded and no longer did justice to their own reality, their choice to use anachronistic tropes represents historically contingent cultural choices that call for explanation. It is important for the discussion that follows to remember that in Late Antiquity even writers blanketed by the heavy weight of the past did not stop thinking about contemporary events. Quite the opposite was the case.

The task is to see how late antique writers reworked and reapplied elements of their own inheritance to questions of their own day. When Woolf speaks, furthermore, of "enduring fictions"[41] to indicate that much of the knowledge formed in the first century CE remained in play well into the Middle Ages and beyond, he sets the stage for the ethnographic innovations of Late Antiquity that reimagined the inhabited world and that continue to influence us today.

In his emphasis on ethnographic writing as a literary construct, Woolf guides us away from the narrow positivism that caused many scholars well into the twentieth century to take surviving textual evidence at face value. By raising the question of how the facts were made, his work encourages examination of how new verities about foreign peoples were hammered out in Late Antiquity. Woolf discusses how various ethnographic paradigms existed in the early Roman Empire that reflected a variety of experiences on the ground as well as writing practices. He makes the important point that these paradigms framed the construction of new knowledge and were not mutually exclusive or competitive, but parallel. We will see that in Late Antiquity the situation was somewhat different: over time, the ethnographic paradigms came together under the influence of Christianity and ignited a revolution in Roman worldview.

Perhaps the salient element in Woolf's discussion is that he ties ethnography to the practice of empire. Without denying the literary constraints that conditioned authorial voices, Woolf sees the production of ethnography as current, in step with the demands of contemporary explanation of events. This was no less true of Late Antiquity than of the early Roman Empire. He does not directly discuss the transformative elements encoded within ethnographic writing, however. Though he deals only with the western provinces, Woolf lets us see that an imperial ethnographic apparatus was in place in the Roman Mediterranean world by the end of the first century CE. Methodologically as well as chronologically, *Tales of the Barbarians* makes one reliable bookend for my discussion.

The second book that frames my study is Anthony Kaldellis's *Ethnography after Antiquity* (2013).[42] It is of chronological significance because it points to the "crashing end" of the classical ethnographic tradition in the seventh century when a new, characteristically Byzantine tradition began.[43] Thus he provides an appropriate bookend to enclose my discussion. Kaldellis's argument for this end date is convincing. His approach differs from mine in several respects, however. The first difference is in the scope of what he considers ethnography to be. In his first chapter, "Ethnography in Late Antique Historiography," he explains his subject matter.[44] He deals with the "classicizing" ethnography, that is, writing that self-consciously mimicked the writings of authors like Thucydides, conventionally found in historical writing in Late Antiquity. He sees this as an essentially secular and primarily literary discourse to be distinguished from explicitly Christian approaches that came to the fore in Late Antiquity and predominated in the Byzantine period. As noted above, my approach views ethnography more broadly. I consider genres other than history writing, taking ethnography beyond the sphere of classicizing literature.

Kaldellis focuses in his first chapter on the ethnographic digressions found in classicizing historical texts of the sixth century (especially Procopius, Agathias, Menander, and Theophylactus Simacotta), and he rightly notes that they were "self-conscious literary artefacts created for a competitive literary scene."[45] Although reliant on traditional modes of description, the late antique authors had considerable room for variation, giving their work a personal stamp, part of a "multi-faceted authorial performance." Thus Kaldellis distinguishes "generic autonomy" and the "textual environments" in which they rested.[46] This is a useful approach to genres other than the historical in the late antique corpus. When he turns to ethnographic description found in the accounts of embassies (Priscus, Peter the Patrician, and others), he notes both the practical uses for which they were originally devised and the wide readership that they found among elite Romans. This gives special force to his observation that the descriptions with all their literary contrivance could be highly political and anything but "a mental straightjacket."[47] Exploiting the differences between Roman and barbarian was central to the ethnographic writing that Kaldellis analyzes. He shows that the contrast lay precisely at the heart of political dispute and subtle commentary on imperial policy. In his hands, ethnography illuminates the thought world of its writers. Just as they had been for Tacitus, the barbarians could be a foil for the Byzantines to view their own society.[48]

If the classicizing approach to ethnography stopped in the seventh century, what came in the new Byzantine tradition? Only a few words can be written here to suggest the complex "after" that followed the seventh-century break. Kaldellis develops a few characteristics, and we will see their gestation to some extent in the pages that follow. Orthodox Christianity, as embodied in the imperial state, had become the chief marker of Byzantine superiority over other of the world's peoples. Christian beliefs would be a lens through which foreigners would be judged and political communities distinguished. As was the case in Late Antiquity, furthermore, ethnographic writing would be a mirror of its writers' self-examination.

CONTINUITY AND CONNECTIVITY

Before describing the chapters of this book, I want to emphasize the truly remarkable chronological depth of the various intellectual and literary traditions drawn upon by authors of all types throughout the late antique centuries. Such men as Homer and Aristotle, who were active centuries before Rome came on the scene, and Ptolemy and Strabo, who flourished as the imperial system took shape, continued to be profoundly influential placeholders in the intellectual universe of Justinian and Isidore of Seville, who lived when Late Antiquity was drawing to a close. Their ethnographic ideas reverberated throughout this enormous time span. In the same way, the Hebrew Bible and the Christian Scriptures remained a constant source of inspiration for late antique Christians. These materials from a far distant time remained as an immanent presence in the thought worlds of late antique writers and the elites who guided affairs. They were a deep and nourishing well from which to draw as need demanded and education permitted. In this sense, the malleable written legacy provided a welcome lifeline of continuity and connectivity to the authoritative voices of the deep past. At the same time, we should also pause to appreciate the equally remarkable ability of late antique writers to adjust this rich literary inheritance to the requirements of an ever-changing present.

This book follows only one red thread through this vast literary canvas, that of ethnographic thought as linked to the Roman Empire. To do this, I have explored many texts written over a long period of time in many genres, all of which contributed to the ethnographic infrastructure. I have not directly investigated visual representations. The voices we will hear have been selected to show how writers of many backgrounds perceived, judged, and accommodated foreign peoples, often ascribing new identities to them. An *index locorum* at the end of the book lists the ancient and early medieval sources mentioned in the following chapters.

In addition to recognizing the remarkable longevity of the written tradition under examination, it is useful to remind ourselves of the astonishing breadth of territory embraced by Roman power. The empire at its greatest extent reached from Morocco to northern Britain and from Cherson to Upper Egypt. Some of its inhabitants of this enormous space knew about Ireland and India, Nubia and China, places they would never visit. Traveling beyond imperial limits was always dangerous, and moving within the borders between major centers of population also meant traversing vast tracts of territory full of recalcitrant populations speaking endless dialects and languages. Access to imperial culture and an interconnected, legible world, eventually a Christian world, meant everything. The writers who generated late antique ethnography knew this disjointed social landscape with all its rough edges very well. For them, isolation and lack of connectivity implied barbarism.

A VARIETY OF ETHNOGRAPHIC DISCOURSES: THE ORGANIZATION OF THE BOOK

Roman ethnography did not offer a single view of society. It was written by people who held a stake in the empire and identified with it in often conflicting ways. We will encounter pragmatic diplomats, ideologically driven courtiers, zealous churchmen, triumphant generals, careful lawyers, and learned historians, setting down their opinions in different modes. The constraints of each genre produced different ethnographic discourses, which, while not incompatible or in conflict with one another, were not interchangeable, either. They maintained separate profiles. As noted above, all shared three basic elements. Each contained descriptions of one sort or another, registers of evaluation, and implicitly the possibility of transformation. In their particular ways they created distance from Rome and Romanness. Together they constituted the empire's loose-limbed ethnographic infrastructure. I treat them separately in the chapters ahead for the sake of discussion, though I am well aware that considerable cross-pollination among them occurred. Christianity challenged and then transformed all of them during Late Antiquity.

Chapter 1, "Conquest and Curiosity: Creating a Roman Imperial Ethnography," discusses the elements of Roman ethnography that would be put to use in Late Antiquity. From the tradition of ethnographic writing begun by Greek scientists in the fifth century BCE, Romans inherited a well-developed contrast

[16] INTRODUCTION

between "civilized" and "barbarian" society. They tailored this literary construct to fit their imperial practices of conquering, governing, and assimilating new populations by developing the idea that contact with the empire would alter the ways of life of their subjects and neighbors. They also maintained a deep-seated antagonism to barbarians as a type, often making them the foil for Roman vice or virtue. In many cases barbarians stood for everything that was not understood to be Roman, such as lawlessness, political instability, or isolation from the rest of the world. Reconciling these contradictory needs to incorporate and exclude created a lasting and invigorating tension in Roman imperial ethnographic thought. The key to understanding this dilemma is to know that distinctions were never absolutely insurmountable in the imperial Roman view of the world, though admittedly resistance could merit the total destruction of a hostile population. Aspects of foreign cultures could be attractive and worth adopting; bridging cultural gaps was always possible and perhaps at times even desirable.[49] Foreigners were not always monsters, after all, just not yet Romans.

This chapter follows the development of the imperial ethnographic toolkit as it took shape from the time of Julius Caesar through the high empire. Sketches of certain representative authors reveal basic ideas in the ethnographic corpus that came into play. We will see how interest in the customs of foreign peoples became intermeshed with imperial self-awareness and purpose. Some aspects of foreign life carried less weight than they would in Late Antiquity. Religious practice, for example, was only one curiosity among many that caught the Roman eye, and religious communities (other than Rome's divinely protected state) had no political agency or place in a religious view of history. The occasional positive judgment of foreigners did not curtail confidence in Rome's superiority that permeated the observations of elite writers. These men claimed center stage morally and politically for Rome in world affairs, and the figure of the emperor emerged as the chief artisan of cultural change. These elements found in literary ethnography would be fundamental to late antique developments. The opposition of Roman civilization and foreign barbarism found in elite writing constitutes the first of the ethnographic dossiers considered in this book.

Chapter 2, "'Hostiles and Friendlies': Diplomacy and Patterns of Subordination to Rome," shows that international relations produced a second ethnographic discourse. Roman diplomatic activity grew in importance and sophistication in Late Antiquity in step with the appearance of formidable new opponents. There emerged an elaborate discourse of friendship and enmity through which questions of the status of negotiating groups relative to Rome were worked out. Hierarchies of friendship and subordination to Rome emerged that were essential in treaty making, where precise evaluation of diplomatic partners was necessary. This chapter focuses on some of the late antique diplomatic arenas in which scenarios of subordination to Rome played out differently: the western European territories, where newcomers, often in league with local populations, developed new political communities in the fifth century;[50] the steppe land that was home to predatory nomad cultures; the Sasanian Persian Empire, Rome's only rival in power and prestige; and Arab groupings on the margins between Rome and Persia that served as proxies for them. When Christianity began to spread beyond Rome's borders, the empire could find a new sort of common ground with some of its neighbors. By rearranging some alliances on religious lines, shared Christianity could be a basis for new modes of interaction.

Chapter 3, "'Include Me Out': Ethnography, Settlement, and Law at the Edges of Empire," turns to the imperial problem of how to settle outsiders on Roman soil. Just as military necessity required Romans to remain vigilant in the face of external neighbors, the practicalities of government required careful management of foreigners settled on imperial lands. The edges of the empire were a particularly vital site of activity, because in Late Antiquity many "barbarians" wished to enter the empire or were forced into it, and identities had to be ascribed to the newcomers as a measure of control. Imperial law, of course, had no direct role to play in the lives of people beyond the borders, but it did provide a somewhat uniform set of terms that provided a recognizable social visage and above all a legal status to outsiders once they had entered the empire. These newly ascribed group identities depended upon tasks the authorities required them to perform after settlement. Every decision made by Roman authorities about the status of newcomers into the empire was a function of the power relations of the moment. Newcomers kept their ethnonyms, but another status category was assigned to them in laws and official documents. The term *barbarian* was not used.

The new formal labels, agreed upon prior to settlement, were applied fairly systematically. They constituted an ethnographic discourse that delineated the extent of participation in the empire in a new way. The terms of differentiation within it were not physical, moral, religious, geographical, or above all ethnic, but had to do with military obligations, legal access, and land. They were occupational labels. The newcomers' responsibilities put them under imperial control, but—and this is the most important point—at the same time deliberately kept them formally apart in some way from the broader provincial populations. In this regard, Roman citizenship continued to play its ancient role as a primary marker of identity and full participation in the state, but now with important modifications. The newly ascribed statuses for incomers to the Empire came only with a partial measure of citizenship, and deliberately so. The late antique terms of inclusion were meant to limit full participation, not enable it.

In this way, Roman law provided a symbolic portal for foreigners to enter Roman space and take on a formal status they did not have before. It enabled and marked transition into Roman society at some determined level of subordination and service. Roman ascription of identifying labels to foreign groups imposed a specific place within the empire's structure, encoded in the law.

[18] INTRODUCTION

This ethnographic representation was in step with the entrenched belief of the Roman governing elite in the transformative and stabilizing power of Roman law within a world in constant flux.

The historical stakes implicit in this discursive system about law and inclusion were high. When Romans lost the power to ascribe identities, that is, to label incoming peoples in terms of their service to the state, the newcomers and their descendants inevitably revised their own identities to form new communities independent of Rome.

Chapter 4, "Divine Providence and the Power of the Stars," and chapter 5, "The Controlling Hand of the Environment," turn to Christianity's contribution to ethnographic thought by examining how Christian writers neutralized ideas about the control exercised by the stars and the geographical environment over human affairs and made God's Providence the operative force instead. They radically recast identity as a choice, not a consequence of astral or geographical influence. Astral and environmental determinism were in dialogue, but were discrete enough to be treated separately.

In antiquity it was widely held that the character of human communities was shaped by the stars and by the earth's terrain. These natural forces were invoked to explain how and why people lived as they did. In Late Antiquity, however, Christian theorists largely discredited astral and environmental determinism. They nevertheless appropriated these ethnographic discourses by pulling the power of the stars and the earthly environment into a Christian realm of explanation. Rough terrain could still be the breeding ground of barbarism, but its force could be overcome by the introduction of Christian worship. At the same time, for many people, inhospitable geography became a site where holiness might be found through ascetic practice. It no longer was simply the breeding ground of barbarism. The stars still shone, but as no more than signs of divine authority. Such changes point to a reimagining of the cosmos in Christian terms and the appearance of new rationales for ethnographic judgment. Displacing old forms of determinism reflected a recentering of humanity's place in a Christian cosmos and provided new possibilities for the creation of communities of Christian belief.

Chapter 6, "Christianity and the Descendants of Noah," is the first of two chapters that address how Christian interpretations of verses in the Book of Genesis significantly contributed to the Roman ethnographic corpus. The biblical story of the Table of Nations (Gen. 10) provided new genealogies for the world's peoples and an explanation of their dispersal and, indirectly, a place in salvation history. Christian writers redrew the mental map of the world and its populations as it was divided among Noah's three sons and their progeny, creating a new narrative of origins for the *oikoumene* that would be a foundational element in medieval historiography.

Chapter 7, "Babel and the Languages of Faith," deals with the account of the Tower of Babel (Gen. 11:1–9), which let Christian thinkers find new

EMPIRES NEED ETHNOGRAPHY [19]

meaning in the world's linguistic diversity. Combined with the Gospel story of Pentecost in which divine instruction was comprehensible in all languages, the story of Babel provided opportunities for the spread of the faith. With speakers of all languages able to receive religious truths, communities of interpretation of sacred texts found voice in different languages. Powerful communities emerged that claimed correct understanding of the faith and jostled for political agency. Consequently, previously marginal languages that were now yoked to expression of belief undercut the primacy of Latin, the language of imperial power. By making language difference a high-profile concern, Christian writers profoundly recast Roman ethnographic certainties.

Chapter 8, "The New Ethnography of Christian Heresy," discusses another far-reaching Christian contribution to the ethnographic corpus. This was the discourse of heresiology, which offered entirely new criteria of differentiation, judgment, and inclusion within the imperial community. Differences about belief and practice had been present in Christian communities since their beginning, but in the hothouse atmosphere of late antique political and religious life, heresiology came into its own. It sprang from Christians' understanding of their sacred texts and fueled endless arguments.

Heresiology was anchored in the idea of correct belief, determined through interpretation of text and formulated in doctrine. By providing distinct criteria of difference among Christian communities, the discourse of heresiology not only politicized heterodoxy, it also provided new definitions of community within the Roman Empire as it came to understand itself as a Christian enterprise. When the state claimed to be the enforcer of Orthodox belief, heresy became a crime. At the same time, heresiology provided a different set of standards for judging and interacting with foreign cultures.

Churchmen were essential in articulating and enforcing these ideas about difference among Christian communities. We can see them as ethnographers, in their own way the equals of Caesar and the other elite writers of the pre-Christian age. In the eyes of pious believers in this reimagined world, heretics became in a sense the new barbarians, beyond the pale of acceptability.

"Conclusion: The Conqueror's Gift" summarizes long-term developments in the Roman ethnographic universe. It reviews the various ethnographic dossiers that Romans used in evaluating foreigners. Together they constituted the imperial ethnographic infrastructure that supported imperial practice and self-awareness.

Next, the chapter reviews the contributions of Christianity. When the religion entered the imperial scene, it deeply affected the existing ethnographic registers, giving them a new focus through a Christian lens. At the same time, the faith brought to the ethnographic table vibrant new possibilities for seeing and evaluating differences among communities and individuals. Roman ethnography was transformed. By the end of our period, the revitalized ethnographic corpus collectively underwrote something not seen before in antiquity, namely a world in which faith became a primary identifier not just for individuals or local groups but for large-scale communities of worship and states as well. The Roman state in identifying itself with certain Christian interpretations of text and belief, took a leading role in shaping a new, sectarian world order.

The chapter turns finally to the question of what constituted the conqueror's gift of this book's title. The ethnographic infrastructure that had developed over the centuries constituted the gift. We will consider it in three ways: as something beneficial to the Romans and well received by them; as an unwelcome set of ideas imposed on outsiders; and finally, as a legacy for us.

CHAPTER ONE

Conquest and Curiosity

CREATING A ROMAN IMPERIAL ETHNOGRAPHY

Each man has a name given him by his enemies.

—ZELDA MISHKOVSKY, "EACH MAN HAS A NAME"[1]

Introduction

As members of the Roman ruling elite competed for mastery of the Mediterranean world and its hinterlands in the late first century BCE, their cultural
and geographical horizons greatly expanded from the Atlantic Ocean to the
Red Sea. During this period of rapid growth, Rome produced generals well
known for their brutality, cunning, and ambition. For these men success in
the domestic political arena went hand in hand with conquest abroad. The
aristocrat Lucius Cornelius Sulla, for example, brought huge tracts of land
under Roman control as far as the foothills of the Atlas Mountain range in
North Africa, while in the next political generation Julius Caesar won Gaul
and briefly led legions into Britain and Germania for the first time. His archrival Pompey the Great campaigned in the Caucasus Mountain region, secured
the Black Sea and the Middle East for Rome, and established a protectorate
in the Crimea, on the edge of Central Asia. In 31 BCE, the craftiest and most
successful politician of them all, Julius Caesar's heir, whom we know as Caesar
Augustus, added Egypt and the Nile's long track into Africa to Rome's domin-
ions as well as territories in the Balkans, Germania, and the Middle East. He
acquired more land for Rome than any other ruler ever would, and he bragged
about the numerous emissaries who came to Rome from India, Scythia, and
other exotic lands to pay their respects.[2]

Rome's new territories and adjacent lands held many peoples with different cultures and often only tenuous prior connections to Rome, if any at all.
Without question, the Roman conquerors had the military and political expertise to engage their new neighbors on a broadly expanding front, but how
were they—as well as the citizens of Rome dazzled by their success—able to
visualize and relate to the newly encountered populations in all their diversity?
Into what imaginative frameworks could they place the deluge of impressions
brought about by Rome's expansion?

[21]

[22] CHAPTER 1

An arsenal of conceptual systems stood ready to assist. Roman leaders could put into action home-grown traditions of viewing and engaging their subjects, allies, and enemies. From an early point in the course of their expansion throughout Italy, there emerged an ideology of incorporation of new peoples into Roman society.[3] Romans could also draw upon a quite varied Greek technical literature, the Greek ethnographic legacy, to help them define their own place among the peoples of the world.[4] Romans may have conquered the world, but they did not entirely invent it; Greek ethnographic writing of different sorts helped them construct their vision of the earth's inhabitants, and so influenced how they carried out the business of empire.

Case Studies: Roman Ethnography before Late Antiquity

Writers in the Roman sphere during the formative early imperial period developed ethnographic concepts that would remain constants in the late antique centuries. Some of their material drew from Greek antecedents, but the Roman hands-on experience of expansion contributed even more. This chapter considers a handful of Roman writers as case studies to illustrate the formation of the imperial Roman ethnographic dossier. These figures, some better known than others, are a mixed fellowship: an astronomer, an architect, a geographer, a polymath career officer, a Stoic philosopher, a Greek and a Roman historian, a successful dynast, and above all, a conquering general with an eye on absolute power, Julius Caesar. They have been selected for the diversity of their literary activity and also because their works survive in more than scraps. Focus is not on how one writer may have influenced another, though some debts are clear, but in how they set in play basic ideas that would continue to shape ethnographic thought into the late antique period. Among them we will see Roman versions of the opposition of barbarism and civilization, the emerging centrality of Rome and the accompanying primacy of the emperor, the capacity of Rome to effect change for good or ill in other societies, and the role of geographical setting and distance from Rome in determining a foreign people's character. Indirectly we will encounter the limits of Roman curiosity about other societies and see what Romans cared to know about the peoples whom they encountered in the creation of their empire.

Julius Caesar

Many of the elements that shaped Roman imperial practice and ideology of rule appear in what is perhaps the most familiar passage of ethnographic writing to have reached us from the Roman world, the first paragraph of Julius

Caesar's notorious *Gallic War*, which began as dispatches from the front and became a brilliantly descriptive and self-aggrandizing legitimation of his conquest of Gaul during the years 58–50 BCE.[5] Caesar epitomized a Roman general in his ruthlessness, ambition, and political acumen, but he was also unusually well educated and evidently curious about peoples beyond the empire, at least those with whom he found himself at war. The famous passage begins:

> Gaul is divided into three parts, inhabited respectively by the Belgae, the Aquitani, and a people who call themselves Celts, though we call them Gauls. All of these have different languages, customs, and laws. The Celts are separated from the Aquitani by the river Garonne, from the Belgae by the Marne and the Seine. The Belgae are the bravest of the three peoples, being farthest removed from the highly developed civilization of the Roman Province, least often visited by merchants with enervating luxuries for sale, and nearest to the Germani across the Rhine, with whom they are continually at war. For the same reason the Helvetii are braver then the rest of the Celts; they are in almost daily conflict with the Germani, either trying to keep them out of Switzerland or themselves invading Germania. The region occupied by the Celts, which has one frontier facing north, is bounded by the Rhone, the Garonne, the Atlantic Ocean, and the country of the Belgae; the part of it inhabited by the Sequani and the Helvetii also touches the Rhine. The Belgic territory, facing north and east, runs from the northern frontier of the Celts to the lower Rhine. Aquitania is bounded by the Garonne, the Pyrenees, and the part of the Atlantic coast nearest Spain; it faces north-west.[6]

With these well-crafted sentences Julius Caesar began his account of his conquest of Gaul.[7] Through his words most students of Latin and Roman history are introduced to the maneuvers of Rome's legions under his command and, perhaps just as daunting, to the careful deployment of Latin grammar in the service of an author's goals. In their early schoolroom encounters, Caesar's readers may easily overlook that the sentences do much more than provide an account of his victories. They also reveal certain essential ideas in play in the second half of the first century BCE at the heart of an emerging Roman imperial ethnography that would last—with many changes but also with a surprising conservatism—through Late Antiquity. By the time Caesar entered Gaul, it had become conventional for Roman writers to include ethnographic excursuses in their work,[8] and he did so with exceptional clarity in his treatment of the Gauls.[9] Ideas like the ones Caesar relied upon helped generate a fully fledged imperial ethnography that could complement and support the practical needs of the state.

[24] CHAPTER 1

Several ideas energize Caesar's initial sentences. First, in his concern for the "different languages, customs, and laws" that distinguish the various peoples of Gaul, Caesar employs standard, descriptive tropes of Greek ethnographic analysis; his debt to Greek practice is undeniable.[10] Nevertheless, it must be emphasized that he gives this literary legacy a Roman imperial spin. Though he may follow Greek convention in some regards, the conquest will be linked to Rome in every way possible in a fully Roman language of power, augmented with much vivid detail drawn from his own experience.

With the careful eye of a general appraising a battlefield, Caesar shows concern for geographical setting. Just as he alerts his readers to differences in culture among the Gauls, he introduces them to the landscape on which the battles were fought. This kind of geographical description had become standard with Roman writers, as we see, for example, in his contemporary Sallust's presentation of the North African terrain of the Jugurthine War.[11] Caesar begins his treatise with the sketch of Gaul's landscape with the double-barreled purpose of informing his readers and making it clear to them just how great was his military achievement in overcoming its constraints. From another perspective, and we cannot fault Caesar for what he does not say, neither in this passage nor elsewhere in his treatise does there appear any vision of a Roman Empire with bounded territorial limits. Such an idea is notable in its absence. Caesar's narrative inadvertently raises the question of how description of foreign peoples who challenged Roman power might help develop ideas of the territorial limits of empire and the eventual emergence of the concept of "barbaricum."[12]

Geographical space carries further explanatory force as well. Caesar presents distance from Rome as a measure of barbarism, making Rome implicitly the hub and source of civilized values and the baseline of the registers of cultural difference upon which Roman ethnography depended. He tells us that the Belgae are the bravest of all the Gauls because they live the farthest away from the civilized life of the Roman province in southern Gaul and because they are closest to the Germani, a people who live across the Rhine with whom they are continually at war.[13] Later in the narrative the savagery of the Germani will play an important role in the unrolling of events and in justifying his war of conquest,[14] and the Rhine will be presented—conveniently if not necessarily accurately—as a cultural barrier between Germani and Gauls.[15] The lands that Caesar describes lie far from the city of Rome, which was not coincidentally the home of the readers of his war reports and the source of the political power that he so ardently pursued. Caesar directs every word of his narrative to an audience in the city of Rome; the city's central focus is practically a combatant in its own right.

It is worth noting in this regard that when Caesar composed his war commentaries, writers had long since begun to establish Rome as the notional center of the world and its affairs, but there had not yet emerged an imperial persona on which to anchor that centrality. Dynasts competed for political primacy in Rome with as much callous vigor as they devoted to imposing their will over foreign peoples.[16] They celebrated their achievements in public art and architecture. For example, Pompey, who was Caesar's greatest rival, commemorated his victories over many peoples on three continents by displaying statues representing them in his theater complex near the Forum in Rome.[17] Though composed in a different medium, Caesar's celebratory account of his victorious wars in Gaul matched Pompey's public expression of foreign expansion. Both men presented themselves as triumphant benefactors of Rome. The figure of the *princeps* as a universal victor and enabler of civilization that Augustus and his advisers invented, however, still lay decades in the future. In Andrew Riggsby's words, "Caesar prefigures in small but important ways the coming imperial order, establishing a link between empire and Empire."[18]

Caesar's commanding authorial voice heard so distinctly in the *Gallic Wars*, as well as his presence at the center of events in Gaul, however, point directly to the manifestation of imperial presence that Augustus and his successors would perfect. Caesar's mention of the Province (modern Provence, in southern France) reminds us that Rome had a very long, home-grown tradition of including peoples within the Roman political system and slowly granting them some degree of citizenship rights.[19] These practices had their origins in the earliest phases of Roman expansion in Italy. Establishing the terms of inclusion and exclusion within the Roman sphere proved to be the source of considerable political strife at Rome, and it was also fundamental to the development of Roman ethnography. Of course, Caesar could not have known that one day all of Gaul would be part of the Roman Empire's heartland. At the moment that he prepared his account of conquest, he could only see the inhabitants of Gaul as sometimes friendly to Rome, but more often hostile and savage to various degrees. Caesar made the most of a discourse of enmity and friendship, turning all possibilities to his advantage.

Caesar fully understood the long-term consequences of his campaigns on the people of Gaul. He knew that Roman culture could transform other peoples, for good or ill. In Gaul's southernmost region, for example, in the territory that Rome had controlled since the previous century, Roman civilization flourished, a positive occurrence in his eyes and his readers'. He accepts a widely held belief in the Hellenistic Age that the intermingling of cultures brings civilization. In the case of the Province, it was the presence of Rome that made the difference. Looking at the other side of the coin, Caesar states that Roman civilization can also have a corrupting and enervating effect on a foreign culture. He notes that the Belgae manage to retain their native courage because they dwell farthest away from the corruption that Roman civilization can bring, in this case through the agency of effeminizing commerce. Caesar's

[26] CHAPTER 1

candid observation suggests that an ambivalent view of the impact of Rome might be found among Rome's governing elite. Later authors would elaborate on this theme well into the late antique period. Eventually, Rome's corruption would play a significant role in some strands of Christian views of the world.

The unimaginable violence of Caesar's war on the peoples of Gaul helped create new knowledge for Romans and Gauls alike.[20] It generated a "middle ground" in which Gauls were disjoined from their pre-Roman pasts and opened possibilities for the creation of new pasts and identities under a mantle of Rome's own celebratory cultural narratives.[21] For Romans, Caesar's account of his astounding successes pulled together many staples of subsequent ethnographic discussion within a Roman frame.[22]

The Greek Backstory

The Greek tradition of description and investigation that lies behind Caesar's work held a venerable pedigree. At least from Homer's day in the early Archaic Age (ca. 750 BCE), as Greek merchants and explorers began to encounter new cultures in their travels, and as ideas and material goods from Asia Minor flooded Greek communities, Greeks developed a new range of ideas about the peculiarities of the different peoples of the world and what they had to offer.[23] In the fifth century BCE, when Rome was still a small community in central Italy, long before Greek intellectuals showed any concern for its existence,[24] Greeks began to put their ideas in writing. There emerged a sophisticated ethnographic literature, often tied to historical and geographical explanation, that described and evaluated the external world. The so-called Classical Age, the era that followed the unexpected victory of a small coalition of Greek forces led by Sparta and Athens against Persian invaders (492–449 BCE), saw the appearance of writers who set the terms of discussion for many centuries to come. Among them was Herodotus, the "Father of History," who traveled to Egypt, Babylon, the Crimea, and many other lands, and incorporated lengthy and sometime fanciful digressions about foreign peoples in his account of the Persian War. Pseudo-Hippocrates, an otherwise unknown author who brought the insights of a physician to, among other things, the question of the influence of natural surroundings on human character and communities. These writers laid the foundations of different forms of ethnographic writing that were still vigorous when Islam entered the picture more than a millennium later.[25]

The conquests of Alexander the Great in the fourth century and the subsequent creation of a Greek cultural, though not politically unified, realm reaching from Gibraltar to the edges of central Asia vastly increased the scope of curiosity and scientific inquiry about foreign societies. Greek became an international language of learning as well as of commerce and political control, and Alexander became the model for all ambitious rulers across the Mediterranean for many centuries to come. Encounters with peoples unfamiliar to Greek culture as well as the development of new centers of power in different Hellenistic kingdoms generated an increasingly complex approach to the world, its inhabitants, and their interrelations. The unequal relation of ruling Greek elites to indigenous populations, constant tensions with peoples beyond the Greek sphere, and rivalry among the Hellenistic Greek kingdoms helped frame ethnographic description and discussion. Also at this time, astrology entered the ethnographic dossier in a significant way.[26] In a hothouse atmosphere, Hellenistic *erudits* produced a fat dossier of useful concepts, organizational questions, and analytical practices that were often taken on board by literate peoples of different heritage—Jews, Egyptians, Babylonians, and Persians— even if sometimes they might write critically about Greek culture.[27] In like fashion, members of the Roman ruling elite gradually adopted much of the Greek conceptual legacy as they extended their own intellectual and geographical field of vision during the late Republican period. They dipped into it as need and interest required, but they always made it their own, suiting the needs of Roman imperial practice as the excerpt from the *Gallic Wars* has suggested, and as we will see below. Caesar and his military colleagues were awash in Greek intellectuals writing various sorts of ethnographic accounts.[28] Roman conquest and curiosity created an environment most amenable to ethnographic writing.

What Was in the Greek Ethnographic Dossier?

Because not all readers of this book will be familiar with the Greek ethnographic toolkit, it may be helpful here to review central topics of interest and discussion. It is worth remembering that, as noted in the Introduction, Greeks had no specific term to match our modern usage of "ethnography" as a specialized kind of investigation,[29] yet ethnographic interest was everywhere. Greg Woolf rightly distinguishes between ethnographic knowledge and writing in an ethnographic mode.[30] We should view ethnography, in his words, "as a set of writing practices, based on traditions of enquiry and interpretation."[31]

Greeks responded strongly to their encounters with foreign peoples and embedded their responses in a wide array of texts in different genres. Their highly judgmental descriptions often included the physical geography of a given area, as well as its climate, agricultural produce, mineral resources, and exotic phenomena of all sorts. They showed interest in the origins of a people as well as the physical features of its members and its political, social, and military organization.[32] They wondered about the causes of the commonalities and the significant differences between themselves and other peoples.

From such concerns there gradually arose in the fifth and fourth centuries a complicated discourse of barbarism and civilization that rested on a polarity between Greek and non-Greek realms.[33] At the simplest level, "barbarian" (βάρβαρος) indicated contrast with a civilized Greek man.[34] This has been the most influential and long-lasting element of Greek ethnography. Sometimes it is treated as the only judgment call, but such was not the case. The cultural polarity of barbarian and civilized instead was a complex literary construct by no means absolutely equivalent to conditions on the ground, and it could be variously interpreted. The opposition was often belied by observable practices and belief. Only in the most extreme literary contexts did it evoke unbridgeable divisions.

Contrasts with the barbarian were a measuring stick that did not rule out appreciation of foreign cultures or prevent drawing and assimilating elements from them. Quite the opposite was true. Appreciation of foreign cultures could be nuanced and positive.[35] In standard use for nearly half a millennium before it came into Roman hands as *barbarus*, the word, with its wide semantic range, was used differently at different times and places throughout the late antique period and beyond.[36]

Causation was a concern, not just in the explanation of events, but in the making of human character. What made a barbarian barbaric? Greeks wondered if nature, by means of geographical location or the position of the stars, shaped the character of communities and individuals.[37] A huge literature developed that explored questions of natural determinism. Taking the next step, some wondered if what nature determines might be altered or circumvented by *human* action. Because the distinction between barbarians and Greeks was cultural, not somatic,[38] the possibility of change within human societies was accepted.

Greek writers wondered about the role of human institutions in shaping the particularity of cultures. Were human institutions capable of determining the character of a people or of an individual? To what extent might the pursuit of *paideia*, a deep education in the fundamentals of Greek moral and intellectual life, be a catalyst of transformation? The institutions of the polis took an instrumental role in these discussions. The possibility of change within communities and an individual's life remained strong, a further indication that the lines between barbarism and civilization were not absolute.

Related questions arose especially in the vast, multiethnic Hellenistic kingdoms that sprang up on the territories conquered by Alexander. What should be the relation between political dominion and cultural and ethnic identity, especially that of subject peoples? What were the limits of participation within the Greek-speaking dominant community? Such concerns lead us to consider the place of ethnography within the theory and practice of empire. They pave the way for consideration of how law and legal status could establish a particular set of terms of inclusion and exclusion from the dominant community and so become an ethnographic discourse.

Rome Enters the Picture and Claims Center Stage

Roman contact with Greek communities in southern Italy and Sicily began as early as the fifth century BCE, with much spillover of Greek ideas. By the late fourth and early third centuries, Romans could refer to their expansion into Italy in terms of the imperialism of the Athenians and Macedonians.[39] It was during the second century BCE, however, as the Roman state rose to preeminence in the Hellenistic Mediterranean world that Greek ethnography and Roman power started to come together in a way that bolstered Roman views of themselves and their place in the inhabited world (*orbis terrarum* or *oikoumene*). The extension of international hegemony provoked for Romans a new consideration of the world's peoples, whether already known, previously unfamiliar, or only on the edges of awareness.[40] In the course of their exposure to broader intellectual horizons that came with contact with foreign cultures, the educated elite that guided Roman affairs absorbed many of the conceptual paradigms developed by Greek scientists to classify and analyze human communities. Arnaldo Momigliano called this an "easy-going absorption of Greek culture."[41]

Romans did not receive this Greek legacy thoughtlessly, however. In their hands ethnographic expression took different turns, changing through the centuries as the empire evolved. In the new international environment that Roman power created across the Mediterranean region, Roman writers (and some Greeks and other provincials in the Roman orbit) mimicked, altered, combined, challenged, and expanded upon the Greek dossier of analytical possibilities. For example, in the early second century, the comic playwright Titus Maccius Plautus (d. 184 BCE) amused his Roman audiences by calling them "barbarians" in several of his works.[42] Others wrote in various genres with as much subtlety as their talent and political circumstances permitted. Roman values and ethical sensibilities, not Greek ones, informed their judgment of foreign peoples. The result was a particularly Roman ethnography well suited to the context and needs of an expanding state. Greek formulations found a place in a Roman worldview in which expansion, conquest, assimilation, and a wide range of diplomatic exchanges were predominant activities. Roman imperialism did not create ethnography nor was ethnography's purpose to initiate or legitimize imperial activity, but the two worked together to shape Roman perceptions of the world during the centuries of greatest expansion. If Rome was to conquer the world and become its center, it would be a world described to a large extent in terms first established in the Greek scientific conceptual repertoire.

The element most strikingly absent from the Greek accounts of the inhabited world, however, was the hard fact of Roman power at the center of world affairs and as the primary agent of change on the international scene. This silence did not last long. Polybius, a Greek intellectual in the Roman sphere (see below) and others, both Greek and Roman, began to analyze Rome's rise in these terms at the mid-second century BCE, following the final defeat of Carthage. The move to writing imperial ethnography was on. Through the eyes of writers of the day, we can watch Roman leaders learning to think of their political community as an imperial state at the forefront of international affairs rather than as a constellation of Hellenistic cities, and they viewed those beyond their community in terms that related them to Roman power and values.

Claiming the Center

Essential to Rome's positioning itself among the nations was claiming center stage, both practically and symbolically. Achieving that would be essential to Roman imperial ethnography in all its forms. "Claiming the center" is shorthand for a series of appropriations and redirections of preexisting patterns of thought, action, and expression. It is the piecemeal accretion of the symbols, practices, justifications, and apparatus of imperial rule. Achieving the center was the sum of countless actions and decisions. "Rome" meant both the Roman way of life in general terms and the city of Rome itself.

We see this centrality played out in the city's topography, in its mundane and red-letter rituals and the architectural spaces in which they were enacted; in the focus on the emperor as prime patron and facilitator of public acts; in the promulgation of laws that set the terms of inclusion within the privileged community of its citizens; and in the fact that what happened in Rome was widely imitated wherever Romans held power and beyond, where it did not.

With centrality came normativity, its reliable accomplice. As the dominant political power, Rome claimed the moral high ground and the right to regularize and control the lives of its subjects. Rome set the rules of conduct through law or custom through which difference might be measured and inclusion within the community determined. Deeply rooted assumptions and practices, even if they changed over time, were the starting point for judging outsiders. As described in the Introduction, a number of registers of difference spun out from the normative center. These were the ethnographic discourses pursued in the chapters of this book.

How did Rome establish its centrality? The first way was by the acquisition of international authority, chiefly by force of arms. The goal of conquerors always was to win glory and political influence as much as it was to defend and extend the state. One natural consequence of their success was that the city of Rome became the focal point of political action across the Mediterranean basin. What happened in Rome, however, did not stay in Rome. Decisions made there about war and peace rolled out to affect millions of lives. On the urban stage, patterns of political behavior, social activity, architectural planning, religious ritual, and a host of other habits of daily existence were imported by lesser cities throughout the empire, serving as a template for urban life throughout the Mediterranean region. Little would-be Romes popped up across the map as members of local elites competed to win power and embellish their towns in emulation of aristocrats in the capital.

Rome's early climb to power in Italy provided lasting mechanisms used during its later expansion into the Mediterranean. From a very early time in their history, according to Nicholas Purcell, Romans had "specialized in centrality,"[43] institutionally and symbolically, as the focal point for the support of allies across Italy. With the establishment of a pan-Mediterranean empire, that specialization took on new significance for them as well as for this book, for the conquest of the center provided the motor for the development of all Rome's ethnographic systems, including their adaptations of the Greek repertoire.

A second way to the center was with the pen. Katherine Clarke has described how, as Rome became the hub of power in the Mediterranean landscape, writers responded by creating a view of the inhabited world that gave Rome a privileged, central position. This was not a deliberate task they set for themselves, and there was no programmatic approach, but as we will see below, they began to position events and places in relation to Rome. That is to say, Roman power provided, or at least suggested the need for, a new rationale for ordering and focusing knowledge about the world. While Clarke does not address ethnography directly, her treatment of geographical and historical writing, in which ethnography consistently appeared, makes a fundamental point: There was an early and intimate connection between the Roman elite's understanding of its power and the description of the people they did and did not yet rule.

Authors wrote Rome into the Hellenistic geographic tradition. For example, in some accounts Rome displaced Rhodes as the center of the map, which it had been since the third century BCE, when Timosthenes, a Greek admiral in the service of Ptolemy II Philadelphus, described his home city, Rhodes, as the center.[44] Other writers who did not originate in the capital city continued to heap praise upon Rome, helping to craft a vision of its centrality. Perhaps the most vivid of these praisemongers was Aelius Aristides, a Greek rhetorician of the second century CE, whose hyperbolically over-the-top "Ode to Rome," presented on a visit to the imperial city in 155, exclaimed that all the world's resources flowed into the city and that Rome was to the entire world as every other city was to its surrounding countryside.[45] For Aristides, the entire world had become peripheral to the capital city.

A third way to claim the center was through the fashioning of the emperor. The emergence of the figure of the emperor that came with the ascendancy of Augustus after 31 BCE proved essential in creating the Roman center. His adoptive father and predecessor Julius Caesar had won control of the political arena and entertained monarchical plans of some sort, but lacked the time before his assassination to develop institutions and political practices that would ensure that his primacy would be passed to an heir. How Augustus and his advisers slowly and carefully contrived the new imperial system that established him as the focus and source of all power is one of history's great tales of a successful political revolution, though one shamelessly posing as a restoration of tradition. Additionally, as will be discussed below, there emerged in the Augustan age the idea of a territorial empire, of which he was the center because he held ultimate, overriding power and the ability to effect change everywhere. Romans often elaborated on the possibility of change and transformation of non-Roman peoples while embracing tradition and ancestral custom. One of the major developments that we will see in the chapters ahead is how the empire and eventually the emperor functioned as legitimate agents of cultural change.

A final means to seizing centrality was to create the apparatus of empire that let new people be included in the system in productive ways. Romans offered a universal language of inclusion and transformation that had legal as well as cultural dimensions. Legal forms helped give shape to this and it let imperial power be felt in the peripheries. This apparatus depended on the participation of provincial cities and contributed to the elaboration of a territorial view of empire. The spread of Roman culture throughout the empire's vast domains happened slowly, but once established it provided a focus of identity. Eventually Christianity would provide another centralizing discourse.

The goal of conquest and imposition of Roman rule was not to compel cultural change through law or any other means. To become Roman remained an option, not an obligation for people under Rome's sway. Emperors held true to Aeneas's promise to respect indigenous traditions that Vergil described in the *Aeneid*.[46] Yet becoming Roman remained a possibility for all, with citizenship a valued prize.

We turn now to the case studies mentioned above to see evidence of the slow buildup of ethnographic ideas that would long remain in force.

Case Studies: Roman Ethnography before Late Antiquity

POLYBIUS, THE GREEK HISTORIAN

In the formative period of Roman imperial ethnography, the first author to consider must be Polybius. Impressed by Rome's success in conquering "nearly the whole inhabited world" in the span of "less than fifty-three years,"[47] Polybius (ca. 200–ca. 118 BCE) made Rome's rise to power in the Mediterranean the subject of a detailed and moralizing inquiry.[48] Born a century before Julius Caesar, he had come to Rome as a political hostage, and he chose to remain there as a privileged observer and commentator on the unfolding of

CONQUEST AND CURIOSITY [33]

events. Roman power fascinated him. His histories focus on political action and constitutional developments in the Roman Republic during this period of dizzying success.

Polybius directed his analysis at an aristocratic audience at Rome, where he was a welcome member of the coterie of Scipio Aemilianus, the victor over Carthage in the Third Punic War (149–146 BCE).[49] He developed for their edification the flattering image of the ideal Roman citizen as an aristocrat who was self-controlled, rational, politically responsible, and mindful of his duty to protect his community from the "forces of disorder and chaos that threatened it everywhere."[50] Doing so entailed placing Rome at the center of the peoples of the world. A sophisticated ethnographic analysis involving distance from a Roman center resulted. Arthur Eckstein explains that Polybius saw civilized life threatened by "several concentric circles of menace."[51] The outermost ring contained the violent and aggressive barbarians who threatened the peace and security of civilized communities. Closer to home were mercenaries, who were uncivilized peoples employed with potentially catastrophic results by civilized states. Next came the urban masses who could disrupt civilized life if not well controlled. The last menace appeared within the aristocratic household itself, posed by women and young aristocratic men, who by nature were undisciplined and needed a firm hand. By mastering these obstacles with courage and firmness, the virtuous aristocrat would stabilize civilization and enjoy its benefits appropriately. Aided by their constitution, the Romans had come to embody these positive virtues and so gained their preeminent place in the world.

Polybius's model of ethical resistance to chaos across a wide spectrum, from irrational forces in the home to the savage atrocities of barbarians on the frontier, is intimately linked to Roman expansion. Barbarians, the embodiment of disorder, became an integral part of his analysis. His notion of the virtuous aristocrat at the center of affairs, combatting chaos in its many forms, anticipates the self-image crafted by Augustus.

POSIDONIUS, THE STOIC PHILOSOPHER

One of the most prominent philosophers of science of the late Hellenistic period and a foundational figure in the emergence of an imperial Roman ethnography was the Stoic polymath Posidonius of Apamea (ca. 135–51 BCE). This Syrian Greek established a school on Rhodes that became the focal point of Stoicism and the leading intellectual center in the eastern Mediterranean. The amazement shown by Polybius at the remarkable speed of Rome's rise had given place in Posidonius's mind to an after-the-fact feeling of inevitability. He saw Rome's preeminence not as the consequence of constitutional, military, or moral factors, but of suprahuman ones. He believed that Rome's rapid ascent could be explained by understanding the interplay of cosmic forces, of which

Rome was one agent, and their effect on human affairs.[52] He wrote on an extraordinarily broad range of subjects, including the natural sciences, moral philosophy, ethnology, and history. His works remained influential through Late Antiquity, but unfortunately none of them survives intact.[53]

Posidonius's *History* in fifty-two books covered the period from 146 BCE, coincidentally the point at which Polybius ended his coverage, to the mid-eighties BCE. In the second half of this century, Roman power continued to expand dramatically. The work embraced the entire Mediterranean world and the peoples surrounding it. In addition to Rome and Greece, major sections dealt with Egypt and Africa, Asia Minor, Spain, the Celtic world, and European peoples not yet in Rome's grasp. He used the wealth of information that he gathered about these different people to help explain events. Posidonius obtained some of his material firsthand while on trips to the western Mediterranean, probably in the nineties, at which time he visited Rome on an embassy and likely consulted its libraries.[54] During his visits to Rome he established ties to many influential men, including Pompey and Cicero.[55]

Katherine Clarke surmises that Posidonius's various studies displayed a unified view of the world in response to the growth of the Roman state.[56] Just as his *History* dealt with the Mediterranean lands, Posidonius's treatise *On Ocean*, she argues, brought together in a particularly potent fashion scientific understanding of the world and the political realities of Roman expansion. Because the Ocean was widely believed to surround the inhabited world, it marked the imagined limits of world conquest attempted by Alexander the Great and his imitators, as well as Pompey and Julius Caesar, whose *Gallic Wars* drew to some degree from Posidonius's writings.[57] Clarke rightly suggests that Posidonius's effort to explain Rome's conquest of the world as far as the Ocean and the many different peoples that came under Roman domination was a "rewriting" of the world in light of new realities. His large-scale objectives must be deduced from the fragments, but it seems likely that he gave Rome a central place in his presentation of the world.[58]

Posidonius knew the Hippocratic treatise *Airs, Waters, Places* and is credited with helping to pass its ideas about environmental and astral determinism to writers in the Roman period,[59] though the extent to which there were direct ties is hard to determine because so much of his writing is lost.[60] He developed a new method of geographical description that involved a significant ethnographical component. He divided terrestrial space in two ways, which resulted in much confusion in later writers. First, he divided the earth into zones, which he believed determined the characteristics of ethnic groups. There were, for example, an Ethiopian zone, a Scythian, and a Celtic zone, the inhabitants of which had different physical and cultural features. Next, he also divided the earth into *klimata*, an idea taken from Greek science, but in a different way from *Airs, Waters, Places*. In his hands, these *klimata*, which had nothing to do with climate in the modern sense, were seven parallel, longitudinal divisions of the earth extending from the mouth of the Dnieper River in the north to Meroe, far south on the Nile River, in modern Sudan.[61] They were geographical descriptors but not cultural or somatic determiners. Posidonius must be reckoned as a major presence in subsequent ethnography, for the information about foreign cultures that he supplied and for his explanations of their differences in scientific terms.

JULIUS CAESAR, AGAIN

Not only did Julius Caesar conquer Gaul, where we left him at the beginning of this chapter, he triumphed in a civil war against the forces marshaled by the Senate in Rome. While consolidating his regime and attempting various reforms in Rome just before his assassination in 44 BCE, he sent scientists to the four corners of his domain. Their mission was to describe the geography and inhabitants of the known world, including all territory under Roman control. The document recording their findings, known as the *Cosmography of Julius Caesar*, took more than thirty years to complete, appearing only during the reign of his heir, the emperor Augustus. Though the *Cosmography* does not survive in its entirety, it does represent an important step in the Roman imperial enterprise at the very end of the Republic and the beginning of the Pax Romana.[62] It shows the Romans staking out an imperial landscape on the ground that proved fundamental for later ethnographic developments.

The specialists who led the expeditions, four otherwise unknown Greek geographers called Nicodemus, Didymus, Theudotus, and Polyclitus, came to the following conclusions: "The inhabited world has 28 oceans, 74 islands, 35 mountains, 70 provinces, 264 towns, 52 rivers, and 129 peoples." We should not be concerned that this list may not in fact be accurate. What does matter is the effort itself to count the physical features of the inhabited world and to include the number of different peoples on that list. For Caesar and his scientists, a complete inventory of the world must contain its peoples as well as its geographical features.

Compiling such a report as this was not a novel enterprise in the classical world, though it was for Romans. Alexander had taken scientists of all sorts on his mission of world conquest, setting the precedent for Caesar and other would-be world conquerors who followed him, such as Napoleon, who brought 150 *savants* on his Egyptian expedition from 1798 to 1801.[63] Caesar's mission of exploration indicates his global ambitions as well as a desire to give a comprehensive order to his realm. As the originator of the project, Caesar was laying claim to mastery of the world for himself and for Rome.

[36] CHAPTER 1

CAESAR AUGUSTUS, THE SUCCESSFUL DYNAST

Standing on the legacy of Julius Caesar, Augustus created the last and most successful monarchy of the Hellenistic world. His reign was a seminal period for Rome, during which a new imperial ethnography coalesced.

A few words must be said about Augustus's genius in comprehending and exploiting the ideological potential of Rome's centrality in the world. He took steps to make the city a symbol of his universal power, and the impact of his actions was revolutionary.[64] He linked an already long tradition of Roman centrality to the new regime, rendering it a staple of imperial self-presentation.[65] He made adept use of monumental construction to further this goal. The complex of buildings around his mausoleum in the Campus Martius best exemplifies his new rhetoric of empire. His tomb imitated that of Alexander the Great in Alexandria, a not very subtle nod from one world conqueror to another. On columns in front of the building Augustus installed bronze tablets onto which his official biography, the *Res Gestae* (*My Accomplishments*), was inscribed. At first glance a straightforward listing of military and political achievements, the document also contains much geographical information that illustrates the full extent of his reach. He describes the world and names many exotic foreign peoples with whom ties have been made through conquest or diplomacy.[66] The point is clear and unequivocal: no lands are too far away to avoid Rome's grasp. Under his command, Rome has won control of the civilized world.[67] In Claude Nicolet's words, "For him . . . the empire was a world, almost a new world which had been discovered, explored, and mastered. It is within a real geographic context that it came about. And it is within this context that the *princeps* should be recognized and admired by his readers."[68] An appreciation of the world's peoples in deference to Roman power is an important element of his self-presentation.

Not far from the mausoleum stood the Altar of Peace, constructed in marble in 13 BCE to replace a temporary structure set up when Augustus returned to the city after establishing peace in the western provinces four years earlier. The altar had an elaborate, carefully developed iconographic program illustrating Augustus's place in Roman history.[69] One of its reliefs, for example, shows Aeneas, the legendary founder of the Roman people and his own direct ancestor, making a sacrifice just as Augustus had done at the celebration of his own return. The marble Altar of Peace linked Aeneas and Augustus together for all time and placed Augustus at the control center of Roman history as well as between gods and men. There are also possible allusions to Rome's central place within the inhabited world. Two children depicted on the altar in foreign clothing have been identified as barbarians from the eastern and western portions of the empire.[70]

Some distance from the mausoleum and the altar stood an obelisk taken from Egypt, which is mentioned in the public biography as evidence of Augustus's control of that great kingdom. This obelisk was put to use as the spine of a huge sundial. The shadow that it cast on Augustus's birthday passed directly through the Altar of Peace and also was in line with the axis of the Mausoleum. In this way, Augustus's horoscope was tied to the topography of the city of Rome and to world rule and world peace.[71] In Nicolet's words, "[Augustus's] achievement was spatial, temporal, and political. It was considered the accomplishment of a divine will that had assigned to Rome the destiny of . . . pacifying and organizing the whole world: *Tu regere imperio populos, Romane, memento* [Remember, Roman, yours will be the rulership of nations]."[72] It was with these words that Vergil famously imagined Anchises instructing his son Aeneas in the Underworld.[73] These were the very tasks undertaken by the Augustan regime.

Another important element in the evolution of an imperial ethnography was the emergence of the idea of a bounded empire. During the latter part of Augustus's reign, the idea of a territorial empire anchored to the figure of the *princeps* came into its own.[74] *Imperium*, which had previously denoted only the authority granted to magistrates to implement their decisions,[75] now meant both the power to control territories and the entirety of the territories themselves. Imperium included the city of Rome and its institutions as the source of authority. Similarly, *provincia* came to mean more than a task or military command given to a magistrate who held imperium. It now indicated the block of land to be governed, a province.[76]

The idea of a permanent territorial empire was something new. Strabo, writing at the end of Augustus's reign and the beginning of Tiberius's ascendancy (see below, on Strabo), and presumably representing views held by the governing elite, viewed the empire as divided into specific areas, the provinces, into which magistrates were sent. Ideally, Augustus's imperium embraced the whole world,[77] but in reality he came to know there were limits, as, according to Tacitus, he explained to Tiberius at the end of his life.[78] That territorial limits existed for the empire gradually came to be accepted in the next centuries.[79]

The expression of these ideas had an immediate effect on ethnography. In Caesar's day, *gentes*, the peoples of the world without Roman citizenship, might be found both inside and beyond Roman boundaries.[80] From the Augustan age, however, as the idea of living inside or outside a territorial empire was coming into being, new parameters for ethnographic discussion were emerging as well. As we will see, by Late Antiquity, people were described in the law as barbarians only if they lived outside the empire; once inside, they received another ascription of identity. The term *barbaricum*, meaning barbarian lands, particularly in northern Europe, seems to have been used first in the early third century.[81]

This approach to the empire found expression on the giant world map commissioned in his will for the people of Rome by Augustus's loyal associate

Marcus Vipsanius Agrippa. Located in the Porticus Vipsania not far from the Forum, it was meant to display the entire inhabited world, not just the city of Rome.[82] Whether it was carved or painted, or perhaps both, is uncertain, and there was probably an accompanying commentary.[83] The tradition of placing maps in public spaces to illustrate the achievements of victorious generals had begun already in the second century BCE, but they were much smaller in scope.[84] This may have been the first large-scale map to show the division of the world into Europe, Asia, and Africa.[85] In its own way, Agrippa's map and its celebration of Roman power was the culmination of Julius Caesar's *Cosmography*. Territory and empire had become inextricably linked. Some twenty years later, Augustus's public list of achievements, the *Res Gestae*, would list Rome's provinces, making a complementary point about the imperial regime.[86]

VITRUVIUS, THE ARCHITECT

A military engineer who had served under Julius Caesar, Vitruvius drew on his own experience as well as the Greek tradition of writing about architecture to compose a treatise called *On Architecture*, which he addressed to Augustus.

Urbanization had progressed rapidly in the Augustan age, marking a new way of life for many of Rome's subjects, particularly in western Europe. In the words of Christian Goudineau, "The city constituted the fullest expression of a well-ordered and magnificent universe, the safety of which was guaranteed by the *princeps*."[87] Vitruvius's treatise tied the civilizing goals of the new regime both to the spread of cities and to the character of Roman subjects throughout the realm. He presents Rome and Italy as occupying a central and perfect place in the natural sphere.

On Architecture enumerates the buildings that an ideal Augustan city required,[88] and it discusses such matters as town planning, the qualifications of an architect, building materials, measuring land, and methods of construction. There is an overtly recognizable ethnographic component as well: Vitruvius provides a wealth of information about the effect of climate on communities and their architecture. The sixth book of the treatise brings environmental determinism into his professional realm. Vitruvius's purpose is practical, as he writes: "we may remedy by art the harm that comes by chance. In other regions also, buildings are to be similarly adjusted to suit the relation of climate to latitude."[89]

He continues, explaining how natural conditions affect the physique of peoples living in different climes:

> For in those regions where the sun pours forth a moderate heat, he keeps the body duly tempered; where he comes near and the earth scorches, he burns out and removes the moisture; whereas in the cold regions, because they are far distant from the south, the moisture

is not drawn out from their complexions, but the dewy air from the sky pours moisture into the body, enlarges the physique and deepens the voice. Hence, also, the races of the north receive nourishment, and are characterised by tall stature, fair complexion, straight red hair, blue eyes, fullness of blood, owing to the abundance of moisture and the cool climate.[90]

In like fashion, peoples in other regions of the earth have different physical characteristics. Romans have the advantage of the best natural conditions:

Since, therefore, the disposition of the world is such by Nature, and all other nations differ by their unbalanced temperament, it is in the true mean within the space of all the world and the regions of the earth, that the Roman people holds its territory. [11]. For in Italy the inhabitants are exactly tempered in either direction, both in the structure of the body, and by their strength of mind in the matter of endurance and courage. For just as the planet Jupiter is tempered by running in the middle between the heat of Mars and the cold of Saturn, in the same manner Italy presents good qualities which are tempered by admixture from either side both north and south, and are consequently unsurpassed. And so, by its policy, it curbs the courage of the northern barbarians; by its strength, the imaginative south. Thus the divine mind has allotted to the Roman state an excellent and temperate region in order to rule the world.[91]

Vitruvius combines environmental determinism (enabled by the position of the planets), a view of cities conditioned by the Augustan regime, and a certainty about the position of the Roman empire at the center of the natural world and at the center of world affairs.

STRABO, THE GEOGRAPHER

Inspired by the triumphant mood of Augustan Rome, Strabo of Amasia (ca. 64 BCE–after 21 CE) brought a deep knowledge of Hellenistic geography to the service of imperial expansion.[92] The son of an aristocratic, pro-Roman family from Pontus that had probably won Roman citizenship, Strabo believed that Augustus and Tiberius had provided the Romans and their allies unprecedented peace and prosperity, and he meant his magnum opus, the *Geography*,[93] to contribute to further imperial success. The treatise deals with "the world which we inhabit and know"[94] and is meant to benefit Rome: "for governmental purposes there would be no advantage in knowing such countries and their inhabitants, and particularly if the people live in islands which are of such a nature that they can neither injure nor benefit us in any way because of their isolation."[95]

According to Strabo, Rome had a mission to raise conquered peoples from their barbaric ways of life. He hoped that knowledge of geography could help Rome do so. This goes well beyond the *Aeneid*'s statement of Rome's task and is a recurrent theme in his discussion. For Strabo, topography and climate may determine the degree of civilization of people, but acculturation tempers the deterministic model: Rome plays a clear civilizing role.

As a young man Strabo studied philosophy and came to know Posidonius, the influential Stoic polymath, on whose work his *Geography* would draw heavily.[96] An avid traveler as well as a scholar, Strabo befriended Aelius Gallus, who served as the prefect of Egypt from 29 to 26 BCE, and with him explored the Nile as far as Syene (mod. Aswan) and then the borders of Ethiopia.[97] A few years later, Strabo joined Gallus on an unsuccessful invasion of Arabia Felix (Yemen), where he learned the hard way about the difficulties of military expansion into unfamiliar terrain.[98] He also traveled to other places in the Mediterranean.

Like so many of his predecessors, Strabo addressed the significant differences separating communities in terms of an opposition between barbarism and civilization,[99] though he did so in a fashion that allowed Romans to be agents of cultural transformation. Because barbarism was not an absolute category, Rome could bridge the distance between the two cultural conditions. Strabo developed a theory about the progress from barbarism to civilization.[100] Natural conditions first might set the stage for agriculture, as they had in Egypt, North Africa, parts of Europe, and the Indus Valley.[101] With agriculture could come the accumulation of wealth and eventually the appearance of cities, which were the true foundation of civilized life. This was the opinion to be expected of an aristocratic, cosmopolitan scholar of the Augustan age.[102]

Geographical setting, however, was not solely responsible for the level of sophistication that a people might reach.[103] That depended as well on their political order and social complexity.[104] Strabo believed that contact with a civilized community could lead to civilized life. Once begun, civilized institutions could spread regardless of terrain, as Strabo explains: "And again, as regards the various arts and faculties and institutions of mankind, most of them, when once men have made a beginning, flourish in any latitude whatsoever and in certain instances even in spite of the latitude; so that some local characteristics of a people come by nature, others by training and habit."[105]

At first reading, Strabo's roster of barbarian attributes appears to be standard and banal. For example, barbarians are always at war, have no laws, and only the lucky ones manage to live even in rude villages. They have no urban life or culture to speak of, and they keep apart from other peoples. Isolation prevented more civilized communities from influencing them. In fact, in Strabo's eyes, the most extreme characteristic of barbarism was the inability or refusal to respond to external, civilizing influences due to social isolation.[106] Desolate mountain regions prohibited agriculture, civilization's base, and so the unfortunate peoples inhabiting such terrain were brutish and crude. The theme of stubborn backwardness and lack of connection to a civilized center will appear in late antique ethnographic thought.

For Strabo, barbarism was an escapable condition susceptible to change, and Romans could be the agent of that change because they were especially effective in establishing connections through contact or conquest.[107] They could break down the barriers of isolation that delayed civilization:

> The quality of intractability and wildness in these [Iberian] peoples has not resulted solely from their engaging in warfare, but also from their remoteness; for the trip to their country, whether by sea or by land, is long, and since they are difficult to communicate with, they have lost the instinct of sociability and humanity. They have this feeling of intractability and wildness to a less extent now, however, because of the peace and of the sojourns of the Romans among them.[108]

Elsewhere he writes in the same vein:

> The Romans, too, took over many nations that were naturally savage owing to the regions they inhabited, because those regions were either rocky or without harbours or cold or for some other reason ill-suited to habitation by many, and thus not only brought into communication with each other peoples who had been isolated, but also taught the more savage how to live under forms of government.[109]

He gives instances elsewhere of conquered peoples who are "are no longer barbarians, but are, for the most part, transformed to the type of the Romans, both in their speech and in their modes of living (τοῖς βίοις), and some of them in their civic life as well."[110] He praises Rome's universal reach: "Now that all peoples have been brought into subjection to a single power, everything is free from toll and open to all mankind."[111]

Strabo followed the Hellenistic geographer Eratosthenes in suggesting that since all peoples had both good and bad qualities, a simple distinction between barbarian and civilized should not be accepted:[112]

> Now, towards the end of his [Eratosthenes's] treatise—after withholding praise from those who divide the whole multitude of mankind into two groups, namely, Greeks and Barbarians, and also from those who advised Alexander to treat the Greeks as friends but the Barbarians as enemies—Eratosthenes goes on to say that it would be better to make such divisions according to good qualities and bad qualities; for not only are many of the Greeks bad, but many of the barbarians are refined—Indians and the people of Ariana,[113] for example, and, further, Romans and Carthaginians, who carry on their governments so admirably.[114]

[42] CHAPTER 1

Strabo added that good and bad qualities might be enhanced by imperial intervention. As did so many of his predecessors, he accepted that the cost of civilization could be very high, and that contact with Rome could have unwelcome consequences:

> And yet our mode of life has spread its change for the worse to almost all peoples, introducing amongst them luxury and sensual pleasures and, to satisfy these vices, base artifices that lead to innumerable acts of greed. So then, much wickedness of this sort has fallen on the barbarian peoples also, on the Nomads as well as the rest; for as the result of taking up a seafaring life they not only have become morally worse, indulging in the practice of piracy and of slaying strangers, but also, because of their intercourse with many peoples, have partaken of the luxury and the peddling habits of those peoples.[115]

We see, then, that Strabo envisaged not an absolute division between civilized and noncivilized conditions of life, but rather a continuum from barbarism to a more advanced stage of human culture in which the good aspects of civilization, especially social and political organization, might be advanced.[116] In his scheme, Rome was the central anchor of civilized life, and distance from Rome was more significant in shaping the character of a people than the latitude in which they lived.[117] In other words, Strabo's deference to environmental determinism only went so far.

The structure of his *Geography* followed this approach. Strabo began his descriptions at the civilized portions of a region and progressed to the least civilized. This generally meant that his descriptions began with cities on the seacoast and moved inland. His treatment of the inhabited world moves from west to east.

Though Strabo's immediate influence was not great, the ideas that he articulated so clearly entered the imperial bloodstream. They resurfaced during Justinian's reign in the sixth century and were recognized by Procopius of Caesarea, who employed to great effect ideas of Rome's civilizing role, a continuum from barbarism to civilization, and the limited force of natural terrain, though in a Christian mode in the service of a Christian emperor.[118] Strabo's ideas helped give voice to a new vision of Christian imperialism.

PLINY THE ELDER, SOLDIER AND SCIENTIST

Born into a wealthy equestrian family from the north of Italy, C. Plinius Secundus, better known as Pliny the Elder, had an illustrious military career that bridged the Julio-Claudian and Flavian dynasties and that provided him with considerable exposure to foreign peoples. He served on the Rhine frontier in the fifties before being posted to Palestine during the Jewish war of 67–70,

CONQUEST AND CURIOSITY [43]

when he befriended the future emperor Titus. Subsequently Pliny's military responsibilities took him to Gaul, North Africa, and Spain before he became commander of the war fleet stationed in the Bay of Naples, where he died in 79 investigating the eruption of Mount Vesuvius.[119] A man of vast intellectual curiosity and energy, Pliny found time during his military service to write treatises on a wide number of topics including the use of the spear by mounted cavalrymen, a biography of his old commander, a rhetorical handbook, and a history of Rome's wars in Germania, all of which are lost.

The treatise on the wars in Germania completed an earlier work on the same topic by Aufidius Bassus, also now lost. Pliny also drew on his own experience as an officer on the Rhine frontier between 46 and 58 CE.[120] In addition to his probable endorsement of Rome's efforts to conquer Germania, Pliny also seems to have accumulated much detailed information about the land and its peoples.[121] It was a valuable source for later writers, including Tacitus.[122]

Pliny's voluminous *Natural History*, his only surviving work, is marvelous to read. In the same spirit with which Julius Caesar sent his scientists to catalog the people and places of his domain, Pliny intended the thirty-seven books of his treatise to provide an inventory of the entire world. Like dynasts of the late republic and early empire, he used geographical imagery to celebrate Rome's conquests.[123] Pliny's introductory material mentions a total of the "sites, nations, seas, towns, harbours, mountain, rivers, dimensions, present and past populations" that he will discuss.[124] His inventory of the world is a statement of possession.[125]

Pliny equates the Roman empire and the inhabited world.[126] His universal vision of the empire indicates the culmination of a long development in which Rome was "written into" the Hellenistic description of the world. He employs the trope of Rome as the central place to which all the produce of the world flows and from which Roman power emanates.[127] Imperial achievement throughout the world is displayed in the city of Rome.[128]

More significantly for the structure of the *Natural History*, Rome is the symbolic high point from which he directs his gaze over all Rome's possessions.[129] His tour of the *oikoumene* takes the form of a voyage along a coastline (a *periplus*) in the manner of Strabo and Greek geographers since the time of Hecataeus, about 500 BCE.[130] Trevor Murphy links Pliny's geographical exposition both to the "survey from on high"[131] and the phenomenon and iconography of the Roman triumph. He notes that Titus's triumph at the end of the Jewish war in 70 CE was an "occasion not only for displaying the bodies and the treasures of the conquered, but for parading captured geographies as well."[132] Pliny cannot claim to have subdued any peoples himself. Instead, he attributes the triumph of Roman arms to the emperor, who bears the ultimate responsibility and honor for each success.[133]

In Pliny's exposition, this survey, catalog, and celebration of knowledge of the inhabited world has been made possible by the benevolence of Roman might which has made the world accessible to everyone, now that "every sea has been opened up and every coast offers a hospitable landing."[134] Titus, an "emperor who so delights in productions of letters and science,"[135] ensures the peace and so makes Pliny's researches possible and purposeful. In presenting the emperor as the facilitator of expansion, peace, inclusion, and scientific enumeration of peoples and landscapes, Pliny demonstrates the full emergence of a truly imperial ethnography. Not only is the city of Rome now the center of the world, but the emperor, as master of Rome, is the builder and patron of civilization. This popular theme recurs in imperial self-presentation well into the sixth century.

Pliny's fascination with alien customs is manifest throughout his treatise. In the geographical books he discusses many different peoples, sometimes in great detail. He relishes their differences and delights in bringing them before the Roman viewer. His seventh book of the *Natural History* is devoted to humanity, "for whose sake great Nature appears to have created all other things";[136] he explains his approach to human communities: "Nor shall we now deal with manners and customs, which are beyond counting and almost as numerous as the groups of mankind; yet there are some that I think ought not to be omitted, and especially those of the people living more remote from the sea; some things among which I doubt not will appear portentous and incredible to many."[137]

Those peoples farthest from the Roman Mediterranean are the most primitive and receive Pliny's greatest attention. For example, he is interested in the Chauci, who live in the extreme northwest of Europe in nearly inaccessible marshes, without the simplest amenities of life.[138] He also maintains a lively curiosity about the marvelous, unusual, and grotesque. In the same book, pushing the limits of credulity, he describes Pygmies and giant people with dogs' heads or feathers; people who are born old and grow younger or who change their sexes; cannibals or people who eat flowers; half-animal tribes of India and Ethiopia.[139] Whether real or fantastic, these people are the necessary periphery to Rome's center. As Murphy shrewdly notes: "You cannot occupy the centre until you acquire something to surround you. Acquiring territory means visiting a new land, fixing it securely in place with an entry in map or gazetteer, and renaming it as a part of your own outskirts. Above all, what you acquire must be solid and immobile—your outskirts must not run away from you twice a day."

Pliny's "empire in the encyclopedia," to borrow Murphy's apt description of the work, contained the chief elements of imperial ethnography, including examination of exotica, geographical context, cultural judgment, and imperial centrality. These were in place at the end of the Julio-Claudian period.

TACITUS, THE HISTORIAN

Cornelius Tacitus, Rome's preeminent historian and best-known ethnographer, was born in Gaul about 56 CE. He pursued an extremely successful public career first under the Flavian emperors and then under Nerva and Trajan, reaching the position of suffect consul in 97. Some years later, from 112 to 113, he served as proconsul of Asia. As a writer, Tacitus is best known for the *Annals*, which covered the years from the accession of Tiberius in 14 to the death of Nero in 69, and the *Histories*, which continued from 69 to 96, when Domitian died and the Flavian dynasty ended. Neither work survives in its entirety, but the substantial portions that remain brilliantly display his trenchant analysis of Roman political life. No one has ever written with greater insight about the effects of imperial might on the Roman character. Evidence of the corrupting force of power, whether in the imperial capital or far afield, never surprised Tacitus. Without moralizing, he looked at events on the frontier and on the Palatine Hill with the same shrewd and unfaltering gaze, displaying a deep concern about the difficulty of living a virtuous life when the political arena is dominated by autocrats. He had the capacity to praise and criticize Roman life as well as that of foreign peoples.

The *Agricola* and the *Germania*, his two earliest works, deserve special attention in this regard because of how they treat foreign peoples and conquest. Both written around 98 following the death of Domitian, the treatises reveal Tacitus's acerbic views on the moral dimensions and political implications of conquest as much as they do the character of Rome's barbarian enemies. The distinctions are far from black-and-white.[140]

Tacitus composed *Germania* against the backdrop of more than a century of war with peoples living between the Rhine and the Elbe Rivers, a region that the Romans called Germania.[141] With great bravado, Julius Caesar's legions had raided across the Rhine in 55 and again in 53 BCE to intimidate the local populations.[142] These forays planted the idea of subduing all of Germania. After the civil war that brought him to power ended, Augustus attempted to create a province of Greater Germania east of the Rhine. His generals pushed to the Elbe River in 9 BCE and by 2 BCE had established an altar on its northern shore to symbolize Germania's entry into the sphere of Roman domination.[143] Hopes of controlling the territory were short-lived, however. In 9 CE, when a coalition of indigenous warriors ambushed and annihilated three legions, Augustus withdrew his armies from Germania and began to think of territorial limits to his domain. In the ensuing decades, some groups beyond the Rhine maintained allegiance to Rome, and in some areas Roman influence remained strong.[144] In the late thirties and the forties, during the reign of Claudius, Roman troops intermittently campaigned against the Chauci and the Frisii, whose territories bordered the North Sea, but without achieving significant victories. Within a few years of seizing power in 69, Vespasian, the first Flavian emperor, reinforced Rome's presence on the Rhine by establishing forts and roads east of the river. Between 83 and 89, his son Domitian campaigned against the Chatti, who lived north of the Main River and threatened Roman settlements in the Rhine valley. Tacitus singled them out for their ferocity, numbers, and rational planning for war, all qualities that made them rather like Romans and so increased the sense of threat.[145] Domitian brought the war to an end and formally established the provinces of Upper and Lower Germany. A defensive line linking the Rhine and Danube frontiers emerged.[146]

By Tacitus's day, Germania had proven to be the greatest barrier to Roman expansion,[147] and we may presume that part of his purpose in writing the treatise was to assess the character and explain the tenacity and military resilience of its inhabitants. In doing so, he indirectly revealed his opinions about the quality of Roman political life and society.

Tacitus wrote the *Germania* as a freestanding ethnographic monograph, not as an excursus embedded in a larger historical narrative.[148] It is the only such essay devoted to a single region and its peoples to have survived from classical antiquity.[149] He intended to present the territory between the Rhine and Elbe as a comprehensible, though internally diverse, unit. Tacitus tells us that the terms *Germani* and *Germania* were a recent coinage, deriving from the name of a single tribe and then taken up by the indigenous peoples themselves.[150]

Where did Tacitus get his information? His description of the different peoples of Germania in chapters 28–46 follows the standard pattern of a periegesis or geographic route, but he had not traveled through these lands himself. His presence in the army on the Rhine frontier remains an unproven possibility.[151] A variety of written sources were available for him to consult, however.[152] He acknowledged Caesar's *Gallic Wars* as his most important source,[153] and he may also have read Pliny the Elder's treatise on the wars in Germania, and Aufidius Bassus's *Germanic War*,[154] both now lost. A considerable amount of unwritten information carried by travelers, soldiers, merchants, and slaves must have been known to him as well. However much he may have drawn from his disparate sources, Tacitus imposed order on a significant amount of information to present his own picture of Germania and its inhabitants as accurately as he could.

While the inhabitants of Germania in Tacitus's eyes were certainly not Romans, and demonstrating this was the point of the treatise, he never presents them uniformly either as unreconstructed barbarians pitted against civilized Romans or as noble savages resisting depraved Romans, as has often been claimed.[155] As Erich Gruen points out, Tacitus's treatment of Germania and its inhabitants contains no such facile contrasts.[156] Such misleading antitheses have led to much abuse. The worst case occurred during the Nazi era when German nationalists reversed the contrast by valorizing the Germani on racial terms at the expense of decadent Romans.[157]

While Tacitus does make generalizations about the Germani, he also distinguishes among different groups possessing their own customs. He is highly judgmental, but is prepared to find praiseworthy traits. He shows interest in the extent of Roman influence upon them. Tacitus praises Germani when they are most like Romans or share the sort of moral code of which he approves. For example, he admires the habit of monogamy among most of the Germani, their hardiness and prowess in war, their modesty in dress and diet, and the sense of justice (among the Chauci).[158] Sometimes he meant by implicit contrast to disparage Roman habits of which he strongly disapproves. His obvious contempt for the shortcomings of his countrymen was sincere and is tangible in all his works, but he never rejects Romanness or suggests that Romans should start acting like Germani.[159]

Tacitus's judgments are rooted in such Roman concepts as *libertas*, which can mean, among other things, freedom from unjust authority. He believes the Roman way of life to be superior but unable to thrive under a tyranny like Domitian's, though it could flourish again under the benign reigns of Nerva and Trajan. Tacitus makes the point that the Germani value a similar sort of freedom that renders them fierce and worthy opponents, even though some of their leaders restrict the autonomy of their subjects.[160] The possibility of such nearness of values among some Germani and some Romans shows that simple ethnic distinctions are not the most important criteria for Tacitus's judgments. As we will see below, when he describes the Britons beginning to accept the customs of the Romans in *Agricola*, he adds that they unwittingly lose their freedom by doing so.

Tacitus employs the term *barbarian* only three times in the *Germania*: when praising their monogamous marriage customs,[161] when condemning human sacrifice among the Semnones,[162] and in noting the sad conditions of life of a remote people, the Aestii. He makes several important points in his description of this primitive people who live near the Baltic Sea, where they gather amber. He emphasizes their geographical remoteness, implying that it is a cause of their barbarism.[163] The theme of remoteness recurs in a more general statement about Germania that echoes Caesar's description of Gaul: "The nearest tribes, through experience of trade, know the value of gold and silver, and recognize and pick out certain types of our currency; the more distant tribes employ the simpler and older practice of bartering goods."[164]

He also asserts that Aestii are typical barbarians in their lack of intellectual curiosity and disinterest in finding underlying causes for natural phenomena. They alone gather amber, but do not recognize its worth and are amazed at the value given it by Romans.[165] He nicely contrasts their naïveté to Roman love of luxury and sneers at both. Then he proceeds to describe how amber is formed, thereby setting himself and his own erudition apart from barbarian indifference to intellectual matters.[166] He makes a point of not being credulous. When he cannot confirm tall tales about people at the very edge of the world with human faces and animal bodies, he pretentiously leaves the matter open.[167]

Remoteness bred isolation. Tacitus describes the Germani as indigenous and stresses their lack of contact with other peoples as an indicator and cause of their difficult lives. He notes that climatic and geographical harshness contributed to their disconnection from a larger world, a very long-lasting ethnographic theme:

> The Germani . . . have in no way been mixed by the arrivals and alliances of other peoples, because in the past those who sought to exchange their old territory for new did not come by land but were carried by fleets, and the Ocean beyond Germania, immeasurable and so to speak hostile, is visited by very few ships from our parts. Moreover, quite apart from the danger of a rough and unknown sea, who would abandon Asia or Africa or Italy and seek out Germania, with its unlovely landscape and harsh climate, dreary to inhabit and behold, if it were not one's native land?[168]

Even though *Germania* is a world in the grip of natural forces, and even though the customs of its inhabitants are often brutal and sometimes the inverse of Roman habits,[169] it is not a timeless region where change never occurs. Tacitus is well aware that their societies are in flux and have histories. They may grow strong or lose their power, as did the Cimbri.[170] They may adopt the customs of non-Germans, as the Veneti took on customs of nomadic Sarmatians.[171] They might also take on the habits of the Romans. To see how Rome might have a hand in such developments, and how Tacitus evaluated this sort of change, we turn to his treatise *Agricola*.

The process and consequences of conquest are more fully developed in the *Agricola* than in the *Germania*. Its primary purpose was not to describe the Britons, but to leave to posterity a record of the illustrious deeds and noble character of his father-in-law, the general Gnaeus Julius Agricola, who had conquered most of Britain from 77 to 84. His fleet circumnavigated Britain, demonstrating that it was an island, and he gathered information about Ireland, perhaps with an invasion in mind. He earned triumphal honors for his victory over the Caledonians at Mount Graupius in southern Scotland. Further glory was not to be won, however. His career was suddenly cut short after his triumph due to the jealousy of the emperor Domitian, and Agricola died of natural causes soon after, in 93. After Domitian was assassinated three years later, Tacitus could praise his father-in-law's character and military exploits more freely. He saw the dawning of a "most happy age" under Nerva and Trajan,[172] a time when men like Agricola could flourish in the service of the empire.

The treatise is full of information about Agricola's successful military strategies over seven years, but what Tacitus says about his father-in-law's role in changing the lives of Britons after their conquest deserves special attention:

> The following winter was devoted to projects of the most admirable sort. By private encouragement he set about persuading men who were scattered, uncultured and thus easily aroused to warfare, to become peaceable and accustomed to the pleasures offered by leisure. In public, he assisted them to build temples, *fora* and residences, praising those who were quick to follow his advice and criticizing those who were slow. A competition for honour thus took the place of compulsion. He went on to give the sons of the nobility a proper education and praised the Britons' intellect above the diligence of the Gauls, so that he aroused an enthusiasm for rhetoric among a people who had recently spurned the Latin language. As a result our national dress, the *toga*, was held in honour and adopted everywhere, and by stages they were led on to the more acceptable vices, public arcades, bathhouses and the sophistication of banquets. In their inexperience they took this for *humanitas* when in fact it was a part of their slavery.[173]

Bringing civilization to the Britons, in Tacitus's eyes, was not only possible but desirable. He can say this while at the same time pointing at the darker consequences of Roman rule.

PTOLEMY, THE ASTRONOMER

Another perspective on the characteristics of human communities and the causes of change among them comes from a second-century Greek scientist, the remarkable Alexandrian scholar Claudius Ptolemaeus, or Ptolemy. He conquered no peoples hostile to Rome, and he held no post in the imperial government. Ptolemy is best known for his contributions to astronomy and geography. Through his treatment of those subjects he also made a most significant contribution to the Roman ethnographic corpus. His explanations of the causes of differences among human communities did not depend on the presence of imperial Rome.

Between 146 and ca. 170 CE, Ptolemy, a polymath like Pliny the Elder, wrote studies of mathematics, geography, optics, and astronomy that would be of great influence in the Roman and later the Byzantine and Islamic worlds. His *Geography* mapped the entire known world, remaining the standard work until the sixteenth century. The *Almagest*, an astronomical textbook, remained canonical for a millennium. Partner to the *Almagest*, the *Tetrabiblos* attempted to apply sound explanations for astrology, which Ptolemy considered to be the application of astronomical methods to the sublunar world of change in which humans live.[174] In this he followed the widely accepted tradition begun by

Plato and Aristotle that the stars and planets were constant and eternal, while human conditions were impermanent. Ptolemy also was steeped in the tradition of natural determinism begun by Pseudo-Hippocrates in the fifth century in the treatise *Airs, Waters, Places*. These two fields of investigation opened a door to ethnography.

The second book of the *Tetrabiblos* divides prognostication into two major fields. The first "relates to whole peoples [ἔθνη], countries, and cities" and the second "relates to individual men."[175] In the course of explaining these two fields, Ptolemy provides an astrological ethnography in which the signs of the zodiac, the stars in different latitudes, and the positions of the celestial bodies play a determining role:[176]

> The demarcation of national characteristics [ἐθνικῶν ἰδιωμάτων] is established in part by entire parallels and angles, through their position relative to the ecliptic and the sun. For while the region we inhabit is in one of the northern quarters, the people who live under the more southern parallels, that is, those from the equator to the summer tropic, since they have the sun over their heads and are burned by it, have black skins and thick, wooly hair, are contracted in form and shrunken in stature, are sanguine of nature, and in habits are for the most part savage because their homes are continually oppressed by heat; we call them by the general name Ethiopians. Not only do we see them in this condition, but we likewise observe that their climate and the animals and plants of their region plainly give evidence of this baking by the sun.
>
> Those who live under the more northern parallels, those, I mean, who have the Bears over the heads, since they are far removed from the zodiac and the heat of the sun, are therefore cooled. . . . they are white in complexion, straight-haired, tall and well-nourished, and somewhat cold by nature; these too are savage in their habits because their dwelling-places are continually cold. The wintry character of their climate, the size of their plants, and the wildness of their animals are in accord with these qualities. We call these men, too, by a general name, Scythians.
>
> The inhabitants of the region between the summer tropic and the Bears, however, since the sun is neither directly over their heads nor far distant at its noon-day transits, share in the equable temperature of the air, which varies, to be sure, but has no violent changes from heat to cold . . .
>
> And now in each of these general regions certain special conditions of character and customs [ἠθῶν καὶ νομίμων] naturally ensue. For as likewise, in the case of the climate, even within the regions that in general are reckoned as hot, cold, or temperate, certain localities and countries have special peculiarities of excess or deficiency by reason of their

situation, height, lowness, or adjacency; and again, as some peoples are more inclined to horsemanship because theirs is a plain country, or to seamanship because they live close to the sea, or to civilization because of the richness of their soil, so also would one discover special traits in each arising from the natural familiarity of their particular climes with the stars in the signs of the zodiac. These traits, too, would be found generally present, but not in every individual. We must, then, deal with the subject summarily, in so far as it might be of use for the purpose of particular investigations.[177]

Like Pliny and Strabo, Ptolemy addressed the entire inhabited world and gave it a place in the heavenly realm among the planets and the stars, fitting humanity into a coherent cosmic scheme. A true scientist, he developed a universal vision supported by careful observation on which he based unifying theories about human diversity. Human societies, and humans themselves, for that matter, he knew always to be in flux because of their place in the sublunar sphere. The stars, however, he believed to be permanent, and he gave them a controlling force over human lives. In a general way, the characteristics of peoples were determined by their proximity to the equator and the heat of the sun. More particular characteristics of communities and individuals themselves were determined by the stars. Most important of all his ideas was that the agency of the heavens, not of the Roman state, determine the direction of change in societies and degrees of civilization.

Conclusion

This chapter has set the stage for late antique developments in ethnographic thought. We have looked at a handful of influential writers of the Republic and early imperial period to see what attitudes about foreignness and cultural difference they developed and how they gave Rome a role in shaping the differences. Their ideas found a lasting place in Rome's imperial ethnographic infrastructure. Some were scholars and scientists on the sidelines of affairs while others stood close to the center of political power and policy. As educated men, they drew deeply from Greek learning, yet they were not isolated academic figures. Their immediate experience of Rome's burgeoning empire gave shape and direction to their thought. The longevity of the ideas they articulated so clearly indicates their broad acceptance by many elements of Roman society. The engagement with foreignness that they embody was a silent ethnography of knowledge commonly accepted and widely shared.

The elements to keep in mind in the chapters ahead fall into several explanatory frames. The first was spatial. Roman writers developed an imperial rationale for ordering the world in which they lived. They put themselves at its center, with the City of Rome taking pride of place. Distance from Rome geographically and from what it represented culturally indicated relative degrees of civilization. Though able to criticize their own society, elite members of Roman society were confident in the superiority of their culture and their imperial system. Their self-ascribed and complacent sense of centrality gave them a starting point for judging others. Within the spatial frame, ideas of bounded territory and the real limits of Roman authority developed, with the emperor as a linchpin. Territory beyond Rome's borders constituted a violent and disordered part of the world.

Another frame was descriptive and involved culture, not space. The Roman ruling elite developed an interest in making an inventory of their diverse subjects who inhabited quite different terrain within imperial borders. At the same time, they had great curiosity about the habits and customs of the peoples beyond their grip, sometimes for very practical reasons related to conquest and defense, and sometimes to support scientific theories about the determining force of climate and the stars. Human diversity fueled their ethnography and views of change in the world.

Imperial agency constituted another conceptual frame. An idea of paramount importance developed that Rome could be a transformational force in the world. Romans knew that imperial expansion profoundly altered the peoples they ruled, and the gradual emergence of the figure of the emperor at the apex of Roman society would lead effortlessly to the idea that he was the chief agent of change. Under his leadership, Romans might include foreign subjects in a civilized, Roman life.

As we have seen in this chapter and will see again in the pages ahead, Roman treatments of foreign peoples can seem very constant, resulting in a conservative feel. Foundations of late antique ethnographic writing were laid early. This apparent conservatism, however, should be distinguished at all times from the circumstances of composition, the problems addressed by each author, and the purposes of each statement. Doing so will show that ethnographic writing was a lively enterprise that continued to evolve in Late Antiquity.

CHAPTER TWO

"Hostiles and Friendlies"[1]

DIPLOMACY AND PATTERNS OF
SUBORDINATION TO ROME

When Attila entered the populous city of Milan, he saw a painting of Roman emperors sitting on golden thrones with Scythians lying before them. He summoned an artist and demanded a rendering of himself on the throne and the Roman emperors pouring gold coins at his feet from leather sacks on their backs.

—*SUIDAE LEXICON*[2]

Introduction: A World in Good Order

In the spring of 359, somewhere in the province of Pannonia Baleria (modern Croatia), the emperor Constantius II met with Zizais, a defeated Sarmatian prince, who had come to learn his fate.[3] The fourth-century soldier and historian Ammianus Marcellinus provides a vivid account of their encounter:

> on the day named for settling the terms . . . Zizais, a tall young man who was even then a royal prince, drew up the ranks of the Sarmatians in battle array to make their petition. And on seeing the emperor he threw aside his weapons and fell flat on his breast, as if lying lifeless. And since the use of his voice failed him from fear at the very time when he should have made his plea, he excited all the greater compassion; but after several attempts, interrupted by sobbing, he was able to set forth only a little of what he tried to ask. At last, however, he was reassured and bidden to rise, and getting up on his knees and recovering the use of his voice, he begged that indulgence for his offences, and pardon, be granted him.[4]

The Sarmatian prince's soldiers, as well as lesser chiefs and nobles, follow his lead in abasing themselves before Constantius. Ammianus tells us that the Sarmatians,

> overjoyed that their lives were spared, offered to make up for their hostile acts by burdensome conditions, and would have willingly submitted themselves with their possessions, their children, their wives,

[53]

and the whole of their territories to the power of the Romans. However, kindness combined with fairness prevailed, and when they were told to retain their homes without fear, they returned all their Roman prisoners. They also brought in the hostages that were demanded and promised from that time on to obey orders with the utmost promptness.[5]

All the participants know their parts in this well-choreographed yet deadly serious enactment of power and submission. The young Sarmatian, pretending to be so overcome that he has lost his ability to speak, provides an award-winning performance because he knows precisely what the Roman audience expects, as do the lesser Sarmatian chiefs who follow him. Zizais and his people have no choice but to offer Constantius everything of value they possess. He in turn graciously allows them to keep their lives and their independence. Ammianus tells the story with considerable gusto but no irony and no comment on stagecraft.

This minor but colorful episode in the long history of Roman diplomacy provides details about the structure of one kind of encounter between imperial forces and defeated barbarian foes. Ammianus employs familiar ethnographic contrasts as he describes the Sarmatians and the emperor. Constantius is compassionate, kind, and fair-minded, while the barbarians are frightened and, above all, vanquished. For Ammianus, his readers, and the soldiers present at the occasion, the primary attribute of barbarians must be their visible acceptance of Roman authority. The ritualized act of submission was an essential part of the deal-making. From an imperial perspective, this story places Rome in a position of absolute control with the world arranged as it should be. The emperor has established an entirely asymmetrical relationship with the defeated Sarmatians.

This chapter suggests that a powerfully enhanced ethnographic discourse of subordination to Roman power emerged in Late Antiquity. The discourse was located in the broad field of diplomatic interactions, its natural home. It began to crystallize under pressure in the third century, when Roman imperial hegemony came under prolonged challenge from powerful and unexpected enemies and keeping up the appearance of universal hegemony became more of a challenge than ever.[6] Men of the governing elite who were involved in imperial diplomacy (there was no formal diplomatic corps) made the best of constantly varying circumstances.[7] They responded by elaborating hierarchies of difference—or we might say in this context hierarchies of deference—to mark distance between themselves and other peoples, whether small war bands or vast empires. They always wanted to think of themselves as holding the upper hand. Romans had a great backlog of experience to draw on, but in Late Antiquity a new phase began in which many old certainties were challenged. A more focused diplomatic ecosystem took shape.

This register of differentiation, unlike other ethnographic discourses, did not evaluate the habits of life of Rome's diplomatic partners. Instead, it placed foreigners in an approximate hierarchy of relative status that expressed heavily weighted power relationships. It needs to be emphasized that this was not an ethnography of knowledge but of relation. By calibrating distance (broadly speaking) from Roman authority, the discourse shaped action and had a strong utilitarian function. Through it Romans projected a deep-seated predilection for hierarchy onto the international order. A great deal was at stake in the delicate business of determining who was hostile and who was friendly and then taking the appropriate next step. The purpose of diplomacy was to help give direction to those steps by establishing, formalizing, and regulating foreign connections in some fashion.[8] There were many scenarios for diplomatic activity. Practically speaking, they might involve such things as establishing an alliance, ending a war, acquiring or ceding territory, engaging one foreign nation to fight another, or even putting a good face on a terrible situation. The percussive events that made diplomacy necessary were so compelling that we may easily overlook underlying ethnographic structures that gave substance to diplomatic efforts.

The episode of Zizais and the Sarmatians was typical of acts of surrender that usually took place in military camps before generals or other imperial representatives to finalize the terms of the deal being struck.[9] Ceremonies of deference would also have been played out in grander settings in Constantinople, where the emperor was more likely to be present. He would observe defeated foes making obeisance in the Hippodrome, and at the palace in a different mode, he would have received gift-bearing ambassadors seeking friendship. The discourse was equally manifest at court in what Jonathan Shepard characterizes as the "incessant grading of gifts, modes of receiving envoys, and addresses to foreign envoys."[10] Calibration of status was essential in diplomacy.

In addition to the ritualized aspects of manifesting power relations wherever they were performed, there was a second, equally important mode of expressing them. That was a two-way traffic in gifts and payments that were essential elements in the diplomatic ecosystem. We turn now to these payments.

Traffic in Gifts: Continuities of Practice and Interpretation

As the Roman empire expanded, an important strategic device in its arsenal was to exchange gifts with its diplomatic partners.[11] Romans made payments to them ("cash out") and also received gifts from them ("cash in"). The exchanges, especially the "cash out" payments, which were often specified in treaties,[12] were asymmetrical and reinforced status relationships. They had great symbolic value and created reciprocal ties and expectations on both sides. Reciprocity did not mean equality, however. For example, Roman emperors always made a point of surpassing the foreigners' gifts with something of greater value. The asymmetry of value reinforced Roman notions of dominance. Romans gained much from making payments. As instruments of policy, payments "out" transformed, however temporarily, enemies into people with whom interaction was possible. In this way they reimagined the character of future interactions. Strings were always attached, yet both sides gained something of value. As Marcel Mauss made clear a century ago, such exchanges, when willingly entered into, reinforce social and political networks both within and between cultures.[13] Already customary in Livy's day,[14] the practice of systematized payment had become a staple of Roman frontier management and reached its apogee by the end of the first century CE. Tacitus took subsidies to lesser powers for granted.[15]

The question of how to interpret the payments raised its head from an early point as well. Because payments (and the act of paying) carried considerable symbolic value, they provoked a wide range of political interpretation. There were two possible approaches. On the one hand, payments could be seen simply as a pragmatic and helpful way to further Rome's interests. Cool-headed emperors with sufficient money in their treasuries kept payment in the Roman diplomatic arsenal, not least as a practical way to avoid the costs of all-out warfare. On the other hand, payments could be interpreted as shameful tribute, whether or not they had actually been coerced.[16] One mark of a good ruler was that he did purchase peace at great expense.[17] These two possibilities of interpretation gave plenty of room for pragmatism to collide with ideology.

Both of these approaches remained operative in Late Antiquity, but under changing circumstances. From the third century, as the defensive lines of the empire deteriorated, subsidies became even more essential as bribes to prevent invasion.[18] Baksheesh at the highest order of business became a "necessary supplement to . . . military strength,"[19] even in the restored Tetrarchic empire with its effectively reorganized army. Constantine and his successors continued the practice.[20] The situation started to change dramatically in the late fourth century. With the arrival of the Goths inside the empire after the Battle of Adrianople and the accompanying confusion in the Balkans in the 370s and '80s, followed by Alaric's depredations that culminated in the sack of Rome in 410, the payment of subsidies without question became the payment of extortion. In 395, Alaric menaced Constantinople but was diverted westward.[21] In 407, when he threatened Italy, 4,000 pounds of gold kept him at arm's length. The western military commander Stilicho, who paid Alaric, tried to deny that the payments were tribute.[22] When Alaric made a push on Rome in 408, he was kept at bay by 5,000 pounds of gold, 30,000 pounds of silver, as well as great quantities of silk tunics, scarlet skins, and pepper, gathered in the city itself.[23]

"HOSTILES AND FRIENDLIES" [57]

By the middle of the fifth century, emperors could no longer call the shots. As we will see, Sasanian Persia and the steppe empires of the Huns and Avars added an additional dimension to payments, namely the regularity with which they wanted them to be paid. Demands on Rome to make the payments on a *regular* basis are often seen in treaties, though the call for such regularity can be overshadowed by the scale of the amounts specified. The thought of annual payments as well as the sums demanded entailed new calculations on Rome's part. There was no place anymore for Tacitus's nonchalance.

In Late Antiquity, tribute came into its own. According to Nicola Di Cosmo, "Tribute is to be understood as a payment extorted in exchange for peace, that is, essentially, protection money. Compared to a purely predatory strategy, tribute obtained by diplomatic means had the advantage of replacing irregular spoils of war with regular yearly collections. It consisted of various forms of wealth, mostly luxuries and precious materials such as silk, gold, silver—that is, commodities that could also be monetized."[24] Di Cosmo is speaking generally of steppe empires (in our case his comments would apply to Huns and Avars), but the same explanation suits Roman relations with Persia, with whom fixed payments over a certain period were often stipulated by treaty. Expectations that both parties would hold to the bargain they had struck regardless of its asymmetry remained present.

The sixth century was a heyday of systematic, often regularized, and always carefully calculated payments of cash used as a diplomatic instrument.[25] The well-documented reigns of Justinian and his immediate successors demonstrate, particularly in dealings with Persians and Arabs, how subsidies, tribute, titles, and gifts played a central role in negotiation and policy formation.[26] The blowback was considerable.[27] More often than not, whatever the benefits accrued, Roman writers decried such transfers of cash as a sign of weakness and dishonor and condemned them as "tribute."

Displaying Subservience: Attila, Constantine, and Theodosius

The story at the head of this chapter about Attila's angry reaction to a standard Roman depiction of steppe nomads as servile barbarians illustrates the register of deference in action. In his own day Attila became the model of the parasitic nomad, a stereotype that would last for a millennium and more. The story comes from an entry in the *Suda*, a quirky amalgamation of all sorts of information compiled at Constantinople around the year 1000. The *Suda* does not name the author of the passage, but the extract might well come from a lost work of Priscus of Panium, a historian who accompanied a Roman embassy to the court of Attila in 448. Curious about the formation of Roman and barbarian identities and their representation, he broke open

FIGURE 1. Gold medallion of Constantine I, struck in 326–27 CE. The medallion reads, "Glory of Emperor Constantine." It memorializes the emperor's complete victory over stereotyped barbarians, who are half naked, in trousers, and with ratty beards. Constantine wears traditional military uniform and carries a trophy of arms. The barbarians have lost everything, and the emperor will decide whether to spare or kill them. This is a moment for Romans to savor. SIS indicates that the medallion was minted in Siscia (Sisak in modern Croatia). © Dumbarton Oaks, Coins and Seals Collection, Washington, DC, Accession no. BZC.1945.6.

many stereotypes.[28] Whether or not the painting he described existed we will never know, but its meaning is clear. Attila has completely turned the tables and barbarians no longer cower in supplication to Rome. Instead, groveling emperors now debase themselves before him.[29] The author imagines an outrageously subversive barbarian perspective on Roman practice.[30] The painting that enraged Attila was only one instance of a ubiquitous image. Representations of barbarian powerlessness and Roman dominance abounded on coins and in the empire's public places.[31]

FIGURE 2. Barberini Diptych, bottom panel. Dating to the reign of Justinian in the sixth century, this ivory panel is at the bottom of a five-piece diptych celebrating the emperor as a triumphant Christian ruler. It shows submissive barbarians in traditional fashion, bringing gifts in homage to the emperor. They are accompanied by fierce beasts. The second barbarian from the left carries a basket of coins. In the lower right corner, a figure of Victory gestures to the barbarians. © Louvre, Paris, France / Bridgeman Images.

In the entirely different fantasy of universal rule preferred by Romans, emissaries from beyond the borders would come before the emperor in a peaceful fashion, in order to establish or maintain diplomatic contacts. Romans considered it proper that foreign political communities (all de facto barbarian in any case) should bring gifts to the emperor in acknowledgment of Rome's power and majesty. These ambassadors and the peoples they represented were "friendlies." Such evidence of Rome's preeminence among the nations was something to celebrate. This imperial premise lasted throughout the centuries. Augustus, Rome's first emperor, boasted in his public memoir of the numerous ambassadors who had come to him from distant lands.[32] Writing in the fourth century, Eusebius described a crush of exotic emissaries at Constantine's court, bringing gifts and seeking the emperor's beneficence,[33] and in the aftermath of Justinian's reign in the sixth century, the panegyrist Corippus repeated the same image.[34] The Byzantine chronicler Theophanes records that an Indian king sent lavish, gem-encrusted congratulatory gifts to Heraclius some three hundred years later.[35] The reception of ambassadors reinforced continuing notions of Roman primacy in the world—the very opposite of the image desired by Attila.

Emissaries bringing gifts did not leave the emperor's presence empty-handed. In conformity with protocol and tradition, after receiving the tokens of barbarian deference, the emperor lavished great gifts upon them to take home, thereby demonstrating Rome's limitless wealth and power. Such largesse strengthened Rome's hand among client states and other peoples beyond the imperial grasp.[36] A brightly colored passage from Bishop Eusebius's *Life of Constantine* illustrates the elaborate arrangements:

There were constant diplomatic visitors who brought valuable gifts from their homelands, so that when we ourselves happened to be present we saw before the outer palace gates waiting in a line remarkable figures of barbarians, with their exotic dress, their distinctive appearances, the quite singular cut of hair and beard; the appearance of their hairy faces was foreign and astonishing, their bodily height exceptional. The faces of some were red, of others whiter than snow, of others blacker than ebony or pitch, and others had a mixed colour in between . . . Each of these in turn, as in a picture, brought their particular treasures to the Emperor, some of them golden crowns, some diadems of precious stones, others fair-haired children, others foreign cloths woven with gold and bright colours, others horses, others shields and long spears and javelins and bows, showing that they were offering service and alliance with these things to the Emperor when he required it. The Emperor received these from those who had brought them and recorded them, and responded with equal gifts, so as to make the bearers very rich all at once. He honoured the most distinguished of them also with Roman titles, so that very many now longed to remain here, forgetting any thought of returning to their homes.[37]

In this account, which is based in part on his own observations, Eusebius emphasizes the exoticism of the emissaries. He points out that they came from the most remote places, bearing as gifts what was most particular to them and offering alliance. Yet the emperor matches his visitors by giving them equally lavish presents and rewarding some with Roman titles and ranks. So convincing are these imperial blandishments, Eusebius states, that many foreigners want to stay. He thus indicates that foreigners can be impressed and transformed by the emperor's endless resources.[38] They can be included in the structures of imperial rule. We have seen the empire's centrality, its inclusiveness, and its transformative powers expressed in other Roman ethnographic systems.

Eusebius indicates that Constantine's generosity gave Rome the upper hand. Like Pliny two centuries earlier, he makes a point of saying that the emperor refused to behave like earlier emperors whose annual gifts to barbarians had made Romans their servants.[39] Instead, Constantine has reversed this practice, compelling and inducing barbarians to become Rome's subordinates. Elsewhere, when describing Constantine's negotiations with Shapur II of Persia, Eusebius introduces a Christian note.[40] An embassy bearing gifts had come from Persia seeking an alliance.[41] Constantine, motivated by a Christian love of peace, welcomed them and gave even more costly presents in return. According to Eusebius, Constantine cares for all the people of the world, especially those many new Christians in the Persian realm, whom he

"HOSTILES AND FRIENDLIES" [61]

FIGURE 3. Obelisk base of Theodosius I, Constantinople, west face. In 390, the emperor Theodosius I erected an obelisk in the Hippodrome of Constantinople. The west side of its base shows the imperial court watching a ceremonial procession of submissive barbarians bringing gifts. The imperial party is represented above them, in rigid hierarchy of authority. Hippodrome, Istanbul, Turkey. © Edifice / Bridgeman Images.

tries to protect in their unhappy condition under tyranny. Just as his god is universal, so, too, Constantine exercises universal concern. This amalgam of Christian and Roman ideas of the emperor's role sets the terms of much future discussion of an emperor-focused ethnography that will continue throughout the late antique period.

When Zizais the Sarmatian abased himself before Constantius, he performed his abject condition, an act that must have occurred countless other times on the frontier. Closer to the center of power, the image of powerlessness was both acted out and memorialized in the Hippodrome in Constantinople.

Sometime between 392 and 395, the emperor Theodosius erected an Egyptian obelisk atop a marble base still visible today.[42] The monument celebrated specifically his recent victory over rivals in the West[43] while complementing the permanent message of imperial victory associated with races in the Hippodrome.[44] All four sides of the column base depict the imperial loge of the Great Palace, from which the royal family and retinue are shown viewing the Hippodrome's spectacle. The northwest side of the base is divided into upper and lower tiers. The emperor sits at the center of the upper tier flanked by his wife and his two sons, the future emperors Arcadius and Honorius. Below them in humiliating postures of subservience are two rows (depicted laterally) of defeated barbarian enemies offering gifts to the royal house. On carefully staged occasions, tens of thousands of viewers in the Hippodrome stands would have joined their emperor watching the live performances of barbarian submission like the one depicted on the obelisk base.[45] The images carved on the base also would have been on permanent display. Yet even more important was the position of the monument itself. Constantinople had become the New Rome, the symbolic center of the world. The Theodosian monument thus stood at the symbolic center of the capital, at the very place where the *populus Romanus* joined with their imperial master to celebrate his eternal victory. Barbarian suppliants, representing the acquiescence of the non-Roman peoples of the world, appear prominently on the base, as part of the imperial order.[46] This is the ethnographic vision implied on the fresco that Attila was said to have rejected in Milan.

The patterns of subordination enacted by tribute payment and gift giving in international relations constituted an ethnographic register of difference. As measures of relative status, coerced payments and diplomatic gifts carried great symbolic value.

———◆———

This chapter is organized around several diplomatic arenas in which the discourse of subordination to Rome took different forms. First, we will look at relations in the East with the empire of Sasanian Persia and with various Arab groups on the fault line between Rome and Persia, acting as satellites to the great powers. The Sasanian state was a constant threat to Rome, but Arab groups in border areas were managed successfully. Next, we look toward the Eurasian steppe land north of the Danube that was home to an array of unanticipated nomad polities that became a constant and costly threat. Their inroads proved costly, but their bases of operation continued to be external to the empire. Finally, we look to the West, where the Roman Empire had long interacted with the many peoples of Germania and then in a dramatic turnabout during the fifth century with "successor states" occupying lands that had once been Roman. Each of these regions required different strategies of diplomatic engagement. In all of them, determining the degree of notional subordination to Rome was a constant element. Interpretation of gifts and payments played a significant part in this. As Eusebius reminded us, the steady growth of Christianity within the empire and abroad eventually affected the tone of diplomatic interaction.[47]

Part I
Rome and Persia: The Dilemma of Equality

The first diplomatic arena lay along Rome's eastern boundary, where the empire of Sasanian Persia stood as Rome's most troublesome rival, a *natio molestissima*.[48] Diplomatic interaction with Persia held a special challenge because of the relative equality of both empires in scale and might, not to mention in self-esteem.[49] Both empires were firmly established over vast territories, and both were in place for the long haul. Even if one or the other monarch were defeated in war, furthermore, neither could realistically hope to absorb and assimilate the other's empire, though peripheral territories quite rich in manpower and resources, and of great strategic value, might change hands. For that reason, competition for the Armenian recruiting grounds, the natural resources of the Caucasus, and the rich cities of Mesopotamia, was always fierce.[50] Persia and Rome recognized their worrying parity, and since neither could afford to be seen as weaker, competitive status anxiety haunted them as their fortunes rose and fell. A long game of constant international rivalry was played out in war, diplomacy, and bellicose rhetoric.

From the beginning of the Sasanian dynasty in the early third century until its defeat in the seventh, Persia and Rome were often at war, but they enjoyed extended periods of peace as well, most notably in the fifth century.[51] In the sixth century their rivalry turned increasingly bitter and culminated in what has been called the last great war of antiquity.[52] On the strength of an elaborate strategic gamble that sent him deep into Persian territory for years at a time, the emperor Heraclius led Roman forces to victory in 628. After humbling the Sasanid royal house, he withdrew to Roman soil. A succession of weak rulers held the Persian throne until the armies of Islam destroyed the kingdom's independence in the middle of the seventh century.

As Matthew Canepa has forcefully explained, during their long period of competitive coexistence, the two empires came to share a symbolic culture, especially in expressing ideas about kingship and universal rule.[53] It is no surprise that the truces and long-term treaties resulting from their frequent diplomatic exchanges reflected this similarity of language even as they established the relative status determined in a specific arrangement. As much as the possibility of material gain existed, the intangible but critical resources of dignity and honor were involved as well, because neither side wished to appear tributary and subordinate to the other. Any sign of diminished power would attract enemies for the regime at home and abroad.

These tensions found expression in highly formalized behavior observable in diplomatic and intercourt communications. Ekaterina Nechaeva has shown with great clarity the existence of an international hierarchy of powers in which position in the pecking order was marked out by gifts, titles, ritual acts, and other specific tokens of status.[54] As the chief players, Rome and Persia effectively established the terms of participation for lesser powers in the informal ranking of mutual regard. The constant challenge for the two superpowers lay in finding a way to represent their relationship to each other and to their internal populations. This entailed a great amount of rhetorical posturing.

Two general scenarios for diplomatic relations between the empires existed. They enacted subordination or parity. In the first, one empire might claim the other was its tributary. We find this unequal relation expressed chiefly in the harsh debate about tribute payments (largely in the sixth century) and depicted in imperial monuments (largely in the third century). Another way to show subordination was through the language of kinship, which could represent an imbalance of power between fathers and sons.

In the second possible scenario, Romans and Persians might wish to claim parity of status. This did not happen often and went in the face of both empires' claims to universal dominance. It usually resulted from a military and diplomatic stalemate. Solutions to the dilemma of representing equality again lay in the language of kinship with evocations of brotherhood between the two monarchs. Less directly, instances of imperial guardianship or adoption across their boundaries indicated a relationship of trust. There were also specific terms to be used, like *isotimia*, that gave equality a special spin. We will look at the two scenarios in turn to see how the diplomatic register of deference found expression in varied circumstances.

The First Scenario: Subordination

The ideology of Sasanian supremacy was represented in monumental sculptural relief and palace architecture in the third century, and in treaties involving tribute payment in the sixth century.[55] The most striking visual representation of Persian attitudes to Rome may still be seen in a series of relief sculptures at Naqsh-e Rostam near Bishapur, the site of the palace of Shapur I, a dynamic ruler who expanded his empire at Roman expense during his long reign (r. 240–70). These carvings celebrate three separate victories over Rome, precisely reversing the standard Roman imagery of the submissive foreigner.[56] Sasanian rulers relished these reliefs, even though no Roman emperor would have seen them.

One relief shows Shapur trampling the Roman emperor Gordian III (r. 238–44), who had died on campaign in Mesopotamia. The carving perhaps is also a metaphor for the eventual triumph of Ohrmazd over the forces of disorder in the form of Ahreman.[57] A second relief depicts Gordian's successor, Philip (r. 244–49), kneeling before the Persian king,[58] to whom he had paid a large sum of money to be allowed to return to Roman territory. The scene presents him as a tribute paying suppliant. A third relief, carved somewhat later, shows Shapur grasping the wrists of the Roman emperor Valerian, whom he had defeated in 260 and taken into captivity.[59]

Sasanian palace architecture and art provide other examples of ritualized status relationships. In the sixth century, Khosro I (r. 531–79) made his title of "King of Kings" tangible in the dais of his throne room in his palace near modern Baghdad. Flanking his own golden throne stood three empty royal chairs intended for his subject kings, namely the rulers of Rome, China, and the Hephthalite Huns.[60] No one else was permitted to sit on these lesser thrones. His entire court sat at an even lower level in fixed positions, turning the throne room into "a ritual map of the known political world."[61] Here, in the symbolic center of the realm, all the great powers of the earth were placed in positions of subordination to the Sasanian ruler. We are reminded both of Eusebius's proud description of emissaries from all lands bringing gifts to Constantine and of the Theodosian obelisk base in Constantinople discussed above. Unlike the obelisk base, however, Khusro's statement of imperial order in the throne room would have been seen by very few people.

In another incident, Khusro took the opportunity to act out his position as King of Kings and simultaneously insult the Romans when he presented himself as the beneficent patron of his Roman "subjects." A Persian source records his voice: "When Caesar deceived me and I assailed him, he was humbled, requested peace, dispatched money to me, and submitted tribute and ransom. I gave in charity to the poor of Rome and to the weak inhabitants of its territories what Caesar had sent to me [in tribute], namely ten thousand dinars."[62] Khusro doubtless enjoyed immensely the opportunity to throw Roman tribute back in their faces by calling it charity on his part. He knew how to twist the knife. At the same time, by reminding Romans of his paramount status with such a public gesture, he demonstrated to his subjects that he was fulfilling his imperial duty.

PERSIAN PERSPECTIVES ON TRIBUTE

Roman and Sasanian imperial attitudes about the payment of tribute were remarkably similar. Persian evidence will be our starting point because it was they who pushed for money from Rome in treaties, not vice versa, especially in the sixth century. How Romans reacted to Persian demands reveals a clash between pragmatism and ideology at the Roman court.

Like the Romans, Sasanian rulers believed that paying tribute to another state, no matter what the circumstances, was a humiliating act of subordination.[63] Although many aspects of Sasanian political thought changed in the late antique centuries, this principle remained constant. Furthermore, Persians believed that all other nations of the world were rightly tributary to them because their King of Kings of the Iranians and non-Iranians, as he styled himself, maintained divine order throughout the world. According to Zoroastrian belief, his effort on behalf of the world's populations required their submission. For a Sasanian ruler, conquest was a duty and necessity because

FIGURE 4. Shapur at Naqsh-e Rostam. In 260, the Sasanian monarch Shapur I captured the Roman emperor Valerian in battle. This monumental relief, carved in a cliff in Iran, commemorates the victory, depicting Valerian kneeling in supplication. In showing the defeat of enemies, the Sasanians and Romans shared a similar iconography. Naqsh-e Rostam, Iran. Luisa Ricciarini / Bridgeman Images.

it demonstrated legitimacy.[64] In the same breath, he needed to be seen by his nobles as the recipient of tribute from vanquished foes. Richard Payne explains, "The acquisition of tribute stood alongside the expansion of agriculture, the construction of cities and the promotion of social justice, among other world-restoring practices, as one of the characteristic activities of a cosmologically effective king realizing the legacy of his primordial predecessors."[65]

TRIBUTE AND TWO TREATIES

In nearly all the known diplomatic exchanges with Rome, demands for payment appeared on the agenda. This was a feature of the heightened tensions of the sixth century. To see what calls for tribute Persian rulers made and how Romans perceived and responded to them, we turn to a few treaties. The

"HOSTILES AND FRIENDLIES" [67]

FIGURE 5. Gold medallion of Constantine I, struck at the mint in Siscia (Sisak in modern Croatia) in 327. It reads, "Virtue of Our Lord Emperor Constantine." The emperor is in full military gear with a sweeping cloak. He carries a spear in his right hand and a trophy of arms over his left shoulder. The figure he steps on wears a Persian hat and clothing, indicating that Constantine is claiming symbolic superiority over the Sasanian kingdom. © Dumbarton Oaks, Coins and Seals Collection, Washington, DC, Accession no. BZC.1949.4.

payments might be presented to the Romans as "cost-sharing" for the defense of Caucasus mountain passes against Hunnic incursions, but in whatever terms they were cast for the Romans, for internal consumption in Persia they were red-letter indications of submission. We can follow the interactions in some detail.

Late in the fifth century, Persian monarchs lost a war with the Hephthalite Huns, whose kingdom extended along Persia's border in Central Asia. The Hephthalites imposed heavy tribute payments on the Persians. In 502, however, a new arrangement between the realms was brokered, which ended

[68] CHAPTER 2

Persia's burden. This enabled the Sasanians to resume a more adventurous policy. Kavadh I began a series of wars with the Romans that spanned almost the entire sixth century (502–32, 540–62, and 572–91). During periods of peace, they continued to struggle against one another through Arab and other proxies. In the treaties that marked the end of each phase of hostilities, terms generally required that Romans pay large sums of gold to Persia, and Roman emperors complied. Some Romans believed that Persian rulers began wars with them in order to refill their treasuries, and many modern scholars share that view, overlooking the symbolic value of receiving tribute.[66] While the sums demanded from Rome were always substantial, however, and certainly would have been welcomed, they were not great enough to restore the Persian treasury.[67] However burdensome the payments may have been, the Roman government evidently considered them preferable to the costs of open warfare. This hints at competing policy-making values between pragmatic cost-benefit analysis and ideologically driven concerns played out at court among bureaucrats, diplomats, military officials, and the emperor. Symbolic value and financial value were at odds.

Many Roman writers of the day censured these payments because, like the Persians, they considered them demeaning. They chose to overlook their "good value" in averting open warfare, preferring to concentrate on the shame accrued by Rome, perhaps because they did not have to make hard budgetary decisions or determine long-term policy. Procopius, the astute historian of Justinian's wars and the best witness for this attitude, took an entirely negative, highly ideological view of tribute payment. In a typically overheated passage in the *Secret History*, for example, he likens Justinian's making payments to barbarians to throwing the wealth of Rome into the sea.[68] When he referred to Persian payments to the Hephthalites in the preceding century, he said that they made the Persians "subjects" of the Huns.[69] We can presume he felt the same way when Romans sent cash to Persia. In his notorious *Secret History*, Procopius explained that Justinian's destructive policies resulted from his demonic nature.[70] Agathias, the historian who continued Procopius's narrative, similarly describes how Justinian imposed tribute on a local population in the Caucasus: "Whereupon Justinian bade him impose upon them a fixed annual tribute to be paid in perpetuity . . . [so] that in this way they should become aware of their position as dependents and realize that they were tributary and absolutely enslaved."[71]

THE TREATY OF 532: THE "ETERNAL PEACE"

The first great war between Rome and Persia during Justinian's reign ended with a treaty in 532 that established a so-called Eternal Peace.[72] Both of the rulers who made the treaty were new to the throne and ambitious, Justinian having come to power in 527 and Khusro in 531. The hostilities that preceded the treaty were complicated, and some background is necessary.[73] Justinian had a full plate of problems that forced him to concentrate on his eastern frontier. A series of earthquakes in 526 had destroyed Antioch, Laodicea, and other towns. Familiar tensions reappeared regarding defense of his north-eastern frontier. At the moment Justinian came to the throne, in the winter of 526–27, Kavadh, the monarch of Persia, had demanded 500 pounds of gold per year from the Romans to help defray the cost of defending the Caucasus mountain passes against nomadic invaders, a not entirely unreasonable request since some of these gateways to the steppe opened into Roman regions as well as Persian territory. His sudden demand caused negotiations to break down, however. Taking advantage of the many uncertainties in the eastern borderlands, Al-Mundhir, the Lakhmid Arab king and Persia's proxy in southern Mesopotamia, led extremely destructive raids into Roman territory between 526 and 529 and again in 536.[74] Costly tasks of reconstruction and building new defensive works to protect against these raids became necessary.[75] Additional problems arose from a major Samaritan revolt that erupted in 532.[76] To meet these challenges, Justinian undertook administrative and military reform of eastern frontier zones.[77]

Al-Mundhir's invasion in the early spring of 529 compelled Justinian to send ambassadors to Kavadh asking for a truce. Malalas records the Persian monarch's reply,[78] which is notable for using celestial imagery to create a parallel between himself and his Roman counterpart, for making claims of traditional brotherhood, and for appealing to Justinian as a Christian monarch:

> Kavadh, King of Kings, of the rising sun, to Flavius Justinian Caesar, of the setting moon. We have found it written in our ancient records that we are brothers of one another, and that if one of us should stand in need of men or money, the other should provide them. From that time till the present we have remained constant in this. Whenever nations have risen against us, against some we have been compelled to fight, whilst others we have persuaded by gifts of money to submit to us, so it is clear that everything in our treasury has been spent. We informed the emperors Anastasius and Justin about this, but we achieved nothing. Thus we have been compelled to mobilize for war, and having become neighbours of Roman territory we have been compelled to destroy the peoples in between on the pretext of their disobedience, even though they had done nothing wrong. But, as pious Christians, spare lives and bodies and give us some of your gold. If you do not do this, prepare yourselves for war. For this you have a whole year's notice, so that we should not be thought to have stolen our victory or to have won the war by trickery.[79]

Justinian demurred, preferring further negotiation, but Kavadh made a surprise attack in force, causing great damage. When negotiations resumed in

530, Kavadh repeated his demand for money to help him defend the Caucasus passes.[80] Before decisions could be reached, however, Persian forces invaded again and the war continued. Finally, renewed negotiations brought a long-desired cessation of hostilities in 532, the "Eternal Peace" that was meant to put an end to the chronic warfare between the two empires.[81] Justinian agreed to hand over 11,000 pounds of gold in one payment. Both sides returned fortresses and territory they had won, hostages were returned, and those who had gone over to the Roman side were permitted to choose whether to return to Persia. The peace was to last for the two emperors' lifetimes (an indication that the peace was between monarchs, not states), and the treaty explicitly stated that the two monarchs "were brothers according to the ancient custom and that if one of them needed military assistance in money or men, they should provide it without dispute."[82] This repeated the Persian's prior argument.

What did the empires gain? The Persians benefited in several ways. There would be immediate financial benefits; Kavadh could boast that the Romans were paying tribute; and Rome's agreement to help in the future might provide an opportunity to make further demands for funds, thereby providing justification for renewed conflict if the Romans refused to pay.[83] Why did Justinian agree to such a large payment? Geoffrey Greatrex rightly suggests that the lump sum avoided the appearance of annual tribute and the ignominy of subordinate status.[84] The Romans could afford it and defending the western Caucasus passes that fed into Lazica was a wise strategic precaution. Not least, it freed him to prepare the invasion of the Vandal Kingdom in North Africa that began the following year. The Eternal Peace lasted until 540, when Khusro, then on the throne for nine years, took advantage of weakened Roman defenses and launched another invasion, which initiated a war that lasted until 562.

In this conflict, neither the forces of Justinian nor Khusro could claim the upper hand, and in 557 they arranged an armistice that recognized the status quo.[85] In 561, discussions began about making a formal treaty. Once again the Persians asked for a long-term arrangement in which the Romans would pay a fixed amount of gold.[86] They demanded, furthermore, thirty years' worth of payments to be made up front. The Romans, on the other hand, wanted a short time period and no payments. A final compromise produced a peace meant to last for fifty years. Rome would receive Lazica in the western Caucasus, and the Persians would be paid 30,000 gold pieces per year, with payment for the first seven years to be made immediately, followed by payment for three more years. They agreed as well to continue defending the Caspian Gates in the eastern Caucasus.[87] They did not receive further Roman payment for their Arab proxies, who had played an important part in the hostilities. A formal treaty was concluded in 562.[88]

While the cost of the treaty for Justinian had been steep, it did not even reach one-half of the sum stipulated in the treaty of 532. This was a victory for

"HOSTILES AND FRIENDLIES" [71]

the pragmatists at court. As it turned out, furthermore, most of the money was never paid. With the death of Justinian in 565, imperial policy regarding the use of payments as a tool in foreign policy abruptly changed.

Justinian's successor, Justin II (r. 565–78), pursued a different foreign policy.[89] Not only did he cease all payments of subsidies to foreign powers, in 572 his armies attacked Persia, provoking a strong counterinvasion. After the great Roman border fortress of Daras in northern Mesopotamia fell in 573, Justin suffered a breakdown and was unable to rule. Tiberius II Constantine (r. 574–82), a family member, assumed power.[90] Negotiations for a truce began in 574. A one-year cessation of hostilities was arranged at the cost of 45,000 nomismata, or 450 pounds of gold, followed by a five-year extension applying to the Mesopotamian frontier at the cost of 30,000 nomismata. Hostilities continued in Armenia, the Caucasus, and Arabia.[91]

THE TREATY OF 576

In late 576, Menander tells us, emissaries of the emperor Tiberius, after a string of Persian defeats, met with representatives of Khusro on the eastern border of the Roman Empire to seek a peace treaty.[92] After fruitless finger-pointing about which side had broken the previous treaty struck in 562 during the reign of Justinian, they decided to move on and discuss what the terms of a peace might be. Mebod, the high-ranking Persian negotiator, spoke first. He suggested a return to the terms of the previous treaty, which would require the Romans to pay 30,000 nomismata annually, return Persarmenia and Iberia, and repatriate Persian fugitives. The Romans immediately rejected the suggestion that they pay anything to the Persians, on the grounds that doing so would make them tributaries and subordinate to Khusro. Furthermore, turning peace into a commodity to be bought and sold would render it neither lasting nor secure.[93] Finally, Mebod played his last card and revealed instructions from Khosro to make peace on the basis of equal terms or *isotimia* (ἰσοτιμία) between the two empires and therefore without any payment. Tiberius, furthermore, was willing to cede Persarmenia and Iberia, though he insisted that any inhabitants of those lands (including rebels) might move without hindrance to Roman territory. A peace based on *isotimia* pleased both sides, so much so that the Persians entered into discussion of their surrendering Daras for a small amount of money.[94]

The word *isotimia*, which means "equality in honor" in Greek, deserves a slight digression. We do not know the equivalent words suggested by the Persian representative, but both sides liked the idea of a treaty on "equal terms" in which neither lost face. Undoubtedly, the word referred to the give-and-take of tribute and land. It also took on an added gloss of legitimacy and dignity for the Romans through patristic associations and more recent doctrinal debates. Church Fathers used *isotimia* to mean the equality of elements of the Trinity and the equality of members within the Church.[95] Beginning in the fourth century, Basil of Caesarea employed *isotimia* to indicate the equal dignity of the Father and the Son in the Trinity.[96] This point was made typically in response to Arian (i.e., heretical) arguments that subordinated the Son or Holy Spirit to the Father. The same honor and veneration was to be given to the Father, the Son, and the Holy Spirit, as stated by the Council of Constantinople of 381.[97] It is striking that the question of the equality or subordination of father and son was precisely the issue at stake between the Persian and Roman rulers.

Another context for *isotimia* was the still controversial discussion of the nature of Christ. In this regard, it is not surprising to find that *isotimia* appears in the concluding document of the Second Council of Constantinople in 553, conducted under Justinian's watchful eye, which sought to resolve various christological issues. An imperative was to deny any sort of inequality between the two natures of Christ.[98] The council issued fourteen canons that anathematized those who held incorrect views. Canon IV notes that anyone who suggests that the union of the Word of God with human flesh was only in respect of equality of honor (*isotimia*), among other things, should be anathema, for Christ's unity was complete even as he was one part of the Trinity.[99] Not only does the possibility of honor equally shared by Rome and Persia recalibrate the register of difference of Roman superiority, it does so with a word highly evocative of Christian meaning.

To return to the treaty of 576, we see that hopes of peace were soon dashed. Roman troops in Armenia, where there had been no cessation of hostilities during the long negotiations, suffered a stinging defeat, which emboldened Khusro to stop discussion of the transfer of Daras and announce, to the alarm of both Roman and Persian ambassadors, that he would break the general truce and invade the Roman Empire again. He also announced that he would return any funds paid by the Romans for the truce currently in effect, prorated against the time that had passed since he broke the truce. Zacharias, the Roman ambassador, scrambled to save the agreement. After hurried secret communications with the emperor in Constantinople, an offer was made to Mebod that the Romans would pay the ransom for Daras plus any outstanding sums owed for the truce. In return, Mebod pledged on oath that if the treaty were agreed upon immediately, and if the Romans evacuated Persarmenia and Iberia, Khusro would give Daras as a gift to the Romans later. The Romans assumed, however, that Mebod had no intention of arranging for the return of Daras and was trying to trick them. Negotiations collapsed once more. Menander tells us that the same Mebod directing the negotiations also was in charge of the renewal of hostilities, yet another indication of Khusro's duplicity.[100]

In this welter of negotiations, control of strategic territories was a critical negotiating point, but so was the payment of treasure. Thirty thousand gold

"HOSTILES AND FRIENDLIES" [73]

pieces (nomismata or solidi) paid annually was an amount as heavy in symbolism as in inherent value. Contemporaries, both Persian and Roman, considered the annual payments to be tribute, and so indicated a lack of equality between the two empires. The risk of subordinate status was built into these negotiations. Demands for the hefty payment of gold in the treaty of 576 indicate that any notion of *isotimia* had broken down.

FATHERS AND SONS: SUBORDINATION
THROUGH KINSHIP

In both Roman and Persian societies, sons owed deference to their fathers. This asymmetrical bond found its way into diplomatic language, but only at moments of dire need for the monarch who called himself the other's son. To be called a "father" by a "son" indicated subordination and a degree of self-abasement. A father-son relationship was invoked in two tense diplomatic exchanges between Rome and Persia. The first played out against the backdrop of civil war in Persia in the last decade of the sixth century, when the Persian ruler needed help from the Romans. The second occurred a dozen years later, when Emperor Heraclius was on the ropes. We will look at them separately.

In 589, the Persian ruler Hormizd IV dismissed his general Vahram Tchobin, who had lost a battle against Roman forces. Vahram decided to rebel, and Persia slid into civil war.[101] Before Vahram could depose Hormizd, however, others at court did so and put Hormizd's son Khusro II on the throne. Refusing to recognize their choice, Vahram defeated Khusro's forces in battle and seized the throne. With nowhere else to run, Khusro escaped to Roman territory and twice beseeched the emperor Maurice to restore him to his throne.[102] In these desperate straits, the royal Persian refugee thoroughly humbled himself by offering to surrender Armenia. Theophylact gives an account:

[11.1] Khusro king of Persians greets the most prudent king of the Romans, the beneficent, peaceful, masterful, lover of nobility and hater of tyranny, equitable, righteous, saviour of the injured, bountiful, forgiving. [2] God effected that the whole world should be illumined from the very beginning by two eyes, namely by the most powerful kingdom of the Romans and by the most prudent sceptre of the Persian state. [3] For by these greatest powers the disobedient and bellicose tribes are winnowed and man's course is continually regulated and guided. And one can see that the sequence of events is consonant with our words. [4] Since, then, there are certain malignant and evil demons abounding in the world, who are eager to confound all God's excellent dispositions, even though their enterprise does not achieve its result, it is right for God-loving men of piety to take the field against these, having received from God a treasury of wisdom and the strong arm and weapons of justice. . . . [10] It is, then, right that you should guide the current irregularity of affairs in the Persian state; for thereby the Romans will receive through you a more glorious reputation. [11] These words which I write, do I, Khusro, address to you as if I were in your presence, I, Khusro *your son and suppliant* [ὁ σὸς υἱὸς καὶ ἱκέτης]. For the chance course of events will not make you disregard what is proper to my rank and title. May the angels of God who grant blessings preserve the kingdom for you free from disgrace and tyranny.[103]

Sebeos, a seventh-century Armenian historian, corroborates this account:

Then king Khosro sent to king Maurice prominent men with gifts, and wrote as follows: "Give me the throne and royal station of my fathers and ancestors; send me an army in support with which I may be able to defeat my enemy; and restore my kingdom; [then] I shall be your son. I shall give you [list of the regions] . . . Let us observe a pact of peace between us until the death of us both; and let this oath be secure between us and between our sons who will reign after us."[104]

Despite objections from his councilors, who were happy to see Persian factions destroy one another,[105] Maurice did not take their advice, preferring long-term security with a victorious Khusro in his debt to the uncertainties of the civil war's results. Roman imperial forces intervened to assist Khusro and his troops in several battles. For the first and last time, Roman and Persian troops fought side by side.[106] When Khusro returned the fortress of Dara to Maurice, the emperor called him "son."[107] Khusro reclaimed his throne in the summer of 591, establishing a period of peace with Rome that lasted twelve years.

Theophylact's remark in the first passage above, that the final treaty of 591 "was made *on equal terms* [ἐν ἴσῃ μοίρᾳ] and thus indeed that great Persian war was brought to a glorious conclusion for the Romans,"[108] has sparked much discussion. Martin Higgins in 1941 wove a fantasy that overstated the significance of the treaty, saying that it marked a turning point in Rome's political ideology[109] in which Rome renounced its claim to exclusive world authority and accepted Persia as a sovereign and equal state.[110] He suggested a Roman policy of cultivating permanent friendship with Persia through diplomacy.[111] Englebert Winter, while noting that the father-son relationship was imagined, suggested that it can be understood as a diplomatic gesture implying equality between the Roman and Persian rulers.[112] Michael Whitby and Mary Whitby rightly point out that "The treaty was equal in the sense that there were no financial payments on either side."[113] A near-contemporary writer, the Armenian compiler of the early-seventh-century *Account of Affairs in Armenia*, interpreted the agreement quite differently.[114] He reports that Khusro "gave all of Armenia, as far as Dvin, to the Emperor Maurice, in return

"HOSTILES AND FRIENDLIES" [75]

for which he was established as king beneath him."[115] Understanding the status differential between the two monarchs that this agreement represented, he saw in Khusro's acknowledgment of Maurice as father a sign not of equality but of subordination.

The Second Scenario: Parity

While many opportunities existed for Roman and Persian monarchs to project their claims of superiority, there were also diplomatic situations that involved equality, as seen in the Treaty of 576 and in other circumstances that we turn to now.

EQUALITY THROUGH KINSHIP, ADOPTION, AND GUARDIANSHIP[116]

Rome and Persia regularly saluted each other as "my brother" in their diplomatic correspondence.[117] They could not have known that the same convention existed among the great Middle Eastern monarchies of the Late Bronze Age, an era when diplomacy and written treaties first appeared in recorded history.[118] In the Roman world, the salutation "my brother" became standard diplomatic practice, perhaps as early as the time of Diocletian.[119] Documentary excerpts are found in histories and chronicles throughout the period, from the third through the sixth century, providing a rich archive.[120] It was also used with formal notification that a new monarch had taken the throne.[121] We do not find it in discussion of tribute demands, which presumed inequality.

As with the monarchs of their forgotten past, Roman and Persian rulers had a brotherhood without open membership. Lesser kings for whom they had contempt could not enter the inner circle. In 520/521, for example, Emperor Justin wrote to Kavadh, alerting him that Zilgibi, a king of the Huns who had betrayed the Romans, was soon to double-cross the Persians, too: "It is necessary . . . for us, brothers as we are, to speak out in friendship and not be made the sport of these dogs."[122] Such fraternal pleasantry did not prevent the Roman and Persian monarchs from heaping insults on one another in written correspondence; from time to time, they cheerfully noted their correspondent's arrogance, duplicity, and above all responsibility for resumption of hostilities.[123]

The Persians also developed terms of address that reflected a rather contradictory strand of political and religious cosmology, in which the sun stood for Persia and the moon for Rome. They were "the two eyes of the earth," ordained by God and meant to share world rule. Matthew Canepa has explored this in fascinating detail.[124] The imagery of parallel power did not rule out competition or cooperation, however.[125] Ammianus Marcellinus was aware of this Persian usage and records it in a letter dated to 358: "I, Sapor, King of Kings, partner with the Stars, brother of the Sun and Moon, to my brother Constantius Caesar offer most ample greeting."[126]

Two centuries later, in an unsuccessful plea for financial assistance, as noted above Kavadh connected the celestial imagery to historical claims of brotherhood in a letter to Justinian: "I, Kavadh, king of kings, of the rising sun, to Flavius Justinian Caesar, of the setting moon. We have found . . . that we are brothers of one another."[127]

GUARDIANSHIP AND ADOPTION

Even more rarely, we find the Roman emperor and the Persian king of kings discussing the possibility of one being the guardian of the other's child. In the first book of his *Wars*, which narrates Roman conflict with Persia, Procopius carefully places three accounts of adoption and guardianship to give structure to his narrative of events. He uses them to describe how cultural differences between nations might play a role in diplomacy. Though scholars have discussed these three episodes individually as moments in political history, they have not discussed them together in terms of Roman ideas of parity with their Persian neighbors or put them in an ethnographic context.

THE FIRST STORY: THE PERSIAN
GUARDIAN OF THEODOSIUS II

Procopius relates that in the year 408, the emperor Arcadius (495–508) on his deathbed in Constantinople had to make hard decisions about the safety of his infant son, Theodosius (r. 408–50).[128] The baby's uncle, Honorius, who was beleaguered in Italy, could not be counted on to support Theodosius's position. Arcadius feared that choosing a regent in Constantinople would guarantee only that the baby would soon be murdered. Forced to look elsewhere for someone to protect his son, the emperor devised an ingenious plan. In his will he named Yazdegerd I of Persia (r. 399–420) to be Theodosius's guardian, urging him to preserve the empire for his son. Fortunately, Procopius relates, the Persian ruler had a very high opinion of Arcadius and accepted his request, promising to go to war against anyone who might plot against young Theodosius.[129] He kept his word, and there was no warfare between Rome and Persia throughout the rest of Yazdegerd's reign.[130]

The idea of finding a guardian for an underage son is certainly not remarkable, but the choice of the foreign guardian needs explanation. Would a Roman emperor ever have contemplated making his archrival the guardian of his infant heir? The decision to do so presumes equal levels of status and a temporary erosion of the standard Roman/barbarian distinction.[131] It would have put a calculated amount of pressure on both the internal system of succession at court and the external system of foreign

"HOSTILES AND FRIENDLIES" [77]

relations in hopes of maintaining stability at home. The stakes could not have been higher.

Unfortunately, early fifth-century sources maintain a puzzling silence regarding the event, though later writers discuss it.[132] Current scholarship considers Procopius generally reliable on the Persians,[133] and we must take his account seriously. This was no literary fiction. Some chronological problems may be found, however. The appeal to Yazdegerd was of such importance that it could scarcely have been a sudden deathbed inspiration, and we know that Arcadius died suddenly.[134] In light of this, the request for guardianship should be seen instead as a carefully considered policy decision based on precedent. The creation of the Persian guardianship probably occurred in 402, shortly after Theodosius's birth, when he was proclaimed Augustus, rather than in 407, when he had grown beyond infancy.[135]

When Yazdegerd assumed his throne in 399,[136] there was no treaty in place between the two powers. The previous treaty of 363 had expired and probably not been renewed.[137] A new treaty resolving border trade disputes was agreed upon late in 400 or shortly thereafter.[138] At the same time, an Armenian bishop named Marutha coincidentally was at the Persian capital. An accomplished physician, he is credited with curing Yazdegerd's invalid son as well as the monarch's migraines. A Syriac source called him "mediator of peace and concord between East and West,"[139] so it is likely he was a member of the Roman embassy negotiating with Yazdegerd. Facing serious problems with his own aristocracy and with the Zoroastrian priesthood, he was in the mood for good relations with Rome. He did not persecute Christians, whom he knew to be a matter of Roman concern, and he repatriated hostages.[140] It was presumably during this period, "the apogee of Roman-Persian relations,"[141] that Arcadius also approached Yazdegerd to suggest guardianship.[142]

Arcadius already had personal experience of guardianship when he approached Yazdegerd. Eight years earlier, in 394, the year before his own death, his father, Theodosius I, had named Stilicho, the commander-in-chief of the western armies (*magister militum per occidentum*), to be the guardian of his nine-year-old son, Honorius. At that time, the emperor was planning to lead an expedition to confront Hunnic and Marcomannic incursions across the Danube. Entrusting the boy to Stilicho, an experienced general and a trusted member of the Theodosian house,[143] made good sense. Because Stilicho's father was a Vandal, he was ineligible for the throne and so all the more trustworthy. It is not likely that Stilicho became guardian of Honorius's brother Arcadius, who at eighteen was well past the legal age of guardianship and was ruling in Constantinople, albeit with the aid of close advisers. For political reasons of his own, after Theodosius's death Stilicho claimed to be the guardian of Arcadius as well as Honorius.[144]

Agathias offers a similar account of the event, but evaluates Arcadius's actions far more harshly:

[78] CHAPTER 2

But whoever expresses admiration for this decision is, in my opinion, judging it in the light of later events and not by the logic of the original situation, since it hardly could have made sense to entrust one's nearest and dearest to a foreigner and a barbarian, the ruler of a bitterly hostile nation, a man who in matters of honour and justice was an unknown quantity and who on top of everything else was the adherent of a false religion. If the infant came to no harm and if, thanks to the care and protection of his guardian, his throne was never in jeopardy though at the time he had not yet even been weaned, then one ought rather to praise the honesty of Yazdegerd than the action of Arcadius.[145]

Agathias is hostile toward Persians in general, full of mistrust and prejudice, but he acknowledges Yazdegerd's "honesty" (εὐγνωμοσύνη). Perhaps he was a bit surprised by it.

THE SECOND STORY: JUSTINIAN AND KHUSRO

Elsewhere in the first book of the *Wars*,[146] Procopius again explores the themes of guardianship, accession to power, and relationships between empires. He tells us that Justin I, Justinian's predecessor, had come to the throne in Constantinople in 518 by pushing aside all of the family of Anastasius, the previous emperor. Upon hearing of this, the Persian monarch Kavadh began to worry that Persian rivals from other aristocratic families might seize the Persian throne when he died and dispose of his sons. He was particularly concerned about his favorite, Khusro. Kavadh hoped to find a solution through diplomacy. Procopius intends his readers to have in mind the story of Arcadius and his vulnerable son. Khusro wrote to Justin offering to end the war between the two empires if Justin would adopt Khusro as his son. Procopius offers a version of Khusro's letter:

> However, I ask of you a certain favour in return for this [putting aside questions of responsibility for the war and making peace], which would bind together in kinship and in the good-will which would naturally spring from this relation not only ourselves but all our subjects, and which would be calculated to bring us to a satiety of the blessings of peace. My proposal, then, is this, that you should make my son Khusro, who will be my successor to the throne, your adopted son [εἰσποιητὸν παῖδα ποιήσαιο].[147]

According to Procopius, Justin and his presumed heir, Justinian, were both initially very pleased at this proposal, and they began drawing up the legal instruments for adoption in accordance with Roman procedure.[148] Proclus, the *quaestor sacri palatii* (quaestor of the sacred palace), the highest legal official at court, however, spoke out forcefully against the adoption. He

"HOSTILES AND FRIENDLIES" [79]

objected to its novelty, claiming it was a trick that could lead to handing over the Roman Empire to the barbarian Persians. If Khusro were to become the adopted son of Justin, Proclus argued, he would be the legal heir to the Roman Empire when Justin died.

Proclus's arguments were contrived and intended to cause fear; Justin may have once been a nobody who forced himself onto the Roman throne, but a Persian emperor was the one person who could never become emperor of Rome through any sort of legitimate process without a victory in war. At the very least, his condition as a Zoroastrian and not a Roman citizen precluded Roman kingship. The legal niceties of a personal adoption by a foreigner, even a foreign emperor, could never elide the fundamental differences between the two empires. By the same token, neither could Justin, a Christian and a Roman, ever be seriously considered as a candidate for the Persian throne. The very cultural differences between Rome and Persia, and the power that their monarchs could wield, would have made Justin a good adoptive father for Khusro, just as Yazdegerd could have been imagined as a capable guardian for Theodosius II, or as Stilicho had been for Honorius. Paradoxically, in these instances, cultural difference functioned in a positive and practical way. Difference became a practical advantage, something upon which an international connection could be built.

A second letter from Kavadh followed, again promising peace and pushing for the adoption. Roman opinion grew more hostile, and it was decided, at Proclus's prompting, to send ambassadors to him, asking for details about how the adoption might be arranged. The Roman emissaries this time were instructed to treat the cultural differences between the two empires not as a helpful factor in arranging the adoption but as an insult. They threw the charge of "barbarism" in the face of their Persian counterparts. Procopius reports that they were instructed to say directly that the adoption "must be of the sort befitting a barbarian, and his [Justin's] meaning was that the barbarians adopt sons, not by a document, but by arms and armour."[149] When the Persians heard the Roman proposal about "adoption . . . befitting a barbarian,"[150] they grew angry at the insult and negotiations broke down with nothing accomplished, neither peace nor adoption. Kavadh immediately began to plan an invasion of Roman territory.[151] Why was "befitting a barbarian" so insulting? The premise of the proposed adoption had presumed an equality between Roman and Persian monarchs. The Roman embassy had deliberately torpedoed that premise.

THE THIRD STORY: KAVADH AND THE HEPHTHALITE HUNS

Procopius tells us how the exiled Persian ruler Kavadh (r. 488–96 and 498–531) took refuge among the Hephthalite Huns, whose king had no qualms about presenting him with one of his daughters in marriage.[152] Then, since Kavadh was now his son-in-law, the Hephthalite king gave him command of an army with which to attack Persia. Practically out of nowhere—it is truly a surprising account—Procopius describes the Hephthalites as being civilized, unlike other Hunnic nomads. They have a settled life, he says, with laws and one ruler, and they "observe right and justice in their dealings both with one another and with their neighbours, in no degree less than the Romans and the Persians."[153]

In these first chapters of his history Procopius has set up a triangle of relations among Romans, Persians, and Hephthalites. He claims that they are civilized in the same basic ways, a remarkable concession, but he never questions Roman superiority. Relations among the rulers of these three empires, despite the constant threat of open warfare, are such that they can establish kinship ties with one another through marriage (as Persians had done with Hephthalites) or adoption and guardianship (as Persians had done with Romans). This is a degree of mutual recognition unimaginable between the great powers and less important peoples.

A dozen years later, in 602, when Phocas deposed Maurice, Khusro again played the filial piety card, claiming to be "upholding the pious memory of the emperor Maurice" when he invaded Roman territory.[154]

SUBORDINATION AGAIN

The last example returns to the display of subordination (p. 73), highlighted by what we have just seen about kinship and adoption. The year 615 saw Heraclius's empire in terrible trouble.[155] The war against Persia was not going well and enemy forces had reached Chalcedon, very near Constantinople. Hoping to negotiate, Heraclius had met with the Persian commander, who claimed not to have the authority to discuss terms. A delegation of Constantinopolitan dignitaries then went to beg for peace from the Persian monarch. They asked Khusro to avenge the murder of Maurice by Phocas, whom Heraclius had deposed but who had formal relations with Persia. In this exchange, Heraclius, truly desperate, humbled himself before his envoys' Persian "father." The *Chronicon Paschale* records his envoys' address to Khusro II as follows:

> [W]e beseech that they be received in appropriate manner by your superabundant Might, and that they shortly return to us, securing for us the peace which is pleasing to God and appropriate to your peace-loving Might. We beg too of your clemency to consider Heraclius, our most pious emperor, *as a true son* [γνήσιον ἔχειν τέκνον], one who is eager to perform the service of your serenity in all things. For if you do this, you will procure a two-fold glory for yourselves, both in respect of your valour in war and in respect of your gift of peace.[156]

Khusro, whose memory was short, rejected Heraclius's abject plea and treated him not as a son but as a usurper. He used the overthrow of Phocas to justify further conflict with Rome, which he ultimately lost.[157]

Arabs

ETHNOGRAPHY AND ARABS
BETWEEN PERSIA AND ROME

Roman rivalry with Persia shaped the profile of Arabs in late antique Roman ethnography. Part of that profile originated centuries before in the "ideology of the pastoral nomad," as Brent Shaw called it, that had resonated in the Near Eastern and Mediterranean world from biblical times.[158] Stubbornly focused on the highly weighted difference between settled and nomadic societies, this ideology coughed up long-lasting judgments about the savagery of nomads as the antithesis of civilized urban life. Though there was space for local particularities in such matters as circumcision, tents, and the beasts they herded and sometimes rode into battle, descriptions of nomads remained predictably similar over time, no matter where they lived. Always on the move, they were considered violent, untrustworthy, and ignorant of settled, civilized life. Eusebius pointed out, aghast, "there is not a banker among them!"[159]

ROMANS AND ARABS[160]

Romans had a long history of relations with the various nomadic and settled groups in the Middle East whom they labeled Saracens (tent dwellers) and we call generically Arabs.[161] When Romans established their presence in the region, they had to cope with bandits on the eastern fringes of the empire who plundered Roman territories and attacked caravans that brought spices and luxury goods into the greater Mediterranean realm. As Rome absorbed client states on the border, confrontation with Arabs became more direct.[162] Roman responses included constructing defensive fortifications, taking punitive military action, nurturing friendships with tribal leaders, and paying bribes as circumstances required.[163] As in the frontier region bordering Germania, complex and distinct societies with regional characteristics slowly developed over several centuries. By the time the weight of the empire had shifted to Constantinople and the Eastern Mediterranean, Romans were old hands on the Arabian frontier.

During Late Antiquity—particularly following the rise to power of the Sasanian dynasty in Persia in the second decade of the third century and the collapse of the kingdom of Palmyra fifty years later—Arab tribes and confederations grew in strategic significance because they became allies of the Roman and Persian empires,[164] which in this region competed for control of Arabian trade routes. Some Arab confederations became strong in their service but, unlike the Goths or the Huns, they never constituted a military threat of the first magnitude to either power. Arab interaction with Rome and Persia was always framed and limited by the larger strategic goals of the great

[82] CHAPTER 2

rivals. By the sixth century, tribal confederations occupied an essential place in Roman defenses, particularly during the wars against Persia.[165] The complex development "from *gentes* to *regna* (peoples to kingdoms)" seen in the Latin West did not occur in precisely the same ways among the various Arab groupings. Against this background, what were the markers that registered difference and how was deference displayed?

EQUALITY

Throughout Late Antiquity, deeply prejudiced Roman policy makers did not consider Arabs or their leaders equal to Romans in any sense.[166] In the diplomatic arena, from the Roman perspective, subordination was taken for granted, both militarily and culturally, and we do not encounter the tense juggling of status markers visible in relations with Persia or the constant belligerence that we will see with the post-Roman polities in Western Europe. An additional factor that contributed to negative views of Arabs was that Christian Arabs often espoused non-Orthodox formulations of the faith, keeping them at a further distance from the Orthodox clerics in Constantinople.

TRUST

In Roman eyes, Arab groups for the most part were either friendly, because they were allies, or hostile, because they were Persia's allies or perhaps raiding independently.[167] They were rarely considered trustworthy. Ammianus Marcellinus went a step further to remark nastily, "The Saracens, however, whom we never found desirable either as friends or as enemies . . . laid waste whatever they could find, like rapacious kites."[168] Nevertheless, his narrative is full of examples of how Romans employed them to Roman ends as best they could.

ALLIANCE

Rome made some Arab groups federate allies (*foederati*).[169] This status involved many tasks, such as protecting caravan routes and settled areas in border provinces, fighting alongside the Roman troops in military campaigns, especially as light cavalry and raiders, controlling other tribes, sometimes helping the Roman army internally, and most of all guarding against Persian attacks. Sometimes groups with allied status lived within Roman borders and their leaders took a place in the Roman army command structure.[170]

Amorkesos, a tribal leader who had once been an ally of Persia, took a different route to a position in the empire.[171] He raided near the Sinai Peninsula from his base on an island in the Gulf of Aqaba, from which he had expelled Roman officials. Leo I (r. 457–74) acceded to his demands for a title and subsidies and invited him to Constantinople, where he received rich gifts, the rank

"HOSTILES AND FRIENDLIES" [83]

of phylarch, and control of several towns in Arabia Petraea, a frontier region in the northern Arabian Peninsula near Petra and the Gulf of Aqaba. Malchus, the fifth-century historian who recorded this visit, condemns the emperor's generosity.[172]

The system of Arab alliances was critically important to the Roman defensive system in the East.[173] One group of Arab federates, perhaps sent by the redoubtable Queen Mavia, helped defend Constantinople from Gothic attack in the aftermath of the Battle of Adrianople in 378.[174] Separate alliances with lesser groups were struck throughout Late Antiquity, but Rome drew its chief allies first from the Tanukh confederation west of the Euphrates, then from the Salih confederation in the Syrian desert, and finally from the Christian Ghassanid confederation in the general area of modern Jordan. The last of these played an important role during Justinian's wars against Persia and its proxies, chiefly the Lakhmids, and against peninsular Arabs. Due to the fact that the Ghassanids followed Monophysite/Miaphysite teachings rather than the Chalcedonian Orthodoxy of imperial Constantinople, during the reigns of Justinian's successors significant tensions developed. Nevertheless they fought on Rome's side against Muslim armies at the Battle of Yarmuk in 628.[175]

ACTS OF DEFERENCE

We have few examples of the "staging" of status relations as Arabs became allies of Rome. One comes from the pen of Ammianus Marcellinus, who, with his appreciative eye for humbled barbarians, records that in March 363 the emperor Julian, advancing through Mesopotamia on his fatal campaign against the Persians, received an embassy of Saracen chieftains (*reguli*).[176] These suppliants approached Julian with heads bowed in great humility to present a golden crown. They hailed him as "lord of the world and of its peoples"—an honorific they might equally have granted the Persian king of kings.[177] Julian was pleased to accept their homage as well as their service as guerilla soldiers. In another passage, Ammianus also notes that Julian's forces had driven off a hostile Arab force which had been allied with Rome but then denied its payment (*salaria* and *munera*). The emperor bragged that he fought with steel, not gold.[178]

Sometimes acts of Arab deference could be seen only as symbolic gestures. During Justinian's reign, an Arab chieftain named Abochorabus (Abu Karib), who controlled territory somewhere on the Arabian coast, gave the emperor an oasis full of palm trees as a token of deference. Both the Roman and the Arab understood that the gift had no practical value and that Justinian could never actually establish Roman government there. In Procopius's words, "Formally, therefore, the emperor holds the Palm Groves, but for him really to possess himself of any of the country there is utterly impossible."[179] Justinian appreciated the intent of the gesture, however, and made Abochorabus the

[84] CHAPTER 2

phylarch of the tribes in Palestine with the responsibility of protecting the province from raids.[180]

These few examples show that the formalities and choreography of approaching the emperor as a suppliant followed the same patterns seen in other diplomatic arenas over the centuries.[181]

SUBSIDIES

Rome paid subsidies to Arab groups determined by degree of friendship. The development of the system in this region is hard to trace.[182] Payments were not referred to as demeaning "tribute"; they were understood to be compensation for services rendered. They indicate Roman control, not a response to extortion. Sometimes paid in gold and sometimes called *salaria et munera*, payments took the form of subsistence allowances that might be withheld or embezzled.[183] Only Heraclius, in the most severe financial and military straits, took severe measures against those of his officials who paid allowances to Arabs. He stopped payments, choosing to view them as extortion, no matter how large or small the amounts might be.[184] Theophanes reports in his *Chronicle* for the year 630/631 that during the reign of Heraclius, when some chieftains arrived at the Syrian village of Mothous (Mu'tah), where the emperor had just won a significant victory, to collect their customary stipends for guarding the approaches to the Syrian desert, the Roman official in charge of distributing funds drove them off, remarking, "The emperor can barely pay his soldiers their wages, much less these dogs!"[185] His action caused much offense, and the Arabs led their fellow tribesmen to Gaza. When the bishop of Alexandria independently made a treaty with approaching Arab forces in 633, meant to buy them off for three years, Heraclius recalled him and sent in his place an official who refused to give them anything.[186] In Mesopotamia, the governor of Osrhoene was condemned and sent into exile for concluding a treaty that involved payment of 100,000 solidi to an Arab general without imperial permission.[187]

TITLES AND RANKS

Romans gave titles and ranks to Arab supporters just as they did to other allies on the empire's perimeter, as we have seen above with Abochorabus. These provided a position within a Roman hierarchy and acknowledged leadership of Arab groups. By Late Antiquity, *phylarch* had become standard as a term applied to Arab leaders in the East, displacing other terms, such as *ethnarch* or *strategos*, that had been used in earlier periods in different regions as well;[188] *tribunus* was their Latin equivalent. The cherished term *basileus* or king was probably given by Justinian to the Ghassanid phylarch Arethas in 529/530 to indicate his considerable power and special ties to the Romans,[189] but it was taken away under Tiberius (see below). No one thought for a moment that the

"HOSTILES AND FRIENDLIES" [85]

title might convey equality with the Roman emperor.[190] Grants of citizenship were not part of the diplomatic reward system. If Arabs lived within a Roman province, they held Roman citizenship after 212. The literary and epigraphic sources do not indicate that citizenship was dangled as a lure or particularly sought after by Arabs beyond Rome's frontier.

CHRISTIANITY

Christianity played a more important role in diplomacy than in the north-western quadrant of the empire because it could indicate a choice of sides. By the early fifth century, baptism had had become a factor in negotiations. For example, when the Arab chieftain Aspebetos allied himself with Rome, he converted to Christianity and took the name Peter. He was given the expected title of phylarch and granted lands in Palestine for himself and his followers, as was the standard Roman practice. He also became a bishop in the region between Jerusalem and Jericho.[191]

Accepting Christianity would make it easier to belong to the Roman enterprise. To some degree it broke the constraints of the anti-nomad ideology through the possibility of shared faith. Christian doctrinal affiliation became a problem in Roman relations with the Ghassanids, however. A break in the treaty between Romans and Ghassanids occurred in 581/582 and lasted for five years.[192] The emperor's attempt to impose Chalcedonian Orthodoxy on the Monophysite/Miaphysite Ghassanids had caused them to revolt. Its leaders were placed under arrest in Constantinople.[193] The treaty was renewed a few years later when a new chieftain, Jafna, reached an accommodation with the emperor on doctrinal matters. His rank was diminished, however. Justinian had granted him kingship in a treaty fifty years earlier, but Heraclius rejected that agreement and ceased calling him king (*basileus*).[194] The appearance of Islam quashed the chances of large-scale Christian expansion. Christian communities, sometimes of significant numbers, would learn to survive in the sea of Muslim believers.

ISLAM

Only with the rise of Islam would perceptions of relative power alter between Romans and Muslim Arabs. The emergence of a lasting Muslim state, as opposed to powerful but dependent tribal confederacies, was due to a combination of the teachings of Islam, military force, internal politics, and voluntary and forced conversion. Consequently, when the Islamic empire took shape in the seventh century, Roman presumptions about diplomatic and military relations with Arabs continued to draw upon a long, shared history, but took a new form shaped by religion as much as by political and military strategy. At that point, a chief marker of difference between their communities would be religious belief.

The Islamic conquests eventually turned the late antique discourse of deference on its head, but the old and new political orders continued to share important links through a connection to Christian history. The followers of Islam, as descendants of Ishmael, located themselves within the Table of Nations tradition that also was so important to Christian views of the world (see chapter 6 below). From the Roman perspective, this gave Muslims a place in the Christian Roman ethnographic frame. For their part, Arab Muslims certainly did not internalize Rome's negative views of Arabs and nomadism. In establishing themselves as a faith-based community, the followers of Islam came to represent a rival sectarian community.

Part II

Rome and the Steppe Peoples: Tables Turned

A third important arena of Roman diplomatic activity in Late Antiquity lay with the steppe polities north of the Danube and farther to the east. Hunnic groups, which started to appear in the grasslands north of the Balkans in the late fourth century, posed a significant threat to the Roman Empire by the middle of the fifth, under the leadership of Attila, who built a far-flung though short-lived empire based in the Great Hungarian Plain. The Avar khaganate plagued the Roman state from the late sixth century and later established a realm in central Europe that lasted until the reign of Charlemagne.[195] With their focus on the figure of the khagan and their own ideology of supremacy, these aggressive empires brought a new level of inclusive political organization to the steppe lands of western Eurasia that set them apart from Rome's other opponents. The imperial nomads upset the geopolitical calculus by testing long-standing Roman claims to hegemony on its northern frontiers. Neither settlers nor conquerors, they posed different challenges in military and diplomatic terms.[196] Romans experienced the newly arrived steppe peoples as predators. What began as modest payments in keeping with old practice turned into painful extortion as the khagans required an increasing intake of gold to maintain the support of their own allies and subordinates.[197] Their growing demands put Romans in the ideologically untenable position of actually being tributary. With Attila, Romans had no choice but to pay. Dealings with him and later nomad rulers provided another context in which the ethnography of status relations could develop.[198]

BEFORE THE HUNS

The Mediterranean world had been well aware of many peoples of the steppe, generically called Scythians, since the time of Herodotus. While acquiring and then protecting Macedonia in the northern Balkans, and also while defending

Greek cities in the Black Sea and Bosporus region, Romans gained considerable experience with different steppe groups. They interacted with the Roman sphere through raiding, migration, and invasion, all of which were quite difficult for Rome to control.[199] Fearing the military strength of steppe confederations, Romans struggled to create defensible lines of demarcation.[200] Romans held steppe peoples in complete contempt because of their savagery and nomadism, not to mention what seemed to be their inability to understand the idea of peace.[201] The nomads epitomized barbarism.

Since military action proved inconclusive, diplomacy played a prominent role in Roman efforts to manage relations with highly mobile nomads.[202] Roger Batty points out that many agreements were struck with steppe chieftains during the first and second centuries because of the volatility of the frontier.[203] Augustus's *Res Gestae* boasts of diplomatic ties with distant steppe peoples.[204] Tacitus describes how, during the reign of Claudius, Romans established diplomatic ties with many peoples of the steppe, some quite new to them, especially in the Pontic region.[205] Batty notes that "As Byzantium was to become in later times, Rome had already become by the middle of the first century an arbiter in the affairs of the steppe tribes. Not the final arbiter, but an important one."[206] The exchange of gifts cemented these ties. By the time Tacitus wrote, Rome was sending gifts to a people who lived beyond the Don River.[207] Roman sources do not complain that the gifts were excessive or unnecessary. All concerned benefited from the networks of dependence that diplomacy enabled. The size of gifts reflected relative status of the negotiating party and their level of autonomy in relation to Roman power.[208] According to Batty, "if not in principle, then in practice, Roman relations with the nomadic peoples had bred some understanding, and even compromise."[209] Rome came to recognize that the nomad threat could not be eliminated but could be somewhat mitigated by maintaining a neutral zone; regulating access to the empire, especially its markets; and by making alliances with different tribes that would limit one another's access to necessary pasturelands.[210] Steppe groupings fought constantly among themselves, and Romans exploited their fractiousness. By the time the situation changed for the worse in Late Antiquity, Roman diplomats had learned a great deal about dealing with steppe peoples.

A LATE ANTIQUE TURNING POINT

The new steppe confederations led by the Huns and then the Avars (and followed by Turks and others), posed a threat that went far beyond the Balkans and the Bosporus. Peoples of the great steppe that reached into Central Asia took a lasting role in shaping European affairs on a grand scale. The Huns were the first to up the ante.[211]

Understanding of how the Huns appeared on the European scene has changed in recent years. As noted above, they did not suddenly appear in large

[88] CHAPTER 2

numbers on the western Eurasian steppe in the late fourth century.[212] Historians now describe a slower process of integration of smaller bands of Huns and various local populations on the western steppe.[213] Archaeologists have found evidence of this complex admixture, particularly in aristocratic graves.[214] We should see the first bands of Huns to arrive not as an "advance guard" of a well-organized empire to the east, but as distinct groups sharing elements of steppe life that would one day coalesce under the more powerful leadership of the khagan, such as that provided by Attila.[215]

The first Hun known by name was Uldin (d. 412), who led a group of Huns on the Danube at the end of the fourth century, a generation after the Battle of Adrianople. Uldin and his forces became embroiled in Roman military affairs and politics in the Balkans. In 400 Uldin captured the rebel Gothic general Gainas and sent his head to Emperor Arcadius as a present.[216] After that, Stilicho employed Uldin's forces in his struggle with Radagaisus, a Gothic warlord in Italy.[217] Uldin had grown strong through alliance and service to Rome. In 408, however, he changed his tune and invaded Moesia. Before he was driven back across the Danube, he rejected the possibility of negotiation.[218] In a passage meant to illustrate the frustration of dealing with Huns, the church historian Sozomen records that he "insolently refused to enter into terms of alliance with the Romans."[219] When the prefect offered terms of peace, Uldin threatened to conquer every nation under the sun. He was willing, however, to accept a huge tribute from the Romans for making peace.[220] Unfortunately for Uldin, his subordinates yielded to Roman bribery and switched sides. Their treachery let Uldin be driven from imperial soil.[221] We see here Uldin's rejection of alliance with Rome, his own claims of world mastery that countered Rome's, his extortionate demands for payments to halt his invasion, and the outrage that they caused. These elements will recur again and again in dealings with Huns and other steppe nomads.

It is worth pointing out that for the first time on record, payments to steppe people were cast as unreasonable extortion and not just the routine cost of doing business. This is the earliest known example of Hunnic extortion on a large scale. Their pressure continued to mount in the course of the fifth century.[222] As their power coalesced, their leaders required a increasing intake of gold to maintain their positions. Attila's uncle Rua received an annual payment of 350 pounds of gold starting in the 420s.[223] When Attila succeeded him in 433, the sum doubled, and in 441 rose to 2,100 pounds annually, supplemented by a lump sum of 6,000 pounds of gold.[224] The success of these demands evidently took a central place in his presentation of kingly authority. The sixth-century Constantinopolitan historian Jordanes, in his description of Attila's funeral, recognized the huge symbolic value of successful extortion. He described the dirge sung by his mourners that gave voice to Hunnic pride at having the upper hand: "King Attila, son of Mundzuk, preeminent among the Huns and master of the mightiest nations, who alone ruled Germania

"HOSTILES AND FRIENDLIES" [89]

and Scythia with previously unheard-of power, who terrified both parts of the Roman Empire by seizing cities, and who mollified by their entreaties lest he plunder them all, accepted an annual tribute."[225] In this encomium, Attila's subversive fantasy (as imagined by another author) in the story about the Milan fresco, had come true.[226] The regular exaction of tribute from Rome demonstrated preeminence in his own eyes and the eyes of his followers.

ROMAN PERCEPTIONS

Late antique Roman writers provide a range of different perceptions of Huns and the exchange of gifts. It is useful to contrast the starkly differing description of Ammianus Marcellinus, in which Huns are presented as barely human, bloodthirsty savages, and the eyewitness account of the mid-fifth-century historian Priscus of Panium, who visited Attila's camp somewhere in Pannonia on a diplomatic mission in 448. As has been shown by Brent Shaw and others, Ammianus's treatment is determined by traditional ethnographic clichés about the barbarity of steppe nomads. Yet he gives the Huns an important role to play in his storytelling.[227] They have driven Goths toward the Roman Empire, where they would destroy the emperor Valens and his army at the Battle of Adrianople, which brings his narrative to a dramatic conclusion.

Priscus, however, has gone far beyond Ammianus's rendition. He has found what Nicola Di Cosmo calls a different "diplomatic voice" with which to address the Huns.[228] His thoughtful observations on his journey survive in fragments, collected in a Byzantine encyclopedic work of the mid-tenth century, the *Excerpta de Legationibus*. Because of the selectivity of the editors of this compendium, we do not know the full range of Priscus's coverage and interests, but among other concerns, he paid close attention to Attila as a political figure. He took an extremely dim view of Attila's extortionate demands for gold and the return of fugitives and of Theodosius II's willingness to accede to them.[229] He describes how the Hun king played the system, repeatedly sending ambassadors to the Roman court on spurious missions in order to collect gifts.[230] He reports a claim made by Attila that by paying tribute, Theodosius had made himself Attila's slave and had surrendered the honor he inherited from his father.[231] Priscus reveals his own opinion when he speaks through the mouth of a Roman in Attila's service, having him say that the title of general given to Attila by the Roman emperor was merely a cover for the fact of having paid tribute.[232] He approved of Theodosius's successor, who refused to pay tribute even at the risk of war but was willing to continue to give gifts as a reward for peace.[233]

Priscus humanizes the Huns without overlooking their violence. Certainly they are terribly destructive enemies, but they also are fully human negotiating partners. His portrait of Attila in the midst of his court shows that he is bound by conventions of international diplomacy and has trust in social relationships.

He is stern but loves his family.[234] For Priscus, Attila is not a monster but a formidable enemy with whom diplomacy is possible and necessary. Priscus's treatment of Attila represents a different ethnographic presentation of steppe peoples.[235] The fragments of Priscus's history that survive show that he was highly ideological in his criticism of tribute and pragmatic about it, too. The Roman register of deference is broken, but Priscus makes no suggestions about how to mend it. Negotiation with him is a step forward in an atmosphere of well-deserved mistrust.

AVARS: A SUDDEN ARRIVAL ON THE WESTERN STEPPE

Avars appeared on the Roman stage in the late sixth century. Probably composed of a mixed group of fighting men, their families, dependents, and allies, they were fleeing the growing Turkic presence on the steppe.[236] Scholars today do not think they constituted a single ethnic group with a continuous history, and how their name was transmitted is unknown.[237] Avars appeared north of the Caucasus in 557 and sent an embassy to Justinian in Constantinople, with whom they made an agreement to fight other tribes in the region in return for payments. Five years later, they controlled a large area north of the Black Sea and the Danube Basin, which made them an immediate threat to the Balkans. Justinian's payments managed to deflect the Avars from attacking Roman territory. In alliance with the Lombards, they then turned their efforts westward to eliminate the Gepids, a powerful Germanic people located in the region of modern Romania. Their khagan's agreement with the Romans collapsed after Justinian's death in 565. Feeling a financial pinch, his successor, Justin II, adopted a new policy of refusing to make payments to Avars and other groups. It is at this stage that the Avars are discussed at length in our sources.

Very few detailed accounts survive of the reception of foreign embassies at the Roman court in this period, whether in Constantinople, Ravenna, or Rome. We have already seen Eusebius's description of barbarians from the four corners of the earth queuing up to make their obeisance at Constantine's throne. Remarkably, there exist three separate sixth-century accounts of the same Avar embassy to the imperial court.[238]

The most colorful of these comes from the pen of the poet Corippus, writing in Constantinople very early in the reign of emperor Justin II, about 566.[239] In his poem *In Praise of Justin the Younger*, Corippus describes in great detail how a delegation of Avars swaggered into Constantinople only to be denied their annual payments by Justin. Corippus's account reveals much about imperial ideology, the staging of deference, and ethnographic attitudes:

> A lofty hall stands in the huge building gleaming with a sun of metal, wondrous in its appearance, and more wondrous in the aspect of the place and proud in its splendour. The imperial throne ennobles

the inmost sanctum . . . When the happy emperor had ascended the lofty throne and settled his limbs high up with his purple robes, the master of offices ordered the Avars to enter and announced that they were before the first doors of the imperial hall begging to see the holy feet of the merciful emperor, and he ordered with gentle voice and sentiment that they be admitted. The barbarian warriors marvelled as they crossed the first threshold and the great hall. They saw the tall men standing there, the golden shields, and looked up at their gold javelins as they glittered with their long iron tips and at the gilded helmet tops and red crests. They shuddered at the sight of the lances and cruel axes and saw the other wonders of the noble procession. And they believed that the Roman palace was another heaven. They rejoiced to be stared at and to appear carefree as they entered: as Hyrcanian tigers when New Rome gives spectacles to her people . . . Tergazis the Avar looked up at the head of the emperor shining with the holy diadem, he lay down three times in adoration and remained fixed to the ground. The other Avars followed him in similar fear and fell on their faces, and brushed the carpets with their foreheads . . . [Justin said to them] . . . So then, the Khagan is preparing to bring his standards against mine, and the Avar people threaten me with trumpets and army camps, if we do not grant their treaty? Do you think my father did it through fear, because he gave gifts to the needy and exiled out of pity? . . . We do not allow arrogance: peoples who are willing to serve we protect, and we raise the humble with gifts and honour.[240]

Corippus's description deserves a close look. It provides a clear view of the staging of entry into the imperial presence.[241] We watch the Avars cooling their heels in the outer court. Then they are given a trip through the palace audience halls intended to impress them with the wealth, power, and stability of the court. The architecture particularly impresses these people of the steppe. Gradually they approach the enthroned emperor, who is specially illuminated. They make public obeisance, kowtowing three times in the formality of subordination that is expected. The emperor, flanked by representatives of the government, finally bids them to speak freely. Then the Avars deliver their message and the discussion begins.

The ceremony in the imperial court is as much about controlling what is seen by the embassy on its carefully planned route to the emperor as it is about the discussion itself. Corippus lets us watch the Avars as they marvel at the palace. They delight at being watched but are cowed by the splendors of the palace and the kind gaze of the emperor. Corippus presents the palace as serene and heavenly. He contrasts this calmness and good order with the bestial aggressiveness of the Avars. The contrast of barbarian ferocity and civilized calmness is an old one, skillfully employed here.

[92] CHAPTER 2

Any thought, however, that the barbarians have been transformed permanently by the emperor's mildness or that they consent to their chains of obedience to him is dispelled by their harsh demands. Justin's admonitory reply combines Vergil's well-known statement of Rome's mission to conquer the proud and spare the suppliant with encouragement to accept Christianity.[242] The emperor says that the Avars should choose servitude and loyalty to Rome, as so many other peoples have done. If they do, they will receive gifts and honor. Corippus acknowledges the broad expanse of the Avar empire of which the khagan boasts, but says that the Roman Empire is superior because it is preferred by God and that its inhabitants wish to serve it; they are not enslaved. The emperor points to Scaldor, an otherwise unknown steppe chieftain in the imperial retinue. This man has allied himself with Rome and demonstrates his loyalty by giving gifts to the emperor, not demanding them. Justin does not convince the Avar khagan, but by the time he is finished explaining his refusal to accede to their demands, the Avars have become terrified and speechless. They return to their barbarous kingdom frustrated though not defeated.

THE SECOND ACCOUNT

Somewhat later in the sixth century, Menander Protector, a historian at the imperial capital, wrote another account of the embassy that agrees with Corippus's version on basic points, though without the emphatically Christian content or the fine appreciation of the staging of the Avars' presence before the emperor.[243] He criticizes Justinian's inertia and gives a clear picture of the mechanisms of subordination through gift-giving, with an emphasis on the reciprocal expectations involved in the payments. He contributes other details about the luxury goods (not cash) that constitute the Avars' gifts.[244] They are willing to acknowledge the emperor as benefactor and will refrain from invading the empire. They will fight Rome's enemies beyond the borders. The Avars insist their continued friendship depends on receiving their "customary gifts." In Menander's version the emperor objects to Avar arrogance and intends to teach "proper moderation," thereby demonstrating Rome's true friendship by saving them from self-destruction. Justin declares further: "I shall never need an alliance with you, nor shall you receive from us anything other than what we wish to give, and that as a free gift for your service, not, as you expect, a tax [φορολογίαν τινὰ] upon us."[245] Menander tells us that the emperor refuses to submit to their extortion, but he does grant them a significant gift: their lives.

THE THIRD ACCOUNT

Another description of the Avar embassy is found in the *Ecclesiastical History* of the Monophysite/Miaphysite bishop John of Ephesus, who wrote some twenty years after the event.[246] He emphasizes the Avars' frequent requests for tribute for spurious reasons and Justinian's willingness to grant their requests. He notes a growing sentiment in Constantinople against Justinian's policy and that Justin shared these beliefs. John describes the interchange: "'Never again shall you be loaded [with gifts] at the expense of this kingdom, and go your way without doing us any service: for from me you shall receive nothing.' And when the Avars began to threaten, he grew angry, and said, 'Do you dead dogs dare to threaten the Roman realm? Learn that I will shave off those locks of yours, and then cut off your heads.'"[247] According to John, Justin imprisoned them in Chalcedon for a few months and then let them go. After a short while, however, Avar ambassadors reappeared at court asking for friendship. They made obeisance and promised to follow the emperor's instructions. The Avars remained Roman allies for the rest of Justin's life.

What do we learn about the connection between tribute and ethnography from these three accounts of the same event? The Roman writers supply many details to show that the Avars are truly barbaric in dress and demeanor. The most telling of these characteristics is their arrogance in refusing to accept their expected subordinate place on the Roman register of deference, even though they went through the motions of obeisance as court ceremonial demanded. They remain adamant in demanding payments and angry that imperial policy had changed. The distant khagan directly challenges the emperor.

When the pageantry is stripped away, we see the basic gears of negotiation turning. The Avar ambassadors are granted the opportunity to speak openly, as was the custom in diplomatic exchanges. They state the views of their absent khagan, whose challenge to the emperor stands out in contrast to the formal ritual of obeisance. If gold is to change hands, the emperor insists on calling it a gift given in reward for service, thereby perpetuating the fond myth of imperial largesse and preeminence. Presumably the Avars were less picky about Roman rhetorical strategies; they just wanted their money. The reception of the Avars at the palace enacted a power dynamic in which the Romans claimed supremacy that the Avars did not accept. They conformed to protocol but in making their demands so unflinchingly, the exotic and violent Avars challenged Roman superiority.

Part III

Western Peoples and Rome: From Barbarians to New Polities

INTRODUCTION

The next diplomatic arena to be considered lay to the north and west of the empire, embracing the many peoples who lived beyond the Rhine and Danube rivers, the *"frons Germaniae."*[248] Some of them entered the empire in significant numbers in the fifth century, changing power relations and ethnography. Gradually, new stakes emerged and an ethnographic discourse developed among Franks and their neighbors in which Romans were the barbarians.[249]

Since the days of the late Republic and Rome's first deep advances to the north, Roman commanders had spared no effort to win renown by seizing territory. In his account of the subjugation of Britain, the historian Tacitus has a defiant British chieftain say in a blistering description of Roman practice, "they make a desolation and they call it peace."[250] In the face of possible genocide, enslavement, and certain loss of their freedom, indigenous peoples vigorously resisted Rome's advance, though with little success.[251]

As Rome turned conquered territories into provinces, those tribal groupings that lived beyond Rome's direct control constantly took new shapes and new names. We do not fully understand the reasons for those internal developments, but contact with Rome played a critical role, politically, economically, and culturally. In Patrick Geary's often quoted words, "[t]he Germanic world was perhaps the greatest and most enduring creation of Roman political and military genius."[252] Roman forces patrolled the western edges of the empire to protect provincials from attack. Sometimes, the border temporarily buckled under external pressures, as in the calamitous third century, but the Roman state had the resources to regain its footing. Some peoples had a long history of interaction with Rome, such as the Quadi and Marcomanni along the Danube, from the second through the fourth century, or the Alamanni along the Rhine through the fifth, but none of them managed to establish an enduring empire like that of Sasanian Persia.[253] Foreign warrior bands might invade or be halted at the front, but scholars understand that Rome's border region was always permeable for people traveling in both directions. Merchants and slave traders with their cargoes, recruits for the army from abroad and veterans returning home, transhumance farmers and shepherds with their flocks, émigrés and exiles seeking asylum; all crossed through border areas every day.

A LATE ANTIQUE CHANGE

During the fifth century, Rome's grip on its western provinces slipped, and by the end of the century, even most of the Italian heartland lay under foreign control. In the place of Roman provinces, new kingdoms gradually took shape, forged from an amalgam of relative newcomers who had been in the empire for at least a generation and existing provincial populations. The new polities confronted a much-reduced Roman realm in the eastern Mediterranean that was based in Constantinople. Throughout this period, Rome's diplomatic relations with the numerous distinct peoples living beyond the northern frontier differed substantially from interactions with the Persians because of their different political structures. Treaties struck reflect the changing status of non-Roman polities in the West. Each carefully negotiated arrangement was tailored to immediate circumstances.[254] The deals made did not conform to an ironclad template of what a treaty should be.[255] Nevertheless, certain basic notions of how diplomatic arrangements might be formally structured remained fairly constant throughout Late Antiquity.

From the Roman imperial perspective, political entities in this arena, whether *gentes* (peoples), *regna* (kingdoms), or something in between, always were envisioned as either still undefeated enemies or politically inferior. Romans insisted on the symbolic subordination of the diplomatic partner as a prerequisite for negotiation and treaty making. Roman insistence on their own preeminence, a pillar of their ethnographic infrastructure, was ideologically driven and often an oversimplification of facts on the ground.

DEFEAT AND ALLIANCE

The act of submission and the acknowledgment of Roman superiority was part of a wide spectrum of forms of *deditio* or surrender that had originated in the Republic. Romans might treat their defeated opponents in several ways. At one extreme, they might decide not to negotiate at all but to kill or enslave them, thereby erasing their community entirely; this had often been Julius Caesar's approach in Gaul.[256] At the other extreme, Rome might enter into an alliance of mutual advantage with them following a token and perhaps even willing act of submission.[257] Historical models and precedents existed for all the possibilities.[258]

When considering the registers of deference contained in these arrangements, we must remember that however the new relationship to Rome took shape and whatever form the submission took, it always included the formal reconstitution of the foreign group.[259] Rome ascribed a new identification to the surrendering group as ally or citizen (see chapter 3). In leaving behind their old condition of being a barbarian enemy and being ascribed a nonhostile place in the Roman scheme, the surrendering people actually were negotiating their identity as demanded by Roman imperial practice. Consequently, they entered the Roman ethnographic infrastructure not as antagonists but as subordinates. The transformation of status was manifested in several stages in the making of a treaty.[260]

First, Romans gauged the condition of the intended diplomatic partner. Perhaps they were an enemy with whom they had not yet crossed swords; perhaps they were a people defeated in war, or an independent group terrified by the fate of a neighbor at Roman hands; perhaps they simply desired alliance instead of Roman invasion or had other reasons of their own. Romans weighed the implications with the information available to them.[261] Some of the most striking examples come from the pages of Ammianus Marcellinus. His narrative of Julian's campaigns against the Alamanni is particularly rich. He illustrates, for example, how sheer terror motivated some of the Alamanni to beg him for peace in 357.[262] Fearing rightly that Julian intended to slaughter them, they sent envoys "with prayers and extreme abasement."[263] After their plea, which was granted for ten months, three extremely savage kings, who trusted that Julian would adhere to the peace even though they had recently aided his enemies, came to his camp and swore oaths "drawn up after the native manner" to do their part in keeping the peace as the Romans wished.[264] In addition, they brought grain to the Roman fortress and stuck to their oaths "since fear curbed their treacherous disposition."[265] This episode reveals a great deal about procedure. Ammianus, who does not provide the precise words of the agreements, presents barbarians as terrified and eager for Rome's protection, an old trope, but undoubtedly true. Access to Julian is neither guaranteed nor immediate, and his reply to their pleas is carefully considered. He ceases hostilities for a limited time only. The specific Roman demands are carefully drawn up but implemented in the most binding fashion, by permitting the Alamanni to take their oaths according to their own customs.[266]

Second, following the decision to enter into a treaty, something not to be taken for granted, came a ritualized act of subordination, an obligatory step in the structuring of formal ties of friendship or alliance. Without such acknowledgment, the other party was understood to be still an undefeated enemy and "barbarian," incapable of civilized interaction. By the fourth century, maintaining ties that might be leveraged with barbarian groups had become an integral part of Roman diplomatic policy.

Third was the deal itself, the *restitutio*, in which the terms of the new relationship were clearly spelled out. Once mutually agreeable decisions were made, the arrangement was solemnized with oaths and other appropriate gestures on both sides, thus combining the customs of each party and the specifics of the current arrangement.

Fourth, through the *foedus*, the subordinate non-Roman diplomatic partner was "reconstituted," transformed, by gaining a new status ascribed by Rome. Often the new status was that of "ally," but the specific obligations of each allied group varied from treaty to treaty. We find gradations of allied status in such things as the Roman titles allotted to their rulers and in the subsidies that each was to receive from Rome.

Romans believed that through its submission (whether token or coerced), the group with which the *foedus* was struck had become dependents of the empire and so in some way part of it, though not necessarily full citizens.[267] Why they had entered the agreement mattered less than their formal acceptance of the preeminence of Rome and the emperor.

TITLES FOR EXTERNAL PEOPLES

The Roman chancery possessed a hierarchical roster of coveted Latin titles and offices to give to non-Roman rulers of western *gentes* (peoples) and *regna* (kingdoms). When emergent kingdoms incorporated Roman lands and some

"HOSTILES AND FRIENDLIES" [97]

elements of the preexisting Roman provincial infrastructure in the fifth and sixth centuries, Constantinople refused to recognize them as equals. The imperial titles, *imperator* and *augustus*, were jealously guarded and never dispersed.[268] The lesser title *rex* was granted to Visigothic, Ostrogothic, Vandal, Burgundian, Frankish, and Lombard kings.[269]

Sometimes foreign rulers chose to refer to themselves with imperial titulature, but this was not approved by any Roman authorities. For example, Masties, a minor leader among the Berbers in sixth-century North Africa, added *imperator* to the title *dux* that had already been granted him by Justinian.[270] For the most part, however, local rulers played by the rules set by the imperial court. It was only in 800 that Charlemagne took imperial titles for himself to become Emperor of the Romans.[271]

Within foreign kingdoms that began to take shape in the fifth century, subjects sometimes referred to their rulers as *dominus noster, dominus*, and even *princeps*, but these honorifics did not necessarily connote imperial sovereignty.[272] There was not absolute consistency in all media. Philip Grierson noted that coins struck by mints controlled by new rulers in the West generally imitated imperial coinage rather mechanically, with standard imperial formulae *Victoria Aug.* and *Victoria Augustorum*, as well as *rex, victor*, and *D(ominus) N(oster)* on the front of coins, but they refrained from using *Augustus*, which was the prerogative of the Roman emperor in Constantinople.[273] During the reign of Theoderic the Ostrogoth (475–526) in Italy, a Roman senator set up an inscription that called his ruler "rex . . . victor ac triumphator semper Augustus (king, Augustus, perpetual victor and conqueror)"; this may be understood as a private gesture,[274] though perhaps done with the tacit approval of the king.

Greek sources often transliterated titles into Greek letters or used Greek equivalents for Latin terms. Most Greek sources refer to the Western kings as *rex* or *phylarch*.[275] *Basileus* (βασιλεύς), the direct translation of the Latin *rex*, was sometimes used.[276] *Basileus* could also mean the Roman emperor, but it did not carry that meaning when applied to subordinate monarchs. However, some writers in the East, like Malalas in mid-sixth-century Constantinople, refrained from using *basileus* to refer to lesser kings, reserving its use instead for the emperor.

Roman authorities did not accord imperial titles to rulers in the West, nor did the kings claim it. When Clovis the Frank was fresh from smashing the Visigoths at the Battle of Vouillé in 508, a victory that served the purposes of the Romans as well, he received an honorary consulship from emperor Anastasius in Constantinople[277] but no further title. Clovis made the most of it and celebrated with a parade that imitated some aspects of imperial ceremonial, but he did not overstep. The most problematic aspect of Clovis's behavior is recorded by Gregory of Tours, some seventy years after the event. Calling Clovis a new Constantine, the Frankish historian comments, "From that day he was hailed as consul or Augustus."[278] There is no evidence to suggest, however, that Anastasius considered Clovis to be of equal status. Bestowing an honorary consulship did not imply this. It shows only that the Roman authorities were consistent in *not* granting imperial status, even if the local king, in this case Clovis, was less punctilious.

Conclusion

This chapter has considered an ethnographic discourse of subordination to Rome, omnipresent and often expressed in diplomatic contexts. It was ethnographic not in its description of foreigners' habits but in its evaluation of their status relative to imperial power. Romans always claimed the top spot. The degree of subjugation was acted out in ceremonies of abasement that took place in various diplomatic encounters and that were memorialized on coins and monumental art. They were the tangible and spatial expression of the international power hierarchy as imagined by Romans.

Status differences were also enacted in the asymmetrical exchange of gifts, which ranged from subsidies paid to influence the actions of smaller communities to the payment of extortion under compulsion. The register of deference, as I have called it, energized and reflected Roman views of their place in the world in relation to their neighbors. The giving and acceptance of gifts was contingent and dynamic, implying mutual recognition of status but not equality. Through them international contacts gained a certain stability, defining and delineating future action. Even the uncompromising Huns acknowledged basic protocols.

The greater the gift, the greater the status of the giver. If the gift were accepted and Roman primacy tacitly acknowledged, Romans saw the deal as honorable. If the payment were seen as unilateral and having been coerced, however, the status relationship was obviously unequal to the point that those coerced could be called slaves. The payment then became tribute, which brought humiliation and loss of honor. All the participants believed that paying tribute was a sign of weakness and an indication of lesser status.

Far more than being solely an ethnography of cultural superiority, then, this ethnographic discourse expressed a self-centered Roman vision of relations among the communities of the world. Through the ethnographic discourse of status and subordination, Romans continually recalibrated their place and the place of others in a growing web of international relations that spread across Eurasia. Understanding this discourse can help us understand the shaping of the medieval world.

CHAPTER THREE

"Include Me Out"[1]

ETHNOGRAPHY, SETTLEMENT, AND
LAW AT THE EDGES OF EMPIRE

What is better than that people should wish to live under the rule of justice? . . . [The law] brings . . . people from their wild state into a civilized community.

—CASSIODORUS, *VARIAE*[2]

Introduction

As their empire grew to its greatest extent in the early second century CE, Romans encountered a kaleidoscopic array of foreign peoples. Some they slaughtered or enslaved, some they fended off with armed force and treaties, but most they incorporated productively (though not gently) within their evolving imperial system. Romans absorbed millions of non-Romans and generally succeeded in turning them into docile provincial populations from which they could draw taxes and soldiers.[3]

Over this long period, foreigners joined the Roman enterprise in two main ways: forcibly through conquest and subjection to the practices of Roman rule; and more or less willingly, through countless arrangements that gave them land inside the empire on which to settle, and with military service before and after settlement frequently part of the deal.[4] Regardless of the quite varied circumstances of entry, however, the influx of new peoples through the centuries was continuous, and for a very long time Roman authorities managed to keep the upper hand. As Rome's first emperor Augustus darkly proclaimed on his publicly displayed record of achievements, "As for foreign nations, those whom I could safely pardon, I preferred to preserve [rather] than destroy."[5]

In Late Antiquity, however, as territorial expansion ended and the edges of the empire began to contract, Romans increasingly found themselves on a defensive footing. The influx of newcomers acquired a different character. Even though Roman authorities managed their arrival successfully (with some notable exceptions) and kept the lid on after they settled down, they had to shift gears. The purposes of settlements took on a greater specificity than in

[99]

earlier centuries, and the settlements were undertaken without the presumption that full integration within the state might be possible or even desirable, setting precedents that would outlast Roman rule in western Europe.[6] As we will see—and this is the red flag—large groups of settlers were deliberately and formally kept apart from the broader provincial populations among whom they found themselves. This change of direction in Roman thinking about settlements was not announced in imperial proclamations, but it gradually became evident in practice.[7]

Generations of scholars have kept a close eye on the settlement of outsiders during Late Antiquity as part of their greater narratives of Roman history. They have tended to focus on five interrelated areas:

1) Military activity and military defense. Because non-Roman (barbarian) units played a highly visible role in military affairs as demand for troops increased, a great deal of attention has been paid to where they were recruited, how they fought, what they contributed to military campaigns, and their numbers in relation to home-grown Roman troops. David Breeze has called for a detailed study of military deployment across the breadth of the empire in Late Antiquity.[8] Peter Brennan noted that while "one-off" recruiting of foreigners was a mainstay of replenishing the army, there were also systemic, internal processes that fed on a steady flow of newcomers for financial reasons.[9] Anthony Kaldellis and Marion Kruse have initiated renewed study of late Roman military organization and the use of foreign troops.[10] In many modern historical accounts, the influx of foreigners is the primary cause of the fall of the western portions of the Roman Empire.[11]

2) Ethnic identity. Who were the "barbarian" settlers before and after they reached their new homes? The question has been of enormous importance in historical discussion, especially to those wishing to demonstrate direct and unbroken continuity (biological as well as cultural) from antiquity to the present, often to justify modern claims of national and ethnic identity. Explanations of barbarian/settler identity have ranged from crude racial theories to the complex understanding of ethnicity as a malleable "situational construct."[12]

3) Economic importance. What economic role did settlers play in the operation of the empire in Late Antiquity? What were the economic rationales for settlement and what were the consequences? Scholars have seen settlers as a sign of imperial weakness, and more recently have paid attention to economic straits that counterintuitively placed a premium on settling migrants. They could be taxed, and Roman landowners as well as the imperial fisc might profit from their labor.[13] The question of how lands were apportioned to the settlers also has received considerable attention.[14]

4) Connection of Roman-era settlers to post-Roman kingdoms. To what extent did the settlers on Roman soil contribute to the formation of new kingdoms in western Europe that supplanted Roman governance? The question of *gentes* to *regna* (peoples to kingdoms), once seen in simple terms of direct continuity from settlers in Roman times to early medieval kingdoms, has now been upended by explanations that see the kingdoms primarily as products of post-Roman conditions.[15]

5) Roman attitudes to the settlers. A rich panoply of usually hostile ancient literary texts illustrates Roman perceptions of the newcomers to the empire (see chapter 1). Though ridden with clichés and biases of all sorts, the writers' opinions put the settlements in living context and make them anything but academic abstractions. Their voices have shaped modern appreciation of events, perhaps unduly so. Christianity came to dominate Roman attitudes by the end of the period discussed here and has colored both ancient and modern interpretation.

The Ethnography of Settlement

Drawing from these necessary discussions, the present chapter takes a different approach. It considers how in Late Antiquity newcomers of diverse origin and condition were labeled and assigned additional group identities on entry into the Roman Empire, depending on what obligations Roman authorities placed on them after settlement. This formal ascription of identity upon entry into Roman administrative space was never casual or arbitrary. It constituted an ethnographic discourse. By providing the terms of inclusion for newcomers to the empire, it was in keeping with the deep-seated habit of creating separate categories for all participants within the state under the umbrella of Roman law. The fundamental Roman legal principle that everyone is either free or a slave[16] underlay this habit, as the newcomers were technically free but also subservient to Rome in many ways. That left a great deal of room for determining the degree to the constraints upon their freedom. (Those countless thousands who were captured and sold into slavery in the empire are not considered in this chapter, though even they had a presence in the law.) Romans had been devising means of including free foreigners and granting them access to Roman law at least since they rose to power in the Mediterranean world centuries before. Late Antiquity witnessed further developments in this process. It must be emphasized, furthermore, that the terms of inclusion—the very labels applied to the new groups of entrants—indicate a register of "occupational" differences only, not the more familiar ethnic, moral, physical, or geographical terms found in other ethnographic discourses.

The newcomers' intended responsibilities within the empire put them firmly in Rome's service and under imperial control, but at the same time deliberately kept them formally apart from the broader provincial population among which they lived. Together, the labels delineated limits of participation in the empire and constitute a register of difference that was similar to those we have seen in other chapters. It was imperial to the core, since the labels indicated a transformation of formal identity, in this case within the parameters of Roman service. The occupational labels carried with them different degrees of access to the law and obligation to the Roman state.[17] Of all the registers of difference considered in this book, the labels come closest to representing an official voice of authority.

The discourse of labeling is particularly notable because it was encoded in the law, which often responded to problems in frontier zones, the site of transition for outsiders entering Roman administrative space.[18] The laws and the labels within them provided a measure of conceptual order in the tangled social field of the Roman frontier. They indicate how the inclusion of new populations was visualized and regulated. The laws enabled and endorsed new sets of relationships with newcomers. They provide a glimpse of the ethnographic footprint coming to life in Late Antiquity.

The historical stakes implicit in this discursive system about law and inclusion were high. When Roman authorities lost the power to control incoming peoples and to ascribe identities to them in terms of their service to the state, the newcomers and their descendants inevitably revised their own identities (whatever they may have been and however they may have understood them). This was the case especially on what had been Roman soil in western Europe, where communities with new identities formed independently of Rome. In the eastern Mediterranean, on the other hand, where imperial authority did not collapse, labels of Christian orthodoxy (and heresy) soon would make the difference in entry and integration within the state. Thus, the labeling discourse of inclusion (or the cessation of it) that had developed in earlier centuries continued to play a significant role in the rearticulation of power and community in the post-Roman provinces and Byzantium.

TERMINOLOGY

A handful of terms (*dediticii, laeti, gentiles, foederati, auxilia*)[19] appear in Roman laws, sometimes supplemented by more anecdotal and not always reliable literary or quasi-official sources that refer to them.[20] Further complications arise from the fact that groups often settled in the empire are mentioned in the nonlegal sources only by an ethnonym. Making sense of them all can be confusing because the written evidence of any sort is not plentiful or always consistent. Some decisions about service and settlement were made on the spot, in response to immediate needs. Circumstances of the terms' application and meaning, furthermore, changed over time, a fact which makes it easy to conflate periods in which they were used differently. Archaeological evidence cannot be tied to specific terms with any precision. Searching for a specific non-Roman ethnicity lurking behind either the terms or the archaeology has proven to be a wild goose chase as well, and indeed is asking the wrong question, because the material culture in the Rhine-Danube border areas was shared so broadly that it cannot be identified with particular groups.[21] Yet, despite the difficulty of pinning down the terms and the realities they represented, we must not think of them as distinctions without a difference.

To make the labels comprehensible, it is helpful to look at them as separate job descriptions for the relatively few kinds of positions the Romans had to fill. The particulars of the job associated with each would change over time, in step with economic, military, and political contingencies. Nevertheless, the sorts of relationships between newcomers and the state fit a general pattern. The labels were part of a much broader system that ascribed a place to all the many elements of imperial populations, Romans and non-Romans alike, within imperial confines. With their job descriptions in hand, the newcomers left behind their place in a Roman ethnographic discourse of hostile barbarism outside the empire and entered a Roman ethnographic discourse of legally defined service within the empire that conveyed rights and privileges. Simply calling them "barbarians within the empire" does not do full justice to the situation. As Alexander Callander Murray puts it, "The term *barbari* commonly appeared in the laws as a synonym for external enemies (*hostes*), but in a more general sense it designated those not subject to Roman rule or bound to Rome by treaty. In law, therefore, there were no internal barbarians."[22]

The basic questions about status and function, on which the newcomers' labels depended, fall into three interrelated areas pertaining to economic roles, military responsibilities, and citizenship rights. 1) When outsiders came inside, were they tied to the land for agricultural labor, and if so, to what extent? Were they granted land as freeholders? Did they have to pay taxes? 2) Were they obliged to supply troops for the army or perform other military services? Were they settled in dangerous or contested areas? 3) Above all, to what extent might they enjoy the rights, privileges, and obligations of Roman citizenship? Could they become citizens at all? Could they intermarry with other status groups, especially Roman citizens?[23] In the answers to these interrelated questions we find meaningful distinctions among groups of newcomers from the perspective of Roman administration.

As noted above, the distinctions were about legal status and work requirements, not ethnicity. The tasks that Romans had in mind were open to any available outsiders, and the newcomers were not compelled to abandon whatever ethnic name they already carried when they acquired their newly ascribed "occupational" identity. Sometimes ethnic names appear in documents in conjunction with the new label.[24] This is seen, for example, in the insecurely dated *Notitia Dignitatum* (*Register of Dignities*), a composite document listing the highest imperial military and administrative offices in the eastern and western parts of the empire, which was put together between the late fourth century and the mid-fifth century.[25]

The entry of foreigners into Roman law was part of a centuries-old discourse of inclusion of outsiders made necessary by imperial expansion and formalized in law. In theory, there was upward social mobility, and even freed slaves might become citizens. The situation was different for settlers in Late Antiquity. The labels permanently froze the newcomers in place. Regardless of the extent of their cultural or religious integration, they found themselves in an intermediate position between barbaric enmity and full Roman integration. The labels were concerned with the limits of inclusion that was based on condition of servility, not ethnicity. In this light, laws reveal an ordered representation of foreigners.

TIME FRAMES

Material discussed in this chapter has two general starting points, one legal and one military. The legal time frame starts with the promulgation of the Antonine Constitution in 212, when most of the inhabitants of the empire gained Roman citizenship.[26] Newcomers consequently acquired a sharper profile in contrast to the citizen population that had now vastly increased in the provinces. It ends with the reign of Justinian (r. 527–65), when the Christian imprint on Roman law became quite strongly marked and entry into the Roman realm, and accompanying service to the Christian empire, acquired a different character. Both Rome's geopolitical position and the character of law took a religious turn that affected the ascription of identities to newcomers within the empire. The more specific terms discussed in this chapter appear during this period.

The military time frame begins a few decades later in the third century, following the end of the Severan dynasty, when imperial borders cracked and then mended for about a hundred years. Pressures continued to intensify, especially in the late fourth and fifth centuries, when the empire faced new military challenges and an increased demand for troops as the western empire unraveled. Controlling the settlement of newcomers took on much greater urgency, as suggested above.[27] It was during these centuries that the new set of ascribed labels developed for the entrants to the empire, who often were settled at different times in strategically important locations, especially in Gaul on the Rhine frontier and in North Africa. They indicate responses to immediate crises, thoughtful planning, and frequent overhauls of military organization. Sometimes the labels were entirely new and sometimes they were reworkings of precedents that existed for non-Romans in military roles. Either way, the labels responded to current circumstances and emphasized both service to Rome and difference from the general Roman provincial population.

Citizenship: A Measure of Belonging

Like the ethnographic dossiers treated in other chapters, the discourse of law and inclusion had a starting place that anchored its particular register of differences. This anchor was citizenship, which had been required for full membership in the Roman state since its humble beginnings. Its long and complicated history was deeply intertwined with the development of Rome and its practices of inclusion of foreigners.[28] Peter Garnsey points out that "[t]he general function of citizenship was and always had been as an enabling mechanism, offering access to the judicial procedures and remedies of the society at different levels," though he notes that in practice relatively few could take advantage of its benefits due to "profound social inequalities."[29] It should come as no surprise that as late Roman society changed, so did ideas about citizenship and access to it. The settlement of outsiders in Late Antiquity marked a change in a very old tradition.

A brief recap of citizenship sets the stage. Citizenship, a juridical status with many advantages, was the prime register of participation in the state, which made it extremely desirable. While anyone might learn to live *like* a Roman, maximum participation had always required *being* a Roman, which required citizenship. Through it came access to Roman civil law.[30] Not everyone ruled by Rome enjoyed citizenship, which was granted sparingly and in different degrees to individuals and communities for their loyalty. Most of the free people who made up the majority of the population did not enjoy it, and slaves were entirely excluded. The system provided a measure of order and was essential in controlling the empire's population. As Garnsey puts it, "the spread of citizenship [after the Social War in the first century BCE] held the key to the prodigious success of Rome as an imperial state."[31]

A significant legal change occurred in 212, when Emperor Caracalla issued the so-called Antonine Constitution, which granted citizenship to nearly all free people within imperial borders, regardless of how rough their habits.[32] After this date, slaves and other groups of very low status did not gain citizenship, and entrants from beyond Rome's borders did not automatically receive full citizenship, either, though they may have enjoyed some of its privileges. They were meant to keep an official profile of separateness, as indicated by the category assigned to them.[33] The new categories of participation carried various degrees of access to Roman law. By keeping certain groups of settlers at arm's length without full access to civil law, and by keeping them in a dependent condition, Romans emphasized their relative lack of civilization and quite deliberately kept them in their place. This was perhaps the most notable turning point in the history of Roman absorption of outsiders.

Before Late Antiquity: Precedents and Models

Three sets of precedents anticipated the emergence of the particular ascription of job-based categories for newcomers to the empire, which found expression in law. They are necessary background for late antique developments.

DEDITICII: SURRENDERED SUBJECTS WITHOUT RIGHTS

The first precedent involved people forced to participate. These people were *dediticii*, a category with a long history. In the Republic and early empire, *dediticii* were enemy peoples who had unconditionally surrendered.[34] Stripped of their possessions, political existence, and land, which was incorporated into the Roman state, they were totally at Rome's mercy. They may be seen as a social blank slate: they waited for a new status to be ascribed to them by their conquerors (see chapter 2, Figure 1). In a society structured around access to Roman law, they stood very nearly at the bottom rung. If they were not immediately enslaved and sold, after swearing allegiance to Rome they could be reconstituted as *peregrini*, which meant they were free persons but nevertheless excluded from full Roman citizenship. They became "inside outsiders," foreigners in regard to the city of Rome and its laws. They were registered in a city (*civitas*) subordinate to Rome, whose laws they followed.[35] Sometimes these cities embodied what had been a tribal formation.[36] The *civitates* were fundamental to Roman provincial organization. This process of conquest, legal transformation, and incorporation was an engine of the growing empire. No longer simply defeated barbarian enemies, *dediticii* were people of a particular legal condition who stood at the threshold of limited participation within the state. They might be of any ethnicity.[37]

The term *dediticii* also could be applied to gladiators and others with dishonorable occupations. In 4 CE, through the *Lex Aelia Sentia*, Augustus created a new class of freed slaves considered unsuitable for citizenship, regardless of their place of origin. According to the second-century jurist Gaius, such individuals had "the lowest form of liberty," *pessima libertas*, due to their shameful professions.[38] Obviously these *dediticii* were not the same as abjectly defeated foreign peoples who had not yet been incorporated within provincial populations, but they had in common an extremely low status that was measured by distance from Roman citizenship. They shared the same abased legal condition (*condicio*) in the hierarchy of Rome's subjects.

In the course of the following two centuries, piecemeal conquest brought huge numbers of people under Roman rule. The bulk of the empire's provincial population did not possess Roman citizenship. They were called *peregrini* and followed the local laws of their *civitas*.[39] When the Antonine Constitution granted Roman citizenship to the free inhabitants of the empire,[40] *dediticii* were explicitly excluded, though precisely to whom this referred and what was entailed are the subjects of continuing discussion. Scholarship has provided several possibilities.

Perhaps *dediticii* refers to those people of *pessima libertas* singled out in the *Lex Aelia Sentia*, which had never been revoked.[41] Another idea is that it refers to internal enemies of the state who had rebelled against imperial power.[42] Third is the widespread and still attractive explanation that it continued to mean defeated, unenslaved barbarians who were settled in the empire but were not yet *peregrini*. C. R. Whittaker rightly notes, "the precise significance of *dediticius* in the later Empire is a puzzle."[43]

Despite the uncertainty, several things remain indisputable: 1) later Roman sources writing about the Antonine Constitution understood that it extended Roman citizenship to all free inhabitants of the empire;[44] 2) that defeated barbarians continued to be brought into the empire, sometimes in very large numbers, where they became an important part of the Roman economic and military structure;[45] 3) that the term *dediticii* is rarely applied to such groups, and that it kept the same pejorative sense at least through the fifth century;[46] 4) not all of the barbarians brought into the empire were called *dediticii*. In the lists of references provided by Geoffrey de Ste. Croix and Yves Modéran, the term is not used by any ancient author except Ammianus[47] to describe defeated barbarians brought into Roman territory and settled or made to fight for Rome.

The quite fragmentary evidence suggests a very general historical development. Beginning in the late third century and continuing through the fourth and fifth, more specific labels and designations start to appear in the sources. This does not mean that barbarians no longer were settled in the empire or that the older sense of *dediticii* as surrendered barbarians has vanished, just that new terms had come into use that were more specific about the purposes of their settlement.[48]

All new entrants into the empire did not become citizens on entry. Yet, as Ralph Mathisen has argued, after 212 being a foreign barbarian did not exclude one from access to some if not all elements of Roman *ius civile* and from other citizen privileges. What counted was not ethnicity or origin but access to civil law. Indeed, the primary distinction in Roman law now was not even between citizen and noncitizen, but between freedom and degrees of legal disability.[49] It is right to call attention to degrees of legal disability as important social markers. Such emphasis was a characteristic late antique extension of the basic legal principle that all men are either free or slaves, which the jurist Gaius articulated in the middle of the second century CE.[50] The labels of settlement indicate that the weight of citizenship was slipping in importance

[108] CHAPTER 3

to the growth of "subjecthood" in Late Antiquity, as dramatically played out in Justinian's conflation of the terms subject and citizen in his legislation in the sixth century, in which he regularly referred to both Roman citizens and conquered barbarians as his subjects.[51]

A well-known example shows how defeated peoples were dragged into new categories. In the year 409, Roman forces on the Danube defeated an extremely large group called Sciri,[52] who before their surrender had been members of a hostile Hun confederacy. Because of special circumstances—namely their great number, combined with a shortage of agricultural workers in Roman fields—the Sciri were immediately settled on Roman lands not as slaves, certainly not as citizens, but as *coloni*, an existing category of agricultural workers who were not enslaved but who worked the land of others and possessed limited rights.[53] A law of 409 that dealt with this settlement tells us, among other things, that landowners could enjoy the free labor of these Sciri captives; that the obligation to provide troops from among them was suspended for twenty years; that they could not be relabeled as slave or citizen or any other category; and that they could be sent to farms in any province across the sea, meaning Africa, as long as that province was not in regions near their place of origin or where Huns were active. Because of the inherent risk implicit in their numbers, they were deliberately scattered widely, and further military use of the Sciri captives was not thought desirable.[54] Keeping them down on the farm was the order of the day.

This is an exceptional case in the Theodosian Code, but whether a "one-off" or not, it illustrates several points: that normally the settled populations would have been expected to provide troops; that labels were carefully chosen and variously ascribed categories were kept distinct; and that appropriate decisions were made on a case-by-case basis.

This situation, with undoubtedly countless variations unnoticed in ancient laws or accounts, takes us to the reign of Justinian, who in 530 abolished the term *dediticia* as an empty label (*vanum nomen*) no longer in use.[55] The law was part of large-scale reconsideration of manumission undertaken by the emperor's lawyers.

PEREGRINI: PROVINCIAL INHABITANTS BUT NOT CITIZENS

The second category, *peregrinus*, was applied to all free residents of the Roman provinces who were not Roman citizens, until the Antonine Constitution did away with the status in 212. In the early empire, *peregrini* constituted the majority of people living in the provinces. Still aliens because of their non-citizen status, *peregrini* could look back to ancestors who had been conquered by Rome or otherwise brought into the imperial system. The status carried numerous disadvantages. Because they were not Roman citizens, *peregrini*

"INCLUDE ME OUT" [109]

did not have access to Roman civil law. Instead, they followed the preconquest laws of their communities, though cases involving a Roman citizen were adjudicated in the court of the Roman governor of their province. They paid direct taxes and a poll tax.[56]

Further disadvantages accrued in military matters. *Peregrini* could serve only in auxiliary regiments, not the legions, which were limited (at least in theory) to Roman citizens. After discharge, an auxiliary veteran would receive Roman citizenship, as would his children. Marriage with a Roman citizen was illegal, so any offspring of a "mixed marriage" were considered illegitimate. They could not inherit property or citizenship. However, some *peregrini* communities (*civitates peregrinae*) were granted *municipium* status, which carried with it Latin rights, and so, legitimate marriages with citizens and inheritance of property and citizenship from the father.[57]

AUXILIA: MILITARY SERVICE FOR PAY

The third set of deeply embedded precedents is found in the *auxilia*, noncitizen troops kept separate from the legions. The term *auxilia* embraced a wealth of circumstances of recruitment and action. During the Republic and early imperial period until 212, these soldiers originated in the provinces (*peregrini* did not yet have citizenship) and sometimes came from lands beyond Roman control. They served as light infantry and cavalry. Recruitment occurred in an irregular fashion. The imperial period, however, saw a standardization of pay and terms of service as well as better organization of fighting units.[58] In the western provinces, auxiliaries often took their names from a tribe or region from which they had originated, while those in the eastern provinces took their names from the city in which they were registered.[59] There were inducements to military service as auxilliaries. When auxiliaries retired after twenty-five years of active service, they and their children, but not their wives, were granted Roman citizenship, and they obtained the right to contract a legal marriage. Unlike citizen legionaries, however, the auxiliary veterans did not receive grants of land. It is estimated that by the mid-second century there were as many auxiliary soldiers as legionaries.[60]

When non-Romans in the provinces first became auxiliary troops, they often used the ethnic names of the groups from which they had been recruited, but the initial ethnic connection eventually faded away as troops were moved to different parts of the empire and nearer sources of manpower were found.[61] It remains possible, however, that some men may have continued to come from the original recruiting ground, even if the unit was stationed far from the province.[62] The ethnonyms remained in use for a long time, regardless of the actual origin of later recruits into a given unit.

Much information about *auxilia* in the imperial period comes from the military diplomas issued to veterans on retirement from active service as proof of the citizenship they had received. About eight hundred survive from antiquity. Diplomas inscribed on large bronze sheets were given to veterans on discharge, and notarized copies were kept in Rome. In addition to the date and the full nomenclature of the emperor who made the grant, they carried a great deal of information about the recipient: his name and that of his commanding officer; his regiment, rank, and origin; the names of his father and wife, with her father and origin, and any of their children who had been granted citizenship.[63] *Auxilia* drawn from the provinces no longer required diplomas following the universal grant of citizenship through the Antonine Constitution. Diplomas indicate, however, that *auxilia*, presumably from outside the empire, continued to be recruited into the navy and the Pretorian Guard in the third century. The tradition of issuing diplomas to auxiliary veterans finally came to an end under the Tetrarchs.[64]

Auxilia in Late Antiquity

Constantine created new infantry formations of *auxilia* in his major restructuring of the army in the early fourth century, and they continued to be created with various assignments and tasks until the fifth.[65] The *Notitia Dignitatum* uses the term to designate infantry units in the eastern (*oriens*) and western (*occidens*) portions of the empire.[66] Regardless of their tactical functions, they continued to maintain a distinct legal profile. The Theodosian Code contains three laws in which the term occurs, dealing with matters such as birth status and tax exemptions.

In 353, Constantius sent instructions to his praetorian prefects regarding recruits:

> Whenever recruits are to be presented for service, they shall not be approved unless their birth status [*origo*] is investigated in the presence of the decurions. The assurance, however, shall be denied to the decurions that any person who is avoiding imperial service may perhaps escape the service by assuming the title of decurion. Leaders of the auxiliary forces shall not be granted license to receive a recruit, of course, unless the judge should first be informed and should write a reply as to whether or not the recruit is a decurion. Recruits shall be chosen for imperial service from their nineteenth year.[67]

The second ruling, sent in the name of Valentinian, Valens, and Gratian in 375, addressed recruits and the tax exemptions they acquired upon enlistment:

> But if they were stationed as auxiliaries on the river patrol, they shall exempt only their wives, along with their own capitation tax, after a period of five years.[68]

A third ruling came in 396, when a law of Arcadius and Honorius distinguished *auxilia* from other sorts of troops:

> When the guardsmen (*scholae*), the cavalry squadrons, either of the field army or of the palatine units, or any legions or auxiliary forces bear to the provinces any kind of written tax warrants for the furnishing of supplies, they shall not be heard if they demand prices beyond those which were established in the general statute of. . . . the elder Valentinian [r. 321–75].[69]

There was no need for auxilia in the western regions when imperial control disappeared in the fifth century. In the eastern territories, other terms for troops from abroad came into regular use.

New Late Antique Categories

GENTILES: TROOPS AND GARRISONS[70]

Gentiles constituted a category of settled foreigners in service to Rome with a distinct profile. In the Theodosian Code, the term *gentilis* does not refer to a specific ethnic group but generically to non-Romans. In the terminology of settlement, it referred specifically to "barbarians" recruited from peoples (Latin: *gentes*) beyond the frontiers of the western provinces, whose primary function was military. These "fighting barbarians" were settled with clear military responsibilities in western provinces.[71] Although they have some characteristics in common with *laeti* and other groups, *gentiles* should not be confused with them.[72]

From at least the time of the Tetrarchy, groups of *gentiles* had been stationed in garrisons in strategically important frontier zones or along routes that led to them.[73] Eventually, some were placed in troublesome internal districts following the wreckage of the early fifth century. They were not intended to be a substitute for border troops of the regular army.[74] Settlements of *gentiles* existed in Gaul, Italy, and North Africa. Their placement suggests long-range strategic planning more than ad hoc recruitment.

Gentiles were under the command of Roman military prefects, who were themselves part of a more extensive military chain of command.[75] In this structure they differed from *foederati*, who since the end of the fourth century, had been led by one of their own group and who followed their own (i.e., not Roman) laws. Instead, in legal affairs *gentiles* were tried by the proconsul of the province in which they were stationed:

> It is Our will that the ancient custom shall be observed in suits which come from appeal, and We add the provision that if an appeal is at any time interposed by [*gentiles*] or their prefects, it shall await, in the customary manner, examination in the sacred imperial court, that is, trial by the proconsul.[76]

[112] CHAPTER 3

This must refer to legal circumstances that involved Roman citizens. There is no information about how *gentiles* managed their internal legal affairs.

Certain legal disabilities distinguished *gentiles* from ordinary soldiers and citizens as well as from *laeti*.[77] As permanent settlers, they could have families, but it has been proposed that only a man could hold the status of *gentilis*, which would be passed on to his sons.[78] This suggestion derives from the fact that their wives are called *barbarae* (barbarian women) in the Theodosian Code.[79] Furthermore, *gentiles* were not permitted to marry a woman who was a Roman citizen.[80] This is known from a marriage law dating to the late fourth century that prohibited unions of provincial Roman women and barbarian men who had military obligations.[81] Regarding this law, Mathisen has shrewdly suggested that "what made marriages between *gentiles* and *provinciales* problematic in the late fourth century was not fears about miscegenation or barbarian disloyalty, but concern over differing legal statuses and obligations. The government was concerned that . . . the *limes* [border] could lose its gentilic sentinels."[82] He goes further to make the general point that "[t]his law is thus one of many laws reflecting Late Roman imperial desires to prohibit marriage between persons of unequal legal and social statuses."[83] The law did not prevent marriages between Roman women and barbarian newcomers without gentilic obligations, many of which occurred.[84] Although the *Notitia Dignitatum*, which drew on material of different dates, mentions settlements in Italy and Gaul, archaeology does not permit specific identification of gentilic sites, so their exact military tasks remain unknown.

In North Africa, on the other hand, archaeology has revealed fortified homesteads, in which *gentiles* may well have lived in the context of military defenses called the *fossatum Africae*, a complex frontier defensive system of noncontiguous ditches, embankments, and short stretches of walls (*clausurae*) running for about 750 km/466 miles.[85] Construction probably began in southern Algeria in Hadrian's day, with a surge of new building in at least some locations in the Severan period and then again in the third quarter of the fourth century. The fortifications also allowed a way to control access of people and goods, including military supplies, through the frontier barrier.[86] Taxing the products of transhumance populations may well have been one of the responsibilities of the troops stationed in these garrisons.[87] Dependent on a complex system of water supply and irrigation that made agriculture possible, these farmer-soldiers cultivated lands and planted olives on both sides of the barriers.[88]

These data complement a law of 409 sent by the emperors Honorius and Theodosius to Gaudentius, the vicar of Africa. The emperors were strengthening African defenses at this time, and all of the western provinces also were in peril. A clearer picture of gentilic settlements on the *fossatum Africae* emerges from the law:

Whereas We have learned that the tracts of land which had been granted by a benevolent provision of our distant predecessors to the settlers [*gentiles*] for the care and protection of the border [*limes*] and of the border fortifications [*fossatum*] are being held by some other people. If such persons are holding these lands because of their cupidity or desire, they shall know that they must serve with zeal and labor in the care of the border fortifications and in the protection of the border, just as did those persons whom past rulers assigned to this task. Otherwise they shall know that these tracts of land must be transferred either to the settlers [*gentiles*] if they can be found, or certainly to veterans, not undeservedly, so that by the observance of this provision there may be no suggestion of fear in any portion of the border fortification and the border.[89]

This law shows that people who were not *gentiles* somehow were acquiring lands that had been granted specifically to *gentiles*. The new proprietors were expected to maintain the military defenses in their place. Mathisen points out that marriages might have been a vehicle for the acquisition of these lands by non-*gentiles*.[90]

Augustine, bishop of Hippo in North Africa, provides further information about the cultural and religious context of the African settlements. In a letter of 419 to Hesychius, bishop of Salona (northeast of Split, in modern Croatia), Augustine responded to a query about the end of the world.[91] He explains that only at some unknown time after the Gospel was proclaimed to all the peoples of the world will the end of the world come, a theme developed at great length in his *City of God*.[92] This leads him to remark that some peoples who had been captured and farmed out to Roman masters in North Africa were ignorant of the Gospel but willing to embrace the faith. He adds that these newcomers are not governed by their own kings but by Roman prefects who are set over them. This probable mention of *gentiles* reminds us that the Roman culture in which they found themselves, and to which some of them were assimilating, was at least partly Christian. The settlers, then, were pulled in several directions: to remain a community set apart in the ambit of Roman law, to join others within the Christian Church, and presumably to assimilate to the local secular Roman culture to some extent.[93]

LAETI: FARMERS THEN FIGHTERS

The *laeti* are not simple to pin down as a category, but it is not impossible to do so. John Drinkwater well observes: "A localized and obscure institution, *laeti* have caused uncertainty and confusion among historians, ancient and modern."[94] Although controversial archaeological evidence makes it impossible to distinguish them from their non-*laeti* neighbors on the basis of material

[114] CHAPTER 3

culture, legal and extralegal sources permit a somewhat fragmentary picture of their function and intended place in the Roman order.

Laeti were settlers of various origins who had entered the empire willingly, not as prisoners of war or conquered enemies.[95] They were settled on abandoned public or imperial lands chosen by Roman authorities, called *terrae laeticae* (laetic lands) located primarily on the Rhine frontier in Gaul and also in Italy.[96] The privileges they enjoyed were similar to those of army veterans: they received a *stipendium* and could get a loan.[97] Émilienne Demougeot observes that *laeti* have an intermediate juridical condition that would develop into the *leti, liti,* or *ledi* found in the post-Roman barbarian law codes.[98]

At the time of their agreement with Rome, *laeti* would have acknowledged their subordination, perhaps in a formal *deditio*. We do not know the precise circumstances of the entry of each group that was settled or have definite information about the number and size of settlements.[99] Their total number must have been constantly refreshed in their several centuries of existence as a category, with new communities created and older ones possibly continuing to draw from their territory of origin, but this cannot be demonstrated. Drinkwater suggests that in the long run some settlements may have prospered more than others.[100] The story that Magnentius, who usurped the imperial throne from 350 to 353, was of non-Roman origin and a *laetus*, was probably a slander.[101]

The first nonlegal source of evidence mentioning the category *laetus/laeti* appears in an anonymous panegyrical poem delivered to the tetrarch Constantius in 297 or 298 in Trier to celebrate his restoration of Britain to Roman rule and to praise the security he has brought to western provinces.[102] The poet remarks that because of Constantius's victories, abandoned lands in Gaul are once again being farmed. Bringing *agri deserti* back into cultivation was a priority of the tetrarchs because the new cultivators would supply recruits for the army and help maintain the tax base. This practice had been going on since Diocletian's military reforms began in the 280s, evidently as a matter of policy that perhaps built on the practices of earlier third-century emperors.[103] The term came into use at about the same time as *gentiles*.

The author also mentions the transfer of inhabitants to abandoned Roman lands by two other tetrarchs, Diocletian (r. 284–305) and Maximian (r. 286–305). He notes that Maximian had settled barbarian Franks on abandoned lands in Gaul and admitted them to a place in Roman law, that is, law as it pertained to *laeti*.[104] At the same time he reports that Maximian brought other unnamed groups (they are not given an ethnonym) to abandoned Roman tracts by the right of *postliminium*. These were surely Romans returning from captivity to reclaim both their citizenship rights, which they had lost when captured, and the property that they had been forced to leave behind.[105] A law issued by Valens, Valentinian, and Gratian in 366 provides a general picture of such circumstances:

If any persons have been led away under the compulsion of captivity, they shall know that if they did not desert to the enemy but were carried away by the force of a hostile invasion, they must hasten to their own lands, and they shall recover by right of *postliminium* the property in either fields or slaves which they had formerly held, whether such property is possessed by Our fisc or has been transferred to anyone by imperial liberality.[106]

Poets are not lawyers, however, and the person who wrote the panegyric to Constantius put Romans in the category of *laetus*, which more appropriately would be applied to the Franks that he mentions, for settling foreign groups (with their ethnonyms given) as *laeti* was common practice and policy.[107] Furthermore, no other source applies the term *laetus* to captured Romans who have regained their fields through the law of *postliminium*. Tetrarchic laws indicate that individuals who invoked *postliminium* did so on a case by case basis, not en masse,[108] and they are not called *laeti*. Perhaps the panegyric's author simply did not understand the legal condition of *laeti* or the particularity of their name.[109] What matters to him is that abandoned fields have gained new cultivators and come back to life through the tetrarch's good efforts.

The *Notitia Dignitatum* gives ethnic names to some communities of *laeti*. It lists prefects as the commanders of a dozen different *laetic* groups.[110] Some of these were the names of peoples who had first encountered Rome centuries before and were still active, like the Batavi. Their names after so long a time, however, may indicate only the old tribal area from which they derived and a vague sense of local identity and custom.[111] Other ethnonyms, like the Franks, were of newer peoples with a strong presence and sense of identity, even though they were admixtures of different groups who accepted their leadership and ethnonym. Some groups of *laeti* are not listed with ethnonyms in the *Notitia Dignitatum*, which has been taken to mean that they were more heterogeneous communities but which more likely means that their name was unknown to the redactor of the *Notitia Dignitatum* or dropped from the manuscript at a later date.[112]

Laetic settlements are not visible in the physical record. Archaeologists agree that ethnic distinctions cannot be securely based on material culture, either in the border zones from which the settlers came or on the abandoned lands where they were placed.[113] Over the generations of settlement, furthermore, they inevitably would have been affected by the presence of their Roman neighbors to some extent. Whatever the precise composition of these *laeti*, and however much their habits of life changed, they were viewed as laetic groups by Roman authorities once they had been settled. Romans were concerned with maintaining formal differences and distinctions for strategic and economic purposes. What must be emphasized is that the legal condition of *laeti* would have continued *despite* the extent of their cultural integration.[114]

The fields assigned to *laeti* were leased to Roman landlords, and the *laeti* worked them in the fashion of *coloni* (but without that formal status), paying a portion of their produce to their landlords, who were in turn required to pay taxes to the imperial government.[115] *Laeti* enclaves lived under the supervision of Roman officials, *praefecti* and *praepositi*.[116] The communities were expected to provide recruits for the army, though we do not know how many.[117] The question of their citizenship is not mentioned in extant sources and is debated today.[118]

By the end of the fourth century, the presence of the *laeti* had become regularized, as demonstrated by three laws from the Theodosian Code. They provide evidence for the status and function of *laeti*, mechanisms of imperial control, and legal problems that arose when *laeti* sometimes tried to take advantage of the system. These imperial regulations point to serious problems on the ground and also delineate the status and obligations of *laeti*.

The first of these three pieces of evidence, an instruction issued by Arcadius and Honorius in April 399, indicates that only through imperial officials could *laeti* obtain lands on which to settle:

> Since persons of many nations seek the good fortune [*felicitas*] of the Romans and have brought themselves to Our Empire, and since laetic lands must be furnished them, no person shall obtain any of these lands except in accordance with Our special written permission [*adnotatio*]. Since some men have either seized more land then they obtained from Us, or by the collusion of the chief decurions or of the municipal defenders, or by rescripts surreptitiously obtained have acquired a measure of land greater than reason demanded, a suitable inspector shall be dispatched who shall recall whatever lands have been either delivered illegally or seized wrongfully by any persons.[119]

Sebastian Schmidt-Hofner paints the general circumstances of this edict. He explains that immigrants have been settled on public lands that are called laetic lands.[120] Roman landlords leased these fields on which the immigrants worked as *coloni*, paying taxes that, he suggests, were probably collected by the landlords. This leads him to conclude that "the situation that prompted the constitution in all probability was not that some *laeti* received more land than others. Rather, it was Roman landlords who had, in collusion with members of the municipal elite, secured for themselves a larger share of the land with its *coloni*, while their Roman peers, who had been outmaneuvered, had countered by soliciting an imperial rescript against their actions."[121] The immigrant workforce, at least at the time of this legislation, was a coveted commodity among elite Roman landholders.

The second law reveals circumstances of a very different nature. At the end of January 400, the emperors Honorius and Arcadius sent a directive to Stilicho, the leading general in the western provinces, about the serious

"INCLUDE ME OUT" [117]

matter of men shirking military service.[122] The problem affected the entire empire, and the political and military situation at Constantinople was especially tense at the time the law was issued. Alaric the Goth was plundering the Balkans and menacing Constantinople.[123] He would not move his forces to Italy until the autumn of the following year. The powerful Hun Uldin was an ominous presence north of the Danube. In the imperial city itself, Gainas, a Gothic general in Roman service, was enjoying a brief and disastrous ascendancy as *magister militum* before fleeing across the Danube where he was killed by Uldin, as noted above. In Italy, the political and military position of Stilicho was insecure. In the face of these many perils, keeping the armies stocked with recruits was of vital concern.[124] The law reads:

> Too many persons are being made veterans by testimonial letters obtained by fraud, although they have never been soldiers, and some are deserting in the beginning of their military service in the very flower of their age. Therefore, if any *laetus*, Alaman, Sarmatian, deserter, son of a veteran, or any person of any group whatever who is subject to conscription and who ought to be enlisted in Our most excellent legions[125] should obtain a testimonial letter conferring the rank of honorary imperial bodyguard or any high rank whatsoever, or if he should obtain those testimonial letters . . . he shall be given training in the recruit camps, so that he may not hide away.[126]

Quite apart from the problem of draft-dodging that the law addresses, it is striking that men of so many different categories are equally subject to the same imperial dragnet. We see the label for a specific sort of settled outsider (*laetus*), ethnonyms (Alaman and Sarmatian),[127] military categories, and a kinship relationship (veteran's son), and then a catch-all for everybody else. The social panorama from which recruits might be drawn was quite diffuse. The need for troops, however, was constant. *Laeti* are one distinct group among many, and their salient characteristic in this rescript is their function as recruits. Ethnicity is ignored.

A novel of Severus Augustus (r. 461–65), issued in September 465, deals with a complaint raised about marriages of *coloni* and household slaves with *laeti* and members of other public corporations (*corpora publica*). The novel states that if they have married without the knowledge of their masters, with the intent of keeping their offspring as *laeti* and not slaves or *coloni*, the children will remain the property of the master of the slave or *colonus* involved.[128] The extent of this problem is not known. What matters is that *laeti* are recognized as constituting *corpora publica* with definite responsibilities, presumably farming and supplying troops. Furthermore, the lines between different status groups are being enforced.[129] *Laeti* are distinguished from *coloni*, which indicates they were not bound to the land and did not have tax obligations of the same sort.[130] Once again, pressing circumstances led to the issuance of the law. When the novel was composed, the general Ricimer held power in the crumbling West, and was struggling to ward off the Vandals and many other lesser foes. Severus lacked real power, and Emperor Leo, ruling at Constantinople, refused to recognize his legitimacy.[131] Even in such difficult circumstances, however, efforts were made to enforce the social and economic order—and the separate place of *laeti* within it.

Nonlegal sources provide glimpses of *laeti* in action, and not always behaving properly. The historian Ammianus, writing toward the end of the fourth century, gives several instances. He reports that in 357, while Julian was leading a large army against the Alamanni, a band of *laeti barbari* made a surprise attack on the city of Lyon, which was unsuccessful.[132] Consequently they ravaged the countryside before being stopped by detachments of Julian's army.[133] Evidently these *laeti* had broken their agreement with Roman authorities. In Ammianus's eyes they are still barbarians.

We find other *laeti* firmly under Roman control, however, in a letter sent by Julian to the emperor Constantius in 361. Julian is trying to assuage Constantius's anger and avoid civil war by promising him troops. He mentions several categories of fighters: "I will furnish Spanish horses for your chariots, and also send some young men of the *laeti*, the sons of barbarians born on this side of the Rhine, or at least I will send some from the *dediticii* who have yielded to us, to be integrated with your *gentiles* and imperial guard [*scutarii*]."[134]

Here Ammianus clearly distinguishes among three groups with barbarian connotations, *laeti*, *gentiles*, and *dediticii*. (A *scutarius* was an armored cavalryman of nonspecific barbarian origin.) The *laeti* are serving as expected. They come from established *laetic* communities, as indicated by reference to their fathers' presence in Roman territories. The *gentiles* of Constantius are not *laeti* but nevertheless are soldiers of non-Roman origin. *Dediticii* would simply be surrendered barbarians whose status had not yet been determined.[135]

GENTILES AND LAETI

The categories of *gentiles* and *laeti* were envisaged by Romans in different ways.[136] Both groups came originally from beyond the limits of the empire, but their settlements functioned differently. The *gentiles* served a primarily military purpose. Their communities were located at hot spots in the immediate face of the enemy, and they were considered "crack regiments of fighting troops" such as those Julian mentions in his letter to Constantius.[137] *Laeti*, on the other hand, were established first of all to be farmers, with their settlements on abandoned agricultural land. Their young men were available for military service as well, and units of *laeti* existed, as seen above. The two categories possessed different legal rights and privileges, and both were viewed in the law as inferior to full citizens. The *Notitia Dignitatum* gives inconclusive evidence for the presence of both categories. It lists units of both *gentiles* and

"INCLUDE ME OUT" [119]

laeti located in different places, not always with an accompanying ethnonym. Only once, in the Spanish province Tarraconensis, does it mention separate *gentilic* and laetic units governed by the same prefect, which suggests that in the administrative system, the two labels were distinguished.[138] The two categories, *laeti* and *gentiles*, may have been introduced at different times, but in the administrative framework the two labels meant different things.

FOEDERATI: ARMIES FOR HIRE

Perhaps the best-known category applied by Romans to foreign groups fighting in Roman service during Late Antiquity is that of federates (*foederati* in Latin; φοιδεράτοι/*phoideratoi* in Greek).[139] The term, which derives from the Latin *foedus*, or treaty, indicates first of all that these outsiders had struck a treaty or made a less formal deal with Roman authorities. They have been called "limited-contract troops who served on ad hoc campaigns in return for rations and gold"[140] and "outsourced armies."[141] Though there are mentions of *foederati* in earlier periods,[142] we find them especially important in Late Antiquity. Our sources preserve only references to treaties made with barbarians, not the treaties themselves.[143]

A contrast with *auxilia* is helpful in understanding the rise to prominence of the *foederati* in Late Antiquity. Romans had used auxiliary units since the days of the Republic as an indispensable force parallel to their regular citizen army. Recruited from noncitizen provincial populations (*peregrini*), the *auxilia* were commanded by Roman officers and granted citizenship after their service, when many of them established homes in imperial territory. In the late third century, however, the venerable system of *auxilia* was largely dismantled in the military reforms of Diocletian.[144] The need for foreign troops did not go away, however, and *foederati* emerged as the main explicitly foreign units in Rome's arsenal.

Foederati had several basic features. The first recurrent element (with rare exceptions)[145] in the agreements was military service to Rome, as noted above. Federate troops fought at different strengths, in different theaters, at different times. Second, living in the empire after military service was a possibility, but not required, and not all did so. Third, bands of *foederati* always came from abroad, since Romans did not make treaties with their own subjects, and we find them collectively often carrying an ethnic name, which they do not lose in the course of their arrangements with Rome. Fourth, *foederati* were led by their own kings or war chiefs, not by Roman commanders. Fifth, *foederati* received payment for their service in cash, food, and supplies, and very often, land on which to settle, which often was a most important part of the bargain.

Foederati took an active part in Rome's wars on the Rhine frontier in the fourth century.[146] They reached their heyday in the fifth century, when the Roman army suffered tremendous losses[147] and needed to rely ever more heavily on barbarian troops.[148] All of the arrangements made by different groups with Rome varied to some extent.[149] As Lucas McMahon puts it, "a clear dictionary definition is simply not possible, given the variety of forms *foederati* took . . . [and] even if the Roman state had a perfectly clear definition of what service parameters produced a *foederatus*, this is obscured from modern scholars."[150] Certain elements recur, however, that give *foederati* their profile and set them apart from the other categories we have looked at.

The settlement option: Sometimes groups of federates pushed their way into the empire and, with grudging imperial permission, they established autonomous settlements.[151] For the Roman government, to allow federate groups onto imperial territory was making the best of a very bad situation. After settlement, *foederati* proved to be more indigestible than *laeti, dediticii*, and other categories of newcomers. Achieving citizenship was not a consideration for the federate rank and file, who continued to follow their own chieftains. They did not pay taxes to Rome, and they still were expected to provide military contingents. Romans expected acknowledgment of imperial superiority and hoped for their good behavior, because the government paid the stipends and provided the territory on which the newcomers settled. If they could begin farming, they might feed themselves, which would lessen the imperial burden of provisioning.

How lands and revenues were distributed to large groups, as to the Visigoths in Aquitania in 418, remains a subject of lively debate.[152] One point not contested is that settlers received no new label. For example, the Visigoths, within a few years of their settlement, established a kingdom of their own in Aquitainia, entirely independent of Roman authority. They paid no taxes to Rome and supplied no troops to the Roman army.[153] While it is true that in some cases Roman authorities often had no choice but to settle *foederati* on Roman soil, they nevertheless manage, at least initially, to retain the upper hand.

Did federates intermarry and assimilate into the general Roman population after settlement? The sources are silent about where small contingents of federate soldiers found homes.[154] In the case of significantly larger groups, such as Visigoths, who ultimately put down roots that led to the creation of new kingdoms, however, change went in a direction away from Roman life. While some of their leaders managed to become high-ranking officers in the Roman military establishment, the rank and file always led an uneasy existence in the midst of Roman provincial populations that vastly outnumbered them. They did not become Romans. Instead, their own ethnic self-identification grew in strength.[155] Roman authorities did not give them another label. Instead the groups developed and fortified their own identities as they settled down, perhaps in combination with other newcomers.

In the law: Imperial laws do not provide much information to help us sort out the parameters of federate service. Only two relevant laws survive from the fifth century. The word *foederatus* first appears in a legal text in 406, in

"INCLUDE ME OUT" [121]

a law saying that slaves owned by federates may be accepted into the Roman army.[156] The law speaks for desperate times.

In mid-winter 405/406, the Gothic general Radagaisus led an army of perhaps twenty thousand men across the Danube and invaded Italy.[157] Before his defeat in the late summer of 406, Roman authorities took extraordinary steps to raise troops to counter the invasion. From his throne in Ravenna, Honorius issued a law that put aside the legal status (*persona*) of recruits and encouraged slaves to enlist in the army with the promise of freedom at the end of their service.[158] This was all the more remarkable because previous legislation had banned slaves from military service.[159] The blanket appeal included slaves not just of Roman masters but also those of *foederati* and even of *dediticii*. These slaves were enrolled, surprisingly enough, in the standing army, not in federate units. It is not clear to which federate groups the law refers. It is also noteworthy that the law distinguishes between *dediticii* and *foederati*; we see indirectly that the system of different ascribed statuses maintains its force.

A law of Theodosius issued in 443 attempted to put an end to the fiscal exploitation of *limitanei* (frontier troops) by Roman officials, who are also forbidden to chisel funds and supplies from those earmarked for federate troops, who constituted a separate category.[160]

The laws remain silent about this category until the sixth century, when Justinian's laws mention *phoideratoi* a dozen times.[161] A major change has occurred, however, in the eastern empire. They are no longer adjunct to Rome by treaty. Instead, they appear as one classification of soldiers among several in the regular army. The government wished to prevent their being employed by private citizens.[162] The fine for doing so was ten pounds of gold, not an inconsiderable sum. Their chief officer was an *optio* (quartermaster).[163] McMahon suggests that this law might indicate that *phoideratoi* were not "entirely integrated within the regular military structure of the day."[164]

Literary sources: The richest literary source of evidence about federates is the historian Ammianus Marcellinus, who provides among other things a detailed discussion of Julian's campaigns on the Rhine frontier against Alamanni in the early 360s, just before he claimed the throne. Peter Heather notes, "Ammianus' account of Julian's campaigns reveals that submissions of Alamannic kings were customarily followed by negotiated agreements which settled the precise terms of the surrender and subsequent relations. These are exactly the kinds of agreements which Ammianus labels *foedera*, and all left established kings in place. Yet these kings nonetheless remained subject to imperial dominion."[165] Further treaties with the same groups would address other issues, with different stipulations regarding border crossings, payments from Rome, and requirements for military service.[166] McMahon concludes that:

> the term's traditional meaning of allied contingents fighting alongside
> Roman regular forces for specific campaigns evolved in the east to be

defined as a regular division of the army . . . Precisely when this change took place will never be known, but the work of Olympiodorus suggests that the transition was already happening by the beginning of the fifth century, whereas by the middle of the sixth century the process was complete. By the time of Maurice's *Strategikon*, the φοιδερᾶτοι [*phoiderati*] were sufficiently well-established as a regular military unit that they were placed in the battle line.[167]

Procopius, who wrote during the reign of Justinian, was aware of this shift, though unreliable on the details. He states in his *Wars*:

> Now at an earlier time only barbarians were enlisted among the foederati, those, namely, who had come into the Roman political system, not in the condition of slaves, since they had not been conquered by the Romans, but on the basis of complete equality. For the Romans call treaties with their enemies "foedera." But at the present time there is nothing to prevent anyone from assuming this name, since . . . men pay little heed to the meaning which they originally attached to a name.[168]

In other words, the term *foederati* was preserved in the sixth century, although its function had changed and the term was applied to mixed units of the regular army.

Conclusion

This chapter has not been about Roman law as a whole, or the cultural identity or ethnicity of foreign groups within the empire, or about the manpower and strategy of the Roman army. It has considered the system of ascribed collective identities by which the newcomers found a place recognized in the law—an ethnographic system.

The introduction to this book suggested that one characteristic of Roman imperial ethnography was that it carried some conceptual way of transforming non-Romans into new categories determined by Romans, a quintessentially imperial act. This possibility of change to an imperial register appears particularly clearly with the material in this chapter. Barbarians were placed in new categories of identification and were given new labels when they were settled on imperial soil. Even though circumstances of entry varied considerably, and obligations for service must have overlapped, Roman patterns of ascription are evident. The new labels remained fully compatible with any ethnic identifications that the settlers may have carried with them. The register of difference from Rome in this discursive ethnographic system was based on military and financial obligations. Denied full citizenship, the new settlers had value for Rome in service as soldiers and farmers.

CHAPTER FOUR

Divine Providence
and the Power of the Stars

[T]he stars cannot be causative, though they may possibly be indicative.
—ORIGEN OF ALEXANDRIA, *PHILOCALIA*[1]

*Assuredly we can easily ascertain how many rulers have changed the laws
and customs of nations which they have conquered and subjected them to
their own laws. This is manifestly done by the Romans, who have brought
under the Roman law and the civil decrees almost the whole world, and
all nations who formerly lived under various laws and customs of their
own. It follows, therefore, that the stars of the nations which have been
conquered by the Romans have lost their climates and their portions.*
—*PSEUDO-CLEMENTINE RECOGNITIONES*[2]

Introduction: An Ethnographic Revolution

In Roman antiquity, the stars, the planets, and the earth's terrain played an
exceptionally vigorous role in human imagination. Men and women at every
station of life believed that their bodies and communities were susceptible
to remote control by these all-powerful natural authorities. Considered by
many to be divinities, the celestial panoply of stars and planets existed as
independent, immanent forces that determined the character and destiny of
individuals and groups. Moreover, in a striking inversion of modern ecological
concerns about humanity's effect *upon* the planet, the earth's natural landscape had the power to shape humanity.[3] Such ideas did not gain complete
acceptance, however. Many non-Christian philosophers sharply challenged
these certainties about the workings of the heavens and the earth. Christian
writers did so as well, and it was their opposition that truly made a difference in popular thought. Their ideas gradually transformed Roman views of
themselves and the world's peoples. Christians offered a reimagined cosmos
operating under new rules that placed a greater burden on human judgment
and action in obedience to an all-powerful yet benign divinity. This change
had profound consequences for ethnographic thinking about the world and
its populations.

[123]

[124] CHAPTER 4

Framed by Roman imperial practice and the rise of Christianity, debates about astral and environmental determinism bred a robust ethnographic discourse in Late Antiquity. This chapter is the first of two that consider the shift from understanding a cosmos determined by natural agency to one in which Christian Providence regulated affairs and in which proper belief indicated the character of human communities, providing new tools for differentiating among them and relating them to the empire.

For non-Christians, whatever unity the disparate celestial and earthbound forces might share derived from the structure of the cosmos itself, which some held to be guided by Fate, a faraway and abstract creative force.[4] In their view, a person's destiny or a people's character might be found in the patterns of the sky's movement. Astrology rested on this possibility.

In contrast, Christians had an aversion to natural determinism of any sort, for if stars and the earth could control humanity independently, God's activity in human history would be nullified. For them, God remained in charge, yet, somewhat paradoxically, it was still up to individuals to make decisions about how to live. Within this developing Christian cosmos, human agency and choice were not only possible but necessary for correct observance of the Christian faith and for the salvation it promised in accordance with God's plan unfolding across time.[5] In the same way, entire communities, with the assistance of clergy, had the option of believing correctly. The stars and the earth no longer made decisions for them, and whatever agency the celestial bodies might retain as signs or symbols derived from God, perhaps with predictive force.[6] One side effect was that with the stars' agency eliminated, the intercession of martyrs took on heightened urgency for individuals seeking access to the divine. The "pitiless stars," as Nicola Denzey Lewis calls them, did not listen to human pleas.[7]

At the same time, the Christianization of the natural world, that is, the disabling of its independent, determining force, affected how people viewed one another.[8] When Christians considered the great human variety in the world around them, they did not see merely a geographer's changing roster of peoples shaped by the landscape in which they lived, nor did they see simply an expanded version of the lists of Noah's many descendants (see chapter 6). Instead, they witnessed proof that God's Providence, not individual stars or the earth, ultimately decided the character of human societies. All humans, regardless of ethnicity, gender, or citizenship had equal access to salvation no matter where they lived. This meant that a person's life and community could change, especially through the medium of Christianity. Slowly but surely, Roman institutions and attitudes began to operate within this reimagined Christian cosmos, and faith became the prime marker of an individual, community, and nation.[9] It is very different to say that the salient characteristics of a group come from belief rather than from the stars or the earth, that is, from the specific characteristics of one's natural environment. The explanatory shift added up to nothing less than an ethnographic revolution.

The ethnographic transformation discussed in this and the following chapter was also part of a much larger and much older discussion of how to understand human agency in an externally determined world. Questions posed long before remained vigorous, but new answers of great consequence developed.[10] In the words of Ken Parry, "The history of the concepts of fate (εἱμαρμένη/*heimarmene*), free choice (προαίρεσις/*prohairesis*) and divine Providence (θεία πρόνοια/*theia pronoia*) between the fifth and the eighth centuries exemplifies the transition from Late Antiquity to the Middle Ages in intellectual terms."[11] Debates about these concepts were the purview of philosophers and theologians, who did not pay direct attention to ethnography. Yet, as these two chapters will show, ancient discussion of the relation of human communities to the stars and the physical environment drew from a larger philosophical inquiry. Investigators wondered how the particularity of human communities might be explained in a unified cosmos in accordance with divine universal law.[12] In turn, we wonder how Roman imperial ethnography was affected by this reimagining of the natural world.

CONNECTIONS TO ROME

To see how Roman concerns found expression in the discussion about the role of the stars and the natural environment in human affairs, it is necessary to consider Roman perspectives on empire. At its core the Roman Empire was a social and political organism hardwired to enable change among its subject populations. In the broadest terms, Romans believed that barbarians could become civilized and included in the Roman social and political order. Romans also created the framework in which Christianity developed. Consequently, two different kinds of inclusion came together in Late Antiquity, namely entry into the empire and entry into the community of Christian believers. They are reflected in ethnography in two related ways. First, an idea came into play in some situations that the power of empire could override the controlling hand of nature,[13] whether that of the celestial bodies or the earth, thereby enabling cultural transformation. The second, and closely related, idea was that the emperor, as God's designated representative, would be the artificer and agent of transformation in society to create a Roman-Christian world.

As will be shown below, the Christian position against astral determinism, based on the idea that the presence of Christians across the Roman map followed the same laws and customs and so could not have had the same horoscope, was only possible in the context of a far-flung, multiethnic empire. To enter the community of Christians and then the Christian imperial community required breaking the natural bonds of the stars and the earth.[14] In this way,

[126] CHAPTER 4

Christianity offered a kind of liberation for people trapped by the stars or geography. We find the emergence of an ethnography in which prayer was efficacious, baptism nullified the influence of the zodiac, conversion to another way of life was possible, and humans could choose whether or not to follow the correct teachings of their faith. These activities could be enabled by the emperor, and were entirely compatible with the Roman state. This was the imperial ethnography of a nondeterministic universe.

TIME FRAME

There is a late antique frame for these developments. Many of the deterministic formulations long predated Roman hegemony in the greater Mediterranean world, and, as in all things, Rome left an imperial stamp on them when they became useful. By the early third century CE, the idea that the stars and the natural environment were determining factors in human lives had become deeply entrenched in the Roman worldview.[15] In particular, astrology was king, though acceptance was not universal, as noted above. Vigorous opposition to natural determinism existed on two fronts, one manned by non-Christians, the other by Christians. The first were non-Christian philosophers, whose arguments reached back to a time before Christianity appeared on the scene. The second attack was made quite successfully by Christian theologians. Argument raged throughout the late antique centuries. By the late sixth century or so, astral determinism had been thoroughly condemned by Christian writers, though not fully eliminated in practice. John Philoponus (ca. 490–570), a Christian theologian and philosopher in Alexandria, said that the greatest proof of Christian piety was to reject astrology.[16] The celestial bodies themselves, however, deprived of their direct agency, remained the subject of astronomical discussion and found safer positions in Christian belief as well.[17] As Origen had put it already in the second century in the *Philocalia*, "the stars cannot be causative, though they may possibly be indicative."[18] In the fourth century, no less a figure than Basil of Caesarea, one of the Greek Church Fathers, said celestial signs are necessary for human life.[19] In short, by the end of Late Antiquity the stars no longer could be independent actors though they still might be symbols of divine intent. Everyone knew that a special star had led the Magi to Bethlehem.[20]

The early seventh century witnessed a considerable change in attitudes about astrology in learned Greek circles in the Roman Empire, now conventionally referred to as Byzantium. This change in attitude about astrology marks the end point of this chapter and this book. As Paul Magdalino has convincingly argued, astrology entered a new phase at about this time in Byzantium, becoming an important medium for the glorification of God the Father.[21] It became so devoid of religious threat that there even could be

DIVINE PROVIDENCE AND THE STARS   [127]

a revival of horoscope astrology in later Byzantine centuries.[22] This was an unexpected development. For it to happen, belief in the independent authority of the stars had to be completely rejected (as heretical),[23] and their presence accepted simply as indicators of God's activity. This possibility had been present in Christian thought for half a millennium but was realized fully only in the seventh century.[24] Magdalino notes that, after having suffered under Justinian, astrology enjoyed imperial favor under Heraclius and entered a new phase.[25]

The same pattern may be noted for environmental determinism, as we will see in the following chapter. It maintained a place in geographical explanation but was disempowered and not seen as a challenge to Christian belief. In fact, sometimes it was used to support Christian arguments. We will find environmental determinism used as an explanation without comment in Byzantine literature and handbooks as well as casual descriptions of the landscape's relation to culture.[26] These changes are witness to a remapping of the interconnections of theology and the natural world in Late Antiquity, outlined in what follows. The rest of this chapter considers astral determinism, while chapter 5 deals with geographical determinism. Although the two phenomena were in dialogue with each other, they warrant separate treatment.

The Power of the Stars

Astrology rests on the certainty that the remoteness of the stars in the heavens does not preclude their immediacy in human life. To ancient sky-watchers, the stars' regular movement suggested predictability, not just among the heavenly bodies but for humans as well. Consequently, over the long term, astrology became hugely popular as a guide to knowing what lay ahead. In the Mediterranean world by the second century CE, as F. E. Robbins, a modern translator of Ptolemy, explained, "[w]ith few exceptions every one, from emperor to the lowliest slave, believed in it."[27] Peter Brown has described astrology's omnipresence in the late Roman world as a "neutral technology of life."[28] Anthony Grafton suggested even more profound significance: "In fact, astrology probably represents the most consistent, unified and durable body of beliefs and practices in the western tradition."[29]

In antiquity, astrology generated intense philosophical study, especially during the Hellenistic age, when Greek scientist-philosophers, who themselves drew from a vast corpus of Babylonian learning, developed a body of astrological theory that would prove foundational for late antique writers.[30] Greek philosophers engaged in a debate about the extent to which, if at all, celestial bodies (stars and planets) and other suprahuman forces like Fate (which might be indicated by the movement of the stars) determine the destinies, characters, and actions of individuals as well as those of the communities in which they lived. Stoic philosophers notably articulated the paradox of human life being both determined and having free will.[31] As we will see, this idea eventually drew heavy Christian fire.

Two general approaches to astrology emerged in response to this difficult puzzle of understanding the extent of Fate's control.[32] The first, "fatalistic astrology," assumed that a person's character and destiny were absolutely determined at the moment of birth by the configuration of celestial bodies. The second approach, "catarchic astronomy," was less absolute but more popular, giving the stars and planets a lesser degree of influence on events, leaving some wiggle room for individuals to make plans. As Frederick Cramer puts it, "Most of those believing in astrology at all preferred the catarchic doctrine permitting man to 'outsmart' the heavens."[33] In step with these developments, scientists gave recognizable shape to the zodiac by the third century BCE, and casting natal horoscopes soon entered everyday life in the Greco-Roman world.

As much as the learned discussions of philosopher-scientists offer a chain of interpretative insights through the scholarly generations, their opinions also gave voice to deep-seated, living concerns of everyday life, both private and political. Would the position of the stars at the time of birth affect an individual's future? Was there anything one might do to ameliorate or sidestep heavenly decisions? Did stars influence the health or the character of one's country or of foreign nations? Such questions mattered. The discussion of astral determinism and fatalism would reverberate throughout Late Antiquity and make an unexpected and largely overlooked contribution to ethnographic thought.[34]

The debate about determinism caught the attention of Romans in the mid-second century BCE, just as their imperial horizons across the Mediterranean were vastly expanding.[35] Roman successes helped frame discussion by bringing a deep roster of new peoples into the imperial orbit. These new faces seemed to require some explanation of their differences and the forces that determined their destiny. In a similar way, several centuries later, Christian thinkers would appropriate and transform debate about determinism by offering a revised universal canvas and new principles of causality. In the emerging Christian worldviews of Late Antiquity, the stars lost ultimate control of human life because faith obliged individuals to make new kinds of choices about how to live. This chapter is not about the modulations of fatalism as they took form in various religious traditions, nor is it about broader principles of fatalism in monotheistic contexts.[36] Instead, it follows the late antique story of determinism through an ethnographic lens.

This chapter is divided into three parts. First, with a few examples, it traces widespread ideas about the controlling force of the stars that came into the Roman dossier to the time of Ptolemy in the second century CE. Then it considers arguments against astrology. Finally, it looks at the consequences of Christian entry into the debate about astrology, noting quite different perspectives among Gnostic and more mainstream Christian communities. The connecting thread will be arguments about *nomima barbarika*, or "customs of the nations," that had been brought into battle against astrology already in the Hellenistic age.

Foundations: Arguments for and against Astrology

In the second century BCE, Greek philosophers carried sophisticated astrological knowledge to Rome. These public intellectuals, who sometimes served on embassies, represented different schools of philosophical thought and pulled Roman intellectuals into broader Hellenistic debates.[37] Astrology found both avid proponents and harsh critics in the Roman realm. Imported Greek ideas framed discussion. In the most important debate of the second century, adherents of Stoicism, "the potent philosophical ally of fatalistic astrology," warred with adherents of the New Academy in Athens over the doctrine of fatalism versus free will.[38] These philosophers struggled with a puzzle: if we live in a completely predetermined world, what room is there for individual agency? Stoics tended to take a "fatalistic" stance to some degree, while New Academicians were astrology's harshest critics.

In Support of Astrology

From the first two centuries BCE onward, the followers of astrological ideas in Rome accepted the organization of the night sky into the twelve segments of the zodiac.[39] With the zodiac came the belief that a person's personality and destiny could be predicted by reading the position of celestial objects at the precise time of birth.[40] Astrological forecasting through the zodiac rapidly spread through every level of Roman society.

A milestone in Rome's involvement with astrology is represented by a remarkable embassy sent to Rome from Athens in 155 BCE to seek reduction of a fine imposed by the Senate.[41] The heads of the three major philosophical schools in Athens led the delegation. They were Carneades, head of the New Academy; Diogenes of Babylon, head of the Stoa; and Critolaus, head of the Peripatetic school. While there is no evidence that they discussed their quite different opinions about astrology during their visit to the city, their presence together in the embassy stands for the different viewpoints to which Romans were exposed by the middle of the second century BCE. Two of these men (and the schools they represented) supported astrology. The Stoic Diogenes thought astrologers could foretell a baby's character, but no more than that,[42] while Critolaus, heir to the Aristotelian tradition, accepted that planets were able to give some order to human affairs.[43] Carneades was a fierce critic. We will return to him in a moment.

[130] CHAPTER 4

Our understanding of the status of astrology in Rome as the Republic drew to a close is well served by Cicero, a major, though skeptical, conduit of many Greek philosophical ideas, writing about a century after the embassy from Athens.[44] His *On Divination*, written in 44 BCE, engages works of many Greek predecessors, especially Stoic philosophers, making the treatise an invaluable source of information about the history of astrological thought as well as its presence among educated Romans of his day.[45] He spoke directly to them: "Did all the Romans who fell at Cannae have the same horoscope?" he asked; "Yet all had one and the same end."[46] He mentions Posidonius as a friend, as well as L. Tarutius Firmanus, who calculated the horoscope of Romulus and the city of Rome.[47] Others of Cicero's friends included the senator G. Nigidius Figulus,[48] a staunch supporter in the Catiline crisis and a scholar whose work on the interpretation of thunder was still studied by John Lydus in Justinian's Constantinople,[49] and the well-known polymath and antiquarian Varro, who asked Tarutius to provide historical horoscopes and composed a now lost treatise on astrology.[50]

The popularity of astral determinism only increased in the Principate. A most important source is Marcus Manilius, a didactic poet writing in the early years of the first century CE, who dedicated his *Astronomica* to Augustus.[51] His ideas were generally in step with those of educated Romans, though not at the cutting edge of astrological thought of the day.[52] He delighted in the orderliness of the stars. Manilius combined an understanding of the power of the zodiac with a broad vision of the inhabited world and produced a forceful ethnography by bringing them together. In his view, the stars completely control every aspect of human life.[53]

In a hundred lines in his fifth book, Manilius explains the relationship between the four divisions of the heavens and the regions of the earth below.[54] He offers a sketch of the world and its peoples, tracing the Mediterranean coast. Manilius is especially important because he brings the signs of the zodiac[55] into his argument, explaining:

> for the creator [*deus*] has divided the world into portions, distributing it among the individual signs. To each guardian power he has given a special region of the world to rule . . . For this reason the human race is so arranged that its practices and features vary: nations are fashioned with their own particular complexions; and each stamps with a character of its own the like nature and anatomy of the human body which all share. Germany, towering high with tall offspring, is blond . . . [56]

He continues:

> Thus is the world for ever distributed among the twelve signs, and from the signs themselves must the laws prevailing among them be applied to the areas they govern; for these areas maintain between

themselves the same relationships as exist between the signs; and just as the signs unite with each other or clash in enmity . . . even so is land joined with land, city with city, and shores are at war with shores, realms with realms. So must every man shun or seek a place to live in, so hope for loyalty or be forewarned of peril, according to the character [*genus*] which has come down to earth from high heaven.[57]

Through his explicit connection of the twelve zodiacal signs and the character of the people each governs (the people of each region have a character sent from heaven) Manilius not only provides an important ethnographic vision shared by others of his era, he also sets the stage for Ptolemy, to whom we will return after surveying anti-astrological arguments.

Opposition to Astrology[58]

CARNEADES AND *NOMIMA BARBARIKA*

To find the arguments against astrology that were put to work in Late Antiquity, we must look back again to the members of the Athenian embassy to Rome in 155 BCE. One of its members, Carneades, head of the so-called New Academy in Athens from about 155 to 136, is credited with developing strong arguments against the stars' control of human destiny.[59] A brilliant speaker, he also presented public lectures that impressed sympathetic Roman listeners and alarmed others.[60] Though Carneades left no writings of his own, one of his students transcribed many volumes of his lectures. From among them, one of his arguments against the stars must be singled out (we do not know if he discussed it in Rome), as it proved to be enormously influential, especially among Christian writers. This argument refers to *nomima barbarika*, or "the customs of the nations." Carneades reasoned that, since a nation of people may follow the same laws and have the same customs despite the fact that every individual member of that group has a different natal horoscope, the stars could not possibly determine its laws, customs, or general characteristics.[61]

Along these same lines, Carneades also pointed out that if a nation, such as that of the Romans, spread across the earth, keeping to its own laws wherever it ruled, the control of the stars over the laws of a particular region within the empire could not be claimed.[62] In their fight against astrology, Christians would expand this argument to include Jews and Christians, peoples who adhered to their own customs and laws in many different lands (see on Bardaisan, below).[63]

Carneades's student Panaetius (185–110 BCE) was another Stoic philosopher from Greece who frequently lived in Rome from the 140s. He attacked the power of the stars more forcefully, though he did accept the role of divine Providence.[64] He joined the entourage of P. Scipio Cornelius Africanus, where his teachings about public service and ethical conduct won him considerable influence among the educated elite that directed Rome's growing empire.[65] Panaetius became the mentor of the polymath Stoic Posidonius, whom Cicero considered a friend, and who had a considerable influence on Julius Caesar and Strabo, as well as Seneca, Tacitus, and later writers of the Principate.[66]

Cicero was the most important transmitter and developer of Carneades's arguments against astrology. In *De Divinatione,* written in 44 BCE, he drew on the ideas of Carneades and Panaetius, whom he mentions often, to offer a scathing attack on astrology and divination.[67] His focus is the horoscopes of individuals, rather than celestial influence on the character of entire peoples. He mocks the assertions of astrologers that they could foretell the character of an individual from the position of the stars at the time of his birth, calling them insane to "insist that all persons born at the same time, regardless of the place of birth, are born to the same fate"[68] and to overlook the importance of local environment[69] and of what we would call genetics in shaping a person's character.[70] He forcefully applies these lessons to Roman history and current events. Pointing out that the questions are of his own making, not derived from Carneades, Cicero asks, "Were all the men eminent for intellect and genius born under the same star? Was there ever a day when countless numbers were not born? And yet there never was another Homer."[71] It is difficult to find fault with his further observation based on his own immediate experience:

> I recall a multitude of prophecies which the Chaldeans [astrologers] made to Pompey, to Crassus and even to Caesar himself (now lately deceased), to the effect that no one of them would die except in old age, at home and in great glory. Hence it would seem very strange to me should anyone, especially at this time, believe in men whose predictions he sees disproved every day by actual results.[72]

Cicero's reservations about astrology helped carry a Greek philosophical tradition into Roman intellectual life, but they did not by any means find universal acceptance. The most influential statement of astrological thought would be written more than a century later.

THE CONTRIBUTION OF PTOLEMY:
IDIOMATIKA ETHNIKA

Ptolemy of Alexandria (ca. 100–ca. 170 CE), who wrote in the Antonine Age, was antiquity's best known and most authoritative student of the stars.[73] His work was the culmination of the Hellenistic astronomical tradition and provides a baseline for subsequent late antique developments because of its clarity and thoroughness. Among his many contributions, he set forth a lasting version of the seven *klimata,* which would become canonical throughout Late

DIVINE PROVIDENCE AND THE STARS [133]

Antiquity and beyond.[74] Aspects of his work can be understood in light of the arguments, pro and con, about astrology that we have seen above.

Like Manilius more than a century before, he combined a very Roman vision of the layout of the earth with data derived from his study of the heavens. He is known for his innovations in mapmaking, such as presenting longitudinal and latitudinal coordinates so that readers might recreate his map from his text, called the *Guide to Drawing a World Map* and better known today as the *Geography*.[75] Not only does it include the Roman Empire from Britain to Ethiopia, Ptolemy has knowledge also of Ceylon, Central Asia, and even China. In another canonical study, called *Apotelesmatika* (*Astrological Influences*), better known today as the *Tetrabiblos*, Ptolemy linked the influence of the heavens, as divided into the signs of the zodiac, to the many nations and peoples of the inhabited world.[76] Viewing Aristotelian belief through a Stoic lens, Ptolemy understood the sublunar realm, Earth, to be influenced to some extent by movements in the heavens,[77] thus leaving a role open for astrological knowledge. The way that he explains astral connections to humanity in the *Tetrabiblos* renders the treatise far more important for the present study than the *Geography*. He does not believe that the stars are absolutely causal in shaping an individual's life. For Ptolemy, noncelestial factors such as an individual's physical strength or cultural influences may play a deciding role.[78]

In this work Ptolemy divides astronomical prediction into two sorts.[79] The first of these, concerning birthday horoscopes (genethlialogical horoscopes), has always received the greater interest.[80] Books 3 and 4 of the *Tetrabiblos* treat the horoscopes of individuals.

The second sort of astronomical prediction (ethno-geographical) appears in the second book of the *Tetrabiblos*[81] in a discussion of the characteristics of the inhabitants of the climes:

> The demarcation of national characteristics is established in part by entire parallels and angles, through their position relative to the ecliptic and the sun ... And now in each of these general regions certain special conditions of character and customs naturally ensue. For as likewise, in the case of the climate, even within the regions that in general are reckoned as hot, cold, or temperate, certain localities and countries have special peculiarities of excess or deficiency by reason of their situation, height, lowness, or adjacency; and again, as some peoples are more inclined to horsemanship because theirs is a plain country, or to seamanship because they live close to the sea, or to civilization because of the richness of their soil, so also would one discover special traits in each arising from the natural familiarity of their particular climes with the stars in the signs of the zodiac. These traits, too, would be found generally present, but not in every individual. We must, then, deal with

the subject summarily, in so far as it might be of use for the purpose of particular investigations.[82]

In this sort of prediction, Ptolemy brought astrological information to bear upon entire peoples, cities, and individuals in general to explain how their character was determined by the configuration of the planets and the stars in the zodiac as well as by the *klimata*.[83]

He divides the northern hemisphere into quarters separated by a latitudinal line crossing through the Mediterranean that reaches to Asia and a longitudinal line running from the Sea of Azov to the Red Sea through the Black Sea and the Aegean. He mentions seventy-two countries,[84] but his groupings of them are not easily rendered on a map, and the limits of his geographical knowledge are disputed. His list of lands includes Serike (the Silk Lands, which must refer to China at the end of the Silk Road) and Azania (the East African coast south of Ethiopia).[85]

The four divisions of the inhabited world reflect four triangular portions of the zodiac.[86] Position N, S, E, W, determines ἐθνικῶν ἰδιωμάτων, or "national characteristics."[87] For example, Europe makes up the NW quarter, and this is how he describes it: "Of these same countries Britain, (Transalpine) Gaul, Germany, and Bastarnia are in closer familiarity with Aries and Mars. Therefore for the most part their inhabitants are fiercer, more headstrong, and bestial."[88] Consider the case of the Scythians, in which environmental as well as astral circumstances play a role:

> Those who live under the more northern parallels, those, I mean, who have the Bears over their heads, since they are far removed from the zodiac and the heat of the sun, are therefore cooled; but because they have a richer share of moisture, which is most nourishing and is not there exhausted by heat, they are white in complexion, straight-haired, tall and well-nourished, and somewhat cold by nature; these too are savage in their habits because their dwelling-places are continually cold. The wintry character of their climate, the size of their plants, and the wildness of their animals are in accord with these qualities. We call these men, too, by the general name, Scythians.[89]

Ptolemy accomplished several important things in the *Tetrabiblos*. He synthesized material about the *klimata*, the zodiac, astronomy, and old environmental theory. He also established a canonical text in astrology that endured for more than a millennium.[90] The structure of the *Tetrabiblos* mirrors his firm distinction between groups and individuals as they are affected by the stars, and it made a clear connection between the peoples and regions of the earth and the configurations of the stars above them. In Ptolemy's hands, the zodiac and the *klimata*, both venerable scientific entities, easily entered a second-century world dominated by Rome. Though he wrote at Alexandria in

DIVINE PROVIDENCE AND THE STARS [135]

a Greek cultural milieu, Ptolemy envisaged an essentially Roman world. His conceptual map would remain standard.[91] It would be for his geographical data in the *Geography* and the *Tetrabiblos* that he made a lasting impression. However, his ideas about the stars determining the character of communities did not find listeners in Late Antiquity.

Scholars debate the source of Ptolemy's ideas about the influence of astrology on peoples and regions, with arguments focused on a debt to Posidonius which cannot be proven.[92] Instead, Ptolemy's and also Manilius's connection to Posidonius should be understood as evidence of Posidonius's popularity.[93]

Other Scientists and Historians

The deep influence of Ptolemy can be seen in the work of men of very different backgrounds and interests. The evidence is scattershot, but its variety indicates the wide spread of his ideas. About the time of Constantine, in the first decades of the fourth century, the mathematician and scientist Pappus of Alexandria (ca. 290–ca. 350) wrote a description of the inhabited world based on Ptolemy's *Geography* that was still being read in Constantinople in the tenth century, though we do not know if he referred to the ethnographic part of the *Tetrabiblos*.[94] An Armenian translation of the work appeared in the first half of the sixth century[95] that apparently drew on Ptolemy, with Pappus as an intermediary.[96]

Ptolemy remained accessible in the Latin West. Ammianus Marcellinus obtained material directly from Ptolemy or through an intermediary source.[97] In the sixth century, Boethius and Isidore of Seville knew his work, as did Cassiodorus, who wrote, "you have the book of Ptolemy who described every place so clearly that you might almost think that he was an inhabitant of all regions."[98] His work remained influential into medieval Byzantium and Arab lands,[99] and later found a good reception in the Renaissance as well.[100]

Julius Firmicus Maternus, a Roman of the senatorial class who lived perhaps in Sicily in the age of Constantine, had a lifelong interest in astrology. He represents a "before and after" in the history of astrology all by himself. He wrote two books about the subject that took very different approaches. The first book, composed in the 330s before he converted to Christianity, was called the *Mathesis*, or *Eight Books of Astrology*, the longest Latin study of astrology to survive from antiquity. It became an authoritative handbook, often as a target for Christian writers.[101] Augustine, for example, harshly criticized its presumption that the stars were divine.[102] In the *Mathesis*, in contrast, Firmicus Maternus explains that the stars determine all of our secondary characteristics:

> We must now take up the question of the complexions and characters of mankind . . . By this it is shown that our essential nature and

the general shape of the naked body are formed from a mixture of the four elements by the skill of the far-sighted Creator. But our individual complexions and our shapes, our character, and our personalities are given us by none other than the constant motion of the planets. For the planets have their own faculties and divine wisdom. Animated by pure reason they tirelessly obey that highest divinity, the ruling God who has organized all things under the rule of law to protect the eternal pattern of creation.[103]

Firmicus Maternus's second book, *The Error of the Pagan Religions*, on the other hand, was composed when he had adopted Christianity in the early 340s. Dedicated to Constantine's sons Constantius II and Constans, the book urged the suppression of all pagan practices, including astrology.[104]

Philosophers in the Sublunar Realm

NEOPLATONISTS

Though well aware of the *Tetrabiblos* and deeply concerned with forces of causality in human affairs, Neoplatonic philosophers showed no interest in how the stars might affect the character of peoples.[105] It was accepted that the Earth and its human institutions existed in the sublunar realm and so were subject to change. Many contingent factors, such as location, government, laws, habits, and cultural disposition might contribute to those changes. The extent to which the celestial bodies were responsible for those contingencies remained an open question.

Plotinus (204–70 CE) roughly followed the approach of Ptolemy. He argued that the stars do have an effect on humans because we live in the malleable sublunar realm. They may influence such things as personal strength or success but will have no effect on other things such as wealth, fame, or occupation.[106] According to A. A. Long, "Overall Plotinus' position seems to be a weakened version of Ptolemaic astrology, but without any commitment to its technical doctrines or interest in horoscopes."[107] For Plotinus, the stars themselves, however, were only a link in a cosmic chain of command, and while they may announce such things as wealth or power, human effort also is a factor in their acquisition.[108] Human activities are themselves influenced by forces lesser than and subordinate to the stars. Plotinus writes in his second *Ennead*:

> And what sort of a life is it for the planets if, when innumerable living beings have been born and continue to exist, they are always effecting something for each one of them, giving them reputation, making them rich or poor or wicked, being themselves responsible for bringing the activities of all the separate individuals to completion. How could they do so much?[109]

For Plotinus and many Neoplatonists who followed him, the stars did not have immediate and absolute control over human achievements or qualities.[110] In Peter Adamson's words, for Plotinus, "[the stars] signify everything but they are not the cause of anything."[111] For this reason Plotinus showed no interest in Ptolemy's ethnographic material in the second book of the *Tetrabiblos*. Such matters were not his concern. According to Plotinus's student Porphyry (ca. 284–ca. 305), who compiled his teacher's *Enneads*, Plotinus's main interest lay in the correct casting of horoscopes and determining if events can be predicted by understanding the stars.[112] Porphyry himself wrote an *Introduction* to the *Tetrabiblos* that meant to clarify astrological terms used by Ptolemy.[113] The work was widely used by later writers, who perhaps wrestled with Ptolemy's Greek.

A close paraphrase of the *Tetrabiblos* exists that has been attributed to the authoritative Proclus (ca. 410–85), who for nearly half a century was head of the Platonic Academy in Athens.[114] He took interest in Ptolemy's astronomy only as much as it enabled calculating the position of planets. He gave the stars no further explanatory function.[115] The need for a simplified version of Ptolemy's text suggests a considerable readership interested in his works.[116]

Imperial Legislation against Astrology[117]

Imperial legislation articulated degrees of opposition to astrology in two phases. The first we might call "pre-Christian." This was not a rejection of astrology but the opposite. Emperors objected to it on the assumption that astrology indeed worked and therefore posed an immediate threat because knowledge of their natal horoscopes could be used against them.[118] Emperors had horoscopes drawn for themselves in the early empire, however, and this practice seems to have lasted intermittently until the fifth century.

In the second phase of legislation, the efficacy of astrology was denied and the practice was demonized by Christian leaders. The Theodosian Code criminalized astrology for Christian reasons, lumping it with heresy, wizardry, Manichaeanism, and "every sect inimical to the Catholics."[119] The laws gathered in the Theodosian Code reveal that astrology was widely practiced.[120]

Casting horoscopes was quite popular, as indicated by imperial legislation and the efforts of churchmen to stamp it out. Opposition by Christians put natal horoscopy in a new context. Ambrosiaster (ca. 366–84) said that "astrologers are the enemy of the truth";[121] Pope Leo I (ca. 400–61), perhaps echoing the Theodosian Code, equated astrology with heresy in his attacks on Priscillianists, who, he said, "deem that men's souls and bodies are bound fast by the fatal stars."[122] The influence of the stars on entire peoples did not motivate the legislation or imperial persecution, however. It was the casting of individual horoscopes that drew fire from Christian authorities. To see Christian attacks on astral determinism, it is necessary to go beyond imperial legislation.

[138] CHAPTER 4

Christians versus Astrology: nomima barbarika

In Late Antiquity, the chief opposition to astral determinism came from Christian theologians engaged in what Tamsin Barton has called "the power struggle between the stars and God."[123] Their objections rested on several interrelated points. First, astrology was pagan. The stars could not possibly be divinities or have causal agency because everything in the heavens and on Earth took direction and could be explained only through God, who had created the entire cosmos. Furthermore, the idea that people's lives, bodies, and minds, or the character of the communities in which they lived, could be determined at birth by the stars was at odds with Christian belief in an omnipotent God. His divine Providence called the shots, not the zodiac.[124] Many believed that if astrology were valid, the consequences for humanity would be dreadful, because belief in astrologically determined destiny undermines human laws and institutions.[125] Augustine thought that it could lead to anarchy.[126] Most important of all, however, it was necessary to deny the influence of the stars because humans had to choose whether or not to sin and so win or lose salvation.[127] Free will entailed making decisions about individual action and salvation, even in a world in which the ultimate course of human history was determined.

In the development of these ideas, the *nomima barbarika* argument attributed to Carneades became very popular among Christian writers.[128] Adjusted and adapted to Christian needs, *nomima barbarika* put into action a powerful vision of a universal Christian community at the expense of the stars' power over specific regions. At the same time, *nomima barbarika* arguments provoked strong opposition among non-Christian astrologers. As H.J.W. Drijvers explained, they attempted to refute the argument by invoking the idea of the seven *klimata* that posited a planetary or zodiacal ruler for each zone on earth.[129]

BARDAISAN

The fullest expression of antiastrological *nomima barbarika* argument was put forward by the Syriac churchman Bardaiṣan/Bardesanes (ca. 154–222), in his widely influential *Book of the Laws of Countries* (*BLC*), or *Dialogue on Fate*, which was set down by his student Philippus.[130] He lived in the independent northern Mesopotamian kingdom of Edessa (Urfa in modern Turkey), which was sandwiched between the Roman and Parthian empires. It was a center of Syriac Christian culture as well as a hub of international trade and a busy marketplace of ideas.[131] Bardaisan's treatise reflected the broad intellectual and geographical horizens of Edessa. Fergus Millar called the *BLC* the "clearest example" of a "fusion of cultures and traditions in this area."[132] It represents a foundational document in Christian Syriac literature. Originally

DIVINE PROVIDENCE AND THE STARS [139]

composed in Syriac, in which it found a considerable audience, the treatise soon was known to theologians in the West in Greek translation.[133]

Bardaisan was a man of high status at the court of Abgar VIII (r. 177–212), and quite knowledgeable about both scientific astronomy and astrology, which he had engaged in before taking up pen to oppose them.[134] Though written to develop theological ideas about human fate and freedom,[135] the *BLC* proved to be a watershed in the inadvertent production of a fresh kind of Christian ethnography.

Cast in the form of a dialogue between Bardaisan and an astrologer called Awida, the *BLC* attacks the idea that the stars have absolute power, though it does not suggest that they have no power.[136] The treatise argues that while Fate, which is expressed in the stars and planets, may influence human life to some extent, perhaps causing misfortunes of different sorts, it is not an independent force nor is its power absolute.[137]

Bardaisan's reluctance to reject astrology completely made him a heretic in later Christian eyes.[138] Nevertheless, Bardaisan poses free will against astrological determinism, arguing that humans are free to choose between performing right and wrong actions. His primary purpose was to explain human choice to sin, not to be an ethnographer or even to fight astrology.[139] Developing his theological points, however, required the rebuttal of the power of the stars and the autonomous control of Fate. He viewed Fate as the expression of divine Providence.[140]

The *BLC* represents a particular Christian appropriation of the *nomima barbarika* arguments.[141] A connection to Carneades is presumed, and Bardaisan could well have been aware of him from many sources.[142] The treatise shows in its first book that in different countries people agree to follow widely different sets of laws and customs, which they frequently change, thereby demonstrating that human freedom to devise laws is stronger than, and independent of, Fate.[143] Furthermore, Bardaisan presents Christians as an international community that observes one law wherever they might be; this is a central argument against astral determinism. He says, regarding Christians:

> What shall we say of the new people of us Christians, that the Messiah has caused to arise in every place and in all climates by his coming? For behold, we all, wherever we may be, are called Christians after the one name of the Messiah . . . But in whatever place they are and wherever they may find themselves, the local laws cannot force them to give up the law of their Messiah, nor does the Fate of the Guiding Signs force them to do things that are unclean for them. But sickness and health, wealth and poverty, that which does not depend on their free-will, comes over them wherever they are.[144]

Consequently, individual horoscopes and astrology in general have no determinative force whatsoever. Ute Possekel shows that, for Bardaisan, who used Carneades's arguments, "[t]he planetary constellations at birth do not determine a person's action, and neither do they determine the customs of people in the various regions (or *klimata*) of the earth."[145] Instead, God-given human liberty counteracts Fate and the power of the stars and planets. In this way Bardaisan demonstrates that the laws of countries are human creations. They have more power than Fate and the power of the stars and planets.

Then Bardaisan says:

> Now listen, and try to understand that not all people over the whole world do that which the stars determine by their Fate and in their sectors, in the same way. For men have established laws in each country by that liberty given them from God, for this gift counteracts the Fate of the Rulers [the stars], who have appropriated something not given to them. I shall now begin to relate these, in so far as I remember them, beginning in the extreme East of the whole world.[146]

In addition to Christian communities, Bardaisan also uses Jews and Romans as examples of how universal communities belie the local power of Fate and the stars. He notes that Jews are found in many lands, yet they all follow the same laws and refrain from violation of religious dictates no matter where they live. The Romans similarly constitute a universal community, though not one defined by religious belief; in fact, it is the empire itself that frames the universal scope of Christians and Jews. Bardaisan's comments on the Romans are particularly important. Fate, he tells us, does not prevent the Romans from always conquering new territories, something at which they excel, or from doing away with the local laws and customs of conquered lands, as he says they have recently done in Arabia.[147] This thought, not further developed, gives a hint of the idea of how a Roman imperial endeavor could enter Christian patterns of explanation of the world.

Bardaisan starts a survey of the inhabited world that for him stretches from China to Britain and about which he provides much exotic ethnographic detail. Where Bardaisan got his data about foreign peoples remains an open question, since there existed no written ethnographic corpus in Syriac to draw on. Perhaps some material came from Greek sources, which he probably could read.[148] Other knowledge must have circulated in the international culture of Edessa. To what ends did he put such information? When he tells us that the Medes throw out their dead to be eaten by dogs,[149] or that in Kushan women dress like men and wear the pants in society, he is not doing so to pass judgment or merely to say that "custom is king," as Herodotus once had done.[150] Instead, his examples are meant to demonstrate that the people in different countries conform to their own peculiar customs by choice. Though they are not all born under the same stars sharing the same zodiacal signs, they all follow the same customs, and their kings often change the laws. The range of change, however, was rather restricted. Some things, like marriage or burial

DIVINE PROVIDENCE AND THE STARS [141]

customs, might be altered, but not basic social relations. For example, he does not mention changes in the relation of masters and slaves or kings and subjects.[151] Bardaisan is saying that human social forms are the product of human device in response to divinely granted freedom to make such choices. He does say, however, that the stars do affect some aspects of human life. For example, in discussion of the laws of the Seres (Chinese):

> The Seres have laws that they shall not kill, shall not commit fornication and shall not worship idols. And in the whole country of the Seres there is no idol, no prostitute, no murderer and no man murdered, although they too are born at all hours and on all days. And not even mighty Mars, standing in midheaven, so forces the liberty of the Seres as to make a man shed the blood of his fellow with an iron sword. Nor does Venus, when in conjunction with Mars, force any of the Serian men to have intercourse with the wife of his neighbour or with any other woman. Yet there are rich and poor there, sick and healthy, rulers and subjects, because these things are given into the power of the Guiding Signs [the stars].[152]

Bardaisan goes on to give similar examples, ranging from the laws of the Brahmans in India to the customs of the Britons.[153] He has a sharp eye for ethnographic detail, which is essential for his argument though secondary to his main point, and his impact on later writers was considerable.

The Influence of Bardaisan

Four Christian writers will be examined in order to illustrate the influence of Bardaisan: Eusebius of Caesarea, Diodorus of Tarsus, Gregory of Nyssa, and the author of the Pseudo-Clementine *Recognitions*.[154]

EUSEBIUS OF CAESAREA

Among the influential figures who appreciated Bardaisan's knowledge of astrology was the biblical scholar Eusebius (ca. 260–339), who was bishop in Caesarea in Palestine from about 314 to 339.[155] This prolific author contributed a great deal to the formation of a Christian canon of writings. In addition to his well-known *Ecclesiastical History* that established a new genre of historical writing by giving Christianity's development an institutional framework, and his *Life* of the Emperor Constantine, which integrated a Christian perspective with imperial Roman panegyric, as well as many other works, Eusebius wrote the *Preparation for the Gospel*, a work of Christian apologetics intended to show, as Aaron Johnson has argued, that Christians constituted a new ethnic group that stemmed from ancient Hebrew roots[156] and that Christianity had a transformative role to play in salvation history. As Johnson writes, "it is the spread of Christ's teaching throughout the world, not the conquest of Rome that causes the profound changes in customs and ways of life that Eusebius depicts."[157] He cites Eusebius:

> [it is] only from his utterances, and from his teaching diffused throughout the whole world, [that] the customs of all nations are now set aright, even those customs which before were savage and barbarous; so that Persians who have become his disciples no longer marry their mothers, nor Scythians feed on human flesh, because of Christ's word which has come even unto them.[158]

It is no surprise, therefore, that Eusebius showed an interest in the cultural variety exhibited in the *oikoumene*, all of which prefigured a world that one day would be made entirely Christian through the spread of the Gospel. Transformation of culture stands out as a consequence of Christian belief.

In the sixth book of the *Preparation for the Gospel*, Eusebius presented extensive extracts from the *BLC*.[159] He offers the extracts in the form of a contrast between wild beasts, which do not vary in their behavior according to species, and humans, who are free to choose the manner in which they live their lives. He borrows the following from Bardaisan:

> A lion is carnivorous and takes revenge if he be injured: and therefore all lions are carnivorous and take revenge. Ewe lambs eat grass, and touch no flesh, and if injured take no revenge: and every lamb's character is the same . . . But men alone, having as their special privilege the mind, and the reason which proceeds from it, in what they have in common follow nature, as I said before, but as to their special gift are not governed by nature. For they do not all even eat the same food: some feed like lions, and others like lambs: they have not one fashion of raiment: there is not one custom, nor one law of civil society among them, nor one impulse of desire for things: but each man chooses a life for himself according to his own will, not imitating his neighbour, except in what he chooses . . . Whence we may understand that man is not altogether led by nature . . . but is borne one way according to nature, and another way according to will. Wherefore he incurs praise and blame and condemnation in matters dependent on will: but in matters dependent on nature he has immunity from blame, not out of pity, but from reason.[160]

Eusebius, who used a Greek translation of Bardaisan's work,[161] was as much drawn to Bardaisan's *nomima barbarika* arguments as he was to the breadth of ethnographic and geographical data that the *BLC* provided. The two churchmen shared a quite similar vision of the *oikoumene*, and the Roman Empire held a special place in that vision. In Eusebius's case, however, the Roman Empire was notable in its failure to complete the kind of civilizing

DIVINE PROVIDENCE AND THE STARS [143]

process that only Christianity could achieve. Elsewhere he argues that God's plan for human salvation required the Roman Empire to impose unity on most of the world so that Christianity could spread more easily;[162] in the *Preparatio Evangelica*, the Roman Empire is replaced by Christianity and the Christian nation as the fulfiller of divine intention.

DIODORUS OF TARSUS

Diodorus, the Orthodox bishop of Tarsus (378–ca. 394), evidently shared with Bardaisan knowledge of the Greek sources concerning *nomima barbarika*.[163] He played a high-profile role in eastern church affairs in the middle half of the fourth century that sometimes earned him imperial displeasure and sometimes favor.[164] The emperor Julian was quite hostile when he came to Antioch, Diodorus's hometown, in 362, while preparing for his ill-fated Persian campaign. After Julian's death, Valens banished Diodorus to Armenia, but when Valens died, Diodorus returned to Antioch and became bishop of Tarsus in Cilicia in 378. Emperor Theodosius I praised him with other bishops as a trustworthy defender of the Nicene Creed at the Second Ecumenical Council at Constantinople in 381.[165] Diodorus probably died before 394,[166] but he did not rest in peace. In 438, no less a force than Cyril of Alexandria wrote a tract accusing him of originating the teaching of Nestorius, and he was finally condemned by a Constantinopolitan synod in 499 in the matter of the Three Chapters.[167] This condemnation, fair or not, resulted in the posthumous destruction of his many writings on religious matters, which now exist only in a few fragments and summaries.[168]

Judging from the titles listed in the tenth-century Byzantine *Suda Lexicon*, Diodorus had a deep interest in astronomy and astrology.[169] Fortunately, Photius, the ninth-century patriarch of Constantinople, wrote an extensive entry (Codex 223) on Diodorus in his *Bibliotheca*, which provides a detailed discussion of *Against Fate*.[170] The codex among other things contains *nomima barbarika* arguments. Judging from the material preserved by Photius, Diodorus was firmly opposed to the idea that a person's destiny is fixed at birth by predestination or fate (εἱμαρμένη),[171] which he considers to be a "fabrication against truth by the enemies of truth."[172] Refutation of astrology and the use of the zodiac naturally follows,[173] and this led to engaging the arguments of Bardaisan. Diodorus knew the *Book of the Laws of Countries* well and attacked it in *Against Fate* even though he was influenced by it. His refutation of astrological determinism employed arguments similar to Bardaisan's, and he gave Bardaisan some credit, but in general his attitude toward him and his followers is quite hostile.[174] Photius writes,

> Indeed, in chapter 51, while he [Diodorus] is demolishing predestination, he also deals a blow to the ideas of Bardisanes, which are half mad

and a kind of half way stage. In fact Bardisanes makes the soul free from predestination and from what is called the horoscope, preserving its free will, but he subjects the body and all that concerns it—I mean wealth or poverty, health or illness, life or death, and everything that is not under our control—to the power of destiny, and he declares that all these matters are the result of predestination.[175]

According to Photius, Diodorus offered three objections to arguments of predestination. The first of these was to question the power of the constellations, which he distinguishes from the signs of the zodiac and the planets:

For each of these constellations by its own activities nullifies that law [of predestination] and its effects, as is shown by what they say. Yet not all of them control the same area of the earth's surface. For example the territory of the Persians and the Georgians, that of the Lazoi and the Romans, or others. How then does one people when compared with another, differ entirely in its life, laws and customs?[176]

Photius notes Diodorus's second point: "[W]hy have most nations, while living in their own territories, adopted Roman customs?"[177]

Diodorus's final point, according to Photius, concerned Jews and Christians. He described how Jews adhered to their laws no matter where they lived:

But even when their [Jewish] nation was led away in captivity to Babylon, and later scattered all over the world, it did not give up its traditions, and no concomitant constellation or law of genesis compelled them to abolish the rules relating to circumcision or the sabbath.[178]

Christians similarly had achieved worldwide presence, facts that clearly denied the power of the zodiac to determine the characteristics of peoples in different regions. He wrote in the sixth book of *Against Fate*:

Our people, I mean the Christians, came into being four hundred years ago and at once conquered the whole of the inhabited world. It detached each nation from their own customs and introduced them to a life of orthodox piety without removing them from their country; it left them inhabiting the same places as before, and it reduced the long-lasting influences of the concomitant constellations to a wretched notion only fit to be laughed at. The ideas which the feeble concept of destiny relied on were brilliantly demolished by the message of men who were illiterate.[179]

In this passage Christian mastery of the inhabited world is described just as the Roman Empire might be described, with change in the customs of a conquered people a consequence of Roman rule. In this case, however, the Christian conquerors bring their own faith instead of Roman law to the peoples of the world. The idea became part of the general imperial Christian repertoire. In the sixth century, Procopius will discuss Justinian's forced conversion of the Tzani in just the same terms, as will be discussed in chapter 5.

Like Bardaisan, Diodorus relished the specific cultural differences among the peoples that he used to demonstrate the falseness of astrologers' claims and the falseness of the zodiac:

> Why, within a single species, does one people wear its hair long, while another cuts it short? Why does one people allow marriage between mother and son, while most consider the idea abhorrent? They are separated by innumerable other differences of law, style of life, and custom. No astral movement crops the long-haired or forces the close-cropped to grow their hair long; nor does it compel others to any form of behaviour which they have not learned from their own local customs.[180]

Again, exotic detail mixes with free will to strike a familiar blow against astrological determinism. As with Bardaisan, ethnography is an essential component of his argument.

GREGORY OF NYSSA

The youngest of the Cappadocian Fathers, Bishop Gregory of Nyssa (372–ca. 394), used *nomima barbarika* arguments in his treatise *Against Fate*.[181] A striking difference between him and Diodorus is found in his presentation of the Jews in his argument.[182] For him, the universal element among Jews scattered across the world was not their commitment to circumcision and the Sabbath but their rejection of Christ:

> The Jewish nation is distributed over just about all parts of the earth; peoples of the east, south, inland, west, north, practically all the nations are mixed in community with the Jews. How therefore does no necessity of the stars prevail over any of them to favour any of the nation with indemnity? But in the myriad combinations of the stars as they come together, for the one who is born it is always the same, according to the ordered cycle of the days, their nature enduring the curse [brought on by the rejection of Christ].[183]

This passage shows how *nomima barbarika* elements could contribute to the growth of anti-Judaism in the late antique Church and in Roman society.

PSEUDO-CLEMENTINE RECOGNITIONES 9.19–29

Written early in the fourth century, the Pseudo-Clementine *Recognitions* are very close to Bardaisan's *Book of the Laws of Countries* in their use of *nomima barbarika* arguments against an independent Fate. They accept human

[146] CHAPTER 4

freedom to choose right from wrong in accordance with the divine Providence that governs all things. The treatises deal with ethnographic data similarly and share a lost third-century source.[184]

Regardless of the texts from which the treatise may have drawn, the *Recognitions* are important for several reasons. The work indicates the broad diffusion of *nomima barbarika* arguments in the fourth century and gives yet another example of how a writer cleverly devised a place for Christians in the Roman conceptual firmament. The *Recognitions* were translated sometime before 410 by Rufinus of Aquileia, a devoted and accurate translator of Greek text for a Latin audience, especially Christian students.[185] Through his translation the *Recognitions* became quite influential. The translation of book 9 of the *Recognitiones* was widely used in attacks on astrological ethnography in the Latin West.[186] Somewhat later they were partially translated into Syriac, Arabic, and Slavonic. The treatise emphasizes the importance of baptism in breaking with astrology in a *nomima barbarika* context, which as shown below also played a part in Gnostic writing.

Clement of Rome, the second or third bishop of Rome, who lived in the last decade of the first century, is the purported author of the *Recognitions*, which is a Christian novel of sorts.[187] In the story, which is told in the first person, Clement converts to Christianity; travels with St. Peter, who had consecrated him bishop; and in the seventh book is eventually reunited with his long-lost family.[188] This restoration of the family is the so-called "recognition."

As Nicole Kelley has pointed out, knowledge of astrology constitutes some of the expertise that establishes the authority of Peter and Clement.[189] The fact that they are so well versed in astrology receives no comment. In the eighth book, Clement and his brothers debate astrology with a certain Faustinianus, who believes that his own sad life has been determined by the stars. Part of the debate with Faustinianus about astrology concerns whether Fate determines national characteristics. Peter of course refutes all the arguments defending astrology, and Faustinianus is eventually won over to Christianity (in book 10) and baptized by Peter at the end of the *Recognitions*.[190] Thus the work may be seen as an extended conversion narrative cast against the background of astrological belief, which is refuted. For Clement, and then Faustinianus, baptism marks the conclusion of the conversion and the defeat of arguments for astrology.

Using *nomima barbarika* arguments, book 9 of the *Recognitions* attacks astrology with many examples of numerous peoples (e.g., Indians, Jews, and others) who possess sharply different customs.[191] In each case the author explains how a particular configuration of the stars and planets does not determine these particular human laws. He calls the power of the stars "genesis." The first direct refutation of astrology begins with a discussion of the customs of the Seres, the world's easternmost people:

DIVINE PROVIDENCE AND THE STARS   [147]

There are, in every country or kingdom, laws imposed by men, enduring either by writing or simply through custom, which no one easily
transgresses. [He mentions their customs] . . . and no man's liberty of
will is compelled, according to your doctrine, by the fiery star of Mars,
to use the sword for the murder of man; nor does Venus in conjunction with Mars compel to adultery . . . But amongst the Seres the fear of
laws is more powerful than the configuration of Genesis.[192]

He illustrates this idea in chapters 20–23 by showing that customs vary enormously among peoples, even though they experience similar configurations of
the celestial bodies.[193] "[E]ach nation," he concludes, "observes its own laws
according to free-will, and annuls the decrees of Genesis by the strictness of
laws."[194]

At 9.26 the author denies the theory of seven *klimata*:

But some one skilled in the science of mathematics will say that Genesis is divided into seven parts, which they call climates, and that over
each climate one of the seven heavenly bodies bears rule; and that
those diverse laws to which we have referred are not given by men,
but by those dominant stars according to their will, and that which
pleases the star is observed by men as a law. To this we shall answer, in
the first place, that the world is not divided into seven parts; and in the
second place, that if it were so, we find many different laws in one part
and one country; and therefore there are neither seven *laws* according to the number of the heavenly bodies, nor twelve according to the
number of the signs, nor thirty-six according to that of the divisions of
ten degrees; but they are innumerable.[195]

The Romans provide his main example:

Assuredly we can easily ascertain how many rulers have changed the
laws and customs of nations which they have conquered, and subjected
them to their own laws. This is manifestly done by the Romans, who
have brought under the Roman law and the civil decrees almost the
whole world, and all nations who formerly lived under various laws and
customs of their own. It follows, therefore, that the stars of the nations
which have been conquered by the Romans have lost their climates and
their portions.[196]

The Pseudo-Clementines reveal a world in which no one, Christian or non-
Christian, ignores the power of the stars. The clarity of discussion on both
sides and the arsenal of well-developed arguments against astrology indicates a battlefield that has seen many days of combat. Particularly notable
is how the prominent discussion of the Roman Empire segues easily from

general *nomima barbarika* discussion, which puts the ethnographic detail of the peoples of the world and their manifestly different customs into a Roman framework. At the same time, it becomes first and foremost a Christian frame. Denial of the power of the stars, the "Genesis," is now from a Christian perspective. We are told that "Genesis" is inconsistent with divine justice. Only God punishes humans who choose to sin.[197] Human fate is not in the hands of the stars.

Baptism and the Stars: The Gnostic Connection[198]

From an early date, Christian ritual offered a means of breaking the control of the stars in a way that found particular resonance in Gnostic contexts and material expression in the carving of some baptismal fonts.[199] The rite of baptism, so essential a part of Christian practice, was understood to cleanse initiates of their sins and to offer a rebirth into a new community of faith. The person baptized began life again.[200] In the words of the Greek Father John Chrysostom (d. 407):

> This bath [baptism] does not merely cleanse the vessel but melts the whole thing down again. Even if a vessel has been wiped off and carefully cleaned, it still has the marks of what it is and still bears the traces of the stain. But when it is thrown into the smelting furnace and is renewed by the flame, it puts aside all dross and, when it comes from the furnace, it gives forth the same sheen as newly-molded vessels.[201]

In the hands of some Gnostic Christians, the rite of baptism was brought into the battle against the stars' power. Gnosticism, an elastic term coined only in the seventeenth century[202] and today applied to a wide variety of religious expression found among non-Christians as well as some Christian groups, stressed spiritual experience that liberates humans from the bonds of materiality in search of redemption. The idea that existence in the sublunar, material world constrains humanity reached back to Plato and took many forms in subsequent centuries.[203]

One commonly found idea in Gnostic cosmology is that humanity is trapped by the control of a malignant Fate.[204] Powerful supranatural figures called archons manage this fate, with agency granted them by the malicious god of material creation, who himself struggles with a benign, saving god of the spirit.[205] In some traditions the archons were associated with the five planetary spheres and sometimes with the twelve zodiac signs that influenced the character of human communities.[206]

Conventional astrology took a central position in Gnostic writings from a very early date. We have looked at the idea of "Genesis" above, namely the power of the stars that held humanity in its grasp. In an explicitly Gnostic context, this sort of zodiac-based astral determinism appeared in the thought

DIVINE PROVIDENCE AND THE STARS [149]

of Basilides, a second-century commentator on the Gospels who taught at Alexandria about 120–40 CE and soon was branded a heretic for various of his arguments.[207] One of these heretical positions ascribed to him was that the angels, who created the lowest of the 365 heavens (which is our heaven), divided and ruled over the different nations and peoples among themselves until the Unborn Father (God the Father) sent the Mind (Nous, i.e., Christ) to break their control.[208]

The celestial archons were, so to speak, cosmic "prison guards,"[209] but their power over humans was not always considered absolute. Some writers believed that humans could transcend this power through acquisition of true knowledge, while some looked for savior figures to redeem them from the bonds of Fate.[210] Other Christians took these ideas about fate and determinism in a different direction by making Christian baptism the means for a prison break. In the late second century, for example, the Gnostic Theodotus, a follower of Valentinus, expressed this idea clearly: "until baptism, fate is real . . . but after it the astrologers no longer speak the truth."[211] In other words, baptism freed Christians from the bonds of astral determinism, though pagans remained subject to its power.[212] The newly baptized individual entered an existing community of believers whose destiny was in the hands of God. Like law, the rite of baptism reinscribed the individual within a new set of personal identifications.

Ethnic origin or place of birth meant nothing in the universal embrace of the Christian community. In the Gospel of Matthew 28:19, Jesus instructed his disciples to make all peoples his disciples through baptism. Nearly four hundred years later, Bishop Zeno of Verona (ca. 300–371) wrote, explaining baptism: "This renewal, this resurrection, this eternal life, this is the mother of all, which when we are united, gathered from every people and nation, eventually makes [us] one body."[213] Not only is baptism instrumental in this new construction of identity, it has a universal application for him. Furthermore, Zeno used the signs of the zodiac in an elaborate allegory about astrology in a sermon on baptism.[214]

Zeno reveals that a new ethnography of the *oikoumene* is emerging in which faith is the main diagnostic element and in which the stars have no power over the community of baptized Christians. In a fascinating transposition, the twelve Apostles became characters in this drama, for in some writings they have replaced the twelve signs of the zodiac.[215] One of the Pseudo-Clementine *Homilies* put it this way: "The Lord had twelve apostles, bearing the number of the twelve months of the sun."[216] After conversion, the newly baptized enter into the control of a new set of heavenly signs.[217] The Apostles govern their rebirth, just as the old signs of the zodiac had before.[218] According to April DeConick, "The Apostles . . . have been substituted for the twelve signs of the zodiac. For, just as birth is regulated by them . . . so too rebirth is directed by the Apostles."[219] By the Middle Ages, different constellations were earmarked for Jews, Christians, and Muslims.

[150] CHAPTER 4

In a late third-century Coptic Gnostic text, the *Pistis Sophia* (lit. Faith Wisdom), probably from Alexandria and full of astrological language, Jesus tells his disciples that he had ascended the heavens and broken Fate's control by grabbing and rotating the zodiac in one direction for six months and in another direction for another six.[220] In consequence, the power of the archons and the zodiac ended and astrologers' predictions were made meaningless. Such descriptions of baptism breaking the grip of the zodiac and the determining power of the stars are not stated so graphically outside of Gnostic texts.

The fifth century registers little significant argumentation regarding astral determinism, though its presence continues to resonate. As witnessed by imperial legislation against them and the hostile comments of various churchmen, astrologers continued to practice their art, and people continued to consult them. I have found no writings that defend astrology on a scientific level. The churchmen who wrote against the practice of astrology did so elegantly and heatedly but offered no new arguments.

Two Christian writers especially stand out. The first is Augustine of Hippo, who addressed astral determinism at some length in the *City of God*, in *On Christian Doctrine*, and in his *Confessions,* with his usual clarity and a special animus that probably stemmed from his own involvement with astrology earlier in his life.[221] In the *City of God* he states that the success of the Roman Empire was due solely to divine Providence.[222] God has not granted any power to the stars to determine what happens on Earth.[223] He asks, "[H]ow is any room left for God to pass judgement on the deeds of men, if they are subject to astrological forces, and God is Lord both of stars and men?"[224] In the *Confessions* he admits to having been an astrology addict before his conversion in Milan.[225] Disquieted by Christian friends who tried to dissuade him, he finally turned from astrology when he heard an anecdote about a dreadful experiment in which two men exchanged information, one about his wife and the other about a slave woman in his possession. Both women bore their children at precisely the same moment, under the same constellation, but their lives, of course, were completely different. The slave child remained in that condition, while the free child had an illustrious career and became Augustine's friend who told him the story. Augustine concluded that identical horoscopes guaranteed nothing about a person's destiny.[226] *On Christian Doctrine* further explains that predicting the character of humans or their fate through astrology is a delusional madness, pointing out the differences between the twins Esau and Jacob, born at the same moment, with Jacob holding the foot of his brother.[227] Elsewhere in his sermons and letters, whenever stars and signs appear in a scriptural passage, he warns his listeners not to mistake this as legitimizing horoscopes. He then provides an alternative reading.[228] Augustine wants his audience to live as Christians in a world designed by God and governed by his Providence, one that is not in any way under the influence of the stars.

DIVINE PROVIDENCE AND THE STARS [151]

On the other side of the Mediterranean world, Theodoret, bishop of Cyrrhus (428–66), Augustine's near contemporary, was active in ecclesiastical politics and doctrinal debate. Though best known for his antiheretical writings following the Council of Chalcedon in 415, Theodoret also addressed astrology.[229] He was deeply learned in the Church Fathers as well as classical literature of different genres. In 442 Theodore witnessed a comet that appeared before an outbreak of plague, and in 451 he saw Halley's Comet when Attila was marauding in Gaul and Italy. Many people believed these comets had foretold the disasters that accompanied them, but Theodore did not. He rejected astrology and the determining power of the stars.[230] That he distinguished astrology from astronomy[231] shows the influence of Ptolemy, and it set a precedent in the Greek East in maintaining astronomical science divorced from astrological additions.

Justinian: The First Responder

As a pious Christian ruler, or *philochristos*, Justinian (r. 527–65) had no patience for individuals who gave credence to the independent power of the stars to determine a person's fate or discern future events, and he persecuted astrologers and those who cast auguries.[232] Astrology and divination proved very hard to dislodge, however, because they were endemic in Roman society and practiced by Christians as well as pagans.

Justinian's punitive actions against people whom he considered pagans were part of a larger campaign begun early in his reign to eliminate all forms of non-Orthodox belief.[233] Pagan practice became a public crime,[234] and, as Pierre Chuvin put it, "From Justinian on, all pagans were condemned to civil death."[235] Justinian's Code kept legislation against astrologers enacted by previous emperors that provided a clear definition of paganism.[236] Anyone who performed sacrifices, libations, or divination in honor of (unnamed) false gods, or abetted those practices in any way, would be severely punished.[237] Violence was forbidden against pagans who gave up their cultic practice and lived quietly, but if any pagan who converted to Christianity were discovered still to be practicing these rites, he might be punished by death. Contemporary writers confirm government persecution.[238] Procopius describes the punishment and public humiliation of men "for no other reason" than their being astrologers learned in astronomical science.[239] Malalas reports cruel actions taken against gamblers, whose offense was to use dice that could also be utilized in divination.[240]

Justinian's crackdown stemmed from his understanding of his obligation to shape a Christian empire in close cooperation with God. Justinian's certainty about his role was expressed by the high-ranking court functionary and poet Paul the Silentiary in his celebration of Justinian's great new church of St. Sophia in Constantinople:

> Is it possible to find a day greater than today, on which both God and Emperor are honoured? It is impossible to name one. We know that Christ is Master; yes, we know it absolutely. For you make this known by your words, Mightiest One, even to barbarians. From this, you have Him to hand as a collaborator in your deeds: in making laws, founding cities, raising temples, taking up arms (should the need arise), arranging truces and checking conflicts. From this, victory is inherent in your labours like an emblem.[241]

In Justinian's eyes, his duty to God involved performing several interrelated labors. First, he must make laws to deal with the changes constantly brought about by Nature in the earthly realm, maintaining order in the world as God does in heaven. His eighty-fourth new constitution explained the task: "It has already been said a number of times, in the preamble to laws, that nature keeps deploying numerous new states of affairs from every direction; and it will go on being repeated for as long as she continues to act in her characteristic way, putting us in need of numerous new laws."[242] The idea of a disruptive Nature, introduced into legislation by Justinian's lawyers,[243] provided a rationale for the emperor to make new laws. Justinian, as God's agent, assumed the mantle of what we might call "first responder" to Nature's constant violence enacted upon an orderly society.

Second, he must enable his version of Orthodox belief throughout the empire and beyond. This entailed excision of deviant belief from the Roman community and motivated his persecution of pagans. The act of creating a community defined by Orthodox faith raised questions about the forces that determine the attributes of a people, which was an ethnographic concern.

Third, the emperor must enforce his mastery over the earth just as God, the sole and ultimate source of power, ruled over the heavens. In that top-heavy structure there was no room for natural forces to determine human life in any way independently of God. In other words, the autonomous authority of the stars in any form was utterly unacceptable in this Christian scheme of the cosmic order. The stars could only be understood within a Christian frame. An unspoken compromise eventually emerged in the sixth century, however, that let the stars find a tame place in Roman society as signs but not agents of divine intent. This made it possible for the beasts of the zodiac, like suppliant barbarians on the Theodosian obelisk base (see Figure 3), to be subservient to greater powers in the Christian cosmic order and represented in churches.

ICONOGRAPHY

The place of the emperor in the Christian cosmic hierarchy that emerged in Justinian's laws was also expressed in imperial iconography.[244] Somewhat paradoxically, at the same time that he was attacking principles of astral determinism, Justinian drew on traditions of imperial representation that had been influenced by astrology. The presence of astrological elements in imperial representation was more than simple testimony to their wide diffusion in late Roman culture. In the Justinianic context they inhabited a subordinate place within the Christian cosmic order. This visual dimension is all the more interesting, therefore, as a feature of tensions in the sixth century because it involves the awkward coming-together of zodiac imagery, imperial iconography, and Christian imperial authority.

The zodiac had a long history in the representation of imperial power. A useful starting point can be the well-known portrait bust of Commodus dressed as Hercules, dating to 191–92, now in the Capitoline Museum in Rome.[245] At its base, in addition to other symbols, it displays the orb of heaven decorated with the signs of the zodiac, indicating what Jas Elsner calls his "cosmic majesty."[246] Somehow the stars endorse or even enable his mastery of the world. At the other, "Byzantine" end of this arc, we can look at a richly illustrated manuscript of Ptolemy's *Handy Tables*, from the eighth or ninth century, now in the Vatican Library.[247] At the center of three concentric bands is a medallion with Helios, the sun, represented as an imperial figure with a solar crown in a four-horse chariot, its yoke in the form of a cross. In his left hand he holds an orb representing imperial power that is covered by a blue cloak. The outer band of the illustration contains the twelve symbols of the zodiac. Regarding this manuscript, Benjamin Anderson concludes that "[t]he result is an image of a cosmos ruled by rational and predictable laws but tempered by grace."[248]

Justinian stands somewhere in the middle of this arc of the development of zodiac-inspired art within the Christian Roman sphere. Perhaps the best example was the mounted statue of himself on a high column at the heart of imperial Constantinople in the Augusteion Square between the Church of Hagia Sophia and the imperial palace. Recently Elena Boeck has discussed this monument in great detail.[249] In his left hand the emperor carried an orb or globe mounted with a cross. Two aspects of this orb are notable, namely its significance in a new sixth-century Christian ideological scheme of empire and its connection to astrological origins.

Roman emperors had long held globes or orbs in their hands as symbols of earthly rule. Often the signs of the zodiac appeared on these orbs.[250] The addition of a cross, however, was a fifth-century innovation that only with Justinian became a regular feature of imperial representation.[251] The orb indicated more than claims to world authority. It now presented a world embedded in a Christian cosmic hierarchy. The image of a globe spread far and wide on his coins, and later rulers continued the use of the orb with a cross on theirs (see Figure 6).[252] The orb with cross (or sometimes with an old-fashioned representation of Victory) indicated that the emperor was a triumphant Christian and that he ruled the world by the grace of God.[253] As we have seen,

FIGURE 6. Solidus of Justinian, obverse and reverse, minted at Constantinople between 538 and 545. This gold coin reads, "Our Lord Justinian, Perpetual Emperor." The obverse of this gold coin shows him holding an orb with a cross that represents the world he rules as a Christian emperor. A mounted figure spearing a barbarian is seen on a shield at his left shoulder. The reverse reads, "Victory of the Emperor." An angel holds a cross. © Dumbarton Oaks, Coins and Seals Collection, Washington, DC, Accession no. BZC1956.6.61.

Justinian's legislation elaborated these same ideas.[254] Eventually images of Christ Pantocrator in Byzantine churches will show the signs of the zodiac at his feet, indicating Christ's mastery of a well-ordered world, the world which the emperor ruled in his name, in the way suggested by the *Handy Tables* image mentioned above.

These developments under Justinian indicate a change underway in the visual representation of the zodiac and its public presence. By the year 700 in Byzantine, Islamic, and European traditions alike, the visual representation of the zodiac had shifted.[255] We have seen the independent authority of the zodiac mastered, directly and indirectly, in the legislation and art of Justinian, who was beloved of Christ, builder of Christian society, and first responder to inevitable change. The stars now were a fixed presence in the palace and the church, so to speak, not as alternatives to God's determining power but as emblems of subordination to it. In these images, God's agency was paramount. Demanding the subservience of the stars and neutering their independence was part of making an imperial Christian world.

UNCERTAIN VOICES

A few writers at Constantinople during Justinian's reign expressed positions not entirely in accord with the emperor's attitudes. Taken together they further indicate a transitional stage in the life of astrology and the zodiac in the sixth century.

DIVINE PROVIDENCE AND THE STARS [155]

John the Lydian, an administrator at Justinian's court, demonstrated how knowledge about the interpretation of celestial events, which he thought could point the way to the future, might find a safe haven in the intolerant atmosphere of the imperial capital.[256] His treatise *On Celestial Signs* is a compendium of writings of much earlier authors about portents, which he translated from Latin to Greek. The ancient authors spoke for their own time and place, of course, but Lydus reveals his goals and opinions as he stitches them together. He states his loyalty to Ptolemy: "These few examples are in reply to those who object to signs and dare to speak against Ptolemy."[257] His interest in Ptolemy was limited, however. He is not concerned with mathematical aspects of astronomy. Instead, he examines how celestial phenomena might presage events. He also includes some information associating different regions and their populations with signs of the zodiac.[258] In the preface to his treatise, Lydus observes that the Bible tells of many signs that transcend nature and are ultimately sent by God.[259] In saying this he echoes Christian attitudes as old as Origen. He calls heavenly phenomena like comets "signs" (σημεῖα), while such things as the plagues endured by the Egyptians in Exodus are "portents" (τέρατα). Both signs and portents give evidence of divine Providence, and they can point the way to the future. At no point, however, does Lydus say that signs or portents *cause* events to occur. For him, as for his emperor, causation is a divine prerogative.

Lydus tells us that he witnessed celestial signs and portents, in particular a "horse-headed" (ἱππέως) comet prefiguring the Persian invasion of Roman territory and the consequent destruction of Antioch in 540.[260] He explains that his experience of the comet led him to compile his treatise.[261] The treatise ends on a telling note. At the very end of *On Celestial Signs*, Lydus places an "astrological geography" that ascribes the regions of the earth to the signs of the zodiac.[262] For example, he says of the first sign that "Britannia, Galatia, Germania, the land of the Bastarnae, Coele Syria, and Idumaea belong to Aries (the Ram)."[263] This portion of his text is based on Ptolemy and is the best evidence available that knowledge of the *Tetrabiblos*'s ethnographic portions was still circulating in the sixth century.[264]

Lydus's comment on this material points to contemporary disagreement. While he makes no direct comments on the lives of the various peoples who live under each sign, he challenges people who think that the signs of the zodiac do not actually (ἐξ ὅλου) impose the same effects on earth in their different zones (κλίματα).[265] This is a remarkable statement that suggests the accommodation of the zodiac, and the astrological principles it represents, within a Christian worldview; that is, the zodiac has effects but is subordinate to God. This is supported by his discussion of eclipses elsewhere in the treatise, in which he observes that it is right to marvel at the providence of God for not having let an eclipse occur during the entire reign of the emperor under the zodiac sign of the Lion.[266] In this way, *On Celestial Signs* illuminates the inconclusive discussion of astrology in the sixth century at Constantinople.[267]

In it, Lydus demonstrates how a Christian could appreciate antique data because it could be justified in biblical terms. Like other figures of his day in the imperial administration or close to the court, he was able to join ancient knowledge and Christian belief without hypocrisy or special pleading.

Lydus's contemporary, the historian Procopius of Caesarea, on whom we have depended for so much information, is relatively quiet on the subject of astrology.[268] As noted above, he did not think that men who studied astrology deserved to be punished. This remark is scarcely an endorsement of astrology, however. It is instead a criticism of Justinian's harsh measures. Can we be more certain of his attitudes? In an influential article on Procopius's "skepticism," Averil Cameron pointed out that his attitude toward the determinism of fate and providence was conventionally Christian, and that he believed that these powers were active, but not independent of Christian divinity.[269] On those occasions in his works in which he refers to providence or chance and fate as though they were autonomous forces, he is simply responding to the demands of the classicizing genres in which he wrote.[270] It may also mean that he has not made up his mind about the autonomy of astral forces and that he is not in lockstep with Justinian.

The work of Lydus and, to a lesser extent, the attitudes of Procopius, suggest that the accommodation of astrology with Christian life was incomplete in the mid-sixth century, despite Justinian's efforts. Paul Magdalino argues that the reign of Heraclius marked the turning point in the Byzantine life of astrology.[271] He points to the activity of Stephanus of Alexandria as an indication of this beginning. Around the year 617, he began to teach the *quadrivium* in Constantinople and to prepare an adjusted edition of Ptolemy's *Handy Tables*.[272] At about the same time, the astrologer Rhetorius of Egypt collated an extensive compendium of excerpts drawn from earlier Greek sources.[273] The breadth of his collection suggests that he consulted a remarkably extensive library. Several epitomes of his work made in the ninth, eleventh, and thirteenth centuries reveal that he drew from many notable treatises, including those of Ptolemy, Vettius Valens, Antiochus, and Paul of Alexandria. His compendium contains many fifth- and sixth-century horoscopes.[274] Once again, these writers were safely within a Christian environment.

Magdalino notes important cross-cultural currents at this time. "Given that the appointment was made at the climax of Heraclius' titanic struggle with the Persian king Khusro II (590–628), a known devotee of Chaldaean astrology, a case can be made for thinking that Heraclius was using Greek science in an attempt to overcome his adversary's advantage in the 'information technology' of 'star wars.'"[275] He suggests that Heraclius's effort was to adapt Persian political astrology to Roman circumstances in the first decades of the seventh century.[276]

Chapter 5 turns to a different sort of determinism, that of the natural environment and geography, reimagined in a Christian cosmology.

CHAPTER FIVE

The Controlling Hand
of the Environment

*The Romans, too, took over many nations that were naturally savage
owing to the regions they inhabited, because those regions were either
rocky or without harbours or cold or for some other reason ill-suited to
habitation by many, and thus not only brought into communication with
each other peoples who had been isolated, but also taught the more savage
how to live under forms of government.*

—STRABO OF AMASEIA, *GEOGRAPHY*[1]

Introduction

The notion that the earth's climates and terrain shape humanity had a long
career in the Greco-Roman world, beginning in Greece in the fifth century
and, with some gaps in the record, proceeding straight through to Late Antiquity, weathering transition to a Christian empire by means of some significant
accommodations. Earth-related forms of determinism received somewhat
less negative attention than astrology, its more dramatic partner in determinist theories, but nevertheless remained extremely influential in how people
understood the impact of the landscapes in which they and their neighbors
lived.[2] The Cappadocian Fathers, for example, appreciated the earthly landscape as reflecting the divine order, an intimation of later developments
within the Christian empire.[3] By the sixth century the earthly landscape
had been radically reimagined in terms of Christian imperial authority. In
this chapter we will see a shift from a straightforward acceptance of identity determined by environmental forces to a bold assertion of identity as a
human choice. There had been a gradual Christian move in this direction, but
the sixth century witnessed a sudden and dramatic intensification of discussion. A greater self-consciousness and certainty in Christian belief led to a
breakthrough in imperial thought about the environment during the period
of Justinian's ascendancy, when questions about the role of environmental
determinism again became a matter of concern. Interpretation of the environment, like that of the stars, was varied in this period, as we will see. The
emperor, however, imagined a connected, accessible world united by his
authority and Christian doctrine. This imperial vision justified conquest and

[157]

the imposition of his will throughout imperial life. To facilitate this Christian, imperial reading of the world, it was necessary to deny the environment's control over human life. If the physical environment were overcome through imperial action, remote peoples could be brought into a new international community defined by faith. Environmental determinism did not vanish after its force had been neutralized by Christianity. The climate and terrain continued to be thought of as factors that could shape culture, but not in any way that challenged the primary authority of Christian Providence. These ideas were reflected in ethnographic thought.

The Greek Background

The initial phase of environmental deterministic theory began in the fifth century BCE, when Greek writers tied the natural environment to the political and cultural character of human communities.[4] Fifty years of conflict with the Achaemenid Persian Empire (499–449 BCE) furthered a long-developing sense of "Greekness" in the face of alien societies that partly explained the dichotomy between themselves and "barbarians" as a function of the natural environment. This was an age in which investigators began to apply general principles of cause and effect to social phenomena just as they did to observable regularities in nature. The work of such men would be foundational for late antique developments. Herodotus stands out among these early researchers for presenting what he considered age-old reciprocal patterns visible in history to explain the great war between the Greeks and the Persians and for relishing the extreme cultural variation among the peoples encountered in his wide travels, who were such an important part of his historical narrative.[5]

Very much in the same spirit of scientific investigation and application of general principles of explanation to human affairs, an unknown doctor composed a treatise called *Airs, Waters, Places* that discussed the nuances of climatic variation and their primary influence on human communities, human character, and of course human health.[6] Probably written sometime in the first half of the fifth century, possibly before Herodotus and certainly before Aristotle addressed similar questions in the middle of the fourth,[7] this treatise was attributed in antiquity to Hippocrates, the so-called "Father of Medicine." In recent times, however, because it is recognized that Hippocrates did not write everything in the Hippocratic corpus, the author is sometimes referred to as Pseudo-Hippocrates. What matters is that in the early days of written analysis of cultural difference, an experienced physician prepared a treatise discussing the effect of climate and geography on human health and character.[8] The work has remained a powerful influence on scientific writers and more indirectly on popular thinking well into the modern age.[9]

THE CONTROLLING HAND OF THE ENVIRONMENT [159]

As a physician, Hippocrates understood that a full diagnostic workup of patients must include consideration of the physical environment in which they lived.[10] Familiar with the human landscape of Greece as well as the habitats of people and places far away, he presented data to show the malleability of human physical characteristics and even human morality within a given environment.[11] The treatise states: "[f]or where the changes of the seasons are most frequent and most sharply contrasted, you will find the greatest diversity in bodily form, in character, and in customs."[12]

Airs, Waters, Places has two parts; the first eleven chapters deal with medical questions and are meant to help a physician arriving in a new town understand its environmental conditions and prevalent diseases.[13] The following twelve chapters address geography and ethnography in three different environmental circumstances: he compares the consequences of living under very hot, very cold, and intermediate temperate conditions.[14] Sometimes cultural as well as geographical elements enter his explanations.

Hippocrates contrasts Asia and Europe, whose peoples he finds completely unalike, especially in their physical characteristics.[15] He positions Asia between the more variable, colder temperatures of northern Europe and the extreme heat of southern lands:

> I hold that Asia differs very greatly from Europe in the natures of everything, of both the things that grow from the earth, and of the human inhabitants. For everything grows to be much more beautiful and grand in Asia; this region is more cultivated than the other one, and the peoples in it are gentler and more cultivated. The cause of this is the blending of the seasons, which occurs because Asia lies toward the east, between the risings of the sun, and farther away from the cold. Growth and cultivation are best furthered when no single force predominates, but an equilibrium of each exists. Although uniformity does not exist all through Asia, the region lying in the middle between the heat and the cold is very fruitful, well-wooded and mild, and it has the very best water, whether coming from the heavens or from the earth.[16]

The temperate conditions have their drawbacks, however:

> With regard to the lack of spirit and bravery of the people, the main reason why Asiatics are so unwarlike in comparison to Europeans, and more gentle in character, is the seasons, which bring no great changes toward heat or cold, but are always much the same.[17]

This tale of contrasts is illustrated by the peoples of Europe:

> The remaining peoples of Europe differ widely among themselves both in size and in bodily form, because of the changes of the seasons, which

are extreme and frequent; there are powerful heat waves, severe winters, copious rains followed by long droughts, and winds causing many changes of various kinds . . . Wildness, unsociability and impetuosity are all engendered in such a natural setting: for the frequent shocks to the mind impart wildness, which displaces tameness and gentleness. Thus I think the inhabitants of Europe are also more courageous than Asiatics.[18]

Hippocrates becomes more precise:

There exist in Europe, then, people differing among themselves in size, appearance and courage, and the factors controlling those differences are those I have described. Let me summarize this plainly. When a people live in a rough, mountainous country, at a high elevation, and well-watered, where great differences of climate accompany the various seasons, there the people will be of large physique, well-accustomed to hardihood and bravery, and with no small degree of fierceness and wildness in their character. On the other hand, in low-lying, stifling lands, full of meadows, getting a larger share of warm than cold winds, and where the water is warm, the people will be neither large nor slight, but rather broad in build, fleshy and black-haired. Their complexions are dark rather than fair, and they are phlegmatic rather than bilious. Bravery and hardihood are not an integral part of their natural characters, although these traits can be created by training . . . The chief controlling vectors, then, are the variability of the weather, the type of country and the sort of water which is drunk.[19]

Hippocrates adds an interesting twist to environmental determinism by describing mutual influences of human custom and natural factors. He tells how, over a long period of time, a legendary people called the Macrocephali, or Long-Headed People, developed the habit of artificially stretching the skulls of their infants.[20] Eventually nature began to emulate this practice, and the physical characteristic of an elongated skull became an inherited, inborn trait. Long-headedness has decreased, he goes on to say, because of interactions between the Macrocephaloi and other peoples.[21] Thus human customs and interactions can also play a role in determining physical characteristics of a people. Environment is not the only force at work.

Another great voice in the development of ideas about determinism was Aristotle (384–322 BCE), antiquity's greatest scientist. He fully participated in the tradition established by *Airs, Waters, Places* and made two major interrelated contributions to the spread of environmental determinism.[22] First, he applied environmental theory, which as we have seen originated in medical thought, to the examination of society and politics. Second, with Greece in mind, he popularized the idea that temperate climates are home to the most civilized nations. He described Greece as having the golden mean of climate and consequently that of culture as well.[23] (Romans would one day eagerly accept this notion and apply it to themselves.) These points come together in the following passage from the *Politics*:

> Having spoken of the number of the citizens, we will proceed to speak of what should be their character. This is a subject which can be easily understood by any one who casts his eye on the more celebrated states of Hellas, and generally on the distribution of peoples in the habitable world. Those who live in a cold climate and in Europe are full of spirit but wanting in intelligence and skill; and therefore they retain comparative freedom, but have no political organization, and are incapable of ruling over others. Whereas the natives of Asia are intelligent and inventive, but they are wanting in spirit, and therefore they are always in a state of subjection and slavery. But the Hellenic people, which is situated between them, is likewise intermediate in character, being high-spirited and also intelligent. Hence it continues free, and is the best-governed of any nation, and, if it could be formed into one state, would be able to rule the world. There are also similar differences in the different peoples (ἔθνη) of Hellas; for some of them are of a one-sided nature, and are intelligent or courageous only, while in others there is a happy combination of both qualities. And clearly those whom the legislator will most easily lead to virtue may be expected to be both intelligent and courageous.[24]

Another work, the *Problems*, is part of the Aristotelian corpus. Its authorship is uncertain, and it may have been compiled as late as the sixth century.[25] The work displays the deep influence of Aristotle across antiquity. One portion is devoted to asking and answering questions about climates (κράσεις):[26]

> Why are those living in conditions of excessive cold or heat beastlike with respect to character and appearance? . . . For the best climate-mix benefits thought, but the excesses disturb it, and just as they distort the body, so too do they affect the temperament of thought [τὴν τῆς διανοίας κράσιν].[27]

We learn as well that Egyptians are bowlegged because their bodies are warped by the heat, that people who dwell at high altitudes live longer because the air is always in movement; that hot lands produce cowards while in cold climates people are brave and wise; warm and cold climates produce different eye colors.[28] Clarence Glacken astutely noted that "The *Problems* are probably representative of the types of questions which were asked and which interested

[162] CHAPTER 5

men for centuries—not only the medical practitioners but those who used these medical speculations as a means of understanding peoples and their environments."[29]

From Greece to the Roman Empire

These basic ideas about environmental determinism slowly entered the Roman world and gained an imperial stamp. A convenient place to begin is with Polybius (ca. 200–ca. 118 BCE), an aristocratic Greek who admired Rome's rise to dominance in the Mediterranean world and became its premier contemporary analyst. Though presumably not the only carrier of ideas about environmental determinism to Italy, Polybius was most articulate in integrating them with explanatory force into a sophisticated historical narrative. Polybius had gone to Rome as a hostage in 167 BCE and soon found a place among the so-called Scipionic Circle, a group of leaders in public life who also were intellectuals with an avid interest in Greek high culture. He went on campaign with Scipio Aemilianus in Africa during the third Punic War and witnessed the destruction of Carthage in 146 BCE. There he saw the futility of resisting Roman force. His travels in Spain and along the North African coast as far as the Atlantic Ocean whetted his curiosity about foreign cultures and their capacity to change, especially in response to Rome. After the war against Carthage, he was sent to Greece with the task of reforming the government of Greek cities to further Roman settlement.[30]

In his *Histories*, Polybius described Rome's rapid expansion up to his own day, giving as the main reason for its success its mixed constitution (partly monarchical, aristocratic, and popular) that kept political forces in balance.[31] He remained keenly interested in the development of institutions in other societies as well. In the course of his narrative, Polybius pays careful attention to the profound effect of cultural and geographical environment on human communities and their political institutions. He stressed the need to maintain Roman aristocratic moral order in the face of barbarians who are "people in chaos."[32] His fond description of Arcadia, his homeland in the central Peloponnese, develops ideas first seen in Hippocrates's *Airs, Waters, Places*. He explains how Arcadians of ancient times civilized themselves by introducing new political institutions and above all by integrating music into every aspect of their lives. In this way they overcame the influences of a rough environment, unlike their neighbors, who remained in a state of cruel and lawless barbarism:

> Now all these practices I believe to have been introduced by the men of old time, not as luxuries and superfluities but because they had before their eyes the universal practice of personal manual labor in Arcadia, and in general the toilsomeness and hardship of the men's lives, as

THE CONTROLLING HAND OF THE ENVIRONMENT [163]

well as the harshness of character resulting from the cold and gloomy atmospheric conditions usually prevailing in these parts—conditions to which all men by their very nature must perforce assimilate themselves; there being no other cause than this why separate nations and peoples dwelling widely apart differ so much from each other in character, feature, and color as well as in most of their pursuits. The ancient Arcadians, therefore, with the view of softening and tempering the stubbornness and harshness of nature, introduced all the practices I mentioned.[33]

This passage represents a milestone in the development of ideas about environmental determinism. It is the first known extended discussion of how what we might call ethnic characteristics can result from environmental factors. Polybius has illustrated with the case of the Arcadians that by means of deliberate effort, people can introduce new institutions and customs to transform their societies and escape the grip of natural forces. Humans can take steps to get beyond climate-induced barbarism.[34] It is a powerful idea that took deep root in Roman imperial views and would flourish well into the sixth century at Constantinople and beyond.

As their power expanded, Romans experienced cultural and geographical diversity in equal measure. They did not always like what they found. In his description of northern lands beyond the empire, the historian Lucius Annaeus Florus (ca. 74–ca. 130 CE), a man of letters of North African descent who spent his career in Rome, wrote, "Nothing is more inclement than this region. The climate is harsh, and the disposition of the inhabitants resembles it."[35]

Figures like Polybius led the way in bringing into the Roman imperial worldview Greek ideas about the shaping hand of the environment. The notion of the superiority of civilization in temperate climes found ready acceptance with Roman empire builders, but with a significant difference. Roman writers adjusted Greek views to the growth of their empire. Tying environmental ideas to empire laid a foundation for the late antique period.

The Age of Augustus, conventionally beginning with his ascendancy in 31 BCE, witnessed the tandem development of natural determinism and empire. Rulers and writers hammered out a new ideology of autocratic world rule based on the authority of the emperor. They dreamed of empire without limit across the inhabited world and wondered about the transformative power of Roman imperial civilization. Could Roman rule elude the proscriptive grasp of nature on the formation of humans and their communities? How might they best deal with subjects in remote and inhospitable lands? Two very different writers show the Roman imperial spin on environmental theory.

First we consider the architect Vitruvius[36] (ca. 80 BCE–ca. 15 CE), who for professional reasons examined the effect of climate on the construction of houses (and architecture generally) and on the character of people in different parts of the world who lived in them. His weighty treatise *On Architecture* demonstrates the diffusion of Hippocratic ideas into many types of literature. In this case it is a practical handbook for architects and planners. He wants to help them build houses "suitable in plan to the peculiarities of nations": "Now if it is a fact that countries differ from one another, and are of various classes according to climate, so that the very nations born therein naturally differ in mental and physical conformation and qualities, we cannot hesitate to make our houses suitable in plan to the peculiarities of nations and peoples, since we have the expert guidance of nature herself ready to our hand."[37]

In this treatise, the different physical characteristics of the peoples of the earth reflect natural conditions. Due to abundant moisture in their homelands, for example, northerners are tall, fair, red-headed, blue-eyed, and barbaric.[38] At the same time, he introduces the possibility of positive development through cultural evolution. Vitruvius believed that humans have developed in stages from bestial ancestors living in crude huts to the highly civilized Romans in elaborate homes by making use of their natural intellect, and along the way adapting houses to environmental conditions.[39] They slowly became better builders of refined society as well as dwelling-places.[40]

Vitruvius links his discussion to Roman imperial concerns. First of all, he shrewdly dedicated the treatise to Rome's new master, whom he calls Imperator Caesar. This suggests a date of composition prior to 27 BCE, when the title Augustus was adopted; Vitruvius is getting in on the ground floor of the new imperial edifice.[41] He ties the civilizing goals of the new regime to the spread of urban life:

> While your divine intelligence and will, Imperator Caesar, were engaged in acquiring the right to command the world, and while your fellow citizens, when all their enemies had been laid low by your invincible valour, were glorying in your triumph and victory,—while all foreign nations were in subjection awaiting your beck and call, and the Roman people and senate, released from their alarm, were beginning to be guided by your most noble conceptions and policies, I hardly dared, in view of your serious employments, to publish my writings and long considered ideas on architecture, for fear of subjecting myself to your displeasure by an unseasonable interruption.[42]

Unsurprisingly, Rome's location takes pride of place in this imperial effort because of its moderate climate:

> Italy, lying between the north and the south, is a combination of what is found on each side, and her preëminence is well regulated and indisputable. And so by her wisdom she breaks the courageous onsets of the barbarians, and by her strength of hand thwarts the devices of the southerners. Hence, it was the divine intelligence that set the city of

the Roman people in a peerless and temperate country, in order that it might acquire the right to command the whole world.[43]

In achieving mastery of the best portions of the inhabited world, Rome has claimed the symbolic and moral center of world affairs. The peoples farthest from Rome suffer the most in their terrible environments and are the least civilized.

Vitruvius cannot boast that Rome can change the climate, but he leads us to wonder if imperial effort can overcome its effects. For an answer to that question, we turn to Strabo.

Strabo

The Greek geographer Strabo (ca. 64 BCE–ca. 24 CE), whose writings straddle the reigns of Augustus and Tiberius, provides the most thoroughgoing treatment of climate, civilization, and geography in the early imperial period.[44] Born to an influential family in Pontus on the Black Sea, he took an interest in Stoic philosophy and came to know Posidonius, the Stoic ethnographer.[45] His many travels in the Roman Empire included a two-year expedition up the Nile as far as Syene and on to the borders of Ethiopia as part of the entourage of his friend Aelius Gallus, the second prefect of Egypt.[46] His journeys found expression in an extensive treatise of seventeen books, the *Geography*. This work represents the pinnacle of Hellenistic geographic science as practiced from a Roman imperial perspective.[47] Strabo demonstrates how scientific investigation might combine with politics and administration. He helped write an expanding Rome into the center of the conceptual universe. Strabo held the empire as well as science in mind when he composed the *Geography*:

> Now my first and most important concern, both for the purposes of science and for the needs of the state, is this—to try to give, in the simplest possible way, the shape and size of that part of the earth which falls within our map, indicating at the same time what the nature of that part is and what portion it is of the whole earth; for this is the task proper of the geographer.[48]
>
> ... for governmental purposes there would be no advantage in knowing such countries and their inhabitants, and particularly if the people live in islands which are of such a nature that they can neither injure nor benefit us in any way because of their isolation.[49]

Strabo's systematic geography was meant to aid Roman commanders and administrators by showing what territories were worth conquering. In this way Strabo, rather like Vitruvius the architect, placed his professional expertise at the service of an expanding empire.

Strabo emphasized the importance of climate, terrain, and especially distance from Rome in shaping the character of peoples. He believed that barbarism could result if the distance from civilization is great and the climate is harsh. This was a question of degree, however. To his mind, there was a continuum between barbarism and civilization, and barbarism was an escapable condition. If a people were to leave their cultural isolation and develop institutions of law and urbanism they might attain a version of civilization. Geography provided the landscapes within which such progress might occur, and help was on the way.

These factors informed Strabo's understanding of Rome's imperial mission. As he explained in the *Geography*, Romans carried the responsibility of bringing distant, barbarous peoples into the civilized space of the empire, and they had often done so. He shows that the force of Roman civilization can override the imperatives of the environment and that cultural change can be brought about through Rome's agency.[50] For him, remoteness from the Roman center joined climate and terrain to shape the character of peoples until Rome chose to intervene.[51] He provides an example:

> The quality of intractability and wildness in these [Iberian] peoples has not resulted solely from their engaging in warfare, but also from their remoteness; for the trip to their country, whether by sea or by land, is long, and since they are difficult to communicate with, they have lost the instinct of sociability and humanity. They have this feeling of intractability and wildness to a less extent now, however, because of the peace and of the sojourns of the Romans among them.[52]

Isolation receives special comment:

> The Romans, too, took over many nations that were naturally savage owing to the regions they inhabited, because those regions were either rocky or without harbours or cold or for some other reason ill-suited to habitation by many, and thus not only brought into communication with each other peoples who had been isolated, but also taught the more savage how to live under forms of government.[53]

The consequences of expansion were not necessarily positive, however. As Caesar had noted before him and Tacitus would in the future, Strabo acknowledged that civilization also could produce ill effects. He comments on its corrupting influence:

> And yet our mode of life has spread its change for the worse to almost all peoples, introducing amongst them luxury and sensual pleasures and, to satisfy these vices, base artifices that lead to innumerable acts of greed. So then, much wickedness of this sort that has fallen on the barbarian peoples also, on the nomads as well as the rest; for as the result

THE CONTROLLING HAND OF THE ENVIRONMENT [167]

of taking up a seafaring life they not only have become morally worse, indulging in the practice of piracy and of slaying strangers, but also, because of their intercourse with many peoples, have partaken of the luxury and the peddling habits of those peoples.[54]

Curiously, despite its undeniable merits, the *Geography* did not find much of a readership in the imperial period until the sixth century,[55] but that does not diminish its importance as a showpiece of ideas about the transformative power of Roman imperial civilization as it was taking shape at the beginning of the millennium. Strabo brilliantly interwove ethnography and geography for the advantage of Rome, articulating a potent idea that would remain in the ethnographic infrastructure.

Such ideas became standard fare. For example, when the naturalist and high-ranking military officer Pliny the Elder (ca. 23–79) described the Chauci, a wretched people at the northern edge of the world whom he had seen while on campaign,[56] he noted that it would be better for them to be conquered, for being spared from Roman rule by Fortune is in fact a punishment.[57] The constant contrast for Pliny is Italy's ideal position in the world, which brought about a pleasant climate and prosperity.[58] As Trevor Murphy puts it, "The land of the Chauci is an inverted Rome."[59] The peoples farthest from Rome in culture and climate suffer the most.

In the next generation, Tacitus (ca. 56–ca. 120) stressed the lack of contact between various northern tribes in Germania and other peoples as an indication of their barbarism. As with Strabo and Pliny, isolation brought about by inhospitable climate and geography as well as distance from Rome were important factors in his analysis. He does not directly address the question of whether contact with Rome could override these limitations, however.[60]

As these few examples have shown, by the end of the first century CE there existed in various genres at Rome a repertoire of ideas about the connection of the physical landscape to imperial civilization and the role of climate and isolation in generating barbarism. One popular idea held that the Roman Empire, because of its favorable geographical and climatic conditions (among other things) was especially suited to rule the world and to bring other peoples to civilization. The environment might determine human characteristics, but Roman rule could overcome those influences. Rome could create the imperial space in which foreigners could change and develop.

In the following centuries, these notions about empire and environmental determinism became widely diffused before finding emphatic expression in Justinian's Constantinople, as we will see. The presence of the ideas in some writers of very different sorts indicates that they have entered the mainstream and become part of the way Romans thought. Two examples illustrate this. The late-fourth-century historian Ammianus Marcellinus, a retired army officer, continued to associate climate with the character of cultures. He made a correlation between savagery and rugged terrain. In his invaluable account of Roman-Gothic conflicts that resulted in the disaster at Adrianople in 378, he stated that the utterly uncivilized Huns set the forces of destruction in motion. In his narrative, Huns who lived "beyond the Maeotic Sea (Azov) near the ice-bound ocean, exceed every degree of savagery"[61] before they began their assault on the Goths. Simply noting their frigid place of origin explains their barbarity. His description of the Huns is in stark contrast to his portrait of the remote but civilized Seres, who live in a mild climate: "The Seres themselves live a peaceful life, for ever unacquainted with arms and warfare; and since to gentle and quiet folk ease is pleasurable, they are troublesome to none of their neighbours. Their climate is agreeable and healthful, the sky is clear, the winds gentle and very pleasant."[62]

Servius, a grammarian and literary scholar who wrote a commentary on Vergil's *Aeneid* in the late fourth century, explained that Africans are crafty, Greeks frivolous, and Gauls lazy because of the nature of the region in which they live.[63] He cited Ptolemy as a source, presumably in reference to the *Tetrabiblos*. In this instance, Servius is commenting on *Aeneid* 6.724, which itself draws from Lucretius's discussion of the transmigration of souls.[64] Servius means to show that when a pure soul enters a new body it adjusts to the character of that body, which is itself influenced by its particular geographical environment.

Avienus, an aristocratic poet of the mid-fourth century, composed an unusual and highly inaccurate iambic poem, *Ora Maritima* (*The Sea Coast*), which describes the Atlantic, Mediterranean, and Black Seas in the form of a *periplus*, that is, a geographical description that follows the coastline.[65] When discussing Ligurians he trots out the old idea that peaceful conditions provided by Rome let them leave their remote highland homes to pursue a happier life: "Afterwards, peace and quiet persuaded them to come down from their lofty homes and descend to the areas around the sea. Security thus bolstered their daring."[66]

After Avienus, no extended discussion of Rome's transformative power appears in any genre until the sixth century, though this may be due simply to the accident of survival.

Christianity Enters the Picture

At the same time that members of Rome's power elite were fashioning an ethnographic frame for their rapidly expanding realm, their Christian subjects began to craft a vision of themselves within that imperial landscape. The imperial map was a necessary ingredient in the development of their ideas about identity and the presence of their religion in the world. Though not immediately felt beyond the communities of believers during the first few centuries of their existence, in the course of the late antique centuries, Christian attitudes became closely intertwined with Roman approaches to the earth, its peoples, and its place in the cosmos.[67] Confronting environmental determinism was one element in that evolution.

From an early date, Christian groups began to understand themselves as having the laws of Christ in common, wherever in the world they might live and however differently they might interpret the message of the Gospels. They moved toward a sense of a collective identity as a people not determined by race or ethnicity in the modern sense. Instead, they were a people set apart from Jews and "pagans" through following the teachings of Jesus.[68]

The sense of belonging to a universal community of Christians spread across the map struck a blow against basic principles of natural determinism. The anonymous *Epistle to Diognetus*, an early example of Christian apologetic written probably in the second century, articulates that special character:

> For Christians cannot be distinguished from the rest of humanity by country or language or customs. They do not live in cities of their own; they do not use a peculiar form of speech; they do not follow an eccentric manner of life . . . This doctrine of theirs has not been discovered by the ingenuity or deep thought of inquisitive men, nor do they put forward a merely human teaching, as some people do. Yet, although they live in Greek and barbarian cities alike, as each man's lot has been cast, and follow the customs of the country in clothing and food and other matters of daily living, at the same time they give proof of the remarkable and admittedly extraordinary constitution of their own commonwealth. They live in their own countries, but only as aliens. They have a share in everything as citizens, and endure everything as foreigners. Every foreign land is their fatherland, and yet for them every fatherland is a foreign land . . . They busy themselves on earth, but their citizenship is in heaven.[69]

The *Letter to Diognetus* made use of *nomima barbarika* arguments designed to refute the power of the stars and the land. This required development of the idea of a universal community. For these arguments, landscapes of the earth and the sky demonstrated the divine order established to nourish and instruct humanity. The door was open for an imperial role in that instruction.

Initially far more humble than imperial in outlook, early Christian writers had little interest challenging secular arguments about environmental determinism. Their ideas found focus in understanding humanity's place in divine creation, and they saw the earth as a manifestation of divine agency.[70] As Clarence Glacken noted in reference to first-century Christian writings, "[t]here is nothing in this literature to compare with the classical speculations on the influences of the physical environment."[71] Yet Christians did have a sense of being a people, but not one determined by space and place.[72]

The most notable expression of such ideas is found in hexaemeral literature, which dealt with explaining the six days of creation described in the first verse of Genesis.[73] This genre drew examples from the natural world to illustrate further how God's creation is orderly. Hexaemeral texts became extremely popular across the Mediterranean in the fourth century, especially in the hands of Basil of Caesarea, Ambrose, and Augustine.[74] As Basil put it in a homily, "I want the marvel of creation to gain such complete acceptance from you that, wherever you may be found and whatever kind of plants you may chance upon, you may receive a clear reminder of the Creator."[75]

In this context, if climate and geographical conditions made a difference in human life, it was due to the providential scheme of God, not geographical determinism. The hardships of existence played an important role in human life after the expulsion from Eden, as God intended. Humans were at the same time given the arts of agriculture and other skills that enabled their survival, and the relationship between the human condition and the natural world remained strong.[76]

Discussion was rich and varied, but several ideas emerge that many theologians and exegetes shared. Of first importance was the idea that God designed the earth, in which his works are manifest. Second was the notion that nature can be read like a book intelligible to all and that it reveals God's creative works.[77] In Augustine's words, "The earth is our big book; in it I read as fulfilled what I read as promised in the book of God."[78] Third was the certainty that the Bible and New Testament provide full explanation of any discordances in nature. Neither the geographical environment nor celestial bodies possessed any notable presence, let alone independent agency, in hexaemeral writings.

Christianity and Roman Environmental Theory in the Age of Justinian

After a long hiatus, writers in the sixth century returned to questions of determinism that had preoccupied men of the Augustan age.[79] Late antique developments suggest some explanations for the revival of their interest. As in the Augustan period, when the presence of the emperor in Roman life was felt for the first time and when the early stages of an imperial ethnography embracing deterministic theories emerged, the Justinianic age witnessed a forceful rearticulation of the imperial position as an expression of Christian faith.[80] Justinianic writers responded to episodes of impressive imperial expansion which gave a further impetus to ethnographic analysis. In both eras Rome confronted new foes; Augustus pushed into Germania and Balkan lands while Justinian reasserted imperial control over North Africa, Italy, and part of Spain and expanded his influence in the Caucasus in his struggle with Persia.

THE CONTROLLING HAND OF THE ENVIRONMENT [171]

New enemies appeared as well, notably Avars and Slavs. The great plague that broke out in 542 also stimulated reflection about uncontrollable natural forces.

There were major differences between the two periods, of course. The most significant was that Christianity had become fully enmeshed in imperial structures by the sixth century. Environmental determinism could be addressed both positively and negatively by Christian writers who were now comfortably settled in Roman society. In fact, they were more likely to be in dispute with other Christians than with non-Christian philosophers or other Christian scholars who were to some extent loyal to non-Christian traditions of explanation. Though modes of discussion of the natural world and its effect on human communities varied in Christian writing, in none of them were the earth and the stars independent of divine control. In the Augustan age, on the other hand, Fate, an entity without a theological dogma, steered imperial events.

Discussion of astrology under Justinian in chapter 4 revealed a fresh wave of attacks on determinism as well as new and positive integration of it within the early Byzantine fabric. Environmental forces played a part in the historical thought of Procopius of Caesarea.

Procopius: Determinism, the Emperor, and the Plague

The adept and complex historian Procopius of Caesarea (ca. 500–ca. 565) takes us to the heart of the reign of Justinian (r. 527–65) in three much-studied works that provide insight into attitudes about empire at the highest levels.[81] Well educated in the Greek classics, Procopius composed the *Wars*, a long historical account of Justinian's reconquests in the western Mediterranean and his backbreaking but ultimately inconclusive struggles with Sasanian Persia. Procopius witnessed much of the action on both fronts as an aide to the general Belisarius. His descriptions of foreigners of all sorts, enemies and allies alike, who exhibited different degrees of barbarism constitute a rich dossier of traditional ethnographic tropes coupled with discerning insights about contemporary events.[82] Throughout the *Wars*, Procopius cultivated a rather old-fashioned, Thucydidean literary style that affected distance from Christianity but did not disguise his knowledge of it.[83]

In stark contrast to the *Wars*, however, were two other compositions. The infamous *Secret History*, a lurid broadside against the emperor, his court, and his policies, is so different in tone and style from the *Wars* that scholars once thought it could not possibly have been written by the same man.[84] The third treatise, *Buildings*, composed in yet another genre, celebrates the emperor's ambitious construction program in Constantinople and the provinces.[85] In this work, Procopius speaks more forthrightly in Christian terms. All three of these works contribute something to our understanding of environmental determinism in Justinian's Constantinople, but it is in the panegyric *Buildings* that environmental theory, Roman imperialism in theory and practice, and Christianity find the clearest synthesis and deliberate expression. As we will see, the great pandemic that broke out in 542 left its mark on Procopius's discussion of these matters.

Procopius probably knew Strabo's *Geography* firsthand. A copy of that long-submerged manuscript had surfaced in Justinian's Constantinople, where it seems to have caught his attention and strongly influenced him.[86] It presumably was known to his literary circle as well.[87] He folded Christian ideas into notions of how imperial agency could transform subject peoples no matter where they lived. Just as Strabo had brought the tradition of Greek geography to bear on this question in the Augustan age, Procopius brought many of the same ideas into play within a Christian Roman worldview.

Procopius's discussion of the distant Tzani,[88] a fiercely independent mountain people located in an inhospitable region at the southwestern edge of the Caucasus Mountains near the Black Sea (see map 3), lets us read portions of the *Wars* in tandem with the *Buildings*, supplemented somewhat by the *Secret History*,[89] and with Strabo always in the wings. Taking into account differences of genre among them, we gain a bird's-eye view of imperial concerns as well as major themes operative in presentation of imperial action. Procopius's discussion also illustrates key elements of the ethnographic infrastructure forming at Constantinople and the international context in which they developed.

Two interconnected themes energize Procopius's treatment of the Tzani. The first is the idea of the malleability of culture, and the second is the challenge of geographical impassability and remoteness. In regard to the first theme, Procopius relies on the word δίαιτα (*diaita*) to mean "way of life" or "culture" in the modern sense.[90] The word has a long pedigree, rooted in a Hippocratic treatise about the regime of eating and exercise that a doctor might prescribe.[91] It is used by other classical authors as well, to mean "mode of living."[92] In Procopius's hands a millennium later, *diaita* can mean many things, ranging from the criminal behavior of one of Justinian's officials to the lifestyle of barbarian peoples, which is the usage of interest here. In this context, for Procopius a people's way of life can be shaped by the physical environment. Just as important, exterior forces can transform it, and they frequently do, because human lifeways are not immutable. Warfare can be an instrument of deleterious change of cultural habits.[93] On the other hand, civilized customs, such as having one king and practicing law and justice, can prevent warfare and its attendant corruption.[94] These attributes of civilization were the very items Justinian offered.

Turning to the second theme, concern with physical impassability enlivened Procopius's geographical descriptions and analysis of political and cultural motivations. For him, remoteness inhibits the development of civilized society because it prevents contact with a larger, more civilized world. The inhabitants in a remote and inaccessible region cannot get out, and civilized

THE CONTROLLING HAND OF THE ENVIRONMENT [173]

outsiders cannot easily get in. The outliers are trapped geographically and culturally. They are barbarians.[95]

Procopius developed the theme of impassibility in the *Wars*, completed in 552, in his discussion of the Tzani.[96] Justinian overcame their resistance in 528 or 529 in his effort to win control of the Caucasus region, a zone of great strategic importance in his greater struggle with Sasanian Persia.[97] Procopius describes the Tzani in this fashion:

> [19] It happened also that a short time before this they [the Romans] had reduced to subjection the Tzanic nation, who had been settled since ancient times in Roman territory as an autonomous people . . . [21] . . . In this place from the beginning lived barbarians, the Tzanic people, subject to no one, called Sani in early times; they made plundering expeditions among the Romans who lived round about, maintaining a most difficult existence [δίαιταν], and always living upon what they stole; for their land produced for them nothing good to eat. [22] Because of this, the Roman emperor sent them each year a fixed amount of gold, with the condition that they should never plunder the country thereabout. [23] And the barbarians had sworn to observe this agreement with their traditional oaths, and then, disregarding what they had sworn, they had been accustomed for a long time to make unexpected attacks and to injure not only the Armenians, but also the Romans who lived next to them as far as the sea; then, after completing their inroad in a short space of time, they would immediately return to their homes. [24] And whenever it so happened that they chanced upon a Roman army, they were always defeated in the battle, but they proved to be absolutely beyond capture owing to the strength of their fastnesses. In this way Sittas had defeated them in battle before this war; and then by many manifestations of kindness in word and in deed he had been able to win them over completely. [25] For they changed their manner of life to one of a more civilized sort, and enrolled themselves among the Roman troops, and from that time they have gone forth against the enemy with the rest of the Roman army. They also abandoned their own religion for a more righteous faith, and all of them became Christians. Such then was the history of the Tzani.[98]

This description, which helps explain Roman policy during their great war with Persia, stresses the mountainous terrain in which the Tzani live and how it determines their fierceness and forces them to become faithless marauders. Most important of all, he explains that their barbarous lives can be changed through Roman intervention. Being conquered by Rome and losing their autonomy are the keys to gaining this new life. Conversion to Christianity additionally brought about a further degree of civilized behavior.

[174] CHAPTER 5

Procopius develops these same ideas more fully in the *Buildings*, completed in the 550s:

Tzanica was a very inaccessible country ... As a result of this it was impossible for the Tzani to mingle with their neighbours, living as they did a life of solitude among themselves in the manner of wild beasts. Accordingly he [Justinian] cut down all the trees by which the routes chanced to be obstructed, and transforming the rough places and making them smooth and passable for horses, he brought it about that they mingled with other peoples in the manner of men in general and consented to have dealings with their neighbours. After this he built a church for them ... and caused them to conduct services and to partake of the sacraments and propitiate God with prayers and perform the other acts of worship, so that they should know they were human beings.[99]

Procopius here emphasizes the remoteness of the Tzani in a slightly different fashion. In this passage, as in the *Wars*, geography and climate engender barbarism by preventing the Tzani from intermingling with other peoples. Isolation is the key retardant element in their way of life. Roman conquest can end that problem, as Strabo and many others would have agreed.[100] Now, however, it is through entry into the much broader community of Orthodox Christians, and by this Procopius means Justinian's empire, that the Tzani can attain full humanity. He envisages something deeper than simple cultural change: it is not just a turn to Rome but a turn to Christian Rome, with its attendant beliefs and customs.

Justinian's own laws confirm Procopius's message. The preamble to *Novel* 1, written in 535, mentions "how the Tzani, newly under the Roman realm, are to take their place among our subjects (something that God has never hitherto granted to Rome even in modern times, except in our reign)."[101] Control of the Tzani is placed side by side with other victories: Persia is quiet, due to a hard-won peace treaty, and the Vandals have been overcome in North Africa. These are all part of what, as Peter Sarris put it, "Justinian regarded as the providential character of his reign."[102] The preface to *Novel* 28 similarly lists the conquest of the Tzani among other God-given victories. Procopius points out that new cities (by which he means garrison towns) are being built in Tzanica.[103] God has overcome their remoteness through the efforts of Justinian, and the Tzani are no longer on the margins of empire. They have joined a vast community of Christian believers.

That overcoming the environment to bring people into an international community and forcing their conversion to Christianity might play a part of imperial policy is supplemented by Procopius elsewhere in the *Wars* in his description of the career of the Heruls,[104] a warlike people of the middle and upper Danube region who in 527 settled in the Balkans south of the Danube

THE CONTROLLING HAND OF THE ENVIRONMENT [175]

River, at Singidunum in the province of Upper Moesia, and whose compli-cated interactions with Justinian lasted to mid-century.[105] He describes the settlement of one group of them in Moesia and their forced conversion. Yield-ing to imperial pressure, their king, Grepes, came to Constantinople with his entourage to be baptized in a magnificent ceremony on the Feast of the Epiphany, January 6, 528. Justinian stood as his sponsor in this politically charged event. The terms of their alliance required that Grepes and his forces must answer imperial summons to war.[106] Procopius describes the conver-sion of the Heruls in terms now familiar to us:

> But when Justinian took over the empire, he bestowed upon them good lands and other possessions, and thus completely succeeded in win-ning their friendship and persuaded them all to become Christians. As a result they adopted a gentler manner of life [δίαιταν] and decided to submit themselves wholly to the laws of the Christians, and in keep-ing with the terms of their alliance they are generally arrayed with the Romans against their enemies.[107]

With some candor, Procopius goes on to say that the Heruls did not com-pletely abandon all of their barbarous habits.[108] Absent from his description of the Heruls is any mention of environment affecting their behavior.

In the *Secret History*, Procopius's vengeful diatribe against Justinian enacts a precisely opposite agenda. He says that the emperor does not just give gifts to barbarians as he did to the Tzani, he actually encourages barbarians to plunder the empire;[109] he does not bring peace and civilization, he destroys them;[110] he does not tame the wilderness by building roads to end isolation; instead, he creates a "Scythian wilderness" through policies that despoiled once-flourishing Roman lands.[111] Procopius describes the emperor no longer as a divinely inspired artisan of imperial civilization but as a diabolical agent of destruction.[112] These negative examples by contrast highlight Procopius's remarks in the *Wars* and the *Buildings*.

The Plague and Determinism

For Procopius, the dreadful plague (*Yersinia pestis*) that struck the empire in 542, called the Justinianic Plague or the FPP/First Plague Pandemic, defied understanding. He could find no plausible human explanations for its cause, and so he looked to God for an answer.[113] His description of the plague emphasizes its unique, universal scope and its indifference to human categories of social or political difference. Most remarkable of all, Procopius indicates that the plague overrode the rules of environmental determinism, for cultural variation due to geographical location in no way influenced the spread of the disease:

[176] CHAPTER 5

But for this calamity it is quite impossible either to express in words or to conceive in thought any explanation, except indeed to refer it to God. For it did not come in a part of the world nor upon certain men, nor did it confine itself to any season of the year, so that from such circumstances it might be possible to find subtle explanations of a cause, but it embraced the entire world, and blighted the lives of all men, though differing from one another in the most marked degree, respecting neither sex nor age. For much as men differ with regard to places in which they live, or in the law of their daily life, or in personality, or in active pursuits, or in whatever else man differs from man, in the case of this disease alone these factors made not the slightest difference.[114]

It is worth juxtaposing Procopius's remarks about the plague's impact with his comments in the *Secret History* about the devastating consequences of barbarian inroads enabled by Justinian. For example, he describes destruction in the Balkans in the following way:

And Illyricum and Thrace in its entirety, comprising the whole expanse of country from the Ionian Gulf to the outskirts of Byzantium, including Greece and the Thracian Chersonese, was overrun practically every year by Huns, Sclaveni and Antae, from the time when Justinian took over the Roman Empire, and they wrought frightful havoc among the inhabitants of that region. For in each invasion more than twenty myriads of Romans, I think, were destroyed or enslaved there, so that a veritable Scythian wilderness came to exist everywhere in this land.[115]

Persians invaded Roman territory four times with similar consequences. Procopius tells us that due to their depredations, "this entire region came to be very sparsely populated, and it will never be possible, I think, for any human being to discover by enquiry the numbers of those who perished in this way."[116]

Procopius's pages show how the great impact of the environment on human communities can be broken by greater power of two sorts, namely the beneficial, Christian agency of the Roman emperor, and the preternatural and inexplicably destructive force of the plague. The barbarians set loose by Justinian's policies were like the plague, for they created a metaphorical Scythian wilderness within the empire, a true sign of the world turned upside-down, in which the emperor and the piety of his subjects were powerless.

Pseudo-Caesarius

Further evidence of sixth century discussion at Constantinople of the limits of environmental determinism comes from the pen of a monk known only as Pseudo-Caesarius. He was probably a member of the Akoimetôn Monastery of the "Sleepless Monks," who celebrated the divine service day and night

THE CONTROLLING HAND OF THE ENVIRONMENT [177]

without interruption.[117] This monk, who lived at about the same time as Procopius, composed a treatise composed of four dialogues in the well-established genre of *erotapokriseis*, a didactic question-and-answer format appropriate to the classroom.[118] In Late Antiquity it became an especially popular and effective way to organize knowledge in a variety of fields, both secular and religious, sometimes bridging them in response to issues of the day, as Pseudo-Caesarius shows.[119] Both astral and environmental determinism found a place in his discussions.

The genre was put to a variety of uses in the sixth century. It is possible that Aristotle's question-and-answer *Problemata* took its final form at this time when his authority was contested, notably by the Monophysite/Miaphysite philosopher John Philoponus in Alexandria.[120] Coming from a quite different direction, Justinian's chief legal officer Junillus Africanus employed the question-and-answer format in a treatise that discussed biblical exegesis against the background of the Three Chapters Controversy.[121] In his own use of question-and-answer discussion, Ps.-Caesarius, a Monophysite/Miaphysite, confronted old determinist ideas in his religious text just as Procopius reacted to them in his historical works.

No evidence suggests that Ps.-Caesarius and Procopius had any direct connection to one another beyond their educated involvement in these older traditions of environmental determinism, about which they held very different opinions shaped by different concerns. Ps.-Caesarius's treatise, which consists of 218 questions and answers on various topics, reveals that he knew the Greek Church Fathers well and had access to a good theological library, presumably in his monastery.[122] What historical or geographical writing he may have consulted is unknown.

As Ioannis Papadogiannakis notes, Ps.-Caesarius could not take for granted "the quality of Christian allegiance"[123] in the unsettled religious environment of his day.[124] He took pains to engage current discussion thereby providing "a priceless glimpse into a debate as ongoing process that highlights all of the contentions, hesitations, doubts and objections of the questioners."[125] Ps.-Caesarius addressed a variety of religious topics, as would be expected, such as the problem of heresy and the nature of the Trinity. He criticized Arian Christians, Origenists, and Jews.[126] Politically, his Monophysitism/ Miaphysitism put him at odds with the official Chalcedonian (Orthodox) Christianity advocated by Justinian and presumably Procopius.[127] He did not, however, take a stand on the calamitous doctrinal reconciliation that the emperor attempted but never achieved.[128]

In the midst of these religious controversies, Slavic groups called Antae and Sclavenes became a significant threat in the Balkans, demanding the emperor's prompt attention. Their violent entry into Roman lands also caught Ps.-Caesarius's eye, perhaps because he had a personal connection to the territory predating his monastic life.[129] The *Dialogues* were composed about 560,[130] which would indicate that he knew about decades of Slavic inroads and imperial countermeasures. With good reason, scholars value his *Dialogues* for the information they provide.[131] Doubtless like thousands of others, he wondered why the Slavs were so fierce. His discussion of that problem brought familiar ideas about environment and the stars into play, with an attack on astrology and the zodiac via *nomima barbarika* arguments:

> *Question*: . . . since seven stars figure into the birth of each one of use, we say that the earth is divided into seven regions and, as you will, each region is ruled by one of these stars, and according to their combination the subjects live and die; this very influence of the stars is called the law.

> *Answer*: If the world is divided into seven regions, how is it that in one region we find many and diverse laws? For not only seven laws exist, according to the number of the stars, nor yet twelve, according to the signs of the zodiac, not even thirty-six after the decani, but innumerable laws are recounted, those long ago forsaken, and those now in effect. How is it that in the same region we see living near one another the Indianthropophagi [Indian Cannibals] and the Brahmans who abstain from all living and enjoyment? . . . Or how is it that in another section of the region (there live together) the Sclaveni [Slavs] and the Physonites, who are also called the Danubians[132] . . . The first mentioned are savage, living by their own law and without the rule of anyone, but . . . the latter . . . obey their leader.[133]

Some of the same venerable tropes that Procopius used appear in this passage. For example, absence of law and political autonomy are indicators of barbarism. The words of the interlocutor in the dialogue indicate furthermore that Ps.-Caesarius had a good understanding of fundamentals of astrology.[134] He knows the entrenched theory of the *klimata*, the seven zones of the earth, each governed by a planet or star according to the zodiac, though he does not mention the theory directly. Every zone determined the customs, laws, and even the features of its inhabitants.[135]

Klimata theory had long provoked considerable opposition among churchmen. As his predecessors had done, Ps.-Caesarius employed *nomima barbarika* arguments against climatic determinism, which would posit that Slavs should not differ in significant ways from their immediate Danubian neighbors. Armed with his firsthand knowledge of the Danubian region, Ps.-Caesarius challenged this idea by emphasizing the differences between Slavs and the people who live near them. He went further to point out that not just in the Balkans but elsewhere in the world, many different peoples with different habits, laws, and customs live side by side in the same region.[136]

Ps.-Caesarius wanted his readers to understand that the environment is not a straitjacket. People in all countries can choose how to live, regardless

THE CONTROLLING HAND OF THE ENVIRONMENT [179]

of the striking differences among their cultures. In his words, "Fate does not force the Seres to commit murder if they do not want to nor the Brahmans to eat meat; it does not prevent the Persians from marrying their daughters and sisters."[137] In noting humanity's freedom to decide whether to live morally, Ps.-Caesarius expressed the fundamental point of Christian opposition to natural determinism.

Another trace of this Constantinopolitan discussion of environment and cultural traits appears in the mostly lost *Ecclesiastical History* of the Syrian churchman John of Ephesus (ca. 507–ca. 588), who wrote in his native Syriac. John, like Ps.-Caesarius, was a leading member of the Monophysite/Miaphysite Christian community in Constantinople during Justinian's reign. He came to Constantinople about 540 and initially enjoyed the emperor's favor. In 542, Justinian made him a bishop and entrusted him with a mission of converting the countryside around Ephesus. John was quite successful. He claimed to have made eighty thousand conversions and built ninety-eight churches and twelve monasteries.[138] Around the year 558 he became a bishop in Syria.[139] The relative security of Monophysite/Miaphysite communities in the empire did not outlive Justinian, however. The emperor's best efforts to reconcile doctrinal differences and reach compromise failed.[140] His successor, Justin II (r. 565–78), adopted a more hostile approach and began to persecute Monophysites/Miaphysites in 571, using force to make them adopt Chalcedonian Orthodox beliefs.

Justinian's inability to protect the Balkans and his successor's hostility to Monophysites/Miaphysites shaped John's ethnography.[141] For him, Slavs were savage and destructive because God had sent them to punish the emperors and their Chalcedonian subjects for persecuting Monophysites/Miaphysites.[142] The geography or climate in which they lived played no part in his explanation of their barbarism. In this way, John's work is one signal of a turning point in the status of environmental determinism in the sixth century.

Another Christian writing in a different genre during the reign of Heraclius gives further evidence of the turning point.[143] The so-called *Chronicon Paschale*, or *Easter Chronicle*, compiled by an anonymous author about 630, gives further evidence of the changing status of environmental determinism. The pious chronicler wrote from a Chalcedonian Christian perspective, relating the history of the world from Adam to his own day. Warren Treadgold suggests he was a well-educated layman serving in the imperial bureaucracy with a special concern for dating documents, religion, and chronology,[144] but there is no evidence that he lived in Constantinople.[145]

Near the beginning of the *Chronicle*, following presentation of Noah and his sons and the contemporary peoples who are their descendants,[146] the author provides a list of seven *klimata* and the cities that lie within them. He ranges from Libya in the West to the Borysthenes (Dnieper River) in the East. His sources are debated,[147] but that is not of direct concern here. What stands out is the matter-of-fact presentation of the *klimata* material within a fully Christian text. The chronicler's list is devoid of any comment either positive or negative about climatic determinism. For him, the *klimata* are not controversial. They are geographical descriptors only as they had been for Ptolemy, who had used them to mark regions for mapping purposes half a millennium before.[148] For the chronicler, they do not challenge divine determination of the characteristics of noteworthy cities. The tacit acceptance of determinism in the *Chronicon Paschale*, however, does not mark the end of the story. The struggle between environmental theory and Christian teaching would persist in Byzantium well into the fourteenth century.[149]

Discussion of environmental determinism in this chapter ends in the eastern Mediterranean with a military handbook. Near the turn of the seventh century, a devoutly Christian military officer composed a handbook of battlefield tactics known as the *Strategikon of Maurice*.[150] The author evidently drew from his own considerable experience on the battlefield as well as from literary sources. The emperor Maurice (r. 582–602) fits that description, and the attribution of authorship to him is as old as the textual tradition. Nevertheless, his authorship "defies demonstration."[151] The treatise begins with an invocation of the Trinity and asks for the intercession of Mary and all the saints.[152] He accepts that God's Providence rules everything, but at the same time, his experience on the battlefield had taught him that military preparedness was essential as well.[153]

The eleventh book of the *Strategikon*, "Characteristics and Tactics of Various Peoples," deals with Rome's chief enemies, namely Persians, Avars, Turks, and Slavs of different sorts.[154] The author can be both precise and general. For example, he calls Avars, Turks, and other steppe peoples Scythians when he is making general comments about nomadic groups who are "one . . . in their mode of life," but he is well aware that their specific characteristics matter a great deal.[155] Joseph Ricci has noted that to distinguish among them the author provides "perhaps the only instance in Roman ethnography when nomadic peoples are titled 'Scythian,' 'Hunnish,' and 'Turks' in the same breath."[156] The author of the *Strategikon* brings a sharp eye to bear on the different fighting skills of his enemies.

Peoples shaped by climate have distinguishing military attributes essential for a general to know so that he could engage them in appropriate fashion and with proper preparation. In this way, peoples become characterized by their style of fighting and successfully challenged on the battlefield. As opponents of Rome and Christ they embody one sort of enmity, and as warriors with known habits, they represent another sort of difference.

The author has combined a Christian sensibility and the lessons of many battles fought with traditional descriptive tropes. Environmental theory is not directly invoked, but the relation between terrain and culture, climate and fighting styles, is deeply embedded in the treatise. The Persians, for example,

THE CONTROLLING HAND OF THE ENVIRONMENT [181]

"[s]ince they have been brought up in a hot climate, they easily bear the hardships of heat, thirst, and lack of food."[157] In the same way, Scythians can endure heat and cold because they are nomads.[158] Their environment makes them greedy, treacherous, and deceitful. The nearly impenetrable forests and marshes in which Slavic peoples live[159] have made them stubborn bandits without benefit of government. They are likewise disorderly in battle. Awareness of such factors makes the *Strategikon* a practical guide for a Christian military officer. The ethnography of warfare suits a Christian empire, but the need for practical fighting information recalls Julius Caesar and the generals who followed him.

After the Empire in the West

It would be from the Latin West that environmental theory entered the modern tradition.[160] Two examples of the different employment of determinist ideas can be seen in the work of Cassiodorus, a sixth-century scholar, statesman, and churchman, and Isidore of Seville, a Spanish bishop. They will stand for broader developments in the Latin West.

Cassiodorus Senator (ca. 485–ca. 585) was an Italian Roman with broad intellectual interests. He conscientiously served the Ostrogothic king Theoderic (r. 493–526) and his successors during the early years of Justinian's invasion of Italy in the 530s. Sometime before 540 Cassiodorus went to Constantinople, where he stayed for twenty years, involved in study and religious discussion with people close to the imperial court. At this time he may well have discussed environmental theory with other intellectuals in the imperial city. About 544, he returned to his hometown Scylletium (modern Squillace), where he founded Vivarium, which Brian Croke has described as "a community of scholars and scribes operating within the framework of a monastic routine with a nearby walled enclave for those who preferred the solitary monastic life."[161] The scholars under his direction were devoted to the preservation of secular as well as religious texts.

The idea for this intellectual center had long been on his mind. While acting as Theoderic's praetorian prefect, Cassiodorus had written to a friend who administered the south Italian region (modern Calabria) in which his hometown lay, complaining that the town was being mismanaged. Cassiodorus lavishly praised the beauty of his beloved birthplace, which "hangs from the hillside like a bunch of grapes."[162] Its temperate climate created the conditions for especially clear thinking. In the same letter he enlarges on the benefits of moderate climate:

> For indeed, a hot country makes men cunning and fickle; a cold one makes them sly and sluggish; it is only the temperate climate that sets human nature in good order by its own quality. Thus it is that the

[182] CHAPTER 5

ancients called Athens the country of the wise; one which, pervaded by the purity of its air, through a happy generosity predisposed the clearest minds to the role of philosophy. For is it really the same thing for a body to gulp down swamp-water as to drink at a sweet and translucent spring? So, the burden of a heavy atmosphere weighs down the vigour of the soul. For we are necessarily subjected to such a state when clouds depress us; and, again, since it is the essence of the heavenly soul to enjoy all that is pure and untainted, we naturally rejoice in bright weather.[163]

Cassiodorus employs conventional climate theory to praise his hometown on the Adriatic coast without concern for its non-Christian associations. It would seem that he already has in mind the seed of an idea that two decades later will take the form of his monastery. Though this letter does not mention plans for founding his community, the rationale for it is well presented. What better place could there be for a community of religious scholars and copyists than a location perfect for the life of the mind? The inhabitants of the community would be monks, but Cassiodorus's ideas are hardly a justification for an ascetic life in a harsh and inhospitable place.

Cassiodorus dismissed astral determinism. In the *Institutions of Divine and Secular Learning*, which he wrote to direct the studies of the monks at Vivarium, he criticizes the idea that the stars determine human actions. Like Augustine more than a century earlier, he feared social anarchy: "If the human race were forced by the inevitability of its birth to various actions, why would good behaviour gain praise or evil behaviour come under the punishment of laws?"[164]

Further west, in the Visigothic court in Spain, there emerged another transmitter of ideas about environmental determinism from the classical to the medieval world and so, on to us. Isidore, who became bishop of Seville in 600 or 601, was born in the 550s. In his infancy, when Justinian's forces invaded Cartagena, Spain, his father moved the family to Seville for safety, and Isidore spent his life there.[165] Educated in the Church, Isidore enjoyed an important ecclesiastical career as bishop of Seville, with influence at the Visigothic court in Spain. Isidore is most important today, however, for his intellectual life and his many writings. Well educated for his time, he knew some Greek and a few words of Hebrew in addition to Latin writers of the classical age and patristic sources. Isidore produced a rich body of work himself.[166] His best-known treatise is the *Etymologies*, which like so many medieval treatises from Spain to Persia, may be viewed as a "compilation of encyclopedias."[167] Such works performed, as Peter Brown has said, "the urgent and deeply existential task of building up a local Christendom."[168] By gathering past knowledge from many different sources, Isidore performed a great service. His book proved to be enormously popular and influential in the Middle Ages and beyond, as evidenced by the more than one hundred manuscripts that survive. Its ninth book deals with, among many other topics, the languages and peoples of the world, what their names mean, and other characteristic elements of their identity, letting us see the cultural diversity of a post-Roman world. Along the way he makes general statements involving environmental determinism: "People's faces and coloring, the size of their bodies, and their various temperaments correspond to various climates. Hence we find that the Romans are serious, the Greeks easy-going, the Africans changeable, and the Gauls fierce in nature and rather sharp in wit, because the character of the climate makes them so."[169]

Isidore's belief that ethnic characteristics result from environmental causes is nothing new and scarcely surprising. The salient point is that he states no opposition to environmental influences in religious terms. Like Cassiodorus and the writers in the East that have been mentioned, Isidore has assimilated environmental theory and neutralized its once controversial character. He echoes developments we have seen in Constantinople. The ethnographic ideas of such long development found a new home in his *Etymologies*. The immense popularity of his compendium of knowledge in the Middle Ages did much to enable the survival of ancient beliefs about the shaping hand of the environment. Isidore and Cassiodorus illustrate the Christian acceptance of determinism without any independent agency that also occurred in Constantinople.

Conclusion

This chapter has described the emergence in Late Antiquity of a new ethnographic discourse centered on the power of the earth to determine the character of individuals and communities. It developed in three phases. Discussion about the controlling hand of the earth's natural environment (and celestial bodies) began in classical Greece, long before Rome entered center stage. Philosophers debated whether the power of Fate held absolute power over human lives or whether at least a measure of choice was possible in shaping human lives. Next, Romans embraced the idea that imperial action could overcome physical limits imposed by terrain and distance, enabling remote peoples to be brought into a larger imperial community. This idea was in place by the first century CE, and it found full expression in the ideology of the Christian emperor Justinian in the sixth century. He saw it as his responsibility to transform his subjects in order to create an accessible and connected empire with one orthodox belief and one law that would override local particularities.

The third phase also emerged during the imperial period. It was the product of successful Christian challenges to the absolute determining power of Fate and the natural force of the celestial bodies and the natural environment. Christians offered a reconceived cosmos in which God's compassionate Providence was ultimately the sole controlling force in human affairs. Humans could exercise their free will to choose whether or not to sin in a Christian world. Natural determinism of any sort was incompatible with this new vision. The previous chapter showed that under Christian pressure the stars lost independent agency and became no more than signs of divine purpose. In a similar way, for sixth-century Christian Romans, the earth retained its formative influence but was no longer independent of God's design. Divine intent was clear: individuals had the ability to choose their spiritual identity and to live and believe correctly. Thus, in a sense, identity became a moral choice and not something determined by the environment. Breaking the controlling hand of the stars and the earth contributed significantly to the development of Christian universalism.

As the Roman earth became a Christian-Roman earth, the new Roman ethnography gave a unique role to the emperor as cultural artificer. New sorts of participation were imagined by those who accepted this ethnographic frame. With the Christian God now as the paramount authority over all natural phenomena as well as human destiny and with the emperor as his agent, the ethnography of environmental determinism found a new place within an imperial Christian field. The empire's role vis-à-vis the nations was recast in a different mode. Geographical remoteness was superceded by spiritual interconnectedness. Everyone might achieve spiritual access to God as humanity found a new spiritual center. From a Christian Roman perspective, the endlessly varied peoples of the world began to inhabit a differently conceived globe and heaven under the watchful gaze of God and the emperor. In the reimagined hierarchy of human and divine power, Romans and barbarians alike now walked differently under the stars and on the earth.

How Christianity provided new communities to enter, new ways to enter them, and new ways to name them is the subject of the next chapter.

CHAPTER SIX

Christianity and the Descendants of Noah

Gog is the Goth.

—AMBROSE OF MILAN, *ON FAITH*[1]

General Introduction to Chapters 6, 7, and 8

From their earliest days in the footsteps of Paul, Christians generated a host of questions that were as ethnographic as they were theological. These questions animated their daily lives as they labored to find their place within the convoluted Roman social environment.[2] How would all the peoples of the inhabited world, Christian and non-Christian alike, be categorized and take a place in a Christian scheme of universal human salvation? What would foreignness mean in a religion that embraced all the world's peoples? At the same time, what were the significant differences among the many local varieties of Christianity that existed, and how would this heterodoxy find a place in a universal vision, especially in the face of imperial claims to orthodoxy?

In grappling with such problems, which produced no single response, Christians revolutionized and reenergized the entire Roman ethnographic vision in Late Antiquity, with momentous consequences. Their answers fundamentally challenged and ultimately transformed Roman views of the inhabited world. Not only did the religion permeate the existing Roman ethnographic paradigms found in law, science, and diplomacy discussed in previous chapters, the book-based faith also brought powerful new Christian analytical approaches to the table. It is not surprising that the new interpretative frameworks were rooted in the Bible and in the interpretation of sacred texts.

The chapters that follow explore the appearance of three powerful new ethnographic approaches to human populations developed by Christian writers. This chapter, "Christianity and the Descendants of Noah," deals with a discourse of biblical origins found in the story of the dispersal of humanity after the Flood, as described in the book of Genesis in the so-called Table of Nations (TN). This discourse offered a new, shared past and a fresh set of historical interconnections to the peoples of the Roman world. It also linked them to salvation history. At the same time, the TN redrew the mental map

[185]

of the world by allocating its lands among the three sons of Noah and their descendants. The importance of this division cannot be overstated. Tristan Major has explained that "the tripartite division of the descendants of Noah outlasts any other ethnic division of the world until the modern period."[3] It provided an elastic template for identifying and accommodating the peoples of the world within a Christian frame. This held true for newcomers as they emerged in changing circumstances. Through the TN, the *oikoumene* was reimagined.

Chapter 7, "Babel and the Languages of Faith," introduces a discourse that let Christian Romans confront the world's linguistic diversity in a biblical frame. It ultimately broke the glass ceiling of Latin, Greek, and Hebrew hegemony, enabling all the languages of the world potentially to be carriers of religious truths. The social force of spoken and written languages changed when they were yoked to the expression of correct belief. Ideas about the TN and Babel spread rapidly among growing communities of believers because they were carried by churchmen, who became influential in affairs at every level, the equivalent of the Roman governing elite before Christianity. When it comes to long-term influence in Late Antiquity, we can safely say that the TN and Babel tales were among the Bible's great success stories.

Chapter 8, "The New Ethnography of Christian Heresy," discusses a discourse of heresy that distinguished among Christian communities, wherever they were on the map, on the basis of creed and interpretation of text. It put forward belief-based criteria of difference and in the process politicized heterodoxy. Interpretation of truth texts (in different languages) played an all-important role in establishing the points of variance. By providing distinct criteria of faith with which to mark differences among groups, Christian writers developed new definitions of community, new terms of inclusion within the Roman Empire (which by the end of the fourth century Christians had come to envisage as a Christian state), and new criteria for judging and interacting with foreign cultures. The ethnography of heresy helped to pave the way for a new religion-based medieval world order.

These three ethnographic dossiers provided fresh ways for Christians to describe, evaluate, and relate to the peoples in the world around them. They gave a new face to entry and transformation within the imperial community. With Christianity's ascendancy, a new rhetoric of difference resting primarily on issues of faith, textual exegesis, and liturgical practice gradually came to the fore. It was not tied to ethnicity, geography, or law, and it rested on a new vision of a global community that did not depend on the Roman state. At the same time, when the imperial government became Christian, the voices of Christian individuals and communities became audible to the state in new ways.

None of these three ethnographic dossiers would have been possible without the efforts of the churchmen and believers of many backgrounds whose writings provide our evidence. The bishops, exegetes, polemicists, chasers of heresy, and laymen who interpreted sacred texts and put their understanding into action constituted a new cadre of ethnographers. They never thought of themselves in this fashion, of course, but in articulating and instrumentalizing core ideas of origin and difference, they acquired power to shape the ideas of millions of people. They understood their influence very well. As describers of culture, they created and slowly imposed a different vision of humanity across the Christian map, responding to lineage, language, and creed. We must not take them for granted. They provide a rich dossier of evidence and stand shoulder to shoulder with Tacitus and Caesar as actors on the ethnographic stage.

The influence of these churchmen was enormous. Over the span of half a millennium between the third and seventh centuries, Christian writers from Syria to Spain slowly brought into focus a Christian vision of the world and its populations that was partly keyed to Roman imperial power—or the absence of it—and partly to theological concerns. Eventually these fused to create what we can call loosely a sectarian medieval vision of the world in which a primary identifier of communities and individuals was faith. Carefully curated systems of belief motivated political activity at the local and imperial level. During this formative period, older descriptions and judgments remained, and old ethnicities continued to flourish, even as new ones appeared. What changed? Established peoples found an additional home within the Christian scheme by being identified as descendants of the sons of Noah and by aligning with a particular Christian creed. Taking pride of place, however, among all the characteristics said to define foreign (and domestic) peoples was religious identification, stated in a fashion that would have been incomprehensible to Augustus, Trajan, and perhaps even Constantine. It would not have needed explaining, however, to Heraclius when he went to war under the banner of Christ against the Zoroastrian Persians and then against the armies of Islam in the early seventh century. Such a sectarian default position had not existed in the High Roman Empire, which exhibited instead an imperial tolerance of pluralism, carefully monitored and highly judgmental, but nonetheless far more accepting of cultural and intellectual variety.

Christianity, Genesis 9–11, and the Peoples of the World

For Greeks and Romans in antiquity, an important way to describe and categorize foreigners was to find an origin for them in mythology or legend. Some great figure, a hero or perhaps a god, could then become the ancestor of an entire people.[4] As Fergus Millar noted, in Greek contexts these identifications were often "taken over and adopted by semi-Greek and non-Greek peoples,

[188] CHAPTER 6

with real consequences for both their self-identification and their activities and attachments in the contemporary world."[5] Millar's point is equally valid for Christian peoples in the late antique world who found biblical origins for themselves and ascribed them to others. Noah, who survived the Flood with his family, was understood to be the progenitor of all humans born subsequently.[6] Descent from Noah produced historical lineages and emerged as a crucial ethnographic marker.

Finding the biblical origins of peoples begins with the book of Genesis. Such discovery happened in two complementary ways in the late antique period. First, contemporary communities could identify themselves as descendants of the sons of Noah (and eventually of the line of Abraham via the TN in Genesis 9–10. The verses provided a basic set of names, genealogies, and locations for the peoples of the world, thereby creating a new map and a new history for humankind. They provided a Christian alternative (but not necessarily a replacement) for the classical tradition of *origines gentium* (origins of peoples) and the populations of the earth. In Late Antiquity, origin narratives of newly emerging cultures, as well as already established political communities within and beyond imperial borders, found a place within the biblical frame. A striking example of the latter is seen in the Christian Roman perception of various Arab groups on the eastern fringes of the empire who would eventually become the Muslim enemies of Christian Byzantium. In the case of Muslim Arabs (discussed below), biblical lineage would become a catalyst for self-definition as well. Rome's old western lands were similarly affected. For example, several documents that were informed by the TN found their way to Merovingian Gaul in the sixth and seventh century, where they played a role in shaping the self-identity of the Frankish kingdom. These texts (discussed below) show that the TN remained an adaptable, living text as Rome left the limelight.[7] For Christians, biblical lineage provided a compelling descriptive tool, and faith served as a decisive instrument of judgment.

The groups that found their place on the Christian map as descendants of the sons of Noah were soon joined by celestial protectors. These were angels, who came to be understood as the guardians of individual peoples.[8] Association with angels added further specificity to the place of human communities within a divinely organized hierarchy.

These tales provided additional historical identifications and geographical locations for groups when they appeared on the Christian horizon, reflecting contemporary circumstances. Furthermore, not only did they reach back to biblical foundations, in Christian hands sometimes they also looked ahead to the End of Days, enabling contemporary events to be interpreted within the broad span of salvation history. Huns, for example, could be both the descendants of Noah through Gog and the precursors of the Apocalypse.

Background: The Book of Genesis

Put in its final form by an unknown redactor probably in the fifth or fourth century BCE, the book of Genesis set the foundation for Christian writers in Late Antiquity on which to build their own picture of the inhabited world.[9] Verses 9–11 became the starting place for Christian discussion. These biblical passages explain the division and diversity of the world's population as part of God's plan, and so, link ethnographic concerns to what would become Christian schemes of history. Verses 9–10 tell how after the Flood the three sons of Noah (Japheth, Ham, and Shem) spread across the world, which was divided among them and their progeny to inhabit. Verse 11 tells the story of the Tower of Babel and the confusion of the world's peoples and languages. These accounts have been interpreted and reworked in many different ways from biblical times until the present day, making them probably the most influential ethnographic statements in the Western tradition that stem from the Bible.

The Table of Nations and the Tower of Babel stories originally were two entirely different tales about the peopling of the earth that were juxtaposed sometime before the book of Genesis took its present form in the fourth century BCE. Today, according to conventional biblical source criticism, the Table of Nations represents the P (or Priestly) tradition, while the Babel story comes from the J (or Yahwist) tradition. The most striking difference is that the TN says that the sons of Noah created communities over the earth, each with its own language, while the Babel narrative relates that until the destruction of the Tower of Babylon, there was only one spoken language.[10] Despite the differences between the verses evident to the modern eye, ancient authors, Jewish and Christian alike, were not prepared to see any contradictions between them. In other words, as far as they were concerned, the Table of Nations and the Tower of Babel story were complementary passages in a divinely inspired narrative of human history. Though the TN and the Babel tales are treated here in two chapters, it is necessary to understand their unity in a late antique context.

The Table of Nations and the Sons of Noah

According to the TN, after the Flood, God divided the lands of the world among Noah's three sons, Shem, Ham, and Japheth:

[9:1] God blessed Noah and his sons, and said to them, Be fertile and increase, and fill the earth.
[9:19] These were the sons of Noah, and from them the whole world branched out.
[10:1] Now these are the lines of Shem, Ham, and Japheth, the sons of Noah: sons were born to them after the flood.

[10:32] These are the groupings of Noah's descendants, according to their origins, by their nations; and from these the nations branched out over the earth after the flood.

The TN tradition developed in several stages. Initially it was simply an intrabiblical matter, involving various writers and redactors within the Jewish exegetical tradition who had limited geographical horizons. We find Jewish writers amplifying the tales already in the book of Ezekiel, written in the sixth century BCE during the Babylonian exile. Later, in another well-known example, the material was reworked in the pseudo-epigraphical text of Jubilees during the Hasmonean period (167–140 BCE) as Jews became entangled in Hellenistic learning and culture.[11] The text draws together classical geographical traditions as well as the text of Genesis and its author may well have referred to a map.[12] Postbiblical Jewish authors like Flavius Josephus in the first century CE continued to find new relevance for the TN in response to current circumstances.[13] In his case, that meant defending Judaism in the aftermath of the failed revolt against Rome in 66–70 CE. He was, in the words of Tristan Major, "eager to show that the tripartite division of the world, along with each part's unique climate, was in accordance with Greek and Roman mental maps."[14] The points to emphasize are, first, that every rearticulation of the text reflected contemporaneous circumstance and cultural challenges; second, that the expansion of geographical information probably derived from non-Jewish sources as well as the personal experience of each redactor; and third, and most important, the TN was constantly changing in application.

The same adaptability appears in Christian contexts from the earliest period. The authors of the New Testament responded directly to the Genesis tale, and its presence is felt in apocryphal and apocalyptic writings.[15] For example, in the early imperial period Christian writers like John, who composed the Book of Revelation, began to integrate TN material into the Christian corpus, a trend that would continue. The Table of Nations appeared in all the earliest Christian biblical compilations in various languages, part of the inheritance from Judaism.[16]

The tales of the sons of Noah and the Tower of Babel continued to resonate in Late Antiquity. The stories were known wherever the growing Christian communities read or heard the Bible. No longer simply the possession of marginal communities that had originated in a province far from the center of international affairs, the TN quickly found global application as the faith spread. Christian writers began to develop the stories and gradually developed a Bible-based Christian ethnography for the inhabited world.[17] Along the way, biblical storylines encountered works of classical geography which helped set the scene. A familiar cast of international peoples with whom Christians intermingled was augmented by some new arrivals from far away, like the Huns and Arabs, who found a place in Christian narratives of origin with scarcely

CHRISTIANITY AND THE DESCENDANTS OF NOAH   [191]

a hitch. The exceptional flexibility of the TN story let them adapt readily to changing circumstances.

The written record of development is spotty, however, and precise lines of transmission are often obscured by the fact that Christians had access to the same, or nearly the same, biblical text. The stories affected perceptions very widely. In Christian communities (as well as Jewish ones) the stories contained a great part of what people know about their pasts. The TN appeared in many sorts of writing and is notably embedded in the traditions of Christian chronography and chronicles or taken for granted by them.[18] The TN found an audience of avid writers and listeners in different languages.

A few examples of Christian texts from across the empire suggest the influence of the Genesis tales upon writers, readers, and then the congregations who heard sermons and saw Bible stories depicted in their churches. The purpose here is not to trace comprehensively the history of any Christian genre or to resolve problems of transmission. Rather, these examples show the ethnographic function of the Genesis tales at moments of their use in different contexts. By the end of Late Antiquity, the Genesis tradition not only had become firmly entrenched in the Roman historical and visual mentality, it had found dramatic expression in Christian perception of foreigners as widespread as steppe peoples, Muslims, and Franks, and sometimes in the foreigners' perception of themselves. A few examples show how newcomers to the Christian Roman world fit into the global picture begun in Genesis.

Beginnings: Christian Chronography and Chronicles

The habit of composing lists of important events in chronological sequence is found already in the remote antiquity of Egypt and Mesopotamia. Much later, and long before Christians entered the picture, such chronographic enterprises flourished in the hands of Greek and Roman authors who wished to keep track of kings' regnal years, the sequence of consuls at Rome, Olympic victors, or other such information. These lists were not meant to be analytical or displace the standard historical writing of the day. The compiler typically provided no causal links between the recorded events. The chronological sequence itself was what mattered. Such works are called chronicles and constitute a specific genre. Important work by Richard Burgess and Michael Kulikowski is forcing reconsideration of many deep-seated notions concerning the chronicle tradition.[19]

Chronicles did not originate in Late Antiquity,[20] but they flourished then and took on a heightened profile and lasting importance in Christian hands.[21] As expected, Christian authors used the stories in Genesis as a point of departure, and they anticipated the End of Days, providing a teleological note missing from non-Christian chronicles. What matters here is how they became a medium for ethnographic information rooted in the Bible. Because of the popularity of the chronicle genre, the stories from Genesis attained a striking presence within Christian communities. They marked a new phase in communities' self-understanding, and there was variety among them. Brian Croke rightly remarks, "Each of the Late Antique chronicles is unique and independent and that is how they must be analysed, not as a monolith."[22] The circumstances of their composition reveal the elasticity of the TN tradition.

We will now look at a sample of chronographic works and chronicles of exceptional influence. They were written in quite different circumstances by churchmen who drew on an array of antecedents, but all carried the freight of Genesis 9–10.

The Book of Genealogy (Liber generationis) *and the* Division of the World (Diamérismos)

In 235 there appeared a composite Greek chronographical text, written by a Christian, that until recently scholars have usually called the *Chronicle of Hippolytus*.[23] The date is known from the final entry in the list of Roman emperors, Alexander Severus, who died in 235.[24] Burgess and Kulikowski have shown, however, that it is a composite text with a difficult lineage, neither a chronicle nor written by Hippolytus, who was an "antipope" in Rome coincidentally martyred in 235.[25] The text has a tortuous history, untangled and clearly explained by Burgess and Kulikowski. Its original title was *A Collection of Chronologies from the Creation of the World to the Present Day*. The title of the Latin rendering is *Liber generationis*,[26] or *Book of Genealogy*. The Latin text survives in various forms.[27] In addition to a revised edition from the tenth or eleventh century, there are two late antique Latin translations. The first of these manuscripts, called *Liber generationis II*, runs to 334, while the second Latin translation, confusingly called *Liber generationis I*, was completed before 460.[28] A Greek text was translated into Armenian around 687. Shortly after that, the Armenian version, with some additions, was translated into Latin and reentered Western discussion in the Merovingian kingdom of the Franks.[29]

In this briar patch of information of many sorts, which has been called a "diverse reference work [that] resembled a modern almanac,"[30] one portion requires special attention. That is the *Diamérismos*, or *Division of the World*, the first surviving Christian interpretation of the TN after Acts.[31] Unlike the author of Acts, however, who drew from a list of Persian provinces, the author of the *Diamérismos* dealt with Roman regions. Because of this, the *Diamérismos* portion of the *Liber generationis* document may be seen as a starting point for late antique developments. It drew material from the Roman Empire into a Christian historical scheme, thereby setting a precedent.[32]

The *Diamérismos* explored the diversity and location of the world's seventy-two peoples (see below) using the TN and the Babel story as

CHRISTIANITY AND THE DESCENDANTS OF NOAH [193]

explanatory templates. The author divided the *Diamérismos* into five broad lists. The first three deal in turn with Noah's sons Japheth, Ham, and Shem, their descendants, and the lands they inhabited. The fourth section considers the seventy-two nations of the story of Babel. The fifth, which considers peoples who came into being after Babel through colonization (*apoikia*),[33] was part of an attempt to address the problem of peoples not mentioned in Gen. 10.[34] In addition to biblical materials, the author drew on out-of-date Greek sources for data on the inhabited regions.[35] He does not consider peoples north of Rome's borders in Europe. New material, furthermore, was not derived from the Jewish tradition of Jubilees. It must be emphasized that the author was the first churchman on record to use Roman provincial names, such as Pannonians, Noricans, and Dalmatians, as names of discrete peoples, overlooking the varied populations that provincial borders might embrace.[36] In this way the Roman provincials were linked to the TN and became participants in a Christian view of history. Hervé Inglebert rightly views this attempt to enumerate the world's populations as a turning point in the convergence of Christian and classical ethnographic traditions.[37]

In the West, the two versions of the *Liber generationis* spawned further responses to the TN in a tangled web of manuscripts. One such offspring, called the *Origo humani generis* (*Origin of Humankind*), probably written at the end of the fourth century or the beginning of the fifth, was a complete translation into Latin of earlier material attributed to Hippolytus, with some additions.[38] The *Origo* accepts the idea found in Jubilees that each of the three sons of Noah received a continent, thus anticipating—or reflecting—the concepts of the T-O *mappa mundi* tradition (see below), but it follows the distribution found in its Greek sources.[39] Still another manuscript, called the *Liber genealogus*, was composed about the same time. The relationship between the two is complicated and disputed.[40] Both carry the Table of Nations, but there are dissimilarities in their lists of Noah's progeny and the lands they occupied.[41] The dissimilarities must reflect either different interpretations of peoples of the Bible in some way we do not understand or, more likely, the use of differing source material.

Still other manuscripts display a reliance on the TN as adapted to contemporary circumstances. Inglebert notes the many-layered character of *Liber genealogus*, which is focused on the interpretation of names for the interpretation of biblical history.[42] Seven manuscripts appeared between 405 and 470 that responded to a fierce and long-lasting religious debate in North Africa known as the Donatist Controversy. Donatists rejected the spiritual authority of priests to give the sacraments if they had turned over holy writings to state authorities during times of persecution. The Donatists' uncompromising position resulted in their own persecution by Roman and Catholic church authorities. The seven manuscripts accordingly reflected either Donatist or Catholic perspectives.[43] Both sorts viewed Roman history in terms of religion

[194]   CHAPTER 6

and eschatology, but they interpreted events quite differently. The Donatist versions treat Rome as the persecutor who will be punished by God. Catholics are seen as the descendants of Cain with whom Donatists, the "true Christians," must struggle.[44] All but one of these Donatist versions include the Antichrist and an outline of Christian persecutions to 405, with Honorius's edicts against the Donatists.[45] The Catholic redactors, on the other hand, see Rome in positive terms and its collapse caused by Arian barbarians, with no connection to the end of the world.[46] It is interesting to note that while the Donatist and Catholic manuscripts do not always agree in their lists of Noah's descendants and their current equivalents, the differences do not in any way suggest doctrinal conflict between them. For example, the Dodanim, who are descendants of Japheth, are identified as Romans or Latins in both Donatist and Catholic manuscripts.[47] This means that the TN itself was not affected by doctrinal struggle.

EXAMPLE 1: EUSEBIUS, FOUNDATIONAL IN THE GREEK WORLD

The *Diamérismos* represented a Christian milestone by bringing Roman populations into the storyline begun in Genesis. Seventy years later, Eusebius of Caesarea took another approach.[48] His *Chronicle*, which appeared in 303 just prior to the persecution of Christians by Diocletian, had two parts. The first, known as the *Chronographia*, contains a careful historical summary of kingdoms of antiquity and a regnal year table. The second, which concerns us here, is called the *Canons* (*Chronici canones*), and provides a set of comparative tables of synchronous history.[49] Eusebius states his debt to previous chronographers throughout the *Canons*.[50] Virtually all of the original Greek text is lost, but an Armenian text from about 600 survives, as does a Latin translation of the *Canons* made by Jerome in the 380s. In this treatise, Eusebius succeeded brilliantly in establishing synchrony between biblical and nonbiblical figures and events, using parallel "lines of kingdoms" (*fila regnorum*).[51] This established a historical sequence of events drawn from biblical and classical sources. It provided a structural model for information concerning the history of Christianity and the Church. He included the history of Chaldaeans, Assyrians, Hebrews, Egyptians, Greeks, and Romans to 325, the year of Constantine's Vicennalia, his twentieth year of rule.[52]

The Table of Nations also makes its appearance several times in the *Chronicle*. In a comparison of Chaldean (i.e., Babylonian) and Hebrew accounts of the Flood, Eusebius repeats the story of Genesis that all of humanity derives only from Noah's progeny, but he locates them geographically in the world known to him. Europe was populated by the offspring of Japheth. Egypt and Libya (and some western lands, i.e., North Africa) he says were the home of Ham's descendants. Shem's offspring filled Assyria and eastern realms.

CHRISTIANITY AND THE DESCENDANTS OF NOAH [195]

Elsewhere in the *Chronicle*, the sons of Noah recur in his comparative summary of the Greek (Septuagint), Hebrew, Samaritan, and versions of biblical chronology.[53] Later he provides a list of the kings of Rome and carries through the Republic to Julius Caesar.[54] Brian Croke sums up his accomplishment: "What Eusebius achieved by this mammoth work was the incorporation of the whole of human history, Christian and pagan, into a single grid."[55] The TN is at the heart of this historical account. It would continue to inform the chronicle tradition and so bring its particular account of the world's peoples to the forefront of ethnographic considerations.

EXAMPLE 2: JEROME, FOUNDATIONAL IN THE LATIN WEST

The Table of Nations received particular attention from the learned Latin churchman Jerome (ca. 342–420), who followed in Eusebius's chronographical footsteps. Jerome's contribution to the exegesis of biblical material in the Latin West was so great that by the sixteenth century he had earned the magnificent sobriquet Doctor Maximus Sacris Scripturis Explanandis (The Most Learned Explainer of Holy Scripture).[56] He frequently treated the TN in his many works that included and ranged far beyond the chronicle tradition. Three of them are closely related and need to be discussed together. These are his translation of the Bible, his translation into Latin of Eusebius's *Canons*,[57] and his *Questions on Genesis*. The biblical vision of the world's peoples that his work made accessible became a reference point in the development of Christian ethnography.

While living in Rome in the early 380s, Jerome became the protégé of Pope Damasus and found himself engaged in various literary projects. He gradually developed a comprehensive plan for shaping Christian knowledge. One part of this was to make a Christian history of the world accessible to Latin readers whose knowledge of Greek could not be taken for granted. To do this, Jerome elegantly translated the *Canons*—the second part of Eusebius's *Chronicle*—into Latin. This rendition maintained the Eusebian chronicle format and became fundamental in the development of Latin Christianity.

An imaginative and assiduous scholar, Jerome was never content merely to translate. In bringing Eusebius's work to his own day, he added considerable new material of two sorts. For the period between the mythical Aeneas and the first part of Constantine's reign, he selected information from Latin authors to build connections with a Latin-speaking audience.[58] The material he added for the period from 325 (the year of Constantine's Vicennalia) to 378 (the Battle of Adrianople) is, in his words, "totum meum est" (entirely my own work).[59]

The TN does not appear in Jerome's *Chronicle* because it was not included in Eusebius's *Canons*. What he did not include in his *Chronicle*, however,

Jerome addressed directly in his later work, *Hebrew Questions on Genesis* (*HQG*),[60] but he did so with a nonchronographic approach, that of commentary. Jerome composed the *HQG* after leaving Rome for Antioch and Palestine in 385. In this last phase of his life (he died in Bethlehem in 420), Jerome immersed himself in studying Hebrew in order to bring Jewish scholarship into the Church. As Charles Hayward puts it, "he sought to prove beyond any reasonable doubt that knowledge and proper use of those Jewish materials was absolutely necessary for a correct understanding of the Scriptures."[61]

The Vulgate Bible is the best-known result of Jerome's immersion in Hebrew. Though Pope Damasus had commissioned this Latin Bible when Jerome still lived in Rome, it was only completed about 405, in Bethlehem. It began as a revision of older Latin versions in circulation (the *Vetus Latina*), some parts of which were included in the final work, but it shows Jerome's determined hand.[62] Dissatisfied with the Greek Septuagint and wishing to go to the source, Jerome prepared the first translation of the Hebrew Bible into Latin. Known since the sixteenth century as the Vulgate, which is short for *versio vulgata*, or "commonly used version," Jerome's work was adopted by the Council of Trent in 1546 as the official version of the Roman Catholic Church.[63]

The *HQG* must be understood as an inseparable part of Jerome's deep commitment to biblical matters,[64] an outgrowth of his rendering of the Hebrew Bible into Latin and a product of his translation of the *Canon*. Completed by 393,[65] the *HQG* once again displays Jerome's scholarship and independence of mind.[66] In the *HQG*, Jerome does not comment on every verse in Genesis. Those that he does choose to explicate therefore deserve special note, as they bring his theological assumptions to the fore. For example, he discusses Gen. 9:27 on the relation of Japheth and Shem, two of Noah's sons, in the following way:

> [9:27] *May God enlarge Japheth, and dwell in the tents of Shem.* From Shem were born the Hebrews, from Japheth the people of the Gentiles. Therefore because the multitude of believers is wide, he received the name *breadth* because of the breadth which is expressed [in Hebrew] as Japheth. And as for what Scripture says, *May he dwell in the tents of Shem*: this is prophesied about us [Christians], who are engaged in the learning and knowledge of the Scriptures after Israel had been cast forth.[67]

Here, Jerome finds in the story of Noah's sons an explanation of the distinction of Jews from Christians, which he locates in TN genealogy and in geography.[68] Jerome also confidently locates the offspring of Noah's sons geographically and identifies them with peoples of his own day.[69] He might as well be looking at an OT map as he comments on Gen. 10:2, "The sons of Japheth were Gomer and Magog and Madai and Javan and Thubal and Mosoch and Thiras":

CHRISTIANITY AND THE DESCENDANTS OF NOAH [197]

[10:2] *The sons of Japheth were Gomer and Magog and Madai and Javan and Thubal and Mosoch and Thiras.* To Japheth the son of Noah were born seven sons who occupied land in Asia from Amanus and Taurus of Coele-Syria and the mountains of Cilicia as far as the river Don. Then in Europe they occupied land as far as Gadira, leaving behind names for places and peoples, most of which were afterwards changed: others remain as they were. So Gomer actually refers to the Galatians; Magog to the Scythians; Madai to the Medes; Javan to the Ionians who are also the Greeks (from which we get "the Ionian Sea"); and Thubal to the Iberians who are also the Spaniards from whom derive the Celtiberians, although certain people suppose them to be the Italians.[70]

The Tower of Babel story makes an appearance, too, in Jerome's pursuit of lines of descent:

[10:24–25] *Arphaxad begat Sela, and Sela begat Heber. Two sons were born from Heber: the name of the one was Phaleg, because in his days the earth was divided; and the name of this brother was Jectan.* Heber, from whom the Hebrews descended, because of a prophecy gave his son the name Phaleg which means "division," on account of the fact that in his days the languages were divided up in Babylon.[71]

Jerome's explanation indicates that the peoples of the world were divided and scattered when God destroyed Babel, and it reveals that lineage and language were primary markers in his understanding of the world's inhabitants.

EXAMPLE 3: AUGUSTINE ON THE SONS OF NOAH

Bishop Augustine of Hippo (354–430) developed central tenets of his theology of history within the framework of the sons of Noah story. In the sixteenth book of *The City of God*, Augustine elaborated his central theory of two human lineages that have been present since Adam, with the first being the community of the righteous, or the City of God, equivalent to Christ and proclaimed from the beginning of human history.[72] The Hebrew Bible prefigures all subsequent history and the presence of Christ, and so Christianity in a sense has been present since Adam.[73] The second city, the City of Man, comprises sinners and non-Christians who will not enjoy salvation and eternal life. Augustine writes in the *City of God*: "We must now turn our attention to the lines of descent from Noah's sons and weave the essential points about them into the pattern of our work, as it depicts the progress in successive periods of both cities, the earthly and the heavenly."[74]

Augustine connects these ideas to the sons of Noah tradition by noting that the generations of the three sons of Noah illustrate the historical progress of the two cities. Specifically, Shem prefigured Christ, because his descendants included the Jews, from among whom Jesus was born. Thus, the presence of the generations after Noah in history helps give him a structure to develop a total history of humanity in terms of salvation. Furthermore, he considers the progeny of Noah's sons not always as individuals but as "nations" (*nationes* or *gentes*), as for example the sons of Ham.[75] He easily progresses from speaking of individual descendants of Noah to the nations that they represent or brought into being, for the families generated by each grew into nations. He makes a calculation of seventy-three peoples in the world. He accounts for the discrepancy between the number of descendants of Noah and the seventy-three peoples by saying that some were not great enough to deserve mention and were absorbed by the group from which they branched.[76]

EXAMPLE 4: ISIDORE OF SEVILLE

A transitional figure in the West who provides a vantage point on TN discussion in Late Antiquity was the deeply learned Isidore, who became bishop of the Spanish city of Seville in 600 or 601 in an environment that combined religious fervor with considerable awareness of the vanished Roman presence.[77] Imperial rule in Spain had ended more than a century and a half earlier, but Roman culture and learning continued in the Visigothic kingdom. King Reccared (r. 586–601) had converted from Arianism to Catholic Christianity in 587, and Catholic learning spread quickly from monastic centers.

A tireless scholar as well as an active bishop, Isidore stood at this cusp of faith, memory, and learning. Admired in his own day for his erudition, Isidore is still acknowledged as one of the main bridges of classical learning (within a Catholic framework) to the Latin Middle Ages and later times.[78] Nearly one thousand manuscripts of his works survive as testimony to his influence on medieval culture.[79] The most important of these treatises is the *Etymologies*, an encyclopedia of sorts with short entries on a very broad range of subjects that quickly became essential reading in monastic libraries.[80]

Isidore is important for the present chapter not only because of the intellectual freight he shipped to the future. He was far more than a transmitter of knowledge, and as a contemporary witness he has particular value. His treatment of the TN and Babel narratives in Genesis offers a serious reflection on historical change and the relation of language to ethnicity in the post-Roman West, and his presentation of the peopling of the earth is thoughtful though not innovative. Furthermore, his discussion of heresy represents a summation and passing on of late antique heresiology into the Latin West. His treatment of Babel will be discussed in chapter 7, and his treatment of heresy will be discussed in chapter 8.

ISIDORE ON THE TABLE OF NATIONS

The ninth book of Isidore's *Etymologies* carries forward a wealth of information rooted in Genesis about the peopling of the earth and the nature and number of human languages.[81] Even though his material is derived from earlier writers and compendia,[82] Isidore's organization indicates an independent, analytical mind and a clear purpose. He is concerned with historical change in peoples and languages, and he attempts to give general explanations for developments over time. Thus, his work is both anchored in the past and contemporary.

Isidore adopts the tripartite division of the world among Noah's three sons and adds to the biblical lists names current in his own time. Moving from a general statement to the particular, he begins discussion of the sons of Noah and their progeny under the rubric *De gentium vocabulis* ("Concerning the names of nations"). He provides a general explanation on which to base his presentation:

> A nation (*gens*) is a number of people sharing a single origin, or distinguished from another nation (*natio*) in accordance with its own grouping, as the "nations" of Greece or of Asia Minor. From this comes the term "shared heritage" (*gentilitas*). The word *gens* is also so called on account of the generations (*generatio*) of families, that is from "begetting" (*gignere*, ppl. *genitus*), as the term "nation" (*natio*) comes from "being born" (*nasci*, ppl. *natus*).[83]

He goes on to explain that there are seventy-two languages in the world, as many as there are nations that fill the lands. Japheth produced fifteen of them, Ham thirty-one, and Shem twenty-seven.[84] The passage of time, however, has transformed the names of the peoples of the world, so that all of them mentioned in Genesis are no longer recognizable, though for a few, such as Assyrians from Assur and Hebrews from Heber, the derivation is quite obvious.[85] He concludes that when all are added up, "there appear to be more names of nations that have been altered than names remaining, and afterwards a rational process has given diverse names to these. So the Indians were named from the river Indus."[86] In this way he effectively accommodates the premise of the TN, which he entirely accepts, to undeniable historical change. The lineages made possible by the Genesis account are not limiting but flexible.

Among the many peoples he discusses in this regard, several deserve mention for their relevance to his own time. For example, he connects the fifth-century Huns and sixth-century Avars to the story of Alexander's Gates in the Caucasus (see below, Example 11).[87] The Goths are noted as well as being associated with Magog, son of Japheth, "because of the similarity of the last syllable. The ancients called them Getae rather than Goths."[88]

How did he perceive Romans in this post-Roman age? Isidore supplies conventional information about Romulus,[89] but pays Romans no special attention as descendants of Japheth.[90] Presumably he is drawing from a non-Christian source. Perhaps he is less interested in Romans as a people than in the knowledge that they generated. On the other side of the Mediterranean, however, a new narrative was forming. In Constantinople in the 570s, the chronicler John Malalas discussed Romus (not Romulus) at length and in largely negative terms as the founder of the city.[91] The anonymous *Easter Chronicle*, put together in the early seventh century drew on Malalas's account of the founders of Rome.[92]

Isidore mentions disagreement about the origin of the Saracens. He identifies them as Ishmaelites, commenting that they stem from Ishmael but are called Saracens in his own day through corruption of the name Sarah, Abraham's wife.[93] He points out that they also are called Agarenes, from Agar (Hagar), Abraham's slave, who, according to the TN was the mother of Ishmael, rather than Sarah.[94] He also says that Saracens have their name either because they believed themselves to be the descendants of Sarah, or as nonbelievers (*gentiles*) say, they are of Syrian origin (*Syriginae*).[95] This shows that a process of self-ascription of biblical lineage is under way among many of the Saracens.

Another etymological point of disagreement between nonbelievers and Christians is found in the name of the Thracians. He explains that Christians understand Japheth's son Tiras to be their ancestor, while pagans say that their ferocious (Lat. *trux*) behavior was the origin of their name.[96]

Finally in this regard, elsewhere in the *Etymologies* Isidore again adjusts the TN to a Christian view:

> [16] Shem means "renowned" . . . for out of him came the patriarchs and apostles and people of God. Also from his stock came Christ, whose name is great among the nations from the rising of the sun to its setting . . . [18] Japheth means "width," for from him were born the pagan nations, and because wide is the multitude of believers from among the gentiles, Japheth was named from that width.[97]

That Isidore casts the etymological history of the names of two contemporary peoples in terms of the TN tradition is not surprising. It shows how firmly entrenched the Christian ethnographic infrastructure had become.

EXAMPLE 5: CLASSICAL CARTOGRAPHY AND THE SONS OF NOAH

In the late antique centuries, a highly influential genre of maps combined basic information from the Table of Nations with information from classical sources. The idea that the world is divided into three parts, Asia, Europe, and Libya/Africa had long been a staple of classical geography and cartography.[98] This tripartite division was easily conflated with the allotment of the

CHRISTIANITY AND THE DESCENDANTS OF NOAH [201]

world to the three sons of Noah. The connection had perhaps been made as early as the time of composition of the pseudoepigraphal Book of Jubilees by an unknown Jewish writer in the mid-second century BCE who, as noted above, probably consulted a map in a Greek treatise.[99] In Late Antiquity, many Christians knew Jubilees well, especially chroniclers,[100] but there is no reason to assume that Jubilees was the sole carrier of the combination of the biblical and classical traditions of the tripartite division of the world or its representation.

Evidence lies in the T-O *mappa mundi* tradition that originated in Late Antiquity and continued throughout the Middle Ages.[101] T-O refers to a map of the world represented as a circle with a T inscribed in it, producing a three-part image. Isidore's *Etymologies*, written about 600 and drawing from unnamed sources, contained a T-O map, found in more than 600 medieval copies,[102] testimony to the enormous popularity of Isidore as well as the importance of the three sons of Noah in late antique and later envisioning of the world.[103]

After Rome: Into the World of the Franks

Awareness of the Bible grew in northern Europe in step with the expansion of Christianity in Late Antiquity. Several important Frankish texts of the sixth and seventh centuries bear the stamp of the TN tradition. In addition to the Bible, these texts reflect the influence of Jerome and Eusebius as well as the *Liber generationis*. Each has a very complicated manuscript history. Perhaps the most remarkable aspect of this material's entry into Frankia is that it likely originated in Greek Byzantium and found its way to the Latin West, probably in the context of diplomatic activity.

EXAMPLE 6: THE *ALEXANDRIAN WORLD CHRONICLE*; *EXCERPTA LATINA BARBARI/BARBARUS SCALIGERI*

The first of these documents goes by several names. Best known as the *Excerpta Latina Barbari* or the *Barbarus Scaligeri*, the work derives from an *Alexandrian World Chronicle* composed in Greek in the late fifth or early sixth century, to which some Roman consular lists were added.[104] Translated into Latin probably in the late sixth century, when diplomatic exchange between Frankia and Constantinople was growing in importance, the document evidently was an attempt to connect Roman and Frankish history. Noah and his progeny appear in the first chapter and are directly tied to the Babel story. As the chronicle explains, "And from the flood of Noah to the building of the tower and the confusion of languages there are six generations, or 558 years. These are the sons of Noah: Shem, Ham, and Japheth."[105]

[202]   CHAPTER 6

This unremarkable information could have come directly from the Bible or from an intermediary. Later in his account, the author easily includes Romans as descendants of Japheth.[106] The compiler had a good source of early Roman history, but his Frankish hand is revealed by the inclusion of the mythical Francus Silvius as one of the Alban kings who ruled Latium after Aeneas and before Romulus.[107]

EXAMPLE 7: THE "FRANKISH TABLE OF NATIONS"

The second document to consider is the so-called *Frankish Table of Nations*.[108] Despite its name, the shaping hand of the biblical TN is only dimly felt. Instead, the table of nations that it offers is that of Germanic peoples of northern Europe divided among the three sons of Mannus, the son of the god Tuisto. The names of the three sons, Eminio, Inguo, and Istio, derive from Tacitus's *Germania*, which was composed around the year 100.[109] The names listed in the Frankish Table, however, refer to populations of the sixth century. The Frankish Table pulls contemporary peoples into an established narrative.

Though its significance lies in Frankish contexts, the text is not itself Frankish. Like the *Excerpta Latina Barbari*, it probably was written in Constantinople in the sixth century.[110] When and how it reached the West is uncertain.[111] Eight versions of the text survive in different manuscripts, leading Walter Goffart to observe that "the Table is a 'texte vivant,' which copyists handled with considerable freedom."[112] The manuscripts contain different catalogues of Roman and Frankish rulers reflecting the status quo when each was composed. Helmut Reimitz observes, "Clearly both manuscripts were shaped by reflections on how to define the relations of Frankish and Roman history in the Carolingian period. It is tempting, however, to see the text that appears in the Carolingian manuscripts as an appropriation and continuation of older efforts, already evident centuries earlier, to synthesize a Roman, Gallic, and Frankish past."[113] Goffart rightly sees the biblical TN in the background of this "Frankish" table. One manuscript makes the connection explicit: "Alanus, from the lineage of Japheth, was the first man to come to Europe."[114]

EXAMPLE 8: THE *CHRONICLE OF FREDEGAR*

Stefan Esders and Helmut Reimitz have recently discussed how the seventh-century Frankish *Chronicle of Fredegar* drew from Jerome's *Chronicle* and the *Liber generationis* as well as other works.[115] The Frankish chronicle, the product of several hands, which went from the beginning of the world to 642, altered Jerome's text, and changed how the material appeared on the page. Its compilers turned their back on the structure originated by Eusebius and continued by Jerome. They deliberately dislodged the Christian Roman Empire as the culmination of historical development of ancient peoples.[116] This represents a most important moment in the Franks' conceptionalization of their history. Frankish elites were starting a new chapter to begin where Rome has ended. The document also demonstrates the adaptability and utility of Jerome's chronicle and the continuity of the chronicle tradition long after the collapse of the Roman West. New peoples could identify themselves and find a place in the chronological narrative even if the biblical Table of Nations itself were not directly invoked.[117]

The Table of Nations in the East

Several Greek and Syriac writers show how the Table of Nations was put to use in the eastern Mediterranean world.

EXAMPLE 9: JACOB OF EDESSA AND THE TABLE OF NATIONS IN THE SYRIAC WORLD

Looking beyond areas of Roman control, we see how the TN was adjusted to contemporary needs in different cultural regions. The TN enjoyed special popularity in Late Antiquity among Christians writing in Syriac.[118] A striking example of how it was adapted to contemporary circumstances occurs in the work of Jacob of Edessa (ca. 540–680), an extremely influential polymath monk who wrote in the years soon after the Islamic conquest of Syria.[119] As the Monophysite/Miaphysite Christian community found its footing under the Muslim regime, a concern to establish its historical identity in biblical terms took on new urgency. In a letter included in a Syriac manuscript now in the British Library,[120] Jacob altered the treatment of the distribution of the land of Canaan found in the Jewish texts that were his sources, by allotting Canaan to the Arameans (and Ludites), whom, as the descendants of Aram, he considered the first Syrians.[121] In doing so he revised older Jewish notions that Arpachshad, the son of Shem and the grandson of Noah, was the progenitor of his people and that Syriac, not Hebrew, was the original human tongue.[122] In this case we see the TN tradition revised—and Jews displaced—in order to legitimate the primacy of the Christian Syriac language and religious culture.

EXAMPLE 10: ISHO'DAD OF MERV

Though considerably beyond the chronological coverage of this book, as an indication of the long-lasting interest in TN and Babel among Christian communities outside the Greek- and Latin-speaking worlds, the Syriac commentaries of Isho'dad of Merv stand out. This mid-ninth-century bishop of Hdatta, in modern Turkmenistan, wrote commentaries on the Old and New Testaments that "present the most expansive form of East-Syriac biblical interpretation."[123] Drawing widely from both Greek and Syriac exegetical sources, Isho'dad had lasting influence in the Syriac world.[124]

[204] CHAPTER 6

Isho'dad follows the tripartite division of world and lists the number of the offspring of Noah's sons: he places Japheth and fifteen of his descendants and their progeny in the North and part of the West.[125] Shem's twenty-four sons are given the East and part of the Southeast of the world; the thirty offspring of Ham inhabit the South and a small part of the West. He mentions the blessing of Shem and his descendants by Noah and the curse of Ham and his descendants (Gen. 9:25–26).[126] This totals seventy-two peoples in the world. The equivalences of the offspring of Noah's sons include many postbiblical peoples, such as Romans, Goths, and Arabs.[127] In these matters, Isho'dad is unexceptional.

His comments on language, however, pertain entirely to his own day. Isho'dad introduces a debate about the original language, stating that while some believe the language in which God spoke to Adam was Hebrew,[128] according to others the original language was Syriac, in a pure and uncontaminated form.[129] He says Hebrew was not one of the seventy-two languages given after Babel. Hebrew was instead a composite language introduced by Abraham, a fusion of his Babylonian/Aramean birth language and the Canaanite spoken in the land where he eventually settled, for the language of immigrants is always corrupted by contact with other languages. In fact, he says, Hebrew and Canaanite are the same language. The pure, original Syriac also had gradually become corrupted in Babylon. In the face of these two adulterated tongues, God decided to give the Scriptures in Hebrew (and not Syriac, Isho'dad implies), not because of the inherent dignity of the language or the extent of its spread, but because it was appropriate for them to be in the language that the Hebrews spoke, and not in the language of some crude and ill-suited group, i.e., barbarians.

External Nations

New peoples confronting Rome on the world stage continued to test the resilience and adaptability of the TN in Late Antiquity. Their presence demanded explanation, and the TN was the perfect means to do so.[130] The entry of newcomers into the Roman sphere required that additional names be ascribed to locate them on the Christian mental map. To illustrate how the TN adjusted to new faces and new political groupings from beyond imperial borders, this chapter looks first at the story of Gog and Magog and the peoples of the steppe who were given a place in Christian apocalyptic writing. Then it examines the emergence of Arabs as the descendants of Ishmael. Finally, it considers the case of the Franks.

EXAMPLE 11: THE GOG AND MAGOG TRADITION: GENEALOGY AND ESCHATOLOGY COMBINE[131]

The biblical names Gog and Magog came to play a significant role in late antique Christian ethnography and were the subject of considerable discussion in the Greek, Latin, and Syriac realms. They were associated with

CHRISTIANITY AND THE DESCENDANTS OF NOAH   [205]

geography and with eschatology, in different combinations[132] and with growing frequency.[133] Late antique usage often conflated the genealogical information in Genesis with eschatological material in Ezekiel. Discussion of Gog and
Magog did much to enliven ethnographic discussion and made a significant
contribution to the Byzantine worldview.[134] Christian writers identified these
names with various contemporary peoples, usually originating on the steppes
and usually in apocalyptic scenarios, though some writers denied such connections. Jews also put the names to use for their own purposes. This range
of application again demonstrates the adaptability and utility of the TN in
various late antique contexts.

BACKGROUND

Genesis 10:2 places Magog in the Table of Nations. It names Magog (Gog is not
mentioned) as one of the three sons of Japheth, the son of Noah whose progeny populated lands to the north and east. The precise locations of the lands
they inhabited are not indicated by the biblical redactor.[135] Magog in Genesis reflects regional Jewish geographical understanding during the monar-
chic period, tenth to ninth century BCE. Greek traditions of ethnography and
geography themselves had not yet matured and played no part in the Genesis
redactor's worldview.

Two centuries later, Ezekiel referred to Gog of the land of Magog, in an
apocalyptic context.[136] Ezekiel was a priest writing in Babylonia in the 570s
BCE, attempting to explain to the exiled Jewish community that the destruction of the Jerusalem Temple in 586 BCE had been God's punishment for
their injustice and impurity of worship. Though aware of Genesis, he shows
no interest in the lineage of Gog. God's power is universal, he explains, and
even the peoples in the farthest corners of the earth (i.e., Gog of the land of
Magog) will be destroyed by divine power if they act against God's plans for
peace. Ezekiel 38:14–15 paints the eschatological scenario:

> Thus said the Lord God: Surely, on that day, when My people Israel
> are living secure, you will "take note," and you will come from your
> home in the farthest north, you and many people with you—all of
> them mounted on horses, a vast horde, a mighty army—and you will
> advance upon My people Israel, like a cloud covering the earth. This
> shall happen on that distant day: I will bring you to My land, that the
> nations may know Me when, before their eyes, I manifest My holiness
> through you, O Gog! . . . [18–23]: On that day, when Gog sets foot on
> the soil of Israel—declares the Lord God—My raging anger shall flare
> up. For I have decreed in my indignation and in my blazing wrath: On
> that day, a terrible earthquake shall befall the land of Israel. The fish
> of the sea, the birds of the sky, the beasts of the field, all creeping things
> that move on the ground, and every human being on earth shall quake

before Me. Mountains shall be overthrown, cliffs shall topple, every wall shall crumble to the ground . . . And every man's sword shall be turned against his brother . . . and they shall know that I am the Lord.

In verse 39, God punishes Gog:

I am going to deal with you, O Gog, chief prince of Meshech and Tubal. I will turn you around and drive you on, and I will take you from the far north and lead you toward the mountains of Israel. I will strike your bow from your left hand and I will loosen the arrows from your bow . . . I will send a fire against Magog.[137]

Several centuries later, in the Hellenistic Age, about 150–120 BCE, the author of the pseudoepigraphal Book of Jubilees brought Jewish and Greek geographical traditions together when he located the land of Gog north of the River Don (8:25–30).[138]

Thus, by the end of the intertestamental period, Gog and Magog offered writers two separate but not incompatible interpretations. They could be identified with specific peoples, and they could be employed in eschatological schemes. Eventually, Christian writers brought these two possibilities together by the end of the late antique period.

Ezekiel served as the "pre-text" for New Testament writings. The apocalyptic symbolism that its author introduced would be picked up and developed by Christian writers. The Book of Revelation, also known as the Apocalypse of John, composed near the end of the first century CE, some six hundred years after Ezekiel, is a full-blown apocalyptic text, but it is no longer concerned with the Babylonian destruction of Solomon's Temple in Jerusalem.[139] Instead, it is keyed to a Christian plan of history in which the Roman destruction of the Second Temple in 70 CE marked a turning point, after which Satan would eventually usher in the End of Days. Gog and Magog have become separate geographical but not ethnic entities: "And when the thousand years are expired, Satan shall be loosed out his prison, and shall go out to deceive the nations which are in the four quarters of the earth, Gog, and Magog, to gather them together to battle: the number of whom is as the sand of the sea."[140] What must be emphasized here is that none of these three texts, Genesis, Ezekiel, or Revelation,[141] identifies Gog and Magog with a specific place or people. That would change, first of all among Jewish writers. The turning point was the failed Jewish rebellion against Rome in 70 CE, which ended with the destruction of Jerusalem and the devastation of the province of Judaea.

Josephus, in his account *Jewish Antiquities*, was the first author known to have identified Magog with Scythians, the generic term for peoples of the Eurasian steppe.[142] He wrote at the very end of the first century, making him a contemporary of the author of Revelation. Josephus, however, is not telling an eschatological story.[143] His mention of steppe peoples carries far less cargo.

CHRISTIANITY AND THE DESCENDANTS OF NOAH [207]

The different task Josephus had set himself was to make Jewish history and culture accessible to a Greco-Roman audience. With a foot in both Jewish and Greco-Roman literary traditions, he could draw freely from Greek ethnography, as for example with his use of "Scythian," a term used by Herodotus half a millennium earlier, when treating biblical material. This is significant, because his attempt to bridge two cultural vocabularies in ethnographic and geographical contexts would be a template of sorts for later Christian writers who needed to identify biblical names with contemporary peoples and places, though obviously for Christian and not Jewish or Roman audiences.

Jewish writers after Josephus were largely uninterested in Roman readers and rarely associated Gog and Magog with groups in the Greco-Roman ethnographic tradition. Sometimes, however, the Roman Empire was labeled Gog because of its hostility to Jews.[144] Nevertheless, the evidence indicates that the theme of Gog and Magog as apocalyptic agents in the End of Days was widespread in Jewish thought of the imperial period, though they were not particularly identified with specific enemies of the day.[145] It was enough for Jews to understand that the Messiah would eventually overcome Gog and Magog.[146]

Christian writers drew on the TN tradition in Genesis and the eschatological tradition emerging from Ezekiel differently than did Jews. The best example, as noted above, comes from the book of Revelation. It integrates Ezekiel's apocalyptic vision with an emerging Christian salvation plan of history, in which Gog and Magog play a role in the End of Days. They are not equated with specific contemporary peoples.[147] Then a curious silence fell. Christian writers did not pay much attention to Gog and Magog through the fourth century.[148] Although many of the Apostolic Fathers held millennial beliefs, they did not refer to Gog and Magog.[149] Even Lactantius (ca. 250–325), who combined details from Ezekiel 38–39 with the vision of the Antichrist and the last war with Gog found in Rev. 20:7–10, did not mention them by name.[150]

By the end of the fourth century, however, the situation began to change as the intensity of external threats to Rome increased. Christian Romans not only wanted to find biblical origins for their new enemies, they sought biblical explanation for their disruptive presence.[151] Eschatological literature accordingly enjoyed a new vogue.[152] Gog and Magog were mentioned with growing frequency, and Gog was sometimes identified as the Antichrist.[153]

The Goths, as well as other peoples of the North, frequently were identified as Gog[154] because of the similarity of the names. Bishop Ambrose of Milan penned a treatise "On Faith" addressed to the Western emperor Gratian (r. 375–83) prior to the Battle of Adrianople in 378, and then he hurriedly revised it after a force of Goths destroyed most of the army of the eastern empire in that battle. In light of the catastrophe, Ambrose readily identified the Goths with Gog, explaining that Ezekiel had foretold the calamitous defeat.[155] "On Faith" went on to attack Arianism, a creed that many Italians had accepted, as well as the Goths, who were causing havoc in the Balkans after Adrianople. The bishop famously declared that "Gog iste Gothus est (Gog is the Goth)" after quoting Ezekiel 38.14, thereby combining a specific identification of a contemporary people and a crisis of his day with a biblical archetype.[156] He places the Goths in an eschatological Christian understanding of history.[157] Ambrose depicted the danger posed by people originating at the western edge of the steppes in the strongest language available to him, that of biblical prophecy.

Many writers accepted this identification of Goths and Gog,[158] but there were important dissenters.[159] Jerome refused to make the connection.[160] Augustine of Hippo also strongly opposed any such identification, but for a different reason.[161] When discussing the End of Days in his *City of God*, he cautions:

> For those nations, called Gog and Magog, are not to be understood as being some barbarian people dwelling in some part of the earth, whether the Getae and Massagetae, as some guess because of the initial letters of their names, or some other peoples, not of our stock and remote from the rule of Rome; for it is indicated that they exist throughout the whole earth, when to the words "the nations that are in the four corners of the earth" it is added that these are Gog and Magog . . . And the words: "And they went up over the breadth of the earth, and encompassed the camp of the saints and the beloved city" surely do not mean that they have come or are to come to a single place, as if the camp of the saints and the beloved city were to be in some single place; for these are nothing else than the church of Christ spread throughout the whole world. Therefore wherever the church shall then be, which is to be among all nations . . . there shall be the camp of the saints.[162]

Augustine meant that at the End of Days, Satan and his minions would appear everywhere to confront an equally universal Church. Gog and Magog stand for all of those demonic forces and should not be identified as individual peoples.[163]

Despite such high-powered opposition, the identification of Gog and Magog with Goths stuck and became widespread among Greek and Latin writers across the Mediterranean.[164] By the sixth century, invoking Gog and Magog had become a staple of explanation among Christian writers. In Greek Constantinople, mention of the biblical figures is lacking in self-consciously classicizing genres, even those written by Christians. We do not find Magog in Procopius, for example. In the seventh century, during the reign of Heraclius, however, the author of the *Easter Chronicle*,[165] drawing from the Table of Nations tradition, related that some people of his day believe that Magog, the son of Japheth and grandson of Noah, was the ancestor of the Goths, Sarmatians, and Scythians, that is to say, all the peoples of the steppe.

CHRISTIANITY AND THE DESCENDANTS OF NOAH [209]

Near the end of the century, on the other side of the Mediterranean, Isidore of Seville identified the Goths as Magog in his *Etymologies*,[166] even though in many other matters he followed Augustine. As noted above, Isidore's synthesis reveals the state of knowledge available to a learned Christian two centuries after Spain had ceased to be a Roman province. His geographical horizons are broad, reaching into Central Asia, and he knows the Alexander Romance, which we will look at more closely in a moment. The chief foundation of his discussion, however, is the Bible, as would be expected of a cleric. He reported that "The Goths are thought to have been named after Magog, the son of Japheth, because of the similarity of the last syllable. The ancients called them Getae rather than Goths. They are a brave and most powerful people, tall and massive in body, terrifying for the kind of arms they use."[167]

As noted above, these remarks are part of his section called "Concerning the names of nations," which combines a survey of peoples with shaky etymological insights. In keeping with Genesis, Isidore reports that Noah's offspring generated seventy-two peoples with an equal number of languages.[168] He adds a wealth of secular learning as well as contemporary events to an extended discussion of the descendants of Noah's sons. His comments on the Avars, for example, show how he brought a variety of nonbiblical traditions up-to-date in his *Etymologies*.[169] He explains that because the Avars are descendants of the Huns (through the name of a king) they are Scythian peoples.[170] They once lived beyond the Maeotic Lake but burst through the Caucasus and Alexander's Gates to terrorize the East for twenty years. In Isidore's hands, the Avars as part of Noah's lineage have found a place in a Christian frame.

Associating steppe peoples with Gog and Magog continued to be irresistible. Syriac writers saw them as Huns and fused them with the story of Alexander's Gate.[171] Theodore the Syncellos, a churchman and chronicler, thought the Avars to be Gog during their siege of Constantinople in 626.[172] Since then, Gog and Magog have been identified as Arabs, Turks, Slavs, Khazars, Magyars, Mongols, and others, even up to the present day.[173]

THE *ALEXANDER ROMANCE*

A third-century novel came to play a significant part in Christian discussion of Gog and Magog. Called the *Alexander Romance*, this entertaining tale, composed by an anonymous Greek author known as Pseudo-Callisthenes, contained many fanciful stories gleaned from many sources, about Alexander the Great.[174] It enjoyed wide popularity and soon was translated into Latin, Armenian, Coptic, Ethiopic, and Arabic. Among the many marvels that it recounts is Alexander's construction of an iron gate somewhere in the Caucasus Mountains to block invasions of savages from the northern steppes.[175] By the fifth century such invaders were identified as the armies of Gog and Magog in the Christian apocalyptic tradition,[176] probably in response to an invasion of Huns through the Caucasus in 395, as mentioned above.[177]

A translation into Syriac appeared about 630, in which Gog and Magog played a role accompanied by a host of demons restrained by Alexander's Gate:[178]

> Alexander said, "Who are the nations within this mountain upon which we are looking?" . . . The natives of the land said, "They are the Huns." He said to them, "Who are their kings?" The old men said: "Gôg and Mâgôg and Nâawâl the kings of the sons of Japhet." . . . The king [Alexander] said, "Let us make a gate of brass and close up this breach."[179]

Alexander then carved a prophecy into the gate:

> The Huns shall go forth and conquer the countries of the Romans and of the Persians, and they shall cast arrows . . . and shall return and enter their own land. Also I have written that, at the conclusion of eight hundred and twenty-six years, the Huns shall go forth by the narrow way which goes forth opposite Halôrâs, whence the Tigris goes forth like the stream which turns a mill, and they shall take captive the nations, and shall cut off the roads, and shall make the earth tremble by their going forth. And again I have written and made known and prophesied that it shall come to pass, at the conclusion of nine hundred and forty years . . . another king, when the world shall come to an end by the command of God the ruler of creation.[180]

The story spread quickly, adjusting to recent events. Across the Mediterranean, for example, a Frankish chronicler around the year 660 suggested that Heraclius had deliberately opened Alexander's Gate to allow barbarian mercenaries from the steppes to join his armies engaged in fighting Muslim Arabs.[181]

Gog and Magog flourished in Byzantine apocalyptic literature. The most significant Byzantine apocalyptic text is that of Pseudo-Methodius, written in the seventh century in Syriac and preserved in Latin, Greek, and Old Church Slavonic versions.[182] It reflects hostility to the enemies of the day and displays a marked anti-Arab attitude by identifying the sons of Ishmael (Arabs) with Gog and Magog. Pseudo-Methodius lists various nations held in check by Alexander's Gate and attributes abominable practices like cannibalism to them. The story says that these barbarians will burst through the gate and play a role in the last phase of human history, leading in different versions to their destruction by God, an archangel, or the last Roman emperor.[183] The text reveals a complete interpenetration of Gog and Magog with biblical genealogy and contemporary events. Its apocalyptic vision became hugely popular in the Middle Ages and placed a distinctively late antique stamp on perception of steppe peoples.[184]

CHRISTIANITY AND THE DESCENDANTS OF NOAH [211]

Steppe nomads found nothing attractive in being called Gog and Magog and did not internalize the identity for themselves. In strong contrast, other nomadic outsiders whom Christian Romans came to call Ishmaelites did accept that label ascribed to them, and it is to them we now turn.

EXAMPLE 12: ISHMAELITES, FROM ASCRIPTION TO SELF-IDENTIFICATION

This section considers how late antique Christians came to perceive the quite distinct groups of nomadic and semi-nomadic peoples living in the Near East as Ishmaelites, the descendants of Ishmael, first mentioned in the book of Genesis.[185] Ishmael was the disavowed eldest son of Abraham and his slave, Hagar,[186] and ultimately descended from Shem, Noah's son.[187] In this way the people who became known as Ishmaelites obtained a common lineage and a place in the elaborated TN scheme of the world's peoples. It gave them a new position in relation to Christians and the Christian Roman state.

The Ishmaelites represent a remarkable Late Antique phenomenon, the acceptance of a label of identity ascribed by an outside group. The name *Ishmaelites* provided many quite diverse groups in Arabia and adjacent lands with a unifying lineage within which to place themselves, centuries before the rise of Islam.[188] Participation in the Abrahamic tradition eventually became a central claim of adherents of Islam. As descendants of Abraham and Hagar, they entered the TN genealogy. This identity was something Christians, Jews, and Muslims could agree on. Muslim self-understanding in this regard proved to be as consequential historically as the adoption of Christianity by the majority of the population of the Roman Empire. The example of the Ishmaelites shows how biblical genealogy became an integral part of the development of late antique identities, Muslim as well as Christian and Jewish. In other words, a place in the TN genealogy, that is, participation in the myth of descent from Noah, had emerged as a key ethnographic marker in the conceptual repertoire of the Christian-Roman state. To understand these developments, we must consider the interconnected story of three ethnonyms: Ishmaelite, Saracen, and Arab.

ARABS, SARACENS, AND ISHMAELITES: HISTORICAL BACKGROUND

The nomadic and semi-nomadic populations of lands from Syria to the Euphrates and the Arabian Peninsula (some were urbanized as well) had contact to different extents with neighboring settled empires for two millennia before Romans appeared on the scene. Arabic in some form had become the predominant language. It is conventional today to refer to these Arabic speakers collectively as Arabs even though this misrepresents a far more complicated

[212] CHAPTER 6

reality.[189] The term *Arab* first appears in the historical records of the Assyrian empire around 1100 BCE, during the reign of Tiglath-Pileser I.[190] By this time Arabic language in various dialects had displaced Aramaic as the tongue of different nomadic and seminomadic groups within the Assyrian sphere of influence from Syria to the Euphrates.[191] Later records show that Tiglath-Pileser III, ca. 738, received tribute from a "Queen of the Arabs." Shortly thereafter, another "Arab" queen, Shamsi, led a federation against him.[192] Whether the term *Arab* at this early point was a tribal self-ascription or a more generic term remains unclear. It may have started as the former and become the latter.[193] While these groups over a broad area may have had much in common linguistically and in terms of lifeways and social organization, there is no evidence of a widespread understanding of common identity as one Arab people. Most scholars today avoid a pan-Arab racial identification that is a product of modern nationalism and outmoded science.[194]

CLASSICAL USAGE

By the classical Greco-Roman period, writers had come to understand as Arabs a wide variety of Arabic-speaking groups on the edges of the Hellenistic kingdoms.[195] Direct Roman involvement in the region continued from the time of the late Republic.[196] How the Romans imposed a degree of conceptual order and descriptive vocabulary upon the variety of peoples and polities within the vast region where Arabic dialects were spoken is the implicit ethnographic question.

In the imperial period, the use of the term *Arab* took on a more limited scope with the establishment of the Roman *provincia Arabia* by Trajan in 106.[197] The inhabitants of the province, regardless of their ethnic background, acquired the name "Arabs," which applied only to them.

At about the same time, the term *Saracen* came into use as another ethnographic label applied to nomads and seminomad peoples living in territories beyond the Roman province of Arabia and the empire.[198] The great scientist Ptolemy (d. ca. 168) provides the first known recorded mention of Saracens (*Sarakenoi/Saraceni*) in his *Geography*,[199] specifically as inhabitants of a portion of the northern Sinai region,[200] but they are just one group among many listed as occupants of the region. As conflict between Saracens and Rome increased due to Roman pressure on the Red Sea region from the late third century onward,[201] references to Saracens appeared more frequently in contemporary sources. The term continued in general, but not exclusive, use throughout Late Antiquity.[202] In the *Notitia Dignitatum* (see discussion in chapter 3), compiled in the late fourth and early fifth centuries, Saracens appear as units in the Roman army, and they are distinguished from Arabs who constitute other units.[203] This indicates specific application of the term in different contexts.

CHRISTIANITY AND THE DESCENDANTS OF NOAH   [213]

A number of writers, both Christian and pagan, drew similar distinctions. For example, early notices appear in works attributed to Hippolytus (above) and Bardaisan (see chapter 4) in the early third century. The shadowy figure Uranius, who probably lived in the fourth century, wrote a treatise called *Arabica*, now known only in fragments but full of timely detail.[204] These men distinguish among three major groups, whom they call Arabs, Saracens, and Taenoi.[205] The Taenoi or Ṭayyi', constituted a large and powerful tribe in pre-Islamic times. Syriac sources used their name (*Tayyāyē*) generically for Arabs.[206]

Ammianus Marcellinus, on the other hand, was content to generalize. Before he began to write history, he had been a well-traveled officer in the Roman army in the 360s and a participant in Julian's eastern campaigns. His historical account contains a wealth of general information about different Saracen groups.[207] A missing portion of his history discussed Saracens during the reign of Marcus Aurelius, but a rather long excursus about Saracens survives with a good deal of ethnographic detail[208] as well as a lengthy geographical description on the Scenitae or "tent-dwelling" Arabs who, he tells us, were later called Saracens.[209] Ammianus is aware of the change of "Arab" to "Saracen" over time. His treatment is all the more important because he was not Christian. Saracen was a religiously neutral term and carried no genealogical implications like those associated with "Ishmaelite."[210] In the sixth century, Procopius of Caesarea, a Christian who wrote in a classicizing style, uses the term *Saracen* for various allies and enemies caught up in the emperor's great struggle with Sasanian Persia.[211]

While the word *Saracen* could be applied quite specifically as well as rather broadly, there has been a difference of opinion since antiquity about the derivation of the word itself.[212] This is where the TN and Ishmael came into play.

ISHMAELITES

As noted, Ishmael appears in the book of Genesis.[213] His offspring are named in chapter 17:25, and the term Ishmaelite was used to refer to their descendants in general by Jewish and Christian writers in the Roman period but never by pagan authors.

JEWISH USE: BIBLICAL AND EXTRABIBLICAL

Arabs and Ishmaelites are both mentioned in the Bible, but they are not treated as equivalents and do not occur concurrently.[214] "Arab" indicates only a nomadic way of life and has no genealogical associations.[215] The story begins in Gen. 17 and 21, which tell how Abraham and his slave Hagar had a son called Ishmael. Mother and son were sent away into the desert by Abraham, who preferred Isaac, his son by his first wife, Sarah. In the Genesis tale, God

[214] CHAPTER 6

reassures Abraham: "And as for Ishmael, I have heard thee: Behold, I have blessed him, and will make him fruitful, and will multiply him exceedingly; twelve princes shall he beget, and I will make him a great nation."[216] We are not told who will constitute that nation or where it will be located. There is no explicit connection made with Arabs in any sense of the term.[217]

Extrabiblical texts also do not make a clear connection between Ishmaelites and Arabs. Jubilees 14–15 might identify Arabs with Ishmaelites,[218] but the text as we have it today is based on later Latin and Ethiopic versions of a Greek text, which itself goes back to a Hebrew original. Because none of the original Hebrew text survives, we cannot be certain that the identification of Arab and Ishmaelite occurred in the original version.

The most important moment in the identification of Arab and Ishmaelite comes with Flavius Josephus, who wrote after the destruction of the Second Temple in Jerusalem in 70. He was the first Jewish writer on record to have developed the identification of Ishmaelites and Arabs. In his *Jewish Antiquities*, according to Fergus Millar, Josephus made a "decisive editorial intervention . . . not only locat[ing] the relevant peoples in the contemporary world but stress[ing] their relationship to Abraham."[219] He elaborates on the Septuagint text by saying that the people of Arabia (Ἀράβων ἔθνος) were the sons of Ishmael[220] and he describes Arab traders as being Ishmaelites.[221] According to him, Ishmaelites in his day inhabited lands from the Euphrates to the Red Sea, far beyond their location in the Bible. Josephus's ideas would have enormous influence on Christian authors and eventually on Islam.[222]

Before the advent of Islam, Jewish writers of the third through sixth centuries showed little interest in the figure of Ishmael. When mentioned, Ishmael and his descendants figured abstractly as an unworthy contrast to the righteous children of Israel. After the rise of Islam in the seventh century, however, Ishmael became "the eponymous prototype of Islam,"[223] which was a dangerous threat to the Roman state.

CHRISTIAN USE

By the middle of the third century, Christian writers had started to wonder about what Fergus Millar has called the "historic religious identity"[224] of the Ishmaelites. Many of them took up the identification of Ishmaelites and Saracens made by Josephus in his *Jewish Antiquities*.[225] "Ishmaelites" became the standard way for Christian writers to refer to Arabs by the late fourth century, a period during which conversion to Christianity among Saracens/Arabs was increasing.[226]

As was so often the case, Eusebius of Caesarea proved to be an important conduit of these ideas. He accepted Josephus's identification of Arabs and the sons of Ishmael. Although his discussion in the *Preparatio Evangelica* (*Preparation for the Gospel*) is quite brief, its influence on subsequent Christian

CHRISTIANITY AND THE DESCENDANTS OF NOAH   [215]

writers was far-reaching. Written in Greek in the early fourth century, the treatise intended to introduce Christianity to a pagan audience by explaining the superiority of the new religion to their worship. Eusebius reports that:

> [Abraham] having taken two wives, the one of his own country and kindred, and the other an Egyptian handmaiden, he begat by the Egyptian twelve sons, who went off into Arabia and divided the land among them, and were the first who reigned over the people of the country: from which circumstance there are even in our own day twelve kings of the Arabians, bearing the same names as the first.[227]

The identification meant something different to Christians than it did to Jews, however. For Christians, the Saracen connection to Ishmael and Abraham was not simply entry into a biblical lineage, it was a key to their conversion. On the part of Christians, this development reflects an attempt to bring the new converts into the grand scheme of Christian ethnographic identification. At the same time, Saracen converts started thinking about themselves in terms of the biblical lineage that came with conversion.[228] Millar suggests that the mounting competition between Rome and Sasanian Persia for the support of Saracen tribes may have influenced the emphasis of their putative relationship to Ishmael and Abraham among Christian writers.[229]

An alternative account of the descent of some Arabs from Abraham appeared in Late Antiquity as well. This version made Chettura, a wife of Abraham after Sarah's death, the ancestor of various peoples, including the Himyarites and Sabaeans of South Arabia.[230]

The fifth century marked a turning point. The Abrahamic lineage of Saracens acquired increased weight in the pious Theodosian era as a passport to Christian conversion. It was more than just a lineage. Millar astutely observed that in two fifth-century church historians,[231]

> We see the fundamental conceptual shift from a mere acceptance of the mythical descent of Saracens, or Ishmaelites, from Abraham to an acknowledgement that this descent gave a special motivation and justification for the preaching of Christianity among them—and by implication the recognition of the justice or appropriateness of any claim by Ishmaelites to the inheritance of Abraham. Both indeed make clear that this proposition was explicitly proclaimed to Ishmaelites by Christians.[232]

In this regard, Sozomen warrants a closer look. He was born near Gaza and knew Arabic and Syriac as well as Greek.[233] In his *Church History*, which continued Eusebius's work from 324 to 425, he showed an interest in the spread of Christianity among non-Roman peoples.[234] He rejected the derivation of "Saracen" from "Sarah," a divergence from the standard lineage that Jerome had accepted.[235] Sozomen wrote:

This is the tribe which took its origin and has its name from Ishmael, the son of Abraham; and the ancients called them Ishmaelites after their progenitor. As their mother Hagar was a slave, they afterwards, to conceal the opprobrium of their origin, assumed the name of Saracens, as if they were descended from Sara, the wife of Abraham. Such being their origin, they practice circumcision like the Jews, refrain from the use of pork, and observe many other Jewish rites and customs. If, indeed, they deviate in any respect from the observations of that nation, it must be ascribed to the lapse of time, and their intercourse with the neighboring nations . . . Some of their tribe, afterwards happening to come in contact with the Jews, gathered from them the facts of their true origin, returned to their kinsmen, and inclined to the Hebrew customs and laws. From that time on, until now, many of them regulate their lives according to the Jewish precepts. Some of the Saracens were converted to Christianity not long before the present reign.[236]

Millar emphasizes that in this passage Sozomen fabricates a religious history for the Ishmaelites in which they maintained a few aspects of their original Jewish practice, such as circumcision and avoidance of pork. He notes that Sozomen also denies the connection to Sarah, and he implies that Saracens have in his own day rediscovered Jewish origins through contact with Jews.[237] More than any other Christian writer of his day, as Millar points out, Sozomen viewed Saracens' lineage from Ishmael as significant in their conversion.[238] Clearly, in Sozomen's mind, Saracens are ripe for conversion on a larger scale.

A century later in the West, we find two conflicting statements of origin for the line of Ishmael, though both are within the Table of Nations tradition. Isidore of Seville, who died in 636, discussed Ishmaelites in his *Etymologies*, which drew on many sources.[239] He gave almost all the earth's people a biblical origin, but for others, like the Romans, Greeks, and Trojans, he must have drawn from a non-Christian source that he did not try to integrate with the TN tradition. He does identify Ishmaelites, however, with Saracens and Hagarenes. He says that the name *Saracen* is a corruption of *Sarah*, or perhaps of *Syrian*. He seems to view Hagarenes as a separate group descending from Hagar.[240] However, he diverges from the usual treatment of the Abrahamic branch of the sons of Noah by calling Arabs the descendants of Ham rather than of Shem.[241] Presumably this is because Ham had been cursed by his father, Noah, and his descendants perpetuated the malediction. Isidore's near contemporary, the unknown compiler of the *Chronicle of Fredegar*, on the other hand, maintains the traditional lineage and says Arabs are the descendants of Shem.[242]

ARAB USE OF "ISHMAELITES"

The examples so far have provided some representative Christian views of Arabs/Saracens/Ishmaelites. We must also consider how these non-Roman populations came to see themselves within the biblical tradition. The process was long, slow, and quite difficult to discern. In the centuries before the rise of Islam, interaction with Jews and Christians in Arabia, Syria, and Mesopotamia heightened awareness of biblical stories, especially the Ishmael story, among local pagan communities.

The late antique Near East was an extraordinarily complex environment, in religious no less than political, economic, or social terms, which makes unraveling the appeal of biblical genealogy to local groups quite difficult. The problem is compounded by the near absence of historical documentation, most of which is, as Fred Donner puts is, "retrospective rather than contemporary," after-the-fact products of established Islamic communities.[243] On the basis of onomastic evidence, René Dagorn has argued that before Islam, the tradition of descent from Hagar and Ishmael was not widespread among Arabs,[244] a conclusion widely shared today. Only during the Islamic period, and not immediately, did the Ishmael story become definitive.[245]

We can say with a certain confidence, however, that during the fourth and fifth centuries, as Christian communities grew, the Abrahamic lineage became more visible and attractive. Millar again provides a succinct description of the phenomenon, suggesting that "a very complex process, which had begun with ethnic ascription by others from within the Judaeo-Christian tradition, and had then developed, hesitantly, into lending, had now shifted to a fateful process of borrowing and appropriation by the 'Arabs', 'Saracens' or Ishmaelites themselves."[246] The developing self-ascription began through contact with Christians and Jews before the rise of Islam and was accomplished finally with the establishment of that religion and an accompanying understanding of Arab identity.

Not only was the original Arab/Ishmael story picked up, in Muslim hands it continued to develop. Robert Hoyland notes one example: "With it [the identification of Arab/Ishmael] they [Muslims] fashioned a religious pedigree for themselves, narrating how Ishmael and his father Abraham had gone to Mecca together and founded the original Muslim sanctuary."[247] The absorption of Abrahamic lineage into Muslim identity was another great success story of the Table of Nations.

Conclusion

The Table of Nations, with its stories of the sons of Noah and their many descendants, gave Christian Romans a remarkably flexible tool for imagining the world's human variety in the light of contemporary circumstances. As a

[218] CHAPTER 6

Christian device, it integrated peoples within a universal system of values, and it provided a new sort of intellectual continuity and connection with the rest of humanity that challenged the centrality of Rome. In this way, the TN enabled a new mental map to be drawn and a new Christian story of humankind to be written. Many of the peoples of the world—both those included among provincial populations and those beyond imperial borders—were already known to Christian Romans. Christian writers did not discard these existing Roman identifications of peoples. Instead, they were given a place in the TN lineage as descendants of one of the sons of Noah.

A second sort of peoples were those new to the late antique scene, such as the Huns, who appeared from the distant reaches of the steppe, or groups of peoples long in place but now with newly formed identities as followers of Islam. Both kinds of newcomers found a place in the Christian scheme of things, with their identities tied to biblical origins. There was a significant difference in the impact of the TN on the two kinds of groups, however. Steppe nomads did not choose to wear the mantle of agents of the Antichrist ascribed to them by Christians. Muslims, on the other hand, eventually internalized the biblical identification ascribed to them as descendants of Ishmael, son of Abraham and Hagar. The adaptability of the TN is demonstrated again in the post-Roman world by the Franks, who were deeply influenced by it as they devised a history for themselves that placed the Romans firmly in the past.

Discussion continues in the following chapter, which looks at another product of the book of Genesis, the story of the Tower of Babel. Like the TN, it offered new paradigms for understanding human diversity, though in terms of language.

CHAPTER SEVEN

Babel and the
Languages of Faith

*Let us, then, go down and confound their speech there, so they shall not
understand one another's speech.*

—GENESIS 11:7

THIS CHAPTER CONSIDERS how Christian understanding of the dispersal
of languages across the inhabited world, and the significance of differences
among them, contributed to late antique ethnography. During this transformative era, Christians began to interact with speakers of many languages and
with their texts from new perspectives.[1] In the polyvocality of their world they
found theological meaning and divine purpose unknown to traditional Roman
thought.[2] In this reevaluation, older Roman paradigms of cultural and linguistic identity were challenged and to some extent dismantled.

The book of Genesis is again the starting place for discussion. In addition to supplying the Table of Nations, which helped late antique Christians
impose order on the world's peoples through genealogy, Genesis contributed
the story of the Tower of Babel, which found order of a different sort among the
world's countless languages. The biblical account of the dispersal of languages
at God's command as interpreted by Christians contributed six interrelated
elements to the ethnographic repertoire. They enabled a fresh approach to
description, judgment, and transformation of communities, adding up to a
new perspective on the peoples of the world.

First, the Babel story provided a framing tale for the world's polyvocality,
especially that of the Roman empire. What had been an unimaginably vast
disarray of spoken tongues and peoples now made sense in a Christian narrative of history and salvation. Second, it imposed a teleology on the world's
cacophony by giving languages meaning within Christian salvation history.
Following God's gift of speech to Adam, Babel and Pentecost became milestones in the unfolding of human destiny. Third, Christian interpretations let
languages play a new role as identifiers of text-based communities of faith.
Identity formation, exegesis of sacred texts, and languages went hand in
hand, and the character of foreignness changed in important ways. Fourth,
the implications of Babel shattered the role of Latin and Greek elites as gatekeepers to the dominant culture. In this way Babel went beyond Rome and

[219]

extended the Christian franchise, enabling a new sort of universalism in which all linguistic communities could participate through the medium of Christian belief. All languages were understood to be spiritually equivalent because religious truths were accessible in any tongue, and so Babel gave new scope to a far wider range of languages than Latin and Greek. It was a worldview that did not privilege Latin and Greek. Fifth, language difference became part of the discussion of heresy, the chief diagnostic category of differentiation among Christian communities, as will be discussed in the next chapter. Sixth, angels entered the Christian ethnographic picture through association with human groups speaking their native languages after the fall of Babel. The number of nations was linked with the number of languages, and an angel guarded each nation. Discussion of each of these six elements follows, with Isidore of Seville as the primary example. His work encapsulates many of the most important late antique ideas about Babel.

Background

To appreciate the impact of Christian responses to polyvocality, some reminders are necessary. First, the Roman Empire had always existed in a fluid and robustly multilingual environment. Much of its internal population probably spoke only their own local tongue, but for a great many people, multilingualism and cross-cultural communication were standard fare.[3] This was especially true in large urban centers, which were magnets for varied populations, as well as in the army, which drew soldiers from throughout the empire and beyond. On the edges of the empire, provincial peoples necessarily dealt with foreign-language speakers and also encountered a jumble of vernaculars within imperial territory. Language in spoken and written form created many kinds of cultural boundaries to traverse. Latin, as the language of law and rule (with assistance from Greek in eastern provinces), had established many of those barriers. It is important to note, however, that even in this complex linguistic matrix, the Roman government never decreed that Latin should be the only language spoken by its subjects. Bruno Rochette sums up the situation well: "While Latin can be considered as the unifying link across the whole Roman Empire, the Romans never established an official language policy ensuring that the subjects of the empire had to learn Latin, which would have been doomed to fail. The complete story of language use during Roman history can be summed up as a compromise between Latin and Greek, while leaving space for other languages, even if there is rarely sufficient evidence to specify the details."[4] The Babel story in Christian hands gave speakers of those excluded languages new opportunities to develop literatures of their own and to find new political legitimacy in the face of the dominance of Latin and Greek power structures.

By the early empire, Latin and Greek were established as the languages of control as well as the prestige tongues that marked entry into the dominant culture.[5] They played another role as well. As Yuliya Minets explains, "They both set up an essential backdrop against which the intricate processes of identity formation unfolded, and this involved various other local languages."[6] This situation continued in Late Antiquity, which remained luxuriantly multilingual. However, as Minets alerts us, Christianity brought a broader range of domestic vernaculars, especially the languages of particular faith communities, to the forefront of imperial concerns.[7] Christian writers confronted this linguistic fragmentation directly,[8] and the story of Babel served them well.

While Late Antiquity continued to be a world of interpreters in everyday discourse and in relations with the representatives of the state,[9] Christianity's rise created the need for an additional sort of translator. Sacred texts required expert explication and rendering into other languages. The exegetes who performed these tasks of taking the truths of their faith and the texts that bore them across linguistic borders were a new kind of dragoman—religious, not just cultural. Their explanations called for a framing tale, and so the Babel story found a new role. Before turning to the ideas that shaped the framing tale, we should look at the text of the Babel story itself.

The Biblical Account of Babel

Gen. 11 provides a foundation narrative for the population of the inhabited world. Originally an independent account, the Babel story at some distant time was sandwiched within the TN story, without making overt reference to the verses that flanked it. The author of the story tells that before the Tower of Babel (Babylon) was built in the land of Shinar (southern Mesopotamia):

> Everyone on earth had the same language and the same words. And as they migrated from the east, they came upon a valley in the land of Shinar and settled there . . . And [they] said to one another, "Come, let us make bricks and burn them hard." . . . And they said, "Come, let us build us a city and a tower with its top in the sky, to make a name for ourselves, else we shall be scattered all over the world. The Lord came down to look at the city and tower that man had built, and the Lord said, "If, as one people with one language for all, this is how they have begun to act, then nothing that they may propose will be out of their reach. Let us, then, go down and confound their speech there, so that they shall not understand one another's speech." Thus the Lord scattered them from there over the face of the whole earth.[10]

[222] CHAPTER 7

The Original Purpose of the Story

The story explains that only after God destroyed the Tower did the human community speak different tongues. Language is seen as a significant marker of difference among people, but its interpretation has varied. Because Genesis makes no attempt to count the languages, and there is no reliance on the progeny of the sons of Noah to identify them, it has been surmised that the purpose of Gen. 11 was to explain the origin of human cultural difference and linguistic diversity at God's hands.[11] A more traditional interpretation, widely accepted in antiquity, gives the story a moral dimension by saying that humans reached too high in building the Tower, and that God accordingly punished their arrogance. What must matter is how late antique writers gave meaning to the story and applied it to their own circumstances.

Isidore of Seville and the Story of Babel

A mirror of late antique responses to the Babel story can be found in the work of Isidore of Seville. As he confronts his multilingual world through post-Roman eyes, we sense the presence of many earlier Christian writers looking over his shoulder who had appropriated the Babel story for their own purposes. An enthusiastic encyclopedist, Isidore was an insightful and thoughtful synthesizer of swaths of Christian and secular knowledge. As a clergyman, he paid considerable attention to the Table of Nations and Babel stories, and his treatment passed into the bloodstream of the medieval Latin world with the rest of the material he gathered. A long passage in his *Etymologies*, written at the beginning of the seventh century, points to several centuries of development of the Babel story:

> The diversity of languages arose with the building of the Tower after the Flood, for before the pride of that Tower divided human society, so that there arose a diversity of meaningful sounds, there was one language for all nations, which is called Hebrew. The patriarchs and prophets used this language not only in their speech, but also in the sacred writings. But at the outset [i.e., starting after the Babel dispersion] there were as many languages as there were nations, and then more nations than languages, because many nations sprang from one language stock . . . There are three sacred languages—Hebrew, Greek, and Latin—which are preeminent throughout the world. On the cross of the Lord the charge laid against him was written at Pilate's command in these three languages (John 19:20). Hence—and because of the obscurity of the Sacred Scriptures—a knowledge of these three languages is necessary, so that, whenever the wording of one of the

languages presents any doubt about a name or an interpretation, recourse may be had to another language.[12]

He continues, "We have treated languages first, and then nations, because nations arose from languages, and not languages from nations."[13] His comments point to a historical ethnography of language developed by late antique Christian writers.

1. Babel as a Framing Tale

Several matters of concern to Isidore help us understand the Babel story as a framing tale. The first of these is the question of the original language.[14] Isidore asserts that until Babel, humanity spoke only one language, Hebrew, which he believed to have been spoken by Adam.[15] Isidore knew Hebrew as the language of the Bible, or, as he put it, of " the patriarchs and prophets."[16] Most Christian authors shared his view,[17] even though the Bible does not name Hebrew as the first language.[18] By saying there was only one tongue spoken until the confusion of Babel, Isidore gave language a point of origin. God's granting speech to Adam, who was "the first to confer names on all the animals . . . [not] in any of the languages of foreign nations, but in that language which, before the Flood, was the language of all peoples, which is called Hebrew."[19] Beginning his story with Adam engages a divinely engineered historical sequence that will be marked later by the milestones of Babel and Pentecost. He establishes Jews as the first bearers of divine instruction, and so the language possesses a moral character and bears a religious message. Isidore corrals the multiplicity of the world's languages within a single narrative frame. This grouping is an act of ethnographic description endorsed by biblical authority.

Though identifying the first language has continued to preoccupy writers into modernity, the attempt is a wild goose chase. What matters far more is the bigger story about language that lies behind Isidore's belief. By Late Antiquity, Christian writers had paired language with a theological message. Languages came to the fore as actors in that story by the very fact of their variety and their capacity to bear Christian truths.

Isidore's remark gives us a glimpse of this story and lets us see how to some extent the character of languages has been reset in his time. In a development of great consequence, all languages have acquired the potential to carry specific divine instruction in the same way as Hebrew. Following this trend, Isidore, like many other Christian writers, gave the world's diverse languages a moral character as well as a historical one.[20] Romans did not historicize or valorize language in this fashion.

Not everyone agreed with Isidore's belief that Hebrew was the first language, however. The Cappadocian bishop Gregory of Nyssa (ca. 335–ca. 395), for example, wrote in opposition to Eunomius, an Arian bishop (d. ca. 393) whose books were burned posthumously as heretical. He said that God does not speak in any human tongue, so the first language could not have been Hebrew,[21] but he did not claim to know what the first language was. Gregory posited further that while God made all languages accessible to the sound of divine instruction, he did not speak human languages to humanity at Pentecost.[22]

THE NUMBER OF PEOPLES AND LANGUAGES

Isidore's comment that "at the outset there were as many languages as there were nations" has a deep backstory.[23] The number of languages mattered and played a part in the emerging Christian ethnographic vision.

First, a word about numbering itself. Though not often looked at in this way, counting the number of peoples and languages may be seen as a descriptive, ethnographic act. Counting imposes order, and that order reflects ideological concerns. In this sense, the person who is counting is also an ethnographer who reveals what is important enough to be counted. Perhaps the order that is created has a practical, if limited, value, such as found in a roster of subjects or a list of military units. In a similar fashion, the Roman understanding that the world's languages were far too many ever to count reveals a particular conception of human diversity.

In Roman imperial hands, the sum of people numbered was proof of power over them. Chapter 1 showed, for example, how Julius Caesar initiated a count of the peoples and geographical features under his control. The final report of his agents, delivered after decades of civil conflict, informed Caesar's heir, Augustus, that there were, among other things, 70 provinces, 52 rivers, and 129 peoples.[24] The languages spoken over this great expanse, let alone beyond it, however, were of no concern to the scientists who compiled the list. Imperial writers knew that a far greater number of peoples than the seventy-two posited by Christians inhabited the world and that far more than seventy-two languages were spoken. Their domain's enormous span and their awareness of the limitless territories beyond their borders made that fact self-evident. Pliny the Elder, for example, writing before 79 CE, marveled at "the number of national languages and dialects and varieties of speech."[25] The governing elite relied on Latin and force of arms to bring a measure of unity to the empire. By their very nature, external languages spoken farther afield were simply barbaric and not of particular interest.

Christians, in contrast, viewed the multiplicity of languages and peoples very differently: they were quantifiable and had biblical significance. It must be noted, however, that the Babel story does not specify the number of languages or name them. It indicates only that before the Tower was built there was one primal language, and after its fall, there were very many. The TN

BABEL AND THE LANGUAGES OF FAITH   [225]

account, however, provided a way to calculate the number of peoples and languages, and in Christian hands the two tales were conflated. Having a set number in accordance with biblical information gave a frame for further discussion. It pulled in the reins on linguistic diversity and at the same time posed the challenge of reconciling the diverse linguistic environment of their own day with Bible-based calculations.

The count of peoples varied, however, causing a further complication. Gen. 10 lists seventy grandsons of Noah, each the father of a nation, to arrive at a total of seventy peoples, each with its own language. This number remained standard among Jews in Late Antiquity, though later rabbinical interpreters would sometimes arrive at a different figure[26] or interpret the significance of "seventy" differently. For example, according to the midrash Genesis Rabbah, dated to the fifth century,[27] each of the seventy nations had its own guardian angel except for that of the Jews, which is protected by God.[28] Another midrash suggested that Hebrew was the noblest of the seventy languages because God spoke it at Creation.[29] (I will return to the association of people and angels in Christian contexts in a moment.)

The Septuagint, however, counts seventy-two grandsons, a number that came to predominate among Christian writers in the East who were reliant on the Greek text.[30] The beginnings of the tradition of seventy-two nations sometime in the Hellenistic age are unclear.[31] Why some Christians adopted this reading is unclear as well. Luke 10:1 accepts the figure in most manuscripts, which is accepted in the late fourth-century Latin Vulgate and would predominate in Latin Christendom.[32]

In accordance with this count, Isidore defines a nation (*natio*) as:

> [A] number of people sharing a single origin, or distinguished from another nation in accordance with its own grouping, as the "nations" of Greece . . . Now, of the nations into which the earth is divided, fifteen are from Japheth, thirty-one from Ham, and twenty-seven from Shem, which adds up to seventy-three,—or rather, as a proper accounting shows, seventy-two. And there are an equal number of languages, which arose across the lands."[33]

He goes on to give the names of their descendants, with each name representing a separate language. Yet Isidore does not believe that there are as many languages as nations. He displays an imperial Roman sensibility when he acknowledges that there are more languages than nations: "[A]t the outset there were as many languages as there were nations, and then more nations than languages, because many nations sprang from one language stock."[34]

This eye-catching observation that languages generate nations allows for an ever-changing roster of peoples in the world. It reveals a way to reconcile knowledge of a vast number of language groups, regions, and peoples with the biblical schemes found in Genesis. Isidore's accomplishment here was not to reconcile the tales of Babel and the sons of Noah (an impossible task) but to bring the Roman understanding of the multiplicity of languages in the world into the Genesis narrative. He cannot increase the number of peoples and languages because the Bible has fixed them at seventy-two. New peoples can be accommodated, however, by saying that languages generate nations. He accommodates the fixed number with an endless number of nations and the emergence of new tongues. This is a major ethnographic statement about human diversity and language change.

Isidore unwittingly presents a contradiction. On the one hand he says that Hebrew was the only language spoken until Babel. On the other he says that the number of languages is equal to the number of progeny of the three sons of Noah, which amounts to seventy-two. But the Flood and the dispersion of the languages occurred before the Tower of Babel fell. Isidore fails to reconcile the two irreconcilable accounts of the spread of languages in the world, and he was typical in being blind to the contradiction.

THE QUESTION OF SACRALITY OF LANGUAGES

Isidore says that of all the languages that came into the world after Babel, only three were sacred, Hebrew, Greek, and Latin.[35] The reason he gives for this claim, citing John 19:20, is that the inscription (the titulus) "Jesus of Nazareth, King of the Jews," was written on the cross in those languages at the command of Pontius Pilate. Hebrew was the language of the Bible, while Greek and Latin were languages into which it was translated. Greek additionally was the language of the New Testament. The titulus authorizes the Latin of the Vulgate to be a holy language. Isidore fails to consider that Pilate's choice of languages may have indicated no more than three languages spoken in his day, Hebrew (which probably means Aramaic), Latin, and Greek, and so did not have anything to do with scriptural languages.

Perhaps Isidore is implying that some languages are somehow inherently holy or that no more than three of them are particularly suitable for carrying God's message. He does not mention where languages such as Armenian or Syriac, in which the Bible had also been translated, fit into this hierarchy of value. Immediately, Isidore's pedantry shines through. With the instinct of an exegete, he notes that having three sacred languages could be of practical advantage. He explains that because of the difficulty (*obscuritas*) of the sacred Scriptures, the languages might be cross-checked against one another for clarification.

Isidore's rather academic comment alerts us, however, to a far more complicated state of affairs relevant to growth in late antique ethnography. It involves the identification of large-scale communities by language and textual interpretation. As Christianity spread among populations that spoke different

BABEL AND THE LANGUAGES OF FAITH   [227]

languages, faith-based communities that had not existed before in the Roman world began to emerge. They were a consequence of regional language differences mixed with ecclesiastical rivalries and divergent doctrinal interpretations. Language and doctrine provided rough contours of new communities that Peter Brown has called "micro-Christendoms."[36]

Unlike the situation with Greeks and Romans, for whom the elite Greek and Latin languages had to be learned for participation in society at the highest level, with Christians, anyone and everyone might enter their communities of faith, perhaps even worship in their own languages. Not every linguistic population produced its own translation of the Gospels or a Christian literature; there were far too many languages and far too much illiteracy for that to happen. The possibility lay open, however, and the field of accessible languages for communities of faith greatly expanded, from Egypt (Coptic) to the Danube (Gothic); from Ethiopia (Ge'ez) to North Africa (Punic); from the Caucasus (Georgian and Armenian) to the Mesopotamian Plateau (Syriac), new linguistic groups joined Greek and Latin communities as legitimate recipients of Christian truths.

The worshippers in these mixed linguistic and theological environments developed priestly hierarchies of their own, which are called "churches," such as the Coptic Church in Egypt; the Monophysite/Miaphysite Churches (some in Persia, beyond Roman reach) that conversed and prayed in Syriac, Greek, and Coptic; or the Arian Church, especially strong among Ostrogothic settlers in Italy (as well as some Italian Arian communities) and the Vandal elite in North Africa, surrounded as they were by Catholic, Latin-speaking populations. Communities of faith were not exclusively based on one language.

In this sense the language communities were spiritually equivalent, but their doctrinal choices might vary enormously and put them at odds. Sometimes the form of Christianity adopted by these groups carried a different doctrinal profile that opponents might consider heretical. In time, various language-religious zones coalesced within and beyond imperial borders. It must be emphasized that no clear boundaries for them may be drawn on a map, though general territorial profiles may be discerned.

Whatever the local configuration of these zones, correct belief as expressed in a "sacred language" attained a powerful social presence within them. For Isidore that had meant Greek and Latin for Christians. Hebrew had force in Christian contexts as the original language of the Bible. We see that two of these sacred languages, Greek and Latin, assumed a role in addition to that of their previous function of imperial administrative control. They had come to exist as well as languages of major faith communities, with texts to explicate and new truths to convey. Christian concerns reordered a polylingual world.

In mentioning that there are three sacred languages, Isidore offers a particularly western Mediterranean perspective. The idea had flourished in the Latin lands of the Roman Empire, where Latin was the language of the Church. Since it was not the language of the Hebrew Bible, the New Testament, or even the Septuagint, however, Latin lacked a suitable pedigree, one which Pontius Pilate's mocking inscription on Jesus's cross fortunately supplied. Isidore's silence about the several liturgical languages of the eastern Mediterranean world is less a deliberate slight than an indication of the shrinking horizons of post-Roman Spain.

2. *Teleology*

A second element pertaining to language that Isidore brings to ethnography is teleological. In his hands the book of Genesis is the starting point of a long sequence of theologically charged events intimately tied to language and known to all Christians. At creation God gave language, specifically Hebrew, to Adam, who then named Eve and other divine creations.[37] After that came the dispersal of human languages as described in the Babel story. The storyline continues in the New Testament with the miracle of Pentecost, which made the teachings of the faith universally accessible, though Isidore does not develop the linguistic potential as did other writers.[38] Babel and Pentecost served as historical milestones on humankind's religious journey to salvation. Pre-Christian Roman ideas about language and the world's diverse populations entirely lacked any such teleological perspective.

THE CONSEQUENCES OF PENTECOST

Acts 2.5 describes the amazement at the Pentecost when the listeners to Jesus's words heard him speaking to them in their own languages—all the languages of the world.[39] As Origen had explained, "For the Lord of all the languages of the earth hears those who pray to Him in each different tongue, hearing, if I may so say, but one voice, expressing itself in various dialects. For the Most High is not as one of those who select one language, barbarian or Greek, knowing nothing of any other, and caring nothing for those who speak in other tongues."[40]

The idea of Pentecost met the needs of the expanding religion as Christian writers well understood. In the middle of the fifth century, the Chalcedonian bishop Basil of Seleucia marveled that Goths, Ethiopians, and Persians, by whom he meant peoples in all corners of the world, could understand "the sound of grace being made known" through the voice of a Jew.[41]

The miracle of Pentecost lent legitimacy and led the way for Christian communities in different regions to translate the Gospels into their own tongues and to develop their own liturgical and exegetical traditions. Pentecost marked a new universality of the Christian community that transcended the effectively bilingual universality of Roman authority. After the diffusion of tongues at

Babel, Pentecost suggested a new unity *despite* language difference. Christians scattered across the world could constitute a new world community regardless of their native tongues. For some churchmen, Babel represented an explosive diversity of peoples and languages, while Pentecost indicated the possibility of a return to unity through the spread of the Christian message, which was accessible to all.[42] The capacity, in fact what was seen as an inevitability, of all peoples receiving divine law was an underpinning of Christian universalism.

The possibility presented by Pentecost in turn became an impetus for missions of conversion, which entailed transformation of individuals and communities to a new set of cultural and religious norms preached in local languages. As Prosper of Aquitaine put it in the early fifth century in his treatise *On the Calling of All Nations*, "today there are in the remotest parts of the world some nations who have not yet seen the light of the grace of the Savior. But we have no doubt that in God's hidden judgment, for them also a time of calling has been appointed, when they will hear and accept the Gospel which now remains unknown to them."[43]

Missions of conversion created new Christian groups with whom Rome might build political relationships based on shared faith. Conversions took place in local languages, though liturgy and texts would be expressed in Greek, Syriac, or Latin, for example, if the converts had no literacy of their own. Eventually, in the ninth century, Cyril and Methodius created a new alphabet for the vernacular Old Church Slavonic, so that translation of religious texts would be possible and desirable.[44] The habit continues.

Fulfilling the possibility of Pentecost carried a price, however. It contributed to multiplication of faith communities and undercut unity. Universal access to the Gospels in separate languages entailed further fragmentation of an already disparate Christian environment.[45] As a result, Late Antiquity witnessed the establishment of language-based Christian communities, such as the Coptic, Syriac, Armenian, Georgian, Ethiopic, and Latin and Byzantine Greek, each able to express ostensibly the same religious truths in its own tongue. Inadvertently, these languages contributed to the disappearance of many other local vernaculars.

3. Identifiers of Text-Based Communities

Through thinking about language communities differently, Christians contributed a third element to the ethnographic mix, a potent redescription of human societies.[46] Chapters 4 and 5 examined beliefs about the effect of the stars and the earth's terrains.

Isidore was sharply aware of the differences among spoken languges, but his observations about sound production have nothing to do with carrying a Christian message. At one level of description, he comments on the qualities of different spoken languages and how different sounds are made, echoing views found in Greek and Roman literature. For example, he reports that: "All the nations of the East—like the Hebrews and the Syrians—crunch together their speech and words in their throats. All the Mediterranean nations—like the Greeks and the people of Asia Minor—strike their speech on the palate. All the western nations—like the Italians and Spaniards—gnash their words against their teeth."[47] Isidore understands, furthermore, that languages can be corrupted by errors or "barbarisms," as Latin had been over time.[48] Language characteristics, however, are not among the physical attributes and character traits that he elsewhere ascribes to climate.[49] He does not tie spoken language to membership in a political community.

Linguistic choices had never conveyed citizenship or granted entry and acceptance into the Roman Empire. Even with Justinian, who forced his subjects to choose between traditional and overtly Christian religious practices on an unprecedented scale, full participation in the state did not require specific language practice, only Orthodox belief. (Being intelligible to representatives of the state in nonreligious matters could be achieved through interpreters or some degree of bilingual expression.) Correct belief expressed in a wider range of languages than ever before would, however, enable participation in the City of God, as Augustine had understood it. In that sense, the spiritual equivalency of languages was profoundly transformative. Reaching far beyond the contrast of Roman civilization and foreign barbarism, it divided the world into those peoples with Christian scriptures and those without, resulting in an ethnographic sea-change. Entry into these scriptural and devotional communities would be the mechanism of transformation to a sectarian world.

4. The Spiritual Equivalency of Languages

The fourth new element in the ethnographic mix is found in the theologically charged story about language that was taking shape in Late Antiquity. It undercut the old Roman ethnographic panorama that privileged Latin and Greek by including the speakers of all languages equally as receivers of a universal message. The implications of Babel shattered the role of Latin- and Greek-speaking elites as gatekeepers of the dominant culture. This expanded Christian field meant that a new kind of participation in the inhabited world was available to everyone. Once the elite cadres of the Roman state identified themselves as Christians, social and political bridges founded on shared belief might be built. These new faith-based opportunities did not exist before Rome understood itself to be a Christian state.

Christians believed that because of the miracle of Pentecost, people speaking all languages, regardless of their coarse sounds, could hear (in some sense) and convey God's words. This capacity made languages spiritually equivalent. In Christian hands, languages no longer were necessarily "barbaric" in the old culturally delimiting way. Isidore's comments suggest that older linguistic

BABEL AND THE LANGUAGES OF FAITH [231]

judgments were being supplanted. Moving to the spiritual equivalency of languages was a major shift because it helped break the mold of the primacy of Latin-speaking culture as diagnostic of civilization and because it lent a transformative aspect to language practice. It enabled entry into a new kind of community with a definite religious profile, perhaps even a language of its own.

5. Heresy

The fifth element lay in the relationship between heresy and language, spoken and written. Did different Christian communities brand one another as acceptable or not on the basis of language of text and worship? That is, did languages per se (as opposed to interpretation of text or creed) become markers of heresy? The following chapter about heresy will discuss how doctrine based on textual exegesis became the base of new judgments about inclusion. Here we examine if there was a language component in such judgments.

That a relationship existed between language and customs was understood well before Isidore.[50] Raf Van Rooy notes that pagan writers had made the connection,[51] and church writers followed their lead. He explains, "The Greek Patristic authors do not only make this link within the context of the confusion of tongues; *lingua* (language) and *mores* (customs) are also used as parameters to characterize a people."[52] He notes that Clement of Alexandria (ca. 150–ca. 215) was perhaps the first Greek patristic writer to make the link, though he referred to habits of speech and not cultural practices or belief: "Thus, the 'dialect' of the Hebrews also has a number of other characteristics, like each of the remaining languages, entailing a way of speech that shows the ethnic character [ἐθνικὸν . . . χαρακτῆρα]. In any case, one defines 'dialect' as a manner of speech that is realized through the ethnic character."[53] Clement did not mention Babel, but he did consider the TN's seventy-two "first and generic dialects of barbarians."[54] This suggests that a sense of languages' diagnostic character was taking hold as Christian communities expanded. Origen (ca. 184–ca. 253), in a passage surviving only in Latin translation by Rufinus of Aquileia (ca. 340–410), provides a strong statement of this idea, though without a nod to Christianity: "Each people, e.g., the Egyptians, the Syrians or the Moabites, is named this or that people in relation with their own borders, their language, their way of life, their customs and their institutions, and the Syrians are never called Egyptians, nor are the Moabites named Idumaeans nor the Arabs Scyths."[55] Similar understanding that language is one of the markers that can define a people is found in Gregory of Nyssa and Theodoret of Cyrrhus.[56]

In the hands of Church writers, heresy inevitably entered the picture. Yuliya Minets notes a gradual development over several centuries of different markers for heretics. Language began to mark, in her words, "confessional otherness,"[57] though not consistently. First, early Christians called heretics

[232]   CHAPTER 7

"Jews"; then "barbarian" came into play as a term of opprobrium; and, finally language difference was noted as a possible sign of heresy.[58] I quote her conclusions at length. She observes:

> [F]rom the last quarter of the third century . . . those who were involved in the inner Church conflict became explicitly compared with Germanic barbarians engaged in the war with the empire. The fertile soil was in place for the further development of rhetorical conventions, according to which a shared language suggests a doctrinal unity and agreement, while *different* [her emphasis] languages, real or metaphorical, signal heterodox opinions. Thus, the age-old rhetoric of alienation of barbarians, i.e. foreign language speakers, was deployed in a brand-new way in the context of theological debates. It would never fall out of vogue again. By the end of the sixth century, its use in Greek Christian writing allowed one to insinuate that any foreign language speaker was a potential heretic, as in the *Life of Daniel the Stylite*, and to equate one who proclaims heterodox ideas to those who talk foreign tongues, as in the *Life of Eutychios* . . . Once the anti-heretic rhetoric that speculated on the importance of actual or perceived speech differences took off in Christian discourse, it was always available, though it was not always used. Both orthodox and heterodox parties contributed to building up associative links between certain languages, ethnic groups, and religious movements: Punic and Donatist; Goths or Vandals and Arians; Syriac and followers of non-Chalcedonian theologies. Writers mentioned language differences, accents, and dialects when they served the polemical purposes of their narratives.[59]

Specific languages came to be associated with certain groups by both orthodox and heterodox churchmen, as was Arianism with Goths and Vandals, Donatism with Punic speakers in North Africa, or Syriac with various non-Chalcedonians in the Near East.[60] Minets wisely notes that these associations were largely rhetorical and meant to create a sense of difference. They were not accurate indicators of actual practice.[61]

A caveat: While the language differences among so many of these communities is striking to us, they often went unremarked upon by contemporaries. Neil McLynn has demonstrated this in a careful analysis of accounts of Ulfila, the primary fourth-century translator of the Bible into Gothic. He shows that the treatments of Ulfila were written by authors who espoused different doctrinal positions.[62] Even though Ulfila was an Arian Christian, and the men who wrote about him were keenly concerned with heresy, they did not comment directly on the Gothic language. The same holds true for Isidore. As he was well aware, doctrine depended on explanation of texts, so the language of the text mattered. As noted, he singled out three of these

BABEL AND THE LANGUAGES OF FAITH [233]

languages as sacred (Greek, Latin, and Hebrew), yet his lengthy description of heresies did not mention the languages spoken and written by different heretical sects.[63]

6. Angels, Languages, and Nations

In Late Antiquity, a direct association of angels with peoples and languages entered the Christian ethnographic equation.[64] This was the sixth element brought to ethnography. The Hebrew Bible indicates that "When the Most High gave nations their homes and set the divisions of man, He fixed the boundaries of peoples in relation to Israel's numbers."[65] The Vulgate accepted this wording, but the Septuagint renders it as "When the Most High divided the peoples, when he separated the sons of Adam, he set the boundaries of peoples according to the number of the angels of God."[66] The Septuagint's rendering of Deuteronomy was taken up by various Church Fathers, first in Greek, then translated into Latin and eventually into other languages.

The guardianship of individual peoples by particular angels cut across religious lines and had broad cultural currency among Christians. Seventy-two nations, as calculated in the Septuagint, meant that there were seventy-two angels.[67] According to Jean Danielou,[68] some Jewish texts accept the idea of guardian angels of nations. He mentions the book of Daniel (10:13–21), which speaks of the angels of Greece and Persia, and Philo's *On the Posterity of Cain*, which said the number of languages, angels, and nations was the same.[69] The idea was current in fifth-century rabbinic texts as well as we have seen above, suggesting broad appeal in Jewish communities.[70]

Although guardian angels had been in the mix for centuries, their entry into Christian thought marked yet another new development in Late Antiquity. Marie-Thérèse d'Alverny noted that the Church Fathers began "les spéculations mystiques sur les peoples et les langues, et le mystère de la dispersion et de la pluralité s'éclaire par l'intervention des anges."[71] "Nations," that is, specific peoples, perhaps with long histories of their own, found themselves reified in biblical terms for Christian purposes, each with its own protecting angel. This located nations in a Christian hierarchy of divine powers and made angels participants in the inhabited world as conceptualized by Christians. Integrating peoples into the heavenly hierarchy was an ethnographic move, another reorientation of the inhabited world that reinforced the legacy of Genesis.

Origen in *Contra Celsum* (ca. 248) wrote that following the destruction of the Tower of Babel angels were variously assigned to the dispersed peoples in accordance with their culpability in building the Tower of Babel and "imprinted on each his native language."[72] Elsewhere he wrote that angels only "inspired" the founders of nations to devise their native languages.[73] Jews were permitted to keep the original language, Hebrew, because with God as their protector, they had no need for an angel to lead them or represent them in heaven.

Origen's belief that angels are critical to the destiny of human nations in salvation history was later expressed by such influential figures as Basil of Caesarea, John Chrysostom, and Pseudo-Dionysius the Areopagite, who stated, "In fact, the Most High has determined the boundaries of the nations according to the numbers of the angels of God."[74] The shadowy figure Severian of Gabala (in Syria) seems to have indicated that languages of humans are not the same as the languages of angels.[75] How the many contemporary nations were apportioned among the seventy-two angels remains unclear, but it was widely accepted that every people had its own language and its particular angel serving as guardian and teacher, leading people to God and salvation.[76] Angels became markers of collective ethnic identity. These celestial beings were everywhere, depicted in churches and on icons and other media, vividly reminding worshippers of their omnipresence and care. They also took an important part in the liturgy.[77] Quite possibly angels as protectors of nations figured more actively in devotional practice than in doctrinal texts. They were reminders of collective identity.

These developments had indirect but significant consequences. The substitution of angels (and also saints in a parallel evolution) as new guardians undercut the old local and national protector gods. This gave a new profile to localities and produced new Christian landscapes for a remodeled Christian world. At the same time, the power of these protector angels, who were agents of divine Providence, struck another blow against the determinism of geography and the stars that we have seen above in chapters 4 and 5, thereby further integrating the entire *oikoumene* in a Christian divine hierarchy.

Conclusion

The story of Babel contributed to another radical revisualization of the world in the ethnographic corpus. Like the TN, it was not visible to or accepted by Romans who were not Christian. Babel enabled a new kind of involvement with the many languages of the Roman world. It let languages (in their diversity) become one element of communities of faith. What the Roman elite had long viewed as a limitless horizon of languages, Christians saw to be a fixed number harnessed to the Babel story and evidence of God's dispersion of languages across the world. Going beyond the book of Genesis, the miracle of Pentecost related in the Christian Gospels gave the world's polyvocality a theological meaning and a strong pulse of its own: Speakers of all languages could "hear" Jesus's message. All people had equal access to the faith no matter what their native tongue. This powerful possibility burst the chains of the old imperial order, which had made Latin and, to some extent, Greek the only languages that mattered to the empire's ruling elites. Furthermore, letting the sacred texts of the Christian faith be put forward in different languages enabled the emergence of language-based communities of faith. These were confessional communities, defined by interpretation of sacred texts in a variety of languages. Greek retained its high status in the Christian world because it was the language of the New Testament. Latin maintained its imperial position in the West because sacred texts were translated into it and because Rome was the center of the Latin Church. The next chapter shows how these changes led to the blossoming of an entirely new ethnography, that of heresy. TN and Babel have helped us see a sectarian world taking shape. In this world the Roman Empire gradually became one confessional entity among many.

CHAPTER EIGHT

The New Ethnography
of Christian Heresy

*There are two kinds of barbarians in the world, that is, heretics
and pagans.*

—SALVIAN OF MARSEILLES, *ON THE GOVERNMENT OF GOD*[1]

Introduction: What Is Heresy?

In the first centuries of Christianity's existence, followers of the developing
religion disagreed about many things.[2] No one version of the faith predominated, no single set of memories or sacred texts stood as canonical,
and no ecclesiastical power structure linked all the many Christian groups.
Every Christian community, however, claimed to be the correct interpreter
of Jesus's message and its only proper practitioner and messenger. Starting in the middle of the second century, by which time diverse Christian
communities had become well established across the Roman Empire,[3] cler-
gymen who claimed truth for themselves and their congregants began to
produce a new literary genre that we call heresiology.[4] It was a discourse
for ascribing identity, in this case based on doctrinal differences, and so it
was fundamentally ethnographic. Heretics, the objects of concern, became
a new "other," a new kind of barbarian beyond the pale of acceptable behavior and belief.

Writers of heresiological literature divided the world into those people
within their community of correct belief, that is, themselves (the orthodox),
and those outside it (the heretical). Churchmen and laymen caught up in the
web of heresiological argument possessed an absolutist mindset, and each
group claimed unambiguous truth. Their screeds armed them for combat
against rival groups by listing beliefs deemed out-of-bounds, naming the leaders and founders of specific heresies, and refuting their errors of interpretation and the incorrect practices that resulted from these errors.[5] Local variations of belief were called out as failures or simply condemned as wrong. In
the Roman ethnographies discussed in earlier chapters, being civilized was a
matter of degree, but heresy was black-and-white.

Some writers also focused on unacceptable habits of life. Their goal was
to bring those in error back into the orthodox fold following repentance.[6] As

[236]

Rebecca Lyman explains, "Through this intellectualization of theological conflict as *hairesis* [heresy] the concrete situation of the conflict, the common sacramental life, or the religious coherence of the dissenting position was effectively hidden beneath a label which condemned, excluded, and distanced the idea or person from orthodox life and teaching."[7] Much was at stake in determining orthodoxy and heresy, for holding incorrect religious belief was understood to preclude salvation.

This chapter discusses several historical phases in the process of Christian heresy. The first was in the early formative centuries of Christianity's growth before the emperor Constantine (r. 306–37) accepted the religion and made it a permissible form of worship. During this period the category of heresy contained different and sometimes contradictory elements, depending on speaker and context. The center of narratives about heresy had no fixed location. Heresies were never static and waxed and waned in different regions.[8] This general circumstance changed at the end of the fourth century when "correct" belief became anchored to imperial government. In this second phase the apparatus of the state began to enforce what it considered to be correct Christian belief. This enabled clerics (of acceptable creed) to define heresies with new confidence and authority. The last phase considered below involves heretical belief (as seen in imperial eyes) in states beyond imperial control, particularly Ostrogothic Italy.

Tia Kolbaba notes that in the years before the Constantinian revolution, early church writers produced "a world divided between orthodoxy and heresy. According to this model, orthodoxy is characterized by apostolic succession, harmony, and agreement regarding the salvation of God, simple teachings, clear biblical exegesis, and separation from Jews and pagans. Those who do not understand every detail need not worry but should rather follow the lead of the bishops and presbyters, who follow directly in succession from the apostles."[9] Averil Cameron goes on to explain, "Heresiology became progressively more important and more necessary as the church struggled to define and formulate a universally valid doctrine, especially after the First Ecumenical Council of Nicaea in 325 C.E."[10] In his 2011 study *Sacred Violence*, Brent Shaw unflinchingly exhumes the "styles and modes of hatred" that motivated attacks and imposed cruel punishments on people thought to be wrong believers.[11] He describes "an obsession with the enemies of true belief who obstinately chose their own perverted way to the truth."[12]

Heresiology's lists of those in error grew longer as what was considered heretical continued to expand. Justin Martyr, the creator of the genre (d. ca. 165), named seven heretical sects, while in the last quarter of the fourth century Epiphanius of Salamis, in his monumental *Panarion* (*Medicine Chest*)—as though heresies were illnesses to be cured—listed eighty.[13] The lists kept growing, and eventually heresiologists included all the world they saw before them—a total view of the world's people cast in terms of religious belief. Heresy came to include Judaism, pagan teachings, Manichaeism, and Islam.

Heresiology was not simply an academic exercise. It demanded action, and zealous churchmen saw much work to be done. While its practitioners often drew evidence and historical examples from the works of their predecessors to build their case, their prime motivation was to address doctrinal struggles of their own day, whether dealing with obscure Adamites (mentioned by Augustine) who imitated Adam's nudity in the Garden of Eden during their religious services,[14] or with Arians, Monophysites/Miaphysites, Nestorians, and other groups that figured so large in the empire's political and religious life in the late antique centuries.[15] By the same token, it was through the process of articulating opposition to heresy that the Orthodox faith could understand itself better. Articulating heresy was the other side of the process of defining Orthodoxy.[16]

A still deeper historical dimension existed as well for many theologians who thought that an essentially orthodox core of belief had been present prior to heretical fragmentation, prior even to the life of Jesus.[17] Christian heresiology could be a truly comprehensive enterprise through time and across the map. These churchmen believed that the universal application of Jesus's teaching and a resulting uniformity of Christian belief and practice in conformity with God's will were goals actively pursued by the emerging Orthodox Church. Heresiology's universalist character ran parallel to imperial ethnography, which as we have seen was developing at the same time, though with different all-embracing categories of differentiation and within a different historical frame. Like imperial ethnography, heresiology also continually responded to change, but in reaction to shifting interpretations of sacred texts.

For these reasons, heresiology properly takes an important place in the late antique ethnographic revolution—an ethnography that helped shape different varieties of Christian community, the growth of their distinctive theologies, and the ugly dissension and repression that followed attempts to control belief. The new Christian ethnography of heresy marked a complex field of identity formation and identification. Within this broad field, some modern scholars focus on matters of theological doctrine, while others consider social, political, economic, and other factors lying behind the orthodoxy versus heresy debates.[18] The scholarly literature on these developments is enormous. I take a different course by treating heresy as a variant of Roman ethnography.

Heresiology as Ethnography

By providing diagnostic criteria for organizing and judging the world's communities on the basis of doctrinal correctness, heresiology looked beyond the confines of the Roman Empire. Clerics writing in the genre of heresiology examined all the Christian (and sometimes non-Christian) communities of the inhabited world in the present and even in the past, because the origins of belief could play a role in their analysis. Decisions were made according to criteria of belief and religious practice, not stature and skin color, geographical location, political institutions, or other of the usual tropes in classical Roman ethnography, though details of habits of life and exotic forms of worship occasionally received attention. Christian registers of variance from a normative base were of a different order. As Salvian of Marseilles described in the fifth century, "There are two kinds of barbarians in the world, that is, heretics and pagans."[19] Exploring heresiology as a form of ethnography has attracted attention in recent years.[20] In the words of Todd Berzon, "The infusion of Christian theology into ethnographic writing fundamentally transformed the landscape for thinking about the peoples of the world. Human unity and difference were recast in the language of theological doctrine, practice, and behavior. Surveying the world now meant mapping the contours of orthodoxy and heresy."[21] Christian heresiology had roots in the broader, universalizing Roman imperial impulse to define, organize, and categorize the inhabited world, but making belief a primary diagnostic factor was something new, another milestone in the growth of Christian perception. Rather than viewing developments in heresiology as an infusion of theology into secular ethnography, we should say that the effort of Christian writers to establish and enforce correct doctrinal belief produced a new ethnographic discourse on the Roman model, not within it. Christian ideas adopted Roman organizing principles.

Heresiology possessed the characteristics of a Roman ethnographic discourse in several now familiar ways. First, it was descriptive, with observations keyed to the truth claims that constituted the normative baseline. Interpretation of sacred texts and doctrinal statements generated these certainties and made heresiology in its first descriptive stages an exegetical exercise. What that truth consisted of varied from group to group; the main point is that heresy indicated distance from something considered central and absolute—and visible in everyday practice.

Second, with its register of differences anchored in absolute truth claims, heresiology was highly judgmental. Any compromise decision about conflicting views and interpretations of text reached in synods resulted in a new definition of absolute truth, not a range of options about it.[22] In addition to the tenets of belief that might be fine-tuned through this sort of debate and negotiation, the register of difference might address forms of worship, habits of life, and the historical lineage of heretical ideas and their exponents. All were subject to an authoritative judgment.

Third, like the other imperial ethnographic discourses we have seen, heresiology offered a passage from "outside" to "inside," from incorrect belief and practice to correct belief and practice. The mechanism was baptism, which enabled crossing to the community of "correct" believers. Baptism itself was often preceded by public renunciation of error and penance. "To confirm the new status of the crossover and to make sure that he could never re-cross to his community of origin, his betrayal was often marked by a public ceremonial of denunciation in the form of a personal confession," explains Brent Shaw concerning Donatist conversions in North Africa.[23] Such transformation was not only possible, it was essential for salvation. Transition from heresy to orthodoxy, furthermore, was one way in which the unity and universality of the Christian empire could be imagined. Thus, heresiology did not merely describe and judge difference, it played an active role in shaping public and personal action and in delineating peripheries around a Christian center. By defining community, it became a pillar of the Christian ethnographic infrastructure.

Christian heresiology differed in one important respect from its other ethnographic counterparts, and this deserves emphasis. Since all forms of human activity would be judged against principles of correct belief and expectations of behavior, the greatest peril of heresy lay not in the geographically distant and exotic but in the familiar surroundings of the family and the local community. The defining principle was distance from correct thought, not distance in space. Unlike the habits of distant peoples conventionally treated in Roman ethnography, heretical error was not necessarily something odd and dangerous from far away. There was plenty to worry about in one's own backyard.

Historical Developments

Imperial authorities did not pay attention to internal Christian debates about heresy in the religion's first centuries. The period before the Roman state entered the picture gave time for different forms of the faith to develop and for heresiology to find its footing in Christian discourse.

BEGINNINGS

The Roman clergyman Justin Martyr, who died around 165, began the genre of Christian heresiology.[24] Though his *Treatise against All Heresies* is now lost, we know that he dealt with seven versions of Christian heresy starting with Simon Magus, a contemporary of Jesus.[25] His search for the origin of heresies unintentionally resulted in giving forms of Christianity that were merely diverse the false status of being variants of an original core of unified belief, a unity that had never existed. This misconception had far-reaching implications. Many varieties of understanding Jesus's words and forms of Christian expression—different Christianities—had existed since the religion began. Justin's writing marks a point at which the local customs of other believers began to be seen as errors. A carapace of Christian universalism and exclusion began to harden. With heresy viewed as a monolithic problem, writers continued to look for its origins in order to explain it. The idea of a diffuse Christian environment with many acceptable interpretations of the faith was inconceivable for such men, who sought to establish universal rules for understanding divinity, and so, two sorts of origin were suggested. One was found in Greek philosophical schools. Another placed the origin of heresy in Satan. Justin drew from both options. The particulars of heresies might differ, he argued, but because heretics blasphemed against God, they must be inspired by Satan or diabolical forces.[26] Justin's own knowledge of Greek philosophy and its schools in which he had participated prior to his conversion to Christianity let him make the analogy between Christian sects that differed among themselves and philosophical schools.[27] This is to say that he began to frame heresiology in a broader Greek intellectual context of competing arguments of which only one could be correct.[28] Justin's work was one of many bridges spanning the gap between insular Christianity and the wider Mediterranean secular world.

An expanded heresiological vision developed in the work of Irenaeus. Born in the first half of the second century in Asia Minor, he became bishop of Lugdunum (mod. Lyon) in Gaul after the end of persecutions under Marcus Aurelius in the 180s[29] and died around 200. During this period Gnostic ideas were spreading throughout the Mediterranean world, and Irenaeus wrote a treatise against them called *Against Heresies*.[30] He drew from Justin's work but made many additions to the list of heresies. Irenaeus chiefly targeted the Gnostic doctrines of the Valentinians but also addressed Marcosians (plentiful in the Rhône Valley), Encratites, Barbeliotes, Ophites, Cainites, and others. Some of these heresies had heresiarchs, leaders who had formulated the error, but not all did. As an exegetical work, *Against Heresies* refutes doctrinal error with quotations from the Apostles, from Jesus as cited in the Gospels, and from other scriptural passages. However, he lacks the historical dimension that will be so important to Epiphanius, as discussed below.

Irenaeus helped create a truly universal view of the emergent church as an institution by supporting the position of bishops as the heirs and successors of the Apostles. Bishops, under the guidance of the Roman church, would be guarantors against error. Thus, the Roman church, by claiming authority at the center of the institution, would verify tradition and make sure that the correct doctrine was taught in all the churches of the world.[31] He dealt with heresies of his own day in the first book of *Against Heresies*. Listing communities of error and the men who initiated them was for Irenaeus part of a centralizing as well as a universalizing function of the Roman church. Though highly ideological in its concern for establishing tradition (at the expense of historical accuracy), his approach had a strong institutional and analytical foundation.[32] He wrote: "You see, my friend, the method which these men employ to deceive themselves, while they abuse the Scriptures by endeavouring to support their own system out of them. For this reason, I have brought forward their modes of expressing themselves, that thus thou mightest understand the deceitfulness of their procedure, and the wickedness of their error."[33]

Seeking sources for heresy led the prominent theologian Hippolytus of Rome (ca. 170–ca. 236) to blame different Greek philosophical schools, which he surveys from the pre-Socratics to Aristotle in his *Refutation of All Heresies*.[34] This controversialist, who wrote in Greek, was possibly the leader of a schismatic group and exiled to Sardinia by imperial order in 235.[35] The *Refutation of All Heresies* resulted partly from his involvement in heated arguments about forgiving individuals who sinned after baptism, itself a reflection of his desire for purity in thought and action among the members of the church. In other words, he was concerned for the authenticity of belief in the heart of the church. Like writers in the secular ethnographic tradition, Hippolytus classified his data in a variety of ways, listing heresies thematically by founder, particular doctrine, their myths, or usages contrary to faith, an approach that ceased by the early fifth century. Like other Christian writers after the beginning of the third century, Hippolytus began to view Jewish groups of the time of Jesus as heretics. He applied what by then erroneously had become an established Christian model of an originally monolithic Christianity that had fragmented into heresies of Judaism, arguing that Jewish sects at the time of Jesus had split off from an originally consistent Jewish core.[35]

The search for distant origins of both correct and incorrect belief led some to the construction of elaborate historical schemes. Philastrius, the bishop of Brescia (d. ca. 397), for example, wrote a history of heresy since Adam called the *Book of Diverse Heresies*,[37] in effect a universal religious history of humanity, with correct belief at its center. The book discussed humanity before the Flood, after Moses, Jews at the time of Jesus, and Christians after Jesus. Hervé Inglebert has noted, however, that by the beginning of the fifth century, using heresiology as a structure for a universal history abruptly ceased, and that subsequent analysts of heresy treated it only as deviation from Christian doctrine.[38] The idea of a normative doctrinal baseline, "the truth," from which registers of doctrinal difference would extend, was by then well established.[39] The established center could then define the margins of belief.

ROME ENTERS THE PICTURE

In the centuries before the age of Constantine, Christian heresy did not have a presence in imperial affairs, and Christian communities did not understand themselves to be tied to the empire in a positive way. During this formative phase, Rome was the Great Whore of Babylon, as the book of Revelation called the empire,[40] and it stood as a hostile force in fact and theory. Defining and combatting heresy began as an intramural activity for Christians alone. With Constantine's conversion, Christianity's inimical relationship to Rome ended. Lactantius reports that making Christianity a *religio licita*, or accepted religion, was Constantine's first official act.[41] The practice of Christianity no longer precluded full participation of Roman citizens in the state, and a close association of Christianity and the government began. This turnabout soon affected the treatment of heresies in the empire. "Heretical" groups were increasingly marginalized or suppressed as the Orthodox church flexed its muscles.

The emperor Constantine's conferral of legitimacy upon Christianity in 313 did not make any reference to internal differences among Christian communities, and there did not yet exist any Roman legal language to describe, let alone penalize, heresy. It is not known if Constantine was even aware of the significance of the idea of heresy in Christian life. Heretical groups, as defined by the bishops who advised Constantine and his successors, did not receive the same imperial favor, however, and "wrong believers" gradually began to be penalized and excluded from Roman society. The imperial government, which had always addressed questions of religion through the law, now started to bring those mechanisms to bear on the question of Christian heresy.

Laws issued by Constantine and his successors that attacked heretics and heresies show how government intolerance grew to match that of church authorities.[42] Each legal measure responded to a specific situation, perhaps to a different heresy that had been brought to imperial attention. Two main strategies were in play. The first was to determine what was Orthodox, and the second was to apply penalties to all sects that were not.[43] When self-proclaimed Orthodoxy melded with the Roman state in the Theodosian age (ca. 379–457), heresy became a public crime, and worldly punishments came into play.[44] Heretics might be forced to pay fines and endure exile, confiscation of property, or far worse, depending on their social status.[45]

The sad record of developments can be found in book 16, "On the Catholic Faith," of the Theodosian Code, which gathers legislation issued between 313 and 437.[46] Very early on, in 326, Constantine determined that only Orthodox Nicene (Catholic) Christians would benefit from imperial religious toleration.[47] Yet the situation was not entirely bleak. Although heresies were forbidden, a constitution of 379 permitted an individual to hold to such doctrines "only for himself but shall not reveal them to others."[48] In 388, heretics were to be expelled from cities: "[Heretics] shall go to places which will seclude them most effectively, as though by a wall, from human association."[49] The harshness of this decision is in sharp contrast to the desirable solitude sought by a monk.[50] The law could not have been enforced on a broad scale, however. Evidently there were still large enough numbers of heretics in cities to worry authorities, and their circumstances continued to worsen under the Theodosian dynasty (379–457).

A little more than a year after being proclaimed emperor, the pious Nicene Christian Theodosius I, with his imperial colleagues in the West, Gratian and Valentinian II, issued the so-called Edict of Thessalonica on February 28, 380.[51] This constitution established (Catholic) Nicene Christianity as the sole acceptable expression of the faith and condemned all variants:

> It is Our will that all the peoples who are ruled by the administration of Our Clemency shall practice that religion which the divine Peter the Apostle transmitted to the Romans, as the religion which he introduced makes clear even unto this day . . . that is, according to the apostolic discipline and the evangelic doctrine, we shall believe in the single Deity of the Father, the Son, and the Holy Spirit, under the concept of equal majesty and of the Holy Trinity. We command that those persons who follow this rule shall embrace the name of Catholic Christians. The rest, however, whom We adjudge demented and insane, shall sustain the infamy of heretical dogmas, their meeting places shall not receive the name of churches, and they shall be smitten first by divine vengeance and secondly by the retribution of Our own initiative, which We shall assume in accordance with the divine judgment.

Enforcing this constitution did not prove to be a simple matter. Imperial lawmakers continued to keep a close eye on bitter struggles and political tensions that continued to arise in different regions. In the following years they repeatedly produced new laws in response to specific problems that whittled away at heretical presence.[52]

Heretics were forbidden to be priests in 381.[53] The next decade saw a new surge of antiheretical legislation. In 395, heretics were forbidden to assemble for worship or hold ecclesiastical office;[54] in September of the same year, they were defined as persons who deviated on even a minor point of doctrine (*levi argumento*) from the tenets of the Catholic religion, and were to be subject to all existing penalties against them.[55] In 398 a law required that heretical books be gathered and burned. Anyone who practiced magic, refused to comply, or hid heretical books would suffer capital punishment.[56]

In 402, heresy itself became a capital crime because any threat to Orthodox religion threatened the entire Roman community. Arcadius and Honorius promulgated a law that read:

> We have recently published Our opinion in regard to the Donatists. Especially, however, do We prosecute with the most deserved severity the Manichaeans and the Phrygians and Priscillianists. Therefore, this class of men shall have no customs and no laws in common with the rest of mankind. 1. In the first place, indeed, it is Our will that

THE NEW ETHNOGRAPHY OF CHRISTIAN HERESY   [245]

such heresy be considered a public crime (*publicum crimen*), since whatever is committed against divine religion redounds to the detriment of us all.[57]

With criminalization came dehumanization. The law considers heretics the crudest sort of barbarians, comparable to those living at the very edges of the world and sharing no attributes of civilized life. In the same breath, persecuting heretics has become necessary for public safety and the welfare of the orthodox community.[58] As Caroline Humfress puts it, "The extant late Roman legislation agrees, in principle, that heresy is detrimental to the peace and security of the Catholic faith; and also recognizes that the safeguarding of the Catholic faith is essential to peace and security of the empire."[59]

The full measure of heretics' marginalization from Roman life is seen in their gradual loss of citizenship rights, their criminal *infamia*, and their exclusion from basic civic activities.[60] Emperor Justinian issued a constitution shortly after coming to the throne in 527 forbidding heretics to be legal advocates because they did not understand divine law correctly.[61] He equated divine law and Orthodoxy, which became necessary for exercising the rights of Roman citizenship.[62]

Rome had a long history of linking citizenship and religious practice, but as Humfress again succinctly notes, "The criminalization of heresy under the Christian empire was a major innovation, and it carried significant social and economic as well as more narrowly religious implications."[63] Heretical Romans became outsiders, virtual barbarians, within the empire. This approach undercut the importance of existing geographical boundaries between Romans and external "barbarians."

Frustration with the continued activity of numerous heretical groups, combined with a bureaucratic impulse to impose order, resulted in a heated law of Theodosius II and Valentinian in 435. This law created a hierarchy of punishments "since not all should be punished with the same severity."[64] It presumes knowledge of the beliefs held by members of each heretical group and so does not explain them. The most lenient treatment was meted to Arians, presumably because they still existed in great numbers, while special opprobrium fell upon Manichaeans, "who have arrived at the lowest depth of wickedness," and so were expelled from cities and forbidden to gather and pray anywhere on Roman soil.[65] The law lists twenty-two heretical groups by name and alludes to others. As Humfress notes, a very high level of theological sophistication would have been necessary to decide about these gradations of error and appropriate punishment.[66] Another ethnographic register of difference had been established that combined religious and legal characteristics. The quantity of sects, the variety of their errors, and the diversity of their punishments indicate how deeply this new ethnographic register found application throughout the empire.

The powerful impulses that turned heresy into a public crime in the context of Roman imperial society also transformed it as an ethnographic tool. As the association between state ideology and heresiology became stronger, heresy provided an ever more nuanced descriptive category, in which every minor point in the interpretation of a sacred text might count. New kinds of identification of local communities within the empire and large states external to it became possible as well, as did new demarcations of distance and new possibilities for shared identities. This happened in three ways.

First, the Roman imperial center that anchored different ethnographic registers became associated with orthodox truth claims, as for example when Nicene Christianity received the imperial imprimatur. Emperors involved themselves and the state apparatus in the determination and elimination of heresy, in actions that ranged from Constantine's rather naïve but insistent summoning of the Council of Nicaea in 324 to Justinian's efforts in the Three Chapters Controversy to determine correct belief.

Second, "heretic" became an adversarial category, like "barbarian" or "pagan," that indicated some degree of opposition to the Roman state. Domestically, this led to the predominance of various communities of belief in certain regions of the empire and beyond it. Powerful bishops who espoused competing orthodoxies, perhaps at odds with the imperial position at Constantinople, were often the focal point of these communities.

Third, in international relations, heresy provided a category for describing foreign powers. As seen from the Roman imperial center, a foreign power that espoused heretical Christian belief could mark hostility or be a pretext for it. By the same token, shared orthodoxy could indicate that Rome and the other power had something in common, that is to say, new possibilities for political interaction because of shared belief. Here lay the seeds of what has been called the "Byzantine Commonwealth."[67] Constantinople faced a different set of problems with the large Christian communities, some of which they considered heretical, that lived safely under Sasanian rule. Sometimes these Christian communities attracted Roman imperial attention and affected interstate relations.[68]

Late Antique Examples

In many respects, heresiology looked and behaved like a Roman ethnographic paradigm, though in Christian garb and put to Christian ends by different writers. A few examples can illustrate how in different contexts heresiology functioned as part of a new late antique ethnographic infrastructure.

EPIPHANIUS: GOD'S PHARMACIST

No one realized the implicit ethnographic potential of heresiology more fully than the combative Epiphanius of Salamis.[69] Born in the early years of the fourth century in Palestine and educated by monks in the Nicene tradition, he founded a monastery near Eleutheropolis, southwest of Jerusalem, around 335 and probably was its abbot at mid-century. He became metropolitan bishop of Salamis in Cyprus, and for the rest of his life kept busy writing doctrinal treatises and participating in church politics, eventually finding himself at odds with the bishops of Jerusalem and Constantinople on matters of doctrine.[70] He died in 402 or 403 while returning from Constantinople after an argument with John Chrysostom.[71] Epiphanius wrote agonistically on many subjects, (e.g., against classical learning, against images) and gained great influence in his own day that continued after his death. His treatises were subsequently translated from Greek into Georgian, Syriac, Arabic, and Old Church Slavonic. An ardent supporter of Nicene orthodoxy, Epiphanius earned a reputation as an opponent of all heretical tendencies.[72] He was particularly eager to root Origenism from monastic life, but he saw the entire community of Christians as his proper subject. He argued his positions forcefully, though contemporaries criticized him for his lack of doctrinal sophistication.[73]

The most consequential of all Epiphanius's works was the *Panarion* (*Medicine Chest*), which contained the "remedies" against the poison of heresy.[74] The treatise addressed an enormous canvas globally and chronologically.[75] He begins the treatise with a table of contents in Proem I, followed by a description of his goals and methods in Proem II.[76] He then lists eighty "sects" that had existed before and after Christ. He uses *hairesis* somewhat loosely to mean both sect and heretical belief.[77] His discussion generally includes consideration of each sect's relation to earlier sects, its particular beliefs; a refutation of the sect's doctrines; and an uncomplimentary comparison with an abhorrent animal. Frank Williams points out that all of the sects that Epiphanius names and describes did not necessarily exist as organized bodies.[78] He explains that the names Epiphanius used to refer to his "sects" were "rarely . . . the ones the group in question gave themselves," and that they "rarely . . . represented organized bodies."[79] In this ascription of identities (whether "accurate" or not), and for every tendency regardless of whether it was manifested in a group, we see another ethnographic aspect of the treatise. For each of the *haireseis*, Epiphanius provides a history including their point of origin, a summary of their beliefs, and a refutation of these beliefs to eliminate the toxin of heresy that threatens human safety. Combatting that threat was the rationale for his compilation.

Epiphanius embraces all of humanity diachronically and synchronically within the larger frame of salvation history. His coverage begins with Adam and continues to heresies of his own day,[80] providing a complete taxonomy of humanity. In his account, everyone since Adam has belonged to a group or "sect." In this way he embraces the entirety of human history, which consists of communities defined by their Christology in the period from Christ to his present day or in earlier historical times by groups that in their actions prefigured Christ. He follows at some length the development of these early communities in terms of heretical belief and sect (he used *hairesis* to mean both). His treatment mixes various lines of discussion.

Epiphanius posits a "sectless" beginning of humanity in Christianity's history, which implies an equation of sin and sect, true faith and unbelief:

> And there was nothing on earth, no sect, no opinion clashing with another one, but only "men" were spoken of, "of one speech and one language" [Gen. 11.1] .... Adam, < the > man who was formed at the first, was not formed with a body circumcised, but uncircumcised. He was no idolater, and he knew the Father as God, and the Son and Holy Spirit, for he was a prophet. Without circumcision he was no Jew and since he did not worship carved images or anything else, he was no idolater ... And we must take this to be the case of Abel, Seth, Enosh, Enoch, Methuselah, Noah and Eber, down to Abraham. Godliness and ungodliness, faith and unbelief, were operative then—a faith which exhibited the image of Christianity and an unbelief which exhibited the character of ungodliness and transgression, contrary to the natural law, until the time I have just mentioned [i.e., that of Abraham].[81]

The *Panarion* then proceeds with the "mothers of all sects" arranged in a kind of developmental order derived from Paul's letters to the Colossians (Col. 3:11) and indirectly from Galatians (Gal. 3:28): "There is neither Jew nor Gentile, neither slave nor free, nor is there male and female, for you are all one in Christ Jesus." Paul meant these words to indicate the world's varied populations. Epiphanius, however, turns each name into that of a "sect," which he places in a historical sequence: Barbarism, followed by Scythianism, Hellenism, and then Samaritanism and Judaism.[82] These are the sources of all other sects. The main characteristics of these groups, such as lawlessness and lack of government, are found in standard Roman ethnography. As Epiphanius describes:

> 1,1 < 1. > The first is Barbarism, a sect which is underived and lasted from Adam's time for ten generations until Noah. (2) It has been called Barbarism because the people of that time had no leader or common consensus. Everyone was in agreement with himself instead and served as a law for himself, according to the inclination of his own will.
>
> 2,1 < 2. > A second is Scythianism, from the time of Noah, and afterwards until the building of the tower and Babylon, and for a few years after the time of the tower, that is until Peleg and Reu. (2) Since they bordered on the latitude of Europe these people were assimilated to Scythia and its peoples from the time of Terah, the ancestor of the Thracians, and afterwards.
>
> 3,1 < 3. > A third is Hellenism, which began from the time of Serug, through idolatry and people's adoption, each in accordance with

THE NEW ETHNOGRAPHY OF CHRISTIAN HERESY   [249]

some superstition, of a more civilized way of life, and of customs and laws . . .<4> And next after these came Judaism . . . [83]

He provides much fuller treatment of each of these "mother sects" in the course of his discussion.

Epiphanius integrates his system of "mother sects" with the Table of Nations story. Somewhat bizarrely, he makes Noah a transitional figure in the passage from Barbarism to Scythianism after the Flood, which had not swept away heresy. He shows quite clearly that in the period after Constantine, heretical groups found a place in narratives of human history devised by churchmen claiming orthodox belief.

In *Panarion* sections 2.8–12, Epiphanius tells how the descendants of Noah took different parts of the earth to inhabit.[84] As his enumeration of sects continued, he often places each in a particular geographical location. Each description contains the beliefs and practices that render the group heretical. For example, Marcionites are described as found in "Rome and Italy, Egypt and Palestine, Arabia and Syria, Cyprus, and the Thebaid—in Persia too moreover, and in other places."[85] His extensive coverage of every "sect" demonstrates his universal scope.[86]

Epiphanius also employs another sort of genealogy, derived not from the Bible but from Hellenistic literature. He provides an intellectual genealogy for the sects, telling from what source they arose whenever he can. For example, he explains, "I have now passed Valentinus' sect by . . . I shall begin to say, one after another, which teacher was the successor of which of the teachers who were derived from Valentinus and yet teach a sowing other than his."[87]

Epiphanius's work brilliantly illustrates one way that the idea of heresy could be used to construct an ethnographic system. His normative baseline is Nicene Christianity as he understands it. The register of difference, which is founded on this interpretation of orthodoxy, embraces all of humanity, and is subdivided into sects or heresies. Each of these groups differs from the Nicene norm first of all in its Christological position and next in specific practices of worship. Sometimes he presents associated habits of life as well. All of this fits within a larger frame of salvation history that involves all of humanity.

AUGUSTINE ON SCHISMATIC SECTS AND HERESIES

Augustine of Hippo wrote and preached extensively against heretical thought throughout his career in the church, but it was only near the end of his life, in the years 428–29 while in the midst of other projects, that he turned his attention to writing a comprehensive study. At the repeated urging of Quodvultdeus, a deacon in Carthage who wanted a short guide for the clergy and laity, Augustine produced *On Heresies*, a list that described and refuted eighty-three deviant expressions of Christianity.[88] Most of the descriptions

[250] CHAPTER 8

are quite short, but they provide much information about major sects with which he had considerable personal experience, such as Manicheans, Donatists, Pelagians, and more obscure groups, like the Abelians, as well.[89] Augustine derived information from a variety of sources, which he followed closely but not uncritically.[90] His death in 430 prevented completion of his plan to address the nature of heresy and answer his own question, "*quid faciat hereticum* (what makes one a heretic?)."[91] His goal was "so that through it every heresy—both known and unknown—may be avoided and so that any that may become known can be correctly assessed."[92] Peter Brown has noted Augustine's complex choices regarding employment of coercion in enforcing religious conformity, particularly in his long struggle with the Donatists, but nonetheless that he could be a "harsh and cold victor."[93] Augustine's activity as a bishop put these distinctions into action, and what stands out is his willingness to use the apparatus of the state to punish heretics. That very willingness marks as vividly as any other predilection of the day just how tightly dovetailed were the impulses behind Theodosian coercive legislation and theological discussion of the greatest sophistication.

THEODORET OF CYRRHUS

Theodoret of Cyrrhus (ca. 393–ca. 466) was a politically nimble theologian deeply involved in fifth-century Christological debate and a beloved bishop who took his responsibilities to the members of his diocese quite seriously.[94] Large numbers of heretics lived in his diocese, and he wished to bring them back to the Orthodox community.[95] Theodoret's *Compendium of the Fables of the Heretics* (*Haereticum fabularum compendium*), written just after the Council of Chalcedon in 451,[96] provides a historical context for his efforts to change the minds of heretical communities in his diocese. He offers a list of heretics beginning with Simon Magus reaching to his own day, with book 4 covering the fourth and fifth centuries.[97] Book 5 provides a careful, systematic treatment of Orthodox doctrine that goes beyond that of any previous heresiology.[98] By condemning all of the heretics, he not only demonstrates his own Orthodoxy and deep knowledge of variant beliefs, he also justifies his own vigilance and hard work to free his diocese from heresy that is constantly provoked by Satan.[99] His listing and classifying of heresies so that their adherents might be brought back to right belief was an ethnography put to immediate use.

ISIDORE OF SEVILLE

Among his many other works, Isidore produced a book *On Heresies* that is now lost (see previous chapter). An abridgement of it is found in the eighth book of his *Etymologies*, called "The Church and sects," with sections like "Heresy and schism," "Heresies of the Jews," "Christian heresies," and other related topics.[100] Though Isidore's organization of material in book 8 (as in the rest of the work) is divided by topic, it nevertheless reveals an all-embracing vision of the world's communities, with everyone belonging to one of three groups, Christians, Jews, and pagans (particularly philosophers). Christians, furthermore, are again divided into two groups, orthodox and heretical. As Isidore puts it:

> These are heresies that have arisen in opposition to the catholic faith, and have been condemned by the apostles and Holy Fathers, or by the Councils. These heresies, although they disagree with each other, differing among themselves in many errors, nevertheless conspire with a common name against the Church of God. But also, whoever understands the Holy Scriptures otherwise than the meaning of the Holy Spirit, by whom they were written, requires, even if he does not depart from the Church, nevertheless can be called a heretic.[101]

Isidore passed on to future generations a remarkably conventional and well-informed total view of humanity in terms of religious belief. His big-picture scheme is not unlike that of Strabo or the Table of Nations.

Epiphanius, Augustine, Theodoret, and Isidore illustrate the painstaking way analytical structures were built on the strength of theological argumentation and analysis. When implemented in law and applied to populations of believers within the empire, they represent a Christian domestic ethnography of categorization and evaluation commensurate with the goals of the Christian government. Inclusion within the Orthodox community, that is, full participation in the state, was the carrot. During the Theodosian age, harsh punishment became the stick. We turn now to see how Christian communities beyond the empire were implicated in these developments.

East and West

In the eastern empire, heretical sects did not become separate states, although separate churches with their own hierarchies and dogmas spun off from the orthodox core. Because the arm of Roman law did not extend beyond imperial borders, non-orthodox Christians viewed as heretical in Roman eyes could thrive in those foreign lands. Monophysites/Miaphysites and Nestorians, for example, established their presence in Sasanian territory, and when Islam first appeared, some Christians were prepared to view it as yet another heresy.[102] The situation was different in the western part of the empire. When imperial government faltered and collapsed there during the course of the fifth century, heresy took on a more emphatic role as a marker of identity for certain groups, particularly Arians.

[252] CHAPTER 8

Arianism from Heresy to Ethnic Marker

Arianism acquired an ethnic and political presence of great weight in international affairs. Two examples show how this occurred. First, there is considerable evidence to show how Arianism became a marker of identity and a political element of significant importance in Gaul in the fifth century. A good example is Salvian of Marseilles, a fifth-century cleric who cast barbarians in a new light through a lens of proper belief. Second, heresy as an ethnic marker played a role in the relations between Constantinople and the Ostrogothic kingdom in Italy in the late fifth and early sixth centuries.

Arianism was a term first imposed in the fourth century by Nicene Orthodox churchmen on a range of Christian beliefs with which they disagreed, and it is much discussed by modern scholars.[103] Arius (ca. 256–336), was an Alexandrian bishop who had made a name for himself in already long-percolating Christological debates. He emphasized the priority of the Father's divinity over that of the Son by saying that they were not coeternal because God the Father had created Christ. Arius was condemned at the Council of Nicaea in 325 but later convinced the emperor Constantine that his views were correct. Arianism became acceptable again, and an Arian bishop, Eusebius of Nicomedia, baptized the emperor on his deathbed in 337.[104] Many found Arius's ideas attractive throughout the empire East and West, especially in the Balkans and Italy.[105] Constantius II, who succeeded his father, Constantine, in 337, encouraged the spread of Arianism beyond imperial borders.[106] At some point in the early decades of the fourth century, Arian doctrines spread among the Gothic peoples north of the Danube, where a bishop and missionary called Ulfilas translated the Bible into the Gothic language in the 370s. Then, in a turnaround, Arianism, along with other heresies within the empire, was condemned at the Council of Constantinople in 381, with the result that most Arians in the eastern empire returned to Nicene Orthodoxy[107] though an Arian community remained in Constantinople at least until about 520.[108] Significant communities of Arians remained in Italy and elsewhere, but these groups were not political entities.

To see how the ethnography of heresiology played a role in Arianism's association with barbarian kingdoms, we turn first to mid-fifth-century Gaul.

SALVIAN OF MARSEILLES

The fifth-century Gallic cleric Salvian of Marseilles wrote a blistering condemnation of Roman responsibility for incurring God's anger and so bringing about the collapse of the empire in the west. His treatise *On the Government of God* was composed sometime in the late 430s or early 440s in post-Roman Gaul, probably at Marseilles. It excoriated Catholic [orthodox Nicene] Romans for their failure to live up to God's law. Salvian described their indifference to the suffering of the Gallic peasantry, their moral depravity, and other lapses of all sorts.[109] He felt they should have known better than to behave as they did because they had been taught divine law properly. According to Salvian, the Visigoths were mere Arians who did not know divine law fully and so were not as blameworthy as the Catholic Romans. Other barbarians who were pagans, such as the Huns or Heruls, whose depredations he knew well, in a rather odd way were even less to blame for their cruelty than the Arian Visigoths because they had no knowledge at all of Christianity. Salvian has constructed a register of difference with Romans as the anchor, but completely in reverse to usual practice. In his inverted scheme of things, his "moral map" of Gaul, as Brown puts it,[110] the center point is corrupt, not pious, and God does not embrace it but brings harsh punishment upon it. Salvian combines political and moral analysis in equal parts. The building blocks of his argument rest on notions of orthodoxy and heresy and the morality that they carry. Traditional ethnic appellations mean little in Salvian's vision. The extent to which people acted justly in adherence to God's law was for him the true measure of a people and their political fate. In his usage, the old contrast of Roman and Barbarian had fallen with the empire.[111]

New political communities began to form on what had been imperial territory in western Europe in the course of the fifth century. During this period barbarian ethnicities began to harden and come to the fore.[112] The new political actors initially were quite mixed groups of chieftains and their followers, not simply the offspring of tribal invaders with a primordial ethnic identity. The ethnic self-identification of the leader may have been adopted collectively by his dependents, regardless of their own mixed origins. The newcomers were always greatly outnumbered by the provincial Roman populations among whom they settled.

Many of the barbarian founders of the new political communities were Arian Christians. Their Arianism, quite apart from its theological content, provided a way for the nascent "successor states" that developed to be "not-Roman." As Peter Brown explains: "For most barbarians in western Europe, Arian Christianity was a truly cosmopolitan religion. A shared Arian faith, which was pointedly different from that of their Roman subjects, linked the Visigoths of Toulouse with the Vandals of Carthage and the Ostrogoths, now firmly established under their king Theodoric, at Ravenna."[113] Arianism helped articulate a Gothic cosmopolitanism alternative to Rome's. In a world in which the military face of Romans and non-Romans was quite similar, and barbarian armies were less ethnic tribes than "private security-firms,"[114] loyalty to a chieftain who could deliver land, booty, and security created a powerful sense of shared enterprise. Legends of common origin and kinship[115] augmented by a shared religious marker, in this case Arianism, cemented the identity. As a successful leader set up shop and developed institutions of government, religious identification helped establish a new, collective identity.

[254] CHAPTER 8

In the initial phases of the development of these new kingdoms, the remnants of Roman provincial elites often collaborated with their new rulers. Most of them remained adherents of Nicene Christianity. This gave them in turn a distinguishing social and political profile in the face of the regime of the Arian Goths. The majority of the populations in the new kingdoms remained Nicene/Catholic as well. That is why the conversions to Catholicism of monarchs like Recared the Visigoth in Spain in 587 or Clovis the Frank in Gaul in 496 were such momentous acts. No longer divided by creed, rulers and ruled could find new unity. The decision to realign with the greater Catholic/Nicene Mediterranean world was made for political, economic, and religious reasons.

The story played out differently in Italy. The sixth century witnessed the identification of the new kingdoms with Arianism in the eyes of both Romans at Constantinople and of the new kingdoms themselves.[116] This is illustrated by the Ostrogoths, from Theoderic's attaining power in Italy in 493 through the reconquest of Italy by the forces of Justinian in the mid-sixth century. After their eventual defeat in 553, Ostrogothic communities fall from sight.

In the late fourth and most of the fifth century, the association of Arianism with Goths had not yet been made.[117] Even in the climate of dread surrounding the Battle of Adrianople in 378, in which Goths destroyed the eastern Roman army, Ambrose, the bishop of Milan, identified the Goths with Gog but did not mention their Arianism.[118] A few years later, in 381, at the First Council of Constantinople, Arianism was condemned again, but Goths were not singled out as its followers.[119] In the fifth century the term *ecclesia gothica* (Gothic Church) was not yet used to refer to the Arian communities in the Balkans and Italy as it would be in the following century.[120]

By the sixth century, however, the story had begun to change, due to the establishment of the Ostrogothic kingdom in Italy by Theodoric. In Thomas Kitchen's words, "The concept of the Arian Goth, complementing the Catholic Roman, was key to Theoderic's Italian regime."[121] The monarch devised a system of *civilitas* in which the Catholic Roman population continued to have its own Nicene churches and follow Roman law and forms of government, while the Goths would have Arian churches and follow their own laws. A Gothic military elite provided the fighting forces. There had been a non-Gothic Arian minority population in Italy prior to the establishment of Theoderic's kingdom. Under circumstances that are still foggy, this population came to identify itself with the Gothic regime, taking on the Gothic heritage.[122] The Bible had been translated into Gothic, which served as the language of the Arian clergy. Theodoric gave generously to the Arian church in Ravenna[123] but did not call it a Gothic church. He refered to "our religion,"[124] perhaps to avoid offending Goths who were not Arians.[125] By this point many Arian churches throughout Italy did use the term *ecclesia gothica*.[126] Catholic churchmen in Italy, perhaps hoping for converts, nevertheless refrained from identifying all Goths as Arians.[127]

A TURNING POINT: THE VIEW
FROM CONSTANTINOPLE

The view from Justinian's Constantinople was quite different.[128] In order to justify his attacking the Arian Ostrogothic kingdom in Italy in 534, Justinian adopted the pose of restoring Orthodoxy. He identified Goths as barbarians and heretic Arians, and he enacted new laws against Arianism.[129] In a spirit of cooperation and to further his own political ends, Pope Vigilius took the same approach in equating Goths and Arians.[130] Procopius, the Constantinopolitan historian who was an eyewitness to much of the fighting in North Africa against the Vandals and in Italy against the Ostrogoths, illustrates the imperial stance in the first book of his history of the Vandal war:

> There were many Gothic nations [ἔθνη] in earlier times, just as also at the present, but the greatest and most important of all are the Goths, Vandals, Visigoths, and Gepids. In ancient times, however, they were named Sauromatae and Melanchlaeni; and there were some too who called these nations Getic. All these, while they are distinguished from one another by their names, as has been said, do not differ in anything else at all. For they all have white bodies and fair hair, and are tall and handsome to look upon, and they use the same laws and practice a common religion. For they are all of the Arian faith, and have one language called Gothic; and, as it seems to me, they all came originally from one nation, and were distinguished later by the names of those who led each group. This people used to dwell above the Ister River from of old. Later on the Gepids got possession of the country about Singidunum and Sirmium, on both sides of the Ister River, where they have remained settled even down to my time . . . And the barbarians . . . became the most cruel of all men.[131]

This well-known passage contains a variety of tropes that appeared in earlier chapters: the physical characteristics of northern peoples; knowledge of names previously used for them; geographical origins; common language and laws; and their barbaric nature. New to the mix, however, is another shared attribute, their Arian Christianity. Procopius equates their heretical beliefs with barbarism and Gothicness. Defeating the Goths in Italy would be a victory for Justinian's version of Orthodox Christian piety and further proof of God's favor. Traditional Roman imperial victory is firmly placed within a Christian cosmos.

JORDANES

Jordanes, an Orthodox historian of Gothic origin, also reflected the imperial position of identification of Goths and Arians. In his *History of the Goths* (*Getica*) written about 551 in Constantinople, he states (incorrectly) that the

[256] CHAPTER 8

spread of Arianism was linked to the spread of the Gothic language.[132] He tells that the Emperor Valens invited Goths into Moesia (a Balkan province south of the Danube) to be a buffer against other peoples:

> And since at that time the Emperor Valens, who was infected with the Arian perfidy, had closed all the churches of our party, he sent as preachers to them those who favored his sect. They came and straightway filled a rude and ignorant people with the poison of their heresy. Thus the Emperor Valens made the Visigoths Arians rather than Christians. Moreover, from the love they bore them, they preached the gospel both to the Ostrogoths and to their kinsmen the Gepids, teaching them to reverence this heresy, and they invited all people of their speech everywhere to attach themselves to this sect.[133]

In this brief passage displaying many familiar ethnographic elements, Jordanes combines stark sectarian divisions between Orthodox Christians and Arians. He speaks of Arian heresy as a poison and couples it with age-old criticism of barbarian ignorance and crudeness. He lets us see that the Gothic language and the doctrinal message of Arianism were not limited to one ethnic group. He provides a vivid snapshot of *barbaricum* as seen from the New Rome. As the following author shows, however, other approaches to barbarians were possible at mid-century in Constantinople.

AGATHIAS

Some years later, during the reign of Justinian's successor, Justin II (r. 565–78), the historian Agathias, also writing at Constantinople, composed a long excursus about the Franks. He described their habits of life, clothing, and hairstyles in considerable detail and in positive terms. His appreciative view comes from the fact that they are Orthodox, or Catholic, Christians.[134] Where Procopius demonized the Ostrogoths as barbarian heretics, Agathias praises the Franks because of their correct beliefs:

> [T]he Franks are not nomads, as indeed some barbarian peoples are, but their system of government, administration and laws are modelled more or less on the Roman pattern, apart from which they uphold similar standards with regard to contracts, marriage and religious observance. They are in fact all Christians and adhere to the strictest orthodoxy. They also have magistrates in their cities and priests and celebrate the feasts in the same way as we do, and, for a barbarian people, strike me as extremely well-bred and civilised and as practically the same as ourselves except for their uncouth style of dress and peculiar language. I admire them for their other attributes and especially for the spirit of justice and harmony which prevails amongst them.[135]

THE NEW ETHNOGRAPHY OF CHRISTIAN HERESY [257]

For Agathias, rather like Jordanes, heresy (or the lack of it) is one of the factors that can help assess a foreign community. Heresy offers a new ethnographic perspective on international relations. We turn now to a glimpse of similar attitudes expressed by churchmen living within a non-Roman polity.

SOPHRONIUS OF JERUSALEM

Sophronius of Jerusalem, born in 560 in Damascus, was patriarch of Jerusalem from 634 until his death in 639, just after the Arab conquest of the province of Palaestina. Active in ecclesiastical politics, he traveled to many monastic centers, including Rome and Alexandria. As an ardent champion of Chalcedonian orthodoxy, he wrote extensively on doctrinal matters, and particularly opposed Monophysitism/Miaphysitism, the Christological position that there is one will in Christ, not two (divine and human). This doctrine was held both by the patriarch of Alexandria and the emperor Heraclius. He explained the cruel advance of Muslim forces as divine punishment for doctrinal discord and error among Christians.[136] After Jerusalem fell in 637 or 638, as archbishop he may have been involved in making an arrangement with the new Arab ruler that guaranteed Christian religious freedom in return for tribute.[137]

While pursuing his career in the midst of these pivotal events in the Middle East, Sophronius composed a list of heresies that he anathematized. Anathema is a religious parallel to the criminalization of heresy in imperial Roman law. In his *Synodical Letter*, read at the Sixth Ecumenical Council of 680, Sophronius presents two lists of heresies. In the first of these he anathematizes more than 120 heresies and heresiarchs and in the second about forty. His contemporary sources are unknown, though he drew material from others, notably Epiphanius and Theodoret.[138] Unlike his sources, he does not treat the history or doctrinal particularities of the heresies he condemns. As Pauline Allen describes, "The closer he comes to his own time, the more expansive and vitriolic he becomes. The whole list is less a theological tour de force and a proof of orthodoxy based on the naming and anathema of scores of sects, many extinct, obscure, and half-remembered, than a polemical exercise directed against eminent anti-Chalcedonians."[139]

Lists of heresies and anathemas were nothing new,[140] yet it is worth seeing how fully Sophronius weaponized them:

All the heresiarchs cited above, therefore, and the most impious heresies and schisms named after them; I anathematize and condemn with soul and heart and mouth, and in mind and speech and words, and every other destructive heresiarch and every other wholly profane heresy, and every other schism pursued by God, as many as our holy catholic church anathematizes. I also anathematize and condemn also all who think like them, those who vie with them in the same impiety and have died unrepentant in them, and those who even at the present time still persist in them and fight the preaching of our catholic church and strike our right and blameless faith. And again I anathematize likewise also all their writings, hostile to God, which they wrote against our right and blameless faith. With the same profane heresies I anathematize also every other heresy hateful to God and unorthodox, which our holy catholic church has been accustomed to anathematize and condemn, and their leaders and begetters, and their loathsome and utterly abominable pamphlets and booklets.[141]

Sophronius's application of anathema to heresy is truly global in scope. He embraces humanity in its entirely and addresses everything that had ever been written, said, or thought contrary to the teachings of the "blameless church." As an ethnographic statement, this passage reveals in the most powerful terms a world conceived as one community of true believers, one with many enemies to eliminate. Sophronius's sectarian vision of the human community is an unpleasant emblem of the emerging medieval world.

JOHN OF DAMASCUS

The seventh-century theologian John of Damascus brought the tradition of late antique Christian heresiology to bear on the new circumstances of the Islamic empire. Like Salvian, he lived in a post-Roman world in which imperial power had dissipated but Roman culture survived. Through John's eyes in those early years, Islam appeared to be yet another heresy in the Christian scheme. He and doubtless others understood Muḥammad to be an Arian.

Born about 650 in Damascus to a Christian family that collected taxes for the Muslim rulers of Syria, John (Yanah ibn Mansur ibn Sargun) became a priest at the St. Saba monastery near Jerusalem, where he produced a large number of religious writings. One of these, the *Fount of Knowledge*, had three parts, an introduction to Christian philosophy, a lengthy and highly influential exposition on dogma called *An Exact Exposition of the Orthodox Faith*, and *On Heresies*, in which he condensed eighty chapters of Epiphanius's *Panarion* and added another twenty derived from other authors.[142]

The 101st heresy in his list, as given in most manuscripts, is Islam.[143] He argued that Muḥammad was an Arian because he did not accept that the Logos and the Holy Spirit were divine. He accuses Muḥammad of devising his own heresy "after speaking with an Arian monk."[144] The Muslims, John believed, were "mutilators" because "they separate God from His Word."[145] As seen in the previous chapter, calling Arabs Ishmaelites and Hagarenes had become habitual among Christian writers. In their hands, these "Arab" peoples acquired a genealogy within a biblical framework, for Ishmael was the son of

THE NEW ETHNOGRAPHY OF CHRISTIAN HERESY   [259]

Abraham and Hagar.[146] Now they have taken on a heretical characterization
as well. The adaptability of the ethnographic discourse of heresy could not be
better demonstrated.

Conclusion

This chapter has considered the concept of doctrinal heresy as a Christian
contribution to the imperial ethnographic dossier. The system of distinguishing among communities had an impact as far-reaching as the ethnographic
dossiers derived from the genealogies of the Table of Nations and the dispersion of languages after the fall of the Tower of Babel. The debates about heresy
provided new criteria and categories for describing and judging the world's
populations. In the hands of Christian groups claiming orthodoxy—that is,
all of them—the accusation of heresy became a new diagnostic category of
ethnographic observation and judgment, and it carried political force. In Late
Antiquity, the debate over heresy contributed to the formation of faith-based
communities with strong self-identification stemming from particular credal
formulations and biblical legitimations.

The problem of divergent belief reached back to the earliest days of the
religion when many different Christian writings and interpretations of them
multiplied independently of the Roman state. The post-Constantinian age
was a turning point. As Christianity became tied to the state, accusations of
heresy gained tremendous force. Imposing "correct" belief became the business of the state, and criminalization of heretical beliefs soon followed. The
alliance of coercive state power with specific doctrinal positions articulated
by theologians made repression of "deviant" belief a terrible possibility. Imperial pressure made acceptance of orthodox Christianity necessary for complete acceptance within the imperial community. Religious criteria had never
been systematically used in this way in the non-Christian Roman world, nor
had an ethnographic register of difference attained such overt and visceral
importance.

The "heresy versus orthodoxy" debates that racked Late Antiquity were
quintessentially Christian because of their concern with biblical explication
and theological truth claims. The judgments implicit in identifying heresy
rested on the exegesis of sacred texts. This was a new way of generating ethnographic information. At the same time, however, as an ethnographic discourse
"heresy versus orthodoxy" followed the paradigm of Roman imperial ethnography. It described, judged, and set terms for inclusion in the same way that
other ethnographic dossiers did, as seen in earlier chapters. Heresy became
another adversarial category, like "barbarian," that indicated opposition to the
Roman state. It also mirrored what it meant to be Roman. Although Christian
exegetes initially raised questions of correct and incorrect belief quite independently of the Roman state, when heresiology first appeared in the second

century its framework was Roman and its content Christian. By the end of the period under consideration here, roughly the late sixth to mid-seventh century, however, in the medium of heresiology Roman and Christian had intertwined to produce a new geopolitical worldview. Grouping the world's populations in terms of their doctrinal choices, that is, their closeness or distance from state-supported orthodoxy, brought new categories of identity into play and helped determine imperial policy toward its neighbors.

CONCLUSION

The Conqueror's Gift

But I reckon I got to light out for the Territory ahead of the rest, because
Aunt Sally, she's going to adopt me and sivilize me and I can't stand it.
I been there before.

—MARK TWAIN, *ADVENTURES OF HUCKLEBERRY FINN*[1]

IN THE COURSE of acquiring and managing their enormous empire, Romans encountered a remarkable assortment of peoples with their own cultures, languages, gods, and political systems. Imperial armies brutally subjected many of them, but an endless number remained beyond their reach in various states of hostility to Roman ambitions. Interaction with these peoples provoked a wide range of responses that reverberated at every level within Roman society.

The challenge faced by Romans, especially the governing classes who managed the empire's affairs, was to impose some sort of conceptual order on this bewildering human array. The challenge for a modern historian is to write a coordinated account of the mix of their perceptions, feelings, and judgments that the encounters provoked among the Romans and to show how they framed imperial experience.

This book has taken up that challenge by examining Roman ethnography, which provided the Romans with "terms of imperial coherence," as Helmut Reimitz puts it,[2] in the face of transformational historical change. The preceding chapters have focused on Roman ethnographic thought primarily during Late Antiquity, roughly the third through seventh centuries. In the midst of a chaotic world full of shifting boundaries and the movement of ideas and peoples, Roman ethnography set terms of order for imperial activity. It offered conceptual guidelines for familiarizing the unknown, and it animated the judgments about non-Roman peoples required in everyday governing. The ancient authors who provided the bulk of evidence examined in the preceding chapters wrote for many reasons and in quite varied circumstances. The differences among them are exciting and provocative. Nevertheless, the excerpts from their texts have revealed certain constants of theme and interpretation in their ethnographic thought. The various forms in which the ethnography was expressed collectively constituted what I have called the ethnographic infrastructure of the Roman Empire. It developed over time and so has a historical dimension. The infrastructure as a whole, that is, the corpus of ideas it sustained, was the conqueror's gift of the book's title.

[261]

[262] CONCLUSION

The conqueror's gift had great value and historical significance. Examining the slow growth of the ethnographic infrastructure has shed new light on the evolution of Late Antiquity. During five centuries of imperial change, the infrastructure supported and nourished Rome's perceptions of non-Roman peoples in many areas of imperial activity. It expressed the gradual reimagining of the inhabited world from the Roman vantage point, and in larger terms it points to the emergence of a new sectarian world order in which Christianity took a significant role in cultural perceptions, identifications, and affiliations. This multifaceted, imaginative shift signifies the end of antiquity.

This final chapter reviews the ethnographic dossiers that the book considered, highlights the particular contributions of Christianity, and then looks at the conqueror's gift in three ways, first as a contribution to Roman imperial society, then as an imposition on others, and finally as a legacy to us.

The Roman Ethnographic Infrastructure

Imperial authors honed a repertoire of analytical tools that were often drawn from the writers and lessons of the past yet were always focused on immediate circumstances and informed by current knowledge. The ethnographic repertoire in its assorted and not always congruent parts provided a rich and growing resource for writers of many backgrounds with many purposes in mind, but all of whom related to Rome's imperial presence in some way. Roman ethnography was dynamic and essential to the functioning of the empire, for it did far more than describe the groups on the other side of the border. By providing frameworks for viewing and judging cultural difference, it helped shape imperial action. Especially in considering the inclusion of foreigners within the imperial community, the repertoire offered possibilities for understanding what it meant to be Roman, an identity always in flux. Furthermore, it solidified a sense of Roman community. For students today, the ethnographic repertoire opens a window on Romans' understanding of themselves.

CENTRALITY

Rome stood at the center of imperial ethnographic activity, not just as the seat of government but as the symbolic site of cultural superiority against which others were judged. Registers of difference emanated from this notional base of Roman centrality. Distance from Rome reckoned in miles as well as *mores* was the basis of cultural and moral evaluation as well as pragmatic decision making. Maintenance of this self-appointed position of superiority entailed placing the world's peoples, even unconquered enemies, within a Roman conceptual frame in which Rome was at the center.

DISTANCE

Evaluating distance from basic Roman norms was essential to setting the terms of inclusion within the Roman enterprise. The distance was marked by traversing both geographical and imaginative space. Registers of differentiation that originated at Rome reached to the limits of the known world, making closeness to Roman life a matter of degree in terms of geographical and cultural distance for both internal and external populations. This book has dealt primarily with Roman views of peoples living outside of the empire, yet Roman imperial ethnography was also directed inward to the populations that had once been external but now were learning to live under Roman control. Roman ethnography responded to their presence as well.

CHANGE

Romans recognized that the world was subject to constant changes, some due to natural causes, some to the gods, and some to human factors. They believed that in human affairs their empire also could be an important agent of change, an idea which found expression in some ethnographic writing. The capacity to envisage and enable transformation of society through Roman agency made the conqueror's gift of ethnography an imperial one. As noted in the chapters above, all the ethnographic dossiers implied ways for outsiders of many sorts to enter the imperial enterprise and imagination. Each dossier had a distinct way of selectively letting non-Romans enter Roman conceptual space, through culture, law, or religious practice.

RECENTERING ROME AND CONSTANTINOPLE

We have seen that the location of Rome, the starting point from which registers of difference emanated, shifted in Late Antiquity. At the beginning of the period, the city and the values that it embodied were in Italy, as Caesar's war commentaries illustrate. As the empire took shape, its core values were acted out in cities throughout the empire that imitated Rome. By the end of the period, the privileged centrality of Rome had relocated symbolically as well as geographically to Constantinople. The city of Rome retained an aura of high prestige, but it had been displaced by the New Rome on the Bosphorus. Christianity emerged from obscurity in the first century CE, at the same time that Augustus's heirs were establishing the system of imperial conquest and autocracy. Christians only slowly came to the attention of the Roman state, but after the third century they were a vocal presence at the imperial level. During Constantine's era, Christian ideas started to intertwine with imperial beliefs, and gradually many imperial values became Christian

[264] CONCLUSION

(and vice versa). By the Age of Justinian in the sixth century, acceptance of Christian Orthodoxy had become the chief measure of participation in the state. The intermingling of Christianity and imperial attitudes generated a new ethnography with new criteria of social judgment. One dramatic consequence was the recentering of the empire within a Christian cosmos. Under the eyes of God, people who had been peripheral and foreign could enter Christian narratives of history and salvation in company with Christian Romans.

The book has suggested several distinct discourses in the imperial ethnographic repertoire through which foreign peoples were viewed. Each was a separate element in the ethnographic infrastructure. Each had come into existence to meet specific needs of government or scientific and historical analysis, and each described, judged, and addressed the possibilities of inclusion in its own way.

The first chapter of the book, "Conquest and Curiosity," discussed the growth of a literary genre that juxtaposed highly mutable notions of barbarism and civilization tied to the Roman political and social order. Chapter 2 described how international diplomacy generated an ethnographic genre of "hostiles and friendlies" in which the degree of subordination to Rome was the key measure of difference. In this highly rhetorical discourse, being *seen* to be paramount was as important as actually possessing paramount power. Communities jockeyed for recognition and tangible signs of status vis-à-vis Rome. Chapter 3, "'Include Me Out,'" examined a set of ascribed identities devised for groups settled by the government within the empire. These labels created new categories of service to the Roman state that were represented in imperial law, but they did not displace preexisting ethnic ascriptions. Chapter 4, "Divine Providence and the Power of the Stars," looked at Christian arguments against astrology and the power of the stars to determine individual and group characteristics and destinies. They envisaged divine Providence playing that role instead. Similarly, chapter 5, "The Controlling Hand of the Environment," considered how Christians attempted to put an end to the independent role of the physical environment in shaping human lives. It was an ethnographic dossier in which geography and climate were no longer thought to determine the character of populations or individuals. Instead, following correct belief and choosing not to sin became the determining factors. Christian communities across the landscape were linked in ways that did not depend on the centrality of Rome. Chapter 6, "Christianity and the Descendants of Noah," considered an ethnographic dossier built on a reimagining of human dispersal across the world. Linking the world's populations to the biblical story of Noah and his sons gave them a new unity and provided identifications for them in biblical terms. Chapter 7, "Babel and the Languages of Faith," revealed another ethnographic breakthrough that resulted from Christian understanding of a tale from the book of Genesis about the dispersal of languages after the fall of Babel, complemented by the possibilities of Pentecost described in the New Testament. Churchmen posited that all the world's languages had become potential carriers of divine instruction, which lent a new aspect to Christian universalism. At the same time, Christian communities of belief could coalesce around interpretation of sacred texts in different languages, which added a vector of fragmentation among them. Chapter 8, "The New Ethnography of Christian Heresy," explored how variant interpretations of sacred texts produced new registers of difference that bitterly divided Christian communities on the basis of perceived heresy. This new ethnography of heresy proved foundational for a world in which sectarian distinctions became extremely important identifiers for communities. There was considerable cross-pollination among the ethnographic discourses treated in these chapters, but nothing compares to the transformative impact that Christianity had on them individually and collectively.

Christianity's Contribution: A Review

Christian Romans devised new ways to understand their place in the empire and look beyond it. These patterns owed much to venerable Roman imperial ethnographic systems that Christians adapted to late antique circumstances. Through their efforts, Christianity revitalized Roman ethnography, setting the groundwork for a new kind of imperial community with terms of inclusion self-avowedly based on faith, text, and doctrine. Two major consequences were the collapse of classical ethnographic thought by the seventh century, as Anthony Kaldellis has discussed,[3] and the accompanying rise of a new world order that rested on religious views of community and foreignness. At the end of our period, Christian Roman ethnography made the faith of foreigners an extremely important factor in diplomatic relations, pointing the way to a sectarian, medieval world. Christianity's specific contributions to Roman ethnography may be summed up briefly.

In the very large scheme of things, Christianity offered an alternative vision of how the world looked and how it was populated. The Bible-based genealogies reaching back to the book of Genesis provided a new organizing template for the peoples of the world, past and present. With the world divided among the sons of Noah and their progeny after the Flood, the world's populations were captured and unified in one Christian frame. The religion introduced a clear teleology lacking in Roman imperial ethnographic visions, thereby linking the peoples of the world and their beliefs to eventual salvation. Christian emperors had a role to play in directing humanity in that direction. In this way, Christian belief imposed a distinctive moral evaluation upon human societies

[266] CONCLUSION

and the differences among them. In addition to "right believing" Christians, the orthodox imperial landscape suddenly was populated by non-believing pagans and wrongly believing heretics. (In Christian eyes, Jews had a special, precarious position.) New labels of identity migrated not in the saddlebags of invading hordes, but through sermons, word of mouth, and circulation of religious texts.

Christian Romans made transformation, in this case conversion to their faith (not just acceptance of Roman norms), an obligation and a necessity for full participation in the imperial community. This altered the face of Roman society. By the end of the fourth century heresy was a crime, paganism was taboo, and Jews were expected one day to convert. In the eastern realm, Orthodox Christianity helped make the Roman Empire "Byzantine." When imperial control of western territories slipped away in the course of the fifth century, post-Roman communities reformulated the mix of power and several forms of the Christian faith.

In this regard the Christian emperor stepped forward to moderate between legal status and spiritual status for the individuals and communities under his direction. Emperors after Constantine played a role as enablers of Christian conversion, and one of them, Justinian, claimed to be a legitimate interpreter of sacred texts.

It must be emphasized that in this emerging sectarian world, expression of belief became a new layer superimposed on ethnicity. Long-existing ethnicities remained influential and vigorous, and some new ones entered Roman history. In this late antique reordering of communities and labels of identity, Christian belief emerged as a diagnostic feature of identity and an important characteristic in judging and interacting with foreign peoples. As Maja Kominko writes, "The advent of Christianity did not cause major changes in the descriptions of barbarian people, but it did reframe the notion of humanity as a whole, bringing a far greater emphasis on its unbreakable unity."[4]

Christianity altered perception and interaction with diplomatic partners. Sometimes the emperor could present himself as protector of Christian communities in foreign lands, as Constantine did with Persia in the fourth century. Sometimes attacking a rival, "heretical" kingdom could be legitimized as an effort to reestablish Orthodoxy, as Justinian did in his wars against Arian Vandals and Ostrogoths in the sixth century.

Christians believed that power over human destiny, as well as human communities and appearance, lay in the hands of God, not the stars or the earth's natural environment. If stars or the earth could determine humanity's fate, salvation by the Christian God was invalidated, an intolerable proposition. Accordingly, Christians deliberately turned their back on natural determinism and developed a new ethnography on different foundations. A neutralized astrology remained a presence in daily life, however.

Landscape remained important as well, though not as an independent, determining force. Terrain and faith were not at odds, and harsh landscapes emerged as sites of ascetic practice, not as generators of barbarism. In the emerging Christian empire, furthermore, angels and saints displaced old local and "national" protector gods. This gave a new profile to city and countryside and led to the creation of Christian landscapes in a remodeled cosmos.

Christianity reshaped the character of communities at the local level. The religion offered sacred core texts in various languages around which new communities could develop. That is, it unwittingly enabled yet another kind of subversion of preexisting local identities. Exegesis of these core texts gave rise to a variety of interpretations of belief. Doctrinal debate, not classical Roman culture, provided the criteria of differentiation in the new Christian discourse of heresiology, and this ethnographic discourse affected the political landscape by identifying and separating Christian communities.

In the same breath, Christianity gave new roles to languages beyond Latin and Greek. In consequence of Pentecost, the religion enabled the formation of Christian communities based on local languages and interpretation of sacred texts in those languages. The members of these communities could hear Christian teaching in Coptic, Georgian, Persian, Ethiopic, and Syriac as well as Latin and Greek, in which the business of empire had been conducted for so long. Some of these languages became associated with specific heresies.

In these ways, Christian ideas eventually came to play an enormously important part in shaping Roman imperial ethnography in Late Antiquity. Christian ideas, however, proved to be a double-edged sword. Although Orthodox Christianity became completely identified with the Roman state, and although this happened through collusion with imperial power, the religion at the same time offered alternative criteria for evaluating cultural difference and determining definitions of community. It is undoubtedly true that Christian Rome stood for another millennium as what we call the Byzantine state, but a critical lesson had been learned especially in the West: it was not necessary for outsiders to be Roman in order to be Christian. The legitimizing power of the religion was not limited to the Roman Empire. The combination of Christianity and ruling power provided the groundwork for many distinct medieval communities around the Mediterranean that integrated Christian identity and ruling power in a different fashion. Examining the development of Roman ethnography in Late Antiquity shows how Christianity through an imperial lens brought the world into focus in a new way and changed visions of the human landscape and the Roman presence on it.

The Conqueror's Gift: Three Aspects

Gifts are never as straightforward as they may seem. They always establish, for better or worse, ties and expectations between the giver and the recipient. As suggested in the introduction, the conqueror's gift, that is, imperial Rome's

[268] CONCLUSION

ethnographic repertoire, can be viewed in three ways. Reviewing them here is a useful way to bring the book to a close.

THE GIFT ONE GIVES ONESELF

Imperial Roman ethnography was devised by Romans for Romans and so was entirely self-serving. It underlay their exercise of power by providing terms in which to evaluate subjects and rivals and to celebrate themselves. Ethnography lubricated the engines of empire. Plastic and adaptable to the needs of the moment, the imperial ethnographic repertoire worked above all for Rome's benefit. It supported imperial expansion and underwrote the Roman sense of superiority. The imperial ethnographic corpus was a welcome gift for practitioners of power because it provided ways to address the peoples of the world and understand Rome's place among them.

THE UNWANTED GIFT

There was a darker side to the conqueror's gift as well, an inevitable and regrettable by-product of Roman imperialism. No one wished to be conquered by Rome or forced into the imperial system. No foreign power desired to have Roman categories imposed on them, particularly a status of inferiority or dependence. James Scott's explanation holds true: "As in any colonial or imperial setting, the experience of the subject was wildly at odds with the ideological superstructure that aimed at ennobling the whole enterprise. The pieties must . . . have seemed to most subjects a cruel joke."[5] Nevertheless, the influence of Roman ideas profoundly affected the lives of millions within and beyond the imperial perimeter. This book has not told their stories, but it has noted a few instances in which groups settled within the empire accepted Roman labels of identity. We have also seen how Christian categories of self-identification originating in the empire were picked up by peripheral populations, notably the followers of Islam, who understood themselves as the descendants of Ishmael. In a notable turnabout, they became great enemies of Rome.

THE GIFT THAT CANNOT BE RETURNED

This third aspect of the conqueror's gift is the Roman ethnographic legacy of which we are the heirs. Like them or not, there is nothing we can do about the Roman ethnographic categories that were forged in brutal expansion long ago but are still part of our world today. The Roman inheritance has remained a touchstone in the European imperialism of recent centuries and in many ways continues to shape the approaches to empire and foreign peoples around the globe. The Roman ethnographic repertoire's failure to pull up stakes and march away centuries ago raises questions. We may not be able to return this gift, but can we exchange it for something else? Is it possible to find new patterns of addressing the diversity of the world's populations without relying on celebratory hierarchies of cultural superiority that are based on geography, military power, or religion? Does the exercise of government require coercive systems of doctrinal or ideological belief built on uncompromising truth claims and in which disagreement with authority is a public crime? The Roman ethnographic repertoire—the conqueror's gift—that provoked these and many other questions provided its own answers. Whether we can stand at the boundaries of civilizations and produce a different set of responses remains to be seen.

LIST OF ABBREVIATIONS

ANF Ante-Nicene Fathers

BAR British Archaeological Reports

BMCR *Bryn Mawr Classical Review* (online)

CAH *Cambridge Ancient History*

CCSL Corpus Christianorum Series Latina

CFHB Corpus Fontium Historiae Byzantinae

CIL *Corpus Inscriptionum Latinarum*

Cod. Just. *Codex Justinianus*

Cod. Th. *Codex Theodosianus*

CSEL Corpus scriptorum ecclesiasticorum latinorum

DOP Dumbarton Oaks Papers

EI *Encyclopedia Islamica*

Exc. de Leg. *Excerpta de legationibus*

Exc. de Leg. Gent. *Excerpta de legationibus gentium*

HAW Handbuch der Altertumswissenschaft

GCS Die Griechischen Christlichen Schriftsteller der Ersten Jahrhunderte

KJV King James Version

LCL Loeb Classical Library

LSJ H. Lidell, R. Scott, and H. S. Jones, eds., *A Greek-English Lexicon*

MGH Monumenta Germaniae Historica

MGHSRM Monumenta Germaniae Historica: Scriptores Rerum Merovingicarum

MGHAA Monumenta Germaniae Historica: Auctores Antiquissimi

Nov. Just. *Novels of Justinian*

NPNF Select Library of Nicene and Post-Nicene Fathers of the Christian Church

OCD4 *Oxford Classical Dictionary*, 4th ed.

PL Patrologia cursus completus, Series latina

PG Patrologia cursus completus, Series graeca

RAC *Reallexikon für Antike und Christentum*

RGA *Reallexikon der Germanischen Altertumskunde*, 2nd ed.

[271]

[272] LIST OF ABBREVIATIONS

RE   *Paulys Realencyclopäedie der Klassischen Altertumswissenschaft*

RIDA   *Revue Internationale des Droits de l'Antiquité*

ODB   *Oxford Dictionary of Byzantium*

TAPA   *Transactions of the American Philological Association*

TTH   Liverpool Translated Texts for Historians

NOTES

Introduction

1. James Clifford, "Introduction: Partial Truths," in *Writing Culture: The Poetics and Politics of Ethnography*, ed. James Clifford and George E. Marcus (Berkeley: 1986), 2.

2. Patrick Amory, *People and Identity in Ostrogothic Italy, 489-554* (Cambridge: 2009), 3, 1-25.

3. Amory, *People and Identity*, 3.

4. Marcel Mauss, "Essai sur le don. Forme et raison de l'échange dans les sociétés archaïques," *L'année sociologique*, n.s. 1 (1923-24): 30-186; Marcel Mauss, *The Gift: Expanded Edition*, trans. Jane I. Guyer (Chicago: 2016).

5. Patrick J. Geary, *The Myth of Nations: The Medieval Origins of Europe* (Princeton: 2002).

6. On the debate about discontinuity, recently Scott Fitzgerald Johnson, "Worlds of Byzantium: Problems, Frameworks, and Opportunities in the Byzantine Near East," in *Worlds of Byzantium: Religion, Culture, and Empire in the Medieval Near East*, ed. Elizabeth S. Bolman, Scott Fitzgerald Johnson, and Jack Tannous (Cambridge: 2024); Averil Cameron, "Bitter Furies of Complexity," review of Anthony Kaldellis's *Romanland*, *Times Literary Supplement* 6077 (Sept. 20, 2019), 28-29, https://www.the-tls.co.uk/articles/byzantium-romanland-kaldellis/.

7. The first attested use of the word is about 220 CE. See Michael Kulikowski, *Rome's Gothic Wars: From the Third Century to Alaric* (Cambridge: 2015), 34 n. 1, citing Tadeusz Sarnowski, "Barbaricum und ein Bellum Bosporanum in einer Inschrift aus Preslav," *Zeitschrift für Papyrologie und Epigraphik* 87 (1991): 137-44.

8. Peter Brown, *The World of Late Antiquity AD 150-750* (London: 1971; repr. 2018), 19-20.

9. Prosper, *De vocatione omnium gentium* 2.16, in PL 51.704A (1844); trans. R. Markus, "Chronicle and Theology: Prosper of Aquitaine," 31-44, in *The Inheritance of Historiography 350-900*, ed. Christopher Holdsworth and T. P. Wiseman (Liverpool: 1986), at 38; see also Gerhart B. Ladner, "On Roman Attitudes toward Barbarians in Late Antiquity," *Viator* 7 (1976): 24-25.

10. According to Vergil, *Aeneid* 12.190-92, Aeneas had promised to respect the "gods and rights" of other Italian peoples. Virgil, *Aeneid*, ed. and trans. H. R. Fairclough, G. P. Goold, LCL 64 (Cambridge, MA: 1918).

11. There were exceptions. The Hellenistic Maccabean state, for example, adopted a religious posture.

12. Margaret L. Antonio et al., "Stable Population Structure in Europe since the Iron Age, Despite High Mobility" (2024), https://doi.org/10.7554/eLife.79714.

13. Greg Woolf, *Tales of the Barbarians: Ethnography and Empire in the Roman West* (Hoboken, NJ: 2011), 5.

14. The steppes did not produce large-scale communities of faith until after the advent of Islam. Much of northern Europe remained non-Christian through the Middle Ages.

15. Han F. Vermeulen, *Before Boas: The Genesis of Ethnography and Ethnology in the German Enlightenment* (Lincoln, NE: 2015), esp. chap. 1, "History and Theory of Anthropology and Ethnology: Introduction," 1-38, and chap. 4, "Ethnography and Empire: G. F. Müller and the Description of Siberian Peoples," 131-218. See also the review by John H. Zammito, in *Critical Philosophy of Race* 4, no. 2 (2016): 263-71; Emma Dench, "Ethnography and History," in *A Companion to Greek and Roman Historiography*, vol. 2, ed. John Marincola (Oxford: 2008), 493-503, at 494-95.

16. Vermeulen, *Before Boas*, 447-54.

17. Vermeulen, *Before Boas*, 23.

[273]

[274] NOTES TO PAGES 7–12

18. *Oxford English Dictionary*, s.v. "ethnography," https://www.oed.com/view/Entry /64809?redirectedFrom=Ethnography&. On the debate of the first use of the term in English, see *The Penny Cyclopedia of the Society for the Diffusion of Useful Knowledge*, cited in Joseph E. Skinner, *The Invention of Greek Ethnography from Homer to Herodotus* (Oxford: 2012), 5 n. 10; Rowe, "Ethnography and Ethnology in the Sixteenth Century," 1–2.

19. Robin Patrick Clair, "The Changing Story of Ethnography," chap. 1 in *Expressions of Ethnography. Novel Approaches to Qualitative Methods*, ed. Robin Patric Clair (Albany, NY: 2003), 3–26. The literature is vast. Clair provides an overview, not reliable for ancient materials but helpful for the discipline in recent years.

20. Dench, "Ethnography and History," 494–95.

21. Skinner, *The Invention of Greek Ethnography*, 3; see Karl Trüdinger, *Studien zur Geschichte der griechisch-römischen Ethnographie* (Basel: 1918) for earlier bibliography.

22. The Greek word is ἱστορίαι (*historiai*).

23. Rowe, 4 and passim; Joannes Aubanus, *Omnium gentium mores leges et ritus ex multis clarissimis rerum scriptoribus . . . nuper collectos . . .* (Augustae Vindelicorum: 1520).

24. In *Agricola*, Tacitus celebrates the virtues of his father-in-law, a successful commander in Britain under Domitian.

25. Woolf, *Tales of the Barbarians*, 13–17.

26. Thomas Hylland Eriksen and Finn Sivert Nielsen, *A History of Anthropology*, 2nd ed. (London: 2013), provides a convenient overview of the development of anthropology.

27. Pliny, *Natural History* 7.6, ed. and trans. H. Rackham, LCL 352 (Cambridge, MA: 1942).

28. Tzvetan Todorov, in *The Conquest of America: The Question of the Other*, trans. Richard Howard (New York: 1984), discusses a "Typology of Relations to the Other," 185; for discussion, see Michael Maas, "Ethnicity, Orthodoxy, and Community in Salvian of Marseilles," in John Drinkwater and Hugh Elton, eds., *Fifth-Century Gaul: A Crisis of Identity?* (Cambridge: 1992), 275–84, at 278–80. See Brent Shaw, "The Exterminating Angel: The Roman Imperial State and Its Indigenous Peoples," in Michael Maas and Fay Yarbrough, eds., *Empires and Indigenous Peoples: Comparing Ancient Roman and North American Experiences* (Norman, OK: 2024), 17–35, for Roman attitudes to eradication of a people when inclusion was not thought desirable.

29. More on this in chap. 1, below.

30. Guy Halsall, *Barbarian Migrations and the Roman West, 376–568* (Cambridge: 2007), 150.

31. James S. Romm, *The Edges of the Earth in Ancient Thought: Geography, Exploration, and Fiction* (Princeton: 1992), 85 and passim.

32. Yves Dauge, *Le Barbare: Recherches sur la conception romaine de la barbarie et de la civilisation* (Brussels: Latomus, 1981), 809, for his concluding summary.

33. See chap. 3, below.

34. Strabo, *Geography* 3.3.8, ed. and trans. Horace Leonard Jones, LCL 50 (Cambridge, MA: 1923).

35. Michael Maas, "'Delivered from Their Ancient Customs': Christianity and the Question of Cultural Change in Early Byzantine Ethnography," in *Conversion in Late Antiquity and the Early Middle Ages: Seeing and Believing*, ed. Kenneth Mills and Anthony Grafton (Rochester, NY: 2003), 152–88, at 160–69.

36. Procopius, *On Buildings* 3.6.12, General Index, ed. and trans. H. B. Dewing and Glanville Downey, LCL 343 (Cambridge, MA: 1940); Maas, "Delivered," 164; Rufinus, in his *Ecclesiastical History* (10.11), notes that when the Georgians begged Constantine to send them priests, the emperor was happier about their conversion than their submission to the empire.

37. Greg Woolf, *Tales of the Barbarians: Ethnography and Empire in the Roman West* (Chichester, UK: 2011).

38. Woolf, *Tales of the Barbarians*, 89.

39. Woolf, *Tales of the Barbarians*, 4.

40. Woolf, *Tales of the Barbarians*, 17.

41. Woolf, *Tales of the Barbarians*, 89–117.

NOTES TO PAGES 13–24 [275]

42. Anthony Kaldellis, *Ethnography after Antiquity: Foreign Lands and Peoples in Byzantine Literature* (Philadelphia: 2013).

43. Kaldellis, *Ethnography after Antiquity*, 1.

44. Kaldellis, *Ethnography after Antiquity*, 1–25.

45. Kaldellis, *Ethnography after Antiquity*, 2.

46. Ibid.

47. Kaldellis, *Ethnography after Antiquity*, 9.

48. Kaldellis, *Ethnography after Antiquity*, 25.

49. This point is much discussed. See, for example, Erich S. Gruen, *Rethinking the Other in Antiquity* (Princeton: 2010), 159–78.

50. Similar patterns are noted with Arab groups. See chap. 2 below.

Chapter One: Conquest and Curiosity

1. Zelda Mishkovsky, "Each Man Has a Name," ed. and trans. T. Carmi, *The Penguin Book of Hebrew Verse* (London: 1981), 558.

2. Augustus, *Res Gestae Divi Augusti* 31, in *Augustus, Res Gestae Divi Augusti: Text, Translation, and Commentary*, ed. and trans. Alison E. Cooley (Cambridge: 2005); on geographical discoveries made by Roman generals from Augustus to Trajan, Claude Nicolet, *Space, Geography, and Politics in the Early Roman Empire* (Ann Arbor: 1991), 85–88; on the use of exotic animals in Late Republican and Early Imperial triumph, see Trevor Murphy, *Pliny the Elder's Natural History: The Empire in the Encyclopedia* (Oxford: 2004) 162–63.

3. Emma Dench, *Romulus' Asylum: Roman Identities from the Age of Alexander to the Age of Hadrian* (Oxford: 2005), esp. 162–73.

4. Greg Woolf, *Tales of the Barbarians: Ethnography and Empire in the Roman West* (Chichester: 2011) refers to a "plurality of paradigms" (32), and "interpretive frames available to those creating . . . new knowledge" (89).

5. James B. Rives, trans., *Tacitus Germania* (Oxford: 1999), 14, surveys ethnography before Caesar, noting that most Latin literature between the mid-second and mid-first century BCE has been lost.

6. Julius Caesar, *The Gallic War* 1.1, trans. S. A. Handford (London: 1951), with some changes.

7. On Caesar in the context of Hellenistic ethnography, see Elizabeth Rawson, *Intellectual Life in the Late Roman Republic* (London: 1985), 259–63. For bibliography on this vast topic, see Andrew M. Riggsby, *Caesar in Gaul and Rome: War in Words* (Austin: 2006).

8. Rives, trans., *Tacitus Germania*, 14.

9. Caesar, *The Gallic War* 6.11, for his ethnographic section on the Gauls and Germani.

10. On his relation to Posidonius: Gerhard Dobesch, "Caesar als Ethnograph," *Wiener Humanistische Blätter* 31 (1989): 16–51; on the influence of Posidonius, see Klaus E. Müller, *Geschichte der antiken Ethnographie und ethnologischen Theoriebildung von den Anfängen bis auf die byzantinischen Historiographen Teil II* (Wiesbaden: 1980), 67–79, at 68; on his interest in exotica in animal life as well as social and political customs, see his excursus contrasting the Gauls and Germani in *The Gallic War* 6.11–28; Hester Schadee, "Caesar's Construction of Northern Europe: Inquiry, Contact and Corruption in *De bello gallico*," *Classical Quarterly* 58, no. 1 (2008): 158–80.

11. Sallust, *The War with Jugurtha* 17.3, in John T. Ramsey, ed., *The War with Catiline: The War with Jugurtha*, ed. and trans. J. C. Rolfe, LCL 116 (Cambridge, MA: 2013); Müller, *Geschichte der antiken Ethnographie*, 2:55–58; Robert Morstein-Marx, "The Myth of Numidian Origins in Sallust's African Excursus (*Iugurtha* 17.7–18.12)," *American Journal of Philology* 122, no. 2 (2001): 179–200.

12. Michael Kulikowski, "Where the Wild Things Are: The Invention of Barbarian Space," in *Empires and Indigenous Peoples: Comparing Ancient Roman and North American Experiences*, ed. Michael Maas and Fay Yarbrough (Norman, OK: 2024), 151–63.

13. Gaius Julius Caesar, *Bellum gallicum* 1.1, ed. Otto Seel (Leipzig: 1961).

[276] NOTES TO PAGES 24–28

14. For a view that counters Caesar's presentation of the frontier, see Sebastian Brather, "Acculturation and Ethnogenesis along the Frontier: Rome and the Ancient Germans in an Archaeological Perspective," in Florin Curta, ed., *Borders, Barriers, and Ethnogenesis: Frontiers in Late Antiquity and the Middle Ages* (Turnhout: 2005), 139–72.

15. Riggsby, *Caesar in Gaul and Rome*, 51–52, 59–60, and esp. 64–71; Roland Steinacher, "Rome and Its Created Northerners: *Germani* as a Historical Term," in Matthias Friedrich and James M. Harland, eds., *Interrogating the 'Germanic': A Category and Its Use in Late Antiquity and the Early Middle Ages* (Berlin: 2021), 31–66; Schadee, "Caesar's Construction," 162–63, 167–70.

16. For Roman savagery, see Brent Shaw, "The Exterminating Angel," in *Empires and Indigenous Peoples*, ed. Maas and Yarbrough, 17–35.

17. Pompey bragged of bringing Roman power to the ends of the earth: Diodorus Siculus, *Library of History, Volume XII: Fragments of Books 33–40*, ed. and trans. Francis R. Walton, LCL 423 (Cambridge, MA: 1967), 40.4; Dio Cassius, *Roman History, Volume III: Books 36–40*, ed. and trans. Earnest Cary and Herbert B. Foster, LCL 53 (Cambridge, MA: 1914), 37.21.2; Murphy, *Pliny the Elder's Natural History*, 154–60, on triumphal display of conquests.

18. Riggsby, *Caesar in Gaul and Rome*, 1–2.

19. The standard introduction remains A. N. Sherwin-White, *The Roman Citizenship*, 2nd ed. (Oxford: 1973).

20. Woolf, *Tales of the Barbarians*, 8–31.

21. Woolf, *Tales of the Barbarians*, passim.

22. Woolf, *Tales of the Barbarians*, 13.

23. Joseph E. Skinner, *The Invention of Greek Ethnography: From Homer to Herodotus* (Oxford: 2012), explains that consideration of Greekness and marking the identity of non-Greeks long predated the development of ethnographic writing.

24. Arnaldo Momigliano, *Alien Wisdom: The Limits of Hellenization* (Cambridge: 1975), 2: "for all practical purposes the Greeks discovered Romans, Celts and Jews only after Alexander the Great." On the Greek ethnographic tradition, from Homer to the Roman Empire, see Woolf, *Tales of the Barbarians*, 13–15, 25–28.

25. Woolf, *Tales of the Barbarians*, 14: "there were no genre-specific varieties of ethnographic writing or knowledge."

26. Woolf, *Tales of the Barbarians*, 49; on Manilius, see Steven J. Green and Katharina Volk, eds., *Forgotten Stars: Rediscovering Manilius' Astronomica* (Oxford: 2011).

27. Rives, trans., *Tacitus Germania*, 11–21.

28. Rawson, *Intellectual Life*, 250–66; Riggsby, *Caesar in Gaul and Rome*, 47–71; Woolf, *Tales of the Barbarians*, 19–24, 59–72.

29. Woolf, *Tales of the Barbarians*, 13–17.

30. Woolf, *Tales of the Barbarians*, 17.

31. Woolf, *Tales of the Barbarians*, 15.

32. Richard F. Thomas, *Lands and Peoples in Roman Poetry. The Ethnographical Tradition* (Cambridge: 1982), 1; Murphy, *Pliny the Elder's Natural History*, 77–87.

33. Emma Dench, *From Barbarians to New Men: Greek, Roman, and Modern Perceptions of Peoples from the Central Apennines* (Oxford: 1995), 11; for modern ways of "seeing" the other, see 21–23.

34. Ilona Opelt and Wolfgang Speyer, "Barbar," *Jahrbuch für Antike und Christentum* 10 (1967): 251–90.

35. Erich S. Gruen, *Rethinking the Other in Antiquity* (Princeton: 2011), 3: "Greeks, Romans, and Jews (who provide us with almost all the relevant extant texts) had far more mixed, nuanced, and complex opinions about other peoples"; Christopher Tuplin, "Greek Racism? Observations on the Character and Limits of Greek Ethnic Prejudice," in Gocha R. Tsetskhladze, ed., *Ancient Greeks West and East* (Leiden: 1999), 47–75, discusses various Greek approaches to the Greek-Barbarian contrast, and at 58–59 introduces the transformative nature of Greek education.

36. Greg Woolf, "The Classical Barbarian: A Discontinuous History," in *Empires and Indigenous Peoples*, ed. Maas and Yarbrough, 91–104; Ilona Opelt and Wolfgang Speyer, "Barbar I," in Theodor Klauser et al., eds., *RAC*, Supplement-Band I (Stuttgart: 2001), 813–95; on

NOTES TO PAGES 28–34 [277]

early Roman usage, see Dench, *Romulus' Asylum*, 305–6, and Dench, *From Barbarians to New Men*, 72–80.

37. On environmental influence in shaping barbarians, see Tuplin, "Greek Racism?," 47–75, at 62–66; Benjamin H. Isaac, *The Invention of Racism in Classical Antiquity* (Princeton: 2004), 55–109; Clarence J. Glacken, *Traces on the Rhodian Shore: Nature and Culture in Western Thought from Ancient Times to the End of the Eighteenth Century* (Berkeley: 1967), 80–115; and chap. 4 below.

38. Dench, *From Barbarians to New Men*, 12.

39. Dench, *From Barbarians to New Men*, 13.

40. Oswyn Murray, "Herodotus and Hellenistic Culture," *Classical Quarterly* 22, no. 2 (1972), 200–13, at 200–202; discussed by Katherine Clarke, *Between Geography and History: Hellenistic Constructions of the Roman World* (Oxford: 1999), 69–76.

41. Momigliano, *Alien Wisdom*, 19.

42. Emma Dench, *From Barbarians to New Men*, 71; Karl Christ, "Römer und Barbaren in der hohen Kaiserzeit," *Saeculum* 10 (1959): 273–88, at 277.

43. Nicholas Purcell, "Urban Spaces and Central Places: The Roman World," in Susan E. Alcock and Robin Osborne, eds., *Classical Archaeology*, 2nd ed. (Malden. MA: 2012), 187.

44. Germaine Aujac, J. B. Harley, and David Woodward, "The Growth of an Empirical Cartography in Hellenistic Greece," in J. B. Harley and David Woodward, eds., *The History of Cartography. Volume One: Cartography in Prehistoric, Ancient, and Medieval Europe and the Mediterranean* (Chicago: 1987), 148–60, at 153; for the Mediterranean as midpoint of the map, see Francesco Prontera, "Karte (Kartographie)," trans. Matthias Perkams, in *RAC: Sachwörterbuch zur Auseinandersetzung des Christentums mit der antiken Welt; Lieferung 154-15. Kanon I (Begriff)—Kastration*, ed. Georg Schöllgen et al. (Stuttgart: Anton Hiersemann, 2001), cols. 187–229, at cols. 192–94.

45. For translation of text and commentary, see James H. Oliver, "The Ruling Power: A Study of the Roman Empire in the Second Century after Christ through the Roman Oration of Aelius Aristides," *Transactions of the American Philosophical Society* 43, no. 4 (1953): 873–1003, at 895–953; for the world as Rome's countryside, 901, section 61: "What another city is to its own boundaries and territory, this city is to the boundaries and territory of the entire civilized world, as if the latter were a country district and she had been appointed common town. It might be said that this one citadel is the refuge and assembly place of all perioeci or of all who dwell in outside demes."

46. Vergil, *Aeneid* 12.187–94.

47. Polybius, *The Histories* 1.1.5, ed. and trans. W. R. Paton, F. W. Walbank, and Christian Habicht, LCL 128 (Cambridge, MA: 2010).

48. Peter Sidney Derow, "Polybius (1)," in Simon Hornblower, Antony Spawforth, and Esther Eidinow, eds., *OCD4* (Oxford: 2012), 1174–75, for overview and bibliography; Arthur M. Eckstein, *Moral Vision in the Histories of Polybius* (Berkeley: 1995); F. W. Walbank, *Polybius* (Berkeley: 1972).

49. Eckstein, *Moral Vision*, 118–60.

50. Eckstein, *Moral Vision*, 119.

51. Ibid.

52. S. C. Humphreys, "Fragments, Fetishes, and Philosophies: Toward a History of Greek Historiography after Thucydides," in Glenn Most, ed., *Collecting Fragments = Fragmente sammeln* (Göttingen: 1997), 207–24, at 214–16; Clarke, *Between Geography and History*, 129–92.

53. None of his works survive intact. The fragments are collected in Ludwig Edelstein and I. G. Kidd, *Posidonius: Volume I, The Fragments*, 2nd ed. (Cambridge: 1989), with full commentary and bibliography; I. G. Kidd, *Posidonius: Volume II, The Commentary* (1988); Willy Theiler, ed., *Poseidonios: Die Fragmente* (Berlin: 1982) is a less reliable collection; Posidonius's historical fragments are edited by Felix Jacoby, ed., "87. Poseidonios von Apamea," in *Die Fragmente der griechischen Historiker: Zweiter Teil [FGH2]; Zeitgeschichte. A. Universalgeschichte und Hellenika* (Berlin: 1926), 222–317; they are translated in Clarke, *Between Geography and History*, 347–73; the best short overview is found in Alexander Hugh McDonald, "Posidonius (Ποσειδώνιος), (1)," in *OCD4*, 1195; on methodological concerns, see I. G. Kidd, "What Is a Posidonian Fragment?," in *Collecting Fragments*, 225–36; on

[278] NOTES TO PAGES 34-37

innovations in ethnographic description, see Christian Jacob, *Géographie et ethnographie en Grèce ancienne* (Paris: 1991), 159.

54. Woolf, *Tales of the Barbarians*, 67.

55. Posidonius refused to write an account of Cicero's consulate: Cicero, *Letters to Atticus* 21(II.1).2, ed. and trans. D. R. Shackleton Bailey, LCL 7 (Cambridge, MA: 1999).

56. Clarke, *Between Geography and History*, 191–92: "One need, as in other post-conquest phases, was for the scope and limits of the new world to be set out; the size, the shape, and the habitable zones of the physical globe which was becoming almost synonymous with Roman imperial aspirations."

57. Daphne Nash, "Reconstructing Poseidonios' Celtic Ethnography: Some Considerations," *Britannia* 7 (1976): 111–26.

58. Clarke, *Between Geography and History*, 186–87; K. Schmidt, *Kosmologische Aspekte im Geschischtswerk des Poseidonius, Hypomnemata* 63 (Göttingen: 1980), 97–104.

59. Glacken, *Traces*, 97; also see further discussion in chap. 5 below.

60. Glacken, *Traces*, 100–103.

61. Glacken, *Traces*, 98, drawing on Ernst Honigmann, *Die sieben Klimata und die ΠΟΛΕΙΣ ΕΠΙΣΗΜΟΙ* (Heidelberg: 1929), 4–9, 25–30.

62. "Cosmographia Iulii Caesaris," and "Cosmographia," in Alexander Riese, ed., *Geographi Latini Minores* (Heilbronn: 1878; repr. 1964), 21–23, 71–103; these sources are discussed in O. A. W. Dilke, "Maps in the Service of the State: Roman Cartography to the End of the Augustan Era," in *History of Cartography*, 1:201–11, at 205–6; see also the thirteenth-century Hereford world map which depicts Caesar ordering his geographers to make the survey, in Valerie I. J. Flint, "The Hereford Map: Its Author(s), Two Scenes and a Border," *Transactions of the Royal Historical Society* 8 (1998): 19–44.

63. For an assessment: Charles Coulston Gillispie, "Scientific Aspects of the French Egyptian Expedition 1798–1801," *Proceedings of the American Philosophical Society* 133, no. 4 (Dec. 1989): 447–74.

64. Purcell, "Urban Spaces and Central Places," 198, notes that Augustus found a "symbolic language" of centrality in place when he took power "suitable for the claim to centrality which he so enhanced." The new ruler "came to shape Rome's public institutions around his own power." Nicolet's *Space, Geography, and Politics* remains the best introduction.

65. See Purcell, "Urban Spaces and Central Places," 190 (on ideology); he does not mention the idea of geographical centrality as on maps.

66. Augustus, *Res Gestae Divi Augusti* 26–27, 31, 30–33, ed. and trans. Alison E. Cooley (Cambridge: 2005), 93, 95–97; for discussion, see Nicolet, *Space, Geography, and Politics*, 20.

67. Nicolet, *Space, Geography, and Politics*, 17–24.

68. Nicolet, *Space, Geography, and Politics*, 23–24.

69. Sophie Crawford-Brown envisages the Ara Pacis in the Campus Martius, in "Down from the Roof: Reframing Plants in Augustan Art," *Journal of Roman Archaeology* 35 (2022): 33–63.

70. Charles Brian Rose, "'Princes' and Barbarians on the Ara Pacis," *American Journal of Archaeology* 94, no. 3 (1990): 453–67.

71. Nicolet, *Space, Geography, and Politics*, 16–17.

72. Nicolet, *Space, Geography, and Politics*, 15, quoting Vergil, *Aeneid* 6.851.

73. Vergil, *Aeneid* 6.679–893.

74. John Richardson, *The Language of Empire: Rome and the Idea of Empire from the Third Century BC to the Second Century AD* (Cambridge: 2008), 117–46, esp. 145.

75. Richardson, *Language of Empire*, 89.

76. Richardson, *Language of Empire*, 115, 137–38.

77. Some preferred the idea of empire without limit (*Aeneid* 1.279, "imperium sine fine"); as discussed by Nicolet, *Space, Geography, and Politics*, 192.

78. Tacitus, *Annals* 1.11, quoted and discussed in Richardson, *Language of Empire*, 147.

79. Richardson, *Language of Empire*, 146–81, and 180 n. 287 for ancient sources on limits of imperium (*termini imperii*).

NOTES TO PAGES 37–40 [279]

80. Richardson, *Language of Empire*, 187–88: In the Republic the "gentes" are simply all those who are not holders of Roman citizenship.

81. Kulikowski, "Where the Wild Things Are," 151–63.

82. Mary T. Boatwright, "Visualizing Empire in Imperial Rome," in *Aspects of Ancient Institutions and Geography: Studies in Honor of Richard J. A. Talbert*, ed. Lee L. Brice and Daniëlle Slootjes (Leiden: 2015), 235–59, esp. 235–43 on the map; Richardson, *Language of Empire*, 144, on how Agrippa's map represents the new approach; Claude Nicolet, *The World of the Citizen in Republican Rome* (Berkeley: 1991), 95–122; but see also Kai Brodersen, *Terra Cognita: Studien zur römischen Raumerfassung; Zweite, durchgesehene Auflage* (Hildesheim: 2003), 251–88; Dilke, "Maps in the Service of the State," 207–9; Dio Cassius, *Roman History* 55.8.4, ed. and trans. Earnest Cary and Herbert B. Foster, LCL 83 (Cambridge, MA: 1917), shows that the map was not completed in 7 BCE.

83. Agrippa's original notes (*Commentarii*) are lost. Some fragments of the explanatory portions probably displayed with the map are collected by Alexander Riese, *Geographi Latini Minores* (Heilbronn 1878, repr. 1995), 1–8; Dilke, "Maps in the Service of the State," 208.

84. Boatwright, "Visualizing Empire," 241–42; Dilke, "Maps in the Service of the State," 208–9.

85. The ninth-century Irish geographer Dicuil claims that "the earth is divided into three sections, named Europe, Asia, and Libya; and this the deified Augustus was first to exhibit by means of his world map." For full text and translation, see Dicuil, "Incipit Prologus Libri de Mensura Orbis Terrae = Dicuil: The Book on the Measurement of the Earth," in J. J. Tierney, ed., *Dicuili Liber de Mensura Orbis Terrae*, Scriptores Latini Hibernae 6 (Dublin: 1967), I.2.

86. Nicolet, *Space, Geography, and Politics*, 189.

87. C. Goudineau, "Gaul," in Alan K. Bowman, Edward Champlin, and Andrew Lintott, eds., *CAH 10, The Augustan Empire, 43 B.C.–A.D. 69* (Cambridge: 1996), 464–502, at 482; see Helen Saradi, "The *Kallos* of the Byzantine City: The Development of a Rhetorical *Topos* and Historical Reality," *Gesta* 34, no. 1 (1995): 37–56, for an overview of "good order" as an attribute of beauty in the description of cities in the imperial and Byzantine periods.

88. Kathryn Lomas, "The Idea of a City: Élite Ideology and the Evolution of Urban Form in Italy, 200 BC–AD 100," in Helen M. Parkins, ed., *Roman Urbanism: Beyond the Consumer City* (London: 1997), 21–41, at 23.

89. Vitruvius, *On Architecture* 6.1.2, ed. and trans. Frank Granger, LCL 280 (Cambridge, MA: 1934).

90. Vitruvius, *On Architecture* 6.1.3.

91. Vitruvius, *On Architecture* 6.1.10–11.

92. Daniela Dueck, *Strabo of Amasia: A Greek Man of Letters in Augustan Rome* (London: 2000), 1–31, on his background; see also Christian Jacob, "Geography," in Jacques Brunschwig and Geoffrey E. R. Lloyd, eds., *Greek Thought: A Guide to Classical Knowledge*, trans. Catherine Porter (Cambridge, MA: 2000), 299–311; Michael Maas, "Strabo and Procopius: Classical Geography for a Christian Empire," in Hagit Amirav and Bas ter Haar Romeny, eds., *From Rome to Constantinople: Studies in Honour of Averil Cameron* (Leuven: 2007), 67–83.

93. Nicholas Purcell, "Strabo," in *OCD4*, 1404: "[B]y far the most important source for ancient geography."

94. Strabo, *Geography* 1.4.6, ed. and trans. Horace Leonard Jones, LCL 49 (Cambridge, MA: 1917).

95. Strabo, *Geography* 2.5.8; on interpretation of this passage, see Dueck, *Strabo of Amasia*, 118; also Jacob, "Geography," 309: "Strabo wanted to be of service to Roman statesmen and provincial administrators who needed information on population, economics, and natural resources."

96. Patrick Thollard, *Barbarie et civilisation chez Strabon: Étude critique des livres III et IV de la Géographie* (Paris: 1987), 22–26; for Stoic background; see also Dueck, *Strabo of Amasia*, 62–69, esp. 62: "Moreover, *contra* Posidonius, Strabo holds that while providence determines order in the natural sphere, it does not determine human character and the nature of the various races. Therefore he thinks that the distribution of races and languages

[280] NOTES TO PAGES 40-43

in the *oikoumene* is accidental, and human character is not natural but is based on habit and custom (2.3.7, C 102–3), thus reducing the role of providence and increasing the role of human freedom and control."

97. Strabo, *Geography* 2.5.12.

98. Strabo, *Geography* 16.4.22–24.

99. Thollard, *Barbarie et civilisation*; D. R. Dicks reviews Thollard's *Barbarie et civilisation* in *The Classical Review* 41, no. 1 (1991): 226; L. A. Thompson, "Strabo on Civilization," *Platon* 31 (1979): 213–30.

100. Thompson, "Strabo on Civilization," 214: "Strabo does not set out a theory of civilization as a formal and complete whole in any particular section of his work."

101. Thompson, "Strabo on Civilization," 215.

102. Thompson, "Strabo on Civilization," 221–29; for Strabo's sources, see Ernst Honigmann, "S.s Quellenbenutzung. Moderne Quellenkritik," in Georg Wissowa, Wilhelm Kroll, and Karl Mittelhaus, eds., *RE: Neue Bearbeitung; Zweite Reihe [R—Z]. Vierter Band. Stoa—Tauris* (Stuttgart: 1932), cols. 97–151.

103. Dueck, *Strabo of Amasia*, 79.

104. Strabo, *Geography* 2.3.7; Francesco Trotta gives case studies of the basic Hellenistic attitude that the marker of a civilized place was a constitution (*politeia*): Francesco Trotta, "Strabone e l'Asia Minore: *Politeiai* e gradi di civilizzazione," in Anna Maria Biraschi and Giovanni Salmeri, eds., *Strabone e l'Asia Minore* (Perugia: 2000), 189–208; Thompson, "Strabo on Civilization," 217.

105. Strabo, *Geography* 2.3.7.

106. Thollard, *"Barbarie et civilisation,"* 19–20; Thompson, "Strabo on Civilisation," 219; Maas, "Strabo and Procopius," 72.

107. Strabo, *Geography* 2.5.26, 4.1.12, and 3.3.8; discussed in Maas, "Strabo and Procopius," 73–75. For other agents of change, like King Masinissa, see also Dueck, *Strabo of Amasia*, 115–22.

108. Strabo, *Geography* 3.3.8.

109. Strabo, *Geography* 2.5.26.

110. Strabo, *Geography* 4.1.12.

111. Strabo, *Geography* 9.4.15.

112. Maas, "Strabo and Procopius," 72–73.

113. Ariana was a region in eastern Iran.

114. Strabo, *Geography* 1.4.9.

115. Strabo, *Geography* 7.3.7.

116. Arthur O. Lovejoy and George Boas, *Primitivism and Related Ideas in Antiquity* (Baltimore: 1935), for lengthy excerpts and discussion of texts.

117. Thompson, "Strabo on Civilisation," 219.

118. Maas, "Strabo and Procopius," passim.

119. Albrecht Dihle, *Greek and Latin Literature of the Roman Empire: From Augustus to Justinian*, trans. Manfred Malzahn (London: 1994), 180–85, offers a convenient summary of his career. See also Murphy, *Pliny the Elder's Natural History*, 77–164; Valérie Naas, *Le projet encyclopédique de Pline l'Ancien* (Rome: 2002).

120. Rives, trans., *Tacitus Germania*, 36; on his service at the Rhine frontier, see the in-depth discussion of Ronald Syme, "Pliny the Procurator," *Harvard Studies in Classical Philology* 73 (1969): 201–36, at 204–8.

121. Rives, trans., *Tacitus Germania*, 37.

122. Rives, trans., *Tacitus Germania*, 36–37.

123. Nicolet, *Space, Geography, and Politics*, 15–24, 37–41; Murphy, *Pliny the Elder's Natural History*, 129–64.

124. Pliny, *Natural History* 1.6. Discussed in Murphy, *Pliny the Elder's Natural History*, 129.

125. Naas, *Le Projet Encyclopédique*, 425–26.

126. Naas, *Le Projet Encyclopédique*, 418–21, discussing the slow conflation of the ideas of *orbis terrarum, orbis romanus*, and *oikoumene*.

NOTES TO PAGES 43–47 [281]

127. Murphy, *Pliny the Elder's Natural History*, 161–64.

128. Murphy, *Pliny the Elder's Natural History*, 160.

129. Murphy, *Pliny the Elder's Natural History*, 131–33; e.g., Pliny, *Natural History* 27.1.3.

130. Felix Jacoby, *Die Fragmente der griechischen Historiker: Erster Teil; Genealogie und Mythographie* (Berlin: 1923), 1–47, with discussion 317–75. On Pliny's work as a *periplus*, see Murphy, *Pliny the Elder's Natural History*, 133–37.

131. Murphy, *Pliny the Elder's Natural History*, 131, 154–64.

132. Murphy, *Pliny the Elder's Natural History*, 155–56.

133. Murphy, *Pliny the Elder's Natural History*, 163, on exploration and discovery as imperial prerogatives.

134. Pliny, *Natural History* 2.118.

135. Pliny, *Natural History* 2.117.

136. Pliny, *Natural History* 7.1.

137. Pliny, *Natural History* 7.6.

138. Pliny, *Natural History* 16.2–7.

139. Pliny *Natural History* 7.21–32; Murphy, *Pliny the Elder's Natural History*, 89–92, for further citations and bibliography on exotic peoples.

140. Rives, trans., *Tacitus Germania*, for introduction.

141. For a summary of Roman interaction with the Germani, see Rives, trans., *Tacitus Germania*, 27–35; and C. Rüger, "Germany," in Alan K. Bowman, Edward Champlin, and Andrew Lintott, eds., *CAH 10, The Augustan Empire, 43 B.C.–A.D. 69* (Cambridge: 1996), 517–34. More recently, Roxana-Gabriela Curcă et al., eds., *Rome and Barbaricum: Contributions to the Archaeology and History of Interaction in European Protohistory* (Oxford: 2020).

142. Erich Gruen, "The Expansion of the Empire under Augustus," in Bowman, Champlin, and Lintott, eds., *CAH 10*, 147–97. Gruen argues that Augustus's military campaigns in Germany were intended to manifest a consistent image of Roman might and not to pursue a consistent policy of conquest and incorporation.

143. C. R. Whittaker, *Frontiers of the Roman Empire: A Social and Economic Study* (Baltimore: 1994), 38–49, for introductory discussion of the western frontier.

144. Rives, trans., *Tacitus Germania* 29.

145. Rives, trans., *Tacitus Germania* 30.1, p. 89.

146. For an introduction to the *limes* between the Rhine and Danube and its major fortifications, see Britta Rabold, Egon Schallmayer, and Andreas Thiel, eds., *Der Limes: Die Deutsche Limes-Strasse vom Rhein bis zur Donau* (Stuttgart: 2000).

147. Rives, trans., *Tacitus Germania*, 55.

148. Rives, trans., *Tacitus Germania*, 50.

149. Gruen, *Rethinking the Other*, 159.

150. Tacitus, *Germania* 1.2.5.

151. Rives, trans., *Tacitus Germania*, 43.

152. Rives, trans., *Tacitus Germania*, 35–41, on Tacitus's sources. For an overview of evidence for Germanic peoples in antiquity and an evaluation of the trends in scholarship: Walter Pohl, *Die Germanen* (Munich: 2000); Gruen, *Rethinking the Other*, 159–61; Herwig Wolfram emphasizes the late antique period in *The Roman Empire and Its Germanic Peoples*, trans. Thomas Dunlap (Berkeley: 1997).

153. Rives, trans., *Tacitus Germania* 28.1, p. 88.

154. Mentioned by Quintilian, *The Orator's Education* 10.1.103, ed. and trans. Donald A. Russell, LCL 127 (Cambridge, MA: 2002); discussed in Rives, trans., *Tacitus Germania*, 35–41, on the Roman sources.

155. Gruen, *Rethinking the Other*, 159–78.

156. Gruen, *Rethinking the Other*, 160.

157. Rives, trans., *Tacitus Germania*, 66–74; Christopher B. Krebs, *A Most Dangerous Book: Tacitus's Germania from the Roman Empire to the Third Reich* (New York: 2011).

158. Gruen, *Rethinking the Other*, 165.

159. Brent Shaw, "The Exterminating Angel: The Roman Imperial State and Its Indigenous Peoples," in *Empires and Indigenous Peoples*, ed. Maas and Yarbrough, 17–35.

[282] NOTES TO PAGES 47–55

160. Tacitus, *Germania* 44.1: Rives, trans., *Tacitus Germania*, 95; Gruen, *Rethinking the Other*, 170–71.

161. Tacitus, *Germania* 18.1: Rives, trans., *Tacitus Germania*, 84.

162. Tacitus, *Germania* 39.1: Rives, trans., *Tacitus Germania*, 93.

163. On distancing from the Other, see Tzvetan Todorov, *The Conquest of America: The Question of the Other* (New York: 1984), 185; discussed by Michael Maas, "Ethnicity, Orthodoxy, and Community in Salvian of Marseilles," in John Drinkwater and Hugh Elton, eds., *Fifth-Century Gaul: A Crisis of Identity?* (Cambridge: 1992), 275–84, at 278–84.

164. Tacitus, *Germania* 5.3: Rives, trans., *Tacitus Germania*, 79, with some modification.

165. Tacitus, *Germania* 45.4: Rives, trans., *Tacitus Germania*, 96; Gruen, *Rethinking the Other*, 161, on these passages.

166. Tacitus, *Germania* 45.5.

167. Tacitus, *Germania* 46.4: Rives, trans., *Tacitus Germania*, 97.

168. Tacitus, *Germania* 2.1: Rives, trans., *Tacitus Germania*, 77; see also *Germania* 4.1.

169. They have no cities, for example (*Germania* 16.1): Rives, trans., *Tacitus Germania*, 83.

170. Tacitus, *Germania* 37.1: Rives, trans., *Tacitus Germania*, 91–92.

171. Tacitus, *Germania* 46.

172. Tacitus, *Agricola* 3, ed. and trans. M. Hutton, W. Peterson, R. M. Ogilvie, et al., LCL 35 (Cambridge, MA: 1914).

173. Tacitus, *Agricola* 21, trans. Greg Woolf, *Becoming Roman: The Origins of Provincial Civilization in Gaul* (Cambridge: 1998), 69.

174. Ptolemy, *Tetrabiblos* 1.1–3, ed. and trans. F. E. Robbins, LCL 435 (Cambridge, MA: 1940).

175. Ptolemy, *Tetrabiblos* 2.1.

176. Ptolemy, *Tetrabiblos* 2.2, p. 121 n. 4 suggests Ptolemy's dependence on the Stoic writer Posidonius.

177. Ptolemy, *Tetrabiblos* 2.2.

Chapter Two: *"Hostiles and Friendlies"*

1. "Hostiles and Friendlies" is taken from a collection of short stories about life on the Nebraska frontier by Mari Sandoz, *Hostiles and Friendlies* (Lincoln, NE: 1959).

2. "2123 Κόρυκος," in Ada Adler, ed., *Suidae Lexicon. Pars III* (Leipzig: 1933), 161, translation M. Maas; Κόρυκος, a Homeric word, means leather sack, or "money bag." The source of the passage may be Priscus of Panium.

3. Peter Heather, *Empires and Barbarians* (London: 2009), 82–85, for fuller discussion.

4. Ammianus Marcellinus, *History* 17.12.9–10, ed. and trans. J. C. Rolfe, LCL 300 (Cambridge, MA: 1950).

5. Ammianus, *History* 17.12.11.

6. Michael Whitby, "Byzantine Diplomacy: Good Faith, Trust and Co-operation in International Relations in Late Antiquity," in Philip de Souza and John France, eds., *War and Peace in Ancient and Medieval History* (Cambridge: 2008), 120–40; A. D. Lee, "Treaty-making in Late Antiquity," in *War and Peace in Ancient and Medieval History*, 107–19; Conor Whately, "Strategy, Diplomacy and Frontiers: A Bibliographic Essay," in Alexander Sarantis and Neil Christie, eds., *War and Warfare in Late Antiquity* (Leiden: 2013), 239–54, at 243–46.

7. Andrew Gillett, *Envoys and Political Communication in the Late Antique West, 411–533* (Cambridge: 2003); for an overview of the role of ambassadors, see Audrey Becker and Nicolas Drocourt, eds., *Ambassadeurs et ambassades au coeur des relations diplomatiques: Rome—Occident médiéval—Byzance (VIIIe s. avant J.-C.—XIIe s. après J.-C.)* (Metz: 2012).

8. For an overview of East Roman diplomacy in Late Antiquity, see Ekaterina Nechaeva, "Late Antique East Roman Diplomacy," in Gordon Martel, ed., *The Encyclopedia of Diplomacy*, vol. 3 (Malden, MA: 2018), 1079–90; Gerhard Wirth, "Rome and Its Germanic Partners in the Fourth Century," in *Kingdoms of the Empire: The Integration of Barbarians in Late Antiquity* (Leiden: 1997), 13–55, esp. on *deditio*.

NOTES TO PAGES 55–56 [283]

9. Walter Pohl, "Ritualized Encounters: Late Roman Diplomacy and the Barbarians, Fifth–Sixth Century," in Alexander Beihammer, Stavrola Constantinou, and Maria G. Parani, eds., *Court Ceremonies and Rituals of Power in Byzantium and the Medieval Mediterranean: Comparative Perspectives* (Leiden: 2013), 67–86, emphasizes the scripted nature of such formal encounters as well as their adjustability as circumstances demanded; Audrey Becker, *Les Relations diplomatiques romano-barbares en Occident au Ve siècle: Acteurs, fonctions, modalités* (Paris: 2013), 143–220, on ambassadorial protocols; Peter the Patrician, Justinian's Master of the Offices, describes the intricate format for receiving foreign embassies at court in Constantine Porphyrogennetos, *The Book of Ceremonies*, ed. and trans. Anne Moffatt and Maxeme Tall (Leiden: 2012), I.88 [R396–98; cod. chap. 97] (embassies from the West) and I.89–90 [R398–410; cod. chap. 98–99] (Persian embassies); on Peter the Patrician, see xxvi–xxvii. The fragments from the lost history of Peter are gathered in Thomas M. Banchich, *The Lost History of Peter the Patrician: An Account of Rome's Imperial Past from the Age of Justinian* (London: 2015); see also Corippus's description of an Avar embassy below, and Flavius Cresconius Corippus, *In laudem Iustini Augusti Minoris, Libri IV*, ed. and trans. Averil Cameron (London: 1976), 190, note on line 234.

10. I thank Jonathan Shepard for this observation.

11. C. D. Gordon, "Subsidies in Roman Imperial Defence," *Phoenix* 3, no. 2 (1949): 60–69.

12. Specific information came from military sources, travelers and merchants, written sources, and experience. Previous treaties found a home in archives in Constantinople that could be consulted by government representatives, though these treaties may not have been consistently filed. In Constantinople, the *magister officiorum*, who often led delegations, supervised the Barbarian Office (*Scrinium Barbarorum*/Σκρίνιον των Βαρβάρων), which handled the affairs of foreigners in the city and provided translators and logistical support for embassies: Otto Seeck, ed., "Notitia dignitatum omnium, tam civilium quam militarium, in partibus Orientis," in *Notitia Dignitatum: Accedunt notitia urbis Constantinopolitanae et Laterculi Provinciarum* (Berlin: Weidmann, 1876), XI (interpreters of different peoples), p. 33. For records of ambassadorial travel expenses, see Peter the Patrician in Constantine Porphyrogennetos, *Book of Ceremonies* 1.89 [R400; cod. chap. 98]; J. B. Bury, *The Imperial Administrative System in the Ninth Century: With a Revised Text of the Kletorologion of Philotheos* (London: 1911), 93; Michael McCormick, "Analyzing Imperial Ceremonies," *Jahrbuch der österreichischen Byzantinistik* 35 (1985): 1–20; Franz Tinnefeld, "Ceremonies for Foreign Ambassadors at the Court of Byzantium and Their Political Background," *Byzantinische Forschungen* 19 (1993): 193–213, at 194–95.

13. Marcel Mauss, "Essai sur le don: Forme et raison de l'échange dans les sociétés archaïques," *L'année sociologique: Nouvelle série* 1 (1923–24): 30–186; Marcel Mauss, *The Gift: Forms and Functions of Exchange in Archaic Societies*, trans. Ian Cunnison (London: 1966; repr. 1974); Marcel Mauss, *The Gift: Expanded Edition*, trans. Jane I. Guyer (Chicago: 2016), 55–198.

14. Livy, *History of Rome* 27.4, ed. and trans. J. C. Yardley, LCL 367 (Cambridge, MA: 2020); and Livy, *History of Rome* 31.9, ed. and trans. J. C. Yardley, LCL 295 (Cambridge, MA: 2017).

15. Tacitus, *Germania* 42.2.

16. For example, Dio Chrysostom, *Discourses* 79.5, ed. and trans. H. Lamar Crosby, LCL 385 (Cambridge, MA: 1951).

17. Pliny the Younger, *Letters, Volume II: Books 8–10. Panegyricus*, ed. and trans. Betty Radice, LCL 59 (Cambridge, MA: 1969), 12.2; see also Edward Gibbon, *The History of the Decline and Fall of the Roman Empire*, 3 vols., ed. David Womersley, (London: 1994), 1:266.

18. Ekaterina Nechaeva, "Late Antique East Roman Diplomacy," 1079–90; Gordon, "Subsidies in Roman Imperial Defence," 63–64, for citations.

19. Gordon, "Subsidies in Roman Imperial Defence," 64.

20. Matthias Hardt, *Gold und Herrschaft: Die Schätze europäischer Könige und Fürsten im ersten Jahrtausend* (Berlin: 2004), 187–96, on tribute in western Europe; for introductions to late antique discussion, with bibliography: R. C. Blockley, *East Roman Foreign*

[284] NOTES TO PAGES 56–58

Policy: Formation and Conduct from Diocletian to Anastasius (Leeds: 1992); Nechaeva, "Late Antique East Roman Diplomacy," in *The Encyclopedia of Diplomacy*, ed. Gordon Martel (Chichester: 2018), 3:1079–90; R. C. Blockley, "Subsidies and Diplomacy: Rome and Persia in Late Antiquity," *Phoenix* 39, no. 1 (1985): 62–74.

21. Claudian, "The Second Book Against Rufinus" 2.74–77, in *Panegyric on Probinus and Olybrius. Against Rufinus 1 and 2, etc.*, ed. and trans. M. Platnauer, LCL 135 (Cambridge, MA: 1922).

22. Zosimus, *New History* 5.26 and 5.29, trans. Ronald T. Ridley (Sydney: 2006).

23. Zosimus, *New History* 5.41; Colin Douglas Gordon, *The Subsidization of Border Peoples as a Roman Policy in Imperial Defence* (PhD diss., University of Michigan, 1948), 91–93.

24. Nicola Di Cosmo, "The War Economy of Nomadic Empires," in Nicola Di Cosmo, Didier Fassin, and Clémence Pinaud, eds., *Rebel Economies: Warlords, Insurgents, Humanitarians* (London: 2021), 103–25, at 113.

25. M. J. Nicasie, "Review of R. C. Blockley, *East Roman Foreign Policy: Formation and Conduct from Diocletian to Anastasius* (ARCA 30)," *Mnemosyne* 49, no. 1 (1996): 118–23; Geoffrey Greatrex, "Procopius and Roman Imperial Policy in the Arabian and Egyptian Frontier Zones," in Jitse H. F. Dijkstra and Greg Fisher, eds., *Inside and Out: Interactions between Rome and the Peoples on the Arabian and Egyptian Frontiers in Late Antiquity* (Leuven: 2014), 249–66.

26. For example, Ze'ev Rubin, "Diplomacy and War in the Relations between Byzantium and the Sassanids in the Fifth Century AD," in Philip Freeman and David Kennedy, eds., *The Defence of the Roman and Byzantine East: Proceedings of a Colloquium Held at the University of Sheffield in April 1986, Part II* (Oxford: 1986), 677–95.

27. Nechaeva, "Late Antique East Roman Diplomacy," 1080–81, for introduction.

28. Michael Maas, "Fugitives and Ethnography in Priscus of Panium," *Byzantine and Modern Greek Studies* 19 (1995): 146–60; for text, see *Suidae Lexicon / Suda*, "2123 Κόρυκος," 161; Priscus's *History* in eight books remains only in fragments and excerpts. They are conveniently gathered and translated into English with historical notes by R. C. Blockley, *The Fragmentary Classicising Historians of the Later Roman Empire*, vol. 2 (Liverpool: 1983). Volume 1 of this work offers a detailed analysis of Priscus's historical work, 48–70; Pia Carolla's *Priscus Panita: Excerpta et Fragmenta* (Berlin: 2008) provides Greek text and detailed history of the text. Priscus's lengthy description of the embassy to Attila as well as other of his diplomatic information appeared in the *Excerpta de Legationibus* compiled at the order of the tenth-century Byzantine emperor Constantine Porphyrogenitus. That work, *Excerpta de Legationibus Iussi Imp. Constantini Porphyrogeniti Confecta*, ed. Carolus de Boor (Berlin: 1903), is a source for both Blockley and Carolla. It is cited in the notes below following the fragment as *Exc. de Leg. Gent. (Excerpts from Legations to Different Peoples)* or *Exc. de Leg. Rom. (Excerpts from Legations to the Romans)*.

29. From about 430, Attila's predecessor Rua (Rugila) received 350 Roman pounds of gold each year. This amount was doubled by the Eastern emperor in the Treaty of Margus in 435. Attila's pressure on the lower Danube region forced the emperor to raise the amount to 2,100 pounds of gold annually. With this arrangement came a further onetime payment of 6,000 pounds of gold. For discussion of these payments, see: Matthias Hardt, "The Nomad's Greed for Gold: From the Fall of the Burgundians to the Avar Treasure," in Richard Corradini, Max Diesenberger, and Helmut Reimitz, eds., *The Construction of Communities in the Early Middle Ages: Texts, Resources, and Artefacts* (Leiden: 2002), 95–108, at 97–98; Jan Iluk, "The Export of Gold from the Roman Empire to Barbarian Countries from the 4th to the 6th Centuries," *Münstersche Beiträge zur Antiken Handelsgeschichte* 4, no. 1 (1985): 79–102, at 87–88; Peter Guest, "Roman Gold and Hun Kings: The Use and Hoarding of Solidi in the Late Fourth and Fifth Centuries," in Aleksander Bursche et al., eds., *Roman Coins Outside the Empire: Ways and Phases, Contexts and Functions; Proceedings of the ESF/SCH Exploratory Workshop, Radziwill Palace, Nieborów (Poland), 3–6 September 2005* (Warsaw: 2008), 295–307; Gordon, "Subsidies in Roman Imperial Defence," 65; Hardt, "The Nomad's Greed," 97, calculates a total amount of over 9 metric tons. Peter Guest, however, doubts that

NOTES TO PAGES 58–62 [285]

such enormous quantities ever crossed Roman borders every year: "Roman Gold and Hun Kings," 300–301.

30. Equally outrageous would have been the possibility of Attila's marrying the Roman princess Honoria, sister of emperor Valentinian III: John of Antioch, "Ἰωάννου Ἀντιοχέως Ἅπαντα τὰ Σωζομενά Ἀποσπάσματα," in Sergei Mariev, ed. and trans., *Ioannis Antiocheni fragmenta quae supersunt omnia*, CFHB (Berlin: 2008), 224 [*EI* 85]; and Priscus, "History," frag. 20.1 and 20.3, in Blockley, *Fragmentary Classicising Historians*, vol. 2 (*Exc. de Leg. Gent.* 7–8); Priscus Panita, *Excerpta* 15–16, ed. Carolla (Berlin: 2008).

31. Treatment of Rome as a "tributary empire" generally also considers the wealth or tribute exacted from the subject peoples *within* the empire, not discussed in this chapter.

32. Augustus, *Res Gestae Divi Augusti* 31–33, in *Augustus, Res Gestae Divi Augusti: Text, Translation, and Commentary*, ed. and trans. Alison E. Cooley (Cambridge: 2005).

33. Discussed further below.

34. Corippus, *In laudem Iustini Augusti minoris libri VI*, pr. 25, trans. Averil Cameron (London: 1976), 85.

35. Theophanes the Confessor, *Chronographia* AM 6123, trans. Cyril Mango and Roger Scott, *The Chronicle of Theophanes Confessor: Byzantine and Near Eastern History; AD 284–813* (Oxford: 1997).

36. Peter Fibiger Bang, "Commanding and Consuming the World: Empire, Tribute, and Trade in Roman and Chinese History," in Walter Scheidel, ed., *Rome and China: Comparative Perspectives on Ancient World Empires* (Oxford: 2009), 100–120, at 102–3: "Tribute was something subjects and outlying barbarian peoples were supposed to remit to Rome, not the other way around. From the point of view of empire, relations with the surrounding world presented themselves in terms of submission and tribute," 103 n. 10; *Digest* 39.4.11 (Paul, *Sententiae*, book 5).

37. Unfinished in 339 at the author's death; Eusebius, *Life of Constantine* 4.7, trans. Averil Cameron and Stuart G. Hall (Oxford: 1999); see also *Life of Constantine* 4.6.

38. Elsewhere in his writings, as Aaron Johnson has discussed, Eusebius attributed cultural change among converts to Christianity as being due not to Rome in any way but to the faith alone: Aaron P. Johnson, *Ethnicity and Argument in Eusebius' Praeparatio Evangelica* (Oxford: 2006), 196.

39. Eusebius, *Life of Constantine* 4.5: "(1) What need is there for me to mention even incidentally how he subjected barbarian races to Roman rule . . . Confident in his Saviour and brandishing the victorious trophy over them too, he very soon subdued them all, sometimes taming the refractory with the military arm, sometimes pacifying the rest by reasonable negotiations, converting them from a lawless animal existence to one of reason and law. In this way the Goths learnt at last to serve Rome."

40. Eusebius, *Life of Constantine* 4.8–14.

41. Eusebius, *Life of Constantine* 4.9–13 for Constantine's letter to Shapur.

42. Linda Safran, "Points of View: The Theodosian Obelisk Base in Context," *Greek, Roman and Byzantine Studies* 34, no. 4 (Winter 1993): 409–35; Jean-Pierre Sodini, "Images sculptées et propagande impériale du IVᵉ au VIᵉ siècle: Recherches récentes sur les colonnes honorifiques et les reliefs politiques à Byzance," in André Guillou and Jannic Durand, eds., *Byzance et les images: Cycle de conferences organisé au musée du Louvre par le Service culturel du 5 octobre au 7 décembre 1992* (Paris: 1994), 43–94; Bente Kiilerich, *The Obelisk Base in Constantinople: Court Art and Imperial Ideology* (Rome: 1998); on tribute processions in Constantinople, Rolf Michael Schneider, "Orientalism in Late Antiquity: The Oriental in Imperial and Christian Imagery," in Josef Wiesehöfer and Philip Huyse, *Ērān ud Anērān: Studien zu den Beziehungen zwischen dem Sasanidenreich und der Mittelmeerwelt; Beiträge des Internationalen Colloquiums in Eutin, 8.-9. Juni 2000, Oriens et Occidens 13* (Munich: 2006), 241–78, at 244–47.

43. Safran, "Points of View," 410.

44. Michael McCormick, *Eternal Victory: Triumphal Rulership in Late Antiquity, Byzantium, and the Early Medieval West* (Cambridge: 1986), 91–93.

45. Safran, "Points of View," discusses the question of visibility.

[286]   NOTES TO PAGES 62–65

46. Jaś Elsner, *Imperial Rome and Christian Triumph: The Art of the Roman Empire AD 100–450* (Oxford: 1998), 75–76, emphasizes that "[e]ven the actual stone of the obelisk is envisaged as Theodosius' obedient servant. The Latin inscription, presented as if the obelisk were itself speaking, reads: 'Formerly reluctant, I was ordered to obey the serene lords and carry the palm of the extinct tyrants. Everything yields to Theodosius and his everlasting offspring. So conquered and vanquished, I was raised to the lofty sky in three times ten days while Proclus was judge.'" For Latin text, see Theodor Mommsen, ed., *CIL* 3.1 *Voluminis Tertii Pars Pior; Inscriptiones Asiae Provinciarum Europae Graecarum Illyrici Latinae* (Berlin: 1873), n. 737.

47. Jonathan Shepard, "Byzantium's Overlapping Circles," in Elizabeth Jeffreys, ed., *Proceedings of the 21st International Congress of Byzantine Studies, London, 21–26 August, 2006. Volume I: Plenary Papers* (London: 2006), 15–55, for discussion of Dimitry Obolensky's arguments for a "Byzantine Commonwealth"; see also George Ostrogorsky, "The Byzantine Emperor and the Hierarchical World Order," *The Slavonic and East European Review* 35, no. 84 (1956): 1–14; Jonathan Shepard, "Superpower to Soft Power, within Overlapping Circles: Byzantium and Its Place in Twenty-First-Century International History," in Michael Gehler and Wolfgang Mueller, eds., *Internationale Geschichte in Theorie und Praxis/ International History in Theory and Practice, Band 4* (Vienna: 2017), 81–122.

48. Ammianus, *History* 23.5.19: Emperor Julian exhorted his troops to destroy this *natio molestissima* at the beginning of his ill-fated invasion in 363.

49. Matthew P. Canepa, "Sasanian Iran and the Projection of Power in Late Antique Eurasia," in *Empires and Exchanges in Eurasian Late Antiquity: Rome, China, Iran, and the Steppe, ca. 250–750*, ed. Nicola Di Cosmo and Michael Maas (Cambridge: 2018), 54–69.

50. Scholars no longer believe that the Sasanians wanted to restore their state to the limits of the Achaemenid empire: Karin Mosig-Walburg, *Römer und Perser: Vom 3. Jahrhundert bis zum Jahr 363 n. Chr.* (Gutenberg: 2009), 19–90, for detailed discussion; Michael Weiskopf's review, "Römer und Perser: Vom 3. Jahrhundert bis zum Jahr 363 n. Chr," *BMCR* 2010.01.33 (2010), https://bmcr.brynmawr.edu/2010/2010.01.33/; on Roman writers who thought that restoration of the Achaemenid empire was a Sasanian goal, see Ze'ev Rubin, "The Sasanid Monarchy," in Averil Cameron, Bryan Ward-Perkins, and Michael Whitby, *CAH 14, Late Antiquity: Empire and Successors, A.D. 425–600* (Cambridge: 2000), 638–61, at 646; Richard Payne, "Cosmology and the Expansion of the Iranian Empire, 502–628 CE," *Past and Present*, no. 220 (August 2013): 3–33, at 10–11, reviews arguments and emphasizes that "the Sasanians saw themselves not as successors of the Achaemenids, who appear only episodically in the Iranian tradition, but as successors of the kings of a Zoroastrian sacred history."

51. Richard Payne, "The Reinvention of Iran: The Sasanian Empire and the Huns," in Michael Maas, ed. *The Cambridge Companion to the Age of Attila* (Cambridge: 2014), 282–300, at 296–98.

52. James Howard-Johnston, *The Last Great War of Antiquity* (Oxford: 2021).

53. Matthew Canepa, *The Two Eyes of the Earth: Art and Ritual of Kingship between Rome and Sasanian Iran* (Berkeley: 2009).

54. Ekaterina Nechaeva, *Embassies—Negotiations—Gifts: Systems of East Roman Diplomacy in Late Antiquity* (Stuttgart: 2014).

55. Matthew P. Canepa, *The Iranian Expanse: Transforming Royal Identity through Architecture, Landscape, and the Built Environment, 550 BCE–642 CE* (Berkeley: 2019), at 333–35; Payne, "Cosmology," 164 n. 41.

56. Canepa, *Two Eyes*, 54, 58–75.

57. Canepa, *Two Eyes*, 60–63.

58. Canepa, *Two Eyes*, 63, notes that later reliefs (Naqsh-e Rostam VI and Bishapur III and IV) show the emperor in more standard Roman postures of supplication.

59. Canepa, *Two Eyes*, 68–71.

60. Guy Le Strange and R. A. Nicholson, eds., *The Fársnáma of Ibnu'l-Balkhí* (London: 1921), 97, cited and translated in Canepa, *Two Eyes*, 143.

61. Canepa, *Two Eyes*, 143.

NOTES TO PAGES 65–70   [287]

62. Ahmad ibn Muhammad ibn Miskawayh, *Tajārib al-umam* [*Experiences of Nations*], ed. A. Emāmi, 8 vols. (Tehran: 2001), i, 190, translated in Payne, "Cosmology," 21.

63. Henning Börm, "'Es war allerdings nicht so, daß sie es im Sinne eines Tributes erhielten, wie viele meinten . . .': Anlässe und Funktion der persischen Geldforderungen an die Römer (3. bis 6. Jh.)," *Historia* 57, no. 3 (2008): 327–46, esp. 341–42; Payne, "The Reinvention of Iran," 298; a Roman perspective is seen in Pacatus Drepanius, *Panegyric to the Emperor Theodosius* 22.4–5, trans. C. E. V. Nixon (Liverpool: 1987): "Persia herself, once a rival to our state and notorious for the deaths of so many Roman leaders, makes amends by her obedience for whatever atrocities she has perpetrated upon our princes. Finally her King himself, who once disdained to concede he was a man, now confesses his fear and worships you in those very temples in which he is worshipped. Then by sending an embassy, and offering gems and silks, and in addition by supplying triumphal animals for your chariots, although in name he is still your ally, in his veneration of you he is a tributary."

64. Payne, "Cosmology," 3–33.

65. Payne, "Cosmology," 16.

66. Beate Dignas and Engelbert Winter, *Rome and Persia in Late Antiquity: Neighbors and Rivals* (Cambridge: 2007), 37, for sources. They say he needed money to pay the Hepthalites and asked Anastasius, who refused and demanded the return of Nisibis. This gave Kavadh a reason to resume hostilities. Payne, "Cosmology," 13, rejects this explanation, emphasizing that Kavadh's request was not to finance his campaigns against the Hephthalites but intended primarily "to renew a tributary relationship that had lapsed."

67. As argued by Börm, "'Es was allerdings nicht so,'" 334–41.

68. Procopius, *The Anecdota or Secret History* 19.15, ed. and trans. H. B. Dewing, LCL 290 (Cambridge, MA: 1935).

69. Procopius, *History of the Wars* 1.4.35, describes how the Persians paid tribute to the Hephthalite Huns in the previous century: "the Persians became subject and tributary to the Ephthalitae, until Cabades had established his power most securely and no longer deemed it necessary to pay the annual tribute to them."

70. On attitudes toward Justinian's payments to barbarians: Procopius, *Secret History* 11.5–13, 19.6, and 19.13–17; on Justinian's demonic nature, see 12.14–27, 18.1–4, and 18.36–37.

71. Agathias, *The Histories* 5.2.3, trans. Joseph D. C. Frendo (Berlin: 1975). For Greek, see Rudolf Keydell, ed., *Agathiae Myrinaei Historiarum Libri Quinque* (Berlin: 1967).

72. Geoffrey Greatrex, *Rome and Persia at War 502–532* (Leeds: 1998), 213–21.

73. Michael Whitby, *The Wars of Justinian* (Barnsley, UK: 2021), 115–72, on wars with Persia.

74. Geoffrey Greatrex and Samuel N. C. Lieu, eds., *The Roman Eastern Frontier and the Persian Wars, Part II: A.D. 363–630* (London: 2008), 86–87, for the 520s, and for the 530s, see Whitby, *Wars of Justinian*, 141–42.

75. Greatrex and Lieu, *Roman Eastern Frontier II*, 86–87.

76. Whitby, *Wars of Justinian*, 126–27; Greatrex, *Rome and Persia at War*, 160–61; Alfredo M. Rabello, *Giustiniano, ebrei e samaritani alla luce delle fonti storico-letterarie, ecclesiastiche e giuridiche I* (Milan: 1987), conveniently gathers sources.

77. Geoffrey Greatrex, "Byzantium and the East in the Sixth Century," in Michael Maas, ed., *The Cambridge Companion to the Age of Justinian* (Cambridge: 2005), 477–509, at 496–500.

78. John Malalas, *The Chronicle of John Malalas* 18.44, trans. Elizabeth Jeffreys, Michael Jeffreys, and Roger Scott (Leiden: 2017); for Greek, Ioannes Thurn, ed., *Ioannis Malalae Chronographia* (Berlin: 2000), 378.

79. Malalas, *Chronicle* 18.44.

80. Procopius, *History of the Wars* 2.10.19–24, has Khusro I, following his sack of Antioch in 540, remark that the Romans pay the Saracens to keep Roman lands from being plundered and that Romans should see their "gifts" to the Persians in the same way.

81. Whitby, *Wars of Justinian*, 139–42.

82. Malalas, *Chronicle* 18.76.

83. Greatrex, *Rome and Persia at War*, 216–17.

[288] NOTES TO PAGES 70-73

84. Greatrex, *Rome and Persia at War*, 216, also listing other sums. This payment to Khusro was readily made.

85. Agathias, *Histories* 4.30.7-10, see Greatrex and Lieu, *Roman Eastern Frontier II*, 130-31.

86. Menander Protector, *The History of Menander the Guardsman*, frag. 6.1.134-54, ed. and trans. R. C. Blockley (Liverpool: 1985).

87. Menander, *History*, frag. 6.1.314-97, further elaborates details of the treaty, involving defense of the Caspian Gates, control of Arab allies, management of trade between the two empires at fixed border points, treatment of ambassadors, the settlement of disputes, and other matters. A separate agreement guaranteed that Christians in Persia might build churches, worship freely, and follow their own burial customs as long as they did not try to convert Persians. They would not be compelled to follow Zoroastrian rites; Greatrex and Lieu, *Roman Eastern Frontier II*, 131-34, for sources and further discussion.

88. Dignas and Winter, *Rome and Persia*, 138-48.

89. Justin's changes in foreign policy: Robert Main, *After Justinian: Foreign Policy in the Byzantine Empire during the Reigns of Justin II and Tiberius II Constantine (565-582)* (DPhil thesis, University of Oxford, 2019), 60-182, 192. Main argues that Justin made changes not because of lack of resources but because of his own coherent strategy; see below, on Avars.

90. On Justin's illness, see Jerome Kroll and Bernard Bachrach, "Justin's Madness: Weak-Mindedness or Organic Psychosis?" *Journal of the History of Medicine and Allied Sciences* 48, no. 1 (1993): 40-67.

91. Dignas and Winter, *Rome and Persia*, 109-15.

92. Menander, *History*, frag. 20.2 (= *Exc. de Leg. Gent.* 24) and frag. 23.1 (= *Exc. de Leg. Rom.* 16).

93. Menander, *History*, frag. 20.2 (= *Exc. de Leg. Gent.* 24), 15-22; on Persian-Roman relations in the second half of the sixth century, see Dignas and Winter, *Rome and Persia*, 41-42.

94. On conceptions of peace and the peace *ex isotimias*, see Maria Grazia Bajoni, "Envoys' Speeches at the Peace Negotiations of 561-562 AD between the Byzantine Empire and the Persian Kingdom," *Diplomacy and Statecraft* 29, no. 3 (2018): 353-71, at 358.

95. G. W. H. Lampe, ed., *A Patristic Greek Lexicon* (Oxford: 1961), 677, "ἰσοτιμία, ἡ, equality of honour, equality," for citations.

96. Basil of Caesarea, *Adversus Eunomium Libri*, in PG 31 (1857), col. 757, line 1.

97. Session 2.14: While the Acts of the Second Ecumenical Council have been lost, its Creed was preserved and quoted in the Acts of the Fourth Ecumenical Council of Chalcedon in 451 CE. See Richard Price and Michael Gaddis, trans., *The Acts of the Council of Chalcedon*, vol. 2 (Liverpool: 2005), 12-13.

98. See Richard Price, trans., *The Acts of the Council of Constantinople of 553* (Liverpool: 2009); Patrick T. R. Gray, "The Legacy of Chalcedon: Christological Problems and Their Significance," in Michael Maas, ed., *The Cambridge Companion to the Age of Justinian* (Cambridge: 2005): 215-38, at 234-35; on Christological statement of the council, see Aloys Grillmeier, in collaboration with Theresa Hainthaler, *Christ in Christian Tradition, Volume Two: From the Council of Chalcedon (451) to Gregory the Great (590-604); Part Two: The Church of Constantinople in the Sixth Century*, trans. John Cawte and Pauline Allen (London: 1975), 443-62.

99. Canon IV, trans. in Price, *The Acts of the Council of Constantinople of 553*, 144: "If anyone says that it was according to grace or operation or merit or equal honour . . . but does not profess that the union of God the Word with flesh ensouled by a rational and intelligent soul was hypostatic and that as a result his composite hypostasis is one, let him be anathema."

100. Menander, *History*, frag. 23 (= *Exc. de Leg. Rom.* 16).

101. Greatrex and Lieu, *Roman Eastern Frontier II*, 172-75; Michael Whitby, *The Emperor Maurice and His Historian: Theophylact Simocatta on Persian and Balkan Warfare* (Oxford: Clarendon Press, 1988), 292-304.

NOTES TO PAGES 73–75 [289]

102. Greatrex and Lieu, *The Roman Eastern Frontier II*, 172, for discussion and sources.

103. Theophylact, *History* 4.11. For Greek, see Carolus de Boor, ed., *Theophylacti Simocattae Historiae* (Leipzig: 1887). Note another document found in the *Chronicon Paschale 284–628 AD*, trans. Michael Whitby and Mary Whitby, (Liverpool: 1989), 735–36, contains a letter from Kavadh, who repeatedly refers to Heraclius as brother in the address and body of the letter; Canepa, *Two Eyes*, 126–27.

104. Sebeos, *The Armenian History Attributed to Sebeos*, chap. 11, trans. Robert W. Thomson, with historical commentary by James Howard-Johnston and Tim Greenwood (Liverpool: 1999); also cited in Greatrex and Lieu, *Roman Eastern Frontier II*, 172, trans. Timothy Greenwood.

105. Sebeos, *Armenian History*, chap. 11: "Then the king gathered all the senate and asked their advice . . . 'Shall we agree? Is it proper to agree, or not?' Then they said: 'It is not proper to agree, because they are an impious nation and altogether deceitful. In their distress they make promises, but when they emerge into calmer [times], they renege. We have suffered many evils from them. Let them slaughter each other, and we shall have relief' . . . But the king rejected the advice of the senate."

106. Engelbert Winter, "Legitimität als Herrschaftsprinzip: Kaiser und 'König der Könige' im wechselseitigen Verkehr," in Hans-Joachim Drexhage and Julia Sünskes, *Migratio et Commutatio: Studien zur alten Geschichte und deren Nachleben* (St. Katharinen, Germany: 1989), 72–92, at 89; Whitby, *The Emperor Maurice*, 292–304.

107. Theophylact, *History* 5.3.11; Evagrius, *Ecclesiastical History: A History of the Church in Six Books, from A.D. 431 to A.D. 594*, ed. and trans. Edward Walford (London: 1846); 6.17 on lavish treatment of Khusro during his visit.

108. Theophylact, *History* 5.15.2; Greatrex and Lieu, *Roman Eastern Frontier II*, 174.

109. Martin J. Higgins, "International Relations at the Close of the Sixth Century," *Catholic Historical Review* 27.3 (1941), 279–315, at 282: "at the end of the sixth century Rome unequivocally recognized the right of Persia to exist as a sovereign and independent state on terms of equality with herself"; and at 314–315: "Previous to 590, Rome claimed exclusive dominance of the earth; thenceforth she agreed to divide the world into two equal shares. She reserved the West for herself; the East she assigned to Persia."

110. Higgins, "International Relations," 308.

111. Higgins, "International Relations," 307.

112. Winter, "Legitimität als Herrschaftsprinzip," 79–92, esp. 84–85 for "equal parts" discussion; Dignas and Winter, *Rome and Persia*, 96–97.

113. Michael Whitby and Mary Whitby, *The History of Theophylact Simocatta* (Oxford: 1986), 153 n. 78.

114. *La Narratio de rebus Armeniae: Édition critique et commentaire*, ed. Gérard Garitte, CSCO 132, subsidia 4 (Louvain: 1952). The Armenian original, written about 700, is lost, but a Greek translation survives, trans. Greatrex and Lieu, *Roman Eastern Frontier II*, 172–74.

115. *Narratio de rebus Armeniae* 94, trans. Greatrex and Lieu, *Roman Eastern Frontier II*, 173.

116. Some of this material appeared in Michael Maas, "The Equality of Empires: Procopius on Adoption and Guardianship across Imperial Borders," in Jamie Kreiner and Helmut Reimitz, eds., *Motions of Late Antiquity: Essays on Religion, Politics, and Society in Honour of Peter Brown* (Turnhout: 2016), 175–86.

117. See below, and Dignas and Winter, *Rome and Persia*, 232–41.

118. Amanda H. Podany, *Brotherhood of Kings: How International Relations Shaped the Ancient Near East* (Oxford: 2010).

119. Canepa, *Two Eyes*, 126; Nina Garsoian, "Byzantium and the Sasanians," in Ehsan Yarshater, ed., *CAH 3* (I), *The Seleucid, Parthian and Sasanian Periods* (Cambridge: 1983), 578.

120. On use of archival and documentary sources in Early Byzantine historians, see Warren Treadgold, *The Early Byzantine Historians* (Basingstoke: 2007): 44 (Eusebius), 76 (Ammianus), 108–9 (Zosimus), 138 and 145 (Socrates), 158ff. (Theodoret of Cyrrhus), 173 (Theodore the Lector), 216 (Procopius), 268–69 (Peter the Patrician), 288 (Agathias), 295–98

[290] NOTES TO PAGES 75-77

(Menander), 338ff. (Theopylact), 345–49 (*Chronicon Paschale*). On access to archives in Constantinople, 354. On "research" practices of historians, see 364–65.

121. They also notified one another when a new monarch took the throne in either empire, for the practice of notifying one another at accession of a new monarch: Theophylact, *History* 3.17.1; John of Ephesus, *The Third Part of the Ecclesiastical History of John Bishop of Ephesus* 6.22, trans. Robert Payne Smith (Oxford: 1860); Martin J. Higgins, "International Relations at the Close of the Sixth Century," *The Catholic Historical Review* 27, no. 3 (Oct. 1941): 279–315, at 305; Rudolf Helm, "Untersuchungen über den auswärtigen diplomatischen Verkehr des römischen Reiches im Zeitalter der Spätantike," *Archiv für Urkundenforschung* 12, no. 1 (1931): 375–436, at 388.

122. Malalas, *Chronicle* 17.10.

123. Ammianus, *History* 17.5, Malalas, *Chronicle* 17.9, Procopius, *History of the Wars* 1.16, Menander, *History*, frag. 6.1 (*Exc. de Leg. Rom.* 3.), esp. lines 100–125.

124. Canepa, *Two Eyes*, passim.

125. Canepa, *Two Eyes*, 126, points out that this was understood to be a real biological connection by the Persians. In their mythology there were two ancient heroes who were both brothers and enemies.

126. Ammianus, *History* 17.5.3; Banchich, *Lost History of Peter the Patrician*, frag. 201 (298 CE), mentions such language used in a Persian embassy to Galerius in 298 (cf. Whitby and Whitby, *The History of Theophylact Simocatta*, 117 n. 40, who propose that this example may be anachronistic). Franz Dölger, *Byzanz und die Europäische Staatenwelt: Ausgewählte Vorträge und Aufsätze* (Ettal: 1953), 60 n. 62, speculates that it could even have emerged after the treaty of 283.

127. See "Malalas 449–450," quoted in Canepa, *Two Eyes*, 294 n. 23.

128. Procopius, *History of the Wars* 1.2.

129. Peter E. Pieler, "L'aspect politique et juridique de l'adoption de Chosroès proposée par les Perses à Justin," *RIDA* 3, no. XIX (1972): 399–433.

130. Maas, "Equality of Empires," 176–80, for further discussion of adoption and its implications for Persian-Byzantine relations.

131. Scott McDonough, "Were the Sasanians Barbarians? Roman Writers on the "Empire of the Persians," in Ralph W. Mathisen and Danuta Shanzer, eds., *Romans, Barbarians, and the Transformation of the Roman World: Cultural Interaction and the Creation of Identity in Late Antiquity* (Farnham: 2011), 55–65.

132. Dignas and Winter, *Rome and Persia*, 95–96, point out that the story of Yazdegerd's adoption of Theodosius II is "not attested in detail before the sixth century," and not in contemporary writers. Greatrex and Lieu, *Roman Eastern Frontier II*, 32, suggest that "Because war broke out once again twelve years later, contemporary historians preferred to omit the story." Other sources on the adoption: George Cedrenus, *Georgii Cedreni Historiarum Compendium*, vol. II, ed. Luigi Tartaglia (Rome: Bardi Edizioni—Editore Commerciale, 2016), 361.1 [586.3–7]; Theophanes, *Chronographia* AM 5900, 407/408 CE.

133. See Geoffrey Greatrex, *BMCR* 2008.05.23 (2008), reviewing Henning Börm, *Prokop und die Perser: Untersuchungen zu den römisch-sasanidischen Kontakten in der ausgehenden Spätantike* (Stuttgart: 2007), regarding Persia: "Börm has amply demonstrated that such a negative view [of Procopius's accuracy] cannot be vindicated."

134. Socrates Scholasticus, *The Ecclesiastical History of Socrates* 6.23, trans. Edward Walford (London: 1853); Malalas, *Chronicle* 13.47.

135. Geoffrey Greatrex and Jonathan Bardill discuss chronological problems in the account: "Antiochus the *Praepositus*: A Persian Eunuch at the Court of Theodosius II," *DOP* 50 (1996): 171–97, at 171–74. For various views on the adoption: Kenneth G. Holum, *Theodosian Empresses: Women and Imperial Dominion in Late Antiquity* (Berkeley: 1982), 83 nn. 18–19; Averil Cameron, "Agathias on the Sassanians," *DOP* 23–24 (1969–70): 67–183, at 149; Greatrex and Lieu, *Roman Eastern Frontier II*, 32–33.

136. Blockley, *East Roman Foreign Policy*, 46–52, on "fraternal cooperation." On "good will and its erosion," see 52–59.

137. On peace treaty of Jovian and its aftermath, see Greatrex and Lieu, *Roman Eastern Frontier II*, 1–13.

NOTES TO PAGES 77–81 [291]

138. See Blockley, *East Roman Foreign Policy*, 48; Greatrex and Lieu, *Roman Eastern Frontier II*, 35–36; sources on Marutha at Persian court cited in Blockley, 196 n. 19.

139. Blockley, *East Roman Foreign Policy*, 49.

140. Ibid.

141. Greatrex, *Rome and Persia at War*, 13.

142. Greatrex and Bardill, "Antiochus the *Praepositus*," 174: "The balance of probabilities thus favors the view that Yazdegerd's undertaking to Arcadius—of whatever type it was—and the dispatch of Antiochus occurred soon after Theodosius' birth, and hence well before Arcadius' death." Blockley, *East Roman Foreign Policy*, 51–52, points out that "a Roman emperor, even a minor, was legally *sui iuris* and could not, therefore, have a guardian; although this difficulty can be removed by assuming that Yezdegerd's position was that of executor of the will and in some respects analogous to that held by Stilicho in respect of Honorius." Blockley presents material about "ἐπίτροπος" as testamentary executor, and mentions other interpretations (*East Roman Foreign Policy*, 197 n. 36). Canepa, *Two Eyes*, 295 n. 31, suggests that the possibility of this guardianship emerged from the two empires' shared diplomatic language.

143. Stilicho married Theodosius's niece.

144. For full discussion, see Alan Cameron, "Theodosius the Great and the Regency of Stilico," *Harvard Studies in Classical Philology* 73 (1969): 247–80; Alan Cameron, *Claudian: Poetry and Propaganda at the Court of Honorius* (Oxford: 1970), 38–39; Blockley, *East Roman Foreign Policy*, 197 n. 36 for sources and discussion of "ἐπίτροπος."

145. Agathias, *Histories* 4.26.6–7, cited and discussed in Greatrex and Lieu, *Roman Eastern Frontier II*, 32.

146. Procopius, *History of the Wars* 1.11.

147. Procopius, *History of the Wars* 1.11.8–9.

148. Procopius, *History of the Wars* 1.11.10–18; What this may have meant in an international context is not precisely known. Could a Persian be adopted under Roman law, for example.

149. Procopius, *History of the Wars* 1.11.22.

150. Procopius, *History of the Wars* 1.11.29–30.

151. Procopius, *History of the Wars* 1.12.1; on adoption by arms, see Herwig Wolfram, "Waffensohn," in Heinrich Beck, Dieter Geuenich, and Heiko Steuer, eds., *RGA* 33 (Berlin: 2006), 49–51.

152. Procopius, *History of the Wars* 1.6.10–11.

153. Procopius, *History of the Wars* 1.3.5–6.

154. Theophylact, *History* 8.15.7; Canepa, *Two Eyes*, 127.

155. Walter E. Kaegi, *Heraclius Emperor of Byzantium* (Cambridge: 2003), 58–99, on the first decade of his reign; Howard-Johnston, *The Last Great War*, 103–33, on military campaign of 615.

156. *Chronicon Paschale* 161–62. For Greek, see Ludwig Dindorf, ed., *Chronicon Paschale: Ad Exemplar Vaticanum*, vol. 1 (Bonn: 1832), 709, line 16.

157. Dignas and Winter, *Rome and Persia*, 45. On peace talks, see Howard-Johnston, *The Last Great War*, 80–81, 105–9, and 112.

158. Brent D. Shaw, "'Eaters of Flesh, Drinkers of Milk': The Ancient Mediterranean Ideology of the Pastoral Nomad," *Ancient Society* 13/14 (1982/1983): 5–31; Conor Whately, "Arabs, Outsiders, and Stereotypes from Ammianus Marcellinus to Theophylact Simocatta," in Jitse H. F. Dijkstra and Greg Fisher, eds., *Inside and Out: Interactions between Rome and the Peoples on the Arabian and Egyptian Frontiers in Late Antiquity* (Leuven: 2014) 215–33: "When stereotypes do emerge, and they do on occasion (particularly in the late sixth century), they tend to coincide with low points in the relationship" (233).

159. Eusebius of Caesarea, *Praeparatio Evangelica (Preparation for the Gospel)* 6.10, trans. E. H. Gifford (1903), Tertullian.org, https://www.tertullian.org/fathers/eusebius_pe _06_book6.htm: "there is not a banker to be seen, nor modeller, nor painter, nor architect, nor geometer, nor singing-master, nor actor of dramatic poems," cited in Robert G. Hoyland, *Arabia and the Arabs: From the Bronze Age to the Coming of Islam* (London: 2001), 96–97.

160. Mark Whittow, "The Late Roman/Early Byzantine Near East," in Chase F. Robinson, ed., *CHI*, vol. 1, *The Formation of the Islamic World: Sixth to Eleventh Centuries* (Cambridge,

UK: 2010), 72–97; See also Whittow's cautionary remarks, Mark Whittow, "Rome and the Jafnids: Writing the History of a 6th-c. Tribal Dynasty," in review of Irfan Shahid, *Byzantium and the Arabs in the Sixth Century*, vol. 1 (Washington, DC: 1995), in J. H. Humphrey, ed., *The Roman and Byzantine Near East*, vol. 2, *Some Recent Archaeological Research* (Portsmouth, RI: 1999): 207–24; Greg Fisher, *Between Empires: Arabs, Romans, and Sasanians in Late Antiquity* (Oxford: 2011), 72–127, 173–212; Ignacio Arce, "Romans, Ghassanids and Umayyads and the Transformation of the *Limes Arabicus*: From Coercive and Deterrent Diplomacy towards Religious Proselytism and Political Clientelarism," in Guido Vannini and Michele Nucciotti, *La Transgiordania nei secoli XII- XIII et le 'frontiere' del Mediterraneo medievale*, BAR International Series 2386 (Oxford: 2012), 55–74; for a more positive assessment of Shahid on Jafnids: Fisher, *Between Empires*, 10–12.

161. On the derivation of "Saracen," David F. Graf, "The Saracens and the Defense of the Arabian Frontier," *Bulletin of the American Schools of Oriental Research*, no. 229 (1978): 1–26, at 14–15; see chap. 6 below, on development of "Arab" identity; the term *Arab* should not be retrojected to earlier times to suggest that there was a unified Arab identity; on knowledge about Arabia in the early empire, Henry I. MacAdam, "Strabo, Pliny the Elder and Ptolemy of Alexandria: Three Views of Ancient Arabia and Its Peoples," in T. Fahd, ed., *L'Arabie Préislamique et son Environnement Historique et Culturel: Actes du Colloque de Strasbourg 24-27 juin 1987* (Leiden: 1989), 289–320; Brent D. Shaw, "Fear and Loathing: The Nomad Menace and Roman Africa," *Revue de l'Université d'Ottawa = University of Ottawa Quarterly* 52, no. 1 (Jan.–Mar. 1982): 25–46, subsequently appeared as a chapter in C. M. Wells, ed., *L'Afrique Romaine: Les Conférences Vanier 1980/Roman Africa: The Vanier Lectures 1980* (Ottawa: 1982), 29–50.

162. Glen Warren Bowersock, *Roman Arabia* (Cambridge, MA: 1983); Lawrence I. Conrad, "The Arabs" in *CAH 14*, (Cambridge: 2000): 678–700.

163. See Graf, "The Saracens and the Defense," 1–26; Lawrence I. Conrad, "Eastern Neighbours: The Arabs to the Time of the Prophet," in Jonathan Shepard, ed., *Cambridge History of the Byzantine Empire c. 500-1492* (Cambridge: 2008) 173–95, at 187–90, on use of tribal allies by Romans and Persians, with further bibliography.

164. Graf, "The Saracens and the Defense," 15–19, discusses the development of regular military auxilia from less formal indigenous units. Seeck, ed., *Notitia Dignitatum Or.* 28.17, 32.27, 32.28, and 34.22 refers to auxilia recruited from Arab tribes during the third century, quoted in Graf, "The Saracens and the Defense," 17.

165. Conrad, "Eastern Neighbours," 186–87, discusses reasons for increased conflict between Persia and Rome involving Arabs, with bibliography.

166. On dismissive Roman attitudes: Hoyland, *Arabia and the Arabs*, 96–102.

167. On raids: e.g., Jerome, *The Principal Works of St. Jerome*, ed. Philip Schaff and Henry Wace, trans. W. H. Fremantle, with the assistance of G. Lewis and W. G. Martley, NPNF, Second Series, vol. 6 (New York: 1893), letter 126.2, "To Marcellinus and Anapsychia," complains about widespread raids. For raids in 447, see Priscus, "History," frag. 10 (*Exc. de Leg. Gent.* 4), 10–15 = Priscus, *Excerpta* 6.4.25–30; Theophanes, *Chronographia* AM 5990 [AD 497/98] mentions several invasions in 498 by "tent-dwelling Arabs," who were allied to Persia.

168. Ammianus, *History* 14.4.1.

169. See chap. 3, below; Irfan Shahid, *Byzantium and the Arabs in the Sixth Century*, vol. 2, part 2 (Washington, DC: 2009), xvii–xix. Following the sources, Shahid employs the terms *foederati* and ἐνσπόνδων (and variants).

170. Procopius, *History of the Wars* 2.19.15–18, 26–30, 46. Belisarius orders his commanders to obey Arethas on campaign across the Tigris. This episode shows Arabs working closely with the Roman army. Though technically an allied people, they dwell inside the *limes*, their leaders are part of the Roman army command, and they also fear that their booty will be confiscated by higher authorities, something that Roman troops worried about, for example, throughout the Balkan campaigns described by Theophylact; on this, see grievances by the army in the winter of 602, as discussed in Whitby, *The Emperor Maurice*, 165–69.

171. His name in Arabic probably was Imru' al-Qays.

NOTES TO PAGES 83–84 [293]

172. Malchus, "Byzantine History," frag. 1, in Blockley, *Fragmentary Classicising Historians*, vol. 2; Shahid, *Byzantium and the Arabs in the Fifth Century*, 82–91; Hoyland, *Arabia and the Arabs*, 79–81.

173. This role was occupied by different tribes in the centuries: fourth c. Tanukhids, fifth c. Salihids, sixth c. Ghassanids; see S. Thomas Parker, *Romans and Saracens: A History of the Arabian Frontier* (Winona Lake, IN: 1986), 131–52; and Fergus Millar, "Rome's 'Arab' Allies in Late Antiquity: Conceptions and Representations from within the Frontiers of the Empire" in Henning Börm and Josef Wiesehöfer, eds., *Commutatio et Contentio: Studies in the Late Roman, Sasanian, and Early Islamic Near East; In Memory of Zeev Rubin* (Düsseldorf: 2010), 199–226.

174. Philip Mayerson, "Mauia, Queen of the Saracens—A Cautionary Note," *Israel Exploration Journal* 30, no. 1/2 (1980), 123–31, at 128–29; Glen W. Bowersock, "Mavia, Queen of the Saracens," in Werner Eck, Hartmut Galsterer, and Hatmut Wolff, eds., *Studien zur antiken Sozialgeschichte: Festschrift Friedrich Vittinghof* (Cologne: 1980), 477–95.

175. On Yarmuk, see John Haldon, *The Byzantine Wars: Battles and Campaigns of the Byzantine Era* (Stroud, UK: 2001), 57–65 and 149–50 for bibliography.

176. Ammianus, *History* 23.3.8.

177. Ammianus, *History* 23.3.8: "mundi nationumnque suarum dominum adorarunt."

178. Ammianus, *History* 25.6.9–10.

179. Procopius, *History of the Wars*, 1.19.12.

180. Procopius, *History of the Wars*, 1.19.8–14; Arce, "Romans, Ghassanids and Umayyads," 59–60; Geoffrey Greatrex, *Procopius of Ceasarea: The Persian Wars; A Historical Commentary* (Cambridge: 2022), 275.

181. Audrey Becker, "La communication symbolique dans les audiences à la cour des rois barbares," in *Dieu, le souverain et la cour: Stratégies et rituels de légitimation du pouvoir impérial et royal dans l'Antiquité tardive et au haut Moyen Âge* (Bordeaux: 2022) 189–216.

182. On tribute payments, see Fisher, *Between Empires*, 98 n. 108, and 126; on status of Arabs in sixth century, see Fisher, *Between Empires*, 120–24.

183. Ammianus, *History* 25.6.9–10 describes denial of payments to an Arab group; administrative abuses: Novels of Theodosius Title 24, trans. Clyde Pharr, *The Theodosian Code and Novels and the Sirmondian Constitutions* (Princeton: 1952).

184. Walter E. Kaegi, *Byzantium and the Early Islamic Conquests* (Cambridge: 1992) 89–91.

185. Theophanes, *Chronographia* AM 6123 [AD 630/31].

186. Theophanes, *Chronographia* AM 6126 [AD 633/34]: "When Kyros, the bishop of Alexandria, had been informed of their onset, he took measures and, fearing their rapacity, concluded a treaty with them, promising that Egypt would pay them every year 200,000 denarii and send them gold in respect of the appointed delay. By providing these sums for three years, he spared Egypt from disaster. Now Kyros was accused before the emperor of giving to the Saracens the gold of Egypt. The emperor, in anger, sent a message to recall him and appointed a certain Manuel, an Armenian by origin, as *augustalis*. At the end of the year the Saracen tribute collectors came to receive the gold, but Manuel drove them away empty-handed, saying, 'I am not unarmed like Kyros that I should pay you tribute. Nay, I am armed.'"

187. Theophanes, *Chronographia* AM 6128 [CE 635/36].

188. Phylarchs: Robert G. Hoyland, "Arab Kings, Arab Tribes and the Beginnings of Arab Historical Memory in Late Roman Epigraphy," in Hannah M. Cotton et al., eds., *From Hellenism to Islam: Cultural and Linguistic Change in the Roman Near East* (Cambridge: 2009), 374–400; Irfan Shahid, *Rome and the Arabs: A Prolegomenon to the Study of Byzantium and the Arabs* (Washington, DC: 1984), 31; Shahid, *Byzantium and the Arabs in the Fourth Century* (Washington, DC: 1984), 516, on various meanings of the term; Thomas Brüggemann, "Εθνάρχος, Φύλαρχος and Στρατηγὸς νομάδων in Roman Arabia (1st–3rd Century): Central Power, Local Administration, and Nomadic Environment," in Ariel S. Lewin and Pietrina Pellegrini, eds., *The Late Roman Army in the Near East from Diocletian to the Arab Conquest: Proceedings of a colloquium held at Potenza, Acerenza and Matera,*

[294] NOTES TO PAGES 84–87

Italy (May 2005), BAR International Series 1717 (Oxford: 2007), 275–84; Fritz Gschnitzer, "Phylarchos," in *RE: Neue Bearbeitung; Supplementband XI* (Stuttgart: 1968), col. 1067–90.

189. Procopius, *History of the Wars* 1.17.47–48: Justinian gave him the "dignity of a king" (ἀξίωμα βασιλέως), something that had never been done before. The term has been much discussed: Hugh Kennedy, "Syria, Palestine and Mesopotamia," in *CAH 14*, 588–611, at 596: "chief phylarch."

190. On conferral and meaning of titles granted to the Ghassanids: Irfan Shahid, *Byzantium and the Arabs in the Sixth Century*, vol. 1, part 1, *Political and Military History* (Washington, DC: 1995), 292.

191. J. R. Martindale, *PRLE*, vol. 2, *A.D. 395–527* (Cambridge: 1980), 169–70: "Aspebetus qui et Petrus"; Cyril of Scythopolis, "Κεφαλαία τῆς περὶ τοῦ μεγάλου Εὐθυμίου συγγραφῆς" [Vita Euthymii], in Eduard Schwartz, ed., *Kyrillos von Skythopoli* (Piscataway, NJ: 1939, repr. 2012), 10 and 15.

192. Irfan Shahid, *Byzantium and the Arabs in the Sixth Century. Volume 1, Part 2: Ecclesiastical History* (Washington, DC: 1995), 922–38.

193. They were released when Phocas seized the throne. See Shahid, *Byzantium and the Arabs 1.2*, 939–41.

194. On shifting attitudes toward Ghassanids, see Shahid, *Byzantium and the Arabs 1.1*, 535–568; on Heraklios, see 634–59.

195. For an overview, Michael Maas, "How the Steppes Became Byzantine: Rome and the Eurasian Nomads in Historical Perspective," in Nicola Di Cosmo and Michael Maas, eds., *Empires and Exchanges in Eurasian Late Antiquity: Rome, China, Iran, and the Steppe, ca. 250–750* (Cambridge: 2018), 19–34; on the Avars, Walter Pohl, *The Avars: A Steppe Empire in Central Europe, 567–822* (Ithaca, NY: 2018).

196. Christopher Kelly, "Neither Conquest Nor Settlement: Attila's Empire and Its Impact," in Michael Maas, ed., *The Cambridge Companion to the Age of Attila* (Cambridge: 2015), 193–208.

197. Di Cosmo, "War Economy," 113–16; Christopher Kelly, "Neither Conquest nor Settlement," in Michael Maas, *The Cambridge Companion to the Age of Attila* (Cambridge: 2015), 193–208, esp. 205–8.

198. Ekaterina Nechaeva, "Patterns of Roman Diplomacy with Iran and the Steppe Peoples," in Di Cosmo and Maas, eds., *Empires and Exchanges*, 357–68, at 368: "These new players challenged the established hierarchies. In different situations nomadic partners put pressure on the Romans, demanding treatment at a higher level than the Romans were accustomed to in dealing with the barbarians. Nomad power made the Roman Empire yield gradually—though not fully. The immediate result of this change was a considerable adjustment of modes of international communication."

199. On destructive Scythian raids with a long-winded discussion: Dio Chrysostom, *Discourses* 36.4–6, ed. and trans. J. W. Cohoon and H. Lamar Crosby, LCL 358 (Cambridge, MA: 1940), 15–16.

200. Roger Batty, *Rome and the Nomads: The Pontic-Danubian Realm in Antiquity* (Oxford: 2007), esp. 423–56 for summary.

201. Florus, *Epitome of Roman History* 2.29, ed. and trans. E. S. Forster, LCL 231 (Cambridge, MA: 1929): "The Sarmatians range on horseback over wide-spreading plains . . . Their territory consists entirely of snow, ice and forest. So barbarous are they that they do not even understand what peace is"; for further discussion, see Batty, *Rome and the Nomads*, 428; Brent D. Shaw, *Rulers, Nomads, and Christians in Roman North Africa* (Aldershot, UK: 1995), "Part Two: Nomads"; see also "'Eaters of Flesh, Drinkers of Milk,'" originally published in *Ancient Society* 13/14 (1982/1983): 5–31; "Fear and Loathing: The Nomad Menace and Roman Africa," originally published in C. M. Wells, ed., *Roman Africa: L'Afrique romaine*, 24–46; and "Autonomy and Tribute: Mountain and Plain in Mauretania Tingitana," originally published in Pierre-Robert Baduel, ed., *Désert et montagne au Maghreb: Hommage à Jean Dresch, Revue de l'Occident Musulman et de la Méditerranée* 41–42 (Aix-en-Provence: 1986), 66–89.

202. Batty, *Rome and the Nomads*, 428–30.

NOTES TO PAGES 87–89 [295]

203. Batty, *Rome and the Nomads*, 428.

204. Augustus, *Res Gestae* 31; for discussion, Batty, *Rome and the Nomads*, 429.

205. Tacitus, *Annals* 12.15–21, ed. and trans. John Jackson, LCL 312 (Cambridge, MA: 1937).

206. Batty, *Rome and the Nomads*, 429.

207. Batty, *Rome and the Nomads*, 430; Dio Cassius, *Roman History* 68.19.2, ed. and trans. Earnest Cary and Herbert B. Foster, LCL 176 (Cambridge, MA: 1925).

208. Shaw, "VIII. Autonomy and Tribute," 77–78, for discussion on Mauretanian context, with Table 4, "The Tribute-Autonomy Continuum."

209. Batty, *Rome and the Nomads*, 438.

210. Batty, *Rome and the Nomads*, 440.

211. For a summary, see Gordon, "Subsidies in Roman Imperial Defence," 65.

212. Peter J. Heather, "The Huns and Barbarian Europe," in Michael Maas, ed., *The Cambridge Companion to the Age of Attila* (Cambridge: 2015), 209–29.

213. They base their arguments on archaeological evidence of the Sîntana de Mures-Černjachov culture which is associated with the Goths of this period: Peter Heather and John Matthews, *The Goths in the Fourth Century* (Liverpool: 1991), 51–101; Michael Schmauder, "The Advance of the Huns: From Asia to the Danube," in Jean-Jacques Aillagon, ed., *Rome and the Barbarians: The Birth of a New World* (Milan: 2008), 236–43.

214. Schmauder, "The Advance of the Huns," 236.

215. Arguing for greater continuity, see Étienne de la Vaissière, "The Steppe World and the Rise of the Huns," in Michael Maas, ed., *The Cambridge Companion to the Age of Attila*, 175–92.

216. Zosimus, *New History* 5.22.1–3.

217. Zosimus, *New History* 5.26.3–5.

218. Sozomen, *The Ecclesiastical History* 9.5, trans. Edward Walford (London: Henry G. Bohn, 1855).

219. Sozomen, *Ecclesiastical History* 9.5.

220. Sozomen does not state the amount.

221. Sozomen, *Ecclesiastical History* 9.5: "insolently refused to enter into terms of alliance with the Romans." Sozomen presents the discussion of bribery as a discussion of the Roman form of government and of the emperor's philanthropy. This recalls Priscus's treatment of his visit to the camp of Attila.

222. For a summary, Gordon, "Subsidies in Roman Imperial Defence," 65.

223. Priscus, "History," frag. 2 (*Exc. de Leg. Rom.* 1) = Priscus, *Excerpta*, ed. Carolla, Exc. 1–1.1.

224. Priscus, "History," frag. 9.3 (*Exc. de Leg. Gent.* 3) = Priscus, *Excerpta*, ed. Carolla, Exc. 5.

225. Jordanes, *Getica* 257, ed. Theodor Mommsen, MGH AA 5.1 (Berlin: 1882), 124.

226. Priscus was one of Jordanes's sources, but there is no way to know if Priscus included a version of this funeral encomium.

227. Ammianus, *History* 31.3, explains how the Huns drove the Goths into the Roman Empire, becoming a catalyst for all the disastrous events leading up to the defeat at Adrianople in 378.

228. Nicola Di Cosmo, *Ancient China and Its Enemies: The Rise of Nomadic Power* (Cambridge: 2002), 202, in reference to two Chinese statesmen's discussion of the Hsiung-nu during the Warring States period.

229. Priscus, *History*, frag. 10 (*Exc. de Leg. Gent.* 4), ed. Blockley, *Fragmentary Classicising Historians*, 2:243: "The Romans heeded his every bidding and obeyed whatever order their master issued . . . Therefore, having been humbled by Attila, they paid him court" = Priscus, *Excerpta*, ed. Carolla, Exc. 6.3–5.

230. Priscus, *History*, frag. 10 (*Exc. de Leg. Gent.* 4), ed. Blockley, *Fragmentary Classicising Historians*, 211: "When the treaty was in force, Attila again sent envoys to the eastern Romans demanding the fugitives. They received the envoys, honoured them with many gift and sent them away . . . Again, he sent others, and, when they had been enriched, he sent a

[296] NOTES TO PAGES 89–95

third embassy and a fourth after it. For the barbarian, mindful of the Romans' liberality . . . sent to them those of his retinue whom he wished to benefit, inventing new reasons and discovering new pretexts." = Priscus, *Excerpta*, ed. Carolla, Exc. 6.1–2.

231. Blockley, *Fragmentary Classicising Historians*, vol. 1, 62–63, discussing Priscus, *History*, frag. 15.2 (*Exc. de Leg. Gent.* 6), line 11 = Priscus, *Excerpta*, ed. Carolla, Exc. 12.2.23.

232. Priscus, *History*, frag. 11.2 (*Exc. de Leg. Rom.* 3), line 629 = Priscus, *Excerpta*, ed. Carolla, Exc. 8.145.10.

233. Blockley, *Fragmentary Classicising Historians*, vol. 1, 66, commenting on Priscus, "History," frag. 20.1 (*Exc. de Leg. Gent.* 7) = Priscus, *Excerpta*, ed. Carolla, Exc. 15.2.24–25.

234. For the embassy to Attila, Priscus, *History*, frag. 11–14, ed. Blockley, *Fragmentary Classicising Historians*, 2:243–303; Priscus, *Excerpta*, Exc. 7–11, ed. Carolla, 13–51; for positive assessment, Jordanes, *Getica* 35.182.

235. Di Cosmo, *Ancient China*, 205, for a parallel Han Chinese response to the Hsiung-nu.

236. Pohl, *The Avars*, for comprehensive discussion.

237. On the name and character of the Avars, see Pohl, *The Avars*, 6, 38–47.

238. Becker, *Dieu, le souverain et la cour*, 151–88, for recent discussion and bibliography on the reception of ambassadors in Constantinople.

239. Jonathan Shepard, "Courts in East and West," in Peter Linehan and Janet L. Nelson, eds., *The Medieval World* (London: 2001), 14–36, at 18.

240. Corippus, *In Laudem Iustini Minoris* III, 191–371.

241. Audrey Becker, "Verbal and Nonverbal Diplomatic Communication at the Imperial Court of Constantinople (Fifth–Sixth Centuries)," *DOP* 72 (2018): 79–92, at 82–83; Walter Pohl, "Ritualized Encounters: Late Roman Diplomacy and the Barbarians, Fifth–Sixth Century," in Alexander Beihammer, Stavroula Constantinou, and Maria Parani, eds., *Court Ceremonies and Rituals of Power in Byzantium and the Medieval Mediterranean: Comparative Perspectives* (Leiden: 2013), 67–86, at 67–69.

242. Vergil, *Aeneid* 6.1151–54.

243. Menander, *History*, frag. 8 [*Exc. de Leg. Gent.* 5].

244. Nechaeva, *Embassies—Negotiations—Gifts*, 180–83.

245. Menander, *History*, frag. 8, lines 54–56.

246. John of Ephesus, *Ecclesiastical History* 6.24.

247. John of Ephesus, *Ecclesiastical History* 6.24, lines 33–40, with some modifications; for discussion, see Pohl, *Avars*, 59–60.

248. Tacitus, *Germania* 42.1: "Germaniae velut frons est." He refers specifically to the area north of the Danube; I am using the term more broadly to include the Rhine as well.

249. Walter Pohl, "Appropriating the Discourse about Barbarians in the Early Medieval West," in Michael Maas and Fay Yarbrough, eds., *Empires and Indigenous Peoples: Comparing Ancient Roman and North American Experiences* (Norman, OK: 2024) 119–36; Audrey Becker, "Romano-Barbarian Treaties and the Redefinition of Identities in Late Antiquity," 105–18 in the same volume.

250. "Ubi solitudinem faciunt, pacem appellant": Cornelius Tacitus, *Agricola* 30, ed. and trans. M. Hutton, W. Peterson, R. M. Ogilvie, et al., LCL 35 (Cambridge, MA: 1914); Brent Shaw, "Exterminating Angel," in *Empires and Indigenous Peoples*, ed. Maas and Yarbrough, 17–35.

251. The literature is gigantic. For a recent introduction with a modern sensibility, David J. Mattingly, *Imperialism, Power, and Identity: Experiencing the Roman Empire* (Princeton: 2011).

252. Patrick J. Geary, *Before France and Germany: The Creation and Transformation of the Merovingian World* (Oxford: 1988), vi.

253. John F. Drinkwater, *The Alamanni and Rome 213–496: Caracalla to Clovis* (Oxford: 2007), traces the long interaction of one people with Rome. They ceased to exist shortly after Roman power collapsed in the West.

254. Peter Heather, "*Foedera* and *Foederati* of the Fourth Century," in *Kingdoms of the Empire: The Integration of Barbarians in Late Antiquity*, ed. Walter Pohl (Leiden: 1997), 57–74, at 66.

NOTES TO PAGES 95–97 [297]

255. Gerhard Wirth, "Rome and Its Germanic Partners in the Fourth Century," 13, notes that "Since then [Mommsen], study of these [legal] concepts has moved with a kind of sublimity, refining terminology in endless ramifications to the point of incomprehensibility"; Conor Whately, "Strategy, Diplomacy and Frontiers: A Bibliographic Essay," in Alexander Sarantis and Neil Christie, ed., *War and Warfare in Late Antiquity: Current Perspectives* (Leiden: 2013), 239–54.

256. Shaw, "Exterminating Angel," 19.

257. Gerhard Wirth, "Rome and Its Germanic Partners," 16–21, on use of *deditio* is essential.

258. Heather, "*Foedera* and *Foederati*," 57–74.

259. Peter Heather, "The Late Roman Art of Client Management," in *The Transformation of Frontiers from Late Antiquity to the Carolingians*, ed. Walter Pohl, Ian Wood, and Helmut Reimitz (Leiden: 2001), 15–68, at 18.

260. Heather, "*Foedera* and *Foederati*," 65: "As far as diplomatic theory of the Roman state was concerned, the Persians excepted, *foederati* were created by an act of surrender (*deditio*) on the part of the people involved, followed by a restitution of the existing social order (*restitutio*) and the making of a negotiated agreement (*foedus*)." This understanding was widely accepted throughout the empire by the ruling class, though practice did not always correspond with this theory.

261. On the gathering and importance of information for diplomacy at the Roman frontiers, see A. D. Lee, *Information and Frontiers: Roman Foreign Relations in Late Antiquity* (Cambridge: 1993).

262. Ammianus, *History* 17.1.

263. Ammianus, *History* 17.1.12.

264. Ammianus, *History* 17.1.13.

265. Ammianus, *History* 17.3; on Ammianus's use of *foedus*, see Heather, "*Foedera* and *Foederati*," 61.

266. Ammianus, *History* 18.2.15–19.

267. Peter Heather has shown that the Latin panegyrics demonstrate that during the fourth century at least "an act of submission meant, in one sense, that the foreign group involved did become part of the Empire, and did so not as full citizens, but as dependent subjects" ("*Foedera* and *Foederati*," 63). He also points out that any area or people brought to submission by the imperial army was afterward considered part of the empire.

268. Evangelos K. Chrysos, "The Title Βασιλευσ in Early Byzantine International Relations," *DOP* 32 (1978): 29–75, at 53.

269. Chrysos, "The Title Βασιλευσ," 52–57.

270. Chrysos, "The Title Βασιλευσ," 53 n. 155, citing Christian Courtois, *Les Vandales et l'Afrique* (Paris, 1955), 333, and Appendix II n. 132.

271. By contrast, in the late sixth century the Constantinopolitan historian Agathias, who was not involved in diplomatic activity for the emperor, could view the Franks on the basis of their orthodoxy and their habits as quite similar to the Romans, showing us that on grounds other than imperial titulature commonalities eventually might be found. See Agathias, *Histories* II.1.6–7. For further discussion, see Michael Maas, "'Delivered from Their Ancient Customs': Christianity and the Question of Cultural Change in Early Byzantine Ethnography," in Kenneth Mills and Anthony Grafton, eds., *Conversion in Late Antiquity and the Early Middle Ages: Seeing and Believing* (Rochester, NY: 2003), 152–88, at 171–74.

272. Chrysos, "The Title Βασιλευσ," 53 n. 154.

273. Chrysos, "The Title Βασιλευσ," 53–54. The Theudebert coin is probably a forgery.

274. Chrysos, "The Title Βασιλευσ," 53 n. 156, cites "H. Dessau, *Inscriptiones Latinae Selectae, I* (Berlin, no. 1892), no. 827."

275. Chrysos, "The Title Βασιλευσ," 54 n. 162, for citations.

276. Another problem involving transliteration and titles occurs in a passage of Procopius, *History of the Wars* 3.9.10–19, in which he discusses an exchange of letters between Emperor Justinian and Gelimer, king of the Vandals, who had just usurped the throne. In a letter to Gelimer, Justinian chides the usurper, "You are not acting in a holy manner nor

[298] NOTES TO PAGES 97–99

worthily of the will of Gizeric, keeping in prison an old man and a kinsman and the king of the Vandals (βασιλέα Βανδίλων)." As Chrysos, "The Title Βασιλευσ," 55, suggests, since Justinian's letter to Gelimer must have been in Latin, Procopius in turn must have been translating *rex* and *regnum* from the Latin as βασιλεύς and βασιλεῖα (*basileos* can mean either king or emperor in Greek).

277. F. K. Haarer, *Anastasius I: Politics and Empire in the Late Roman World* (Cambridge: 2006), 94–97; on Clovis: Raymond Van Dam, "Merovingian Gaul and the Frankish Conquests," in Paul Fouracre, ed., *The New Cambridge Medieval History*, vol. 1, *c. 500–c.700* (Cambridge: 2005), 93–231, at 197–98; Michael McCormick, "Clovis at Tours: Byzantine Public Ritual and the Origins of Medieval Ruler Symbolism," in Evangelos K. Chrysos and Andreas Schwarcz, *Das Reich und die Barbaren* (Vienna: 1989), 155–80; Chrysos, "The Title Βασιλευσ," 55.

278. Gregory of Tours, *The History of the Franks* 2.28(38), trans. O. M. Dalton (Oxford: 1927): "Clovis received letters from the emperor Anastasius conferring the consulate, and in the church of the blessed Martin he was vested in the purple tunic, and in a mantle, and set the diadem upon his head. Then, mounting his horse, he showered with his own hand in the generosity of his heart pieces of gold and silver among the people all along the road between the gate of the atrium of the holy Martin's church, and the church of the city. From that day he was hailed as consul or Augustus [*tamquam consul aut augustus*]. He left Tours and came to Paris, where he established the seat of the government." For Latin text, see Bruno Krusch and Willhelm Levison, eds., *Gregorii Episcopi Turonensis Libri Historiarum X, MGHMM*, Vol. I, 2nd ed. (Hannover: 1951), II.38. For detailed discussion, see Ralph W. Mathisen, "Clovis, Anastasius, and Political Status in 508 C.E.: The Frankish Aftermath of the Battle of Vouillé," in Ralph W. Mathisen and Danuta Shanzer, eds., *The Battle of Vouillé, 507 CE: Where France Began* (Boston: 2012), 79–110.

Chapter Three: "Include Me Out"

1. Samuel Goldwyn, a reported malapropism, 1937.

2. Cassiodorus, *Variae* 4.33.

3. A few interesting examples from the immense literature: Emma Dench, *Romulus' Asylum: Roman Identities from the Age of Alexander to the Age of Hadrian* (Oxford: 2005); Greg Woolf, *Becoming Roman: The Origins of Provincial Civilization in Gaul* (Cambridge: 1998); G. E. M. de Ste. Croix, "Appendix III. The Settlement of 'Barbarians' within the Roman Empire," in *The Class Struggle in the Ancient Greek World from the Archaic Age to the Arab Conquests* (London: 1981), 509–18; Mary T. Boatwright, "Acceptance and Approval: Romans' Non-Roman Population Transfers, 180 B.C.E.–ca. 70 C.E.," *Phoenix 69*, no. 1 (2015): 122–46, for earlier periods, in terms of competition for honor and prestige; for Late Antiquity, see Patrick Périn and Michel Kazanski, "Identity and Ethnicity during the Era of Migrations and Barbarian Kingdoms in the Light of Archaeology in Gaul," in Ralph W. Mathisen and Danuta Shanzer, eds., *Romans, Barbarians, and the Transformation of the Roman World* (Farnham: 2011), 299–330, at 304–10; for individual immigrants, see Ekaterina Nechaeva, "International Political Hospitality and Non-hospitality in Late Antiquity: High-profile Strangers between Asylum and Extradition," in Claire Fauchon-Claudon and Marie-Adeline Le Guennec, eds., *Hospitalité et régulation de l'altérité dans l'antiquité méditerranéenne* (Bordeaux: 2022), 235–47; Yves Modéran, "L'établissement de barbares sur le territoire romain à l'époque impériale," in Claudia Moatti, ed., *La mobilité des personnes en Méditerranée de l'Antiquité à l'époque moderne: Procédures de contrôle et documents d'identifications* (Rome: 2004), 337–97, gives an overview of the period before Romans lost control of the process of settlement; Raymond Van Dam, *Rome and Constantinople: Rewriting Roman History during Late Antiquity* (Waco, TX: 2010), 53–54, indicates that there was more movement of internal populations in the late empire than there was of invaders.

4. A. H. M. Jones, *The Later Roman Empire 284–602: A Social Economic and Administrative Survey* (Norman, OK: 1964), 619–20, and de Ste. Croix, *Class Struggle*, 247.

5. Augustus, *Res Gestae* 3: "Externas gentes, quibus tuto ignosci potuit conservare quam excidere malui": *Res Gestae Divi Augusti, Text, Translation, Commentary*, ed. Allison E.

NOTES TO PAGES 100–102 [299]

Cooley (Cambridge: 2009); on *clementia* in Augustan propaganda: Melissa Barden Dowling, *Clemency and Cruelty in the Roman World* (Ann Arbor: 2006), 126–68.

6. C. R. Whittaker, "The Use and Abuse of Immigrants in the Later Roman Empire," in *Rome and Its Frontiers: The Dynamics of Empire* (London: 2004), 199–218, at 202: "The majority of the migrants, apart from the élites, are portrayed as working on the land or serving as recruits in the army, or both."

7. Yves Modéran, "L'établissement de barbares," 337–97, stresses the variety of circumstances of entry into the empire and manner of settlement.

8. David Breeze, "In Defence of the Late Empire," in Rob Collins, Matt Symonds, and Meike Weber, eds., *Roman Military Architecture on the Frontiers: Armies and Their Architecture in Late Antiquity* (Oxford: 2015), 140–42, at 142.

9. Peter M. Brennan, "The Last of the Romans: Roman Identity and the Roman Army in the Late Roman Near East," *Mediterranean Archaeology* 11 (1998) 191–203, at 201.

10. Anthony Kaldellis and Marion Kruse, in *The Field Armies of the East Roman Empire, 361–630* (Cambridge: 2023), at xiv and passim; Conor Whately reviews Kaldellis and Kruse in *Plekos* 26, (2024): 77–85, https://www.plekos.uni-muenchen.de/2024/r -kaldellis_kruse.pdf.

11. For a recent overview of evidence and problems from 250 to 400: Conor Whately, "Making Sense of the Frontier Armies in Late Antiquity: An Historian's Perspective," in Collins, Symonds, and Weber, eds., *Roman Military Architecture on the Frontiers*, 6–17.

12. Patrick J. Geary, "Ethnic Identity as a Situational Construct in the Early Middle Ages," *Mitteilungen de Anthropologischen Gesellschaft in Wien* 113 (1983): 15–26; see the remarks of Périn and Kazanski, "Identity and Ethnicity during the Era of Migrations," 304–10. See also essays in Walter Pohl, ed., *Kingdoms of the Empire: The Integration of Barbarians in Late Antiquity* (Leiden: 1997), and Hans-Werner Goetz, Jörg Jarnut, and Walter Pohl, eds., *Regna and Gentes: The Relationship between Late Antique and Early Medieval Peoples and Kingdoms in the Transformation of the Roman World* (Leiden: 2003).

13. Sebastian Schmidt-Hofner, "Barbarian Migrations and Socio-Economic Challenges to the Roman Landholding Elite in the Fourth Century CE," *Journal of Late Antiquity* 10, no. 2 (2017): 372–404, at 389–91.

14. Review of scholarship in Guy Halsall, *Barbarian Migrations and the Roman West* (Cambridge: 2007), 417–54; Yves Modéran, *Les Vandales et l'Empire romain*, ed. Michel-Yves Perrin (Paris: 2014), 155–80, on distribution of land in Vandal North Africa.

15. Hans-Werner Goetz, "Introduction," in Goetz, Jarnut, and Pohl, eds., *Regna and Gentes*, 1–11, as well as other essays in the same volume; Thomas F. X. Noble, ed., *From Roman Provinces to Medieval Kingdoms* (London: 2006); Walter Pohl, "Introduction: The Empire and the Integration of Barbarians," in Pohl, ed., *Kingdoms of the Empire*, 1–11.

16. The Law of Persons was articulated by Gaius, *Institutes* 1.9: "Et quidem summa divisio de iure personarum haec est, quod omnes homines aut liberi sunt aut servi."

17. Cf. Whittaker, "Use and Abuse," 206, on the relative unimportance of the juridical status of immigrants.

18. Sven Rugullis, *Die Barbaren in den spätrömischen Gesetzen: Eine Untersuchung des Terminus* barbarus (Frankfurt am Main: 1992), 55–91, seeks to link the constitutions to specific events; see Alexander Callander Murray, review of Sven Rugullis, *Die Barbaren in den spätrömischen Gesetzen; Eine Untersuchung des Terminus* barbarus," *Gnomon* 67, no. 7 (1995): 649–50, at 650; for the use of *hostis*/enemy in the Theodosian Code, Alain Chauvot, *Les "barbares" des romains: Representations et confrontations*, ed. A. Becker and H. Huntzinger (Metz: 2016), 103–17.

19. For an overview, see Chauvot, *Les "barbares" des romains*, 301–25; Evangelos Chrysos, "Legal Concepts and Patterns for the Barbarians' Settlement on Roman Soil," in Evangelos K. Chrysos and Andreas Schwarcz, eds., *Das Reich und die Barbaren* (Vienna: 1989), 13–23; Evangelos Chrysos, "Conclusion: De Foederatis Iterum," in Pohl, ed., *Kingdoms of the Empire*, 185–206; Peter Heather, *Goths and Romans 332–489* (Oxford: 1991), 164–65 (on Romans conceding some level of "semi-autonomy" to settlers); Halsall, *Barbarian Migrations*, 152–53; C. R. Whittaker, *Frontiers of the Roman Empire: A Social and Economic Study* (Baltimore: 1994), 158; Rosario Soraci, *Ricerche sui Conubia tra Romani e Germani nei*

secoli *IV-VI*, 2nd ed. (Catania: 1974), 83–110, on *gentiles* in the fourth century, with review of scholarship.

20. Chrysos, "Legal Concepts and Patterns," 18, notes (in discussing *foederati*) "the diversity of legal conditions established between the empire and the barbarians in Late Antiquity." See also Chrysos, "Conclusion," 189 n. 39; Ziegler, "Das Völkerrecht der römischen Republik," 68ff.; and Ziegler, "Tradition und Wandel im Völkerrecht der römischen Spätantike." See, now, Kaser, *Ius gentium*, and Whittaker, "Use and Abuse," 202: "The actual vocabulary referring to immigrants, terms such as *laeti*, *dediticii*, *gentiles*, tributary and others, is varied and inconsistent, probably reflecting their many diverse statuses and conditions. Even the differences between those who settled on negotiated terms, *dediticii* and *foederati*, are unclear and overlap." For the *Notitia Dignitatum*, see *Notitia Dignitatum: Accedunt Notitia Urbis Constantinopolitanae et Laterculi Provinciarum*, ed. Otto Seeck (Berlin: 1876); *La Notitia Dignitatum: Nueva edición critica y commentario histórico*, ed. Concepción Neira Baleiro (Madrid: 2006), for historical commentary and extensive bibliography.

21. Walter Pohl, "Conclusion: The Transformation of Frontiers," in Walter Pohl, Ian Wood, and Helmut Reimitz, eds., *The Transformation of Frontiers: From Late Antiquity to the Carolingians* (Leiden: 2001), 247–60; Peter J. Heather, "The Huns and Barbarian Europe," in Michael Maas, ed., *The Cambridge Companion to the Age of Attila* (Cambridge: 2014), 209–29; for a general introduction to late Roman archeology, see Simon Esmonde Cleary, *The Roman West, AD 200–500: An Archaeological Study* (Cambridge: 2013).

22. Murray, "Sven Rugullis: *Die Barbaren in den spätrömischen Gesetzen*," 649.

23. Chauvot, *Les "barbares" des romains*, 301–25; for discussion of law and citizenship, see n. 28 below; Whittaker, "Use and Abuse," 207: "The juridical personality of the citizen was almost eliminated as frontier controls relaxed and as immigrants were accommodated in ever greater numbers."

24. Peter Brennan, "Units in the *Notitia Dignitatum*," in Yann le Bohec, ed., *The Encyclopedia of the Roman Army* (Chichester, UK: 2015), 1049–54; Gerhard Wirth, "Rome and Its Germanic Partners in the Fourth Century," in Pohl, ed., *Kingdoms of the Empire*, 13–55 at 37 n. 104, on ethnic homogeneity of certain settled groups.

25. The generally accepted date for the material concerning the western part of the empire is around 420 and for the eastern about 395. Anthony Kaldellis and Marion Kruse, in *The Field Armies of the East Roman Empire, 361–630* (Cambridge: 2023), redate the eastern portion to the 440s (esp. at 152–79); Michael Kulikowski, "The 'Notitia Dignatum' as a Historical Source," *Historia: Zeitschrift für Alte Geschichte* 49.3 (2000): 358–77, at 368, is more confident of an earlier date for the eastern list.

26. See Peter Alois Kuhlmann, ed. and trans., *Die Giessener literarischen Papyri und die Caracalla-Erlasse, 217–239* [P. Giss. 40] (Giessen: 1994); for commentary, see Arnaud Besson, *Constitutio Antoniniana: L'universalisation de la citoyenneté romaine au 3e siècle* (Basel: 2020); Alex Imrie, "Appendix," in *The Antonine Constitution: An Edict for the Caracallan Empire* (Leiden: 2018), 139–53, for text, translation, and commentary; Christoph Sasse, *Die Constitutio Antoniniana* (Wiesbaden: 1958); Karl-Heinz Ziegler, "Tradition und Wandel im Völkerrecht der römischen Spätantike," in *Idee und Realität des Rechts in der Entwicklung internationaler Beziehungen: Festgabe für Wolfgang Preiser*, ed. Alexander Böhm, Klaus Lüderssen, and Karl-Heinz Ziegler (Baden-Baden: 1983), 11–31, at 24–25 on *deditio* in Late Antiquity.

27. Overview: Michael Whitby, "Emperors and Armies, AD 235–395," in Simon Swain and Mark Edwards, eds., *Approaching Late Antiquity: The Transformation from Early to Late Empire* (Oxford, UK: 2006), 156–86; Peter M. Brennan, "The Last of the Romans: Roman Identity and the Roman Army in the Late Roman Near East," *Mediterranean Archaeology* 11, *Identities in the Eastern Mediterranean in Antiquity: Proceedings of a Conference held at the Humanities Research Centre in Canberra 10-12, November, 1997* (1998): 191–203, at 196: Brennan makes an important point regarding recruitment, that it is necessary to differentiate between normative and ad hoc responses to different sorts of pressures over time. In the second half of the fourth century, established patterns of recruitment worked well, but in the early fifth century many decisions had to be made on the spot. He notes that scholars often muddle the two sets of circumstances by lumping together law codes and other written sources.

NOTES TO PAGES 105–106 [301]

28. Convenient introductory discussions of Roman law: Wolfgang Kunkel, *An Introduction to Roman Legal and Constitutional History*, 2nd ed., trans. J. M. Kelly (Oxford: 1973); Peter Stein, *Roman Law in European History* (Cambridge: 1999); for Late Antiquity: Peter Garnsey, "Roman Citizenship and Roman Law in the Late Empire," in Swain and Edwards, eds., *Approaching Late Antiquity*, 133–55; for summary, Adrian N. Sherwin-White, "The Roman Citizenship: A Survey of Its Development into a World Franchise," in Hildegard Temporini, ed., *Aufstieg und Niedergang der Römischen Welt [ANRW]* 1.2 (Berlin: 1972), 23–58, at 55–58; Jill Harries, "Roman Law from City State to World Empire," in Jeroen Duindam, Jill Diana Harries, Caroline Humfress, and Hurvitz Nimrod, eds., *Law and Empire: Ideas, Practices, Actors* (Leiden: 2013) 45–61; Ralph W. Mathisen, "*Peregrini, Barbari*, and *Cives Romani*: Concepts of Citizenship and Legal Identity of Barbarians in the Late Roman Empire," *American Historical Review* 111, no. 4 (Oct. 2006): 1011–40, at 1025–26, on legal rights of barbarian auxiliaries; Jean Gaudemet, "L'étranger dans le monde romain," *Studii Clasice* 7 (1965): 37–47, remains a useful introduction.

29. Garnsey, "Roman Citizenship and Roman Law," 155.

30. Garnsey, "Roman Citizenship and Roman Law," passim, and 139; Ralph W. Mathisen, "Concepts of Citizenship," in Scott Fitzgerald Johnson, ed., *The Oxford Handbook of Late Antiquity* (Oxford: 2012), 744–63.

31. Garnsey, "Roman Citizenship and Roman Law," 137, notes: "we can see that the spread of citizenship [after the Social War] held the key to the prodigious success of Rome as an imperial state."

32. See n. 26 above.

33. For other changes in ideas of citizenship: William S. Thurman, "The Application of *Subiecti* to Roman Citizens in the Imperial Laws of the Later Roman Empire," *Klio* 52 (1970): 453–63; Clifford Ando, "Sovereignty, Territoriality and Universalism in the Aftermath of Caracalla," in Clifford Ando, ed., *Citizenship and Empire in Europe 200–1900: The Antonine Constitution after 1800 Years* (Stuttgart: 2016), 7–27.

34. In Latin, *deditio* means an act of surrender. On forms of *deditio*, Raimund Schulz, *Die Entwicklung des römischen Völkerrechts im vierten und fünften Jahrhundert n. Chr* (Stuttgart: 1993), 141–48; Guillaume Sartor, *Recherches sur les fédérés et l'armée romaine (de la fin du IIe siècle après J.-C. au début du VIIe siècle après J.-C.), Volume III: Analyses et conclusion générale* (Doctoral thesis, Université de recherche Paris Sciences et Lettres = PSL Research University, 2018), 111–12.

35. A. H. M. Jones, "The Dediticii and the Constitutio Antoniniana," in *Studies in Roman Government and Law* (Oxford: 1960), 129–40, at 130–31, 139; Jones, *Later Roman Empire*, 619–20; Gaius, *The Institutes of Gaius* 1.14 [V. De peregrinis dediticiis], trans. W. M. Gordon and O. F. Robinson, with the Latin text of Emil Seckel and Bernhard Kuebler (Leipzig: 1908) 144: "Vocantur autem peregrini dediticii hi qui quondam aduersus populum Romanum armis susceptis pugnauerunt, deinde uicti se dediderunt [The peregrini dediticii are those who once had taken up arms against the Roman people and had surrendered when they were conquered]"; Claudia Moatti, "The Notion of *Res Publica* in the Age of Caracalla," in Ando, ed., *Citizenship and Empire*, 63–98, at 91; Adrian N. Sherwin-White, *The Roman Citizenship*, 2nd ed. (Oxford: 1973), 283–87 and 380–94; Hugh Elton, *Warfare in Roman Europe, AD 350–425* (Oxford: 1996), 129–33.

36. An excellent case study is Ton Derks, "Ethnic Identity in the Roman Frontier," 239–82. It is almost impossible to avoid using the word *tribe* to describe populations that understood themselves to be bound by ties of kinship, political or military allegiance, geographical proximity, common goals, language, or leadership. In using the term, I do not wish to imply racial uniformity.

37. Mathisen, "*Peregrini, Barbari*, and *Cives Romani*," 1020; Sasse, *Die Constitutio Antoniniana*, 69, on the extent and differentiation of the various categories of *dediticii*, in particular those of the so-called *peregrini dediticii*.

38. Gaius, *Institutes* 1.26. These were individuals who had fought in the arena, or been branded or tortured, and were unworthy of citizenship. See Gaius, *Institutes* 1.13–15:

[I. 13] By the L. Aelia Sentia it is provided that slaves who by way of punishment have been put in bonds by their masters or have been branded, or have been

[302] NOTES TO PAGE 107

questioned under torture on account of some wrongdoing and have been found guilty of the same, also those who have been handed over to fight (in the arena) with men or beasts or who have been cast in a gladiatorial school or into prison—that such slaves, if afterwards manumitted whether by the same or another master, shall become free men of the same status as peregrini dediticii [*cuius condicionis sunt peregrini dediticii*]. [14.] Are called peregrini dediticii those who in the past have taken up arms and fought against the Roman people and being defeated have surrendered (at discretion). [15.] Slaves disgraced in the manner mentioned, by whatever method and at whatever age they are manumitted, and though they were in the full ownership of their masters, never become either Roman citizens or Latins, but are always ranked as dediticii.

For analysis, see Mathisen, "Concepts of Citizenship," 746; on branding, C. P. Jones, "*Stigma*: Tattooing and Branding in Graeco-Roman Antiquity," *Journal of Roman Studies* 77 (1987): 139–55; see also Jones, "Dediticii," 139 and passim; Moatti, "The Notion of *Res Publica*," 91; Michael Crawford, "Dediticii," in Hornblower, Spawforth, and Eidinow, eds., *OCD4*, 423.

39. Michael Maas, "*Mores et Moenia*: Ethnography and the Decline in Urban Constitutional Autonomy in Late Antiquity," in Walter Pohl and Maximilian Diesenberger, eds., *Integration und Herrschaft: Ethnische Identität und soziale Organisation im Frühmittelalter* (Vienna: 2002), 25–35, with further bibliography.

40. For further discussion: W. W. Buckland, *A Text-Book of Roman Law from Augustus to Justinian*, ed. Peter Stein, 3rd ed. (Cambridge: 1963), 98–100; Sherwin-White, "The Roman Citizenship," 57, suggests that the exclusion of *dediticii* does not have to do with the citizenship grant; Garnsey, "Roman Citizenship and Roman Law," 143, points out that after 212 there were still *peregrini*, both from the old system and those newcomers who came in large numbers to serve in the army. On the special case of Egyptians, see Jones, "Dediticii," 139.

41. Mathisen, "*Peregrini, Barbari*, and *Cives Romani*," 1020.

42. Moatti; see n. 36 above.

43. Whittaker, "Use and Abuse," 206 and 207: "we should not assume any single bundle of rights for all *deditici*, but that their conditions were negotiated according to circumstances. That is why it is also difficult to separate them from *foederati*."

44. For a list of passages, see Sasse, *Die Constitutio Antoniniana*, 9–11; this includes Justinian, *Nov. Just* 78.5. For translation, see David J. D. Miller and Peter Sarris, trans., *The Novels of Justinian: A Complete Annotated English Translation*, 2 vols. (Cambridge: 2018).

45. Wirth, "Rome and Its Germanic Partners," 34–35; Schmidt-Hofner, "Barbarian Migrations," esp. 372–74.

46. Sasse, *Die Constitutio Antoniniana*, 111–20, notes differing opinions about meaning of *barbari dediticii*; that it had a general connotation of contempt for those who had surrendered: "der Begriff 'dediticii' noch im 5. Jh. ebenso lebendig ist wie um die Zeitenwende und mit denselben charakteristischen Merkmalen beschrieben warden kann" (119–20). He emphasizes that insisting on a difference between *barbari dediticii* and *peregrini dediticii* is a function of modern theory, not ancient usage.

47. de Ste. Croix, "Appendix III," 509–18; Modéran, "L'établissement de Barbares," 393–94, with supplemental material; Julian's campaigns are notable for their mentions of *dediticii* in the Roman army, as described by Ammianus, *History* 20.8.13 and 21.4.8; John F. Drinkwater, *The Alamanni and Rome 213–496* (Oxford: 2007), 160 and 166: "The fine line between the two sorts of communities, especially in later generations, may have led to both eventually being treated as laetic"; Elton, *Warfare*, 129–30.

48. Drinkwater, *The Alamanni and Rome*, 162, places weight on circumstances of recruitment rather than assigned status after entry; Mathisen, "Concepts of Citizenship," 751–52, points out that newcomers (post-212) were under the umbrella of Roman law and interacted with Romans in many legal matters, particularly related to landholding and taxation. On problems of understanding the legal status of newcomers after 212, see p. 749: "One of the great hitherto unanswered questions of Roman law relates to the status of *peregrini*—foreign 'barbarians'—who settled in the empire after Caracalla's grant. Just how were they treated under Roman law? Did they then (1) constitute a new class of noncitizens, (2) 'become'

NOTES TO PAGES 107–109 [303]

citizens by some as yet undefined process, (3) gain access to Roman civil law by some other means, or (4) likewise become covered by the Antonine Constitution? These are issues that have been rarely discussed in the scholarship and never answered."

49. Mathisen, "Concepts of Citizenship, 754–55.

50. Gaius, *Institutes* 1.9.

51. See Charles Pazdernik, "Procopius and Thucydides on the Labors of War," *Transactions of the American Philological Association* 130 (2000): 149–87, at 157.

52. Sozomen, *The Ecclesiastical History* 9.5; *Cod. Th.* 5.6.3.

53. Modéran, "L'établissement de Barbares," 367, on their juridical status.

54. *Cod. Th.* 5.6.3; Elton, *Warfare*, 130 and 132; Modéran, "L'établissement de Barbares," 367–68; Brennan, "The Last of the Romans," 197–98; Schmidt-Hofner, "Barbarian Migrations," esp. 372–74 and passim.

> We have subjected the Scyrae [Sciri], a barbarian people, to Our power after defeating a very great force of Huns with whom they had allied themselves. Therefore We grant to all persons the opportunity to supply their own fields with men of the aforesaid people. But all persons shall know that they shall hold those whom they have received by no other title [*alio iure*] than that of colonus, and that no one shall be permitted either fraudulently to take anyone of this class of coloni away from the person to whom he had once been assigned or to receive such a one as a fugitive, under the penalty which is inflicted upon those who harbor persons that are registered in the tax rolls of others or coloni who are not their own. Moreover, the owners of lands may use the free labor of such captives . . . but no one shall be forced to undergo a tax equalization for the tax rolls . . . and no one shall be permitted to transfer such persons, as though they had been given to him, from the obligations of the tax rolls to that of slavery, or to assign them to urban duties . . . Those who receive such persons shall be permitted, because of the shortage of farm produce, to retain them for a two-year period in any provinces they please, provided that these provinces are across the sea, and thereafter to place them in permanent homes, for which purpose their residence in the regions of Thrace and Illyricum shall be absolutely prohibited to them. Only within a five-year period shall it be permitted to make a transfer openly and freely within the confines of the same province. The furnishing of recruits also shall be suspended during the aforesaid twenty-year period. The distribution of these people throughout the transmarine provinces shall be made to those who so wish through petitions to apply to your court. (*Cod. Th.* 5.6.3.)

55. *Cod. Just.* 7.5.1: "The condition of prisoner of war [*dediticia condicio*] shall not be permitted to trouble Our state in any manner in the future but shall be entirely abolished, because We find it no longer in use, and the empty name of this kind of freedom is used deceptively" (AD 530). Discussion in Buckland, *A Text-Book of Roman Law*, 82 and 381; Adolf Berger, "Encyclopedic Dictionary of Roman Law," *Transactions of the American Philosophical Society* 43, no. 2 (1953): 333–809, at 427.

56. Clifford Ando, "Legal Pluralism in Practice," in Paul J. Du Plessis, Clifford Ando, and Kaius Tuori, eds., *The Oxford Handbook of Roman Law and Society* (Oxford: 2016), 283–94.

57. Chauvot, *Les "barbares" des romains*, 310–21, for recent overview.

58. Lawrence Keppie, *The Making of the Roman Army: From Republic to Empire* (London: Batsford, 1984), 182–86, for overview on auxiliaries; a comprehensive study: Ian Haynes, *Blood of the Provinces: The Roman Auxilia and the Making of Provincial Society from Augustus to the Severans* (Oxford: 2013), 1–27 on recruitment; Catherine Wolff and Patrice Faure, eds., *Les auxiliaires de l'armée romaine: Des alliés aux fédérés* (Lyon: 2016).

59. Keppie, *The Making of the Roman Army*, 182.

60. Haynes, *Blood of the Provinces*, vii and passim; Hartmut Wolff, "Die Entwicklung der Veteranenprivilegien vom Beginn des 1. Jahrhunderts v. Chr. bis auf Konstantin d. Gr.," in Werner Eck and Hartmut Wolff, eds., *Heer und Integrationspolitik: Die römischen Militärdiplome als historische Quelle* (Cologne: 1986), 44–115, for an overview.

61. Noted already by G. L. Cheesman, *The Auxilia of the Roman Imperial Army* (Oxford: 1914), 138–39; Keppie, *The Making of the Roman Army*, 185; Haynes, *Blood of the Provinces*,

[304] NOTES TO PAGES 109–112

121–34, however, says they were not usually moved, esp. at 134; See also Richard Talbert, "Natives Naming Themselves? Rome's Veterans Speak," in Michael Maas and Fay Yarbrough, eds., *Empires and Indigenous Peoples: Comparing Ancient Roman and North American Experiences* (Norman, OK: 2024) 212–26.

62. Michael P. Speidel, "The Soldiers' Homes," in *Roman Army Studies*, vol. 2 (Stuttgart: 1992), 313–27, at 313 and 316.

63. Haynes, *Blood of the Provinces*, 57, 84, 333, 343–50; Wolff and Faure, eds., *Les auxiliaires de l'armée romaine*; Talbert, "Natives Naming Themselves?"

64. Michael Alexander Speidel, "The Roman Army," in *The Oxford Handbook of Roman Epigraphy*, ed. Christer Bruun and Jonathan Edmondson (Oxford: 2015), 319–44, at 339–40.

65. Jones, *Later Roman Empire*, 98–99 and "Appendix II: Table VIII," 1437; Peter Brennan, "Units in the *Notitia Dignitatum*," in *The Encyclopedia of the Roman Army*, ed. Yann Le Bohec (Chichester: 2015), 1054 = Wiley Online Library, https://doi.org/10.1002/9781118318140.wbra1562.

66. Brennan, "Units in the *Notitia Dignitatum*," at 1 and 3–4; for references to auxiliary troops stationed on the Danube frontier, see Jones, *Later Roman Empire*, "Appendix I: Table VIII," 1437; for difficulties in determining their numbers, see Warren Treadgold, *Byzantium and Its Army 284–1081* (Stanford, 1995) 44–49.

67. *Cod. Th.* 7.13.1.

68. *Cod. Th.* 7.13.7.4.

69. *Cod. Th.* 7.4.22.

70. On late antique military architecture: Collins, Symonds, and Weber, eds., *Roman Military Architecture on the Frontiers*, esp. Rob Collins and Meike Weber, "Late Roman Military Architecture: An Introduction," 1–5.

71. Jean Gaudemet, "Les romains et les 'autres,'" in *La nozione di "romano" tra cittadinanza e universalitá* (Naples: 1984), 7–37, at 26, points out that *gentiles* appear only in western provinces; Ralph Mathisen, "*Provinciales, Gentiles*, and Marriages between Romans and Barbarians in the Late Roman Empire," *Journal of Roman Studies* 99 (2009): 140–55, at 151, for discussion of locations; *Notitia Dignitatum*, 42.34–44, ed. Otto Seeck (1876; repr. 1962), has inconsistent information and should be used with caution.

72. Jean Gaudemet, "Les romains et les 'autres,'" 26, for similarities and differences; Soraci, *Ricerche sui Conubia*, 83–110, discusses *gentiles* in the fourth century, with a helpful review of literature prior to 1974; Audrey Becker, "Romano-Barbarian Treaties and the Redefinition of Identities in Late Antiquity," in Maas and Yarbrough, eds., *Empires and Indigenous Peoples, 105–118*; Chauvot, *Les "barbares" des romains*, 269–72; Ammianus, *History* 16.11.4 and 20.8.13; Sartor, *Recherches sur les fédérés*, 111–17; Sartor summarizes his dissertation: Guillaume Sartor, "Les fédérés (*foederati*) dans les guerres imperiales (IIIe–VIe siècles)," in Wolff and Faure, eds., *Les auxiliaires de l'armée romaine*, 527–73.

73. Modéran, "L'établissement de barbares," 380–81; Émilienne Demougeot, *L'empire romain et les barbares d'Occident (IVe–VIIe siècle): Scripta Varia* (Paris: 1988), 61–73, at 70–71 = Demougeot, "À propos des lètes gaulois du IVe siècle," in Ruth Stiehl and Hans Erich Stier, eds., *Beitäge zur alten Geschichte und deren Nachleben: Festschrift für Franz Altheim zum 6.10.1968*, vol. 2 (Berlin: 1970), 101–13, at 110–11. She remarks that fourth-century emperors and their commanders settled *gentiles* to confront military threats: Demougeot, "Laeti et Gentiles dans la Gaule du IVe siècle," in *Actes du Colloque d'Histoire Sociale 1970* (Paris: 1972), 101–12, at 101.

74. Jones, *Later Roman Empire*, 651–52.

75. For prefects: *Cod. Th.* 11.30.62. They answered to the Master of Soldiers; we know of one exceptional case in which an Alaman in Roman service briefly held command of *gentiles*. Drinkwater, *The Alamanni and Rome*, 146–48, for Agilo's career.

76. *Cod Th.* 11.30.62.

77. Whittaker, *Frontiers*, 295 n. 7, arguing that *gentiles* were recruited from within the empire as well as beyond the frontier.

78. Mathisen, "*Provinciales, Gentiles*, and Marriages," 151.

79. Mathisen, "*Provinciales, Gentiles*, and Marriages," 151; Mommsen, ed., *Theodosiani Libri XVI*, 3.14.1.

NOTES TO PAGES 112–114 [305]

80. For overview of literature: Chauvot, *Les "barbares" des romains*, 301–25.

81. *Cod. Th.* 3.14.1: "No provincial, of whatever rank or class he may be, shall marry a barbarian wife (*barbara*), nor shall a provincial woman be united with any foreigner. But if there should be any alliances between provincials and foreigners through such marriages and if anything should be disclosed as suspect or criminal among them, it shall be expiated by capital punishment."

82. Mathisen, "*Provinciales, Gentiles*, and Marriages," 154.

83. Mathisen, "*Provinciales, Gentiles*, and Marriages," 154 and passim. See also John B. Bury, *History of the Late Roman Empire from the Death of Theodosius I to the Death of Justinian*, vol. I (New York: 1958), 40 and n. 1, on the inability of *gentiles* to marry Roman women.

84. Mathisen, "*Provinciales, Gentiles*, and Marriages," 154, notes that marrying a citizen woman might gain the foreigner the status of a *provincialis*, and with that new status would come tax obligations, which were evidently a burden worth enduring.

85. Jones, *Later Roman Empire*, 652. For overview of imperial fortification, see Alexander Sarantis with Neil Christie, "Fortifications in the West: A Bibliographic Essay," "Fortifications in Africa: A Bibliographic Essay," and "Fortifications in the East: A Bibliographic Essay," in Alexander Sarantis and Neil Christie, eds., *War and Warfare in Late Antiquity: Current Perspectives* (Leiden: 2013), 255–370. For the *fossatum Africae*: Richard J. A. Talbert, ed., *Barrington Atlas of the Greek and Roman World* (Princeton: 2000), 33, coordinates B4; Jean Baradez, *Vue-aerienne de l'organisation romaine dans le Sud-Algerien: Fossatum Africae* (Paris: 1949) remains the starting place for discussion; G. D. B. Jones and D. J. Mattingly, "Fourth-Century Manning of the 'Fossatum Africae,'" *Britannia* 11 (1980), 323–26; R. G. Goodchild and I. A. Richmond, review of "Jean Baradez, Fossatum Africae" (1949), *Journal of Roman Studies* 40, no. 1–2 (1950), 162–65, at 163, notes similarities to Hadrian's Wall.

86. For a comparative approach, see Peter Spring, *Great Walls and Linear Barriers* (Barnsley, UK: 2015), 70, 79–80, 82, 252, and 292–94; for overview of long-term social and economic conditions in Roman North Africa, Susan T. Stevens and Jonathan P. Conant, eds., *North Africa under Byzantium and Early Islam* (Washington, DC: 2016), esp. chap. 3, Elizabeth Fentress and Andrew Wilson, "The Saharan Berber Diaspora and the Southern Frontiers of Byzantine North Africa," 41–64; chap. 6, Philipp von Rummel, "The Transformation of Ancient Land- and Cityscapes in Early Medieval North Africa," 105–18; and chap. 15, Peter Brown, "Byzantine and Early Islamic Africa, ca. 500–800: Concluding Remarks," 295–302; Whittaker, *Rome and Its Frontiers*, 10–11 and 101, on purpose of the *fossatum* and movement of supplies; the only known reference is the *Cod. Th.* 7.15.1; Pol Trousset, "Pénétration romaine et organisation de la zone frontière dans le prédésert tunisien," *L'Africa romana* 15, no. 1 (2004): 59–88, stressing the *fossatum's* role in facilitating exchange and communication; Christian Hünemörder, "Fossatum," *Brill's New Pauly*, http://dx.doi.org/10.1163/1574-9347_bnp_e414400.

87. David Cherry, *Frontier and Society in Roman North Africa* (Oxford: 1998), 58–66.

88. Jones, *Later Roman Empire*, 652, believes these are the lands mentioned in the law.

89. *Cod. Th.* 7.15.1.

90. Mathisen, "*Provinciales, Gentiles*, and Marriages," 153–54, for fuller discussion.

91. Augustine, "Letter 199," in *Letters 156–210 (Epistulae)*, ed. Boniface Ramsey, trans. Roland Teske (Hyde Park, NY: 2004), 199.46.

92. U. Dionisi, "Hesychius of Salona," in Angelo di Berardino, ed., *Encyclopedia of the Early Church*, vol. 1, trans. Adrian Walford (Cambridge: 1992), 379.

93. For multiple allegiances and self-identifications: Brent D. Shaw, "Keti, Son of Maswalat: Ethnicity and Empire," in Jonathan J. Price, Margalit Finkelberg, and Yuval Shahar, eds., *Rome: An Empire of Many Nations; New Perspectives on Ethnic Diversity and Cultural Identity* (Cambridge: 2021), 58–83.

94. Drinkwater, *The Alamanni and Rome*, 166; Demougeot, "Laeti et Gentiles," 101, understands the category as "le genre de servitude spécifiquement militaire"; Chauvot, *Les "barbares" des romains*, 259–99, for overview.

95. Schmidt-Hofner, "Barbarian Migrations," 389–91; Whittaker, "Use and Abuse," 204–5: "Military contingents of *laeti* are recorded in over half the *civitates* of Gaul north of the

[306] NOTES TO PAGES 114–115

Loire, quite apart from other contingents of Sarmatians, *gentiles*, and so on," citing A. L. F. Rivet, "The *Notitia Galliarum*: Some Questions," in R. Goodburn and P. Bartholomew, eds., *Aspects of the Notitia Dignitatum: Papers Presented to the Conference in Oxford, December 13 to 15, 1974*, BAR Supplementary Series 15 (Oxford: 1976), 119–41; on relationship between designations of groups of subjects (including *laeti*) and the growth of imperial power, see Chauvot, *Les "barbares" des romains*, 279–80; see also Demougeot, "À propos des lètes gaulois," 103–13 = Demougeot, *L'empire romain*, 63–73; Jones, *Later Roman Empire*, 1077 n. 38, sees them as transplanted tribal groups.

96. *Cod. Th.* 13.11.10 (369 CE); on *praefecti laetorum*, *Cod. Th.* 7.20.10 (369 CE); Jones, *Later Roman Empire*, 620; Mathisen, "*Peregrini, Barbari*, and *Cives Romani*," 1025–26; "Panegyric of Constantius," in C. E. V. Nixon and Barbara Saylor Rodgers, trans., *In Praise of Later Roman Emperors: The Panegyrici Latini* (Berkeley, CA: 1994), 104–44 (at 141–43 nn. 75 and 76).

97. Demougeot, "À propos des lètes gaulois," 101–13 = Demougeot, *L'empire romain*, 61–73.

98. Gabriele von Olberg-Haverkate, "Liten," in Albrecht Cordes et al., eds., *Handwörterbuch zur deutschen Rechtsgeschichte (HRG), Band III, 2: Völlig überarbeitete und erweiterte Auflage* (Berlin: 2004), 1013–15, https://www.hrgdigital.de/HRG.liten. I thank Helmut Reimitz for this reference. Demougeot, "À propos des lètes gaulois," 101–3 = Demougeot, *L'empire romain*, 61–63.

99. Drinkwater, *The Alamanni and Rome*, 168–69.

100. Ibid.

101. Zosimus, *New History* 2.54.1, trans. Ronald T. Ridley (Canberra: 1982). See Zosime, *Histoire Nouvelle: Tome I (Livres I et II)*, ed. and trans. François Paschoud (Paris: 1971), 261–62 n. 69. Zosimus was perhaps drawing from Eunapius. I thank Michael Kulikowski for this observation.

102. Pan. Lat. VIII. 21, ed. and trans. R. A. B. Mynors: Nixon and Rodgers, ed., *In Praise of Later Roman Emperors: The Panegyrici Latini* (Berkeley: 2004): on the date, 105–6; Domenico Lassandro, "I 'cultores barbari' (Laeti) in Gallia da Massimiano alla fine del IV secolo d.C.," in Marta Sordi, ed., *Conoscenze etniche e rapporti di convivenza nell'antichità*, Contributi dell'Istituto di storia antica 6 (Milan: 1979), 178–88, at 180–82, on use of legal terminology (*postliminium*), and 185–87 on the origin of the status of the *laeti* (not as homogeneous ethnic groups), and 187 on the problem of their possible origin as *dediticii*.

103. Abandoned lands were a constant problem in Late Antiquity. For an overview: Jones, *Later Roman Empire*, 812–23. He notes, p. 816, that in the 420s, for example, more than half of the land was deserted in Byzacena and other parts of North Africa. Lands that required constant maintenance of water resources and irrigation were particularly hard hit; Cam Grey, "Revisiting the 'Problem' of *agri deserti* in the Late Roman Empire," *Journal of Roman Archaeology* 20 (2007): 363–76, stresses the variety and flexibility of Roman responses to deserted lands.

104. Some Frankish *laeti* are mentioned in the *Notitia Dignitatum Occ.* 42.36.

105. "Panegyric to Constantius," 21.1: "And so as formerly on your orders, Diocletian Augustus, Asia filled the deserts of Thrace by the transfer of inhabitants, and as later, at your bidding, Maximian Augustus, the *laeti*, restored by right of *postliminium*, and the Franks, admitted to our laws, have cultivated the empty fields of the Arvii and the Treveri, so now though your victories, Constantius, invincible Caesar, whatever land remained abandoned to the territory of the Ambiani, Bellovaci, Tricasses, and Lingones turns green again under cultivation by the barbarian"; *postliminium*: *Cod. Th.* 5.7.1–2, Justinian, *Institutes* 1.12.5; H. Kreller, "Postliminium," in Georg Wissowa et al., *RE: Dreiundvierzigster Halbband; Pontarches bis Praefectianus* (Stuttgart: 1953), cols. 863–73; *postliminium* and citizenship rights: Mathisen, "*Peregrini, Barbari*, and *Cives Romani*," 1025–26.

106. *Cod. Th.* 5.7.1.

107. Seeck, ed., *Notitia Dignitatum Occ.* 42.36, "Praefectus laetorum Francorum," at 217.

108. *Cod. Just.* 8.50.5, 8.50.12. See Maria Virginia Sanna, *Ricerche in tema di redemptio ab hostibus* (Cagliari: 1998) 148–51.

NOTES TO PAGES 115–116 [307]

109. Alain Chauvot, *Opinions romaines face aux barbares au IVe siècle ap. J.-C.* (Paris: 1998), 48–50.

110. Seeck, ed., *Notitia Dignitatum Occ.* 42.33–44.

111. For example, see Franz Theuws, "Grave Goods, Ethnicity, and the Rhetoric of Burial Rites in Late Antique Northern Gaul," in Ton Derks and Nico Roymans, eds., *Ethnic Constructs in Antiquity: The Role of Power and Tradition* (Amsterdam: 2009), 283–319, at 314–15; for the Batavi, Ammianus, *History* 16.12.45.

112. Wirth, "Rome and Its Germanic Partners," at 37 n. 104; Alain Chauvot, *Opinions romains face aux barbares*, 48–50, for various explanations and clear statement of where scholars have taken wrong turns.

113. For example: Patrick Périn and Michel Kazanski, "Identity and Ethnicity during the Era of Migrations and Barbarian Kingdoms in Light of Archaeology in Gaul," in Ralph W. Mathisen and Danuta Shanzer, eds., *Romans, Barbarians, and the Transformation of the Roman World: Cultural Interaction and the Creation of Identity in Late Antiquity* (Farnham: 2011), 299–329, for a particularly clear and up-to-date overview and statement of main questions. They point out (324–27) that Germanic graves marked, by weapons and ornaments, from the later fourth century to the Merovingian period are mixed in with those of the late Roman population, pointing to a high degree of integration and even a blurring of identities, leading to the emergence of a "common style of prestige for military elites" by 500. Other summaries of archaeological material are Whittaker, *Frontiers*, 301 n. 68; Peter Heather, *Empires and Barbarians* (London: 2009), 311–17, reviews archaeological evidence and previous theories, suggesting the emergence of a discontinuous, non-Roman social order; Halsall, *Barbarian Migrations*, 152–57; Nico Roymans and Stijn Heeren, "Introduction: New Perspectives on the Late Roman Northwest," in Nico Roymans and Stijn Heeren, eds., *Social Dynamics in the Northwest Frontiers of the Late Roman Empire: Beyond Decline or Transformation* (Amsterdam: 2017), 1–10. For example, see Franz Theuws, "Grave Goods, Ethnicity, and the Rhetoric of Burial Rites in Late Antique Northern Gaul," in *Ethnic Constructs in Antiquity*, ed. Derks and Roymans, 283–319, at 314–15.

114. On the longevity of the legal condition in Frankia: Gabriele von Olberg-Haverkate, "Liten," 1013–15; Guy Halsall, *Settlement and Social Organization: The Merovingian Region of Metz* (Cambridge: 1995), 41, 57, 258; Whittaker, *Frontiers*, 275: "In the sixth century there were still units of *laeti* in the Auvergne"; see also Bernard S. Bachrach, *Merovingian Military Organization, 481–571* (Minneapolis: 1972), 14–15; C. J. Simpson, *"Laeti* in Northern Gaul: A Note on Pan. Lat. VIII, 21," *Latomus* 36, no. 1 (Jan.-Mar. 1977): 169–70, at 170, notes that "There is no evidence here [in this passage] that *laeti* were ever prisoners of war captured by the Romans," *contra* the opinions of Erich Zöllner, *Geschichte der Franken bis zur Mitte des sechsten Jahrhunderts* (Munich: 1970), 13, and Jones, *Later Roman Empire*, 157.

115. Schmidt-Hofner, "Barbarian Migrations," 390–91; Wirth, "Rome and Its Germanic Partners," 38:

> There is no clear picture about the number and size of the *laeti* settlements. What the Notitia Dignitatum shows is without doubt no more than a remnant, and archaeological remains only leave us guessing. It is very probable that there was military training in the handling of Roman weapons in order to facilitate their integration into other units, as well as the use of individuals in barbarian units with their own tactics. It is clear that the imported way of life was still practiced, especially as there was no romanised substratum of the population in which they could quickly be integrated, or because that substratum had already lost the necessary density. Members of the elite and the successful will have adapted more quickly than the masses, who, together with their families, went on living as they were accustomed to at home. To what extent colonies of *laeti* were different from other barbarian settlements remains unclear.

116. Still useful: Eugène Léotard, *Essai sur la condition des barbares établis dans l'empire romain au Quatrième Siècle* (Paris: 1873), 103–28; these officers were monitored; on their responsibilities: *Cod Th.* 7.20.10, promulgated by Valens and Gratian to Probus, praetorian prefect (369):

[308] NOTES TO PAGES 116–118

If any person should serve as provost (*praepositus*) of an armory or of the fleet or of the *laeti* or likewise if he should serve as provost of the Roman largesses or as tribune of a cohort, or if he should perhaps be in charge of those administrative positions to which individuals do not come except with reliable persons as sureties, and if the aforesaid person should be discovered neither to have served within the palace with suitable service nor to have toiled in the armed imperial service, he shall forfeit those special privileges which are granted to soldiers and palatines.

See also *Cod. Th.* 13.11.10; other sources: Zosimus, *New History*, 2.54.1; Ammianus, *History* 20.8.13–14.

117. Drinkwater, *The Alamanni and Rome*, 168–69; *Cod. Th.* 7.12.1.pr.

118. On evolution of the concept up to the year 400 and a review of literature, see Chauvot, *Les "barbares" des romains*, 259–68.

119. *Cod. Th.* 13.11.10.

120. Schmidt-Hofner, "Barbarian Migrations," 389–91.

121. Schmidt-Hofner, "Barbarian Migrations," 390, and his n. 44.

122. *Cod. Th.* 7.20.12.

123. Peter Heather, *The Goths* (Oxford: 1996), 144–46, on court politics and military tensions; Alan Cameron, Jacqueline Long, and Lee Sherry, *Barbarians and Politics at the Court of Arcadius* (Berkeley: 1993), 199–211.

124. For concise accounts of these exciting events, see Heather, *The Goths*, 146, and Stephen Mitchell, *A History of the Roman Empire, AD 284–641*, 2nd ed. (Chichester: 2005), 101–2.

125. *Legio* here must mean the army in general, since *laeti* would not have been placed in regular units.

126. *Cod. Th.* 7.20.12.pr.; for *vagus* as deserter: *Cod. Th.* 13.6.1.

127. Drinkwater, *The Alamanni and Rome*, 80–116, on Alamannic settlements.

128. "The Novels of the Sainted Severus Augustus," in Pharr, trans., *The Theodosian Code* 2.1 (465 CE); Jones, *Later Roman Empire*, 620 and 1257 n. 26.

129. Ernest Stein, *Histoire du Bas-Empire II: De la disparition de l'empire d'Occident à la mort de Justinien (476–565)*, ed. Jean-Remy Palanque (Paris: 1949), 42 n. 2, believed the *laeti* in question were Alamans or Taifals.

130. Mathisen, "*Provinciales, Gentiles*, and Marriages," 151–52.

131. On Libius Severus, see Ralph Mathisen, "Libius Severus (461–465 A.D.)," *Roman Emperors—An Online Encyclopedia of Roman Rulers and Their Families*, http://www.roman-emperors.org/libius.htm (last modified July 28, 2022).

132. Ammianus, *History* 16.11.4–8. Regarding this passage, Drinkwater, *The Alamanni and Rome*, 166–67, disagrees with Rolfe's Loeb translation of this band as "*Laeti*, a savage tribe," which "by-pass[es] the issue of the existence of a semi-servile population in Gaul," and he dismisses the idea of these *laeti* being Alamanni: "They are just 'barbarian *laeti*': certainly not a tribe, probably not Alamannic, perhaps not principals in the events of 357, and maybe not hostile to Rome."

133. On barbarian raiding as an ethnographic trope, see Harmut Ziche, "Barbarian Raiders and Barbarian Peasants: Models of Ideological and Economic Integration," in *Romans, Barbarians, and the Transformation of the Roman World: Cultural Interaction and the Creation of Identity in Late Antiquity*, ed. Ralph W. Mathisen and Danuta Shanzer (Farnham: 2011), 199–219.

134. Ammianus, *History* 20.8.13 (trans. M. Maas).

135. Whittaker, *Frontiers*, 275, on continuity of *laeti* in Gaul after Roman rule and their giving allegiance to Frankish rulers: "In the sixth century there were still units of *laeti* in the Auvergne." See also Bachrach, *Merovingian Military Organization*, 14–15; Zöllner, *Geschichte der Franken*, 13; Jones, *Later Roman Empire*, 157; *contra* Zöllner and Jones: Simpson, "*Laeti* in Northern Gaul," 170, notes that "There is no evidence here [in this passage] that *laeti* were ever prisoners of war captured by the Romans."

136. Chauvot, *Les "barbares" des romains*, 280; Demougeot, "Laeti et Gentiles," 101–4, suggesting coexistence and then displacement, and that *gentiles* were effectively inferior to the *laeti*.

NOTES TO PAGES 118–120 [309]

137. Ammianus, *History* 20.8.13.

138. Seeck, ed., *Notitia Dignitatum Occ.* 42.34.

139. Ralf Scharf, *Foederati: Von der völkerrechtlichen Kategorie zur byzantinischen Truppengattung*, TYCHE, Supplementband 4 (Vienna: 2001) discusses in detail their evolution from the fifth century in the West to the eleventh century in Byzantium. Two more recent theses review the question of federates in the eastern and western parts of the empire. For the West, see the voluminous study of Guillaume Sartor (above, n. 34); and for the East, the unpublished University of Ottawa Master's thesis of Lucas McMahon, "The Foederati, the Phoideratoi, and the Symmachoi of the Late Antique East (ca. A.D. 400–650)" (April 2014). McMahon traces changes in the word *phoideratos* (φοιδεράτος) in Late Antiquity in legal and other written sources, between the fourth and sixth century. Through his examination of only the Greek sources, he shows how the Greek term differs from the Latin *foederatus*. This was already noted in antiquity. In the age of Justinian it acquired a new meaning. Avshalom Laniado, *Ethnos et droit dans le monde protobyzantin, Ve-VIe siècle: Fédérés, paysans et provinciaux à la lumière d'une scholie juridique de l'époque de Justinien* (Geneva: 2015); Timo Stickler, "The *Foederati*," in Paul Erdkamp, ed., *A Companion to the Roman Army* (Oxford: 2007), 495–514; Walter Pohl, "The Empire and the Lombards: Treaties and Negotiations in the Sixth Century," in Pohl, ed., *Kingdoms of the Empire*, 75–133, at 78–87; Chrysos, "Legal Concepts and Patterns," 13–24 and "Conclusion," 185–206; Alexander Sarantis, *Justinian's Balkan Wars: Campaigning, Diplomacy and Development in Illyricum, Thrace and the Northern World; A.D. 527–65* (Prenton, UK: 2016), 47 and passim; Guillaume Sartor, "Les fédérés (*foederati*) dans les guerres impériales (IIIe-Vie siècles)," in *Les auxiliares de l'armée romaine: Des alliés aux fédérés*, ed. Catherine Wolff and Patrice Faure (Paris: 2016), 527–73, at 527–32 for definitions.

140. C. R. Whittaker, "Foederati," in G. W. Bowersock, Peter Brown, and Oleg Grabar, eds., *Late Antiquity: A Guide to the Postclassical World*, 451–52.

141. Brennan, "The Last of the Romans," 193, for "outsourcing" armies.

142. Romans had, of course, been making treaties with external communities for many centuries. Stickler, "The *Foederati*," 495–97, discusses federates in the Republic and continuity from the Principate. He notes, "However, no certainty can be attained as to whether the term *foederati* really describes a coherent concept that was created in the fourth century and that was universally employed for the integration of barbarian soldiers into the military of the late empire. In fact, the military structures in Late Antiquity seem to have varied as much as the challenges the imperial administrations in the West and in the East had to face" (509–10).

143. Chrysos, "Legal Concepts and Patterns," 17.

144. Constantin Zuckerman, "Les 'Barbares' romains: Au sujet de l'origine des *auxilia* tétrarchiques," in Françoise Vallet and Michel Kazanski, eds., *L'armée romaine et les barbares du IIIe au VIIe siècle* (Paris: 1993), 17–20; auxiliaries sometimes appear in late antique sources; the difference between them and *foederati* is sometimes blurry.

145. Goths, for example, in a second treaty had no military obligations, but this was rare, if not exceptional: Heather, *Goths and* Romans, 116–18.

146. Peter Heather emphasizes that in the fourth-century treaties with groups beyond the frontiers varied considerably: Heather, "*Foedera* and *Foederati* of the Fourth Century," in Pohl, ed., *Kingdoms of the Empire*, 57–74, esp. 72–74.

147. Jones, *Later Roman Empire*, 198–99.

148. Halsall, *Barbarian Migrations*, 417–54, esp. 437–39.

149. On conditions for recruitment in the army, see Elton, *Warfare*, 128–54; on *foederati* regiments, see 91–94.

150. McMahon, "The Foederati, the Phoideratoi, and the Symmachoi," 11.

151. Halsall, *Barbarian Migrations*, 153, notes that in the fourth century "[f]oederati who turned out to be losers in barbarian politics might be admitted into the Empire as refugees in reward for their support, but in so doing they became *dediticii*." This statement blurs two different categories of barbarians in the empire.

152. The best overview of historiography about the terms of settlement is found in Halsall, *Barbarian Migrations*, 417–54.

153. Heather, *Goths and Romans*, 115–224, on the long journey and internal evolution of Goths from before the Huns to their settlement in Gaul.

[310] NOTES TO PAGES 120–124

154. For an overview of Roman marriage law: Jean Gaudemet, "Justum Matrimonium," *RIDA* 2 (1949): 309–66, at 344–66 for Late Antiquity; Chauvot, *Les "barbares" des romains*, 301–25.

155. For overview: Goetz, "Introduction," 1–12, and the collected essays in the volume Goetz, Jarnut, and Pohl, eds., *Regna and Gentes*.

156. *Cod. Th.* 7.13.16 (406 CE).

157. Jeroen W. P. Wijnendaele, "Stilicho, Radagaisus, and the So-Called "Battle of Faesulae" (406 CE)," *Journal of Late Antiquity* 9, no. 1 (2016): 267–84; Zosimus, *New History* 5.26.3, exaggerates the size of his army at 400,000.

158. *Cod. Th.* 7.13.16 (406 CE); Jones, *Later Roman Empire*, 184, for other examples of enrolling slaves.

159. *Cod. Th.* 7.13.8 (380 CE) prohibited slaves from enlistment in the army.

160. *Nov. Th.* 24.1–6 (443 CE); McMahon, "The Foederati, the Phoideratoi, and the Symmachoi," 15–16. For its reference to Saracen *foederati*, McMahon argues against Irfan Shahîd, *Byzantium and the Arabs in the Sixth Century I*, xx. See also Geoffrey Greatrex, "Les Jafnides et la défense de l'Empire au VIe siècle," in Denis Genequand and Christian Julien Robin, eds, *Les Jafnides: Des rois arabes au service de Byzance (VIe siècle de l'ère chrétienne); Actes du colloque de Paris, 24–25 novembre 2008* (Paris: 2015), 121–54, here 136–37 n. 51, arguing that different groups of Arabs had different sorts of ties to Rome; on the proconsul of Palestine, see *Nov. Just.*, 103.pr.

161. Laniado, *Ethnos et droit*, 35–127; McMahon, "The Foederati, the Phoideratoi, and the Symmachoi," 29–31; on Justinian's army, Warren Treadgold, *Byzantium and Its Army 284–1081* (Stanford, CA: 1995), 15–19; Alexander Sarantis, *Justinian's Balkan Wars*; for a survey of army structure in the Age of Justinian, see Michael Whitby, *The Wars of Justinian* (Barnsley, UK: 2021), 85–114; on military culture among the East Roman ruling elite, see Conor Whately, "Militarization, or the Rise of a Distinct Military Culture? The East Roman Ruling Elite in the 6th Century AD," in Stephen O'Brien and Daniel Boatright, eds., *Warfare and Society in the Ancient Eastern Mediterranean Papers Arising from a Colloquium Held at the University of Liverpool, 13th June 2008* (Oxford: 2013), 49–57.

162. McMahon, "The Foederati, the Phoideratoi, and the Symmachoi," 29.

163. Justinian, *Nov. Just.* 116.1.

164. McMahon, "The Foederati, the Phoideratoi, and the Symmachoi," 30.

165. Ammianus, *History* 25.4.25; Heather, "*Foedera* and *Foederati*," 64.

166. Heather, "*Foedera* and *Foederati*," 66–68.

167. McMahon, "The Foederati, the Phoideratoi, and the Symmachoi," 71.

168. Procopius, *History of the Wars II (Vandalic War)* 3.11.3–5, ed. and trans. H. B. Dewing, LCL 81 (Cambridge, MA: 1916); for discussion, see McMahon, "The Foederati, the Phoideratoi, and the Symmachoi," 28–29; on the changed meaning of *foederati* in the sixth century, see Jones, *Later Roman Empire*, 663.

Chapter Four: Divine Providence and the Power of the Stars

1. Origen, *The Philocalia of Origen: A Compilation of Selected Passages from Origen's Works Made by St. Gregory of Nazianzus and St. Basil of Caesarea*, trans. George Lewis (Edinburgh: 1911), 23.16.

2. Pseudo-Clement, *Recognitiones* IX.27, trans. Thomas Smith, in Alexander Roberts and James Donaldson, eds., *Ante-Nicene Fathers*, vol. 8: *The Twelve Patriarchs, Excerpts and Epistles, The Clementina, Apocrypha, Decretals, Memoirs of Edessa and Syriac Documents, Remains of the First Ages* (Edinburgh: 1886, repr. 1989).

3. Robin Attfield, "Christian Attitudes to Nature," *Journal of the History of Ideas* 44, no. 3 (Jul.–Sep. 1983): 369–86.

4. David Amand, *Fatalisme et liberté dans l'Antiquité grecque: Recherches sur la survivance de l'argumentation morale antifataliste de Carnéade chez les philosophes grecs et les théologiens chrétiens des quatre premiers siècles* (Louvain: 1945).

5. And sometimes an abstract creative force, "deus," among the Stoics; see Manilius, *Astronomica* I.483–85, ed. and trans. G. P. Goold, LCL 469 (Cambridge, MA: 1977): "I find

NOTES TO PAGES 124–126   [311]

no argument so compelling as this to show that the universe moves in obedience to a divine power and is indeed the manifestation of God, and did not come together at the dictation of chance."

6. Molly Whittaker, "'Signs and Wonders': The Pagan Background," *Studia evangelica Vol. 5: Papers Presented to the Third International Congress on New Testament Studies Held at Christ Church, Oxford, 1965* (1968), 155–58. There was no agreement about astrology in Jewish circles: Alexander Altmann, "Astrology," in Michael Berenbaum and Fred Skolnik, eds., *Encyclopaedia Judaica 2*, 2nd ed. (Beit Shemesh, Israel: 2007), 616–20; James H. Charlesworth, "Jewish Astrology in the Talmud, Pseudepigrapha, the Dead Sea Scrolls, and Early Palestinian Synagogues," *Harvard Theological Review* 70, no. 3–4 (Jul.–Oct. 1977): 183–200.

7. Nicola Denzey Lewis, *Cosmology and Fate in Gnosticism and Graeco-Roman Antiquity: Under Pitiless Skies* (Leiden: 2013); on the role of stars in early patristic writings, see Kocku von Stuckrad, "Jewish and Christian Astrology in Late Antiquity—A New Approach," *Numen* 47, no. 1 (2000): 1–40, at 31.

8. Attfield, "Christian Attitudes to Nature," 369–86, stressing the diversity of Christian opinions and the theme of human responsibility to God. This article provides an overview of modern literature, especially useful on patristic writers; Clarence Glacken, *Traces on the Rhodian Shore: Nature and Culture in Western Thought from Ancient Times to the End of the Eighteenth Century* (Berkeley: 1990), 176–265.

9. On the Christian idea of themselves as a "third race," see David M. Olster, "Classical Ethnography and Early Christianity," in Katharine B. Free, ed., *The Formulation of Christianity by Conflict through the Ages* (Lewiston, NY: 1995), 9–31; Oskar Skarsaune, "Ethnic Discourse in Early Christianity," in James Carleton Paget and Judith Lieu, eds., *Christianity in the Second Century: Themes and Developments* (Cambridge: 2017), 250–64; Erich S. Gruen, "Christians as a 'Third Race': Is Ethnicity an Issue?," in *Christianity in the Second Century*, 235–49; Denis Kimber Buell, *Why This New Race: Ethnic Reasoning in Early Christianity* (New York: 2005).

10. For Clitomachus of Carthage, see Tim Hegedus, *Early Christianity and Ancient Astrology* (New York: 2007), 23–24, and Amand, *Fatalisme et liberté*; Malcolm Schofield, "Academic Epistemology," in Keimpe Algra, Jonathan Barnes, Jaap Mansfeld, and Malcolm Schofield, eds., *The Cambridge History of Hellenistic Philosophy* (Cambridge: 1999), 323–51; Franz Boll, *Sternglaube und Sterndeutung: Die Geschichte um das Wesen der Astrologie* (Leipzig: 1931), 24–29, for general comments on debates about fate, free will, and the sympathy between the heavens and the earth.

11. Ken Parry, "Fate, Free Choice, and Divine Providence from the Neoplatonists to John of Damascus," in Anthony Kaldellis and Niketas Siniossoglou, eds., *Cambridge Intellectual History of Byzantium* (Cambridge: 2017), 341–60, at 341. Parry surveys the main actors in these debates from Plotinus to the early Islamic period.

12. Carl Andresen, *Logos und Nomos: Die Polemik des Kelsos Wider das Christentum* (Berlin: 1955), shows that already in the second century the Christian idea of universal law, as espoused by Origen, contested the arguments of Celsus.

13. Michael Maas, "The Shaping Hand of the Environment: Three Phases of Development in Classical Antiquity," in Lee L. Brice and Daniëlle Slootjes, eds., *Aspects of Ancient Institutions and Geography: Studies in Honor of Richard J. A. Talbert* (Leiden: 2015), 333–46.

14. On universality of Christianity, see Hegedus, *Early Christianity and Ancient Astrology*, 98–100; on role of baptism, see below; Peter Brown, *The Cult of the Saints: Its Rise and Function in Latin Christianity* (Chicago: 1981), 58: "Baptism canceled the influence of the stars that had first formed the personality, by giving him a new protective spirit, in such a way to free him from a personality in which the quality of the original *genius* itself had been woven into a tangled web by the conflicting influence of the planets"; Peter Brown, *The Making of Late Antiquity* (Cambridge, MA: 1978), 73–77.

15. Important introductions to different aspects of Roman astrology, with further bibliography, include: Kocku von Stuckrad, *Geschichte der Astrologie: Von den Anfängen bis zur Gegenwart* (Munich: 2007), 90–124; Hegedus, *Early Christianity and Ancient Astrology*, 1–23; S. J. Tester, *A History of Western Astrology* (Woodbridge, Suffolk: 1987), 1–97; Frederick H. Cramer, *Astrology in Roman Law and Politics* (Philadelphia: 1954).

[312] NOTES TO PAGES 126-127

16. See John Philoponus, *De Opificio Mundi Libri VII*, IV.20, ed. Walter Reichardt (Leipzig: 1897); Averil Cameron, "The 'Scepticism' of Procopius," *Historia* 15, no. 4 (Nov. 1966): 466–82, at 476 n. 71: "Cf. also Agathias, I. I, p. 15. 7f."; see also Panayiotis Tzamalikos, *Origen: Philosophy of History & Eschatology* (Leiden: 2007), 132, and esp. no. 15.

17. Paul Magdalino, "The Byzantine Reception of Classical Astrology," in Catherine Holmes and Judith Waring, eds., *Literacy, Education and Manuscript Transmission in Byzantium and Beyond* (Leiden: 2002), 33–58, on continuity throughout the Byzantine period.

18. Origen, *Philocalia* XXIII.16: "Now let us look at our second undertaking, and try to show how it is that the stars cannot be causative, though they may possibly be indicative. In the vast multitude of nativities we may possibly get at the incidents of one man's life; but this is only an assumption; we concede the point that it is possible for men to gain a knowledge of them." Here Origen is commenting on Gn. 1.14: "And God said, Let there be lights in the firmament of the heaven to divide the day from the night; and let them be for signs, and for seasons, and for days, and years" (KJV); Speaking of "the philosophers," Origen, "Homily on Genesis XIV," in *Homilies on Genesis and Exodus*, trans. Ronald E. Heine (Washington, DC: 1982), writes: "They disagree with us when they appraise the lives of those being born by the courses of the stars." *Origéne: Homélies sur la Genèse*, Homily XIV.3, ed. and trans. Louis Doutreleau, 2nd ed., Sources Chrétiennes 7 (Paris: 1976), discusses points of agreement and disagreement with moral and natural philosophy; Alan Scott, *Origen and the Life of the Stars: A History of an Idea* (Oxford: 1991), 112–49; Annette Reed, "Abraham as Chaldaean Scientist and Father of the Jews," *Journal for the Study of Judaism in the Persian, Hellenistic, and Roman Period* 35, no. 2 (2004): 119–58.

19. Basil of Caesarea, *Homélies sur L'Hexaéméron*, Homily 6.4, ed. Stanislas Giet (Paris: 1949); for his rebuttal of astrology, see Homily 6.5–7. Basil interprets God's desire for the sun and moon to act as "signs" for weather forecasting useful in farming. He warns, however, that casting nativities through the signs of the zodiac is wrong and he mocks the claims of astrologers to predict personal characteristics or whether individuals will be virtuous or sinful. Finally, he emphasizes that astrology does not recognize personal liberty and action.

20. Tim Hegedus, "The Magi and the Star in the Gospel of Matthew and Early Christian Tradition," *Laval théologique et philosophique* 59, no. 1 (2003): 81–95; Nicola Denzey, "A New Star on the Horizon: Astral Christologies and Stellar Debates in Early Christian Discourse," in Scott Noegel, Joel Walker, and Brannon Wheeler, eds., *Prayer, Magic, and the Stars in the Ancient and Late Antique World* (University Park, PA: 2003), 207–21, at 215–20 for late antique debate; see also Clement of Alexandria, "Excerpts from Theodotus," LXXIV.1–2: "It is for this reason that the lord descended: in order to bring the peace from heaven to those on earth, as the apostle says, 'peace on earth and glory on high.' This is why a strange and new star arose, bringing to an end the old astral order and shining with a new, not worldly light, tracing new and salvific courses, (just like) the lord himself, the guide of humanity, the one who descended to earth in order to transfer those who have faith in the anointed (Christ) from fate into his forethought."

21. Paul Magdalino, *L'orthodoxie des astrologues: La science entre le dogme et la divination à Byzance (VIIe–XIVe siècle)* (Paris: 2006), 10; Benjamin Anderson, *Cosmos and Continuity in Early Medieval Art* (New Haven: 2017), 8–9 and 107–43, notes a marked decline in zodiac-related representations at the same time.

22. Hervé Inglebert, *Interpretatio Christiana: Les mutations des savoirs (cosmographie, géographie, ethnographie, histoire) dans l'Antiquité chrétienne 30–630 après J.-C.* (Paris: 2001), 229 and 232–33; Magdalino, "The Byzantine Reception," 33–58.

23. See chap. 8 below, on heresy.

24. Lucetta Desanti, "Astrologi: eretici o pagani? Un problema esegetico," *Atti dell'Accademia Romanistica Costantiana* 10 and 687–96, at 695–96, for discussion and citations; Philaster of Brescia: "Alia est haeresis, quae dicit secundum duodecim Zodiaci signa nasci hominis," in *Liber de Haeresibus*, in PL 12, cols. 1248–49; Magdalino, "The Byzantine Reception," 34: "Like the ancients, the Byzantines did distinguish between astronomy and astrology, between the pure and the applied science of celestial observation, but the distinction was mainly theoretical. It was important in religious terms, since it served to reconcile

NOTES TO PAGES 127–129 [313]

the Church's objections to astrology with the undeniable fact that God had created celestial phenomena to be observed, used and admired: in the words of Genesis 1.14, 'to be for signs of the times and the seasons.' Otherwise, no strict separation between astronomy and astrology was maintained in linguistic, educational or professional practice." And: "Christian critics well into the Middle Ages equated astral determinism with belief in the animate nature of the sun, moon and stars" (37).

25. Magdalino, "The Byzantine Reception," 38.

26. For example, Maurice, *Strategikon: Handbook of Byzantine Military Strategy* XI.1, trans. George T. Dennis (Philadelphia: 1984): "Since they [the Persians] have been brought up in a hot climate, they easily bear the hardships of heat, thirst, and lack of food"; *Das Strategikon des Maurikos*, ed. George T. Denns, trans. [German] Ernst Gamillscheg (Vienna: 1981).

27. Ptolemy, *Tetrabiblos*, ed. and trans. F. E. Robbins, LCL 435 (Cambridge, MA: 1940), xii.

28. Peter R. L. Brown, "Art and Society in Late Antiquity," in Kurt Weitzmann, ed., *Age of Spirituality: A Symposium* (New York: 1980), 17–27, at 23.

29. Anthony Grafton, "Starry Messengers: Recent Work in the History of Western Astrology," *Perspectives on Science* 8, no. 1 (2000): 70–83, at 72.

30. For a detailed survey of the rise of Hellenistic astrology, see Cramer, *Astrology in Roman Law and Politics*, 9–44. Still helpful: Karl Trüdinger, *Studien zur Geschichte der griechisch-römischen Ethnographie* (Basel: 1918), 81–89; Glen M. Cooper, "Astrology: The Science of Signs in the Heavens," in Paul T. Keyser and John Scarborough, eds., *The Oxford Handbook of Science and Medicine in the Classical World* (Oxford: 2018), 381–408, provides a historical introduction to classical astrology.

31. For overview, A. A. Long, "Astrology: Arguments Pro and Contra," in Jonathan Barnes, Jacques Brunschwig, Mylse Burnyeat, and Malcolm Schofield, *Science and Speculation: Studies in Hellenistic Theory and Practice* (Cambridge: 1982), 165–92; for Stoic interest in Fate, see Cramer, *Astrology in Roman Law and Politics*, 50–58; Trüdinger, *Studien zur Geschichte der griechisch-römischen Ethnographie*, 81–89, reviews astrological ethnography; Amand, *Fatalisme et liberté*, 6–13 and passim.

32. Cramer, *Astrology in Roman Law and Politics*, 19.

33. Ibid.

34. For discussion, see von Stuckrad, "Jewish and Christian Astrology in Late Antiquity," 1–40. He argues (esp. at 1–5) that astrology in Late Antiquity became part of Christian and Jewish belief and were not incompatible with monotheism.

35. Cramer, *Astrology in Roman Law and Politics*, chap. 2, "The Conversion of Republican Rome to Astrology (250–44 B.C.)," 44–80; Auguste Bouché-Leclercq, "L'astrologie dans le monde romain," *Revue historique* 65, no. 2 (1897): 241–99.

36. Von Stuckrad, "Jewish and Christian Astrology in Late Antiquity," 23.

37. Von Stuckrad, *Geschichte der Astrologie*, 90–98; for succinct review, see Giuseppe Cambiano, "Philosophy, Science and Medicine," in Algra, Barnes, Mansfeld, and Schofield, eds., *The Cambridge History of Hellenistic Philosophy*, 585–613, at 595–99.

38. Cramer, *Astrology in Roman Law and Politics*, 50; on debate, see 50–58; Cambiano, "Philosophy, Science and Medicine," 595–99; Amand, *Fatalisme et liberté*, 18–21.

39. John Vanderspoel, "Zodiac," in Graham Shipley, John Vanderspoel, David Mattingly, Lin Foxhall, eds., *The Cambridge Dictionary of Classical Civilization* (Cambridge: 2008), 960–62, at 960: "A band of the night sky 8° on either side of the ecliptic, the imaginary line depicting the Sun's apparent path through the heavens. The zodiac is divided into a dozen 30° segments, each named from a constellation in the sector and representing approximately one month"; Cicero, "On Divination" II.89, in *On Old Age: On Friendship; On Divination*, ed. and trans. W. A. Falconer, LCL 154 (Cambridge, MA: 1923), 42; Lucretius, *On the Nature of Things*, book 2, ed. and trans. W. H. D. Rouse and Martin F. Smith, LCL 181 (Cambridge, MA: 1924), argues for free will vs. fatalism.

40. Bouché-Leclercq, "L'Astrologie," 241–99.

41. Cramer, *Astrology in Roman Law and Politics*, 52–54; Aulus Gellius, *Attic Nights Volume II: Books 6–13*, VI.14.8–10, ed. and trans. J. C. Rolfe, LCL 200 (Cambridge, MA: 1927);

Polybius, *The Histories* VI.33.2, ed. and trans. W. R. Paton, S. Douglas Olson, F. W. Walbank, and Christian Habicht, LCL 128, 6 vols. (Cambridge, MA: 2010), 137–38, 159–61.

42. Tamsyn Barton, *Ancient Astrology* (New York: 1994), 34; Cicero, "On Divination" 1.6 [3], 1.84 [38–39], and 2.101–6 [49–51].

43. Chris Brennan, *Hellenistic Astrology: The Study of Fate and Fortune* (Denver: 2017), 148. Brennan refers to the Pseudo-Aristotelian work *De mundo*, which is perhaps as late as the fourth century BCE. He refers to Gad Freudenthal, "The Astrologization of the Aristotelian Cosmos: Celestial Influences on the Sublunary World in Aristotle, Alexander of Aphrodisias, and Averroes," in Alan C. Bowen and Christian Wildberg, eds., *New Perspectives on Aristotle's De caelo* (Leiden: 2009), 239–81.

44. The literature on Cicero is vast. A particularly engaging treatment is Yelena Baraz, *A Written Republic: Cicero's Philosophical Politics* (Princeton: 2012).

45. See Cicero, "On Divination" 2.88 [42], where he names Panaetius and other Stoics who rejected astrology.

46. Cicero, "On Divination" 2.97 [47].

47. Cicero, "On Divination" 1.6 [3], on the acceptance of astrology by the Roman elite; on Tarutius, see II.98 [47]; for discussion of ancient sources, see A. T. Grafton and N. M. Swerdlow, "The Horoscope of the Foundation of Rome," *Classical Philology* 81, no. 2 (Apr. 1986): 148–53; Stephan Heilen, "Ancient Scholars on the Horoscope of Rome," *Culture and Cosmos* 11 (2007): 43–68. More generally, see Bouché-Leclercq, "L'Astrologie," 245–47, for an overview; for general survey of astrology in the Late Republic and the transition to the Principate, see Barton, *Ancient Astrology*, 37–41; Cramer, *Astrology in Roman Law and Politics*, 65–66.

48. Mentioned in Cicero, "Brutus," in *Brutus, Orator*, ed. and trans. G. L. Hendrickson and H. M. Hubbell, LCL 342 (Cambridge, MA: 1939), 79 [20], and Cicero, *Timaeus*, ed. C. F. W. Mueller (Leipzig: 1900), 1.

49. John Lydus, *Liber de ostentis et calendaria graeca omnia*, ed. Curt Wachsmuth (Leipzig: 1897), 27–38; *On Celestial Signs (De Ostentis)*, ed. and trans. Anastasius C. Bandy (Lewiston: 2013); Nigidius drew from Etruscan materials to prepare his Latin brontoscopic calendar, which Lydus translated into Greek. See Jean MacIntosh Turfa, "The Etruscan Brontoscopic Calendar and Modern Archaeological Discoveries," *Etruscan Studies* 10 (2007): 163–73; for further bibliography, Stuckrad, *Geschichte der Astrologie*, 13–14, and his notes.

50. Barton, *Ancient Astrology*, 37; Lydus, *De ostentis*, 27–38; for Nigidius Figulus's influence on Varro and Roman astrology, see Cramer, *Astrology in Roman Law and Politics*, 62–65; on Cicero's friendship with Varro, see T. P. Wiseman, "Cicero and Varro," in *Remembering the Roman People: Essays on Late-Republican Politics and Literature* (Oxford: 2009), 107–30.

51. Manilius, *Astronomica* I.7, ed. and trans. G. P. Goold, LCL 469 (Cambridge, MA: 1977).

52. On Manilius, see Katharina Volk, "'Heavenly Steps': Manilius 4.119–121 and Its Background," in Ra'anan S. Boustan and Annette Yoshiko Reed, eds., *Heavenly Realms and Earthly Realities in Late Antique Religions* (Cambridge: 2004), 34–46.

53. Long, "Astrology," 186; e.g. Manilius, *Astronomica*, II.57ff.; Volk, "'Heavenly Steps,'" 34–46.

54. Manilius, *Astronomica* IV.587.

55. Vettius Valens, *Anthologies* I.2, ed. and trans. Jöelle-Frédérique Bara (Leiden: Brill, 1989), gives a detailed description of the zodiacal signs; Semíramis Corsi Silva and Vinícius de Oliveira da Motta, "Astrologia e poder no Império Romano: A adivinhação do Destino na *Antologia*, de Vettius Valens (século II d.C.)," *Romanitas: Revista de Estudos Grecolatinos* 9 (2017): 115–37, discusses how astrological knowledge can provide understanding of the cosmic order through a mystical union.

56. Manilius, *Astronomica* IV.697–99 and 711–15.

57. Manilius, *Astronomica* at IV.807–17 translates *genus* as character; Volk, "'Heavenly Steps,'" 102 as "ethnicity"; Manilius, *Astronomica* IV.595–695, begins with a leisurely description of the *oikoumene*, following the shorelines of the Mediterranean. He then explains

NOTES TO PAGES 131–133 [315]

(IV.696–743) that the ethnic and national difference among the peoples of the earth are due to the fact that different signs of the zodiac dominate different regions, crucially influencing the appearance and lifestyle of their inhabitants: IV.817: "ut *genus* in terram caelo descendit ab alto" = "according to the way *his ethnicity* comes to him from high heaven."

58. Amand, *Fatalisme et liberté*, 573–81, is the place to start. Note especially his thumbnail sketch of each writer's position and how each relates to the foundational antifatalistic arguments advanced by Carneades.

59. Cramer, *Astrology in Roman Law and Politics*, 55–58; Gisela Striker, "Carneades," *OCD4* (Oxford: 2012), 282; K. E. Wilkerson, "Carneades at Rome: A Problem of Sceptical Rhetoric," *Philosophy & Rhetoric* 21, no. 2 (1988): 131–44; he had, in his characteristic fashion, lectured both for and against justice, raising the alarm among men like Cato the Censor.

60. Wilkerson, "Carneades at Rome," 131–44; Striker, "Carneades," 282; for different modern interpretations of his speech, see Gruen, *The Hellenistic World*, vol. I, 341–42.

61. His arguments are summarized by Cramer, *Astrology in Roman Law and Politics*, 55–56; Carneades was not alone among philosophers in arguing against astrology; Eusebius of Caesarea, *Eusèbe du Césarée: La préparation évangélique*, ed. J. Sirinelli and Éduard des Places, Sources Chrétiennes 206 (Paris: Éditions du Cerf, 1974), VI.7–9, mentions people as diverse as the Cynic Oenomaus of Gadara, Diogenianus the Epicurean, and the Peripatetic Alexander of Aphrodisias; also Long, "Astrology," 191; on the *nomima barbarika* argument, Hegedus, *Early Christianity and Ancient Astrology*, 91–107, for Christian authors.

62. Cramer, *Astrology in Roman Law and Politics*, 55–56.

63. Cramer, *Astrology in Roman Law and Politics*, 55: "the anti-astrological argumentation of Carneades not only was destined to become the standard system of attacking astrology in pagan and Christian times, but also in all likelihood may have been presented at least in part to his Roman hearers in 155 B.C."

64. Brad Inwood, "Panaetius," *OCD4*, 1073; Cramer, *Astrology in Roman Law and Politics*, 57–58; Modestus van Straaten, *Panétius, sa vie, ses écrits et sa doctrine avec une édition des fragments* (Amsterdam: 1946), esp. 63–94.

65. Gordon Campbell, "Philosophy," in *The Cambridge Dictionary of Classical Civilization*, 677–80, here 678–79.

66. Posidonius's ideas are summarized by Strabo, *Geography* II.2; see above, chap. 1; Franz Cumont, *Astrology and Religion among the Greeks and Romans* (New York: 1912), 82–89; Cicero, "On Divination" 1.3; J. J. Tierney, "The Celtic Ethnography of Posidonius," *Proceedings of the Irish Academy: Archaeology, Culture, History, Literature* 60 (1959/1960): 189–275, at 198–201, on his ethnographical method; on Julius Caesar's use of Posidonius, 211–18; for Strabo, see 207–11; on his influence, 201–24; I. G. Kidd, "Posidonius (2)," *OCD4*, 1195–96.

67. Cicero, "On Divination" 2.41–47 at 2.43: "O delirationem incredibilem! [what unbelievable madness!]"; Barton, *Ancient Astrology*, 35–36, comments on the limits of his understanding of astrology.

68. Cicero, "On Divination" 2.44.

69. Cicero, "On Divination" 2.46.

70. Cicero, "On Divination" 2.45.

71. Cicero, "On Divination" 2.47.

72. Ibid.

73. Long, "Astrology," 178–83; Teri Gee, "Strategies of Defending Astrology: A Continuing Tradition," PhD diss., University of Toronto, 89–93, on determinism in the *Tetrabiblos*, 89–92; G. J. Toomer, "Ptolemy," in Charles Coulston Gillispie, ed., *Dictionary of Scientific Biography*, vol. 11 (New York: 1981), 186–206, for overview.

74. Ptolemy, *Almagest* II.12 [H172–73], trans. G. J. Toomer (London: 1984).

75. Ptolemy, *Ptolemy's Geography: An Annotated Translation of the Theoretical Chapters*, trans. J. Lennart Berggren and Alexander Jones (Princeton: 2000), 3–4, esp. 4: "The core of the *Geography* consists of three parts necessary for Ptolemy's purpose: instructions for

[316] NOTES TO PAGES 133–135

drawing a world map on a globe and on a plane surface using two new map projections (Book 1.22–24), a catalogue of localities to be marked on the map with their coordinates in latitude and longitude (2.1–7.4), and a caption or descriptive label (*hypographe*) to be inscribed on the map (7.5)."

76. Ptolemy, *Tetrabiblos* II.2–3; summarized in Glacken, *Traces*, 111–14; Ptolemy, *Ptolemy's Geography*, 21.

77. Long, "Astrology," 179; Freudenthal, "The Astrologization of the Aristotelian Cosmos," 262–63, on Alexander of Aphrodisias and general developments at the turn of the third century.

78. Long, "Astrology," 178–83. He notes that "By denying that astrology identifies complete causal conditions for an individual's life Ptolemy undermines Cicero's criticism of the omission of genetics and nurture" (183).

79. Ptolemy, *Tetrabiblos* II.1–3; Glacken, *Traces*, 112.

80. Ptolemy does not believe that astrology is absolutely causal in shaping an individual's life; non-celestial factors (such as an individual's physical strength or cultural influences) may play a deciding role (Long, "Astrology," 178–83). The purpose of Ptolemy's organization of this material is to aid in making predictions about events, where and when they will take place, what the event will affect, and the nature of the event itself. See Ptolemy, *Tetrabiblos* II.4.

81. Ptolemy, *Tetrabiblos* II.3; Hephaistion of Thebes (fl. 415), drew much from Ptolemy, but not his discussion of determinism; for passages of Ptolemy used by Hephaistion, see Hephaistion of Thebes, *Apotelesmaticorvm* VI-VII, ed. David Pingree (Leipzig: 1973); see also Herbert Jennings Rose, "Hephaistion of Thebes and Christianity," *Harvard Theological Review* 33, no. 1 (Jan. 1940): 65–68.

82. Ptolemy, *Tetrabiblos* II.2; see chap. 1, n. 178.

83. Ptolemy, *Tetrabiblos* II.2–3.

84. On the number of languages in Genesis, Jubilees, etc., see chap. 7 below; Kaufmann Kohler and Isaac Broydé, "Nations and Languages, The Seventy," in Cyrus Adler et al., eds., *The Jewish Encyclopedia*, vol. IX (New York: 1901), 188–90; Eric Burrows, "The Number Seventy in Semitic," *Orientalia*, Nova Series 5 (1936): 389–92.

85. Ptolemy, *Ptolemy's Geography*, 21.

86. Ptolemy, *Tetrabiblos* II.3.

87. Ptolemy, *Tetrabiblos* II.2.

88. Ptolemy, *Tetrabiblos* II.3.

89. Ptolemy, *Tetrabiblos* II.3.

90. For history of the text, see Ptolemy, *Tetrabiblos*, xii–xxiv.

91. O. A. W. Dilke, "Cartography in the Ancient World: A Conclusion," in J. B. Harley and David Woodward, eds., *Cartography in Prehistoric, Ancient, and Medieval Europe and the Mediterranean* (Chicago: 1987), 276–79, at 277, notes that "Ptolemy worked within the framework of the early Roman Empire"; Pappus survives only in an Armenian abridgement: Ptolemy, *Ptolemy's Geography*, 50; the Neoplatonist Plotinus, *Ennead* 2.3.14, ed. and trans. A. H. Armstrong, LCL 441 (Cambridge, MA: 1966), followed Ptolemy's approach to some extent, arguing that the stars have an effect on humans only in the malleable sublunar realm. They may influence such things as personal strength or success but will have no effect on other things such as wealth, fame, or occupation; Long, "Astrology," 187–91; M. L. W. Laistner, "The Western Church and Astrology during the Early Middle Ages," *Harvard Theological Review* 34, no. 4 (1941): 251–75, at 255.

92. Robbins suggests that he drew from Posidonius (Ptolemy, *Tetrabiblos*, ix), while Trüdinger, *Studien zur Geschichte der griechisch- römischen Ethnographie*, 81–89, esp. 88; Klaus E. Müller, "Klaudios Ptolemaios," in *Geschichte der Antiken Ethnographie und Ethnologischen Theoriebildung: Von den Anfängen bis auf die byzantinischen Historiographen II* (Wiesbaden: 1980), 167–75, at 174 n. 652, notes that scholars like Boll and Trüdinger are uncertain about the sources, which could have been of a Hellenistic/Egyptian origin, which he probably accessed in the Library of Alexandria; on Posidonius as a source, see Trüdinger, *Studien zur Geschichte der griechisch-römischen Ethnographie*, 81; Glacken, *Traces*, 113 n. 78; Wilhelm Gundel and Hans Georg Gundel, *Astrologumena: Die Astrologische Literatur in der*

NOTES TO PAGES 135–137 [317]

Antike und ihre Geschichte (Wiesbaden: 1966), 202–16, esp. 207–16, on the *Tetrabiblos* and its commentaries; they doubt Poseidonius is the source (209 n. 15).

93. On editions of the text: Ptolemy, *Tetrabiblos*, xii–xvii. On *Geography*, see Ptolemy, *Ptolemy's Geography*, 52–53.

94. Catharine Roth and David Whitehead, eds., "pi,265. Pappos, Pappus," *Suda Online (SOL)*, http://www.cs.uky.edu/~raphael/sol/sol-entries/pi/265, mention his *Chorographia/ Description of the Inhabited World.*

95. Robert H. Hewsen, trans., "The *Geography* of Pappus of Alexandria: A Translation of the Armenian Fragments," *Isis* 62, no. 2 (Summer 1971): 186–207.

96. Hewsen, "The *Geography*," 186.

97. Ptolemy, *Ptolemy's Geography*, 50–51, for sources.

98. Cassiodorus, *Institutions of Divine and Secular Learning* 25.2, trans. James W. Halporn (Liverpool: 2004), *Institutions* 7.3 also mentions (erroneously) Ptolemy's *Greater* and *Lesser Astronomy* (see also *Institutions*, 227 n. 240); for a discussion, see Ptolemy, *Ptolemy's Geography*, 51; on astrology in the Latin West in the sixth century, R. Bonnaud, "Notes sur l'astrologie latine au VIe siècle," *Revue belge de philologie et d'histoire* 10, no. 3 (1931): 557–77, pointing to its diminishing importance and the willingness of some churchmen to see the stars as indications of divine will. Boethius wrote an *Astronomy* based on the *Almagest* of Ptolemy; Pierre Courcelle, *Les lettres grecques en Occident: De Macrobe à Cassiodore* (Paris: 1948), 262–64; see Bonnaud, "Notes sur l'astrologie," 562–64, on ideas of Ptolemy found in Boethius; Cassiodorus, *Variae* 1.45.4, trans. S. J. B. Barnish (Liverpool: 1992), mentions that Boethius also composed a translation of Ptolemy.

99. Ptolemy, *Ptolemy's Geography*, 51.

100. Zur Shalev and Charles Burnett, eds., *Ptolemy's Geography in the Renaissance* (London: 2011).

101. Julius Firmicus Maternus, *Matheseos Libri VIII*, ed. Karl Sittl (Leipzig: 1894); Marie Theres Fögen, *Die Enteignung der Wahrsager: Studien zum kaiserlichen Wissensmonopol in der Spätantike* (Frankfurt am Main: 1997), 278–84, on his linking of the stars to the figure of the emperor.

102. For example, Augustine, *On Christian Teaching* 2.21.32–2.24.37, trans. R. P. H. Green (Oxford: 1997).

103. Firmicus Maternus, *Ancient Astrology: Theory and Practice; Matheseos Libri VIII*, I.5.1–7, trans. Jean Rhys Bram (Park Ridge, NJ: 1975).

104. Firmicus Maternus, *L'erreur des religions païennes*, ed. and trans. Robert Turcan (Paris: 1982).

105. Marilynn Lawrence, "Hellenistic Astrology," in James Fieser and Bradley Dowden, eds., Internet Encyclopedia of Philosophy, https://iep.utm.edu/hellenistic-astrology/#H7.

106. Plotinus, *Ennead* II.3.14; Laistner, "Western Church and Astrology," 255, for other pagan rebuttals of astrology. For an overview of Neoplatonism, see Christian Wildberg, "Neoplatonism," in Edward N. Zalta, ed., *The Stanford Encyclopedia of Philosophy*, Winter 2021 edition, https://plato.stanford.edu/archives/win2021/entries/neoplatonism/.

107. Long, "Astrology," 188.

108. Plotinus, *Ennead* II.3.14.

109. Plotinus, *Ennead* II.3.6.

110. Plotinus, *Ennead*, II.3.14; Long, "Astrology," 187–91; Laistner, "Western Church and Astrology," 255, on other pagan rebuttals of astrology; Peter Adamson, "Plotinus on Astrology," *Oxford Studies in Ancient Philosophy* 35 (Winter 2008): 265–92.

111. Adamson, "Plotinus on Astrology," 287.

112. Porphyry, "On the Life of Plotinus" 15.22–26, in Plotinus, *Ennead, Volume I: Porphyry on the Life of Plotinus. Ennead I*, ed. and trans. A. H. Armstrong, LCL 440 (Cambridge, MA: 1969); Adamson, "Plotinus on Astrology," 265–92; on Porphyry, see Paul Kalligas, *The Enneads of Plotinus: A Commentary* (Princeton: 2014), 3–7. The technical glossary meant to introduce the *Tetrabiblos* attributed (probably wrongly) to Porphyry (234–ca. 305) does not truly engage with Ptolemy's work; Giuseppe Bezza, "Introduction à l'Apotélesmatique de Ptolémée (Εἰσαγωγὴ εἰς τὴν Ἀποτελεσματικὴν τοῦ Πτολεμαίου) [58]," in Richard Goulet,

[318] NOTES TO PAGES 137–138

ed., *Dictionnaire des philosophes antiques Vb. de Plotina à Rutilius Rufus* (Paris: 2012), 1381–84, at 1384, doubts that it is an original work by Porphyry.

113. Porphyry, "Porphyrii Philosophi Introductio in Tetrabiblum Ptolemaei," in Stephen Weinstock and Emilie Boer, eds., *Catalogus codicum astrologorum graecorum: Codicum romanorum tomi V pars IV* (Brussels: 1940), 185–231; James Herschel Holden, trans., in his preface to *Porphyry the Philosopher*, Introduction to the Tetrabiblos, *and Serapio of Alexandria*, Astrological Definitions (Tempe, AZ: 2010), suggests that the work was a composite probably of the tenth century; Bezza, "Introduction," 1381–84. I thank Christophe Erismann for this reference.

114. Stephan Heilen, "Ptolemy's Doctrine of the Terms and Its Reception," in Alexander Jones, ed., *Ptolemy in Perspective: Use and Criticism of his Work from Antiquity to the Nineteenth Century* (New York: 2010), 45–93, at 62–63. Heilen doubts the attribution to Proclus.

115. Christoph Helmig and Carlos Steel, "Proclus," in Edward N. Zalta, ed., The Stanford Encyclopedia of Philosophy, Fall 2020 Edition, https://plato.stanford.edu/archives/fall2020 /entries/proclus/.

116. Heilen, "Ptolemy's Doctrine of the Terms," 62–63.

117. Cramer, *Astrology in Roman Law and Politics*, 44–80, for material through the first century CE. For later centuries, see 146–231.

118. James J. O'Donnell, *Pagans: The End of Traditional Religion and the Rise of Christianity* (New York: 2015), 94.

119. *Cod. Th.* 9.16; 16.5.64. On astrology as heterodoxy, see Hegedus, *Early Christianity and Ancient Astrology*, 146–47.

120. *Cod. Th.* 9.16.

121. Ambrosiaster, "Questio 63," in Alexander Souter, ed., *Pseudo-Augustini Quaestiones veteris et novi testamenti*, CSEL 50 (Vienna: 1908), 112; Hegedus, *Early Christianity and Ancient Astrology*, 205, for citation and discussion; for introduction to Ambrosiaster, "Introduction," in *Ambrosiaster, Contre les païens and sur le destin*, ed. Marie-Pierre Bussières (Paris: 2007), 29–109.

122. Leo the Great, "Epistola XV," in PL 54.679A-B (1850), trans. Laistner; "Western Church and Astrology," 264.

123. Tamsyn S. Barton, *Power and Knowledge: Astrology, Physiognomics, and Medicine under the Roman Empire* (Ann Arbor: 1994), 62.

124. Laistner, "Western Church and Astrology," 256. On the astrological ethnography of the *Tetrabiblos* and its reception, see Franz Boll, *Studien über Claudius Ptolemäus* (Leipzig: 1894), 181–235.

125. Laistner, "Western Church and Astrology," 259.

126. Augustine, "Letter No. 57 (Ep. CCXLVI): Augustine to Lampadius," in *Select Letters*, ed. and trans. James Houston Baxter, LCL 239 (Cambridge, MA: 1930).

127. Barton, *Power and Knowledge*, 64, for summary.

128. Other Christian writers, not associated with Bardaisanes, also invoked *nomima barbarika*: Hegedus, *Early Christianity and Ancient Astrology*, 94–96.

129. For fuller discussion, Drijvers, *Bardaisan of Edessa*, 21–22.

130. Hendrik J. W. Drijvers, "Bardesanes," in Gerhard Krause and Gerhard Müller, eds., *Theologische Realenzyklopädie. Band V. Autokephalie–Biandrata* (Berlin: 1980), cols. 206–12; Javier Teixidor, *Bardesane d'Edesse: La première philosophie syriaque* (Paris: 1992) places Bardaisan at the beginning of Syriac Christian literature. H. J. W. Drijvers, *Bardaisan of Edessa* (Assen: 1966), 69–109, summarizes arguments; at 21–22 and 70 he reviews discussion about regarding the influence of Carneades. For text and translation of *BLC*, see Bardaisan of Edessa, *The Book of the Laws of Countries: Dialogue on Fate of Bardaisan of Edessa* [*BLC*], trans. H. J. W. Drijvers (Piscataway, NJ: 2007). For Bardaisan's influence on later writers, esp. in the Syriac tradition, see Drijvers, *Bardaisan of Edessa*, 207–22; Ilaria L. E. Ramelli, *Bardaisan of Edessa: A Reassessment of the Evidence and a New Interpretation* (Piscataway, NJ: 2009), 56; Ute Possekel, "Bardaisan and Origen on Fate and the Power of the Stars," *Journal of Early Christian Studies* 20, no. 4 (Winter 2012): 515–41, for a survey of his life and works and relation to Origen; Alberto Camplani, "Bardesane et les Bardesanites," *Annuaires de l'École pratique des hautes études* 112 (2003): 29–50.

NOTES TO PAGES 138–139 [319]

131. Teixidor, *Bardesane d'Edesse*, 29–63, discusses Edessa as a hub of international trade; Steven K. Ross, *Roman Edessa: Politics and Culture on the Eastern Fringes of the Roman Empire, 114–242 C.E.* (London: 2001), xi, 74, 171 n. 39, 175 n. 29, complements Teixidor and sometimes disagrees with him.

132. Fergus Millar, "Empire, Community and Culture in the Roman Near East: Greeks, Syrians, Jews and Arabs," *Journal of Jewish Studies* 38, no. 2 (1987), 143–64, at 160.

133. Bardaisan put this new kind of Christian antiastrological argument in the hands of influential Christian writers listed by Hegedus, *Early Christianity and Ancient Astrology*, 94–96, whose list comes from Adolf Hilgenfeld, *Bardesanes, der Letzte Gnostiker* (Leipzig: 1864), 92–123. On Bardaisan's influence, see Drijvers, *Bardaisan of Edessa*, 173–85. Greek theologians understood him differently than Latin ones, and both groups were at a distance from the Syriac world. Bardaisan (or a predecessor) was widely known, and evidently available to the author of the Ps.-Clementine *Recognitiones* 9.19–29 and Ps.-Caesarius, *Dialogue* (see Hegedus, *Early Christianity and Ancient Astrology*, 94).

134. Possekel, "Bardaisan and Origen," 522–23, discusses how he sought to distance himself from astral determinism.

135. Hegedus, *Early Christianity and Ancient Astrology*, 261; see also Amand, *Fatalisme et liberté*, 244–49.

136. Hegedus, *Early Christianity and Ancient Astrology*, passim.

137. Evidently it was not his position on this point that caused him later to be judged a heretic: Eusebius, *Ecclesiastical History* 4.30, for his opinions on other doctrinal matters, ed. and trans. Kirsopp Lake, LCL 153 (Cambridge, MA: 1926); on the zodiac: Hegedus, *Early Christianity and Ancient Astrology*, 265, and Drijvers, *Bardaisan of Edessa*, 37; see also Possekel, "Bardaisan and Origen," 536.

138. Cf. F. Stanley Jones, "The Astrological Trajectory in Ancient Syriac-Speaking Christianity (Elchasai, Bardaisan, and Mani)," in Luigi Cirillo and Alois van Tongerloo, eds., *Atti del Terzo Congresso Internazionale di Studi "Manicheismo e Oriente Cristiano Antico": Arcavata di Rende—Amantea 31 agosto—5 settembre 1993* (Turnhout: 1997), 183–200, at 194.

139. Possekel "Bardaisan and Origen," 525, citing Bardaisan, *Book of the Laws of Countrie*, 12.

140. Ramelli: *Bardaisan of Edessa*, 141.

141. Hegedus, *Early Christianity and Ancient Astrology*, 94: "For example, in his commentary on Gen 1.14 Origen refers to the practice of circumcision of male Jews on the eighth day after birth, circumcision of male Ishmaelites in Arabia at age thirteen, the removal of kneecaps among certain people in Ethiopia, and the Amazons who remove one of their breasts: 'How do the stars do such things to groups of people?' he asks (*Philocalia* 23.16)." See also Origen, *Philocalia*, 23.16; Kathleen Gibbons, "Who Reads the Stars? Origen of Alexandria on Ethnic Reasoning and Astrological Discourse," in Rebecca Futo Kennedy and Molly Jones-Lewis, eds., *The Routledge Handbook of Identity and the Environment in the Classical and Medieval Worlds* (Abingdon: 2016), 230–46.

142. Amand, *Fatalisme et liberté*, 250–57, argued that Bardesanes owed a debt to Carneades. He transposed some of his ideas about *nomima barbarika* to a Christian context but did not follow Carneades's arguments against Fate extensively. This opinion is widely accepted. Teixidor, *Bardesane d'Edesse*, 101–2, however, rejects the possibility of a direct connection between Bardaisan and Carneades's philosophy on the grounds that he had no familiarity with the Stoic philosopher's work and that the *BLC* does not actually reflect close ties with Carneades's thought, as much as it can be reconstructed. Instead, Teixidor points to Bardaisan's originality as a Christian thinker. He suggests that the *BLC* is not exactly Bardaisan's work since it was composed by his student, who may have wished to cast it in the light of Greek philosophy; hence the resemblance to Carneades (143). Ross, *Roman Edessa*, 137 and 178–79 n. 7, disagrees about Bardaisan's knowledge of Greek writers, i.e., Carneades; Hegedus, *Early Christianity and Ancient Astrology*, 94, argues that the idea of νόμιμα βαρβαρικά originated with Carneades, but we do not know how the ideas reached Bardaisan; see Ramelli, *Bardaisan of Edessa*, 22 and 56, for connection to Carneades.

143. Bardaisan, *BLC*, 41–43.

144. Bardaisan, *BLC*, 59–61.

[320] NOTES TO PAGES 140–143

145. Ute Possekel, "Bardaisan and Origen on the Origin of the Stars," *Journal of Early Christian Studies* 20, no. 4: 515–41, at 530 n. 62, for bibliography on Carneades.

146. Bardaisan, *BLC*, 41.

147. Bardaisan, *BLC*, 57.

148. Ross, *Roman Edessa*, 137.

149. On the so-called "argument of common destinies," see Hegedus, *Early Christianity and Ancient Astrology*, 85–89.

150. Herodotus, *The Persian Wars* 3.38, ed. and trans. A. D. Godley, LCL 118 (Cambridge, MA: 1921): "or if it were proposed to all nations to choose which seemed best of all customs, each, after examination made, would place its own first; so well is each persuaded that its own are by far the best."

151. I thank Peter Brown for this observation.

152. Bardaisan, *BLC*, 41–43.

153. Drijvers, *Bardaisan of Edessa*, 193, says it is "largely traditional material" but his knowledge of India might come in part from interaction with an Indian delegation to Elagabalus's court.

154. For other Christian writers not associated with Bardaisanes who also invoked *nomima barbarika*: Hegedus, *Early Christianity and Ancient Astrology*, 94–96.

155. Eusebius, *Praeparatio Evangelica* 6.9.32. Eusebius praises Bardaisan's knowledge of astrology.

156. Aaron P. Johnson, *Ethnicity and Argument in Eusebius'* Praeparatio Evangelica (Oxford: 2006); on the question of connection to the ancient Hebrews, see 94–125.

157. Johnson, *Ethnicity and Argument*, 185.

158. Johnson, *Ethnicity and Argument*, 185, citing E. H. Gifford, *Preparation for the Gospel* (Grand Rapids: 1981), 1.4.6.

159. Eusebius, *Praeparatio Evangelica* 6.10.

160. Eusebius, *Praeparatio Evangelica*, 6.10.2–10.

161. Eusebius, *Ecclesiastical History* 4.30. For discussion of the complicated ancient translation history see Drijvers, *Bardaisan of Edessa*, 74–75.

162. On Eusebius's conception of the role of the Roman Empire in salvation history, see F. Edward Cranz, "Kingdom and Polity in Eusebius of Caesarea," *Harvard Theological Review* 45, no. 1 (1952): 47–66, at 55–57. A summary and critique of this dominant reading of Eusebius in scholarship is offered in Christopher Bonura, "Eusebius of Caesarea, the Roman Empire, and the Fulfillment of Biblical Prophecy: Reassessing Byzantine Imperial Eschatology in the Age of Constantine," *Church History* 90 (2021), 509–36.

163. Hegedus, *Early Christianity and Ancient Astrology*, 95 and 99–100; Drijvers, *Bardaisan of Edessa*, 183, notes that the Greek Fathers knew little about Bardaisan.

164. Photius, "223. Diodoros of Tarsus," in *The Bibliotheca*, trans. N. G. Wilson (London: 1994), 194–219; for Greek text, see Photius, *Bibliothèque. IV ("Codices" 223–229)* 223 [208b–222a], ed. and trans. René Henry (Paris: 1965); Johannes Quasten, "Diodore of Tarsus," in *Patrology. III. The Golden Age of Greek Patristic Literature from the Council of Nicaea to the Council of Chalcedon* (Westminster, MD: 1960), 397–401, at 397–98; Manlio Simonetti, "Diodore of Tarsus," in Angelo Di Berardino, ed., *Encyclopedia of the Early Church. I*, trans. Adrian Walford (Cambridge: 1992), 236–37; Hegedus, *Early Christianity and Ancient Astrology*, 99–100.

165. *Cod. Th.* 16.1.3.

166. Quasten, "Diodore," 397.

167. John Behr, ed. and trans., *The Case against Diodore and Theodore: Texts and Their Contexts* (Oxford: 2011), 83–129; Quasten, "Diodore," 397–98; Simonetti, "Diodore of Tarsus," 236.

168. Quasten, "Diodore," 398–401, on his writings.

169. Catharine Roth, David Whitehead, and Oliver Phillips, eds., "delta,1149. Diodoros, Diodorus, Diodore," Suda Online (SOL), http://www.cs.uky.edu/~raphael/sol/sol-entries /delta/1149: "He wrote a variety of things . . . They are as follows: . . . Against Astronomers and Astrologers, and Fate, About the [heavenly] Sphere and the Seven Zones and of the

NOTES TO PAGES 143–146   [321]

Contrary Motion of the Stars, About Hipparchus's Sphere, About Providence . . . Against Aristotle concerning Celestial Body, How Hot is the Sun, Against Those Who Say the Heaven is a Living Being."

170. Photius, *Bibliotheca* 223.

171. Photius, *Bibliotheca* 223 [220a]: "In chapter 46 he [Diodorus] says that the fanatical believers in astrology even make the creator of all things subject to its laws. In fact, they say that just as correct behaviour derives from the law of genesis, so do the success of prayer, inspiration through the presence of God, and initiation into the higher mysteries of revelation. And so their audacious claim makes God into a servant of the law of genesis and a benefactor of those whom the law in its course may have favoured with good fortune. Can there be any more atheistical and impious doctrine?" For Greek text, see Photius, *Bibliothèque* 223 [220a]; on translating "γένεσις," which Diodorus uses in his attack on astrology: Photius, *Bibliotheca*, 218 n. 4.

172. Photius, *Bibliotheca* 223 [216a].

173. Photius, *Bibliotheca* 223 [210b–211a].

174. Photius, *Bibliotheca* 223 [208b] tells us that "in chapter 51, while he is demolishing predestination, he also deals a blow to the ideas of Bardisanes, which are half mad and a kind of half way stage. In fact Bardisanes makes the soul free from predestination and from what is called the horoscope, preserving its free will, but he subjects the body and all that concerns it—I mean wealth or poverty, health or illness, life or death, and everything that is not under our control—to the power of destiny, and he declares that all these matters are the result of predestination." He continues at 223 [221b]: "[Diodorus] proceeds to the fifty-first chapter, in which he confutes the heretical followers of Bardisanes. They claim to accept the authority of the prophets; they make the soul free from any law of genesis and allow that it has free will, but they subject the body to that law; they say that wealth, poverty, illness, health, life, death and all things outside our control, are the work of predestination."

175. Photius, *Bibliotheca* 223 [208b].

176. Photius, *Bibliotheca* 223 [218a].

177. Photius, *Bibliotheca* 223 [218a].

178. Photius, *Bibliotheca* 223 [218a].

179. Photius, *Bibliotheca* 223 [218a].

180. Photius, *Bibliotheca* 223 [217b].

181. James Andrew McDonough, *The Treatise of Gregory of Nyssa Contra Fatum: A Critical Text with Prolegomena* (Cambridge, MA: 1952); Hegedus, *Early Christianity and Ancient Astrology*, 100; J. Gribomont, "Gregory of Nyssa," in Angelo Di Berardino, ed., *Encyclopedia of the Early Church. I*, trans. Adrian Walford (Cambridge, UK: 1992), 363–65, at 364; Donald L. Ross, "Gregory of Nyssa (c. 335–c. 395 C.E.)," in James Fieser and Bradley Dowden, eds., *Internet Encyclopedia of Philosophy*, https://iep.utm.edu/gregoryn/.

182. Noted by Hegedus, *Early Christianity and Ancient Astrology*, 100; translation is from McDonough, cited and discussed by Hegedus.

183. McDonough, 57.9–17, quoted and translated by Hegedus, *Early Christianity and Ancient Astrology*, 100; for Greek, see 107 n. 67.

184. Nicole Kelley, *Knowledge and Religious Authority in the Pseudo-Clementines* (Tübingen: 2006), 83, following F. Stanley Jones, "Eros and Astrology in the Περίοδοι Πέτρου: The Sense of the Pseudo-Clementine Novel," *Apocrypha* 12 (2001): 53–78, believes that *BLC* was an influence on the common source or *Grundschrift* of the Ps.-Clementine *Recognitions*: "*Hom* 19.23.5 (cf. *Rec* 9.7.1–6) preserves the *Grundschrift*'s agreement with Bardaisan: it suggests that astral determinism is in control from a person's birth until the moment of baptism, at which point baptism allows one to escape the grip of fate. This idea resembles views expressed by other ancient Christians, and gives at least a limited role to the power of fate." Kelley, 83 n. 7 gives as examples Clement of Alexandria's *Exc. Theodot.* 78.1: "Until baptism, they say, Fate is real, but after it the astrologers are no longer right." For the influence of the text in later centuries, see William Adler, "Did the Biblical Patriarchs Practice Astrology? Michael Glykas and Manuel Komnenos I on Seth and Abraham," in Paul Magdalino and Maria Mavroudi, eds., *The Occult Sciences in Byzantium* (Geneva: 2006), 245–63, at 256–58.

[322] NOTES TO PAGES 146–148

185. Nicola Pace, *Ricerche sulla traduzione di Rufino del "De principiis" di Origine* (Florence: 1990), 13–17, for discussion of his method of translation; I thank Louise Loehndorff for helpful discussion of Rufinus. He was "pro-Origen" but unsuccessful in his attempts to defend him. See also Elizabeth A. Clark, *The Origenist Controversy: The Cultural Construction of an Early Christian Debate* (Princeton: 1992), 187–88.

186. Rufinus chose to make this translation probably in 497, when he was in the south of Italy, in flight from the barbarians causing havoc around Milan; Laistner, "Western Church and Astrology," 260; Leo the Great, "Epistola XV," col. 679.A–B, condemned (Priscillianist) heretics whom he accused of believing that human souls and bodies are "bound fast (*obstringi*) by the fatal stars" (Laistner, "Western Church and Astrology," 264); on the Pseudo-Clementines and Jewish Christianity, see Everett Ferguson, *Baptism in the Early Church: History, Theology, and Liturgy in the First Five Centuries* (Grand Rapids: 2009), 248–65.

187. For a summary of the narrative, see Kelley, *Knowledge and Religious Authority*, 8–11; on its relation to a hypothetical, earlier *Grundschrift*, 11–13.

188. Kelley, *Knowledge and Religious Authority*, 7: "The subplot of Clement losing and later finding his family members belongs to a specific genre known as the *romance of recognitions*, of which the Pseudo-Clementines are the first extant Christian example."

189. Kelley, *Knowledge and Religious Authority*, 88.

190. Kelley, *Knowledge and Religious Authority*, 9–11, for summary.

191. Pseudo-Clement, *Recognitions* 9.19–30, in Bernhard Rehm and Georg Strecker, eds., GCS (Berlin: 1994).

192. Pseudo-Clement, *Recognitions* 9.19.

193. Pseudo-Clement, *Recognitions* 9.20–25.

194. Pseudo-Clement, *Recognitions* 9.25.

195. Pseudo-Clement, *Recognitions* 9.26.

196. Pseudo-Clement, *Recognitions* 9.27.

197. Pseudo-Clement, *Recognitions* 9.30.

198. Nicola Denzey Lewis, *Cosmology and Fate in Gnosticism and Graeco-Roman Antiquity: Under Pitiless Skies* (Leiden: 2013). On Gnostic interest in astrology: von Stuckrad, "Jewish and Christian," 21–22, speaking of "an extraordinary discourse."

199. On the relation of the twelve signs of the zodiac and the twelve Apostles; Jean Daniélou, "Les Douze Apôtres et le Zodiaque," *Vigiliae Christianae* 13, no. 1 (Apr. 1959): 14–21; April D. DeConick, "Apostles as Archons: The Fight for Authority and the Emergence of Gnosticism in the Tchacos Codex and Other Early Christian Literature," in April D. DeConick, ed., *The Codex Judas Papers: Proceedings of the International Congress on The Tchacos Codex Held at Rice University, Houston Texas, March 13–16, 2008* (Leiden: 2009), 241–88.

200. Matt. 28.19 tells how after Jesus's resurrection he instructed his disciples to "make disciples of all nations, baptizing them in the name of the Father and of the Son and of the Holy Spirit."

201. John Chrysostom, *Baptismal Instructions* IX.21, trans. Paul W. Harkins (Westminster, MD: 1963). The bibliography ancient and modern is colossal. Helpful recent studies are: Peter Cramer, *Baptism and Change in the Early Middle Ages, c. 200–c. 1150* (Cambridge: 1993); Ivan Roletti and Serena Romano, eds., *Fons vitae: Baptême, baptistères et rites d'initiation (IIe- VIe siècle)* (Rome: 2009); for John Chrysostom's views on baptism, see Ferguson, *Baptism in the Early Church*, 533–63; Bryan D. Spinks, *Early and Medieval Rituals and Theologies of Baptism: From the New Testament to the Council of Trent* (London: 2006).

202. Ismo Dunderberg, *Beyond Gnosticism: Myth, Lifestyle, and Society in the School of Valentinus* (New York: 2008), 16: "The problems with the term 'Gnosticism' itself are now well known. It does not appear in ancient sources at all." Birger A. Pearson, *Gnosticism and Christianity in Roman and Coptic Egypt* (New York: 2004), 210: "As Bentley Layton points out, the term *Gnosticism* was first coined by *Henry More* (1614–87) in an expository work on the seven letters of the Book of Revelation. More used the term *Gnosticisme* to describe the heresy in Thyatira." Werner Foerster, *Gnosis: A selection of Gnostic Texts. I. Patristic Evidence*, trans. R. McL. Wilson (Oxford: 1972), 1–26, for overview.

NOTES TO PAGES 148–149 [323]

203. Cramer, *Baptism and Change*, 21: "The diversity of the Gnostic groups is the result of the different ways in which these absolute terms—knowledge, salvation, the good, evil—were given practical, this-worldly expression."

204. Horace Jeffery Hodges, "Gnostic from Liberation Astrological Determinism: Hipparchan 'Trepidation' and the Breaking of Fate," *Vigiliae Christianae* 51, no. 4 (1997), 359–73, at 359–62; Barton, *Power and Knowledge*, 62–69, provides an overview of the church's attitude to astrology. See Denzey Lewis, nn. 8 and 21 above; Utto Riedinger, *Die Heilige Schrift im Kampf der griechischen Kirche gegen die Astrologie von Origenes bis Johannes von Damaskos* (Innsbruck: 1956), 15.

205. For example, the third-century text *The Reality of the Archons* from Nag Hammadi, which offers a Gnostic myth of creation: see Michel Roberge and Bernard Barc, eds., *L'Hypostase des Archontes: Traité gnostique sur l'origine de l'homme, du monde et des archontes (NH II, 4)*, Section "Textes 5" (Quebec: 1980); Denzey Lewis, *Cosmology and Fate*, 54–55.

206. DeConick, "Apostles as Archons," passim.

207. Irenaeus of Lyon, *Irénée de Lyon: Contre les hérésies* I.24, ed. and trans. Adelin Rousseau and Louis Doutreleau (Paris: 1979).

208. Barton, *Ancient Astrology*, 74; he seems to draw on J. P. Arendzen, "Basilides," in Charles G. Herbermann et al., eds., *The Catholic Encyclopedia*, vol. 2 (New York: 1907), 327–29, at 327; cf. Birger A. Pearson, "Basilides the Gnostic," in Antti Marjanen and Petri Luomanen, eds., *A Companion to Second-Century Christian "Heretics"* (Leiden: 2005), 1–31, at 20–21.

209. DeConick, "Apostles as Archons," 245: "The Gnostic literature . . . is obsessed with mapping the correspondences between the heavens and the earth. The reason for this is that the Gnostic Christian systems of salvation depend upon altering the cosmic structures, physically changing the universe from a cage that traps the spirit to a portal that frees it . . . The prison guards are the celestial beings, the rulers or archons, who reside in the planetary spheres above the earth and in the sublunar realm where the abyss or Hades was believed to be. . . . The various Gnostic systems play with the number of these archons, but all of them are built from astrological speculation about the numbers seven and twelve commonly assumed in the Greco-Egyptian and Hermetic environments in which these Gnostic systems originated. The number seven reflects the seven planets . . . The number twelve is a correspondence with the twelve signs of the Zodiac" (and see 250 for twelve disciples . . . twelve tribes of Israel, etc.). On parallelism between signs of the Zodiac and the apostles, Wolfgang Hübner, *Zodiacus Christianus: Jüdisch-christliche Adaptationen des Tierkreises von der Antike bis zur Gegenwart* (Königstein: 1983), 37–39.

210. Hodges, "Gnostic Liberation," 362.

211. Clement of Alexandria, "Excerpts from Theodotus," 78.1.

212. Barton, *Ancient Astrology*, 76: Clement of Alexandria, "Excerpts from Theodotus," 78.1; Marius Victorinus Afrus, "In Epistolam Pauli ad Galatias," in PL VIII (1844), commentary on 2 Gal. 2:5, cols. 1175–76.3–4.

213. Zeno of Verona, *Tractatus* 1.55, ed. Bengt Löfstedt, *Zeno Veronensis Tractatus*, CCSL 22 (Turnhout: 1971), 130. Zeno was bishop of Verona from ca. 362 to 370/371. For parallels with other authors, see Hegedus, *Early Christianity and Ancient Astrology*, 102 n. 26: "The following parallels are listed by Paul Wendland, *Philos Schrift über die Vorsehung* (Berlin: 1892), 30–32: Philo, *On Providence* 1.84–86 (Jews, Scythians, Egyptians); Origen in *Philocalia* 23.16 (Jews, Ishmaelites, Ethiopians, Amazons); Procopius (Jews, Ishmaelites, Amazons, Christians); the *Book of the Laws of the Countries* (Persians, Jews, Christians)."

214. DeConick, "Apostles as Archons," 250–54, on the identification of the zodiac with the Apostles in Gnostic writings; Wolfgang Hübner, "Das Horoskop der Christen: (Zeno 1,38 L.)," *Vigiliae Christianae* 29, no. 2 (1975): 120–37, esp. 137, noting that the Christian horoscope is not limited to one sign but includes all signs. On Zeno's baptismal sermon: Hegedus, *Early Christianity and Ancient Astrology*, 353–70.

215. On the relation of the twelve signs of the zodiac and the twelve Apostles, see Jean Daniélou, "Les douze Apôtres," 14–21; DeConick, "Apostles as Archons," 241–88; Hübner, *Zodiacus Christianus*, 37–39, and on association with Christ, 120–21.

[324] NOTES TO PAGES 149–151

216. Ps.-Clement, "Homily II," trans. Thomas Smith, in Alexander Roberts and James-Donaldson, eds., *Ante-Nicene Fathers*, vol. 8, *The Twelve Patriarchs, Excerpts and Epistles, The Clementina, Apocrypha, Decretals, Memoirs of Edessa and Syriac Documents, Remains of the First Ages* (Edinburgh: 1886, repr. 1989), II.23; DeConick, "Apostles as Archons," 251.

217. DeConick describes an early-fifth-century lamp, now in Geneva, which has Jesus at the center, surrounded by the twelve Apostles. She suggests that they have replaced the signs of the zodiac and were, like the *Homilies*, part of a "widely circulating tradition": DeConick, "Apostles as Archons," 251–52. An image of the lamp appears at 252. On mixing of Christian and non-Chrisitan astrological elements in Zeno of Verona, see Hübner, "Das Horoskop der Christen," 120–37.

218. DeConick, "Apostles as Archons," 268, on Theodotus to Valentinan (mid- to late second century): "the Apostles were substituted for the twelve signs of the Zodiac, for, just as birth is directed by them, so is rebirth by the Apostles." For a parallel, see Clement of Alexandria, "Excerpts from Theodotus" 25.2: "The apostles—he (Theodotus) says—have been substituted for the twelve signs of the Zodiac. For just as birth is regulated by them (the signs of the Zodiac), so too rebirth is directed by the apostles."

219. Clement of Alexandria, "Excerpts from Theodotus" 25.2. See DeConick, "Angels as Archons," 252.

220. *Pistis Sophia* I.15–16, ed. Carl Schmidt, trans. Violet Macdermot (Leiden: 1978); Hodges, "Gnostic Liberation," 366–73, understands this as based on various astrological calculations regarding the oscillation of the equinoxes.

221. Augustine, *City of God. II: Books 4–7*, ed. and trans. William M. Green, LCL 412 (Cambridge, MA: 1963); Augustine, *Confessions. I: Books 1–8*, ed. and trans. Carolyn J.-B. Hammond, LCL 26 (Cambridge, MA: 2014); Augustine, *On Christian Teaching*.

222. Augustine, *City of God* 5.15.

223. Augustine, *City of God* 5.1.

224. Augustine, *City of God* 5.1. See François Dolbeau, "Le combat pastoral d'Augustin contre les astrologues, les devins et les guérisseurs," in Pierre-Yves Fux, Jean-Michel Roessli, and Otto Wermelinger, eds., *Augustinus Afer. Saint Augustin: Africanité et universalité; Actes du colloque international, Alger-Annaba, 1–7 avril, 2001, Paradosis* (Freiburg: 2003), 167–82; Brent Shaw, *Sacred Violence: African Christians and Sectarian Hatred in the Age of Augustine* (Princeton: 2011), 210.

225. Augustine, *Confessions* 4.3.5.

226. Augustine, *Confessions* 7.6.8–10.

227. Genesis 25:25; Augustine, *On Christian Teaching* 2.XXII33.

228. Éric Rebillard, "Religious Sociology. Being Christian in the Time of Augustine," in Mark Vessey and Shelley Reid, eds., *A Companion to Augustine* (Malden MA: 2012), 40–53, here 47–48.

229. Theodoret of Cyrus, "A Cure of Greek Maladies," in *Theodoret of Cyrus*, trans. Istvan Pasztori Kupan (London/New York: 2006), 89–108, Frederick W. Norris, "Greek Christianities," in Augustine Casiday and Frederick W. Norris, eds., *The Cambridge History of Christianity: Constantine to c. 600* (Cambridge: 2007), 70–117, at 93–94.

230. Theodoret of Cyrus, "The Questions on Genesis," in John F. Petruccione, ed., *The Questions on the Octateuch. I. On Genesis and Exodus*, trans. Robert C. Hill (Washington, DC: 2007), 15; Riedinger, *Die Heilige Schrift*, 72–74, for the comets and his views on astrology.

231. Riedinger, *Die Heilige Schrift*, 74.

232. On *philochristos* (Christ loving): Michael Maas, *John Lydus and the Roman Past: Antiquarianism and Politics in the Age of Justinian* (London: 1992), 15; Gerhard Rösch, *ONOMA ΒΑΣΙΛΕΙΑΣ: Studien zum offiziellen Gebrauch der Kaisertitel in spätantiker und frühbyzantinischer Zeit* (Vienna: 1978), 65, 103.

233. Edward Watts, "Justinian, Malalas, and the End of Athenian Philosophical Teaching in A.D. 529," *Journal of Roman Studies* 94 (2004), 168–82, esp. 171–74, on astronomy; Maas, *John Lydus and the Roman Past*, 67–77.

234. Justinian, *The Codex of Justinian* 1.11.8, trans. Fred H. Blume and Bruce W. Frier (Cambridge: 2016) [Leo and Anthemius, 472 CE].

NOTES TO PAGES 151–153 [325]

235. Pierre Chuvin, *A Chronicle of the Last Pagans*, trans. B. A. Archer (Cambridge, MA: 1990), 134.

236. *Cod. Just.*, e.g., 1.4.10; 9.18.2; Magdalino, *L'orthodoxie des astrologues*, 27–29. Dice-playing may have been connected to zodiacal signs and augury; see Watts, "Justinian, Malalas, and the End of Athenian Philosophical Teaching," *Journal of Roman Studies* 94 (2004): 168–82, at 171–73 (with 171 n. 24), explaining how "the teaching of philosophy and astronomy in Athens could be prohibited by a law that more generally forbade the use of dice" (173).

237. Maas, *John Lydus and the Roman Past*, 69.

238. Procopius of Caesarea, *The Anecdota or Secret History* 11.37, ed. and trans. H. B. Dewing, LCL 290 (Cambridge, MA: 1935); John Malalas, *The Chronicle of John Malalas* 18.47, trans. Elizabeth Jeffreys, Michael Jeffreys, and Roger Scott (Leiden: 1986): "During the consulship of Decius, the emperor issued a decree and sent it to Athens ordering that no-one should teach philosophy nor interpret the laws; nor should gambling be allowed in any city, for some gamblers who had been discovered in Byzantion had been indulging themselves in dreadful blasphemies. Their hands were cut off and they were paraded around on camels"; Watts, "Justinian, Malalas, and the End of Athenian Philosophical Teaching," 171, translates the passage as ". . . nor interpret astronomy; nor in any city should there be lots cast using dice . . ."; for his discussion of Malalas, see 171–77.

239. Procopius, *Secret History* 11.37.

240. Watts, "Justinian, Malalas, and the End of Athenian Philosophical Teaching," 173–74, suggests that the victims mentioned by Malalas may have been the astrologers mentioned by Procopius, who suffered similar humiliating punishments.

241. Paul the Silentiary, "Description of the Church of Hagia Sophia," l.1–11, in *Three Political Voices from the Age of Justinian*, trans. Peter N. Bell (Liverpool: 2009), and on Paul the Silentiary, 14–18; for discussion of these triumphal sentiments in visual imagery, see Henry Maguire, *Earth and Ocean: The Terrestrial World in Early Byzantine Art* (University Park, PA: 1987), esp. 76–80, on San Vitale in Ravenna.

242. *Nov. Just.* 84, pr. (539 CE), in *The Novels of Justinian* trans. David J. D. Miller and Peter Sarris, vol. 1. (Cambridge: 2018), 277–78.

243. *Cod. Just.* 1.17.2.18 (533 CE); Michael Maas, "Roman History and Christian Ideology in Justinianic Reform Legislation," *DOP* 40 (1986): 17–31, at 29 notes its origin lay in the old understanding of the malleability of human affairs in the sublunar realm; Giuliana Lanata, *Legislazione e natura nelle Novelle giustinianee* (Naples: 1984), 165–87 and 189–204; W. S. Thurman, "A Juridical and Theological Concept of Nature in the Sixth Century A.D.," *Byzantinoslavica* 32, no. 2 (1971): 77–85, at 82–85, for precedents in philosophical and patristic thought.

244. For an overview of Christian monarchy in the work of Eusebius: Raffaele Farina, *L'impero e l'imperatore Cristiano in Eusebio di Cesarea: La prima teologia politica del Cristianesimo* (Zurich: 1966), esp. 107–205.

245. Jaś Elsner, *Imperial Rome and Christian Triumph: The Art of the Roman Empire AD 100–450* (Oxford: 1998), 201–2.

246. Elsner, *Imperial Rome and Christian Triumph*, 202.

247. Anderson, *Cosmos and Continuity*, 114–26, cites Vaticanus Graecus 1291, Biblioteca Apostolica Vaticana, fol. 9r, https://digi.vatlib.it/view/MSS_Vat.gr.1291.

248. Anderson, *Cosmos and Continuity*, 123; See also H. P. L'Orange, *Studies on the Iconography of Cosmic Kingship in the Ancient World* (Oslo: 1953), 139–70, esp. 153; for images of Justinian in other media, 140 and 145–47.

249. Elena N. Boeck, *The Bronze Horseman of Justinian in Constantinople: The Cross-Cultural Biography of a Mediterranean Monument* (Cambridge: 2021). I am grateful to Prof. Boeck for sharing the manuscript before publication. On Justinian's Christianization of the imperial image, see Boeck, *The Bronze Horseman*, 28–32; Percy Ernst Schramm, *Sphaira, Globus, Reichsapfel: Wanderung und Wandlung eines Herrschaftsbezeichens von Caesar bis zu Elisabeth II. Ein Beitrag zum "Nachleben" der Antike* (Stuttgart: 1958), 20–54, and Tables 1–16, offers a thorough discussion of orbs as well as many illustrations.

250. Boeck, *The Bronze Horseman*, 31; on the appearance of the zodiac cycle in fourth- and fifth-century synagogue mosaics as a symbol of the divine order: Jodi Magness, "Heaven

[326] NOTES TO PAGES 153–156

on Earth: Helios and the Zodiac Cycle in Ancient Palestinian Synagogues," *DOP* 59 (2005): 1–52, at 27. She finds analogies in Christian church decoration and in Sasanian imperial art (16). The zodiac served as a frame in the anonymous late antique Hebrew lament for the destruction of the Temple in Jerusalem in 70 A.D. See "Dirge for the Ninth of Av," in T. Carmi, ed., *The Penguin Book of Hebrew Verse* (London: 1981), 204–6: "How long will there be weeping in Zion and lamentation in Jerusalem? Have mercy on Zion and build anew the walls of Jerusalem! Because of our sins the Temple was destroyed . . . The Ram, first of all, wept bitterly, for his sheep were being led to the slaughter. The Bull howled on high, for we were all driven hard, with yokes upon our necks." George Foot Moore, "Fate and Free Will in the Jewish Philosophies According to Josephus," *Harvard Theological Review* 22, no. 4 (Oct. 1929): 371–89, at 386–87, on rabbinic discussion of the zodiac and whether Israel is bound by astral fate.

251. Boeck, *The Bronze Horseman*, 31.

252. For example, a gold solidus (MET 17.190.147) of the emperor Maurice (582–602) shows him in a chariot, with an orb in his right hand, on which stands a victory figure (Anderson, *Cosmos and Continuity*, 123–26 for illustrations and discussion). Another solidus (DOK BZC.1948.17.2430), of Theodosius III, dating to 715–17, has a portrait bust of the emperor on the obverse. In his right hand there is an orb with a cross: Anderson, *Cosmos and Continuity*, 125.

253. Boeck, *The Bronze Horseman*, 31–32.

254. Maas, "Roman History and Christian Ideology," 30–31; zodiac signs at the feet of Christ Pantokrator appear in Byzantine churches. L'Orange, *Studies on the Iconography of Cosmic Kingship*, 114–16 and 165–70, addressed the question of Christ Pantocrator, seated in the heavens, sometimes with the signs of the zodiac at his feet.

255. Anderson, *Cosmos and Community in Early Medieval Art*, 8.

256. Maas, *John Lydus and the Roman Past*, 105–18; Michael Maas, "Preface" in Anastasius C. Bandy et al., eds. and trans., *On Celestial Signs* (Lewiston: 2013).

257. Lydus, *De ostensis* 8: "Τοσαῦτα μὲν οὖν πρὸς τοὺς ταῖς διοσημείαις ἐνισταμένους καὶ Πτολεμαίῳ τολμῶντας ἀντιλέγειν ἐκ πολλῶν ὀλίγα λελέχθω." Trans. M. Maas.

258. Lydus, *De ostensis* 53.

259. Lydus, *De ostensis*, pr.

260. Lydus, *De ostensis* 1.

261. Lydus, *De ostensis* 1: other signs he witnessed.

262. Lydus, *De ostensis* 71.

263. Lydus, *De ostensis* 71: "κριῷ Βρεταννία, Γαλατία, Γερμανία, Βαστάρναι, Κοίλη Συρία, Ἰδουμαία."

264. Lydus, *De ostensis*, xlvi; see also Ptolemy, *Tetrabiblos* II.2–3.

265. Lydus, *De ostensis* 71.

266. Lydus, *De ostensis* 9. The emperor is probably Justinian, and not Anastasios as Wachsmuth surmises, in Lydus, *De ostensis* 9 [p. 20]; on complications with chap. 71, attributing it to Lydus, see xix–xx and xlvi: he accepts the reading of the manuscript (Codex Caseolinus) and ordering of the fragments. It is possible that this passage was composed by a completely different and earlier source and tacked onto Lydus's text at a later date, but no scholars have pursued this.

267. Magdalino, *L'orthodoxie des astrologues*, 27–31, on reception of astrology in the sixth century.

268. For a recent discussion of Procopius, see Henning Börm, "Procopius, His Predecessors, and the Genesis of the *Anecdota*: Antimonarchic Discourse in Late Antique Historiography," in Henning Börm, ed., *Antimonarchic Discourse in Antiquity* (Stuttgart: 2015), 305–46, esp. 311 on his Christianity, and 323–26 on his background; Geoffrey Greatrex, "L'historien Procope et la vie à Césarée au VIe siècle," in Geoffrey Greatrex and Sylvain Janniard, eds., *Le monde de Procope / The World of Procopius* (Paris: 2018), 15–38; Mischa Meier and Federico Montinaro, eds., *A Companion to Procopius of Caesarea* (Leiden: 2022). The bibliography is expanding rapidly.

269. On Procopius's identification of God and Fortune: Averil M. Cameron, "The "Skepticism" of Procopius," *Historia* 15, no. 4 (1966), 466–82, at 478.

NOTES TO PAGES 156–158 [327]

270. Cameron, "The 'Skepticism' of Procopius," 482; Anthony Kaldellis, *Procopius of Caesarea: Tyranny, History, and Philosophy at the End of Antiquity* (Philadelphia: 2004), 165–222, argues that such use of non-Christian concepts by Procopius indicates a firmly non-Christian, even anti-Christian, perspective throughout his works. For Kaldellis, 221, Procopius lived in a world "ruled by chance and tyrany," not divine Providence.

271. Magdalino, "The Byzantine Reception," 40–46, suggests this history falls into four phases, beginning in the reign of Heraclius; see also Paul of Alexandria, *Pauli Alexandrini Elementa Apotelesmatica* β' [Περὶ τῶν δώδεκα ζῳδίων], ed. Ae. Boer, with commentary by O. Neugebauer (Leipzig: 1958).

272. Magdalino, *L'orthodoxie des astrologues*, 10–11 and 19–20.

273. David Pingree, "Rhetorios of Egypt," in Alexander P. Kazhdan et al., eds., *ODB*, vol. 3 (New York: 1991), 1790.

274. Pingree, "Rhetorios of Egypt," 1790; David Pingree, "Antiochus and Rhetorius," *Classical Philology* 72, no. 3 (1977), 203–23; David Pingree, "From Alexandria to Baghdad to Byzantium: The Transmission of Astrology," *International Journal of the Classical Tradition* 8, no. 1 (2001): 3–37; see also Frantz Grenet, "The Circulation of Astrological Lore and Its Political Use between the Roman East, Sasanian Iran, Central Asia, India, and the Türks," in Nicola Di Cosmo and Michael Maas, eds., *Empires and Exchanges in Eurasian Late Antiquity: Rome, China, Iran, and the Steppe, ca. 250–750* (Cambridge: 2018), 235–52.

275. Magdalino, "The Byzantine Reception," 40.

276. Magdalino, "The Byzantine Reception," 40–41. The second phase of Byzantine astrology begins in the mid-eighth century, at the time of the rise and fall of the Abbasid Caliphate, beyond the time frame of this book.

Chapter Five: The Controlling Hand of the Environment

1. Strabo, *Geography* 2.5.26, ed. and trans. Horace Leonard Jones, LCL 49 (Cambridge, MA: 1917).

2. A selection of excerpts from ancient texts on environmental questions can be found in Rebecca F. Kennedy, C. Sydnor Roy, and Max L. Goldman, eds. and trans., *Race and Ethnicity in the Classical World: An Anthology of Primary Sources in Translation* (Indianapolis: 2013), 35–51; Clarence J. Glacken, "Changing Ideas of the Habitable World," in William L. Thomas Jr., ed., *Man's Role in Changing the Face of the Earth*, vol. 1 (Chicago: 1956), 70–92; for introduction to the Renaissance and Early Modern reception of Classical environmental determinism, see Clarence J. Glacken, *Traces on the Rhodian Shore: Nature and Culture in Western Thought from Ancient Times to the End of the Eighteenth Century* (Berkeley: 1967), 355–74; survey of modern treatments in David N. Livingstone, "Changing Climate, Human Evolution, and the Revival of Environmental Determinism," *Bulletin of the History of Medicine* 86, no. 4 (2012): 564–95.

3. Michael J. Decker, "What Is a Byzantine Landscape?," in Myrto Veikou and Ingela Nilsson, eds., *Spatialities of Byzantine Culture from the Human Body to the Universe* (Leiden: 2022), 243–61. Note that the most meaningful characteristic of landscape changed from distance from Rome in a literal or qualitative sense, to relative position in a heavenly hierarchy.

4. Rebecca Futo Kennedy, "Airs, Waters, Metals, Earth: People and Land in Archaic and Classical Greek Thought," in Rebecca Futo Kennedy and Molly Jones-Lewis, eds., *The Routledge Handbook of Identity and the Environment in the Classical and Medieval Worlds* (Abingdon: 2016), 9–28. Cf. Joseph E. Skinner, *The Invention of Greek Ethnography: From Homer to Herodotus* (Oxford: 2012), 3–8, 233–58, esp. 255: "The fifth-century origins of ethnographic prose have also encouraged the assumption that ethnography itself was a fifth-century phenomenon. However, even a limited survey of this wider discourse of identity and difference demonstrates that this was not in fact the case." J. L. Heiberg, "Théories antiques sur l'influence morale de climat," *Scientia* 28 (1920), 453–64; Mario Pinna, "Ippocrate: Fondatore della Teoria dei Climi," *Rivista Geografica Italiana* 95 (1988): 3–19; Hippocrate, *Airs, eaux, lieux*, ed. Jacques Jouanna (Paris: 1996), 7–82; Wilhelm Backhaus, "Der Hellenen-Barbaren-Gegensatz und die Hippokratische Schrift Περὶ ἀέρων ὑδάτων τόπων," *Historia* 25, no. 2 (1976): 170–85; Hyun Jin Kim, "The Invention of the 'Barbarian' in

[328] NOTES TO PAGES 158–160

Late Sixth-Century BC Ionia," in Eran Almagor and Joseph Skinner, eds., *Ancient Ethnography: New Approaches* (London: 2013), 25–48.

5. Herodotus, *The Persian Wars* 2.122, ed. and trans. A. D. Godley, LCL 120 (Cambridge, MA: 1925): Cyrus, the first Persian king of kings, convinces his followers to choose "rather to be rulers on a barren mountain side than slaves dwelling in tilled valleys." Kennedy, "Airs, Waters, Metals, Earth," 9–28, and Clara Bosak-Schroeder, "The Ecology of Health in Herodotus, Dicaearchus, and Agatharchides," in Kennedy and Jones-Lewis, eds., *The Routledge Handbook of Identity and the Environment*, 29–44; Rosalind Thomas, *Herodotus in Context: Ethnography, Science and the Art of Persuasion* (Cambridge: 2000), 75–101.

6. Hippocrate, *Airs, eaux, lieux*, 7–10; Hippocrates, *Airs, Waters, Places*, ed. and trans. Paul Potter, *Ancient Medicine: Airs, Waters, Places. Epidemics 1 and 3. The Oath. Precepts. Nutriment*, LCL 147 (Cambridge, MA: 2022); Pinna, "Ippocrate," 3–19; Charles Chiasson, "Scythian Androgyny and Environmental Determinism in Herodotus and the Hippocratic περὶ ἀέρων ὑδάτων τόπων," *Syllecta Classica* 12 (2001): 33–73.

7. Heiberg, "Théories antiques sur l'influence morale," 434, discusses the impossibility of assigning a precise date to the treatise, suggesting that its author was earlier than Hippocrates; Oliver Thomas, "Creating *Problemata* with the Hippocratic Corpus," in Robert Mayhew, ed., *The Aristotelian Problemata Physica: Philosophical and Scientific Investigations* (Leiden: 2015), 79–99.

8. Pinna, "Ippocrate," 3–4; Glacken, *Traces*, 82–88.

9. Glacken, *Traces*, esp. 3–149, and 91–95 on influences between Hippocrates and Aristotle.

10. Pinna, "Ippocrate," 7.

11. I use "climate" in the modern sense. The Greek term *klima* also meant a band of land that was a parallel of latitude. The concept of seven *klimata* would be developed only much later than Ps.-Hippocrates. Daniela Dueck, *Geography in Classical Antiquity* (Cambridge: 2012), 84–90, describes varying numbers of *klimata*; Eratosthenes (276–194 BCE) is credited as the originator of the seven *klimata* system by Ernst Honigmann, *Die Sieben Klimata und die ΠΟΛΕΙΣ ΕΠΙΣΗΜΟΙ: Eine Untersuchung zur Geschichte der Geographie und Astrologie im Altertum und Mittelalter* (Heidelberg: 1929), 10–24, and more recently Dmitriy A. Shcheglov, "Ptolemy's System of Seven Climata and Eratosthenes' Geography," *Geographia Antiqua* 13 (2004), 21–37; while D. R. Dicks, "The ΚΛΙΜΑΤΑ in Greek Geography," *Classical Quarterly* 5, no. 3–4 (July–Oct. 1955): 248–55, argues for Hipparchus. Ptolemy made the seven *klimata* canonical, as Shcheglov, 26, points out: "The Ptolemaic system should be called canonical not because it was accepted by the most of his successors, but as the first system in which a strict distinction was drawn between the seven climata and the infinite number of all other possible latitudes." On the beginnings of astrological use of *klimata*, see Dicks, "The ΚΛΙΜΑΤΑ," 251–52.

12. Hippocrates, *Airs, Waters, Places* 24.6; Backhaus, "Der Hellenen-Barbaren-Gegensatz, 170–85, at 178–85. He notes the importance of Hippocrates's systematic treatment of the relation between the geographical characteristics of a region and its inhabitants and locates him in the *nomos-physis* debate (70). He points out that the treatise is the first scientific climate theory to justify Greek superiority and Barbarian inferiority (185).

13. Glacken, *Traces*, 83, discussing Ludwig Edelstein, *Peri Aerōn und die Sammlung der Hippokratischen Schriften* (Berlin: 1931), 1–4; discussion of the unity of the two parts, see Hippocrate, *Airs, eaux, lieux* 2.2.

14. Glacken, *Traces*, 84.

15. Hippocrates, *Airs, Waters, Places* 12–14.

16. Hippocrates, *Airs, Waters, Places* 12.53–54.

17. Hippocrates, *Airs, Waters, Places* 16.63–64.

18. Hippocrates, *Airs, Waters, Places* 23.83–84.

19. Hippocrates, *Airs, Waters, Places* 24.87–90.

20. Hippocrates, *Airs, Waters, Places* 14.

21. Ibid.

22. Glacken, *Traces*, 93.

NOTES TO PAGES 161–165 [329]

23. Glacken, *Traces*, 93–94; on the idea of the "golden mean," see Aristotle, *Nicomachean Ethics* 2.7.2–16, ed. and trans. H. Rackham, LCL 73 (Cambridge, MA: 1926), [1107b–1108b]; Aristotle, *Politics* 7.6.1–3 [1327b.19–39], ed. and trans. H. Rackham, LCL 264 (Cambridge, MA: 1932); see Aristotle, *Problems* 14, ed. and trans. Robert Mayhew, LCL 316 (Cambridge, MA: 2011), for discussion of environmental effects on human characteristics; Daniel S. Richter, *Cosmopolis: Imagining Community in Late Classical Athens and the Early Roman Empire* (Oxford: 2011), 21–54.

24. Aristotle, *Politics* 7.7, ed. and trans. Richard McKeon, *The Basic Works of Aristotle* (New York: 1941). For Greek text, see Aristotle, *Politics* 7.6.1–3 [1327a–1328a], ed. and trans. H. Rackham, LCL 264 (Cambridge, MA: 1932).

25. For discussion of the difference between the ancient Ps.-Aristotelian *Problems* and the anonymous *Problemata Aristotelis* composed in the thirteenth or fourteenth century, see Ann Blair, "Authorship in the Popular 'Problemata Aristotelis,'" *Early Science and Medicine* 4, no. 3 (1999): 189–227, at 189–90; for discussion of a possible fifth- or sixth-century date of composition, see Ann Blair, "The *Problemata* as a Natural Philosophical Genre," in Anthony Grafton and Nancy Siraisi, eds., *Natural Particulars: Nature and the Disciplines in Renaissance Europe* (Cambridge, MA: 1999), 171–204, at 171 and 190 n. 1 for bibliography on estimates as to when the *Problems* were completed; Glacken, *Traces*, 94.

26. Κρᾶσις (*krasis*) can mean both mixture and climate.

27. Aristotle, *Problems* 14.1.

28. Aristote, *Problèmes* 14, ed. Pierre Louis (Paris: 1993).

29. Glacken, *Traces*, 95.

30. Christian Jacob, "Polybius," in Jacques Brunschwig, Geoffrey E. R. Lloyd, and Catherine Porter, eds., *Greek Thought: A Guide to Classical Knowledge*, trans. Elizabeth Rawlings and Jeannine Pucci (Cambridge, MA: 2000), 712–20.

31. Polybius, *The Histories*, esp. 4.21, ed. and trans. W. R. Paton and S. Douglas Olson, F. W. Walbank, and Christian Habicht, LCL, vol. 2. (Cambridge, MA: 2010).

32. Arthur M. Eckstein, *Moral Vision in the Histories of Polybius* (Berkeley: 1995), 118–25 (esp. 123, for "people in chaos"), on the barbarian threat to the social order. The threat of disorder, however, not only menaces foreign enemies but can be found at the heart of Roman society itself.

33. Polybius, *Histories* 4.21.2.

34. Glacken, *Traces*, 96, on Polybius 4.20–21: "This is the first full exposition known to me of the idea that an environment produces a certain kind of ethnic character, which by conscious, purposive, and hard work, can be counteracted by cultural institutions (such as music) which are all-pervasive. Here the transition from a primordial state (probably of barbarism, induced by the environment) to civilization is made by the conscious decision of a body of culture-heroes or elders."

35. Lucius Annaeus Florus, *Epitome of Roman History* 1.37.2, ed. and trans. Edward S. Forster, LCL 231 (Cambridge MA: 1929).

36. Vitruvius, *The Ten Books on Architecture*, trans. Morris Hicky Morgan, 2nd ed. (Cambridge, MA: 1926; repr. 2014); Vitruve, *De l'Architecture / De Architectura*, ed. Pierre Gros (Paris: 2015); Pierre Gros, "Les composantes environnementales de la qualité d'un projet dans le *de architectura* de Vitruve," in Jacques Jouanna, Christian Robin, and Michel Zink, eds., *Vie et climat d'Hésiode à Montesquieu* (Paris: 2018), 165–84; Glacken, *Traces*, 106–10.

37. Vitruvius, *Architecture* 6.1.12.

38. Vitruvius, *Architecture* 6.1.1 and 6.1.10–11.

39. Vitruvius, *Architecture* 2.1.1–7; Glacken, *Traces*, 107–8.

40. Vitruvius, *Architecture* 2.1.6.

41. Vitruve, *De l'Architecture / De Architectura*, ed. Gros, 2 n. 2.

42. Vitruvius, *Architecture* 1.pr.1.

43. Vitruvius, *Architecture* 6.1.11; Pliny the Elder, *Natural History* 37.202, ed. and trans. D. E. Eichholz, LCL 419 (Cambridge, MA: 1962), shares these views; see Trevor Murphy, *Pliny the Elder's Natural History: The Empire in the Encyclopedia* (Oxford: 2004), 172.

[330] NOTES TO PAGES 165–169

44. Michael Maas, "Strabo and Procopius: Classical Geography for a Christian Empire," in Hagit Amirav and Bas ter Haar Romeny, eds., *From Rome to Constantinople: Studies in Honour of Averil Cameron* (Leuven: 2007), 67–83, at 67–75.

45. J. J. Tierney, "The Celtic Ethnography of Posidonius," *Proceedings of the Royal Irish Academy: Archaeology, Culture, History, Literature* 60 (1959/1960), 189–275.

46. Maas, "Strabo and Procopius," 70.

47. For unknown reasons, Strabo did not complete the *Geography*; Maas, "Strabo and Procopius," 67–68.

48. Strabo, *Geography* 2.5.8.

49. Strabo, *Geography* 2.5.8; Daniela Dueck, *Strabo of Amasia: A Greek Man of Letters in Augustan Rome* (London: 2002), 118, 154, and 204 n. 28; Maas, "Strabo and Procopius," 71.

50. For example, Strabo, *Geography* 3.3.8.

51. Maas, "Strabo and Procopius," 71–75; Glacken, *Traces*, 103–5.

52. Strabo, *Geography* 3.3.8; Maas, "Strabo and Procopius," 73.

53. Strabo, *Geography* 2.5.26; Dueck, *Strabo of Amasia*, 115–22; Maas, "Strabo and Procopius," 74.

54. Strabo, *Geography* 7.3.7; Maas, "Strabo and Procopius," 74–75; Dueck, *Strabo of Amasia*, 79 and 119; on negative results of conquest: Benjamin Isaac, *The Invention of Racism in Classical Antiquity* (Princeton: 2004), 239–47.

55. Maas, "Strabo and Procopius," passim and 67–68; on the reception of the *Geography* until the sixth century, see Aubrey Diller, *The Textual Tradition of Strabo's Geography* (Amsterdam: 1975), 9–11.

56. Pliny, *Natural History* 16.1.1–4, ed. and trans. H. Rackham, LCL 370 (Cambridge, MA: 1945).

57. Pliny, *Natural History* 16.1.4; Murphy, *Pliny the Elder's Natural History*, 166–74, for extended discussion.

58. Pliny, *Natural History* 37.202.

59. Murphy, *Pliny the Elder's Natural History*, 173.

60. For example, Tacitus, *Agricola* 29–32, ed. and trans. M. Hutton, W. Peterson, R. M. Ogilvie, et al., LCL 35 (Cambridge, MA: 1914), in a well-known speech he puts in the mouth of the British leader Calgacus.

61. Ammianus Marcellinus, *History* 31.2.1, ed. and trans. J. C. Rolfe, LCL 331 (Cambridge, MA: 1939).

62. Ammianus Marcellinus, *History* 23.6.67, ed. and trans. J. C. Rolfe, LCL 315 (Cambridge, MA: 1940); E. H. Bunbury, *A History of Ancient Geography among the Greeks and Romans from the Earliest Ages till the Fall of the Roman Empire*, vol. 2, 2nd ed. (London: 1932, repr. 1959), 682, notes Ammianus's debts to Pliny and Ptolemy.

63. Servius, *Commentaire sur l'Énéide de Virgile. Livre VI*, ed. and trans. Emmanuelle Jeunet-Mancy (Paris: 2012), 164, commenting on lines 724ff. of the *Aeneid*; at 252 n. 730, she makes the connection to Ptolemy, *Tetrabiblos* 2.2.8–9, following Germaine Aujac, *Claude Ptolémée: Astronome, astrologue, géographe; Connaissance et représentation du monde habité* (Paris: 1993), 286, and she notes the similarity of language between Servius and his contemporary Firmicus Maternus, citing Aldo Setaioli, *La vicenda dell'anima nel commento di Servo a Virgilio* (Frankfurt am Main: 1995), 26–27; Glacken, *Traces*, 114–15.

64. Virgil, *Aeneid* 6.724–35, ed. and trans. H. R. Fairclough, G. P. Goold, LCL 63 (Cambridge, MA: 1916).

65. Rufus Festius Avienus, *Ora Maritima: A Description of the Seacoast from Britanny to Marseilles [Massilia]*, ed. Adolph Schulten (Berlin: 1922); repr. trans. John P. Murphy (Chicago: 1977).

66. Avienus, *Ora Maritima*, lines 142–45; Gregory Hays, "Avienius," in Oliver Nicholson, ed., *Oxford Dictionary of Late Antiquity* (Oxford: 2018), 187.

67. Glacken, *Traces*, 168.

68. Finding the right vocabulary to describe their corporate identities was not an easy matter for early Christians. Denise Kimber Buell, *Why This New Race? Ethnic Reasoning in Early Christianity* (New York: 2005) emphasizes the fluidity of ancient concepts of ethnicity

NOTES TO PAGES 169–171 [331]

and the difficulties in using modern terms like ethnicity and race for the period before Constantine. In the following centuries, she suggests new possibilities arose for Christian self-definition in the imperial frame.

69. Glacken, *Traces*, 182; see *The Letter to Diognetus* 5 in Bart D. Ehrman, ed., *The Apostolic Fathers*, vol. 2, LCL 25N (2003), 121–61.

70. Utto Riedinger, *Die Heilige Schrift im Kampf der griechischen Kirche gegen die Astrologie* (Innsbruck: 1956); Tim Hegedus, *Early Christianity and Ancient Astrology* (New York: 2007), 12, 49, and 157–62; Stephen C. McCluskey, *Astronomies and Cultures in Early Medieval Europe* (Cambridge: 1998), 29–48.

71. Glacken, *Traces*, 167.

72. See discussion of Bardaisan above.

73. Glacken, *Traces*, 163: "[Hexaemeral literature] was started by Philo, cultivated with charm by St. Basil, disseminated by the Latin prose of St. Ambrose, who borrowed much from Basil. Since Genesis I left so many questions unanswered, the hexaemeral writings, whether apologetics, exegesis, or homiletics, thus made use of knowledge for religious ends." On the Christian geographical tradition, see Glacken, *Traces*, 174–75; on Basil, 189–96; on Augustine, 196–203.

74. Augustine, *Confessions* 13; Glacken, *Traces*, 189, on Basil, Ambrose, and Augustine. He highlights that Ambrose "kept alive and passed on the conception of man as a partner of God in improving the earth" (196).

75. Basil of Caesarea, "Homily 5. The Germination of the Earth (on the Hexaemeron)," in *Exegetic Homilies*, trans. Agnes Clare Way (Washington, DC: 1963), 5.2.

76. Glacken, *Traces*, 177–205, for discussion of hexameral literature.

77. Glacken, *Traces*, 202–3; for later materials, see Natalia Lozovsky, *The Earth Is Our Book: Geographical Knowledge in the Latin West ca. 400–1000* (Ann Arbor: 2000).

78. Augustine of Hippo, *Epistulae* 43.9.25.10–11, ed. A. Goldbacher, CSEL 34 (Prague and Leipzig: 1895), trans. and discussion in Lozovsky, "*The Earth Is Our Book*," 142; on the need to study the visible world and the role of Roman geographical writing, 141–55; for overview of Christianization, particularly in medieval Europe, see Richard C. Hoffmann, *An Environmental History of Medieval Europe* (Cambridge: 2014), 91–94.

79. The reasons for this hiatus are difficult to explain. As just described, Christian writers were preoccupied with other approaches to the environment, primarily its place in God's creation. Perhaps environmental determinism was so deeply rooted in the minds of secular writers that it did not warrant extended discussion.

80. Maas, "Strabo and Procopius," passim.

81. Greatrex, "L'historien Procope et la vie à Césarée au vie siècle," in *Le monde de Procope*, ed. Geoffrey Greatrex and Sylvain Janniard (Paris: 2018), 15–38; Geoffrey Greatrex, *Procopius of Caesarea, Persian Wars: A Historical Commentary* (Cambridge: 2021).

82. Alexander Sarantis, "Procopius and the Different Types of Northern Barbarian," in Greatrex and Janniard, eds., *Le monde de Procope*, 355–78; Geoffrey Greatrex, "Procopius' Attitude towards Barbarians," in Greatrex and Janniard, eds., *Le monde de Procope*, 327–54, at 340: "But not all non-Roman peoples were barbarians or necessarily enemies."

83. On the much-discussed question of Procopius's Christianity, see Averil Cameron, *Procopius and the Sixth Century* (London: 1996), 113–33; Anthony Kaldellis, *Procopius of Caesarea: Tyranny, History, and Philosophy at the End of Antiquity* (Philadelphia: 2004), 165–73, Greatrex, *Procopius of Caesarea*, 13–14 and passim; on his Thucydidean style, see Charles F. Pazdernik, "Procopius and Thucydides on the Labors of War: Belisarius and Brasidas in the Field," *TAPA* 130 (2000): 149–87.

84. Tamás Mészáros, "Notes on Procopius' *Secret History*," in E. Juhász, ed., *Byzanz und das Abendland: Begegnungen zwischen Ost und West* (Budapest: 2013), 285–304, esp. 287–88, for discussion of authorship and bibliography; Procopius's authorship of the *Anecdota* was demonstrated definitively by Jakob Haury, in "Zu Prokops Geheimgeschichte," *Byzantinische Zeitschrift* 34 (1934): 10–14, and in *Procopiana: Programm des Königlichen Realgymnasiums Augsburg für das Studienjahr 1890/1891* (Augsburg: 1891), 9–27.

[332] NOTES TO PAGES 171-175

85. Procopius, *On Buildings*, ed. and trans. H. B. Dewing and Glanville Downey, LCL 343 (Cambridge, MA: 1940).

86. Maas, "Strabo and Procopius," 67–83, for discussion and further bibliography; Diller, *The Textual Tradition*, 9–11, summarizes the reception history of the *Geography*.

87. Claudia Rapp, "Literary Culture under Justinian," in Michael Maas., ed., *The Cambridge Companion to the Age of Justinian* (Cambridge: 2005), 376–97.

88. Procopius, *History of the Wars*, ed. and trans. H. B. Dewing, LCL 48, 5 vols. (Cambridge, MA: 1914–28), 81, 107, 173, and 217, here 1.15.19–25.

89. Michael Maas, "'Delivered from Their Ancient Customs': Christianity and the Question of Cultural Change in Early Byzantine Ethnography," in Kenneth Mills and Anthony Grafton, eds., *Conversion in Late Antiquity and the Early Middle Ages: Seeing and Believing* (Rochester, NY: 2003), 152–88, at 160–69.

90. For example, Procopius, *History of the Wars* 1.15.21–25, 6.14.34, 6.15.23, 7.14.28, etc.

91. Hippocrates, *Du régime*, ed Robert Joly (Paris: 1967), ix–xxxiv; a second edition, by Joly and Simon Byl, appeared in 1984 = *Corpus medicorum Graecorum* 1.2.4.

92. Henry George Liddell and Robert Scott, "δίαιτα, ἡ," in Henry Stuart Jones and Roderick McKenzie, eds., *LSJ* (Oxford: 1940), 396.

93. Procopius, *Wars* 2.10.11–12: "One might say that such a state of affairs that it is nothing else than the transformation of the habits of men into those of beast. For in a time when no treaties at all are made there will remain certainly war without end, and war which has no end is always calculated to estrange from their proper nature those who engage in it."

94. Cf. Procopius, *Wars* 2.2.2. Note that Romans, Persians, and Hephthalite Huns have these institutions.

95. For example, Procopius, *Wars* 8.2.15–16.

96. On the date of the *Wars*: Geoffrey Greatrex, "Recent Work on Procopius and the Composition of *Wars* VIII," *Byzantine and Modern Greek Studies* 27 (2003): 45–67.

97. For background, Henning Börm, *Prokop und die Perser: Untersuchungen zu den römisch-sasanidischen Kontakten in der ausgehenden Spätantike* (Stuttgart: 2007); Geoffrey Greatrex, "Byzantium and the East in the Sixth Century," in M. Maas, ed., *Cambridge Companion to the Age of Justinian* (New York: 2005) 477–509; Greatrex, *Procopius of Caesarea*.

98. Procopius, *Wars* 1.15.19–25; *Wars* 8.1.9–10 on difficulty of terrain; compare 8.14.6–7 for the Dolomites, a group in Persia that inhabits inaccessible mountains and have continued to live autonomously.

99. Procopius, *Buildings* 3.6.9–13; for comparison, see Calgacus's speech in Tacitus, *Agricola* 31.1: "life and limb themselves are worn out in making roads through marsh and forest to the accompaniment of gibes and blows." Procopius describes the difficulty of passage through the heavily forested land of Lazica. The Lazi tell Chosroes, in Procopius, *Wars* 2.15.33, that "the way through the country would be easy for the whole Persian army, if they cut the trees and threw them into the places which were made difficult by precipices."

100. Procopius, *Wars* 8.13.5: the Persians also can force entry into seemingly impassable terrain.

101. *Nov. Just.* 1.pr.; see also 54 n. 3.

102. *Nov. Just.* 54 n. 3.

103. *Nov. Just.* 28.pr.; see also 305 n. 3, for a list of the centers of Roman authority in the region.

104. Procopius, *Wars* 6.14–15.

105. Sarantis, "Procopius and the Different Types of Northern Barbarian," 366–68; Roland Steinacher, "The Heruls: Fragments of a History," in Florin Curta, ed., *Neglected Barbarians* (Turnhout: 2010), 319–60.

106. Malalas, *The Chronicle* 18.6, ed. Elizabeth Jeffries, Michael Jeffries, and Roger Scott (Melbourne: 1986).

107. Procopius, *Wars* 6.14.33.

108. Procopius, *Wars* 6.15.35–42.

109. Procopius, *Secret History* 21.27.

110. Procopius, *Secret History* 1.3–7.

111. Procopius, *Secret History* 18.21.

NOTES TO PAGES 175–178 [333]

112. Procopius, *Secret History* 12.19–32 and 18.1–45.

113. Procopius, *Wars* 2.22.3.

114. Procopius, *Wars* 2.22.3–5.

115. Procopius, *Secret History* 18.20–21.

116. Procopius, *Secret History* 18.22.

117. Rudolf Riedinger, *Pseudo-Kaisarios: Überlieferungsgeschichte und Verfasserfrage* (Munich: 1969), 301–29.

118. Ioannis Papadogiannakis, "Didacticism, Exegesis, and Polemics in pseudo-Kaisarios's *erotapokriseis*," in Marie-Pierre Bussières, ed., *La littérature des questions et réponses dans l'antiquité profane et chrétienne: De l'enseignement à l'exégèse; Actes du séminaire sur le genre des questions et réponses tenu à Ottawa les 27 et 28 septembre 2009* (Turnhout: 2013), 271–89; Yannis Papadogiannakis, "Instruction by Question and Answer: The Case of Late Antique and Byzantine *Erotapokriseis*," in Scott F. Johnson, ed., *Greek Literature in Late Antiquity: Dynamism, Didacticism, Classicism* (Aldershot: 2006), 91–105, at 95–96, on Ps.-Caesarius; Stephanos Efthymiadis, "Questions and Answers," in Anthony Kaldellis and Niketas Siniossoglou, eds., *Cambridge Intellectual History of Byzantium* (Cambridge: 2017), 47–62, at 47–51; Jean Andrieu, *Le dialogue antique: Structure et présentation* (Paris: 1954), 283–344; Michael Maas, *Exegesis and Empire in the Early Byzantine Mediterranean: Junillus Africanus and the Instituta Regularia Divinae Legi* (Tübingen: 2003), 20–25.

119. Papadogiannakis, "Instruction by Question and Answer," 91–92.

120. Richard Sorabji, ed., *Philoponus and the Rejection of Aristotelian Science* (Ithaca, NY: 1987); Leslie S. B. MacCoull, "Philoponus' Letter to Justinian (CPG 7264)," *Byzantion* 73, no. 2 (2003): 390–400, describing the letter as a "well-made anticipatory summary of the highlights of Philoponus' theological learning" (400).

121. Maas, *Exegesis and Empire*.

122. Riedinger, *Pseudo-Kaisarios*, 283–300, on his sources.

123. Papadogiannakis, "Didacticism, Exegesis, and Polemics," 275.

124. Papadogiannakis, "Didacticism, Exegesis, and Polemics," 286.

125. Papadogiannakis, "Didacticism, Exegesis, and Polemics," 275.

126. On his polemics, particularly against Jews: Riedinger, *Pseudo-Kaisarios*, 373–82; Papadogiannakis, "Didacticism, Exegesis, and Polemics," 275–77 and 283; on his exegesis, 279–281; on other sixth-century collections of arguments, 286–88.

127. Cf. Kaldellis, *Procopius of Caesarea*, 165–222.

128. On background of theological controversies in the age of Justinian, see Patrick T. R. Gray, "The Legacy of Chalcedon: Christological Problems and Their Significance," in Maas, ed., *Cambridge Companion to the Age of Justinian*, 215–38, and Maas, *Exegesis and Empire*, passim and 47–52 on the Three Chapters Controversy.

129. Alexander Sarantis, *Justinian's Balkan Wars: Campaigning, Diplomacy and Development in Illyricum, Thrace and the Northern World; A.D. 527–565* (Prenton, UK: 2016) for discussion, esp. 65–88, on the origins of the Slavs; Florin Curta, *The Making of the Slavs: History and Archaeology of the Lower Danube Region; C. 500–700,* (Cambridge: 2001); R. Benedicty, "Die Milieu-Theorie bei Prokop von Kaisareia," *Byzantinische Zeitschrift* 55, no. 1 (1962): 1–10.

130. Curta, *Making of the Slavs*, 44; Riedinger, *Pseudo-Kaisarios*, 301–2, 305–7.

131. For example, Sarantis, *Justinian's Balkan Wars*; Curta, *Making of the Slavs*.

132. Pseudo-Caesarius equates the Danube with the unidentifiable river Pishon mentioned in Gen. 2:11.

133. Pseudo-Kaisarios, *Die Erotapokriseis*, ed. Rudolf Riedinger (Berlin: 1989), 2.109 [87]; translation taken from Jakov Bacic, *The Emergence of the Sklabenoi (Slavs), Their Arrival on the Balkan Peninsula, and the Role of the Avars in These Events: Revised Concepts in a New Perspective* (PhD diss., Columbia University, 1983), 152.

134. Papadogiannakis, "Didacticism, Exegesis, and Polemics," 277–79, 282: Questions 106, 107, 108, 110, 111, 116, and 117 are directed against magic and astrology.

135. Dueck, *Geography in Classical Antiquity*, 84–90; Heiberg, "Théories antiques sur l'influence morale," 453–64; Honigmann, *Die Sieben Klimata*, 10–24 and passim; Hegedus, *Early Christianity and Ancient Astrology*, 91–100.

[334] NOTES TO PAGES 178–180

136. Curta, *Making of the Slavs*, 44; Ivan Dujčev, "Le Témoignage du Pseudo-Césaire sur les Slaves," *Slavia Antiqua* 4 (1953): 193–209; trans. Bacic, *The Emergence of the Sklabenoi*, 152.

137. Pseudo-Kaisarios, *Erotapokraseis* 985.2 [lines 104–5].

138. Susan A. Harvey, "Yuḥanon of Ephesus. John of Asia (ca. 507–589). [Syr. Orth.]," in Sebastian P. Brock et al., eds., *Gorgias Encyclopedic Dictionary of the Syriac Heritage* (Piscataway, NJ: 2011), 445.

139. Jan Jacob van Ginkel, *John of Ephesus: A Monophysite Historian in Sixth-Century Byzantium* (PhD diss., University of Groningen, 1995), 27–44, for summary of his life and career.

140. Monophysites (or Miaphysites) differed from Orthodox Chalcedonians in their belief that God had only one nature, not two separate human and divine natures that were distinct yet unified; Gray, "The Legacy of Chalcedon," 215–38.

141. Harvey, "Yuḥanon of Ephesus," 445.

142. Curta, *Making of the Slavs*, 48.

143. Text: Ludwig Dindorf, *Chronicon Paschale* (Bonn: 1832); Karl Krumbacher, *Geschichte der Byzantinischen Litteratur von Justinian bis zum Ende des Oströmischen Reiches*, ed. A. Ehrhard and H. Gelzer, 2nd ed. (Munich: 1897), 337–39; Warren Treadgold, *The Early Byzantine Historians* (Hampshire, UK: 2010), 340–49; *Chronicon Paschale 284–628 AD*, trans. Michael Whitby and Mary Whitby (Liverpool: 1989), ix–xxix.

144. Treadgold, *Early Byzantine Historians*, 342.

145. Treadgold, *Early Byzantine Historians*, 341–42.

146. Dindorf, *Chronicon Paschale*, 62–64, for the climates; Honigmann, *Sieben Klimata*, 61–71 and 81–92 for text and discussion.

147. Krumbacher, *Geschichte der Byzantinischen Litteratur*, 337–339; Honigmann, *Sieben Klimata*, 61–71 and 81–92, discusses the text and sources within the Christian tradition at length. The origin of *klimata* theory is a different matter: He believes that Eratosthenes introduced the system of seven *klimata* (10–24); see the reservations of Shcheglov, "Ptolemy's System of Seven Climata," 31–37; Dicks, "The ΚΛΙΜΑΤΑ," 248–55, argues for Hipparchus.

148. Florian Mittenhuber, "The Tradition of Texts and Maps in Ptolemy's *Geography*," in *Ptolemy in Perspective: Use and Criticism of His Work from Antiquity to the Nineteenth Century*, ed. Alexander Jones, *Archimedes* 23 (Heidelberg: 2010), 95–120, at 98–99 for *poleis episemoi*.

149. Alexander Kazhdan, "Klima," in Kazhdan, ed., *ODB*, vol. 2 (New York: 1991), 1133; for a survey of the continuity of the theory of *klimata* in the Muslim world, see A. Miquel, "Iḳlīm," in Peri Bearman et al., *Encyclopaedia of Islam*, 2nd ed. (Leiden: 2012), http://dx.doi.org/10.1163/1573-3912_islam_SIM_3519. The Persian word *'iqlīm* derives from the Greek *klima* and was used by al-Masudi in the tenth century to refer to the regions of seven great kingdoms of the world, at the center of which was Iran; in the Iranian tradition, another Persian theory divides the earth into seven concentric "climes" called *kešvars*. The Iranian concept of seven climes was combined with the Greek theory of seven in Islamic geographical and cosmographical works. See also Aḥmad Tafażżolī, "Clime," in *Encyclopaedia Iranica. Volume V, Fasc. 7* (New York: Columbia University Press, 1982), 713.

150. Maurice, *Das Strategikon des Maurikios*, ed. George T. Dennis, trans. Ernst Gamillscheg (Vienna: 1981); trans. George T. Dennis, *Maurice's Strategikon: Handbook of Byzantine Military Strategy* (Philadelphia: 1984); Philip Rance, "Maurice's *Strategicon* and 'the Ancients': The Late Antique Reception of Aelian and Arrian," in Philip Rance and Nicholas V. Sekunda, eds., *Greek Taktika: Ancient Military Writing and Its Heritage: Proceedings of the International Conference on Greek Taktika Held at the University of Toruń, 7–11 April 2005* (Gdansk: 2017), 217–55, at 217–22 on style, language, sources, and attribution to Maurice.

151. Rance, "Maurice's Strategicon and the Ancients," 219–20; *The Ethnika in Byzantine Military Treatises* (PhD diss., University of Minnesota, 1977), 15–49, argues for Maurice's general Philippicus (ca. 580–ca. 610) as the author of the treatise.

152. Maurice, *Strategikon*, "Praefatio" [68].

153. Maurice, *Strategikon*, "Praefatio" [68–69].

NOTES TO PAGES 180–188   [335]

154. Maurice, *Strategikon* 11.

155. Maurice, *Strategikon* 11.2; Giuseppe A. Ricci, *Nomads in Late Antiquity: Gazing on Rome from the Steppe; Attila to Asparuch (370–680 C.E.)* (PhD diss., Princeton University, 2015), 233.

156. Ricci, *Nomads in Late Antiquity*, 234; see also 233–41 on Maurice, *Strategikon* 11.2.

157. Maurice, *Strategikon* 11.1.

158. Maurice, *Strategikon* 11.2.

159. Maurice, *Strategikon* 11.4.

160. Glacken, *Traces*, 171–287.

161. Brian Croke, "Cassiodorus," in Oliver Nicholson, ed., *Oxford Dictionary of Late Antiquity*, 299–300, at 300; James J. O'Donnell, *Cassiodorus* (Berkeley: 1979), 177–222.

162. Cassiodorus, *Variae* 12.15.1; For Latin text, see Cassiodorus, *Variarum Libri XII*, ed. Å. J. Fridh (Turnhout: 1973).

163. Cassiodorus, *Variae* 1215.3.

164. Cassiodorus, *Institutions of Divine and Secular Learning* 2 and conclusion 2, trans. James W. Halporn, TTH 42 (Liverpool: 2004), 229–30; for Latin text, see Cassiodorus, *Institutiones Divinarum et Saecularium Litterarum* 2.7 and conclusion 2.15–18, ed. R.A.B. Mynors (Oxford: 1937).

165. Peter Brown, *The Rise of Western Christendom: Triumph and Diversity, A.D. 200–1000*, rev. ed. (Chichester: 2013), 364–68; J. Fontaine, "Isidore of Seville," in Angelo Di Berardino, ed., *Encyclopedia of the Early Church. Volume I*, trans. Adrian Walford (Cambridge: 1992), 418–19, at 418; see also articles in Andrew Fear and Jamie Wood, eds., *A Companion to Isidore of Seville* (Leiden: 2020)

166. For a survey of his works, see Humphry Ward, "Isidorus (18)," in Henry Wace and William C. Piercy, eds., *A Dictionary of Christian Biography and Literature* (London: 1911), 541–45; Andrew Fear and Jamie Wood, eds., *A Companion to Isidore of Seville* (Leiden: 2020), for discussion and bibliography.

167. Isidore of Seville, *Etymologies*, ed. and trans. Stephen A. Barney et al. (Cambridge: 2006), 11. See also Fontaine, "Isidore of Seville," 418; and Ward, "Isidorus," 542; Brown, *Rise of Western Christendom*, 364–68, on the widespread "encyclopedic tendency."

168. Brown, *The Rise of Western Christendom*, 365.

169. Isidore, *Etymologies* 9.2.105.

Chapter Six: Christianity and the Descendants of Noah

1. Ambrose of Milan, *De fide [ad Gratianum]*, ed. and trans. by Christoph Markschies (Turnhout: Brepols, 2003.)

2. The Apostle Paul had confronted the problem of different interpretations of Jesus's teachings; see 1 Cor. 11:19. For recent discussion and citation of other texts: Todd S. Berzon, *Classifying Christians: Ethnography, Heresiology, and the Limits of Knowledge in Late Antiquity* (Berkeley: 2016), 12.

3. Tristan Gary Major, *Literary Developments of the Table of Nations and the Tower of Babel in Anglo-Saxon England* (PhD diss., University of Toronto, 2010), 118.

4. Elias J. Bickerman, "Origines Gentium," *Classical Philology* 47, no. 2 (Apr. 1952): 65–81, is foundational; helpful recent discussions: Fergus Millar, "Hagar, Ishmael, Josephus and the Origins of Islam," *Journal of Jewish Studies* 44, no. 1 (Spring 1993): 23–45, esp. 24–25; Walter Pohl, "Narratives of Origin and Migration in Early Medieval Europe: Problems of Interpretation," *The Medieval History Journal* 21, no. 2 (Oct. 2018): 192–221.

5. Millar, "Hagar, Ishmael, Josephus," 25.

6. Augustine, *The City of God* 15.11, ed. and trans. Philip Levine, LCL 414 (Cambridge, MA: 1966), on the problem of Methusaleh's living beyond the Flood.

7. Walter Goffart, "The Supposedly 'Frankish' Table of Nations: An Edition and Study," *Frühmittelalterliche Studien* 17, no. 1 (1983): 98–130; Helmut Reimitz, *History, Frankish Identity and the Framing of Western Ethnicity, 550–850* (Cambridge: 2015), 82–83, 118, 216–17.

8. See chap. 7 for discussion of angels.

[336]   NOTES TO PAGES 189–192

9. Scholars debate the circumstances and purpose of the first redaction of Genesis. Joseph Blenkinsopp, *The Pentateuch: An Introduction to the Five Books of the Bible* (New Haven: 1992), reviews scholarship.

10. See Theodore Hiebert, "The Tower of Babel and the Origin of the World's Cultures," *Journal of Biblical Literature* 126, no. 1 (2007): 29–58 for an introduction to conflicting interpretations. For further differences, compare Gen. 4:17–26 and Gen. 5:1–32, which both try to explain the same progression of generations but are written by different authors. The two accounts of creation found in Genesis are well known.

11. James M. Scott, *Geography in Early Judaism and Christianity: The Book of Jubilees* (Cambridge: 2002); Philip S. Alexander, "Notes on the *'Imago Mundi'* of the Book of Jubilees," *Journal of Jewish Studies* 33 (1982), 197–213, arguing that the author of Jubilees "interpreted the Bible in the light of the non-Jewish 'scientific' knowledge of his day" (210); Young Richard Kim, *Epiphanius of Cyprus: Imagining an Orthodox World* (Ann Arbor: 2015), 46–48.

12. Alexander, "Notes on the *'Imago Mundi*,'" 213; Jub. 8:11–30 seem to describe a map: Francis Schmidt, "Jewish Representations of the Inhabited Earth during the Hellenistic and Roman Periods," in A. Kasher, U. Rappaport, and G. Fuks, eds., *Greece and Rome in Eretz Israel: Collected Essays* (Jerusalem: 1990), 119–134, at 128.

13. Sabrina Inowlocki, "Josephus' Rewriting of the Babel Narrative (Gen 11:1–9)," *Journal for the Study of Judaism in the Persian, Hellenistic, and Roman Period* 37, no. 2 (2006): 169–91. Considering *Jewish Antiquities* 1.120–21, Inowlocki argues that Josephus criticizes Greek imperialism for "imposing Greek names on conquered peoples" (187).

14. Major, "Literary Developments of the Table of Nations," 118; see also 119: "Especially after Josephus had strengthened the bond between the tripartite division of the world with the three sons of Noah by syncretizing the names in the Table of Nations with contemporary ethnic groups, the Christians of Late Antiquity and the Middle Ages were unable to view the world in any other manner: Sem's descendants inhabited Asia, Japheth's Europe, and Ham's Africa." See 119 n. 13 for references.

15. Schmidt, "Jewish Representations," 119–34.

16. Arno Borst, *Der Turmbau von Babel: Geschichte der Meinungen über Ursprung und Vielfalt der Sprachen und Völker; Band I. Fundamente und Aufbau* (Stuttgart: 1957), 218–27, on early Christianity.

17. Hervé Inglebert, *Interpretatio Christiana: Les mutations des savoirs (cosmographie, géographie, ethnographie, histoire) dans l'Antiquité chrétienne (30–630 après J.-C.)* (Paris: 2001), 189–92.

18. See below on Hippolytus, Eusebius, Jerome, etc.

19. For a revisionist introduction, see Richard W. Burgess and Michael Kulikowski, *Mosaics of Time: The Latin Chronicle Traditions from the First Century BC to the Sixth Century AD*, vol.1: *A Historical Introduction to the Chronicle Genre from Its Origins to the High Middle Ages* (Turnhout: 2013). The history and historiographical review in their first chapter, 1–62, is the best starting point. See also Brian Croke, *Count Marcellinus and His Chronicle* (Oxford: 2001), 1–13.

20. Burgess and Kulikowski, *Mosaics*, 63–131.

21. For general introduction, Alden A. Mosshammer, *The Chronicle of Eusebius and the Greek Chronographic Tradition* (Lewisburg: 1979); Burgess and Kulikowski, *Mosaics*, 99–132.

22. Croke, *Count Marcellinus*, 3.

23. Most of his writings in Greek no longer survive because of his heretical Christology and because knowledge of Greek was rapidly declining in the West. Much of his work survives in the East in Syriac, Coptic, Arabic, Ethiopic, Armenian, Georgian, and Slavonic, an indication of widespread interest in his considerable output: Johannes Quasten, "Hippolytus of Rome" in *Patrology*, vol. 2, *The Ante-Nicene Literature after Irenaeus* (Utrecht: 1953), 163–207, at 176–77, on the *Chronicle*.

24. Burgess and Kulikowski, *Mosaics*, 118; Inglebert, *Interpretatio*, 125–59.

25. Burgess and Kulikowski, *Mosaics*, 117–19; "antipope," though now in standard usage, is an anachronism, because the papacy as we now understand it did not emerge until the sixth century.

NOTES TO PAGES 192–194 [337]

26. The Greek title: Συναγωγὴ χρόνων καὶ ἐτῶν ἀπὸ κτίσεως κόσμου ἕως τῆς ἐνεστώσης ἡμέρας; Burgess and Kulikowski, *Mosaics*, 117: The first words in manuscripts B (Berlin, Staatsbibliothek, MS Phillipps 1829) and F (Paris, BN, MS lat. 10910), from Matt. 1:1.

27. Burgess and Kulikowski, *Mosaics*, 117 n. 74, for references to edition.

28. Umberto Roberto, "Liber generationis mundi," in Graeme Dunphy and Cristian Bratu, eds., *Encyclopedia of the Medieval Chronicle*, http://dx.doi.org/10.1163/2213-2139 _emc_SIM_01691. The *Liber generationis II*, the better of the Latin translations according to Roberto, is preserved in the *Chronograph* of 354; for edition, see "Chronographvs Anni CCCLIIII," in Theodor Mommsen, ed., MGHAA IX. *Chronicorum Minorum Saec. IV. V. VI. VII. Vol. I* (Berlin: 1892), 13–196.

29. See Burgess and Kulikowski, *Mosaics*, 117–18; Helmut Reimitz, *History, Frankish Identity and the Framing of Western Ethnicity, 550–850* (Cambridge: 2015), 81–83.

30. Steven Muhlberger, *The Fifth-century Chroniclers: Prosper, Hydatius, and the Gallic Chronicler of 452* (Leeds: 1990), 14.

31. Inglebert, *Interpretatio*, 126; Justin Taylor, "The List of the Nations in Acts 2:9–11," *Revue Biblique* 106, no. 3 (Jul. 1999): 408–20, at 419: "Luke used a list of the central and western lands of the Persian Empire, which was ultimately derived from the Behistun inscription, to represent 'every nation under heaven.'"

32. Inglebert, *Interpretatio*, 159–65, 177; R. W. Burgess, "The Date, Purpose, and Historical Context of the Original Greek and the Latin Translation of the So-called *Excerpta Latina Barbari*," *Traditio* 68 (2013): 1–56, at 9–11 on the *Diamérismos*; for a standard, authoritative view of Hippolytus's *Chronicle*: Quasten, "Hippolytus of Rome," 176–77.

33. Inglebert, *Interpretatio*, 127, 129–33.

34. Inglebert, *Interpretatio*, 156.

35. Inglebert, *Interpretatio*, 127, 141.

36. Inglebert, *Interpretatio*, 149; he mentions Cappadocians, Pannonians, Dalmatians, and Noricans (see chart on 150; this does not deal with how Roman provincial names reflected the names of various peoples who lived in each province).

37. Inglebert, *Interpretatio*, 156.

38. Inglebert, *Interpretatio*, 161, for discussion of its complex textual history.

39. Inglebert, *Interpretatio*, 162.

40. Inglebert *Interpretatio*, 161, and Hervé Inglebert, *Les romains chrétiens face à l'histoire de Rome: Histoire, Christianisme et romanités en Occident dans l'antiquité tardive (IIIe-Ve siècles)* (Paris: 1996), 603–4.

41. Inglebert, *Interpretatio*, 162: In the *Origo*, as in the *Diamérismos*, the descendants of Ham possess Africa from Egypt to the Ocean, the descendants of Japheth stretch from Media to Cadiz, and the descendants of Shem from Persia to India. Inglebert, *Interpretatio*, 160, Table 18, lists the various descendants of Noah in different manuscripts of the *Origo generis* and the *Liber genealogus*. He lists the manuscripts under the rubrics Shem, Ham, and Japheth and indicates their identification of biblical names with contemporary peoples.

42. Inglebert, *Les romains*, 603–4; discussed in detail by Richard Rouse and Charles McNelis, "North African Literary Activity: A Cyprian Fragment, the Stichometric Lists and a Donatist Compendium," *Revue d'histoire des textes* 30 (2001): 189–238, at 212.

43. Inglebert, *Interpretatio*, 160; Rouse and McNelis, "North African Literary Activity," 219–24.

44. Rouse and McNelis, "North African Literary Activity," 212, 224.

45. *Cod. Th.* 16.5.37–38; Richard W. Burgess, "*Liber genealogus*," in Dunphy and Bratu, eds., *Encyclopedia of the Medieval Chronicle*, http://dx.doi.org. /10.1163/2213-2139_emc_ SIM_01690; Inglebert, *Les romains*, 601.

46. Richard Burgess, "*Liber genealogus*," in Dunphy and Bratu, *Encyclopedia of the Medieval Chronicle*, for the quite complicated manuscript tradition; Rouse and McNelis, "North African Literary Activity," 189–238; Inglebert, *Les romains*, 599–604.

47. Inglebert, *Interpretatio*, 160.

48. Burgess and Kulikowski, *Mosaics*, 119–26, is basic; Richard W. Burgess and Shaun Tougher, "Eusebius of Caesarea," in Dunphy and Bratu, eds., *Encyclopedia of the Medieval Chronicle*, http://dx.doi.org/10.1163/2213-2139_emc_SIM_00970.

[338] NOTES TO PAGES 194–196

49. Nearly all of the original Greek text is lost, except for a few fragments; Eusebius, *Die Chronik des Eusebius*, ed. and trans. Josef Karst, *Die Chronik: Aus dem armenischen Übersetzt mit textkritischem Commentar* (Leipzig: 1911); for English translation, see Eusebius, "Eusebius' Chronicle," trans. Robert Bedrosian, Archive.org, https://ia800702.us .archive.org/26/items/EusebiusChroniclechronicon/Eusebius_Chronicle.pdf; and Kevin P. Edgecomb, "Eusebius of Caesarea, The Gospel Canon Tables," Tertullian.org, https://www .tertullian.org/fathers/eusebius_canon_tables_01.htm; Muhlberger, *The Fifth-century Chroniclers*, 15–19.

50. Burgess and Kulikowski, *Mosaics*, 119–21.

51. At first there were three columns, for Hebrews, Assyrians, and Egyptians. The number increased to accommodate Persians, Greeks, and Romans. Burgess and Kulikowski, *Mosaics*, 119–26; Brian Croke, "Origins of the Christian World Chronicle," in Brian Croke and Alanna M. Emmett, eds., *History and Historians in Late Antiquity* (Sydney: 1983), 116–31, at 123–25.

52. Burgess and Kulikowski, *Mosaics*, 126–31; Croke, "Origins," 123–25.

53. Eusebius, *Die Chronik*, 38–43.

54. Eusebius, *Die Chronik*, 125–43, 154–55; Romans appear in the Canon tables, 197–227.

55. Croke, "Origins," 125.

56. Noted by Edward Mathews, "Jerome's Hebrew Questions on Genesis," review of Robert Hayward, *Saint Jerome's Hebrew Questions on Genesis* (1995), BMCR (1996.02.12); Muhlberger, *The Fifth-Century Chroniclers*: he gives Jerome's *Chronicle* and its continuation in Latin by Eusebius in his *Canons* as models for these chronicles: "as a complete but relatively brief summary of world and Christian history, [Jerome's translation of Eusebius's *Canons*] had no Latin rival, and thus it was quickly adopted and long treasured by western readers. It was an attractive basis for the Christian writer who wished to link an annalistic account of his own times to the important secular and religious events of the past" (9).

57. For current overview of his translation of the *Canons*: Burgess and Kulikowski, *Mosaics*, 126–31.

58. Mosshammer, *Chronicle of Eusebius*, 37. For further discussion, see Rudolf Helm, *Hieronymus' Zusätze in Eusebius' Chronik und ihr Wert für die Literaturgeschichte* (Leipzig: 1929).

59. Mosshammer, *Chronicle of Eusebius*, 37; possibly Jerome stopped coverage in 378 to highlight the Battle of Adrianople and the death of the emperor Valens in that year at the hands of the Goths: Jerome, *Hebrew Questions on Genesis*, trans. C. T. R. Hayward (Oxford: 1995), 139–40.

60. Jerome, *Hebrew Questions on Genesis*. This is a translation of the edition of Dominic Vallarsi, *S. Eusebii Hieronymi Stridonensis Presbyteri Liber Hebraicorum Quaestionum in Genesim*, in PL 22.1 (1883), cols. 983–1062. Jerome, *Hebrew Questions* 27 points to problems in the more recent edition of Hieronymus, "Hebraicae quaestiones in libro Geneseos," in Paul de Lagarde, G. Morin, and M. Adriaen, eds, *Hebraicae quaestiones in libro Geneseos: Liber interpretationis hebraicorum nominum; Commentarioli in psalmos. Commentarius in Ecclesiasten*, CCSL 72 (Turnhout: 1959), itself a reprint of Hieronymus, *Quaestiones Hebraicae in Libro Geneseos*, ed. Paul de Lagarde (Leipzig: 1868).

61. Jerome, *Hebrew Questions*, 23.

62. Aline Canellis, "Introduction," in Aline Canellis, ed., *Jerome: Préfaces aux Livres de la Bible*, rev. ed. (Paris: 2017), 53–355, for detailed discussion of the historical context in which Jerome created the Vulgate.

63. Terrence G. Kardong, "Vulgate," in Everett Ferguson, ed., *Encyclopedia of Early Christianity*, 2nd ed. (New York: 1998), 1167–69.

64. For his sources, see Jerome, *Hebrew Questions*, 15–23.

65. Jerome, *Hebrew Questions*, 23–27.

66. On influence of Targumim: Jerome, *Hebrew Questions*, 22.

67. Jerome, *Hebrew Questions*, commentary on Gen. 9:27, p. 38; for consistency, I have changed his Sem to Shem.

68. For Japheth as a type of the church, see Jerome, *Hebrew Questions*, 137, citing for example, Justin, *Dial.* 139.2–3; Irenaeus, *Demonstratio* 21, *Adv. Haer.* 3–5.3, 5.34.2.

NOTES TO PAGES 196–199 [339]

69. He drew extensively from Josephus, but omits some information: Jerome, *Hebrew Questions*, 141, e.g., on verse 3, drawing from Josephus, *Jewish Antiquities* 1.126, ed. and trans. H. St. J. Thackeray, LCL 242 (Cambridge, MA: 1930).

70. Jerome, *Hebrew Questions*, commentary on Gen. 10:2, p. 39; see discussion of Gog/Magog, below; Jerome continues: "I know that a certain man [Ambrose] has referred to Gog and Magog, both as regards the present verse and in Ezekiel, to the account of the Goths who were recently raging in our land: whether this is true is shown by the outcome of the actual battle [recorded in Ezekiel 38–9]. But in fact all learned men in the past had certainly been accustomed to calling the Goths Getae rather than Gog and Magog. So these seven nations, which I have related as coming from the stock of Japheth live in the region of the North." Hayward, *Saint Jerome's Hebrew Questions on Genesis*, 140–41: "Jerome's comment seems to have in mind the battle of Adrianople (378), whose definitive character may be marked by the fact that it is the last event which he records in his translation of Eusebius' *Chronicon*. He was, however, familiar with the Jewish identification of Magog with the Goths, attested in the Jerusalem Talmud: in the *In Esa.* 10.30:27–9 and *In Hiez.* II.38: 1–23 he notes that they think Gog and Magog come from Scythia, the very region which he and Josephus identify with Magog in this verse!"

71. Jerome, *Hebrew Questions*, commentary on 10:24–25, p. 42.

72. Augustine, *City of God* 16, ed. and trans. Eva M. Sanford, LCL 415 (Cambridge, MA: 1965).

73. Augustine, *City of God* 15.17: Adam as progenitor of both the earthly and heavenly cities.

74. Augustine, *City of God* 16.3.

75. Augustine, *City of God* 16.3. On the curse of Ham's son Canaan: David M. Goldenberg, *The Curse of Ham: Race and Slavery in Early Judaism, Christianity, and Islam* (Princeton: 2005), 157–77; Augustine uses both *nationes* and *gentes* to refer to the peoples who descended from Noah's sons.

76. Augustine, *City of God* 16.3 and 15.8, on the growth of numbers of Hebrews.

77. For recent discussions, see Sabne Panzram and Paulo Pachá, eds., *The Visigothic Kingdom: The Negotiation of Power in Post-Roman Iberia* (Amsterdam: 2020).

78. For an introduction to Isidore's life, works, and times: Isidore of Seville, *The Etymologies* 3–28, ed. and trans. Stephen A. Barney et al. (Cambridge: 2006).

79. Isidore, *Etymologies* 24–26.

80. M. L. W. Laistner, *Thought and Letters in Western Europe: A.D. 500 to 900* (London: 1957), 124, cited in Christopher Heath, "Hispania et Italia: Paul the Deacon, Isidore, and the Lombards," in Andrew Fear and Jamie Wood, eds., *Isidore of Seville and His Reception in the Early Middle Ages: Transmitting and Transforming Knowledge* (Amsterdam: 2016), 159–76, at 160: "The *Etymologiae* far surpassed (in demand) any other of his [Isidore's] books in popularity; for this encyclopaedia was a *sine-qua-non* in every monastic library of any pretensions. Its use by a long list of writers from the seventh to the tenth century is easily demonstrable, it appears constantly in medieval library catalogues, and the number of extant manuscripts is exceedingly great."

81. Isidore, *Etymologies* 9.

82. He often drew from Jerome's *Hebrew Questions on Genesis*: Isidore, *Etymologies*, 192 n. 5.

83. Isidore, *Etymologies* 9.2.1; the translators have added the verbal forms of *gignere* and *nasci*. Isidore writes: "Gens autem appellata propter generationes familiarum, id est a gignendo, sicut natio a nascendo."

84. Isidore, *Etymologies* 9.2.2; On the division of languages at Babel, see Valentina Izmirlieva, *All the Names of the Lord: Lists, Mysticism, and Magic* (Chicago: 2008), 84–92.

85. Isidore, *Etymologies* 9.2.38: "Indeed, the names for many nations have partially remained, so that their derivation is apparent today, like the Assyrians from Assur and the Hebrews from Heber (i.e. Eber). But partly, through the passage of time, they have been so altered that the most learned people, poring over the oldest historical works, have not been able to find the origin of all nations from among these forebears, but only of some, and these with difficulty."

[340] NOTES TO PAGES 199–201

86. Isidore, *Etymologies* 9.2.40.

87. Isidore, *Etymologies* 9.2.66, mentions Huns, Avars, Massagetes: "Then, with their nimble horses, they burst forth from the crags of the Caucasus, where Alexander's Gates had been keeping the fierce nations back. They held the East captive for twenty years, and exacted an annual tribute from the Egyptians and the Ethiopians."

88. Isidore, *Etymologies* 9.2.89.

89. Isidore, *Etymologies* 9.2.84.

90. Isidore, *Etymologies* 9.2.36, does not equate the Romans with the Dodanim/Rodanim, or Rhodians, as descendants of Japheth.

91. John Malalas, *Chronographia* 7.1–7, ed. Johann Thurn, CFHB Series Berolinensis 35 (Berlin: 2000); Dominique Briquel, *Romulus vu de Constantinople: La réécriture de la légende dans le monde byzantin; Jean Malalas et ses successeurs* (Paris: 2018), 29–38 text and translation, and 101–77 for discussion.

92. Briquel, *Romulus*, 190.

93. Isidore, *Etymologies* 9.2.57.

94. Isidore, *Etymologies* 9.2.6.

95. Isidore, *Etymologies* 9.2.57.

96. Isidore, *Etymologies* 9.2.82.

97. Isidore, *Etymologies* 7.6.16 and 7.6.18.

98. Herodotus, *The Persian Wars* 2.16, ed. and trans. A. D. Godley, LCL 117 (Cambridge, MA: 1920), criticizes the Ionians for their tripartite division, suggesting that they have left out a fourth part, the Egyptian delta. Romans generally accepted the three continents: e.g., Pomponius Mela, *Description of the World* (ca. 43–44 CE), trans. F. E. Romer (Ann Arbor: 1998), 1.8 and passim; Pomponius Mela, *Kreuzfahrt durch die Alte Welt: Zweisprachige Ausgabe*, trans. Kai Brodersen (Darmstadt: 1994). For overviews of Greek and Roman cartography to Ptolemy: J. B. Harley and David Woodward, eds., *The History of Cartography. I: Cartography in Prehistoric, Ancient, and Medieval Europe and the Mediterranean* (Chicago: 1987), 130–76; Daniela Dueck, *Geography in Classical Antiquity* (Cambridge: 2012), 99–110; in a much broader context, see Martin W. Lewis and Kären E. Wigen, *The Myth of Continents: A Critique of Metageography* (Berkeley: 1997).

99. Philip S. Alexander, "Notes on the 'Imago Mundi" of the Book of Jubilees, *Journal of Jewish Studies* 33 (1982): 197–213. Jubilees is not canonical in the Jewish tradition; it is one of the pseudoepigrapha in the Greek Orthodox, Catholic, and later Protestant churches. In Late Antiquity, many Christian writers knew Jubilees well.

100. Among them were Epiphanius of Salamis, Origen, Isidore of Seville, Eutychius of Alexandria, and John Malalas.

101. Zonal maps continued to be used in Late Antiquity. They are known as Macrobian maps because they derived from Macrobius's commentary on Cicero's *Dream of Scipio* (Macrobius, *Commentarii in Somnium Scipionis*, ed. James Willis [Leipzig: 1963]), written in the fifth century, itself with a long pedigree. In the hands of Christian writers, such maps enjoyed long currency. See David Woodward, "Medieval *Mappaemundi*," in Harley and Woodward, eds., *History of Cartography*, 1:286–370, at 299–302.

102. Sometime before the eighth century the Sea of Azov was added to the map. Woodward, "Medieval *Mappaemundi*," 299–302, discusses Macrobius to Isidore; for a later period with helpful bibliography, see Marcia Kupfer, "The Noachide Dispersion in English Mappae Mundi c. 960–c. 1130, *Peregrinations: Journal of Medieval Art and Architecture* 4, no. 1 (2013): 81–106.

103. For a database of the pre-1000 manuscripts of Isidore's *Etymologiae*, see Evina Steinova, "etymologiae.ms: a database of the pre-1000 manuscripts of the Etymologiae of Isidore of Seville," Academia.edu, https://www.academia.edu/video/gjE5Wj?email_video _card=title&pls=RVP.

104. For discussion of the complicated history of the *Excerpta Latina barbari*, known also as the *Barbarus Scaligeri*, see R. W. Burgess, "The Date, Purpose, and Historical Context of the Original Greek and the Latin Translation of the So-called *Excerpta Latina Barbari*," *Traditio* 68 (2013), 1–56. Burgess argues for a historical compendium assembled in Alexandria

NOTES TO PAGES 201–202 [341]

between 476 and 527, to which was added a Greek translation of Latin consular lists, followed by a translation into Latin in a Frankish monastery at the middle of the eighth century. On 41–42, he rejects the arguments of Benjamin Garstad in various works, cited at 41 n. 94; on later witnesses in Greek, Latin, and Armenian, see Burgess and Kulikowski, *Mosaics*, 117; Benjamin Garstad develops his argument in "Apocalypse" of Pseudo-Methodius, *An Alexandrian World Chronicle* (Cambridge, MA: 2012), xxviii–xxx; Benjamin Garstad, "Barbarian Interest in the *Excerpta Latina Barbari*," *Early Medieval Europe* 19 (2021): 3–42. Helmut Reimitz, "Pax inter utramque Gentem: The Merovingians, Byzantium and the History of Frankish Identity," in Stefan Esders, Yaniv Fox, Yitzhak Hen, and Laury Sarti, eds., *East and West in the Early Middle Ages: The Merovingian Kingdoms in Mediterranean Perspective* (Cambridge: 2019), 45–63, at 58 n. 60, argues that "Given the integration of the Franks into early Roman history and the chronicle's stress on the empire's role as defender of orthodox Christianity, the chronicle seems more likely to be contemporary with Agathias' *Histories*," and he counters Garstad: "It is thus more likely that the historiographical exchange between Byzantium and the Merovingian kingdoms took place in the context of the intensified diplomatic contacts between Byzantium and the Merovingian kingdoms in the last decades of the sixth century": Helmut Reimitz, *History, Frankish Identity and the Framing of Western Ethnicity, 550–850* (Cambridge: 2015), 82.

105. *Alexandrian World Chronicle*, 147; chap. 1, 142–48; the division of the lands among Shem, Ham, and Japheth, chap. 2, 148–67.

106. *Alexandrian World Chronicle* 2.2.

107. *Alexandrian World Chronicle* 2.6. Reimitz, *History, Frankish Identity*, 81–82 = Burgess, "The Date, Purpose, and Historical Context," 33–38.

108. Goffart, "The Supposedly 'Frankish' Table of Nations," 98–130.

109. On the history of the *Germania*: J. B. Rives, *Tacitus Germania* (Oxford: 1999), 66–74; Christopher B. Krebs, *A Most Dangerous Book: Tacitus's "Germania" from the Roman Empire to the Third Reich* (New York: 2011); Cassiodorus knew of it: Goffart, "The Supposedly 'Frankish' Table of Nations," 118.

110. Reimitz, *History, Frankish Identity*, 81–83; Goffart, "The Supposedly 'Frankish' Table of Nations," 98–130; for Latin text, see "Appendix VI. Excerpta Latina Barbari Post Scaliagerum. E Libro Parisino Denuo Edita," in Alfred Schoene, ed., *Eusebi Chronicorum Liber Prior* (Berlin: 1875), 174–239. For translation, see *Alexandrian World Chronicle*, 141–395.

111. Reimitz, *History, Frankish Identity*, 83.

112. Goffart, "The Supposedly 'Frankish' Table of Nations," 119.

113. Reimitz, *History, Frankish Identity*, 83.

114. Goffart, "The Supposedly 'Frankish' Table of Nations," 110, manuscript h: "Primus homo uenit ad Europam de genere Iafeth: Alanus." For background, see 98: "Seven manuscripts, as well as the ninth-century Historia Brittonum, contain a brief genealogy of peoples that, in essentials, proceeds from Tacitus's threefold division of the Germans into Ingaevones, Herminones, and Istaevones. Although some of the names are Tacitean, the *gentes* mentioned belong to the neighborhood of the sixth century; they include Goths and Vandals, Thuringians and Lombards, Bretons and Franks. This document has, in modern times, customarily been called the 'Frankish Table of Nations' ('fränkische Völkertafel'). Each of the eight versions varies in some respects from the others and is found in different contexts." He shows, at 107–9, that some of its material is also derived from Isidore's *Etymologies*: "The wider framework of this genealogy is that of the biblical/Hippolytan table of nations beginning with Noah" (109).

115. Stefan Esders and Helmut Reimitz, "Legalizing Ethnicity: The Remaking of Citizenship in Post-Roman Gaul (Sixth–Seventh Centuries)," in Cédric Brélaz and Els Rose, eds., *Civic Identity and Civic Participation in Late Antiquity and the Early Middle Age* (Turnhout: 2021), 295–329. I thank Professors Esders and Reimitz for sharing this article with me prior to its publication; Burgess and Kulikowski, *Mosaics*, 377–78, for the varied material contained in the *Chronicle of Fredegar*.

116. Esders and Reimitz, "Legalizing Ethnicity," 303.

[342] NOTES TO PAGES 203–205

117. Burgess and Kulikowski, *Mosaics*, 240–43; Reimitz, *History, Frankish Identity*, 217–22 on the *Chronicle of Fredegar* in relation to Eusebius/Jerome.

118. Daniel A. Machiela, "Some Jewish Noah Traditions in Syriac Christian Sources," in Michael E. Stone, Aryeh Amihay, and Vered Hillel, *Noah and His Book(s)* (Atlanta: 2010), 237–52, at 245: "It is among Syriac exegetes, however, that the tradition of Noah's division of the earth seems to gain the strongest foothold, reflecting a vibrant interest in material associated with the Table of Nations." Burgess and Tougher, "Eusebius of Caesarea": "In Syriac, translations of Eusebius likewise inspired an explosion of chronicle writing that continued even into later Arabic traditions, including such works as those of Jacob of Edessa, Pseudo-Dionysius and Michael the Syrian." For various other fourth- to sixth-century continuators that no longer survive, see Burgess and Tougher, "Eusebius of Caesarea."

119. A. G. Salvesen, "Ya'qub of Edessa," in *Gorgias Encyclopedic Dictionary of the Syriac Language* (Piscataway, NJ: 2011), 432–33.

120. Machiela, "Some Jewish Noah Traditions," 246–47.

121. Machiela, "Some Jewish Noah Traditions," 247. Gen. 22:20–24 lists the children of Abraham's brother Nahor. The identification with Syria was made by exegetes in the Syriac tradition.

122. Isidore, *Etymologies* 9.2.3, says Syrians descended from Aram, descendant of Shem; Yonatan Moss, "The Language of Paradise: Hebrew or Syriac? Linguistic Speculations and Linguistic Realities in Late Antiquity," in Markus Bockmuehl and Guy G. Stroumsa, eds., *Paradise in Antiquity: Jewish and Christian Views* (Cambridge: 2010), 120–37; Machiela, "Some Jewish Noah Traditions," 251–52.

123. Lucas Van Rompay, "Isho'dad of Merv," in *Gorgias Encyclopedic Dictionary of the Syriac Heritage*, 216–17; Isho'dad, *Commentaire d'Išo'dad de Merv sur l'Ancien Testament. I. Genèse*, ed. J.-M. Vosté, trans. Ceslas Van den Eynde, Corpus Scriptorum Christianorum Orientalium Scriptores Syri 67 (Louvain: 1955).

124. Van Rompay, "Isho'dad of Merv," 216–17.

125. Isho'dad, *Commentaire*, commentary on Gen. 9:27, 130; translation, 140.

126. Isho'dad, *Commentaire*, commentary on Gen. 9:25–26, 129; translation, 139.

127. Inglebert, *Interpretatio*, 190.

128. Isho'dad, *Commentaire*, on Gen. 11:1, translation, 146. Isho'dad alludes to many authorities, including Epiphanius.

129. Eynde notes that Isho'dad alludes to Theodoret: *Questions on Genesis* 10 (165A), p. 147.

130. Walter Pohl, "Introduction—Strategies of Identification: A Methodological Profile," in Walter Pohl and Gerda Heydemann, eds., *Strategies of Identification: Ethnicity and Religion in Early Medieval Europe* (Turnhout: 2013), 1–64, at 32–38.

131. Andrew Runni Anderson, *Alexander's Gate, Gog and Magog, and the Inclosed Nations* (Cambridge, MA: 1932), 3–14; Sverre Bøe, *Gog and Magog: Ezekiel 38–39 as Pretext for Revelation 19, 17–21 and 20, 7–10* (Tübingen: 2001); Emeri van Donzel and Andrea Schmidt, *Gog and Magog in Early Eastern Christian and Islamic Sources: Sallam's Quest for Alexander's Wall* (Leiden: 2010).

132. Paul J. Alexander, *The Byzantine Apocalyptic Tradition*, ed. Dorothy de F. Abrahamse (Berkeley: 1985), 184–92; Paul Magdalino, "The History of the Future and Its Uses: Prophecy, Policy and Propaganda (with Postscript)," in Jonathan Shepard, ed., *The Expansion of Orthodox Europe* (Aldershot: 2007), 28–63, at 29–31.

133. Bøe, *Gog and Magog*, 218.

134. Michael Maas, "How the Steppes Became Byzantine: Rome and the Eurasian Nomads in Historical Perspective," in Nicola Di Cosmo and Michael Maas, eds., *Empires and Exchanges in Eurasian Late Antiquity: Rome, China, Iran, and the Steppe, ca. 250–750* (Cambridge: 2018), 19–34, for overview.

135. The name may refer to the kingdom of Gyges in Lydia (716–678 BCE); *The New Interpreter's Study Bible: New Revised Standard Version with the Apocrypha*, ed. Walter J. Harrelson (Nashville: 2003), 23, on Gen. 10:2.

136. Ezekiel 38–39.

NOTES TO PAGES 206–208 [343]

137. *Tanakh, A New Translation of the Holy Scriptures According to the Traditional Hebrew Text*, ed. Jewish Publication Society (Philadelphia: 1985), 959–60.

138. Jubilees is a narrative rendition of Genesis and part of Exodus (as far as chap. 14); see Van Donzel and Schmidt, *Gog and Magog in Early Eastern Christian and Islamic Sources*, 6–7; Alexander, "Notes on the '*Imago Mundi*,'" 213.

139. Bøe, *Gog and Magog*, esp. 235–345.

140. Rev. 20:8.

141. Bøe, *Gog and Magog*, 14–18, summarizes scholarship on identity of Gog and Magog in Rev. 20:8.

142. Josephus, *Jewish Antiquities* 1.6.1, trans. H. St. J. Thackeray; see Anderson, *Alexander's Gate*, 8 n. 2, for other citations of later authors.

143. Josephus, *Jewish Antiquities* 1.6.1; Bøe, *Gog and Magog*, 47–48; Van Donzel and Schmidt, *Gog and Magog*, 9–11.

144. Bøe, *Gog and Magog*, 20, for biblical and intertestamental mentions of Gog and Magog.

145. The eschatological use of Gog and Magog predominated in Jewish writings. The destruction of the Temple in 70 and failure of the Bar Kochba revolt in 136 spurred Jewish writers to reconsider eschatological theories. Ezekiel 38–39 was the most significant text for them. Accordingly, there is frequent mention of Gog and Magog, "the last great eschatological enemies of Israel" (Bøe, *Gog and Magog*, 206) in many different ways in many sources. The Messiah, understood as the figure who will eventually destroy Gog and Magog, was variously construed in the Jewish sources. These were the Targumim (Aramaic translations of the Hebrew Bible), numerous rabbinic sources that are notoriously difficult to date, and apocryphal texts like 3 Enoch, composed probably in the fifth century (Bøe, *Gog and Magog*, 207–8). Ezekiel 38–39 provides the main textual points of departure for the Gog and Magog tradition, while mention in Gen. 10 plays a much less significant role, though Magog's Japhetic descent is always assumed. Rome is sometimes identified with Gog and Magog (as it never was in Christian texts of the post-Constantinian period). For Gog and Magog in the Targumim and related Jewish sources: Bøe, *Gog and Magog*, 189–207.

146. Bøe, *Gog and Magog*, 50–75; Van Donzel and Schmidt, *Gog and Magog*, 6–8.

147. Rev. 20:7–8.

148. Bøe, *Gog and Magog*, 211 and 214–15; for summary, see his excursus 3 on 210–18.

149. Bøe, *Gog and Magog*, 211–13.

150. Bøe, *Gog and Magog*, 214–15, citing Lactantius's *Divine Institutes* 7.26; see also Lactantius, *Divine Institutes*, trans. Anthony Bowen and Peter Garnsey (Liverpool: 2003), 19.

151. Pohl, "Introduction," 32–38.

152. See n. 117 above.

153. Bøe, *Gog and Magog*, 218.

154. Bøe, *Gog and Magog*, 216–18, on the combination of Gog, with whom eschatological expectations are associated, and Magog, who is associated with the genealogies springing from the Genesis 10 account. Their combination reflects mixing Greek ethnography with biblical genealogy and eschatology. Jerome, like Augustine, opposed the identification (see below); see also Van Donzel and Schmidt, *Gog and Magog*, 13–14.

155. Ambrose of Milan, "In Libros de Fide Admonitio," in Ambrosius von Mailand, *De fide* 2.16.138, ed. and trans. [German] Christoph Markschies, vol. 2 (Turnhout: 2005), citing Ezekiel 38–39; Ambrose revised the letter, written to the Western emperor Gratian before the battle, in 379.

156. Mark Humphries, "'Gog is the Goth': Biblical Barbarians in Ambrose of Milan's *De fide*," in Christopher Kelly, Richard Flowers, and Michael Stuart Williams, eds., *Unclassical Traditions. I: Alternatives to the Classical Past in Late Antiquity* (Cambridge: 2010), 44–57; Wolfram Brandes, "Gog, Magog und die Hunnen: Anmerkungen zur eschatologischen 'Ethnographie' der Völkerwanderungszeit," in Walter Pohl, Clemens Gantner, and Richard Payne, eds., *Visions of Community in the Post-Roman World: The West, Byzantium and the Islamic World, 300–1100* (Farnham: 2012), 477–98.

157. Maas, "How the Steppes Became Byzantine," 31–33.

[344] NOTES TO PAGES 208–210

158. Ambrose of Milan, "In Libros de Fide Admonitio" 2.16; for other writers, Anderson, *Alexander's Gate*, 9–11.

159. Anderson, *Alexander's Gate*, 10.

160. Jerome, *Hebrew Questions on Genesis* 10.2; Bøe, *Gog and Magog,* 216.

161. Bøe, *Gog and Magog*, 213.

162. Augustine, *The City of God* 20.11; Bøe, *Gog and Magog*, 216, citing translation of William B. Green, *Saint Augustine: The City of God against the Pagans*, LCL 416 (Cambridge, MA: 1960), 321 and 323.

163. Augustine, *The City of God* 20.11.

164. Anderson, *Alexander's Gate*, 10–14.

165. Ludwig Dindorf, ed., *Chronicon Paschale* (Bonn: 1832), 1.46.11–12.

166. Isidore of Seville, *Isidori Hispalensis episcopi, Etymologiarum sive Originum Libri XX*, ed. W. M. Lindsay (Oxford: 1911), 9.2.89; for English translation, Isidore, *Etymologies* 9.2.89.

167. Isidore, *Etymologies* 9.2.89.

168. Isidore, *Etymologies* 9.2.1-2. On divergences in his account from Genesis and Chronicles, see Isidore, *Etymologies*, 192 n. 5: "The number of nations was traditionally seventy-two, taking Eber and Phaleg as progenitors of a single nation. In several particulars Isidore departs from the accounts in Genesis 10 and Paralipomenon (Chronicles) 1. Often he follows Jerome's *Liber Quaestionum Hebraicarum in Genesim.*"

169. Van Donzel and Schmidt, *Gog and Magog*, 4–8, summarize Gog and Magog in Jewish sources; see also 14: "Up to the 7th century, Josephus, St. Jerome and Isidore can be considered as primarily responsible for acquainting readers in the Western Roman Empire with the idea of a barrier-gate built by Alexander at the Caspian or Caucasian Gates. From the 7th century onwards, however, ideas in the West about Alexander's gates were more generally inspired by Syriac traditions translated into Latin."

170. Isidore, *Etymologies* 9.2.66.

171. Van Donzel and Schmidt, *Gog and Magog*, 21–24, on the Syriac Alexander poem, and 24–26 on the Syriac "Sermon on the Last Days" of Pseudo-Ephrem Syrus, which identifies Gog and Magog with Huns.

172. Roger Pearse, "Theodore the Syncellus, Homily on the Siege of Constantinople in 626 AD (2007)," Tertullian.org, https://www.tertullian.org/fathers/theodore_syncellus_01_homily.htm, XL-XLVI; Ferenc Makk, *Traduction et commentaire de l'Homélie écrite probablement par Théodore le Syncelle sur le Siège de Constantinople en 626* (Szeged: 1975), contains French introduction, translation, and notes, followed by the Greek text, 73–121, reprinted from Leo Sternbach, "Analecta Avarica," *Rozprawy Akademii Umiejętności: Wydział Filologiczny* Series 2, no. 15 (1900), 297–365.

173. Anderson, *Alexander's Gate*, 12–14; Bøe, *Gog and Magog*, 215-17.

174. For description of the manuscript tradition: Reinhold Merkelbach, *Die Quellen des griechischen Alexanderromans* (Munich: 1977) 93–108 and 201–214; Van Donzel and Schmidt, *Gog and Magog*, 16; Sebastian P. Brock, "Alexander Cycle," in Brock, Butts, Kiraz, and Van Rompey, eds., *Gorgias Encyclopedic Dictionary of the Syriac Heritage*, 16.

175. "The History of the Dariali Gorge," in Eberhard W. Sauer et al., *Dariali: The 'Caspian Gates' in the Caucasus from Antiquity to the Age of the Huns and the Middle Ages: The Joint Georgian-British Dariali Gorge Excavations & Surveys of 2013-2016*, vol. 2 (Oxford: 2020), 857–929, esp. 858, on foundation stories.

176. Anderson, *Alexander's Gate*, 18, cites "Andreas, Commentar. in Apocalypsin, ed. Sylburg, 94, 45," in PG 106. cols. 215–458 and 1387–94, at 94.45 (1857–66) = Andrew of Caesarea, *Commentary on the Apocalypse*, trans. Eugenia Scarvelis Constantinou (Washington, DC: 2011).

177. See Anderson, *Alexander's Gate*, 18–19; Alexander, *The Byzantine Apocalyptic Tradition*, 185–92, on Gog and Magog; Bøe, *Gog and Magog*, 20, on Alexander's Gate and his Excursus 4, 219–30.

178. Van Donzel and Schmidt, *Gog and Magog*, 16–21.

179. Pseudo-Callisthenes, *The History of Alexander the Great*, trans. Ernest A. Wallis Budge (Cambridge: 1889), 150–53; Bøe, *Gog and Magog*, 223.

NOTES TO PAGES 210-212 [345]

180. Pseudo-Callisthenes, *The History of Alexander the Great*, 154.

181. Fredegar, "Chronicarum quae Dicuntur Fredegarii Chronicae Scholastici Libri IV cum Continuationibus," in Bruno Krusch, ed., MGHSRM II (1888), 4.64; James T. Palmer, *The Apocalypse in the Early Middle Ages* (Cambridge: 2014), 112.

182. *Alexandrian World Chronicle*, 141–395; Alexander, *The Byzantine Apocalyptic Tradition*, 13–60; Bøe, *Gog and Magog*, 225–26.

183. Bøe, *Gog and Magog*, 226, for citations and references to different ancient translations and related texts; Alexander, *The Byzantine Apocalyptic Tradition*, 185–92, on Gog and Magog; Emeri Van Donzel and Andrea Schmidt, *Gog and Magog*, 9–14, on Jewish and early Christian writers; Jerome also identifies them as Scythians and probably is referring to Huns; Isidore of Seville, *History of the Goths, Vandals and Suevi*, trans. Guido Donini and Gordon B. Ford (Leiden: 1966), 3: "It is certain that the Goths are a very old nation. Some conjecture from the similarity of the last syllable that the origin of their name comes from Magog, son of Japheth, and they deduce this mostly from the work of the prophet Ezekiel. Formerly, however, the learned were accustomed to call them Getae rather than Gog and Magog. The interpretation of their name in our language is 'tecti' [protected], which connotes strength; and with truth, for there has not been any nation in the world that has harassed Roman power so much. For these are the people who even Alexander declared should be avoided." On the last Roman emperor: Alexander, *Byzantine Apocalyptic Tradition*, 151–84; P. J. Alexander, "The Diffusion of Byzantine Apocalypses in the Medieval West and the Beginnings of Joachimism," in Ann Williams, ed., *Prophecy and Millenarianism: Essays in Honour of Marjorie Reeves* (Harlow, UK: 1980), 55–106, at 56–65.

184. Maas, "How the Steppes Became Byzantine," 30–34; Alexander, *The Byzantine Apocalyptic Tradition*, 13–60; Alexander, "The Diffusion of Byzantine Apocalypses," 53–106; *Alexandrian World Chronicle*, vii–xxxix; Palmer, *The Apocalypse in the Early Middle Ages*, 115–16.

185. The sons of Ishmael are listed: Gen. 25:13–16; 1 Chron. 1:29–31. See discussion of I. Eph'al, "Ishmael' and 'Arab(s)': A Transformation of Ethnological Terms," *Journal of Near Eastern Studies* 35, no. 4 (Oct. 1976): 225–35. He observes that "there is no biblical reference to the Ishmaelites (or to Ishmael, their *pater eponymos*) later than about the mid-tenth century B.C.E." (226). For the appearance of Ishmael in extrabiblical Jewish sources from the fourth century BCE and early Islamic Arab sources use of the term again, see 226–27.

186. Gen. 16:3.

187. Gen. 11:26.

188. On the much-discussed importance of lineages in Arab contexts, see the remarks of Daniel Mahoney, "The Political Construction of a Tribal Genealogy from Early Medieval South Arabia," in Eirik Hovden, Christina Lutter, and Walter Pohl, eds., *Meanings of Community across Medieval Eurasia: Comparative Approaches* (Leiden: 2016) 165–82.

189. Other terms were used as well: see Jan Retsö, *The Arabs in Antiquity: Their History from the Assyrians to the Umayyads* (London: 2002), 505–25, for discussion of the name as used by various authors.

190. Retsö, *The Arabs in Antiquity*, 122.

191. See Peter Webb, *Imagining the Arabs: Arab Identity and the Rise of Islam* (Edinburgh: 2016), 24–31.

192. J. Spencer Trimingham, *Christianity among the Arabs in Pre-Islamic Times* (Beirut: 1990), 11–12.

193. Eph'al, "'Ishmael and 'Arab(s),'" 227, for Arabs in Assyrian sources; 228 suggests that *Arab* was their self-designation.

194. The literature is vast. Two recent overviews: Webb, *Imagining the Arabs*, especially useful here on the problem of "Arab" origins; and Robert G. Hoyland, *Arabia and the Arabs: From the Bronze Age to the Coming of Islam* (London: 2001).

195. Robert G. Hoyland, "Arab Kings, Arab Tribes and the Beginnings of Arab Historical Memory in Late Roman Epigraphy," in Hannah M. Cotton, Robert G. Hoyland, Jonathan J. Price, and David J. Wasserstein, eds., *From Hellenism to Islam: Cultural and Linguistic Change in the Roman Near East* (Cambridge: 2009), 374–400, at 392–93.

[346] NOTES TO PAGES 212–214

196. For the growth of Rome's presence: Glen W. Bowersock, *Roman Arabia* (Cambridge, MA: 1983); Fergus Millar, *The Roman Near East: 31 B.C.–A.D. 337* (Cambridge, MA: 1993) is indispensable.

197. Bowersock, *Roman Arabia*, 76–89.

198. Millar, "Hagar, Ishmael, Josephus," 41, provides further citations; Retsö, *The Arabs in Antiquity*, 505–25.

199. Ptolemy, *Geography* 6.7.41, ed. Susanne Ziegler (Wiesbaden: 1998).

200. See n. 173 above.

201. Retsö, *The Arabs in Antiquity*, 512–21, for Arabs and Romans in the fourth century; Webb, *Imagining the Arabs*, 44–49 and 74–77; Hoyland, "Arab Kings," 374–400; Hoyland, *Arabia and the Arabs*, 234–47.

202. In the Middle Ages it became synonymous with Muslim.

203. *Notitia Dignitatum*, ed. Otto Seeck (1876): Saraceni: *Oriens.* 28.17; 32.27–28; Arabes: *Oriens.* 28.24; 36.35; 37.34.

204. On Uranius: J. M. I. West, "Uranius," *Harvard Studies in Classical Philology* 78 (1974), 282–84, for a summary of his unavailable 1973 Harvard dissertation, *Uranius*; text: F. Jacoby, *Die Fragmente der griechischen Historiker*, no. 675; cited appreciatively by Stephanos of Byzantium (early sixth century) in his *Ethnika*; Retsö, *The Arabs in Antiquity*, 505.

205. On Taenoi/Tayye, see Retsö, *The Arabs in Antiquity*, 505; Irfan Shahîd, "Ṭayyiʾ or Ṭayy," in *Encyclopaedia of Islam*, ed. P. Bearman, Th. Bianquis, C. E. Bosworth, E. van Donzl, and W. P. Heinrichs, http://dx.doi.org/10.1163/1573-3912_islam_SIM_7471.

206. Shahîd, "Ṭayyiʾ or Ṭayy."

207. Retsö, *The Arabs in Antiquity*, 513–17.

208. Ammianus Marcellinus, *History* 14.4.1–6, ed. and trans. J. C. Rolfe, LCL 300 (Cambridge, MA: 1950).

209. Ammianus Marcellinus, *History* 22.15.2: "Scenitas praetenditur Arabas, quos Sarracanos nunc apellamus" and 23.6.13: "Scenitas Arabas quos Saracenos posteritas apellavit."

210. Millar, "Hagar, Ishmael, Josephus," 41.

211. For example, Procopius, *History of the Wars* 1.17.45–47, 1.18.30, 1.18.35–36, 1.18.46, 1.19.7–8, 1.19.15, 2.10.23, 2.16.18, 2.16.5, 2.19.10–12, 2.27.30, and 2.28.12–14, ed. and trans. H. B. Dewing, LCL 48 (Cambridge, MA: 1914); Henning Börm, *Prokop und die Perser: Untersuchungen zu den römisch-sasanidischen Kontakten in der ausgehenden Spätantike* (Stuttgart: 2007).

212. Retsö, *The Arabs in Antiquity*, 505–20, for detailed overview.

213. Gen. 16–17.

214. Eph'al, "'Ishmael' and 'Arab(s),'" 227, concludes "the term 'Arab' was clearly introduced only after 'Ishmael' had become obsolete."

215. Ibid.

216. Gen. 17:20.

217. On appearance of Ishmaelites in the Bible, see Eph'al, "'Ishmael' and 'Arab(s),'" 225 and 229: "Thus the list of the 'Sons of Ishmael' is not based in historical fact but is more in the nature of an ethnological 'midrash' on Ishmael." See also 231: "the gentilicon Ishmael is no longer to be seen in the biblical world-picture after the ninth century B.C.E."

218. Millar, "Hagar, Ishmael, Josephus," 37.

219. Millar, "Hagar, Ishmael, Josephus," 31; see also 28–37 for detailed discussion.

220. Josephus, *Jewish Antiquities* 1.221; Eph'al, "'Ishmael' and 'Arab(s),'" 232–33, on Josephus and other Jewish exegetes; e.g., 233: "the Palestinian Talmud (Ta'anit 4, 69b), where the country of the Ishmaelites is called 'Arabia.'"

221. Josephus, *Jewish Antiquities* 2.32.

222. Millar, "Hagar, Ishmael, Josephus," 45.

223. Carol Bakhos, *Ishmael on the Border: Rabbinic Portrayals of the First Arab* (Albany, NY: 2006), 2.

224. Millar, "Hagar, Ishmael, Josephus," 40.

225. Millar points out that in the mid-third century Christians began the habit of direct association: "Hagar, Ishmael, Josephus," 40–45; Fergus Millar, "Empire, Community and Culture in the Roman Near East: Greeks, Syrians, Jews, and Arabs," *Journal of Jewish*

NOTES TO PAGES 214-216 [347]

Studies 38, no. 2 (1987): 143–64; Fergus Millar, "The Theodosian Empire (408–450) and the Arabs: Saracens or Ishmaelites?," in Erich S. Gruen, ed., *Cultural Borrowings and Ethnic Appropriations in Antiquity* (Stuttgart: 2005), 297–314, here 305–6; see also a similar story in Origen, "Ex origene selecta in Genesim," in PG 12 (1862), cols. 91–146, here cols. 119–20.

226. Millar, "Hagar, Ishmael, Josephus," 41–43.

227. Eusebius, *Preparatio Evangelica* 9.19, trans. E. H. Gifford (Oxford: 1903; repr. 1981), book 9; Millar, "Hagar, Ishmael, Josephus," 40–41; Retsö, *The Arabs in Antiquity*, 510–11 and 286–87, on Nabataean Arabs; Jerome, "The Life of Malchus, the Captive Monk," in NPNF ser. 2, vol. 6, 315–18, calls Saracens "Ishmaelites"; Irfan Shahîd, *Byzantium and the Arabs in the Fourth Century* (Washington, DC: 1984), 284–86.

228. The question of the influence of Christianity on pre-Islamic populations is controversial and has generated an enormous bibliography. See Shahîd, *Byzantium and the Arabs*, 152–58, on the proselytizing Arab holy man Moses, a Monophysite/Miaphysite Christian, among Saracen groups; Sozomen, *The Ecclesiastical History* 6.38; Hoyland, *Arabia and the Arabs*, 149–50.

229. Millar, "The Theodosian Empire," 312.

230. Gen. 25; Greg Fisher, *Between Empires: Arabs, Romans, and Sasanians in Late Antiquity* (Oxford: 2011), 166–68, for discussion and sources on Chettura.

231. Millar, "The Theodosian Empire," 305–6, mentions Sozomen (ca. 400–after 445) and Theodoret, bishop of Cyrrhus (393–after 460).

232. Millar, "The Theodosian Empire," 305.

233. Peter Van Nuffelen, "Sozomen," in Oliver Nicholson, ed., *The Oxford Dictionary of Late Antiquity* (Oxford: 2018), 1406. He wrote an epitome of Eusebius's *Church History* that is now lost.

234. Barry Baldwin, "Sozomenos," in *ODB* (1991), 1932–33.

235. Fisher, *Between Empires*, 166–67: "[Jerome] accuses the Saracens of falsely assuming Sara's name, so as to attach themselves to a free descendant instead of suffering the ignominy of descent from the slave, Hagar." He cites, at 166 n. 144: "Jer. Com. In Ezech. 8.25.1–7 (CCSL 75, 335)"; see also Retsö, *The Arabs in Antiquity*, 486–87; Curiously, this faulty etymology found its way into the *Etymologies* of Isidore of Seville, in early-seventh-century Spain: Isidore, *Etymologies* 9.2.57.

236. Sozomen, *Ecclesiastical History* 6.38 = NPNF ser. 2, vol. 2, cited in Millar, "The Theodosian Empire," 310–11; Millar, "Hagar, Ishmael, Josephus," points out, at 43, that the link to Sara is unique to Sozomen; Fisher, *Between Empires*, 167–68.

237. Millar, "The Theodosian Empire," 311: "The unique features of this passage are, first, its imaginative reconstruction of the religious history of the Ishmaelites, slowly drifting away from their originally Jewish observances, while apparently still maintaining—or re-adopting?—circumcision and abstention from pork; second, the explanation of 'Sarakēnos' as embodying a (false) relationship to Sarah; and third, and by far the most significant, the assertion, which seems to have no parallel, that (at some unspecified time) some Saracens had learnt of their true origins from Jews with whom they had contact, came back into relationship with them, and now observed Jewish customs."

238. Millar, "The Theodosian Empire," 309–12; Millar, "Hagar, Ishmael, Josephus," 42–43.

239. Isidore, *Etymologies* 9.2.6; on source, see *Etym.* 10–17.

240. Isidore, *Etymologies* 9.2.57: "The Saracens are so called either because they claim to be descendants of Sarah or, as the pagans say, because they are of Syrian origin, as if the word were *Syriginae*." See also 9.2.6: "A son of Abraham was Ishmael, from whom arose the Ishmaelites, who are now called, with corruption of the name, Saracens, as if they descended from Sarah, and the Agarenes, from Agar (i.e. Hagar)."

241. Isidore, *Etymologies* 9.2.2: "Now, of the nations into which the earth is divided, fifteen are from Japheth, thirty-one from Ham, and twenty-seven from Shem, which adds up to seventy-three—or rather, as a proper accounting shows, seventy-two. And there are an equal number of languages, which arose across the lands and, as they increased, filled the provinces and islands."

[348] NOTES TO PAGES 216-221

242. Fredegar, *Chronicle* 1.5 and 2.2; Ekkehart Rotter, *Abendland und Sarazenen: Das okzidentale Araberbild und siene Entstehung im Frümittelalte* (Berlin: Walter de Gruyter, 1986), 67–82 contrasts Isidore and the *Chronicle of Fredegar* (ca. 613 or 616/17). Isidore (ca. 560–70) says Arabs are the descendants of Ham, while the *Chronicle of Fredegar* says they are the descendants of Shem; see also his diagrams on 76 and 81.

243. Fred M. Donner, "The Background to Islam," in Michael Maas, ed., *The Cambridge Companion to the Age of Justinian* (Cambridge: 2005), 510–33, at 511.

244. René Dagorn, *La geste d'Ismaël d'après l'onomastique et la tradition arabes* (Geneva: 1981) for extended discussion.

245. Fisher, *Between Empires*, 167, on when Abrahamic descent was internalized by the Arabs. He cites note 151, "R. Dagorn, *La geste d'Ismaël d'après l'onomastique et la tradition arabes* (Paris, 1981), cf. Shahid, *Fifth Century*, 382–3"; while known to Jews and Christians earlier, Abrahamic descent was not internalized by Arabs until the Islamic period; Eph'al, "Ishmael" and "Arab(s)," 234: "Arab sources divide the inhabitants of the peninsula into those descended from 'Adnān, the son of Ishmael, and Qaḥtān (the biblical Joktan), descendant of Shem . . . none of the sources connect 'the True Arabs' with Ishmael; they all agree that the descendants of 'Adnān, the son of Ishmael, are not to be regarded as 'Arabs' but merely as 'arabized' (musta'riba)."

246. Millar, "The Theodosian Empire," 313.

247. Hoyland, *Arabia and the Arabs*, 243.

Chapter Seven: Babel and the Languages of Faith

1. For a sociolinguistic overview of the late antique Mediterranean world, see the remarkable study of Yuliya Minets, *The Slow Fall of Babel: Languages and Identities in Late Antique Christianity* (Cambridge: 2021), to which I am much indebted. I also wish to thank Professor Minets for sending me her dissertation, *The Slow Fall of Babel: Conceptualization of Languages, Linguistic Diversity and History in Late Antique Christianity* (PhD diss., Catholic University of America, 2017), prior to the publication of the monograph.

2. Minets, *The Slow Fall of Babel*, 330: "Christian elites demonstrated increasing interest in other peoples and their languages. Many felt an urge to comprehend the world in its diversity and to explain it in a theologically meaningful way. In literary accounts, speaking in foreign languages was no longer primarily a feature of marginalized characters, but appeared as a positive quality that could be instrumental in fulfilling divine purposes."

3. Arietta Papaconstantinou, *The Multilingual Experience in Egypt, from the Ptolemies to the 'Abbāsids* (Farnham: 2010); Alex Mullen and Patrick James, eds., *Multilingualism in the Graeco-Roman Worlds* (Cambridge: 2012); Alex Mullen, *Southern Gaul and the Mediterranean. Multilingualism and Multiple Identities in the Iron Age and Roman Periods* (Cambridge: 2013); Minets, *The Slow Fall of Babel*, 18–52.

4. Bruno Rochette, "Language Policies in the Roman Republic and Empire," in James Clackson, ed., *A Companion to the Latin Language* (Malden, MA: 2011), 549–63, at 562–63.

5. J. N. Adams, *Bilingualism and the Latin Language* (Cambridge: 2003), 758: "There does not seem to have been an explicit official policy (based on the sort of linguistic nationalism which has often surfaced in the history of Europe) that subject peoples should learn Latin." Discussed in Minets, *The Slow Fall of Babel*, 20–25; emphasized by Rochette, "Language Policies in the Roman Republic and Empire," 549, 562–63.

6. Minets, *The Slow Fall of Babel*, 25.

7. Minets, *The Slow Fall of Babel*, 328–29:

> Compared to their colleagues in the pre-Christian era, Christian writers seem to care more about the multilinguality of the world around them. They acquired a better notion of such languages as Hebrew and Aramaic and started to pay greater attention to non-classical idioms previously dismissed as "barbarian." The spread of Christianity stimulated the appearance of Syriac, Coptic, Armenian, Georgian, Ge'ez (Ethiopic), and Gothic as literary languages and encouraged some adventurous proponents of the new religion to convey the gospel message

NOTES TO PAGES 221–224 [349]

in multiple Aramaic, Arabic, Iranian, Turkic, Germanic, Celtic, and Slavic vernaculars. All this had a significant impact on the subsequent history of languages and speech communities around the Mediterranean.

8. On the process of linguistic fragmentation, and the awareness of Christian authors of it, see Minets, *The Slow Fall of Babel*, 18–52.

9. A. D. Lee, *Information and Frontiers: Roman Foreign Relations in Late Antiquity* (Cambridge: 1993), 47–48, 66–67, and 164; Yuliya Minets, "'Rushing Noise' and 'Mingled Clamor': The Persian Language and Its Speakers from the Perspective of Their Western Neighbours in Late Antiquity" (paper presented at *Migration and Mobility across the Roman-Persian Frontier, 3rd–7th c. A.D*, Eberhard Karls Universität Tübingen, December 2018). I thank Prof. Minets for sending me this paper before publication.

10. Gen. 11:1–8, *Tanakh, A New Translation of the Holy Scriptures According to the Traditional Hebrew Text* (Philadelphia: 1985).

11. Theodore Hiebert, "The Tower of Babel and the Origin of the World's Cultures," *Journal of Biblical Literature* 126, no. 1 (2007): 29–58; for a contrary view: André Lacocque, "Whatever Happened in the Valley of Shinar? A Response to Theodore Hiebert," *Journal of Biblical Literature* 128, no. 1 (2009): 29–41; on the Priestly and Jahwist traditions, see chap. 6 above.

12. Isidore, *Etymologies* 9.1.1 and 9.1.3, *The Etymologies*, ed. and trans. Stephen A. Barney et al. (Cambridge: 2006).

13. Isidore, *Etymologies* 9.1.14.

14. Minets, *The Slow Fall of Babel*, 99–169, for detailed overview of discussion in antiquity; on the considerable debate that has continued since antiquity regarding the identity of the first language, see Maurice Olender, *The Languages of Paradise: Race, Religion, and Philology in the Nineteenth Century*, trans. Arthur Goldhammer (Cambridge, MA: 1992), which provides a magisterial survey of major figures in the discussion from antiquity to the early twentieth century; Josef Eskhult, "Augustine and the Primeval Language in Early Modern Exegesis and Philology," *Language & History* 56, no. 2 (2013): 98–199, treats patristic exegesis and Augustine; John McWhorter's popularizing book *The Power of Babel: A Natural History of Language* (New York: 2001), 10, uses the idea of "most likely one original language" as a starting point. See also Raf Van Rooy, "Πόθεν οὖν ἡ τοσαύτη διαφωνία: Greek Patristic Authors Discussing Linguistic Origin, Diversity, Change and Kinship," *Beiträge zur Geschichte der Sprachwissenschaft* 23, no. 1 (2013): 21–54, at 21.

15. Isidore, *Etymologies* 12.1.2.

16. Isidore, *Etymologies* 12.1.

17. He accepts and transmits Augustine's authoritative opinion; Minets, *The Slow Fall of Babel*, 99–169 for historical overview; Van Rooy, "Πόθεν οὖν ἡ τοσαύτη διαφωνία," 27–35; Borst, *Der Turmbau von Babel*, vol. 1: *Fundamente und Aufbau* (Stuttgart: 1957), 227–57, for broader overview; Gregory of Nyssa was an exception: Minets, *The Slow Fall of Babel*, 139–43; on Gregory: Milka Rubin, "The Language of Creation or the Primordial Language: A Case of Cultural Polemics in Antiquity," *Journal of Jewish Studies* 49, no. 2 (1998): 306–33, at 320–21.

18. Van Rooy, "Πόθεν οὖν ἡ τοσαύτη διαφωνία," 27.

19. Isidore, *Etymologies* 12.1–2.

20. For a survey of patristic authors' views on linguistic origin, diversity, change, and kinship, see Van Rooy, "Πόθεν οὖν ἡ τοσαύτη διαφωνία," 21–54.

21. Grégoire de Nysse, *Contre Eunome* II, ed. Raymond Winling, Sources Chrétiennes 551 (Paris: 2013), 253–55.

22. Charles A. Sullivan, "An Analysis of Gregory of Nyssa on Speaking in Tongues," posted June 7, 2020, https://charlesasullivan.com/7212/analysis-gregory-nyssa-speaking-tongues/: "Gregory Nazianzus recognized the theory of a one sound emanating and multiplying during transmission into real languages. He . . . posited this against the miracle of speaking in foreign languages . . . These two positions by Nyssa and Nazianzus set the stage for an ongoing debate for almost 900 years."

23. Isidore, *Etymologies* 9.1.

[350] NOTES TO PAGES 224–228

24. "Cosmographia Iulii Caesaris," in Alexander Riese, ed., *Geographi Latini Minores* (Heilbronn: 1878), 21–23.

25. Pliny, *Natural History* 7.6, ed. and trans. H. Rackham, LCL 352 (Cambridge, MA: 1942): "tot gentium sermones, tot linguae, tanta loquendi varietas."

26. Kaufmann Kohler and Isaac Broydé, "Nations and Languages, The Seventy," in *The Jewish Encyclopedia. Volume IX* (New York: 1901), 188–90, at 189.

27. Eyal Ben-Elyahu, Yehudah Cohn, and Fergus Millar, eds., *Handbook of Jewish Literature from Late Antiquity. 135–700 CE* (Oxford: 2012), 81, on date and introduction.

28. The third-century Palestinian scholar Jonathan of Bet Gubrin famously remarked: "There are four fine languages that ought to be used by the whole world: Greek for poetry, Latin for war; Aramaic for the dirge; and Hebrew for general speech" (Kohler and Broydé, "Nations and Languages," 189).

29. *Genesis Rabbah*, xiii and xxxi (Kohler and Broydé, "Nations and Languages," 189, with other Talmudic comments on the significance of the seventy).

30. See Augustine, *City of God* 16.3; Tristan Major, "The Number Seventy-two: Biblical and Hellenistic Beginnings to the Early Middle Ages," *Sacris Erudiri* 52 (2013): 7–46, at 33–35, on Augustine's discussion and influence; *The Book of Jubilees*, trans. James C. Vanderkam (Louvain: 1989), 8:10: "At the beginning of the thirty-third jubilee they divided the earth into three parts—for Shem, Ham, and Japheth—each in his own inheritance." Kohler and Broydé, "Nations and Languages."

31. Major, "Literary Developments of the Table of Nations," 12: "The origins of the tradition of seventy-two names in the Table of Nations start to appear, albeit unclearly, in the Hellenistic world during the third and second centuries before Christ. Initially, the number 72 was important astrologically among the Greeks, Romans, Egyptians, and Babylonians. It is often repeated that the heavens were divided into seventy-two parts, or that there were seventy-two stars that are able to influence the world." See also 12 n. 37: "See Burrows, 'The Number Seventy in Semitic' 389–90."

32. Most Vetus Latina translations accept that there were seventy-two translators of the Septuagint: Major, "Literary Developments of the Table of Nations," 17–18; Tristan Major, *Undoing Babel: The Tower of Babel in Anglo-Saxon Literature* (Toronto: 2018), 50–77, for overview.

33. Isidore, *Etymologies* 9.2.1–2.

34. Isidore, *Etymologies* 9.1.1; at 9.2.2 he says that there are an equal number (seventy-two) of languages as descendants of Noah's sons.

35. Isidore, *Etymologies* 9.1.3.

36. Peter Brown, *The Rise of Western Christendom: Triumph and Diversity, A.D. 200–1000*, rev. ed. (Malden, MA: 2013), 355–80.

37. Isidore, *Etymologies* 12.1.1.

38. Isidore, *Etymologies* 5.37.4 and 6.18.4.

39. *Acts* 2.5–11:

> And there were dwelling at Jerusalem Jews, devout men, out of every nation under heaven. Now when this was noised abroad, the multitude came together, and were confounded, because that every man heard them speak in his own language. And they were all amazed and marvelled, saying one to another, Behold, are not all these which speak Galilæans? And how hear we every man in our own tongue, wherein we were born? Parthians, and Medes, and Elamites, and the dwellers in Mesopotamia, and in Judæa, and Cappadocia, in Pontus, and Asia, Phrygia, and Pamphylia, in Egypt, and in the parts of Libya about Cyrene, and strangers of Rome, Jews and proselytes, Cretes and Arabians, we do hear them speak in our tongues the wonderful works of God.

Van Rooy, "Πόθεν οὖν ἡ τοσαύτη διαφωνία," 40: "the diversity of languages is transcended by the unifying power of Christianity which began with the speaking in tongues at Pentecost . . . which most of them [Greek patristic writers] interpret as the biblical counterpart of the Babelic confusion of tongues." Cf. Borst, *Der Turmbau von Babel*, vol. 1, 227–57 and passim.

NOTES TO PAGES 228–233 [351]

40. Origen, *Contra Celsum* 8.37, trans. Frederick Crombie, *The Writings of Origen. Volume II. Origen Contra Celsum* (Edinburgh: 1872).

41. Basil of Seleucia, "Homilia I. De Sancta Pentecoste," in PLG 64 (1862), cols. 417424, at cols. 421–22 (Homily I.5), trans. Charles A. Sullivan, "Basil of Seleucia's Explanation of Pentecost," https://charlesasullivan.com/5083/fifth-century-basil-of-seleucia-on-pentecost /#easy-footnote-bottom-22-5083: "A Hebrew was uttering a sound, and foreigner being educated. The sound of grace being made known, and the hearer understanding the word. Goths were recognizing the sound. The Ethiopians recognized the language. Persians were marveling about this one speaking, and who was teaching foreign nations by the ascendency of one language."

42. Acts 2:1–13; 1Cor. 12.7–11, 12.28–31, 14, 14.2, 14.13, 14.27–8; discussed in Minets, *The Slow Fall of Babel*, 170–219.

43. Prosper of Aquitaine, *The Call of All Nations* II.17, trans. P. De Letter (New York: 1952).

44. Sergey A. Ivanov, *"Pearls before Swine": Missionary Work in Byzantium*, adapted from a translation from Russian by Deborah Hoffman (Paris: 2015), 213: "We know next to nothing as to how Byzantine mission was structured and the language of mission is a complicated issue. To all appearances Greeks did not study barbarian languages, but used local or imported barbarians as interpreters."

45. Minets, *The Slow Fall of Babel*, 18–52.

46. Minets, *The Slow Fall of Babel*, 326, for discussion of the concept of "communities of linguistic sensitivities."

47. Isidore, *Etymologies* 9.1.8.

48. Isidore, *Etymologies* 9.1.7: "Then Mixed, which emerged in the Roman state after the wide expansion of the Empire, along with new customs and peoples, corrupted the integrity of speech with solecisms and barbarisms" = Isidore, *Etymologiarum sive Originum* 9.1.7: "integritatem verbi per soloecismos et barbarismos corrumpens."

49. Isidore, *Etymologies* 9.2.105.

50. Van Rooy, "Πόθεν οὖν ἡ τοσαύτη διαφωνία," 41–42.

51. Van Rooy, "Πόθεν οὖν ἡ τοσαύτη διαφωνία," 41–42, with nn. 34–37 for citations.

52. Van Rooy, "Πόθεν οὖν ἡ τοσαύτη διαφωνία," 41–42.

53. Clement of Alexandria, *Stromata* VI.15.129. 2, trans. Van Roy, "Πόθεν οὖν ἡ τοσαύτη διαφωνία," 42.

54. Noted in Minets, *The Slow Fall of Babel*, 333.

55. Rufinus, *In Epistulam Pauli ad Romanos explanationum libri secundum translationem Rufini*, VIII.5, Library of Latin Texts Online (2010) http://clt.brepolis.net/llta/Default .aspx, quoted and trans. in Van Rooy, "Πόθεν οὖν ἡ τοσαύτη διαφωνία," 42. He notes that Gregory of Nyssa and Theodoret also made the connection.

56. Van Rooy, "Πόθεν οὖν ἡ τοσαύτη διαφωνία," 41–42, with nn. 36 and 37 for citations.

57. Minets, *The Slow Fall of Babel*, 343.

58. Minets, *The Slow Fall of Babel*, 342–44.

59. Minets, *The Slow Fall of Babel*, 344–45, with accompanying bibliography. The passage continues: "Orthodox Greek and Latin intellectuals represented by far the most prestigious cultural and literary traditions in the Mediterranean. Their remarks on linguistic peculiarities in the speech of their doctrinal opponents were used in order to create an alienating effect on the rhetorical plane. They did not faithfully describe social practices, and they did not mean to."

60. Minets, *The Slow Fall of Babel*, 345.

61. Minets, *The Slow Fall of Babel*, 345.

62. Neil McLynn, "Little Wolf in the Big City: Ulfila and His Interpreters," *Bulletin of the Institute of Classical Studies* 50, Supplement 91 (2007): 125–35, https://doi.org/10.1111/j .2041-5370.2007.tb02383.x.

63. Isidore, *Etymologies* 8.5.

64. Drawing on Jewish precedents, angelic guardianship of nations derives from the Septuagint, which altered the Hebrew text. See Jean Danielou, *Origen*, trans. Walter Mitchell (Eugene: 1955), 224–37. For the representation of angels in Late Antiquity (but not as

guardians), see Glenn Peers, *Subtle Bodies: Representing Angels in Byzantium* (Berkeley: 2002); György Geréby, "The Angels of the Nations: Is a National Christianity Possible?," in Tamás A. Bács, Ádám Bollók, and Tivadar Vida, eds., *Across the Mediterranean—Along the Nile: Studies in Egyptology, Nubiology and Late Antiquity; Dedicated to László Török on the Occasion of His 75th Birthday*, vol. 2 (Budapest: 2018), 819–47, at 826–30 and 837–41.

65. Deut. 32:8, Jewish Publication Society, *Tanakh, A New Translation of the Holy Scriptures*.

66. Deut. 32.8, lines 5–8: "ὅτε διεμέριζεν ὁ ὕψιστος ἔθνη, / ὡς διέσπειρεν υἱοὺς Αδαμ, / ἔστησεν ὅρια ἐθνῶν / κατὰ ἀριθμὸν ἀγγέλων θεοῦ" (trans. M. Maas): "Deuteronomium," in Alfred Rahlfs, ed., *Septuaginta: Id est Vetus Testamentum graece iuxta LXX interpretes*, ed. Robert Hanhart, rev. ed. (Stuttgart: 2006).

67. Jewish calculation and tradition was seventy (see n. 26), while Christians following the Septuagint accepted seventy-two (see nn. 31 and 34).

68. Jean Danielou, *The Angels and Their Mission According to the Fathers of the Church*, trans. David Heimann (South Bend, IN: 1957), 14–23; Michele Nicoletti, "The Angel of the Nations," in T. Faitini, F. Ghaia, and M. Nicoletti, eds., *Theopopedia: Archiving the History of Theologico-political Concepts* (Trento: 2015), 1–11.

69. Philo, *On the Posterity and Exile of Cain* XXVI.91–94, ed. and trans. F. H. Colson and G. H. Whitaker, LCL 227 (Cambridge, MA:, 1929), 323–442, at 378–80; Nicoletti, "The Angel of the Nations," 2–3 for citations of other sources.

70. Jean Danielou, "Les sources juives de la Doctrine des Anges des Nations chez Origéne," *Recherches de Science Religieuse* 38 (1951): 132–37. Nicoletti, "The Angel of the Nations," 2–3.

71. Marie-Thérèse d'Alverny, review of "Arno Borst, *Der Turmbau von Babel*," in *Cahiers de Civilisation Médiévale* 3, no. 12 (Oct.–Dec. 1960): 492–94, at 492.

72. Origen, *Contra Celsum* 5.30; discussed in Minets, *The Slow Fall of Babel*, 122–23; Origen, *Homily on Genesis* 9.3: God divided the nations according to the number of angels.

73. Minets, *The Slow Fall of Babel*, 123; Origen, *De Principiis* 3.3.3, translated in Danielou, "Les sources juives," 137.

74. Danielou, *The Angels and Their Mission*, 15–17, cites earlier sources; for a résumé, see: Erik Peterson, *Der Monotheismus als politisches Problem: Ein Beitrag zur geschichte der politischen Theologie im Imperium romanum* (Leipzig: 1935)=trans. Michael J. Hollerich, "Monotheism as a Political Problem: A Contribution to the History of Political Theology in the Roman Empire," in Erik Peterson, *Theological Tractates* (Stanford: 2011), 68–105, on the Hellenistic idea of the immutability of the "national" religions, and 89–90 on Origen's response to Celsus; Jean Danielou, "Les sources juives," 132.

75. Minets, *The Slow Fall of Babel*, 153–54.

76. Danielou, *The Angels and Their Mission*, 15–16.

77. Erik Peterson, "The Book on the Angels: Their Place and Meaning in the Liturgy," trans. Michael J. Hollerich, in Erik Peterson, *Religious Tractates*, 106–42.

Chapter Eight: The New Ethnography of Christian Heresy

1. Salvien de Marseille, *Du Gouvernement de Dieu* 4.61, ed. Georges Lagarrigue (1975), 262.

2. 1 Cor. 11:19; Todd S. Berzon, *Classifying Christians: Ethnography, Heresiology, and the Limits of Knowledge in Late Antiquity* (Berkeley: 2016), 12, for other texts contemporary with the Gospels.

3. Lewis Ayres, "The Question of Orthodoxy," *Journal of Early Christian Studies* 14, no. 4 (2006): 395–98, on influence of Walter Bauer, *Orthodoxy and Heresy in Earliest Christianity*, ed. Robert A. Kraft and Gerhard Krodel (Philadelphia: 1979)=Walter Bauer, *Rechtgläubigkeit und Ketzerei im ältesten Christentum*, 2nd ed. (Tübingen: 1964).

4. Heinrich Von Staden, "*Hairesis* and Heresy: The Case of the *haireseis iatrikai*," in B. F. Meyer and E. P. Sanders, eds., *Jewish and Christian Self-Definition*, vol. 3 (London: 1982), 76–100 and 199–206 (notes); Averil Cameron, "Heresiology," in G. W. Bowersock, Peter

NOTES TO PAGES 236–239 [353]

Brown, and Oleg Grabar, eds., *Late Antiquity. A Guide to the Postclassical World* (Cambridge, MA: 1999), 488–90.

5. Hervé Inglebert, "L'histoire des hérésies chez les hérésiologues," in *L'historiographie de l'Église des premiers siècles*, ed. Bernard Pouderon and Yves-Marie Duval = *Théologie Historique* 114 (2001), 105–25, at 106; Averil Cameron, "How to Read Heresiology," *Journal of Medieval and Early Modern Studies* 33, no. 3 (Fall 2003): 471–92.

6. Brent D. Shaw, *Sacred Violence: African Christians and Sectarian Hatred in the Age of Augustine* (Cambridge: 2011), 339–42, for discussion of practices in North Africa.

7. Rebecca Lyman, "A Topography of Heresy: Mapping the Rhetorical Creation of Arianism," in Michel R. Barnes and Daniel H. Williams, eds., *Arianism after Arius: Essays on the Development of the Fourth Century Trinitarian Conflicts* (Edinburgh: 1993), 45–62, at 47. On the gradual evolution of the neutral sense of the term in the Hellenistic age to its use by Church Fathers as a hostile label for those who had adopted doctrinally incorrect views, and for how this usage "soon gave rise to elaborate new taxonomies of doctrinal and institutional error (in which *hairesis* played a central role), and to a substantial body of canon law," see Von Staden, "Hairesis and Heresy," 97–98.

8. Young Richard Kim, "Epiphanius of Cyprus and the Geography of Heresy," in Harold Allen Drake, ed., *Violence in Late Antiquity: Perceptions and Practices* (Burlington: 2006), 235–51; Shaw, *Sacred Violence*, 310–11.

9. Tia M. Kolbaba, *Inventing Latin Heretics: Byzantines and the Filioque in the Ninth Century* (Kalamazoo: 2008), 16.

10. Cameron, "Heresiology," 489.

11. Shaw, *Sacred Violence*, 6; see also especially chap. 7, "Little Foxes, Evil Women," 307–47, on heresy.

12. Shaw, *Sacred Violence*, 307.

13. Eighty also happened to be the number of concubines in Solomon's Song of Songs, a disquieting coincidence: Cameron, "Heresiology," 489. See below for further discussion of Justin and Epiphanius.

14. They are mentioned by both Augustine, *Heresies* 31, and Epiphanius, *Panarion* 2.4.52. Augustine, *De haeresibus*, ed. R. vander Plaetse and C. Beukers, CCSL 46 (Turnhout: 1969), 283–385. This is translated by Roland J. Teske, *Arianism and Other Heresies: The Works of Saint Augustine; A Translation for the 21st Century*, ed. Roland J. Teske et al., part 1, vol. 18 (New York: 1995); the *Panarion* is translated by Frank Williams (Leiden: 2013).

15. For recent discussion and bibliography, see Berzon, *Classifying Christians*; Aline Pourkier, *L'hérésiologie chez Épiphane de Salamine* (Paris: 1992); A. Le Boulluec, *La notion d'hérésie dans la litterature grecque aux IIe—IIIe siècles, I.1 De Justin à Irénée* (Paris: 1985).

16. Averil Cameron, "The Violence of Orthodoxy," in Eduard Iricinschi and Holger M. Zellentin, eds., *Heresy and Identity in Late Antiquity* (Tübingen: 2008), 102–14, at 104.

17. Walter Bauer, in *Orthodoxy and Heresy*, challenged the idea of an original unity among Christians that became fragmented and corrupted by heresy. For discussion and bibliography, see Kolbaba, *Inventing Latin Heretics*, 12–13.

18. Averil Cameron, "The Violence of Heresy," in Iricinschi and Zellentin, *Heresy and Identity*, 102–14.

19. Salvien de Marseille, *Du Gouvernement de Dieu* 4.61, ed. and trans. Georges Lagarrigue 1975), 262; for a convenient English translation, though with different organization of the text, see Eva M. Sanford, *On the Government of God* (New York: 1930), IV.13.

20. Berzon, *Classifying Christians*, for overview and recent discussion; Michael Maas, "'Delivered from Their Ancient Customs': Christianity and the Question of Cultural Change in Early Byzantine Ethnography," in Kenneth Mills and Anthony Grafton, eds., *Conversion in Late Antiquity and the Early Middle Ages: Seeing and Believing* (Rochester, NY: 2003), 152–88.

21. Berzon, *Classifying Christians*, 257.

22. For example, Justinian's attempts at rapprochement with Monophysites/Miaphysites: Patrick T. R. Gray, "The Legacy of Chalcedon: Christological Problems and Their Significance," in Michael Maas, ed., *The Cambridge Companion to the Age of Justinian* (Cambridge: 2005), 215–38, at 227–36.

[354] NOTES TO PAGES 240–243

23. Shaw, *Sacred Violence*, 339; see also his discussion at 339–42.

24. Pourkier, *L'hérésiologie*, 56; Cameron, "How to Read Heresiology," 471–92; Antti Marjanen and Petri Luomanen, eds., *A Companion to Second-Century Christian 'Heretics'* (Leiden: 2008), for helpful essays.

25. Pourkier, *L'hérésiologie*, 53–59.

26. Justin Martyr, *Dialogue with Trypho*, ed. Michael Slusser, trans. Thomas B. Falls, Thomas P. Halton (Washington, DC: 2003), 35.5; for discussion, see Pourkier, *L'hérésiologie*, 56: "[L]es hérétiques sont toujours suscités et inspirés par les démons et, au-delà, par le diable."

27. Le Boulluec, *La notion d'hérésie*, 60–61.

28. Von Staden, "Hairesis and Heresy," 97–98.

29. Mary T. Clark, "Irenaeus," in Everett Ferguson, ed., *The Encyclopedia of Early Christianity*, 2nd ed. (New York: 1998), 587–88.

30. Irenaeus, *Against Heresies*, in Alexander Roberts and James Donaldson, eds., rev. A. Cleveland Coxe, *Ante-Nicene Fathers*, vol. 1, *The Apostolic Fathers, Justin Martyr, Irenaeus* (Grand Rapids: 1885), 315–567.

31. Clark, "Irenaeus," 588. For a more general background of the creation of the work and its purposes, see Alexander Roberts and James Donaldson, "Introductory Note to Irenæus Against Heresies," in Roberts and Donaldson, eds., *Ante-Nicene Fathers* 1, 309–13.

32. Berzon, *Classifying Christians*, 13: "Scholars now regard Irenaeus's history of Christianity and Christian traditions, where truth always preceded falsity and heresy was conceptualized as an adulteration of a uniform, stable, continuous chain of tradition, as an ideological representation rather than a historical reality." For general introduction, see 11–14.

33. Irenaeus, *Against Heresies* 1.9

34. He wrote in Greek, and much of his work survives only in Latin. For editions: Everett Fergusen, "Hippolytus," in Ferguson, ed., *Encyclopedia of Early Christianity*, 2nd ed., 531–32; Ferguson notes controversy about whether Hippolytus as known today was one person or several who have been conflated.

35. See chapter 8 on Hippolytus.

36. Inglebert, "L'histoire des hérésies," 117–19.

37. Inglebert, "L'histoire des hérésies," 121–22: Philastrius of Brescia presented a history of heresy since Adam in a series of steps. Philastrius of Brescia, *"Liber de Haeresibus,"* in Migne, ed., PL 12 (1845), cols. 1111–1302, at 1113–38.

38. Inglebert, "L'histoire des hérésies," 124.

39. Inglebert, "L'histoire des hérésies," 124, on successors to Epiphanius and Philastrius.

40. Rev. 17.

41. Lactantius, "On the Death of the Persecutors," in *Lactantius: The Minor Works*, trans. Mary Francis McDonald (Washington, DC: 1965), 117–203, at 168; Ilaria Ramelli, "Constantine: The Legal Recognition of Christianity and Its Antecedents," *Annuario de Historia de la Iglesia* 22 (2013): 65–82, reviews evidence including Galerian's recognition of Christianity in 262 or earlier.

42. On the exclusion of heretics from some imperial service but not from their curial or bureaucratic obligations, see Caroline Humfress, "Citizens and Heretics: Late Roman Lawyers on Christian Heresy," in Iricinschi and Zellentin, *Heresy and Identity*, 128–42, at 134–35; Caroline Humfress, "Roman Law, Forensic Argument and the Formation of Christian Orthodoxy (III–VI Centuries)," in Susanna Elm, Éric Rebillard, and Antonella Romano, eds., *Orthodoxie, christianisme, histoire = Orthodoxy, Christianity, History* (Rome: 2000), 125–47.

43. Caroline Humfress, "Heretics, Laws on," in Bowersock, Brown, and Grabar, eds., *Late Antiquity*, 490–91, at 490.

44. Humfress, "Heretics," 490–91; Laurette Barnard, "The Criminalisation of Heresy in the Later Roman Empire: A Sociopolitical Device?" *Journal of Legal History* 16, no. 2 (1995): 121–46; Jean Gaudemet, "Politique ecclésiastique et legislation après l'édit de Théodose 1 de 380," in Jean Gaudemet, *Droit et société aux derniers siècles de l'empire romain* (Naples: 1992), 175–96.

45. Barnard, "The Criminalisation of Heresy," 128, for discussion of penalties; Humfress, "Citizens and Heretics," 128–42, discusses the criminalization of heresy in the Christian empire.

NOTES TO PAGES 243–247   [355]

46. *Cod. Th.* 16.

47. *Cod. Th.* 16.5.1: "Emperor Constantine Augustus to Dracilianus [a vicar]. The privileges that have been granted in consideration of religion must benefit only the adherents of the Catholic faith. It is Our will, moreover, that heretics and schismatics shall not only be alien from these privileges but shall also be bound and subjected to various compulsory public services" [Sept 1. 326].

48. *Cod. Th.* 16.5.5; Humfress, "Citizens and Heretics," 133–34.

49. *Cod. Th.* 16.5.14.

50. For example, *Cod. Th.* 16.3.1, issued by Valentinian, Theodosius, and Arcadius in 390: "If any persons should be found in the profession of monks, they shall be ordered to seek out and to inhabit desert places and desolate solitudes."

51. *Cod. Th.* 16.1.2; Theodosius was proclaimed emperor on January 19, 379, following the disaster at Adrianople.

52. *Cod. Th.* 16, arranged in order of issuance.

53. *Cod. Th.* 16.1.3.

54. *Cod. Th.* 16.5.5.26: "None of the heretics, who are now restrained by innumerable laws of Our sainted father, shall dare to assemble unlawful gatherings and to contaminate with profane mind the mystery of Almighty God, either publicly or privately, secretly or openly. None shall dare to appropriate the title of bishop or, with polluted mind, to arrogate to himself the ecclesiastical order and their most sacred titles" [Constantinople, March 30, 395].

55. *Cod. Th.* 16.5.28: "Those persons who may be discovered to deviate, even in a minor point of doctrine [qui vel levi argumento iudicio catholicae religionis], from the tenets and the path of the Catholic religion are included under the designation of heretics and must be subject to the sanctions which have been issued against them. Your Experience, therefore, shall recognize that Heuresius shall be considered a heretic and not among the number of most holy bishops." [Constantinople, Sept. 3, 395].

56. *Cod. Th.* 16.5.34.1.

57. *Cod. Th.* 16.5.40.1.

58. *Cod. Th.* 16.5.40.1: "it is Our will that it [their heresy] shall be considered a public crime, since whatever is committed against divine religion redounds to the detriment of all"; Humfress, "Citizens and Heretics," 131.

59. Humfress, "Citizens and Heretics," 133.

60. Humfress, "Citizens and Heretics," 136–41, on how the loss of citizenship rights became a standard legal punishment for heresy; see chap. 3 above.

61. *Cod. Just.* 1.5.12.8, ed. Bruce W. Frier, trans. Fred H. Blume (Cambridge: 2016).

62. Humfress, "Citizens and Heretics," 141.

63. Ibid.

64. *Cod. Th.* 16.5.65.2.

65. *Cod. Th.* 16.5.65.2; Peter Brown has pointed out to me that Manichaeism was in many ways an extreme example of the use of religious criteria in defining communities. In spreading their message, Manichaeans did not meet peoples, only dogmas. See Jason BeDuhn, "Mani and the Crystallization of the Concept of 'Religion' in Third Century Iran," in Iain Gardner, Jason D. BeDuhn, and Paul Dilley, eds., *Mani at the Court of the Persian Kings: Studies in the Chester Beatty Kephalaia Codex* (Leiden: 2015), 247–75, at 272–75.

66. Humfress, "Heretics," 490.

67. The term is much debated. For an overview, see Günter Prinzing, "Byzantium, Medieval Russia and the So-called Family of Kings: From George Ostrogorsky to Franz Dölger's Construct and Its Critics," in Alena Alshanskaya, Andreas Gietzen, and Christina Hadjiafxenti, eds., *Imagining Byzantium: Perceptions, Patterns, Problems* (Mainz: 2018), 15–30.

68. Joel Walker, "From Nisibis to Xi'an: The Church of the East in Late Antique Eurasia," in Scott Fitzgerald Johnson, ed., *Oxford Handbook of Late Antiquity* (Oxford: 2012), 994–1052.

69. For "spiritual pharmacy," see Young Richard Kim, *Epiphanius of Cyprus: Imagining an Orthodox World* (Ann Arbor: 2015), 31; Andrew S. Jacobs, *Epiphanius of Cyprus: A Cultural Biography of Late Antiquity* (Berkeley: 2021).

70. John II Bishop of Jerusalem, 387–417; John Chrysostom (d. 407).

[356] NOTES TO PAGES 247–250

71. Epiphanius of Salamis, *The Panarion of Epiphanius of Salamis: Book I (Sects 1–46)*, trans. Frank Williams, 2nd revised and expanded ed. (Leiden: 2009), xi–xx, for his life and writings.

72. He attacked Apollinarianism and Melitianism, condemned at the councils of Ephesus in 431 and Chalcedon in 451. On his influence on Apollinarianism: Charles Kannengiesser, "Apollinaris of Laodicea," in Ferguson, ed., *Encyclopedia of Early Christianity*, 2nd ed., 79–81; on Melitianism, a form of Arianism: Barry Baldwin and Alice-Mary Talbot, "Epiphanios," in Alexander P. Kazhdan, ed., *ODB* (Oxford: 1991), 714; more generally: J. Rebecca Lyman, "Heresiology: The Invention of 'Heresy' and 'Schism,'" in Augustine Casiday and Frederick W. Norris, eds., *The Cambridge History of Christianity. Volume 2. Constantine to c. 600* (Cambridge: 2007), 296–313.

73. Socrates Scholasticus, *Socrates' Ecclesiastical History* 6.10; 12; 14, ed. Robert and William Bright (Oxford: 1893); Socrates Scholasticus, *The Ecclesiastical History*, trans. A. C. Zenos, *Nicene and Post-Nicene Fathers*, ser. 2., vol. 2 (Buffalo: 1890; repr. 1979); cf. Basil the Great, "Letter CCLVIII. To Bishop Epiphanius," in *Letters, Volume IV: Letters 249–368; On Greek Literature*, ed. and trans. Roy J. Deferrari and M. R. P. McGuire, LCL 270 (Cambridge, MA: 1934), 35–47, at 38–39.

74. Epiphanius, *Panarion*, xvi.

75. For a list of his sources: Epiphanius, *Panarion*, xxv–xxvii.

76. For summary of structure, Epiphanius, *Panarion*, xx–xxiv.

77. Epiphanius, *Panarion*, xxi.

78. Epiphanius, *Panarion*, xxiii.

79. Epiphanius, *Panarion*, xxiii.

80. This included contemporary holy men who had come to have been considered as heretics: "Heresy was both external opposition and a lurking internal poison within the tradition in seemingly holy men" (Lyman, "Heresiology," 303).

81. Epiphanius, *Panarion* 1.2.3–7 ["Scythianism"].

82. Epiphanius, *Panarion* 1.1–4 ["Barbarism"].

83. Epiphanius, *Panarion* 1.1–4 ["Anacephalaeosis I"].

84. Epiphanius, *Panarion* 1.2.8–12 ["Scythianism"].

85. Epiphanius, *Panarion* 1.42.1.1 ["Against Marcionites"].

86. E.g., Epiphanius, *Panarion* 1.42.3 ["Against Marcionites"].

87. Epiphanius, *Panarion* II, 1.32.1.1–3 "[Against Secundians," with whom Epiphanes and Isidore are associated].

88. Augustine, *De haeresibus*, ed. R. vander Plaetse and C. Beukers, CCSL 46 (Turnhout: 1969), 283–385.

89. The Abeloim were a community of Christian peasants who practiced abstinence and perpetuated their community through adoption. See Shaw, *Sacred Violence*, 310–11 and 431–33.

90. Gustave Bardy, "L'Indiculus de Haeresibus' du Pseudo-Jérome," *Recherches de science religieuse* 19, no. 1 (1929): 385–405; Judith McClure, "Handbooks against Heresy in the West, from the Late Fourth to the Late Sixth Centuries," *The Journal of Theological Studies* 30, no. 1 (Apr. 1979): 186–97.

91. Augustine, *De haeresibus*, Proem 7.

92. Augustine, *De haeresibus*, Proem 7; McClure, "Handbooks against Heresy," 192.

93. Peter R. L. Brown, "St. Augustine's Attitude to Religious Coercion," *Journal of Roman Studies* 54, nos. 1–2 (1964): 107–16, at 116.

94. Paul B. Clayton, Jr., *The Christology of Theodoret of Cyrus: Antiochene Christology from the Council of Ephesus (431) to the Council of Chalcedon (451)* (Oxford: 2007), esp. 3–14, for an overview of his career and works.

95. Clayton, *The Christology of Theodoret of Cyrus*, 3; Theodoret of Cyrrhus, "Epistolae," in *Theodoreti Cyrensis Episcopi Opera Omnia*, in PG 83 (1864), cols. 1171–1494, esp. epistles 81, cols. 1259–64; 113, cols. 1311–18; and 116, cols. 1327–28.

96. Theodoret of Cyrrhus, *Haereticarum fabularum compendium*, in PG 83 (1864), 335–556. See Clayton, *The Christology of Theodoret of Cyrus*, 5–6 and 273–82 for general discussion; Glenn Melvin Cope, *An Analysis of the Heresiological Method of Theodoret of Cyrus in the Haereticarum Fabularum Compendium* (PhD diss., Catholic University of America, 1990).

NOTES TO PAGES 250–254 [357]

97. Cope, "Analysis," 77; for text, see 171–206, on the unchanged character of his Christology in the 450s; see also Clayton, *The Christology of Theodoret of Cyrus*, 282.

98. Cope, "Analysis," 58; for text, see 207–355.

99. Cope, "Analysis," 357–70, demonstrates that Theodoret knew the heresiological tradition well, but he did not intend, as Cope, points out (55–56), to give a detailed account of every heresy. He preferred to condemn them all in order to demonstrate his own orthodoxy, which was coming under attack.

100. Isidore of Seville, *Etymologies* 8.3–5, ed. and trans. Stephen A. Barney et al. (Cambridge: 2006). His material on heresies draws from many sources, including Augustine.

101. Isidore, *Etymologies* 8.5.70.

102. See below on John of Damascus.

103. Ralph W. Mathisen, "Barbarian 'Arian' Clergy, Church Organization, and Church Practice," in Guido M. Berndt and Roland Steinacher, eds., *Arianism: Roman Heresy and Barbarian Creed* (Farnham: 2014), 145–91, at 146–47; Yitzhak Hen, "Conclusion: The Elusive Nature of an Orthodox Heresy," in Berndt and Steinacher, eds., *Arianism*, 311–15.

104. Eusebius, *Life of Constantine* 4.62, ed. and trans. Averil Cameron and Stuart G. Hall (Oxford: 1999).

105. On the heterogeneity of Arianism: Patrick Amory, *People and Identity in Ostrogothic Italy, 489–554* (Cambridge: 1997), 238–39.

106. Fergus Millar, "Ishmael, Hagar, Josephus and the Origins of Islam," *Journal of Jewish Studies* 44, no. 1 (Spring 1993): 23–45, at 40, mentions a reference of Philostorgius to a mission sent by Constantius II to the Sabaeans, "now called Homeritae," in the southwest of Arabia.

107. Mathisen, "Barbarian 'Arian' Clergy," 147 n. 7: *Cod. Th.* 16.1.2 (p. 380) and *Cod. Th.* 16.5.6 (p. 381).

108. Mathisen, "Barbarian 'Arian' Clergy," 153–54; Thomas E. Kitchen, *Contemporary Perceptions of the Roman Empire in the Later Fifth and Sixth Centuries* (PhD thesis, Cambridge University, 2008), 147, on the continuation of a nonbarbarian Arianism after 381.

109. Salvien, *Du gouvernement de Dieu*; see now Peter Brown, *Through the Eye of a Needle: Wealth, the Fall of Rome, and the Making of Christianity in the West* (Princeton: 2012), esp. chap. 26, "*Romana respublica vel iam mortua:* With the Empire Now Dead and Gone: Salvian and His Gaul, 402–450," 434–54; Michael Maas, "Ethnicity, Orthodoxy and Community in Salvian of Marseilles," in John Drinkwater and Hugh Elton, eds., *Fifth-Century Gaul: A Crisis of Identity?* (Cambridge: 1992), 275–84.

110. Brown, *Eye of a Needle*, 445.

111. Maas, "Ethnicity, Orthodoxy and Community," 275–84.

112. The topic has produced an enormous, contentious literature. See Hans-Werner Goetz, "Introduction," in Hans-Werner Goetz, Jörg Jarnut, and Walter Pohl, eds., *Regna and Gentes: The Relationship between Late Antique and Early Medieval Peoples and Kingdoms in the Transformation of the Roman World* (Leiden: 2003), 1–11; Pohl has discussed an "ethnic turn" in the Early Middle Ages: Walter Pohl, "Christian and Barbarian Identities in the Early Medieval West: Introduction," in Walter Pohl and Gerda Heydemann, eds., *Post-Roman Transitions: Christian and Barbarian Identities in the Early Medieval West* (Turnhout: 2013), 1–46, at 8–17.

113. Peter Brown, *The Rise of Western Christendom: Triumph and Diversity, A.D. 200–1000*, rev. ed. (Chichester: 2013), 136.

114. Walter Pohl, "The Transformation of the Roman World Revisited," in Jamie Kreiner and Helmut Reimitz, eds., *Motions of Late Antiquity: Essays on Religion, Politics, and Society in Honour of Peter Brown* (Turnhout: 2016), 45–61, at 53.

115. For discussion of this idea, Amory, *People and Identity*, 236–76, as well as 308; and Peter Heather, "Merely an Ideology?—Gothic Identity in Ostrogothic Italy," in Sam J. Barnish and Federico Marazzi, eds., *The Ostrogoths from the Migration Period to the Sixth Century: An Ethnographic Perspective* (Woodbridge, NY: 2007), 31–80.

116. Hanns Christof Brennecke, "Introduction: Framing the Historical and Theological Problems," in Berndt and Steinacher, eds., *Arianism*, 1–19, and Hen, "Conclusion," 311–15 in the same volume.

117. Amory, *People and Identity*, 237–47, on the Gothic church.

[358] NOTES TO PAGES 254–258

118. Ambrose of Milan, *Sancti Ambrosii, Mediolanensis Episcopi, De Fide ad Gratianum Augustum, Libri Quinque* 2.16.138, in Migne, ed., PL 14 (Paris: 1845), cols. 527–698, at col. 588A: "Gog iste Gothus est, quem jam videmus exisse"; Amory, *People and Identity*, 238; Michael Maas, "How the Steppes Became Byzantine," 30–33.

119. Amory, *People and Identity*, 241–42.

120. Amory, *People and Identity*, 243.

121. Kitchen, "Contemporary Perceptions," 263; Amory, *People and Identity*, 43–85.

122. Amory, *People and Identity*, 256–57, suggests that the Italian Arian clergy may have begun to identify with the Gothic Arianism to differentiate themselves from Italian Catholics even before the arrival of Theodoric. He notes also, at 246, that Theoderic "never connected his Arian belief with the Goths. The only thing that we can assume is that Theoderic, some of his family, and some of his followers were Arian because they came from the Balkans, where Arians still maintained a strong presence, as in Italy," and, at 251, that "Arianism always existed in Italy; Arian churchmen gradually made the Arian Gothic heritage their own, and the process was underway before Theoderic came to Italy."

123. Deborah M. Deliyannis, *Ravenna in Late Antiquity* (Cambridge: 2014), 177–87, on the Baptistry of the Arians and Sant'Apollinare Nuovo.

124. Amory, *People and Identity*, 258 and n. 91.

125. Amory, *People and Identity*, 259.

126. Amory, *People and Identity*, 247–76.

127. Amory, *People and Identity*, 261.

128. Ibid.

129. Amory, *People and Identity*, 254.

130. Amory, *People and Identity*, 261.

131. Procopius, *History of the Wars* 3.2.2–11, ed. and trans. H. B. Dewing, LCL 81 (Cambridge, MA: 1916); discussed in Amory, *People and Identity*, 141–42.

132. Jordanes, *Romana et Getica*, ed. Theodor Mommsen, MGHAA 5.1 (Berlin: 1882), 25: "Omnem ubique linguae eius nationem ad culturam huius sectae invitaverunt," cited in Amory, *People and Identity*, 245 n. 42; Maya Maskarinec, "Clinging to Empire in Jordanes' *Romana*," in Helmut Reimitz and Gerda Heydemann, eds., *Historiography and Identity II: Post-Roman Multiplicity and New Political Identities* (Turnhout: 2020), 71–93, for discussion of Jordanes's views of the Christian Roman Empire; Andrew Gillett, "The Mirror of Jordanes: Concepts of the Barbarian, Then and Now," in *A Companion to Late Antiquity*, ed. Philip Rousseau (Chichester: 2009), 392–408, for Jordanes's views of barbarism in broad historical context.

133. Charles C. Mierow, *The Gothic History of Jordanes* (Princeton: 1915), 25.132–33 [88].

134. Maas, "'Delivered from Their Ancient Customs': Christianity and the Question of Cultural Change in Early Byzantine Ethnography," in *Conversion in Late Antiquity and the Early Middle Ages: Seeing and Believing*, ed. Kenneth Mills and Anthony Grafton (Rochester: 2003), 152–88, at 172.

135. Agathias, *Agathiae Myrinaei Historiarum Libri Quinque* 1.2.3–5, ed. Rudolf Keydell (Berlin: 1967); Agathias, *The Histories*, trans. Joseph D. C. Frendo (Berlin: De Gruyter, 1975).

136. Robert Hoyland, *Seeing Islam as Others Saw It: A Survey and Evaluation of Christian, Jewish and Zoroastrian Writings on Early Islam* (Princeton: 2019), 54–59, for sources and discussion.

137. Pauline Allen, *Sophronius of Jerusalem and Seventh-Century Heresy: The Synodical Letter and Other Documents* (Oxford: 2009).

138. Allen, *Sophronius*, 54–55.

139. Allen, *Sophronius*, 62.

140. On anathema in the sixth century: Michael Maas, *Exegesis and Empire in the Early Byzantine Mediterranean: Junillus Africanus and the Instituta Regularia Divinae Legis* (Tübingen: 2003), 58–60 and 63–64.

141. Sophronius of Jerusalem, "Synodical Letter" 2.6.4, trans. in Allen, *Sophronius*, 148–49.

NOTES TO PAGES 258–268 [359]

142. George C. Berthold, "John of Damascus," in Ferguson, ed., *Encyclopedia of Early Christianity*, 625–26; Daniel J. Sahas, *John of Damascus on Islam: The "Heresy of the Ishmaelites"* (Leiden: 1972); John Meyendorff, "Byzantine Views of Islam," *DOP* 18 (1964): 113–32, at 116–20; Peter Schadler, "Heresy and Heresiology in Late Antiquity," in Peter Schadler, *John of Damascus and Islam: Christian Heresiology and the Intellectual Background to Earliest Christian-Muslim Relations* (Leiden: 2018), 20–48, on the question of whether John understood Islam to be a Christian heresy, his answer is "yes and no."

143. Some place it at 100; Sahas, *John of Damascus*, 58–60. He argues (60–66) that it was a genuine part of John's work and not a later interpolation.

144. John of Damascus, *De haeresibus liber*, in PG 94 (1864), cols. 578–788, at col. 765A; translated in Sahas, *John of Damascus*, 68.

145. Sahas, *John of Damascus*, 69–70.

146. Fergus Millar, "Hagar, Ishmael, Josephus and the Origins of Islam," *Journal of Jewish Studies* 44, no. 1 (Spring 1993): 23–45; Robert G. Hoyland, *Arabia and the Arabs: From the Bronze Age to the Coming of Islam* (London: 2001), 243.

Conclusion: The Conqueror's Gift

1. Mark Twain, *Adventures of Huckleberry Finn* (London: 1884).

2. Helmut Reimitz, private communication, October 9, 2023.

3. Anthony Kaldellis, *Ethnography after Antiquity: Foreign Lands and Peoples in Byzantine Literature* (Philadelphia: 2013), provides a bookend for this book's coverage, as noted in the introduction of this book.

4. Maja Kominko, "Changing Habits and Disappearing Monsters—Ethnography between Classical and Late Antiquity," in Koray Durak and Ivana Jevtić, eds., *Identity and the Other in Byzantium: Papers from the Fourth International Sevgi Gönül Byzantine Studies Symposium* (Istanbul: 2019), 53–70, at 57.

5. James C. Scott, *The Art of Not Being Governed: An Anarchist History of Upland Southeast Asia* (New Haven: 2009), 118.

BIBLIOGRAPHY

Primary Sources

The Acts of the Council of Chalcedon. Translated by Richard Price and Michael Gaddis. 3 Volumes. TTH 45. Liverpool: Liverpool University Press, 2007.

The Acts of the Council of Constantinople of 553. Translated by Richard Price. TTH 51. Liverpool: Liverpool University Press, 2009.

Aelius Aristides. "The Ruling Power: A Study of the Roman Empire in the Second Century after Christ through the Roman Oration of Aelius Aristides." Edited by James H. Oliver. *Transactions of the American Philosophical Society.* Vol. 43, no. 4 (1953): 873–1003.

Agathias. *Agathiae Myrinaei Historiarum libri quinque.* Edited by Rudolf Keydell. Berlin: Walter de Gruyter, 1967.

———. *The Histories.* CFHB, Series Berolinensis, Vol. 2A. Translated by Joseph D. C. Frendo. Berlin / New York: Walter de Gruyter, 1975.

Alexandrian World Chronicle. Edited and translated by Benjamin Garstad. Dumbarton Oaks Medieval Library 14. Cambridge, MA: Harvard University Press, 2012.

Ambrose of Milan. *De fide [ad Gratianum].* Edited and translated by Christoph Markschies. 3 vols. Turnhout: Brepols, 2003.

Ambrosiaster. *Contre les païens et Sur le destin.* Edited and translated by Marie-Pierre Bussières. Paris: Éditions du Cerf, 2007.

Ammianus Marcellinus. [*History*]. Translated by John C. Rolfe. 3 vols. LCL 300, 315, 331, 1950–1972.

Andrew of Caesarea. *Commentary on the Apocalypse.* Translated by Eugenia Scarvelis Constantinou. Fathers of the Church 123. Washington, DC: Catholic University of America Press, 2011.

Antonine Constitution. Die Giessener Literarischen Papyri und die Caracalla-Erlasse, Pp. 217–239 [P. Giss. 40]. Edited, translated, and with commentary by Peter Alois Kuhlmann. Giessen, Universitätsbibliothek, 1994.

The Antonine Constitution. An Edict for the Caracallan Empire. Brill: Leiden and Boston, 2018.

[The Antonine Constitution]: "Appendix" by Alex Imrie. *The Antonine Constitution: An Edict for the Caracallan Empire* (Leiden: 2018), 139–53

Die Constitutio Antoniniana: eine Untersuchung über den Umfang der Bürgerrechtsverleihung auf Grund des Papyrus Giss. 40 I. Edited by Christoph Sasse, Wiesbaden: Harrassowitz, 1958.

Apocalypse of Pseudo-Methodius. Edited by Benjamin Garstad. Dumbarton Oaks Medieval Library 14. Cambridge, MA / London: Harvard University Press, 2012.

Aristote. *Problèmes: Sections XI à XXVII.* Edited and translated by Pierre Louis. Vol. 2. Paris: Les Belles Lettres, 1993

Aristotle. *Nichomachean Ethics.* Translated by H. Rackham. LCL 73. Cambridge, MA: Harvard University Press, 1926.

———. *Politics.* Translated by H. Rackham. LCL 264. Cambridge, MA: Harvard University Press, 1932.

———. "Politics." In *The Basic Works of Aristotle,* translated by Benjamin Jowett, and edited by Richard McKeon, 1114–1316. New York: Random House, 1941.

———. *Problems: Books 1–19.* Edited and translated by Robert Mayhew. LCL 316, Vol. 1. Cambridge, MA: Harvard University Press, 2011.

Pseudo-Aristotle. *See below*

Arrian. *Anabasis of Alexander.* Translated by P. A. Brunt. 2 vols. LCL 236, 269. Cambridge, MA: Harvard University Press, 1976–1983.

[361]

[362] BIBLIOGRAPHY

Augustine. *City of God, Vol. 2: Books 4–7*. Translated by William M. Green. LCL 412. Cambridge, MA: Harvard University Press, 1963.

———. *City of God, Vol. 4: Books 12–15*. Translated by Philip Levine. LCL 414. Cambridge, MA: Harvard University Press, 1966.

———. *City of God, Vol. 5: Books 16–18.35*. Translated by Eva M. Sanford. LCL 415. Cambridge, MA: Harvard University Press, 1965.

———. *City of God, Vol. 6: Books 18.36–20*. Translated by William Chase Greene. LCL 416. Cambridge, MA: Harvard University Press, 1960.

———. *Confessions, Vol. 1: Books 1–8*. Edited and translated by Carolyn J.-B. Hammond. LCL 26. Cambridge, MA: Harvard University Press, 2014.

———. *De Haeresibus*. Edited by Michael P. J. van den Hout, Ernest Evans, Johannes Bauer, Roel vander Plaetse, S. Dominic Ruegg, Marie Vianney O'Reilly, and Clemens Beukers. CCSL 46. Turnhout: Brepols, 1969.

———. *The "De haeresibus" of Saint Augustine: A Translation with an Introduction and Commentary*. Translated by G. Liguori Müller. Washington, DC: Catholic University of America Press, 1956.

———. *Epistulae*. Edited by Alois Goldbacher. CSEL 34, no. 1. Prague/Vienna: F. Tempsky, 1895.

———. "Heresies." In *De haeresibus ad Quodvultdeum liber unus*, edited by Roel vander Plaetse and Clemens Beukers, 263–351. Turnhout: Brepols, 1969.

———. "Letter 199." In *Letters 156–210 (Epistulae)*, edited by Boniface Ramsey and translated by Roland J. Teske. Hyde Park, NY: New City Press, 2004.

———. "Letter No. 57 (Ep. CCXLVI): Augustine to Lampadius." In *Select Letters*, translated by James Houston Baxter, 482-483. LCL 239. Cambridge, MA: Harvard University Press, 1930.

———. *On Christian Teaching*. Translated by R. P. H. Green. Oxford: Oxford University Press, 1997.

———."Question 63." In *Pseudo-Augustini Quaestiones Veteris et Novi Testamenti*, edited by Alexander Souter, 112. CSEL 50. Vienna: F. Tempsky, 1908.

Augustus. *Res Gestae Divi Augusti: Text, Translation, and Commentary*. Edited by Allison E. Cooley. Cambridge: Cambridge University Press, 2009.

Aulus Gellius. *Attic Nights, Vol. 2: Books 6–13*. Translated by John C. Rolfe. LCL 200. Cambridge, MA: Harvard University Press, 1927.

Avienus, Rufus Festius. *Avieno ora maritima periplo massaliota del siglo VI.a. de J.C.* Edited by Adolph Schulten. Berlin: Libreria Universitaria de A. Bosh, 1922.

———. *Ora Maritima: A Description of the Seacoast from Britanny to Marseilles [Massilia]*. Translated by John P. Murphy. Chicago: Ares Publishers, 1977.

Bardaisan of Edessa. *The Book of the Laws of Countries: Dialogue on Fate of Bardaiṣan of Edessa*. Translated by H. J. W. Drijvers. Assen: 1965. Reprinted with new introduction by Jan Willem Drijvers. Piscataway, NJ: Gorgias Press, 2007.

Basil of Caesarea. "Adversus Eunomium Libri." *S.P.N. Basilii Opera Omnia Quae Exstant*, edited by J.-P. Migne. PL 31. Paris: 1857.

———. *Homélies sur l'Hexaéméron*. Edited by Stanislas Giet. Sources Chrétiennes, vol. 26. Paris: Les Éditions du Cerf, 1949.

———. "Homily 5: The Germination of the Earth (on the Hexaemeron)." In *Exegetic Homilies*, translated by Agnes Clare Way, 67–82. Fathers of the Church 46. Washington, DC: Catholic University of America Press, 1963.

———. "Letter CCLVIII: To Bishop Epiphanius." In Vol. 4: *Letters 249–368; On Greek Literature*, translated by Roy J. Deferrari and M. R. P. McGuire, 35–47. LCL 270. Cambridge, MA: Harvard University Press, 1934.

Basil of Seleucia, "Basil of Seleucia's Explanation of Pentecost." Translated by Charles A. Sullivan, 2014. https://charlesasullivan.com/5083/fifth-century-basil-of-seleucia-on-pentecost/.

———. "Homilia I: "Εἰς τὴν ἁγίαν Πεντηκοστήν." / Homilia I. De Sancta, edited by J.-P. Migne. PG 64, cols. 417–24. Paris: 1862.

Bible. *The New Interpreter's Study Bible. New Revised Standard Version with the Apocrypha*. Edited by Walter J. Harrelson. Nashville: Abingdon Press, 2003.

BIBLIOGRAPHY [363]

Bible. *Septuaginta: Id est Vetus Testamentum graece iuxta LXX interpretes*. Edited by Alfred Rahlfs. Rev. ed. Stuttgart: Deutsche Bibelgesellschaft, 2006.

Bible. *Tanakh: A New Translation of the Holy Scriptures According to the Traditional Hebrew Text*. Edited by Jewish Publication Society. Philadelphia / New York / Jerusalem: Jewish Publication Society, 1985.

Blockley, R. C., ed and trans. *The Fragmentary Classicising Historians of the Later Roman Empire: Eunapius, Olympiodorus, Priscus and Malchus*. 2 vols. Ottawa: Francis Cairns, 1981–83.

Boemus, Joannes [Aubanus]. *Omnium gentium mores leges et ritus ex multis clarissimis rerum scriptoribus a ioanne boemo aubano sacerdo e teutonicae militia deuto nuper collectos*. Augustae Vindelicorum: In officium Sigismundi Grimm medici, ac Marci Vuirsung, 1520.

Caesar, Gaius Julius. *Bellum gallicum*. Edited by Otto Seel. Leipzig: B. G. Teubner Verlag, 1961.

———. *The Gallic War*. Translated by S. A. Handford. London: Penguin Books, 1951.

Cassiodorus. *Institutiones divinarum et saecularium litterarum*. Edited by R. A. B. Mynors. Oxford: Clarendon Press, 1937.

———. *Institutions of Divine and Secular Learning and On the Soul*. Translated by James W. Halporn. TTH 42. Liverpool: Liverpool University Press, 2004.

———. *Variae*. Translated by S. J. B. Barnish. TTH 12. Liverpool: Liverpool University Press, 1992.

———. *Variarum Libri XII*. Edited by Å. J. Fridh. CCSL 96. Turnhout: Brepols, 1973.

Cedrenus, George. *Georgii Cedreni Historiarum Compendium*. Bolletino dei Classici, edited by Luigi Tartaglia. Vol. 2. Accademia Nazionale dei Lincei 30. Rome: Bardi Edizioni, 2016.

Chronicon Paschale. *Chronicon Paschale 284-628 AD*. Translated by Michael Whitby and Mary Whitby. TTH 7. Liverpool: Liverpool University Press, 1989.

———. Edited by Ludwig Dindorf, 2 vols. Bonn: Weber, 1832.

Chronograph of 354. "*Chronographus Anni CCCLIIII*." Edited by Theodor Mommsen, MGHAA Tomus IX. Chronicorum Minorum Saec. IV. V. VI. VII. Vol. 1:13–196. Berlin: Weidmann, 1892.

Chrysostom, John. *Baptismal Instructions*. Translated by Paul W. Harkins. Westminster, MD / London: Newman Press / Longmans, Green and Co., 1963.

———. *Huit catéchèses baptismales inédites*. Edited by Antoine Wenger. Sources Chrétiennes 50. Paris: Éditions du Cerf, 1957.

Cicero. "Brutus." In *Brutus, Orator*, translated by G. L. Hendrickson and H. M. Hubbell, 18–296. LCL 342. Cambridge, MA: Harvard University Press, 1939.

———. *Letters to Atticus, Volume I*. Edited and translated by D. R. Shackleton Bailey. LCL 7. Cambridge, MA: Harvard University Press, 1999.

———. "On Divination." In *On Old Age. On Friendship. On Divination*, translated by W. A. Falconer, 222–329. LCL 154. Cambridge, MA: Harvard University Press, 1923.

———. "Scipio's Dream." In *De Re Publica (VI 9-29)*, translated and edited by Clinton Walker Keyes, 260–83. LCL 213. Cambridge, MA: Harvard University Press, 1928.

———. *Timaeus*. Edited by C. F. W. Mueller. Leipzig: B. G. Teubner Verlag, 1900.

Claudian. "The Second Book Against Rufinus." In *Panegyric on Probinus and Olybrius. Against Rufinus 1 and 2. War against Gildo. Against Eutropius 1 and 2. Fescennine Verses on the Marriage of Honorius. [. . .]*, translated by M. Platnauer, 74–77. LCL 135. Cambridge, MA: Harvard University Press, 1922.

Clément d'Alexandrie. *Les Stromates. Stromate VI*. Edited and translated by Patrick Descourtieux. Sources Chrétiennes 446. Paris: Éditions du Cerf, 1999.

Clement of Alexandria. "Clement of Alexandria's Excerpts from Theodotus." In *The Gnostic Scriptures*, 2nd ed., edited by Bentley Layton and David Brakke, LXXIV–LXXVIII. New Haven: Yale University Press, 2021.

Codex Theodosianus. Theodosiani Libri XVI cum Constitutionibus Sirmondianis. Edited by Theodor Mommsen. Vol. 2. Hildesheim: Weidmann, 1905.

The Theodosian Code and Novels and the Sirmondian Constitutions: A Translation with Commentary, Glossary, and Bibliography. Translated by Clyde Pharr. Princeton: Princeton University Press, 1952.

[364] BIBLIOGRAPHY

Constantine Porphyrogennitos [Constantinus Porphyrogenitus]. *The Book of Ceremonies.* Edited and translated by Anne Moffatt and Maxeme Tall. Byzantine Australiensia 18. Leiden/Boston: Brill, 2012.

———. *De cerimoniis aulae byzantinae libri duo graece et latine: Volumen I.* Edited by Johan Jakob Reiske and B. G. Niebuhr. Corpus Scriptorum Historiae Byzantinae. Bonn: E. Weber, 1829.

Corippus, Flavius Cresconius. *In Laudem Iustini Augusti Minoris Libri IV.* Edited and translated by Averil Cameron. London: Athlone Press, 1976.

Corpus Inscriptionum Latinarum, Vol. 3.1: Inscriptiones Asiae, Provinciarum Europae Graecarum, Illyrici Latinae. Edited by Theodor Mommsen. Berlin: Georg Reimer, 1873.

Cosmography of Julius Caesar. "Cosmographia Iulii Caesaris." In *Geographi latini minores*, 21–23. Edited by Alexander Riese. Heilbronn: Henninger Fratres, 1878. Reprint, Hildesheim: Georg Olms, 1995.

Cyril of Scythopolis. "Κεφαλαία τῆς Περὶ τοῦ Μεγάλου Εὐθυμίου Συγγραφῆς" [Vita Euthymii]. In *Kyrillos von Skythopolis*, edited by Eduard Schwartz. Classics in the History of Early Christian Literature 87. Piscataway, NJ: Gorgias Press, 1939.

Dicuil. *Liber de Mensura Orbis Terrae.* Edited by J. J. Tierney. With contributions by L. Bieler. In *Scriptores Latini Hiberniae*, vol. 6. Dublin: Dublin Institute for Advanced Studies, 1967.

Dio Cassius. *Roman History, Volume III.* Translated by Earnest Cary and Herbert B. Foster. LCL 53. Cambridge, MA: Harvard University Press, 1914.

Dio Chrysostom. *Discourses 31–36.* Translated by J. W. Cohoon and H. Lamar Crosby. LCL 358. Cambridge, MA: Harvard University Press, 1940.

———. *Discourses 61–80. Fragments. Letters.* Translated by H. Lamar Crosby. LCL 385. Cambridge, MA: Harvard University Press, 1951.

Diodorus Siculus. *Library of History, Volume XII: Fragments of Books 33–40.* Translated by Francis R. Walton. LCL 423. Cambridge, MA: Harvard University Press, 1967.

Diodorus of Tarsus. *See* Behr, John.

"Dirge for the Ninth of Av." In *The Penguin Book of Hebrew Verse*, edited and translated by T. Carmi, 204–6. London: Penguin Books, 1981.

Epiphanius of Salamis. "Against Adamians 32, but 52 of the Series." In *The Panarion of Epiphanius of Salamis, Books II and III. De Fide*, translated by Frank Williams. Nag Hammadi and Manichaean Studies 79. Leiden/Boston: Brill, 2013.

———. *The Panarion of Epiphanius of Salamis. Book I (Sects 1–46).* Rev. ed. Translated by Frank Williams. Nag Hammadi and Manichaean Studies 63. Leiden/Boston: Brill, 2009.

Eusebius. *Die Chronik: Aus dem armenischen Übersetzt mit textkritischem Commentar.* Edited and translated by Josef Karst. Eusebius Werke 5. Leipzig: J. C. Hinrichs'sche Buchhandlung, 1911.

———. *Die Praeparatio evangelica.* Edited by Karl Mras. Eusebius Werke 8. Berlin: Akademie Verlag, 1954–1956.

———. *Ecclesiastical History.* Translated by Kirsopp Lake and J. E. L. Oulton. LCL 246, 248. Cambridge, MA: Harvard University Press, 1926.

———. *Eusèbe de Césarée: La Préparation évangélique.* Edited by J. Sirinelli and Éduard des Places. Sources Chrétiennes 206. Paris: Éditions du Cerf, 1974.

———. *Eusebii Pamphili Praeparationis evangelicae libri XV.* Edited by Fredrich Adolf Heinichen. Leipzig: Serigiana Libraria, 1842.

———. "Eusebius' Chronicle." Translated by Robert Bedrosian. Archive.org. https://ia800702 .us.archive.org/26/items/EusebiusChroniclechronicon/Eusebius_Chronicle.pdf.

———. *Eusebius of Caesarea: Praeparatio Evangelica (Preparation for the Gospel).* Translated by E. H. Gifford. Oxford: Oxford University Press, 1903.

———. *Life of Constantine.* Translated by Averil Cameron and Stuart G. Hall. Clarendon Ancient History Series. Oxford: Clarendon Press, 2006.

Evagrius. *Ecclesiastical History: A History of the Church in Six Books, from A.D. 431 to A.D. 594.* Edited and translated by Edward Walford. London: Samuel Bagster and Sons, 1846.

"Excerpta Latina Barbari," see *An Alexandrian World Chronicle.* Edited by Alfred Schöne. In *Eusebi Chronicorum liber prior*, 174–239. Berlin: Weidmann, 1875.

BIBLIOGRAPHY [365]

Filastrius [Philastrius] of Brescia. *Filastrii Brixiensis Diversarum hereseon liber.* Edited by F. Heylen. CCSL 9. Turnhout: Brepols, 1957.

———. "Liber de Haeresibus." In *Sancti Eusebii Episcopi Vercellensis Opera Omnia* [. . .] *Firmici Materni Necnon Sancti Philastrii Opera Omnia*, edited by J.-P. Migne, PL 12. cols. 1111–1302. Paris: Vrayet, 1845.

Firmicus Maternus, Julius. *Ancient Astrology Theory and Practice: Matheseos Libri VIII.* Translated by Jean Rhys Bram. Park Ridge, NJ: Noyes Press, 1975.

———. *L'erreur des religions païennes.* Edited and translated by Robert Turcan. Paris: Les Belles Lettres, 1982.

———. *Matheseos libri VIII.* Edited by Wilhelm Kroll and Franz Skutsch. 1897. Reprint, Stuttgart: B. G. Teubner Verlag, 1968.

Florus, Lucius Annaeus. *Epitome of Roman History.* Translated by E. S. Forster. LCL 231. Cambridge, MA: Harvard University Press, 1929.

Fragments of Greek Historians. *Die Fragmente Der Griechischen Historiker. Erster Teil. Genealogie Und Mythographie.* Edited by Felix Jacoby. Berlin: Weidmann, 1923

Fredegar. "Chronicarum quae dicuntur Fredegarii Scholastici libri IV cum Continuationibus." In *Fredegarii et Aliorum Chronica: Vitae Sanctorum*, edited by Bruno Krusch. *MGHSRM* 2. Hannover: Hahnsche Buchhandlung, 1888.

Gaius. *The Institutes of Gaius.* Translated by Francis de Zulueta. Oxford: Clarendon Press, 1946.

Geographi Latini Minores. Edited by Alexander Riese. Heilbronn: Henninger Fratres, 1878. Reprint, Hildesheim: Georg Olms, 1995.

Gnosis: A Selection of Gnostic Texts. See Foerster

Grégoire de Nysse. *Contre Eunome II.* Edited by Raymond Winling. Sources Chrétiennes 551. Paris: Les Éditions du Cerf, 2013.

Gregory of Nyssa. *The Treatise of Gregory of Nyssa Contra Fatum: A Critical Text with Prolegomena.* Edited and translated by James Andrew McDonough. Cambridge, MA: Harvard University Press, 1952.

Gregory of Tours. *Gregorii Episcopi Turonensis Libri Historiarum X.* Rev. ed. Edited by Bruno Krusch and Wilhelm Levison. MGHSRM 1.1. Hannover: Hahnsche Buchhandlung, 1951.

———. *The History of the Franks.* 2 vols. Translated by O. M. Dalton. Oxford: Clarendon Press, 1927.

Hephaistion of Thebes. *Apotelesmaticorum libri tres.* Edited by David Pingree. Vol. 1. Leipzig: B. G. Teubner Verlag, 1973.

Herodotus. *The Persian Wars.* Translated by A. D. Godley. 4 vols. LCL 117–120. Cambridge, MA: Harvard University Press, 1920–1925.

Hippocrate/Hippocrates. *Airs, eaux, lieux.* Edited and translated by Jacques Jouanna. 2nd ed. Vol. 2.2. Paris: Les Belles Lettres, 1996.

———. "Airs, Waters, Places." In *Hippocrates, Volume I: Ancient Medicine. Airs, Waters, Places. Epidemics 1 and 3. The Oath. Precepts. Nutriment*, edited and translated by Paul Potter. LCL 147. Cambridge, MA: Harvard University Press, 2022.

———. *Du régime.* Edited and translated by Robert Joly. Paris: Les Belles Lettres, 1967.

L'Hypostase des archontes: Traité gnostique sur l'origine de l'homme, du monde et des archontes (NH II, 4). Edited by Bernard Barc. Bibliothèque Copte de Nag Hammadi. Section "Textes 5". Québec/ Louvain: Les Presses de l'Université Laval / Éditions Peeters, 1980

Inscriptiones latinae selectae. Edited by Hermann Dessau. 3 vols. Berlin: Weidmann, 1892.

Irenaeus of Lyons. "Against Heresies." In *The Apostolic Fathers*, edited by Alexander Roberts and James Donaldson, 315–567. ANF 1. New York: Christian Literature Publishing, 1885.

Irénée de Lyon. *Contre les hérésies.* Edited and translated by Adelin Rousseau and Louis Doutreleau. Vol. 2, no. 1. Paris: Les Éditions du Cerf, 1979.

Isho'dad. *Commentaire d'Išoʿdad de Merv sur l'Ancien Testament: I. Genèse.* Edited by J.-M. Vosté. Translated by Ceslas Van den Eynde. Corpus Scriptorum Christianorum Orientalium: Scriptores Syri 67. Louvain: Imprimerie Orientaliste L. Durbecq, 1950.

Isidore. *The Etymologies of Isidore of Seville.* Translated by Stephen A. Barney, W. J. Lewis, J. A. Beach, and Oliver Berghof. Cambridge: Cambridge University Press, 2006.

[366] BIBLIOGRAPHY

Isidore. *History of the Goths, Vandals and Suevi*. Translated by Guido Donini and Gordon B. Ford. Leiden: Brill, 1966.

——. *Isidori Hispalensis Episcopi, Etymologiarum sive Originum libri XX*. Edited by W. M. Lindsay. 2 vols. Oxford: Clarendon Press, 1911.

Jerome/Hieronymus. *Chronicon*. In *Die Chronik Des Hieronymus; Hieronymi Chronicon*, 2nd ed., edited by Rudolf Helm. Eusebius Werke 7. GCS 47. Berlin: Akademie Verlag, 1956.

——. "Hebraicae quaestiones in libro geneseos." In *Hebraicae quaestiones in libro geneseos: Liber interpretationis hebraicorum nominum. commentarioli in psalmos; Commentarius in Ecclesiasten*, edited by Paul de Lagarde, G. Morin, and M. Adriaen, 1–56. CCSL 72. Turnhout: Brepols, 1959.

——. "The Life of Malchus, the Captive Monk." In *Jerome: Letters and Select Works; Second Series*, edited by Philip Schaff and Henry Wace, translated by W. H. Fremantle, 315–18. NPNF 6. Edinburgh / Grand Rapids: T&T Clark / W.M.B. Eerdmans Publishing Company, 1988.

——. *The Principal Works of St. Jerome*. Edited by Philip Schaff and Henry Wace. Translated by W. H. Fremantle. NPNF 6. New York: Christian Literature Company, 1893.

——. *Saint Jerome's Hebrew Questions on Genesis*. Translated by C. T. R. Hayward. Oxford Early Christian Studies. Oxford: Clarendon Press, 1995.

John Malalas. *Chronographia*. Edited by Ioannes Thurn. CFHB, Series Berolinensis 35. Berlin / New York: Walter de Gruyter, 2000.

John of Antioch. *Ioannis Antiocheni fragmenta quae supersunt omnia*. Edited and translated by Sergei Mariev. CFHB, Series Berolinensis 47. Berlin / New York: Walter de Gruyter, 2008.

John of Ephesus. *The Third Part of the Ecclesiastical History of John Bishop of Ephesus*. Translated by Robert Payne Smith. Oxford: Oxford University Press, 1860.

John Philoponus. *De opificio mundi libri VII*. Edited by Walther Reichardt. Leipzig: B. G. Teubner Verlag, 1897.

Jordanes. *The Gothic History of Jordanes*. Translated by Charles C. Mierow. Princeton: Princeton University Press, 1915.

——. *Jordanes: Romana and Getica*. Translated by Peter Van Nuffelen and Lieve Van Hoof. TTH 75. Liverpool: Liverpool University Press, 2020.

——. *Romana et Getica*. Edited by Theodor Mommsen. MGHAA 5.1. Berlin: Weidmann, 1882.

Josephus. *Jewish Antiquities, Vol. 1: Books 1–3*. Translated by H. St. J. Thackeray. LCL 242. Cambridge, MA: Harvard University Press, 1930.

——. *Jewish War, Volume 3: Books 5–7*. Translated by H. St. J. Thackeray. LCL 210. Cambridge, MA: Harvard University Press, 1928.

Jubilees, Book of. Translated by James C. Vanderkam. Corpus Scriptorum Christianorum Orientalium 511. Louvain: Peeters, 1989.

Justin. *Dialogue with Trypho*. Edited by Michael Slusser. Translated by Thomas B. Falls. Fathers of the Church 3. Washington, DC: Catholic University of America Press, 2003.

——. *Iustini Martyris Apologiae pro Christianis. Iustini Martyris Dialogus cum Tryphone*. Edited by Miroslav Marcovich. Patristische Texte und Studien Vol. 38/47. Berlin: de Gruyter, 2005.

Justinian. *Codex Iustinianus*. In *Corpus iuris civilis*, Vol. 2, 11th ed., edited by Paul Krueger. Berlin: Weidmann, 1954.

——. *The Codex of Justinian*. 3 Volumes. Translated by Bruce W. Frier et al. Cambridge: Cambridge University Press, 2016.

——. *Institutiones* and *Digesta*. In *Corpus iuris civilis*, Vol. 1, 16th ed., edited by Paul Krueger. Berlin: Weidmann, 1954.

——. *Justinian's Institutes*. Translated by Peter Birks and Grant McLeod. Ithaca, NY: Cornell University Press, 1987.

——. *Novellae*. In *Corpus iuris civilis*, Vol. 3, 6th ed., edited by Rudolf Schöll and Wilhelm Kroll. Berlin: Weidmann, 1954.

BIBLIOGRAPHY [367]

———. *The Novels of Justinian: A Complete Annotated English Translation.* 2 Volumes. Translated by David J. D. Miller and Peter Sarris. Cambridge: Cambridge University Press, 2018.

Lactantius. *De Mortibus Persecutorum / On the Death of the Persecutors.* Edited and translated by J. L. Creed. Oxford: Oxford University Press, 1984.

———. *Divinarum institutionum libri septem.* Edited by Eberhard Heck and Antonie Wlosok. 4 vols. Berlin / New York: de Gruyter, 2005–2011.

———. *Divine Institutes.* Translated by Anthony Bowen and Peter Garnsey. TTH 40. Liverpool: Liverpool University Press, 2003.

———. "On the Death of the Persecutors." In *Lactantius: The Minor Works*, translated by Mary Francis McDonald, 117–203. Fathers of the Church Patristic Series. Washington, DC: Catholic University of America Press, 1965.

Leo the Great. "Epistola XV." In *Sancti Leonis Magni Romani pontificis opera omnia, tomus primus*, edited by J.-P. Migne. PL 54.679A-B, cols. 677–695. Paris: 1850.

"Letter to Diognetus." In *The Apostolic Fathers, Volume II*, edited by Bart D. Ehrman, 121–61. LCL 25. Cambridge, MA: Harvard University Press, 2003.

Livy. *History of Rome, Volume VII: Books 26–27.* Edited and translated by J. C. Yardley. LCL 367. Cambridge, MA: Harvard University Press, 2020.

———. *History of Rome, Volume IX: Books 31–34.* Edited and translated by J. C. Yardley. LCL 295. Cambridge, MA: Harvard University Press, 2017.

Lucretius. *On the Nature of Things.* Translated by W. H. D. Rouse and Martin F. Smith. LCL 181. Cambridge, MA: Harvard University Press, 1924.

Lydus, John. *Liber de ostentis et calendaria graeca ommia.* Edited by Curt Wachsmuth. Leipzig: B. G. Teubner Verlag, 1897.

———. *Ioannes Lydus. On Celestial Signs (De Ostentis).* Edited and translated by Anastasius C. Bandy. Lewiston, NY: Edwin Mellen Press, 2013.

Macrobe/Macrobius. *Commentaire au songe de Scipion.* Edited and translated by Mireille Armisen-Marchetti. 2 vols. Paris: Les Belles Lettres, 2003.

Macrobe/Macrobius. *Commentarii in somnium Scipionis.* Edited by James Willis. Leipzig: B. G. Teubner Verlag, 1963.

Malalas, John. *The Chronicle of John Malalas.* Translated by Elizabeth Jeffreys, Michael Jeffreys, and Roger Scott. Byzantina Australiensia 4. Leiden/Boston: Brill, 2017.

Manilius. *Astronomica.* Edited and translated by G. P. Goold. LCL 469. Cambridge, MA: Harvard University Press, 1977.

Marius Victorinus. *In epistulam Pauli ad Galatas.* Edited by Franco Gori. CSEL 83, no. 2. Salzburg: Verlag der Österreichischen Akademie der Wissenschaften, 1986.

———. *Marius Victorinus' Commentary on Galatians.* Translated by Stephen Andrew Cooper. Oxford: Oxford University Press, 2005.

Maurice. *Das Strategikon des Maurikios.* Edited by George T. Dennis. CFHB 17. Vienna: Verlag der Österreichischen Akademie der Wissenschaften, 1981.

———. *Maurice's Strategikon: Handbook of Byzantine Military Strategy.* Translated by George T. Dennis. Philadelphia: University of Pennsylvania Press, 1984.

Mela. *See* Pomponius Mela

Menander Protector. *The History of Menander the Guardsman.* Edited and translated by R. C. Blockley. Liverpool: Francis Cairns, 1985.

Miskawayh, Ahmad ibn Muhammad ibn. *Tajārib al-umam* [Experiences of nations]. Edited by A. Emāmi. Tehran: Soroush Press, 2001.

La Notitia dignitatum: Nueva edición crítica y commentario histórico. Edited by Concepción Neira Baleiro. Madrid: Consejo Superior de Investigaciones Científicas, 2006.

"Notitia dignitatum omnium, tam civilium quam militarium, in partibus orientis." In *Notitia dignitatum: Accedunt notitia urbis constantinopolitanae et laterculi provinciarum.* Edited by Otto Seeck. Berlin: Weidmann, 1876.

Origen. *Contra Celsum.* Edited and translated by Henry Chadwick. Cambridge: Cambridge University Press, 1980.

———. "Homily on Genesis XIV." In *Homilies on Genesis and Exodus*, translated by Ronald E. Heine, 196–202. Fathers of the Church 71. Washington, DC: Catholic University of America Press, 1982.

[368] BIBLIOGRAPHY

Origen. *The Philocalia of Origen: A Compilation of Selected Passages from Origen's Works Made by St. Gregory of Nazianzus and St. Basil of Caesarea.* Translated by George Lewis. Edinburgh: T&T Clark, 1911.

Origène. *Philocalie 1–20 Sur les Écritures et La Lettre à Africanus sur l'histoire de Suzanne.* Edited and translated by Marguerite Harl and Nicholas de Lange. Sources Chrétiennes 302. Paris: Éditions du Cerf, 1983.

Origines. *Die Homilien zum Buch Genesis.* Edited by Peter Habermehl. Vol. 1, no. 2, of *Origenes: Werke mit deutscher Übersetzung.* Berlin/Boston/Freiburg: De Gruyter, 2011.

Orose. *Histoires: Contre les païens.* Edited and translated by Marie-Pierre Arnaud-Lindet. 3 vols. Paris: Les Belles Lettres, 1990–1991.

Orosius, Paulus. *Seven Books of History Against the Pagans: The Apology of Paulus Orosius.* Edited by Irving W. Raymond. New York: Columbia University Press, 1936.

Pacatus. *Panegyric to the Emperor Theodosius.* Translated by C. E. V. Nixon. TTH 3. Liverpool: Liverpool University Press, 1987. For Latin text, see Nixon and Rogers, *In Praise of Later Roman Emperors*, no. 7.

Panegyrics. *In Praise of Later Roman Emperors: The Panegyrici Latini; Introduction, Translation and Historical Commentary, with Latin Text of R.A.B. Mynors.* Translated by C. E. V. Nixon and Barbara Saylor Rodgers. Berkeley: University of California Press, 1994.

———. "Panegyric of Constantius." In *In Praise of Later Roman Emperors: The Panegyrici Latini; Introduction, Translation and Historical Commentary, with Latin Text of R.A.B. Mynors*, 104–44. Berkeley: University of California Press, 1994.

Panétius. *Sa vie, ses écrits et sa doctrine avec une édition des fragments.* Edited by Modestus van Straaten. Amsterdam/Paris: H. J. Uitgeverij, 1946.

Pappus of Alexandria. [*Chorographia*] "The Geography of Pappus of Alexandria: A Translation of the Armenian Fragments." Translated by Robert H. Hewsen. *Isis* 62, no. 2 (Summer 1971): 186–207.

Papyrus Giessen 40. See Antonine Constitution

Paul of Alexandria. *Pauli Alexandrini elementa apotelesmatica.* Edited by A. E. Boer. Leipzig: B. G. Teubner Verlag, 1958.

Paul the Silentiary. "Description of the Church of Hagia Sophia." In *Three Political Voices from the Age of Justinian*, translated by Peter N. Bell, 1–18. TTH 52. Liverpool: Liverpool University Press, 2009.

———. *Un tempio per Giustiniano: Santa Sofia di Costantinopolu e la Descrizione di Paolo Silenziario.* Edited and translated by Maria Luigia Fobelli. Rome: Viella, 2005.

Peter the Patrician. *The Lost History of Peter the Patrician: An Account of Rome's Imperial Past from the Age of Justinian.* Edited and translated by Thomas Banchich. Routledge Classical Translations. London / New York: Routledge, 2015.

Philo. "On the Posterity and Exile of Cain." In *On the Cherubim. The Sacrifices of Abel and Cain. The Worse Attacks the Better. On the Posterity and Exile of Cain. On the Giants*, translated by F. H. Colson and G. H. Whitaker, 323–442. LCL 227. Cambridge, MA: Harvard University Press, 1929.

Philoponus. *See* John Philoponus

Photius. *The Bibliotheca.* Translated by N. G. Wilson. London: Duckworth, 1994.

———. *Bibliothèque.* Edited and translated by René Henry. 9 vols. Paris: Les Belles Lettres, 1965.

Pistis Sophia. Edited by Carl Schmidt. Translated by Violet Macdermot. Nag Hammadi Studies 9. Leiden: E. J. Brill, 1978.

Pliny. *Natural History,* Translated by H. Rackham and W. H. S. Jones. 10 vols. LCL. Cambridge, MA: Harvard University Press, 1938–1963.

Pliny the Younger. *Letters, Volume II: Books 8–10. Panegyricus.* Translated by Betty Radice. LCL 59. Cambridge, MA: Harvard University Press, 1969.

Plotinus. *Ennead II.* Translated by A. H. Armstrong. LCL 441. Cambridge, MA: Harvard University Press, 1966.

Polybius. *The Histories.* 2nd ed. Edited by F. W. Walbank and Christian Habicht. Translated by W. R. Paton. 6 vols. LCL. Cambridge, MA: Harvard University Press, 2010–2012.

BIBLIOGRAPHY [369]

Pomponius Mela. *Description of the World*. Translated by Frank E. Romer. Ann Arbor: University of Michigan Press, 1998.

———. *Kreuzfahrt durch die Alte Welt*. Translated by Kai Brodersen. Darmstadt: Wissenschaftliche Buchgesellschaft, 1994.

Porphyry. "On the Life of Plotinus." In *Porphyry on the Life of Plotinus: Ennead I* by Plotinus, translated by A. H. Armstrong, 15.22–26. LCL 440. Cambridge, MA: Harvard University Press, 1969.

———. "Porphyrii Philosophi: Introductio in Tetrabiblum Ptolemaei." In *Codicum Romanorum*, edited by Emilie Boer and Stephen Weinstock, 185–231. Vol. 5, no. 4, of *Catalogus Codicum Astrologum Graecorum*. Brussels: In Aedibus R. Academiae Belgicae, 1940.

Posidonius. "87. Poseidonios von Apamea." In *Die Fragmente der griechischen Historiker* II: *Zeitgeschichte: A Universalgeschichte und Hellenika*, edited by Felix Jacoby, 222–317. Berlin: Weidmannsche Buchhandlung, 1926.

———. *Vol. 1, The Fragments*. Edited by Ludwig Edelstein and I. G. Kidd. Cambridge Classical Texts and Commentaries 13. 2nd ed. Cambridge: Cambridge University Press, 1972.

———. *Vol. 2, The Commentary*. Edited by I. G. Kidd. Cambridge Classical Texts 14B. Cambridge: Cambridge University Press, 1988.

Priscus. "History." In *The Fragmentary Classicising Historians of the Later Roman Empire*. Translated by R. C. Blockley, Vol. 2. Liverpool: Francis Cairns, 1983.

Priscus Panita. *Excerpta et fragmenta*. Edited by Pia Carolla. Bibliotheca scriptorum Graecorum et Romanorum Teubneriana 136. Berlin / New York: Walter de Gruyter, 2008.

Procopius. *The Anecdota or Secret History*. Translated by H. B. Dewing. LCL 290. Cambridge, MA: Harvard University Press, 1935.

———. *History of the Wars*. Translated by H. B. Dewing and Glanville Downey. 5 vols. LCL. Cambridge, MA: Harvard University Press, 1914–1928.

———. *On Buildings*. Translated by H. B. Dewing and Glanville Downey. LCL 343. Cambridge, MA: Harvard University Press, 1940.

Prosper of Aquitaine. *The Call of All Nations*. Translated by P. De Letter. New York / Ramsey, NJ: Paulist Press, 1952.

———. *De vocatione omnium gentium*. Edited by Roland Teske and Dorothea Weber. CSEL 97. Vienna: Verlag der Österreichischen Akademie der Wissenschaften, 2009.

Pseudo-Aristotle. *De Mundo (On the Cosmos)*. Edited by Pavel Gregorić and George Karamanolis. Cambridge: Cambridge University Press, 2020.

Pseudo-Callisthenes. *The Greek Alexander Romance*. Edited by Richard Stoneman. London / New York: Penguin Classics, 1991.

Pseudo-Clement. "Homily II." In *The Twelve Patriarchs, Excerpts and Epistles, The Clementina, Apocrypha, Decretals, Memoirs of Edessa and Syriac Documents, Remains of the First Ages*, edited by Alexander Roberts and James Donaldson, translated by Thomas Smith. ANF 8. Edinburgh / Grand Rapids: T&T Clark / Wm. B. Eerdmans Publishing Company, 1886.

———. "Recognitiones." In *The Twelve Patriarchs, Excerpts and Epistles, The Clementina, Apocrypha, Decretals, Memoirs of Edessa and Syriac Documents, Remains of the First Ages*, edited by Alexander Roberts and James Donaldson, translated by Thomas Smith. ANF 8. Edinburgh / Grand Rapids: T&T Clark / Wm. B. Eerdmans Publishing Company, 1886.

———. "Recognitions." In GCS, edited by Bernhard Rehm and Georg Strecker. Berlin: Akademie Verlag, 1994.

Pseudo-Kaisarios. *Die Erotapokriseis*. Edited by Rudolf Riedinger. GCS 29. Berlin: Akademie Verlag, 1989.

Ptolemy. *Almagest*. Translated by G. J. Toomer. London: Duckworth, 1984.

———. *Claudii Ptolemaei opera quae exstant omnia*. Edited by J. L. Heiberg. 2 vols. Leipzig: B. G. Teubner Verlag, 1898–1903.

———. *Geography: Book 6, Part 1; Text and English/German Translation*. Edited by Suzanne Ziegler. Wiesbaden: Reichert Verlag, 1998.

———. *Ptolemy's "Geography": An Annotated Translation of the Theoretical Chapters*. Translated by J. Lennart Berggren and Alexander Jones. Princeton/Oxford: Princeton University Press, 2000.

[370] BIBLIOGRAPHY

Ptolemy. *Tetrabiblos*. Translated by F. E. Robbins. LCL 435. Cambridge, MA: Harvard University Press, 1940.

Quintilian. *The Orator's Education, Volume IV: Books 9-10*. Edited and translated by Donald A. Russell. LCL 127. Cambridge, MA: Harvard University Press, 2002.

The Reality of the Archons. See Bernhard Barc, *L'Hypostase des Archontes*

Rufinus. *Historia ecclesiastica*. Edited by Eduard Schwarz and Theodor Mommsen. 2nd ed. by F. Winkelmann, in *Eusebius Werke*, II.1-3, *Die Kirchengeschichte*. GCS NF 6.1-3. Berlin, 1999.

———. *In Epistulam Pauli ad Romanos explanationum libri: Secundum translationem Rufini*. Turnhout: Brepols, 2021. Library of Latin Texts Online. http://clt.brepolis.net/llta/Default .aspx.

Sallust. "The War with Jugurtha." In *The War with Catiline. The War with Jugurtha*, edited by John T. Ramsey, translated by John C. Rolfe, 150-418. LCL 116. Cambridge, MA: Harvard University Press, 2013.

Salvian of Marseilles. *On the Government of God*. Translated by Eva M. Sanford. New York: Columbia University Press, 1930.

Salvien de Marseilles. *Oeuvres: Du gouvernement de Dieu*. Edited and translated by Georges Lagarrigue. Vol. 2. Sources Chrétiennes 220. Paris: Éditions du Cerf, 1975.

Sebeos. *The Armenian History Attributed to Sebeos: Part I; Translation and Notes*. Edited by James Howard-Johnston and Tim Greenwood. Translated by Robert W. Thomson. TTH 31. Liverpool: Liverpool University Press, 1999.

Septuagint. *See* Bible

Servius. *Commentaire Sur l'Énéide de Virgile: Livre VI*. Edited and translated by Emmanuelle Jeunet-Mancy. Collection des universités de France. Paris: Les Belles Lettres, 2012.

Socrates Scholasticus. *The Ecclesiastical History of Socrates, surnamed Scholasticus, or the Advocate: comprising a history of the church, in seven books, from the accession of Constantine, A.D. 305, to the 38th year of Theodosius II., including a period of 140 years*. Translated by Edward Walford. London: Henry G. Bohn, 1853.

Sophronius of Jerusalem. "Synodical Letter." In *Sophronius of Jerusalem and Seventh Century Heresy: The Synodical Letter and Other Documents*, translated by Pauline Allen, 148-49. Oxford Early Christian Texts. Oxford: Oxford University Press, 2009.

Sozomen. *Ecclesiastical History*. Edited by Chester D. Hartranft. NPNF, 2nd ser, vol. 2. Edinburgh: T&T Clark, 1890.

———. *The Ecclesiastical History, Comprising a History of the Church: From A.D. 324 to A.D. 440*. Translated by Edward Walford. London: Henry G. Bohn, 1855.

———. *Kirchengeschichte*. 2nd ed. Edited by Günther Christian Hansen, GCS n.s., 4. Berlin: Akademie Verlag, 1995.

Strabo. *Geography*, Translated by Horace Leonard Jones. 8 vols. LCL. Cambridge, MA: Harvard University Press, 1917-1932.

Suidae Lexicon / Suda. Edited by Ada Adler. 5 Vols. Leipzig: B. G. Teubner, 1933.

Tacitus. *Agricola. Germania. Dialogue on Oratory*. Edited by R. M. Ogilvie, E. H. Warmington, and Michael Winterbottom. Translated by M. Hutton and W. Peterson. LCL 35. Cambridge, MA: Harvard University Press, 1914.

———. "Agricola." In *Agricola. Germania. Dialogue on Oratory*, edited by R. M. Ogilvie, E. H. Warmington, and Michael Winterbottom, translated by M. Hutton and W. Peterson, 3-118. LCL 35. Cambridge, MA: Harvard University Press, 1914.

———. *Annals: Books 4-6, 11-12*. Translated by John Jackson. LCL 213. Cambridge, MA: Harvard University Press, 1937.

———. *Germania: With Translation, Introduction, and Commentary*. Edited and translated by James B. Rives. Oxford: Clarendon Press, 1999.

Theodore of Mopsuestia. *See* Behr, John

Theodore the Syncellus. "Homily on the Siege of Constantinople in 626 AD." Translated by Roger Pearse. Tertullian.org, 2007. https://www.tertullian.org/fathers/theodore_syncellus _01_homily.htm. *See esp.* XL-XLVI.

———. *Traduction et commentaire de l'homélie écrite probablement par Théodore le Syncelle sur le siège de Constantinople en 626*. Translated by Ferenc Makk. Acta Universitatis de Attila József Nominatae: Acta Antiqua et Archaeologica 19. Szeged: JATE, 1975.

BIBLIOGRAPHY [371]

Theodoret of Cyrrhus. "A Cure of Greek Maladies." In *Theodoret of Cyrus*, translated by Istvan Pasztori Kupan, 89–108. London / New York: Routledge, 2006.

———. "Epistolae." In *Theodoreti, Cyrensis Episcopi, opera omnia*, edited by J.-P. Migne, PG 41, cols. 1171–1494. Paris: 1864.

———. "Graecarum Affectionum Curatio." In *Theodoreti, Cyrensis Episcopi, opera omnia*, edited by J.-P. Migne, PG 83, cols. 783–1152. Paris: 1864.

———. "The Questions on Genesis." In *The Questions on the Octateuch, Volume I: On Genesis and Exodus*, edited by John F. Petruccione, translated by Robert C. Hill, 15. Library of Early Christianity. Washington, DC: Catholic University of America Press, 2007.

Theodosian Code, ed. *Theodosiani Libri XVI Cum Constitutionibus Sirmondianis. 2 Volumes in Three. Textus cum Apparatu*. Edited by Theodor Mommsen. Hildesheim: Weidmann, 1905.

———. *The Theodosian Code and Novels and the Sirmondian Constitutions: A Translation*. Edited and translated by Clyde Pharr. Princeton: Princeton University Press, 1952.

Theophanes the Confessor. *The Chronicle of Theophanes Confessor. Byzantine and Near Eastern History: AD 284–813*, translated by Cyril Mango and Roger Scott. Oxford: Clarendon Press, 1997.

Theophylact. *The History of Theophylact Simocatta*. Translated by Michael Whitby and Mary Whitby. Oxford: Oxford University Press, 1986.

———. *Theophylacti Simocattae Historiae*. Edited by Carolus de Boor. Leipzig: B. G. Teubner Verlag, 1887.

Vaticanus Graecus 1291. Bibliotheca Apostolica Vaticana, 2023. https://digi.vatlib.it/view/MSS _Vat.gr.1291. *See esp.* fol. 9r.

Velleius Paterculus. *Compendium of Roman History: Res Gestae Divi Augusti*. Translated by Frederick W. Shipley. LCL 152. Cambridge, MA: Harvard University Press, 1924.

Vettius Valens. *Anthologies, Livre I*. Edited and translated by Jöelle-Frédérique Bara. Leiden: Brill, 1989.

Virgil. *Aeneid*. Translated by H. R. Fairclough, revised by G. P. Goold. 2 Vols. LCL. Cambridge, MA: Harvard University Press, 1916/2001.

Vitruve. *De l'architecture: De architectura*. Edited by Pierre Gros. Paris: Les Belles Lettres, 2015.

Vitruvius. *On Architecture, Volume 2: Books 6–10*. Translated by Frank Granger. LCL 280. Cambridge, MA: Cambridge University Press, 1934.

———. *The Ten Books on Architecture*. Translated by Morris Hicky Morgan. 2nd ed. Cambridge, MA: Harvard University Press, 1926.

Zeno of Verona. *Tractatus*. Edited by Bengt Löfstedt. CCSL 22. Turnhout: 1971.

Zosime. *Histoire Nouvelle: Livres I et II*. Edited and translated by François Paschoud. Vol. 1. Paris: Les Belles Lettres, 1971.

Zosimus. *New History*. Translated by Ronald T. Ridley. Byzantina Australiensia 2. Leiden: Brill, 1982. Reprint, Sydney: Australian Association of Byzantine Studies, 2006.

Secondary Sources

Adams, J. N. *Bilingualism and the Latin Language*. Cambridge: Cambridge University Press, 2003.

Adamson, Peter. "Plotinus on Astrology." *Oxford Studies in Ancient Philosophy* 35 (Winter 2008): 265–92.

Adler, William. "Did the Biblical Patriarchs Practice Astrology? Michael Glykas and Manuel Komnenos I on Seth and Abraham." In *The Occult Sciences in Byzantium*, edited by Paul Magdalino and Maria Mavroudi, 245–63. Geneva: La Pomme d'or, 2006.

Alexander, Paul J. *The Byzantine Apocalyptic Tradition*. Edited by Dorothy deF. Abrahamse. Berkeley: University of California Press, 1985.

———. "The Diffusion of Byzantine Apocalypses in the Medieval West and the Beginnings of Joachimism." In *Prophecy and Millenarianism: Essays in Honour of Marjorie Reeves*, edited by Ann Williams, 55–106. Harlow, UK: Longman, 1980.

Alexander, Philip S. "Notes on the '*Imago Mundi*' of the Book of Jubilees." *Journal of Jewish Studies* 33 (1982): 197–213.

BIBLIOGRAPHY

Altmann, Alexander. "Astrology." In *Encyclopaedia Judaica*, edited by Michael Berenbaum and Fred Skolnik, 616–20. Vol. 2. Beit Shemesh, Israel: Keter, 2007.

Alverny, Marie-Thérèse d'. Review of *Der Turmbau von Babel: Geschichte der Meinungen über Ursprung und Vielfalt der Sprachen und Völker*, by Arno Borst. *Cahiers de Civilisation Médiévale* 3, no. 12 (December 1960): 492–94.

Amand, David. *Fatalisme et liberté dans l'Antiquitè grecque: Recherches sur la survivance de l'argumentation morale antifataliste de Carnéade chez les philosophes grecs et les théologiens chrétiens des quatre premiers siècles.* Amsterdam: Hakkert, 1945.

Amory, Patrick. *People and Identity in Ostrogothic Italy.* Cambridge: Cambridge University Press, 2009.

Anderson, Andrew Runni. *Alexander's Gate, Gog and Magog, and the Inclosed Nations.* Monographs of the Mediaeval Academy of America 5. Cambridge, MA: Medieval Academy of America, 1932.

Anderson, Benjamin. *Cosmos and Community in Early Medieval Art.* New Haven: Yale University Press, 2017.

Ando, Clifford, ed. *Citizenship and Empire in Europe 200–1900: The Antonine Constitution after 1800 Years.* Stuttgart: Franz Steiner Verlag, 2016.

———. "Legal Pluralism in Practice." In *The Oxford Handbook of Roman Law and Society*, edited by Paul J. Du Plessis, Clifford Ando, and Kaius Tuori, 283–94. Oxford: Oxford University Press, 2016.

———, ed. "Sovereignty, Territoriality and Universalism in the Aftermath of Caracalla." In *Citizenship and Empire in Europe 200–1900: The Antonine Constitution after 1800 Years*, 7–27. Stuttgart: Franz Steiner Verlag, 2016.

Andresen, Carl. *Logos und Nomos: Die Polemik des Kelsos wider das Christentum.* Berlin: De Gruyter, 1955.

Andrieu, Jean. *Le Dialogue antique: Structure et présentation.* Collection d'Études Latines. Série Scientifique 29. Paris: Les Belles Lettres, 1954.

Antonio, Margaret L., et al. "Stable Population Structure in Europe since the Iron Age, despite High Mobility." bioRxiv, January 1, 2022, 2022.05.15.491973. https://doi.org/10.1101/2022 .05.15.491973.

Arce, Ignacio. "Romans, Ghassanids and Umayyads and the Transformation of the Limes Arabicus: From Coercive and Deterrent Diplomacy towards Religious Proselytism and Political Clientelarism." In *La Transgiordania nei secoli XII-XIII et le "frontiere" del Mediterraneo medievale*, edited by Guido Vannini and Michele Nucciotti, 55–74. BAR International Series 2386. Oxford: BAR, 2012.

Arendzen, J. P. "Basilides." In *The Catholic Encyclopedia*, edited by Charles G. Herbermann, Edward A. Pace, Condé B. Pallen, Thomas J. Shahan, and John J. Wynne, 327–29. Vol. 2. New York: Robert Appleton Company, 1907.

Attfield, Robin. "Christian Attitudes to Nature." *Journal of the History of Ideas* 44, no. 3 (September 1983): 369–86.

Aujac, Germaine. *Claude Ptolémée: Astronome, astrologue, géographe; Connaissance et représentation du monde habité.* Paris: Éditions du CTHS, 1993.

Aujac, Germaine, J. B. Hartley, and David Woodward. "The Growth of an Empirical Cartography in Hellenistic Greece." In *The History of Cartography, Volume One: Cartography in Prehistoric, Ancient, and Medieval Europe and the Mediterranean*, edited by J. B. Hartley and Woodward, 148–60. Chicago: University of Chicago Press, 1987.

Ayres, Lewis. "The Question of Orthodoxy." *Journal of Early Christian Studies* 14, no. 4 (2006): 395–98.

Bachrach, Bernard S. *Merovingian Military Organization, 481–571.* Minneapolis: University of Minnesota Press, 1972.

Bacic, Jakov. "The Emergence of the Sklabenoi (Slavs), Their Arrival on the Balkan Peninsula, and the Role of the Avars in These Events: Revised Concepts in a New Perspective." PhD diss., Columbia University, 1983.

Backhaus, Wilhelm. "Der Hellenen-Barbaren-Gegensatz und die Hippokratische Schrift Περὶ Ἀέρων Ὑδάτων Τόπων." *Historia* 25, no. 2 (1976): 170–85.

BIBLIOGRAPHY [373]

Bajoni, Maria Grazia. "Envoys' Speeches at the Peace Negotiations of 561–562 AD between the Byzantine Empire and the Persian Kingdom." *Diplomacy & Statecraft* 29, no. 3 (2018): 353–71.

Bakhos, Carol. *Ishmael on the Border: Rabbinic Portrayals of the First Arab*. SUNY series in Judaica: Hermeneutics, Mysticism, and Religion. Albany: State University of New York Press, 2006.

Baldwin, Barry. "Sozomenos." In *ODB 1: Aero-Eski*, edited by Alexander P. Kazhdan, 1932–33. Oxford: Oxford University Press, 1991.

Baldwin, Barry, and Alice-Mary Talbot. "Epiphanios." In *ODB 1: Aero-Eski*, edited by Alexander P. Kazhdan, 714. Oxford: Oxford University Press, 1991.

Banchich, Thomas M., ed. and trans. *The Lost History of Peter the Patrician: An Account of Rome's Imperial Past from the Age of Justinian*. London / New York: Routledge, 2015.

Bang, Peter Fibiger. "Commanding and Consuming the World: Empire, Tribute and Trade in Roman and Chinese History." In *Rome and China: Comparative Perspectives on Ancient World Empires*, edited by Walter Scheidel, 100–120. Oxford / New York: Oxford University Press, 2009.

Baradez, Jean. *Vue-aerienne de l'organisation romaine dans le Sud-Algerien: Fossatum Africae*. Paris: Arts et Métiers Graphiques, 1949.

Baraz, Yelena. *A Written Republic: Cicero's Philosophical Politics*. Princeton: Princeton University Press, 2012.

Barc, Bernard, ed. *L'hypostase des archontes: Traité gnostique sur l'origine de l'homme, du monde et des archontes (NH II, 4)*. Bibliothèque Copte de Nag Hammadi, sec. "Textes" 5. Québec, Canada / Louvain: Les Presses de l'Université Laval / Éditions Peeters, 1980.

Bardy, Gustave. "L'*Indiculus de Haeresibus* du Pseudo-Jérome." *Recherches de Science Religieuse* 19, no. 1 (1929): 385–405.

Barnard, Laurette. "The Criminalisation of Heresy in the Later Roman Empire: A Sociopolitical Device?" *Journal of Legal History* 16, no. 2 (1995): 121–46.

Barton, Tamsyn S. *Ancient Astrology*. New York: Routledge, 1994.

———. *Power and Knowledge: Astrology, Physiognomics, and Medicine under the Roman Empire*. Ann Arbor: University of Michigan Press, 1994.

Batty, Roger. *Rome and the Nomads: The Pontic-Danubian Realm in Antiquity*. Oxford: Oxford University Press, 2007.

Bauer, Walter. *Orthodoxy and Heresy in Earliest Christianity*. Edited by Robert A. Kraft and Gerhard Krodel. Philadelphia: Fortress Press, 1979.

———. *Rechtgläubigkeit und Ketzerei im ältesten Christentum*. 2nd ed. Tübingen: J. C. B. Mohr (Paul Siebeck), 1964.

Becker, Audrey. *Dieu, le souverain et la cour: Stratégies et rituels de légitimation du pouvoir impérial et royal dans l'Antiquité tardive et au haut Moyen Âge*. Scripta Antiqua 151. Bordeaux: Ausonius Éditions, 2022.

———. *Les relations diplomatiques romano-barbares en Occident au Ve siècle: Acteurs, fonctions, modalités*. Collections de l'Université de Strasbourg. Études d'archéologie et d'histoire ancienne. Paris: De Boccard, 2013.

———. "Romano-Barbarian Treaties and the Redefinition of Identities in Late Antiquity." In *Empires and Indigenous Peoples: Comparing Ancient Roman and North American Experiences*, edited by Michael Maas and Fay Yarbrough, 105–18. Norman, OK: University of Oklahoma Press, 2024.

———. "Verbal and Nonverbal Diplomatic Communication at the Imperial Court of Constantinople (Fifth–Sixth Centuries)." *DOP* 72 (2018): 79–92.

Becker, Audrey, and Nicolas Drocourt, eds. *Ambassadeurs et ambassades au coeur des relations diplomatiques: Rome—Occident médiéval—Byzance (VIIIe s. Avant J.-C.-XIIe s. Après J.-C.)*. Collection du CRULH 47. Metz: Centre de Recherche Universitaire Lorrain d'Histoire, 2012.

BeDuhn, Jason. "Mani and the Crystallization of the Concept of 'Religion' in Third Century Iran." In *Mani at the Court of the Persian Kings: Studies in the Chester Beatty Kephalaia*

[374] BIBLIOGRAPHY

Codex, edited by Iain Gardner, Jason D. BeDuhn, and Paul Dilley, 247–75. Nag Hammadi and Manichaean Studies 87. Leiden/Boston: Brill, 2015.

Behr, John, *The Case against Diodore and Theodore: Texts and Their Contexts*. With texts edited and translated by John Behr. Oxford: Oxford University Press, 2011.

Bell, Peter N. *Social Conflict in the Age of Justinian: Its Nature, Management, and Mediation*. Oxford Early Christian Texts. Oxford: Oxford University Press, 2013.

Benedicty, Robert. "Die Milieu-Theorie bei Prokop von Kaisareia." *Byzantinische Zeitschrift* 55, no. 1 (1962): 1–10.

Ben-Eliyahu, Eyal, Yehudah Cohn, and Fergus Millar, eds. *Handbook of Jewish Literature from Late Antiquity, 135–700 CE*. Oxford: Oxford University Press, 2012.

Berger, Adolf. "Encyclopedic Dictionary of Roman Law." *Transactions of the American Philosophical Society* 43, no. 2 (1953): 333–809.

Berthold, George C. "John of Damascus." In *The Encyclopedia of Early Christianity*, edited by Everett Ferguson, 625–26. New York / London: Garland Publishing, 1998.

Berzon, Todd S. *Classifying Christians: Ethnography, Heresiology, and the Limits of Knowledge in Late Antiquity*. Berkeley: University of California Press, 2016.

Besson, Arnaud. *Constitutio Antoniniana: L'universalisation de la citoyenneté romaine au 3e siècle*. Schweizerische Beitrage zur Altertumswissenschaft 52. Basel: Schwabe Verlag, 2020.

Bezza, Giuseppe. "Introduction à l'Apotélesmatique de Ptolémée (Εἰσαγωγὴ Εἰς Τὴν Ἀποτελεσματικὴν Τοῦ Πτολεμαίου) [58]." In *Dictionnaire des philosophes antiques V: De Paccius à Rutilius Rufus. 2e Partie—Vb. De Plotina à Rutilius Rufus*, edited by Richard Goulet, 1381–84. Paris: CNRS Éditions, 2012.

Bickerman, Elias J. "Origines Gentium." *Classical Philology* 47, no. 2 (April 1952): 65–81.

Billerbeck, Margarethe, ed. and trans. *Stephani Byzantii Ethnica*. Berlin: Walter de Gruyter, 2006.

Blair, Ann. "Authorship in the Popular 'Problemata Aristotelis.'" In *Early Science and Medicine* 4, no. 3 (1999): 189–227.

———. "The Problemata as a Natural Philosophical Genre." In *Natural Particulars: Nature and the Disciplines in Renaissance Europe*, edited by Anthony Grafton and Nancy Siraisi, 171–204. Cambridge, MA: MIT Press, 1999.

Blenkinsopp, Joseph. *The Pentateuch: An Introduction to the Five Books of the Bible*. The Anchor Bible Reference Library. New Haven / London: Yale University Press, 1992.

Blockley, R. C. *East Roman Foreign Policy: Formation and Conduct from Diocletian to Anastasius*. Leeds: Francis Cairns, 1992.

———. "Subsidies and Diplomacy: Rome and Persia in Late Antiquity." *Phoenix* 39, no. 1 (1985): 62–74.

Boatwright, Mary T. "Acceptance and Approval: Romans' Non-Roman Population Transfers, 180 B.C.E.–ca 70 C.E." *Phoenix* 69, no. 1 (2015): 122–46.

———. "Visualizing Empire in Imperial Rome." In *Aspects of Ancient Institutions and Geography: Studies in Honor of Richard J. A. Talbert*, edited by Lee L. Brice and Daniëlle Slootjes, 235–59. Leiden: Brill, 2015.

Bøe, Sverre. *Gog and Magog: Ezekiel 38–39 as Pre-Text for Revelation 19,17–21 and 20,7–10*. Tübingen: Mohr Siebeck, 2001.

Boeck, Elena N. *The Bronze Horseman of Justinian in Constantinople: The Cross-Cultural Biography of a Mediterranean Monument*. Cambridge: Cambridge University Press, 2021.

Boll, Franz. *Sternglaube und Sterndeutung: Die Geschichte und das Wesen der Astrologie*. Leipzig: B. G. Teubner Verlag, 1931.

———. *Studien über Claudius Ptolemäus*. Leipzig: B. G. Teubner Verlag, 1894.

Bonnaud, R. "Notes sur l'astrologie latine au VIe siècle." *Revue belge de Philologie et d'Histoire* 10, no. 3 (1931): 557–77.

Bonura, Christopher. "Eusebius of Caesarea, the Roman Empire, and the Fulfillment of Biblical Prophecy: Reassessing Byzantine Imperial Eschatology in the Age of Constantine." *Church History* 90 (2021): 509–36.

Börm, Henning. "Es war allerdings nicht so, dass sie es im Sinne eines Tributes erhielten, wie viele meinten . . .': Anlässe und Funktion der persischen Geldforderungen an die Römer (3 bis 6 Jh.)." *Historia* 57, no. 3 (2008): 327–46.

BIBLIOGRAPHY [375]

———. "Procopius, His Predecessors, and the Genesis of the Anecdota." In *Antimonarchic Discourse in Antiquity*, edited by Henning Börm, 305–46. Stuttgart: Franz Steiner Verlag, 2015.

———. *Prokop und die Perser: Untersuchungen zu den römisch-sasanidischen Kontakten in der ausgehenden Spätantike*. Oriens et Occidens 16. Stuttgart: Franz Steiner Verlag, 2007.

Borst, Arno. *Der Turmbau von Babel: Geschichte der Meinungen über Ursprung und Vielfalt der Sprachen und Völker; Fundamente und Aufbau*. Vol. 1. Stuttgart: Hiersemann, 1957.

Bosak-Schroeder, Clara. "The Ecology of Health in Herodotus, Dicaearchus, and Agatharchides." In *The Routledge Handbook of Identity and the Environment in the Classical and Medieval Worlds*, edited by Rebecca Futo Kennedy and Molly Jones-Lewis, 29–44. Abingdon: Routledge, 2015.

Bouché-Leclercq, Auguste. "L'astrologie dans le monde romain." *Revue Historique* 65, no. 2 (1897): 241–99.

Bowersock, Glenn W. "Mavia, Queen of the Saracens." In *Studien zur antiken Sozialgeschichte: Festschrift Friedrich Vittinghoff*, edited by Werner Eck, Hartmut Galsterer, and Hartmut Wolff, 477–95. Kölner Historische Abhandlungen 28. Köln / Vienna: Böhlau Verlag, 1980.

———. *Roman Arabia*. Cambridge, MA: Harvard University Press, 1983.

Bowersock, Glenn W., Peter Brown, and Oleg Grabar, eds. *Late Antiquity: A Guide to the Postclassical World*. Cambridge: Harvard University Press, 1999.

Brandes, Wolfram. "Gog, Magog und die Hunnen: Anmerkungen zur Eschatologischen 'Ethnographie' der Völkerwanderungszeit." In *Visions of Community in the Post-Roman World: The West, Byzantium and the Islamic World, 300–1100*, edited by Walter Pohl, Clemens Gantner, and Richard Payne, 477–98. Farnham / Burlington, VT: Ashgate, 2012.

Brather, Sebastian. "Acculturation and Ethnogenesis along the Frontier: Rome and the Ancient Germans in an Archaeological Perspective." In *Borders, Barriers, and Ethnogenesis: Frontiers in Late Antiquity and the Middle Ages*, edited by Florin Curta, 139–72. Turnhout: Brepols, 2005.

Breeze, David. "In Defence of the Late Empire." In *Roman Military Architecture on the Frontiers: Armies and Their Architecture in Late Antiquity*, edited by Rob Collins, Matt Symonds, and Meike Weber, 140–42. Oxford / Philadelphia: Oxbow Books, 2015.

Brennan, Chris. *Hellenistic Astrology: The Study of Fate and Fortune*. Denver: Amor Fati Publications, 2017.

Brennan, Peter. "The Last of the Romans: Roman Identity and the Roman Army in the Late Roman Near East." In "Identities in the Eastern Mediterranean in Antiquity: Proceedings of a Conference Held at the Humanities Research Centre in Canberra," special issue, *Mediterranean Archaeology* 11 (1998): 191–203.

———. "Units in the *Notitia Dignitatum*." In *The Encyclopedia of the Roman Army*, edited by Yann le Bohec et al., 1049–54. Vol. 3, Pol-Z. Chichester: John Wiley & Sons, 2015.

Brennecke, Hanns Christof. "Introduction: Framing the Historical and Theological Problems." In *Arianism: Roman Heresy and Barbarian Creed*, edited by Guido M. Berndt and Roland Steinacher, 1–19. Farnham: Ashgate, 2014.

Briquel, Dominique. *Romulus vu de Constantinople: La réécriture de la légende dans le monde byzantin; Jean Malalas et ses successeurs*. Paris: Hermann, 2018.

Brock, Sebastian P. "Alexander Cycle." In *Gorgias Encyclopedic Dictionary of the Syriac Heritage*, edited by Sebastian P. Brock, Aaron M. Butts, George A. Kiraz, and Lucas Van Rompay. Piscataway, NJ: Gorgias Press, 2011.

Brodersen, Kai. *Terra cognita: Studien zur römischen Raumerfassung*. 2nd ed. Hildesheim / Zürich / New York: Georg Olms Verlag, 2003.

Brown, Peter. "Art and Society in Late Antiquity." In *Age of Spirituality: A Symposium*, 17–28. New York: Metropolitan Museum of Art, 1980.

———. "Byzantine and Early Islamic Africa, ca. 500–800: Concluding Remarks." In *North Africa under Byzantium and Early Islam*, edited by Susan T. Stevens and Jonathan P. Conant, 295–302. Washington, DC: Dumbarton Oaks Research Library and Collection, 2016.

———. *The Cult of the Saints: Its Rise and Function in Latin Christianity*. Chicago: University of Chicago Press, 1981.

———. *The Making of Late Antiquity*. Cambridge, MA: Harvard University Press, 1978.

[376] BIBLIOGRAPHY

Brown, Peter. *The Rise of Western Christendom: Triumph and Diversity, A.D. 200–1000.* 10th anniversary rev. ed. Malden, MA / Chichester: Wiley-Blackwell, 2013.

———. "St. Augustine's Attitude to Religious Coercion." *Journal of Roman Studies* 54, no. 1–2 (1964): 107–16.

———. *Through the Eye of a Needle: Wealth, the Fall of Rome, and the Making of Christianity in the West, 330–550 AD.* Princeton: Princeton University Press, 2012.

———. *The World of Late Antiquity: From Marcus Aurelius to Muhammad, A.D. 150–750.* London: Thames & Hudson, 1971.

Brüggemann, Thomas. "Ἐθνάρχος, Φύλαρχος and Στρατηγὸς νομάδων in Roman Arabia (1st–3rd Century): Central Power, Local Administration, and Nomadic Environment." In *The Late Roman Army in the Near East from Diocletian to the Arab Conquest: Proceedings of a colloquium held at Potenza, Acerenza and Matera, Italy*, edited by Ariel S. Lewin and Pietrina Pellegrini, 275–84. BAR International Series 1717. Oxford: BAR Publishing, 2007.

Buckland, W. W. *A Text-Book of Roman Law from Augustus to Justinian.* Revised by Peter Stein. 3rd ed. Cambridge: Cambridge University Press, 1963.

Buell, Denise Kimber. *Why This New Race: Ethnic Reasoning in Early Christianity.* New York: Columbia University Press, 2005.

Bunbury, E. H. *History of Ancient Geography among the Greeks and Romans from the Earliest Ages Till the Fall of the Roman Empire.* 2nd ed. Vol. 2. London: Constable & Co., 1932.

Burgess, Richard W. "The Date, Purpose, and Historical Context of the Original Greek and the Latin Translation of the So-called Excerpta Latina Barbari." *Traditio* 68 (2013): 1–56.

———. "Liber Genealogus." In *Encyclopedia of the Medieval Chronicle*, edited by Graeme Dunphy and Cristian Bratu. http://dx.doi.org/10.1163/2213-2139_emc_SIM_01690.

Burgess, Richard W., and Michael Kulikowski. *Mosaics of Time: The Latin Chronicle Traditions from the First Century BC to the Sixth Century AD. Vol.1 of A Historical Introduction to the Chronicle Genre from Its Origins to the High Middle Ages.* Turnhout: Brepols, 2013.

Burgess, Richard W., and Shaun Tougher. "Eusebius of Caesarea." In *Encyclopedia of the Medieval Chronicle*, edited by Graeme Dunphy and Cristian Bratu. Leiden/Boston: Brill, 2010. http://dx.doi.org/10.1163/2213-2139_emc_SIM_00970.

Burrows, Eric. "The Number Seventy in Semitic." *Orientalia*, Nova Series 5 (1936): 389–92.

Bury, John B. *History of the Later Roman Empire: From the Death of Theodosius I to the Death of Justinian.* Vol 1. New York: Dover Publications, 1958.

———. *The Imperial Administrative System in the Ninth Century: With a Revised Text of the Kletorologion of Philotheos.* London: British Academy, 1911.

Cambiano, Giuseppe. "Philosophy, Science and Medicine." In *The Cambridge History of Hellenistic Philosophy*, edited by Keimpe Algra, Jonathan Barnes, Jaap Mansfield, and Malcolm Schofield, 585–613. Cambridge: Cambridge University Press, 1999.

Cameron, Alan. *Claudian: Poetry and Propaganda at the Court of Honorius.* Oxford: Clarendon Press, 1970.

———. "Theodosius the Great and the Regency of Stilico." *Harvard Studies in Classical Philology* 73 (1969): 247–80.

Cameron, Alan, Jacqueline Long, and Lee Sherry. *Barbarians and Politics at the Court of Arcadius.* Berkeley: University of California Press, 1993.

Cameron, Averil. "Agathias on the Sassanians." *DOP* 23–24 (1969–70): 67–183.

———. "Bitter Furies of Complexity." *The Times Literary Supplement*, no. 6077, September 20, 2019. https://www.the-tls.co.uk/articles/byzantium-romanland-kaldellis/.

———. "Heresiology." In *Late Antiquity: A Guide to the Postclassical World*, edited by G. W. Bowersock, Peter Brown, and Oleg Grabar, 488–90. Cambridge, MA: Harvard University Press, 1999.

———. "How to Read Heresiology." *Journal of Medieval and Early Modern Studies* 33, no. 3. (Fall 2003): 471–92.

———. *Procopius and the Sixth Century.* London: Routledge, 1996.

———. "The 'Scepticism' of Procopius." *Historia* 15, no. 4 (November 1966): 466–82.

———. "The Violence of Orthodoxy." In *Heresy and Identity in Late Antiquity*, edited by Eduard Iricinschi and Holger M. Zellentin, 102–14. Tübingen: Mohr Siebeck, 2008.

BIBLIOGRAPHY [377]

Campbell, Gordon. "Philosophy." In *The Cambridge Dictionary of Classical Civilization*, edited by Graham Shipley, John Vanderspoel, David Mattingly, and Lin Foxhall, 677–80. Cambridge: Cambridge University Press, 2008.

Camplani, Alberto. "Bardesane et les Bardesanites." *Annuaires de l'École pratique des hautes études* 112 (2003): 29–50.

Canellis, Aline. "Introduction." In *Jerome: Préfaces aux livres de la Bible*, Rev. ed., edited by Aline Canellis, 53–355. Paris: Éditions du Cerf, 2017.

Canepa, Matthew P. *The Iranian Expanse: Transforming Royal Identity through Architecture, Landscape, and the Built Environment, 550 BCE–642 CE*. Berkeley: University of California Press, 2019.

———. "Sasanian Iran and the Projection of Power in Late Antique Eurasia." In *Empires and Exchanges in Eurasian Late Antiquity: Rome, China, Iran, and the Steppe, ca. 250–750*, edited by Nicola Di Cosmo and Michael Maas, 54–69. Cambridge: Cambridge University Press, 2018.

———. *The Two Eyes of the Earth: Art and Ritual of Kingship between Rome and Sasanian Iran*. Berkeley: University of California Press, 2009.

Charlesworth, James H. "Jewish Astrology in the Talmud, Pseudepigrapha, the Dead Sea Scrolls, and Early Palestinian Synagogues." *Harvard Theological Review* 70, no. 3–4 (October 1997): 183–94.

Chauvot, Alain. *Les "barbares" des romains: Representations et confrontations*. Edited by A. Becker and H. Huntzinger. Metz: Centre de Recherche Universitaire Lorrain d'Histoire, 2016.

———. *Opinions romains face aux barbares au IVe siècle ap. J.-C.* Paris: De Boccard, 1998.

Cheesman, G. L. *The Auxilia of the Roman Imperial Army*. Oxford: Clarendon Press, 1914.

Cherry, David. *Frontier and Society in Roman North Africa*. Oxford: Clarendon Press, 1998.

Chiasson, Charles. "Scythian Androgyny and Environmental Determinism in Herodotus and the Hippocratic Περὶ Ἀέρων Ὑδάτων Τόπων." *Syllecta Classica* 12 (2001): 33–73.

Christ, Karl. "Römer und Barbaren in der hohen Kaiserzeit." *Saeculum* 10 (1959): 273–88.

Chrysos, Evangelos. "Conclusion: De foederatis iterum." In *Kingdoms of the Empire: The Integration of Barbarians in Late Antiquity*, edited by Walter Pohl, 185–206. Leiden / New York: Brill, 1997.

———. "Legal Concepts and Patterns for the Barbarians' Settlement on Roman Soil." In *Das Reich und die Barbaren*, edited by Evangelos K. Chrysos and Andreas Schwarcz, 13–23. Wien/Köln: Böhlau Verlag, 1989.

———. "The Title Βασιλευσ in Early Byzantine International Relations." *DOP* 32 (1978): 29–75.

Chuvin, Pierre. *A Chronicle of the Last Pagans*. Translated by B. A. Archer. Revealing Antiquity. Cambridge, MA / London: Harvard University Press, 1990.

Clair, Robin Patric. "The Changing Story of Ethnography." In *Expressions of Ethnography: Novel Approaches to Qualitative Methods*, edited by Robin Patric Clair, 3–26. Albany: State University of New York Press, 2003.

Clark, Elizabeth A. *The Origenist Controversy: The Cultural Construction of an Early Christian Debate*. Princeton Legacy Library 146. Princeton: Princeton University Press, 1992.

Clark, Mary T. "Irenaeus." In *The Encyclopedia of Early Christianity*, edited by Everett Ferguson, 587–88. New York / London: Garland Publishing, 1998.

Clarke, Katherine. *Between Geography and History: Hellenistic Constructions of the Roman World*. Oxford: Oxford University Press, 1999.

Clayton, Jr., Paul B. *The Christology of Theodoret of Cyrus: Antiochene Christology from the Council of Ephesus (431) to the Council of Chalcedon (451)*. Oxford Early Christian Studies. Oxford: Oxford University Press, 2007.

Clifford, James. "Introduction: Partial Truths." In *Writing Culture: The Poetics and Politics of Ethnography*, edited by George E. Marcus and James Clifford, 1–26. University of California Press, 1986.

Collins, Rob, Matt Symonds, and Meike Weber, eds. *Roman Military Architecture on the Frontiers: Armies and Their Architecture in Late Antiquity*. Oxford/Philadelphia: Oxbow Books, 2015.

Collins, Rob, and Meike Weber. "Late Roman Military Architecture: An Introduction." In *Roman Military Architecture on the Frontiers. Armies and Their Architecture in Late Antiquity*, edited by Rob Collins, Matt Symonds, and Meike Weber, 1–5. Oxford/Philadelphia: Oxbow Books, 2015.

Conrad, Lawrence I. "The Arabs." In *CAH 14: Late Antiquity; Empire and Successors, A.D. 425–600*, edited by Averil Cameron, Bryan Ward-Perkins, and Michael Whitby, 678–700. Cambridge: Cambridge University Press, 2000.

———. "Eastern Neighbours: The Arabs to the Time of the Prophet." In *The Cambridge History of the Byzantine Empire c. 500–1492*, edited by Jonathan Shepard, 173–95. Cambridge: Cambridge University Press, 2008.

Cooper, Glen M. "Astrology: The Science of Signs in the Heavens." In *The Oxford Handbook of Science and Medicine in the Classical World*, edited by Paul T. Keyser and John Scarborough, 381–408. Oxford: Oxford University Press, 2018.

Cope, Glenn Melvin. "An Analysis of the Heresiological Method of Theodoret of Cyrus in the Haereticarum Fabularum Compendium." PhD diss., Catholic University of America, 1990.

Courcelle, Pierre. *Les lettres grecques en Occident: De Macrobe à Cassiodore*. Paris: Boccard, 1948.

Courtois, Christian. *Les Vandales et l'Afrique*. Paris: Arts et Métiers Graphiques, 1955.

Cramer, Frederick H. *Astrology in Roman Law and Politics*. Memoirs of the American Philosophical Society 37. Philadelphia: American Philosophical Society, 1954.

———. "The Conversion of Republican Rome to Astrology (250–44 B.C.)." In *Astrology in Roman Law and Politics*, 44–80. Memoirs of the American Philosophical Society 37. Philadelphia: American Philosophical Society, 1954.

Cramer, Peter. *Baptism and Change in the Early Middle Ages, c. 200–c. 1150*. Cambridge: Cambridge University Press, 1993.

Cranz, F. Edward. "Kingdom and Polity in Eusebius of Caesarea." *Harvard Theological Review* 45, no. 1 (1952): 47–66.

Crawford, Michael. "Dediticii." In *OCD4*, edited by Simon Hornblower, Antony Spawforth, and Esther Eidinow, 423. Oxford: Oxford University Press, 2012.

Crawford-Brown, Sophie. "Down from the Roof: Reframing Plants in Augustan Art." *Journal of Roman Archaeology* 35 (2022): 33–63.

Croke, Brian. "Cassiodorus." In *Oxford Dictionary of Late Antiquity, Vol. 1*, edited by Oliver Nicholson, 299–300. Oxford: Oxford University Press, 2018.

———. *Count Marcellinus and His Chronicle*. Oxford: Oxford University Press, 2001.

———. "The Origins of the Christian World Chronicle." In *History and Historians in Late Antiquity*, edited by Brian Croke and Alanna M. Emmett, 116–31. Sydney: Pergamon Press, 1983.

Cumont, Franz. *Astrology and Religion among the Greeks and Romans*. New York / London: Knickerbocker Press, 1912.

Curcă, Roxana-Gabriela, Alexander Rubel, Robin P. Symonds, and Hans-Ulrich Voß, eds. *Rome and Barbaricum: Contributions to the Archaeology and History of Interaction in European Protohistory*. Archaeopress Roman Archaeology 67. Archaeopress, 2020.

Curta, Florin. *The Making of the Slavs: History and Archaeology of the Lower Danube Region. c. 500–700*. Cambridge: Cambridge University Press, 2001.

Curta, Florin, ed. *Neglected Barbarians*. Turnhout: Brepols, 2010.

Dagorn, René. *La geste d'Ismaël d'après l'onomastique et la tradition arabes*. Geneva: Librairie Droz, 1981.

Daniélou, Jean. *The Angels and Their Mission: According to the Fathers of the Church*. Translated by David Heimann. South Bend, IN: Newman Press, 1957.

———. "Les douze Apôtres et le zodiaque." *Vigiliae Christianae* 13, no. 1 (April 1959): 14–21.

———. "Les sources juives de la doctrine des anges des nations chez Origéne." *Recherches de Science Religieuse* 38 (1951): 132–37.

———. *Origen*. Translated by Walter Mitchell. Eugene, OR: Wipf and Stock Publishers, 2016.

Dauge, Yves. *Le barbare: Recherches sur la conception romaine de la barbarie et de la civilisation*. Brussels: Latomus, 1981.

BIBLIOGRAPHY [379]

Decker, Michael. "What Is a Byzantine Landscape?" In *Spatialities of Byzantine Culture from the Human Body to the Universe*, edited by Myrto Veikou and Ingela Nilsson, 243–61. The Medieval Mediterranean 133. Leiden/Boston: Brill, 2022.

DeConick, April D. "Apostles as Archons: The Fight for Authority and the Emergence of Gnosticism in the Tchacos Codex and Other Early Christian Literature." In *The Codex Judas Papers: Proceedings of the International Congress on the Tchacos Codex Held at Rice University, Houston, Texas, March 13–16, 2008*, edited by April D. DeConick, 241–88. Leiden/Boston: Brill, 2009.

de la Vaissière. *See* la Vaissière

Deliyannis, Deborah M. *Ravenna in Late Antiquity*. Cambridge: Cambridge University Press, 2014.

Demougeot, Émilienne. "À propos des lètes gaulois du IVe siècle." In *Beiträge zur alten Geschichte und deren Nachleben: Festschrift für Franz Altheim zum 6.10.1968.*, edited by Ruth Stiehl and Hans Erich Stier, 101–13. Vol. 2. Berlin: Walter De Gruyter, 1970.

———. "Laeti et Gentiles dans la gaule du IVe siècle." In *Actes du colloque d'histoire sociale 1970*, 101–12. Annales Littéraires de l'Université de Besançon 128. Paris: Les Belles Lettres, 1972.

———. *L'Empire romain et les barbares d'Occident (IVe-VIIe siècle): Scripta varia*. Paris: Publications de la Sorbonne, 1988.

Dench, Emma. "Ethnography and History." In *A Companion to Greek and Roman Historiography*, edited by John Marincola, Vol. 2: 493–503. Oxford: Blackwell Publishing, 2008.

———. *From Barbarians to New Men: Greek, Roman, and Modern Perceptions of Peoples from the Central Apennines*. Oxford Classical Monographs. Oxford: Clarendon Press, 1995.

———. *Romulus' Asylum: Roman Identities from the Age of Alexander to the Age of Hadrian*. Oxford: Oxford University Press, 2005.

Denzey, Nicola. "A New Star on the Horizon: Astral Christologies and Stellar Debates in Early Christian Discourse." In *Prayer, Magic, and the Stars in the Ancient and Late Antique World*, edited by Scott Noegel, Joel Walker, and Brannon Wheeler, 207–21. University Park, PA: Pennsylvania State University Press, 2003.

Denzey Lewis, Nicola. *Cosmology and Fate in Gnosticism and Graeco-Roman Antiquity: Under Pitiless Skies*. Nag Hammadi and Manichaean Studies 81. Leiden/Boston: Brill, 2013.

Derks, Ton (A. M. J.). "Ethnic Identity in the Roman Frontier: The Epigraphy of Batavi and Other Lower Rhine Tribes." In *Ethnic Constructs in Antiquity: The Role of Power and Tradition*, edited by Ton Derks and Nico Roymans, 239–382. Amsterdam: Amsterdam University Press, 2009.

Derow, Peter Sidney. "Polybius (1)." In *OCD4*, edited by Simon Hornblower, Antony Spawforth, and Esther Eidinow, 1174–75. Oxford: Oxford University Press, 2012.

Desanti, Lucetta. "Astrologi: eretici o pagani? Un problema esegetico." *Atti Dell'Accademia Romanistica Costantiniana* 10 (1995): 687–96.

Di Cosmo, Nicola. *Ancient China and Its Enemies: The Rise of Nomadic Power in East Asian History*. Cambridge: Cambridge University Press, 2002.

———. "The War Economy of Nomadic Empires." In *Rebel Economies: Warlords, Insurgents, Humanitarians*, edited by Nicola Di Cosmo, Didier Fassin, and Clémence Pinaud, 103–25. London: Lexington Books, 2021.

Di Cosmo, Nicola and Michael Maas, eds., *Empires and Exchanges in Eurasian Late Antiquity: Rome, China, Iran, and the Steppe, ca. 250-750*. Cambridge: Cambridge University Press, 2018.

Dicks, D. R. "The ΚΛΙΜΑΤΑ in Greek Geography." *Classical Quarterly* 5, no. 3–4 (1955): 248–55.

———. Review of *Barbarie et civilisation chez Strabon: Étude critique des livres III et IV de la Géographie*, by Patrick Thollard. *The Classical Review* 41, no. 1 (April 1991): 226.

Dignas, Beate, and Engelbert Winter. *Rome and Persia in Late Antiquity: Neighbours and Rivals*. Cambridge: Cambridge University Press, 2007.

Dihle, Albrecht. *Greek and Latin Literature of the Roman Empire: From Augustus to Justinian*. Translated by Manfred Malzahn. London / New York: Routledge, 1994.

[380] BIBLIOGRAPHY

Dilke, O. A. W. "Cartography in the Ancient World: A Conclusion." In *Cartography in Prehistoric, Ancient, and Medieval Europe and the Mediterranean*, edited by J. B. Harley and David Woodward, 276–79. Chicago/London: University of Chicago Press, 1987.

———. "Maps in the Service of State: Roman Cartography to the End of the Augustan Era." In *The History of Cartography: Cartography in Prehistoric, Ancient, and Medieval Europe and the Mediterranean*, edited by J. B. Hartley and David Woodward, 201–11. Vol. 1. Chicago: University of Chicago Press, 1987.

Diller, Aubrey. *The Textual Tradition of Strabo's "Geography."* Amsterdam: Adolf M. Hakkert, 1975.

Dionisi, U. "Hesychius of Salona." In *Encyclopedia of the Early Church*, edited by Angelo di Berardino, translated by Adrian Walford. Vol. 1: 379. Cambridge: James Clarke & Co., 1992.

Dobesch, Gerhard. "Caesar als Ethnograph." *Wiener Humanistische Blätter* 31 (1989): 16–51.

———. "Caesar als Ethnograph (Erstmals: Wiener Humanistische Blätter 31, 1989, 16–51)." In *Ausgewählte Schriften Vol. 1: Griechen und Römer*, edited by Herbert Heftner and Kurt Tomaschitz, 453–505. Cologne/Weimar/Vienna: Böhlau Verlag, 2001.

Dolbeau, François. "Le combat pastoral d'Augustin contre les astrologues, les devins et les guérisseurs." In *Augustinus Afer: Saint Augustin, africanité et universalité; Actes du colloque international, Alger-Annaba, 1–7 avril, 2001*, edited by Pierre-Yves Fux, Jean-Michel Roessli, and Otto Wermelinger, 167–82. Paradosis: Études de Littérature et de Théologie Anciennes 45, no. 1. Freiburg: Éditions Universitaires, 2003.

Dölger, Franz. *Byzanz und die Europäische Staatenwelt: Ausgewählte Vorträge und Aufsätze*. Ettal: Buch-Kunstverlag, 1953.

Donner, Fred M. "The Background to Islam." In *The Cambridge Companion to the Age of Justinian*, edited by Michael Maas, 510–33. Cambridge: Cambridge University Press, 2005.

Doutreleau, Louis, ed. *Origéne: Homélies sur la Genèse*. 2nd ed. Translated by Louis Doutreleau. Sources Chrétiennes 7. Paris: Les Éditions du Cerf, 1976.

Dowling, Melissa Barden. *Clemency and Cruelty in the Roman World*. Ann Arbor: University of Michigan Press, 2006.

Drijvers, H. J. W. *Bardaiṣan of Edessa*. Assen: Van Gorcum, 1966.

———. "Bardesanes." In *Theologische Realenzyklopädie*, edited by Gerhard Krause and Gerhard Müller, 206–12. Vol. 5. Berlin / New York: Walter de Gruyter, 1980.

Drinkwater, John F. *The Alamanni and Rome 213–496: Caracalla to Clovis*. Oxford: Oxford University Press, 2007.

Dueck, Daniela. *Geography in Classical Antiquity*. Cambridge: Cambridge University Press, 2012.

———. *Strabo of Amasia: A Greek Man of Letters in Augustan Rome*. London / New York: Routledge, 2000.

Dujčev, Ivan. "Le témoignage du Pseudo-Césaire sur les Slaves." *Slavia Antiqua* 4 (1953): 193–209.

Dunderberg, Ismo. *Beyond Gnosticism: Myth, Lifestyle, and Society in the School of Valentinus*. New York: Columbia University Press, 2008.

Eckstein, Arthur M. *Moral Vision in the Histories of Polybius*. Berkeley: University of California Press, 1995.

Edelstein, Ludwig. *Peri aerōn und die Sammlung der hippokratischen Schriften*. Berlin: Weidmannsche Buchhandlung, 1931.

Edgecomb, Kevin P. "Eusebius of Caesarea, The Gospel Canon Tables." Tertullian.org. Accessed August 9, 2023. https://www.tertullian.org/fathers/eusebius_canon_tables_01.htm.

Efthymiadis, Stephanos. "Questions and Answers." In *The Cambridge Intellectual History of Byzantium*, edited by Anthony Kaldellis and Niketas Siniossoglou, 47–62. Cambridge: Cambridge University Press, 2017.

Elsner, Jaś. *Imperial Rome and Christian Triumph: The Art of the Roman Empire AD 100–450*. Oxford / New York: Oxford University Press, 1998.

Elton, Hugh. *Warfare in Roman Europe, AD 350–425*. Oxford Classical Monographs. Oxford: Clarendon Press, 1996.

Eph'al, I. "'Ishmael' and 'Arab(s)': A Transformation of Ethnological Terms." *Journal of Near Eastern Studies* 35, no. 4 (1976): 225–35.

BIBLIOGRAPHY [381]

Eriksen, Thomas Hylland, and Finn Sivert Nielsen. *A History of Anthropology*. 2nd ed. Anthropology, Culture, and Society. London: Pluto Press, 2013.

Esders, Stefan, and Helmut Reimitz. "Legalizing Ethnicity: The Remaking of Citizenship in Post-Roman Gaul (Sixth-Seventh Centuries)." In *Civic Identity and Civic Participation in Late Antiquity and the Early Middle Ages*, edited by Cédric Brélaz and Els Rose, 295–329. Cultural Encounters in Late Antiquity and the Middle Ages 37. Turnhout: Brepols, 2021.

Eskhult, Josef. "Augustine and the Primeval Language in Early Modern Exegesis and Philology." *Language & History* 56, no. 2 (2013): 98–199.

Esmonde Cleary, Simon. *The Roman West, AD 200–500: An Archaeological Study*. Cambridge: Cambridge University Press, 2013.

"Ethnography." In *Oxford English Dictionary*, 2014. https://www.oed.com/dictionary /ethnography_n.

Farina, Raffaele. *L'impero e l'imperatore Cristiano in Eusebio di Cesarea: La prima teologia politica del Cristianesimo*. Zurich: Pas Verlag, 1966.

Fear, Andrew, and Jamie Wood, eds. *A Companion to Isidore of Seville*. Companions to the Christian Tradition 87. Leiden/Boston: Brill, 2020.

Fentress, Elizabeth, and Andrew Wilson. "The Saharan Berber Diaspora and the Southern Frontiers of Byzantine North Africa." In *North Africa under Byzantium and Early Islam*, edited by Susan T. Stevens and Jonathan P. Conant, 41–64. Washington, DC: Dumbarton Oaks Research Library and Collection, 2016.

Ferguson, Everett. *Baptism in the Early Church: History, Theology, and Liturgy in the First Five Centuries*. Grand Rapids: William B. Eerdmans Publishing Company, 2009.

———. "Hippolytus." In *The Encyclopedia of Early Christianity*, edited by Everett Ferguson, 531–32. New York / London: Garland Publishing, 1998.

Fisher, Greg. *Between Empires: Arabs, Romans, and Sasanians in Late Antiquity*. Oxford Classical Monographs. Oxford / New York: Oxford University Press, 2011.

Flint, Valerie I. J. "The Hereford Map: Its Author(s), Two Scenes and a Border." *Transactions of the Royal Historical Society* 8 (1998): 19–44.

Foerster, Werner, ed. *Gnosis: A Selection of Gnostic Texts; Patristic Evidence*. Edited and translated by R. McL. Wilson. Vol. 1. Oxford: Clarendon Press, 1972.

Fögen, Marie Theres. *Die Enteignung der Wahrsager: Studien zum kaiserlichen Wissensmonopol in der Spätantike*. Suhrkamp Taschenbuch Wissenschaft 1316. Frankfurt am Main: Suhrkamp, 1997.

Fontaine, J. "Isidore of Seville." In *Encyclopedia of the Early Church*, edited by Angelo Di Bernardino, translated by Adrian Walford, 418–19. Vol. 1. Cambridge: James Clarke & Co., 1992.

Freudenthal, Gad. "The Astrologization of the Aristotelian Cosmos: Celestial Influences on the Sublunary World in Aristotle, Alexander of Aphrodisias, and Averroes." In *New Perspectives on Aristotle's "De caelo,"* edited by Alan C. Bowen and Christian Wildberg, 239–81. Leiden/Boston: Brill, 2009.

Garitte, Gérard. *La narratio de rebus Armeniae: Édition critique et commentaire*. (CSCO) Corpus Scriptorum Christianorum Orientalium 132, Subsidia 4. Louvain: Imprimerie Orientaliste L. Durbecq, 1952.

Garnsey, Peter. "Roman Citizenship and Roman Law in the Late Empire." In *Approaching Late Antiquity: The Transformation from Early to Late Empire*, edited by Simon Swain and Mark Edwards, 133–55. Oxford: Oxford University Press, 2006.

Garsoïan, Nina. "Byzantium and the Sasanians." In *The Cambridge History of Iran 3.1: The Seleucid, Parthian and Sasanian Periods*, edited by Eshan Yarsharer. Cambridge: Cambridge University Press, 1983.

Garstad, Benjamin. "Barbarian Interest in the Excerpta Latina Barbari." *Early Medieval Europe* 19, no. 1 (2011): 3–42.

Gaudemet, Jean. "Justum matrimonium." *RIDA* 2 (1949): 309–66.

———. "Les romains et les 'autres.'" In *La nozione di "romano" tra cittadinanza e universalità*, 7–37. Naples: Edizione Scientifiche Italiane, 1984.

———. "L'étranger dans le monde romain." *Studii Clasice* 7 (1965): 37–47.

BIBLIOGRAPHY

Gaudemet, Jean. "Politique ecclésiastique et legislation religieuse après l'édit de Théodose I de 380." In *Droit et société aux derniers siècles de l'empire romain*, 175–96. Naples: Jovene, 1992.

Geary, Patrick J. *Before France and Germany: The Creation and Transformation of the Merovingian World*. Oxford: Oxford University Press, 1988.

——. "Ethnic Identity as a Situational Construct in the Early Middle Ages." *Mitteilungen der Anthropologischen Gesellschaft in Wien* 113 (1983): 15–26.

——. *The Myth of Nations: The Medieval Origins of Europe*. Princeton: Princeton University Press, 1992.

Gee, Teri. "Strategies of Defending Astrology: A Continuing Tradition." PhD diss., University of Toronto, 2012.

Geréby, György. "The Angels of the Nations: Is a National Christianity Possible?" In *Across the Mediterranean - Along the Nile: Studies in Egyptology, Nubiology and Late Antiquity; Dedicated to László Török on the Occasion of His 75th Birthday*, edited by Tamás A. Bács, Ádám Bollók, and Tivadar Vida, Vol. 2: 819–47. Budapest: Institute of Archaeology, Research Center for the Humanities, Hungarian Academy of Sciences and Museum of Fine Arts, 2018.

Gibbon, Edward. *The History of the Decline and Fall of the Roman Empire: 180 A.D.-395 A.D.* Edited by David Womersley. Vol. 1. London: Penguin Press, 1994.

Gibbons, Kathleen. "Who Reads the Stars? Origen of Alexandria on Ethnic Reasoning and Astrological Discourse." In *The Routledge Handbook of Identity and the Environment in the Classical and Medieval Worlds*, edited by Rebecca Futo Kennedy and Molly Jones-Lewis, 230–46. Abingdon: Routledge, 2015.

Gifford, E. H. *Preparation for the Gospel*. Grand Rapids: Baker Book House, 1981.

Gillett, Andrew. *Envoys and Political Communication in the Late Antique West, 411–533*. Cambridge: Cambridge University Press, 2003.

——. "The Mirror of Jordanes: Concepts of the Barbarian, Then and Now." In *A Companion to Late Antiquity*, edited by Philip Rousseau, 392-408. Chichester: Wiley-Blackwell, 2009.

Gillispie, Charles Coulston. "Scientific Aspects of the French Egyptian Expedition 1798–1801." *Proceedings of the American Philosophical Society* 133, no. 4 (December 1989): 447–74.

Ginkel, Jan Jacob van. "John of Ephesus: A Monophysite Historian in Sixth-Century Byzantium." PhD diss., University of Groningen, 1995.

Glacken, Clarence J. "Changing Ideas of the Habitable World." In *Man's Role in Changing the Face of the Earth*, edited by William L. Thomas, Jr., 70–92. Vol. 1. Chicago/London: University of Chicago Press, 1956.

——. *Traces on the Rhodian Shore: Nature and Culture in Western Thought from Ancient Times to the End of the Eighteenth Century*. Berkeley: University of California Press, 1967.

Goetz, Hans-Werner. "Introduction." In *Regna and Gentes. The Relationship between Late Antique and Early Medieval Peoples and Kingdoms in the Transformation of the Roman World*, edited by Hans-Werner Goetz, Jörg Jarnut, and Walter Pohl, 1–11. Leiden/Boston: Brill, 2003.

Goetz, Hans-Werner, Jörg Jarnut, and Walter Pohl, eds. *Regna and Gentes. The Relationship between Late Antique and Early Medieval Peoples and Kingdoms in the Transformation of the Roman World*. Leiden/Boston: Brill, 2003.

Goffart, Walter. "The Supposedly 'Frankish' Table of Nations: An Edition and Study." *Frühmittelalterliche Studien* 17, no. 1 (1983): 98–130.

Goldenberg, David M. *The Curse of Ham: Race and Slavery in Early Judaism, Christianity, and Islam*. Jews, Christians, and Muslims from the Ancient to the Modern World. Princeton: Princeton University Press, 2005.

Goodchild, R. G., and I. A. Richmond. Review of *Fossatum Africae*, by Jean Baradez. *Journal of Roman Studies* 40, no. 1–2 (1950): 162–65.

Gordon, Colin D. "Subsidies in Roman Imperial Defence." *Phoenix* 3, no. 2 (Autumn 1949): 60–69.

——. "The Subsidization of Border Peoples as a Roman Policy in Imperial Defence." PhD diss., University of Michigan, 1948.

Goudineau, C. "Gaul." In *CAH 10: The Augustan Empire, 43 B.C.-A.D. 69*, 2nd ed., edited by Alan K. Bowman, Edward Champlin, and Andrew Lintott, 464–602. Cambridge: Cambridge University Press, 1996.

BIBLIOGRAPHY [383]

Graf, David F. "The Saracens and the Defense of the Arabian Frontier." *Bulletin of the American Schools of Oriental Research* 299 (1978): 1–26.

Grafton, Anthony. "Starry Messengers: Recent Work in the History of Western Astrology." *Perspective on Science* 8, no. 1 (2000): 70–83.

Grafton, Anthony T., and Noah M. Swerdlow. "The Horoscope of the Foundation of Rome." *Classical Philology* 81, no. 2 (April 1986): 148–53.

Gray, Patrick T. R. "The Legacy of Chalcedon: Christological Problems and Their Significance." In *The Cambridge Companion to the Age of Justinian*, edited by Michael Maas, 215–38. Cambridge: Cambridge University Press, 2005.

Greatrex, Geoffrey. "Byzantium and the East in the Sixth Century." In *The Cambridge Companion to the Age of Justinian*, edited by Michael Maas, 477–509. Cambridge: Cambridge University Press, 2005.

————. "Les Jafnides et la défense de l'Empire au VIe siècle." In *Actes du colloque de Paris, 24–25 novembre 2008*, edited by Denis Genequand and Christian Julien Robin, 121–54. Paris: Boccard, 2015.

————. "L'historien Procope et la vie à Césaréé au VIe siècle." In *Le monde de Procope / The World of Procopius*, edited by Geoffrey Greatrex and Sylvain Janniard, 15–38. Paris: Éditions de Boccard, 2018.

————. "Procopius and Roman Imperial Policy in the Arabian and Egyptian Frontier Zones." In *Inside and Out: Interactions between Rome and the Peoples on the Arabian and Egyptian Frontiers in Late Antiquity*, edited by Jitse H. F. Dijkstra and Greg Fisher, 249–66. Late Antique History and Religion 8. Leuven/Paris/Walpole, MA: Peeters, 2014.

————. "Procopius' Attitude towards Barbarians." In *Le monde de Procope / The World of Procopius*, edited by Geoffrey Greatrex and Sylvain Janniard, 327–54. Paris: Éditions de Boccard, 2018.

————. *Procopius of Caesarea: Persian Wars; A Historical Commentary.* Cambridge: Cambridge University Press, 2021.

————. "Recent Work on Procopius and the Composition of Wars VIII." *Byzantine and Modern Greek Studies* 27 (2003): 45–67.

————. Review of *Prokop und die Perser: Untersuchungen zu den römisch-sasanidischen Kontakten in der ausgehenden Spätantike*, by Henning Börm. *Bryn Mawr Classical Review*, May 23, 2008.

————. *Rome and Persia at War, 502–532*. ARCA: Classical and Medieval Texts, Papers and Monographs 37. Leeds: Francis Cairns, 1998.

Greatrex, Geoffrey, and Jonathan Bardill. "Antiochus the Praepositus: A Persian Eunuch at the Court of Theodosius II." *DOP* 50 (1996): 171–97.

Greatrex, Geoffrey, and Samuel N. C. Lieu, eds. *The Roman Eastern Frontier and the Persian Wars: Part II, A.D. 363–630; A Narrative Sourcebook*. London / New York: Routledge, 2008.

Green, Steven J. and Katharina Volk, eds., *Forgotten Stars: Rediscovering Manilius' "Astronomica."* Oxford: Oxford University Press, 2011.

Grenet, Frantz. "The Circulation of Astrological Lore and Its Political Use between the Roman East, Sasanian Iran, Central Asia, India and the Türks." In *Empires and Exchanges in Eurasian Late Antiquity: Rome, China, Iran, and the Steppe, ca. 250–750*, edited by Nicola Di Cosmo and Michael Maas, 235–52. Cambridge: Cambridge University Press, 2018.

Grey, Cam. "Revisiting the 'Problem' of *Agri Deserti* in the Late Roman Empire." *Journal of Roman Archaeology* 20 (2007): 363–76.

Gribomont, J. "Gregory of Nyssa." In *Encyclopedia of the Early Church*, edited by Angelo Di Bernadino, translated by Adrian Walford, 363–65. Vol. 1. Cambridge: James Clarke & Co., 1992.

Grillmeier, Aloys, and Theresa Hainthaler. *Christ in Christian Tradition: From the Council of Chalcedon (451) to Gregory the Great (590–604); The Church of Constantinople in the Sixth Century.* Vol. 2, no. 2. Translated by John Cawte and Pauline Allen. London: Mowbray, 1975.

Gros, Pierre. "Les composantes environnementales de la qualité d'un projet dans le *De architectura* de Vitruve*.*" In *Vie et climat d'Hésiode à Montesquieu*, edited by Jacques Jouanna, Christian Robin, and Michel Zink, 165–84. Paris: De Boccard, 2018.

Gruen, Erich S. "Christians as a 'Third Race': Is Ethnicity an Issue?" In *Christianity in the Second Century: Themes and Developments*, edited by James Carleton Paget and Judith Lieu, 235–49. Cambridge: Cambridge University Press, 2017.

———. "The Expansion of the Empire under Augustus." In *CAH 10: The Augustan Empire, 44 B.C.–A.D.70*, 2nd ed., edited by Alan K. Bowman, Edward Champlin, and Andrew Lintott, 147–97. Cambridge: Cambridge University Press, 1996.

———. *The Hellenistic World and the Coming of Rome*. Vol. 1. Berkeley: University of California Press, 1984.

———. *Rethinking the Other in Antiquity*. Martin Classical Lectures. Princeton: Princeton University Press, 2011.

Gschnitzer, Fritz. "Phylarchos." *RE* Suppl. 11: 1067–90. Stuttgart: Alfred Druckenmüller Verlag, 1968.

Guest, Peter. "Roman Gold and Hun Kings: The Use and Hoarding of Solidi in the Late Fourth and Fifth Centuries." In *Proceedings of the ESF / SCH Exploratory Workshop, Radziwill Palace, Nieborów (Poland), 3–6 September 2005*, edited by Aleksander Bursche, Renata Ciołek, and Reinhard Wolters, translated by Nicholas Sekunda, 295–307. Collection Moneta 82. Warsaw/Wetteren: Institute of Archaeology, University of Warsaw / Moneta, 2008.

Gundel, Wilhelm, and Hans Georg Gundel. *Astrologumena: Die astrologische Literatur in der Antike und ihre Geschichte*. Wiesbaden: Franz Steiner Verlag, 1966.

Haarer, Fiona K. *Anastasius I: Politics and Empire in the Late Roman World*. Cambridge: Francis Cairns, 2006.

Haldon, John. *The Byzantine Wars: Battles and Campaigns of the Byzantine Era*. Stroud, UK / Charleston, SC: Tempus Publishing, 2001.

Halsall, Guy. *Barbarian Migrations and the Roman West, 376–588*. Cambridge Medieval Textbooks. Cambridge: Cambridge University Press, 2007.

———. *Settlement and Social Organization: The Merovingian Region of Metz*. Cambridge: Cambridge University Press, 1995.

Hardt, Matthias. *Gold und Herrschaft: Die Schätze europäischer Könige und Fürsten im ersten Jahrtausend*. Europa im Mittelalter, edited by Michael Borgolte, Wolfgang Huschner, and Barbara Schlieben. Vol. 6. Berlin: Akademie Verlag, 2004.

———. "The Nomad's Greed for Gold: From the Fall of the Burgundians to the Avar Treasure." In *The Construction of Communities in the Early Middle Ages: Texts, Resources, and Artefacts*, edited by Richard Corradini, Max Diesenberger, and Helmut Reimitz, 95–108. Leiden/Boston: Brill, 2003.

Harley, J. B., and David Woodward, eds. *The History of Cartography: Cartography in Prehistoric, Ancient, and Medieval Europe and the Mediterranean*. Vol. 1. Chicago/London: University of Chicago Press, 1987.

Harries, Jill. "Roman Law from City State to World Empire." In *Law and Empire: Ideas, Practices, Actors*, edited by Jeroen Duindam, Jill Harries, Caroline Humfress, and Nimrod Hurvitz, 45–61. Leiden/Boston: Brill, 2013.

Harvey, Susan A. "Yuḥanon of Ephesus." In *Gorgias Encyclopedic Dictionary of the Syriac Heritage*, edited by Sebastian P. Brock, Aaron M. Butts, George A. Kiraz, and Lucas Van Rompay. Piscataway, NJ: Gorgias Press, 2011.

Haury, Jakob. "Procopiana." In *Programm des Königlichen Realgymnasiums Augsburg für das Studienjahr 1890 / 1891*, 9–27. Augsburg: Druck des Litterarischen Instituts von Haas & Grabherr, 1891.

———. "Zu Prokops Geheimgeschichte." *Byzantinische Zeitschrift* 34 (1934): 10–14.

Haynes, Ian. *Blood of the Provinces: The Roman Auxilia and the Making of Provincial Society from Augustus to the Severans*. Oxford: Oxford University Press, 2013.

Hays, Gregory, and Oliver Nicholson. "Avienius." In *Oxford Dictionary of Late Antiquity*, Vol. 1: 187. Oxford: Oxford University Press, 2018.

BIBLIOGRAPHY [385]

Heath, Christopher. "Hispania et Italia: Paul the Deacon, Isidore, and the Lombards." In *Isidore of Seville and His Reception in the Early Middle Ages: Transmitting and Transforming Knowledge*, edited by Andrew Fear and Jamie Wood, 159–76. Amsterdam: Amsterdam University Press, 2016.

Heather, Peter. *Empires and Barbarians: The Fall of Rome and the Birth of Europe*. London: Macmillan, 2009.

———. "Foedera and Foederati of the Fourth Century." In *Kingdoms of the Empire: The Integration of Barbarians in Late Antiquity*, edited by Walter Pohl, 57–74. Leiden: Brill, 1997.

———. *The Goths*. The Peoples of Europe. Oxford: Blackwell, 1996.

———. *Goths and Romans 332–489*. Oxford: Oxford University Press, 1991.

———. "The Huns and Barbarian Europe." In *The Cambridge Companion to the Age of Attila*, edited by Michael Maas, 209–29. Cambridge: Cambridge University Press, 2014.

———. "The Late Roman Art of Client Management." In *The Transformation of Frontiers: From Late Antiquity to the Carolingians*, edited by Walter Pohl, Ian Wood, and Helmut Reimitz, 15–68. Transformation of the Roman World 10. Leiden: Brill, 2001.

———. "Merely an Ideology?—Gothic Identity in Ostrogothic Italy." In *The Ostrogoths from the Migration Period to the Sixth Century: An Ethnographic Perspective*, edited by Samuel J. Barnish and Federico Marazzi, 31–80. Woodbridge / Rochester, NY: Boydell Press, 2007.

Heather, Peter, and John Matthews, trans. *The Goths in the Fourth Century*. TTH 11. Liverpool: Liverpool University Press, 1991.

Hegedus, Tim. *Early Christianity and Ancient Astrology*. New York: Peter Lang, 2007.

———. "The Magi and the Star in the Gospel of Matthew and Early Christian Tradition." *Laval théologique et philosophique* 59, no. 1 (February 2003): 81–95.

Heiberg, Johan Ludvig. "Théories antiques sur l'influence morale du climat." *Scientia* 28 (1920): 453–64.

Heilen, Stephan. "Ancient Scholars on the Horoscope of Rome." *Culture and Cosmos* 11, no. 1 and 2 (2007): 43–68.

———. "Ptolemy's Doctrine of the Terms and Its Reception." In *Ptolemy in Perspective: Use and Criticism of His Work from Antiquity to the Nineteenth Century*, edited by Alexander Jones, 45–93. New York: Springer Dordrecht, 2010.

Helm, Rudolf. *Hieronymus' Zusätze in Eusebius' Chronik und ihr Wert für die Literaturgeschichte. Philologus*. Supplementband 21.2. Leipzig: Dieterich'sche Verlagsbuchhandlung, 1929.

———. "Untersuchungen über den auswärtigen diplomatischen Verkehr des römischen Reiches im Zeitalter der Spätantike." *Archiv für Urkundenforschung* 12, no. 1 (1931): 375–436.

Helmig, Christoph, and Carlos Steel. "Proclus." In *The Stanford Encyclopedia of Philosophy*. Stanford University, 2020. https://plato.stanford.edu/archives/fall2020/entries/proclus/.

Hen, Yitzhak. "Conclusion: The Elusive Nature of an Orthodox Heresy." In *Arianism: Roman Heresy and Barbarian Creed*, edited by Guido M. Berndt and Roland Steinacher, 311–15. Farnham: Ashgate, 2014.

Hiebert, Theodore. "The Tower of Babel and the Origin of the World's Cultures." *Journal of Biblical Literature* 126, no. 1 (2007): 29–58.

Higgins, Martin J. "International Relations at the Close of the Sixth Century." *Catholic Historical Review* 27, no. 3 (October 1941): 279–315.

Hilgenfeld, Adolf. *Bardesanes: Der letzte Gnostiker*. Leipzig: T. O. Weigel, 1864.

Hodges, Horace Jeffery. "Gnostic Liberation from Astrological Determinism: Hipparchan 'Trepidation' and the Breaking of Fate." *Vigiliae Christianae* 51, no. 4 (1997): 359–73.

Hoffmann, Richard C. *An Environmental History of Medieval Europe*. Cambridge: Cambridge University Press, 2014.

Holum, Kenneth G. *Theodosian Empresses: Women and Imperial Dominion in Late Antiquity*. Berkeley: University of California Press, 1982.

Honigmann, Ernst. *Die sieben Klimata und die ΠΟΛΕΙΣ ΕΠΙΣΗΜΟΙ: Eine Untersuchung zur Geschichte der Geographie und Astrologie im Altertum und Mittelalter*. Heidelberg: Carl Winter's Universitätsbuchhandlung, 1929.

———. "S.s Quellenbenutzung: Moderne Quellenkritik." *RE* 4.2. Stuttgart: J. B. Metzlersche Verlagsbuchhandlung, 1932.

Howard-Johnston, James. *The Last Great War of Antiquity*. Oxford: Oxford University Press, 2021.

Hoyland, Robert G. *Arabia and the Arabs: From the Bronze Age to the Coming of Islam*. London / New York: Routledge, 2001.

——. "Arab Kings, Arab Tribes and the Beginnings of Arab Historical Memory in Late Roman Epigraphy." In *From Hellenism to Islam: Cultural and Linguistic Change in the Roman Near East*, edited by Hannah M. Cotton, Robert G. Hoyland, Jonathan J. Price, and David J. Wasserstein, 374–400. Cambridge: Cambridge University Press, 2009.

——. *Seeing Islam as Others Saw It: A Survey and Evaluation of Christian, Jewish and Zoroastrian Writings on Early Islam*. Princeton: Gorgias Press, 2019.

Hübner, Wolfgang. "Das Horoskop der Christen: (Zeno 1,38 L.)." *Vigiliae Christianae* 29, no. 2 (1975): 120–37.

——. *Zodiacus Christianus: Jüdisch-christliche Adaptationen des Tierkreises von der Antike bis zur Gegenwart*. Königstein/Ts.: Verlag Anton Hain, 1983.

Humfress, Caroline. "Citizens and Heretics: Late Roman Lawyers on Christian Heresy." In *Heresy and Identity in Late Antiquity*, edited by Eduard Iricinschi and Holger M. Zellentin, 128–42. Tübingen: Mohr Siebeck, 2008.

——. "Heretics, Laws On." In *Late Antiquity: A Guide to the Postclassical World*, edited by G. W. Bowersock, Peter Brown, and Oleg Grabar, 490–91. Cambridge MA: Harvard University Press, 1999.

——. "Roman Law, Forensic Argument and the Formation of Christian Orthodoxy (III–VI Centuries)." In *Orthodoxie, Christianisme, Histoire* [Orthodoxy, christianity, history], edited by Susanna Elm, Éric Rebillard, and Antonella Romano, 125–47. Collection de l'École Française de Rome 270. Rome: École Française de Rome, 2000.

Humphreys, S. C. "Fragments, Fetishes, and Philosophies: Toward a History of Greek Historiography after Thucydides." In *Collecting Fragments* [Fragmente sammeln], edited by Glenn W. Most, 207–24. Göttingen: Vandenhoeck & Ruprecht, 1997.

Humphries, Mark. "'Gog is the Goth': Biblical Barbarians in Ambrose of Milan's *De fide*." In *Unclassical Traditions: Alternatives to the Classical Past in Late Antiquity*, edited by Christopher Kelly, Richard Flowers, and Michael Stuart Williams, 44–57. Vol. 1. Cambridge: Cambridge University Press, 2010.

Hünemörder, Christian. "Fossatum." In *Brill's New Pauly*. http://dx.doi.org/10.1163/1574-9347_bnp_e414400.

Iluk, Jan. "The Export of Gold from the Roman Empire to Barbarian Countries from the 4th to the 6th Centuries." *Münstersche Beiträge zur antiken Handelsgeschichte* 4, no. 1 (1985): 79–102.

Imrie, Alex. *The Antonine Constitution: An Edict for the Caracallan Empire*. Leiden/Boston: Brill, 2018.

Inglebert, Hervé. *Interpretatio christiana: Les mutations des savoirs (cosmographie, géographie, ethnographie, histoire) dans l'Antiquité chrétienne, 30–630 après J.-C*. Paris: Institut d'études augustiniennes, 2001.

——. *Les romains chrétiens face à l'histoire de Rome: Histoire, christianisme et romanités en Occident dans l'Antiquité tardive (IIIe-Ve siècles)*. Paris: Institut d'études augustiniennes, 1996.

——. "L'histoire des hérésies chez les hérésiologues." In *L'historiographie de l'Église des premiers siècles*, ed. Bernard Pouderon and Yves-Marie Duval. *Théologie Historique* 114 (2001): 105–25.

Inowlocki, Sabrina. "Josephus' Rewriting of the Babel Narrative (Gen 11:1–9)." *Journal for the Study of Judaism in the Persian, Hellenistic, and Roman Period* 37, no. 2 (2006): 169–91.

Inwood, Brad. "Panaetius." In *OCD4*, edited by Simon Hornblower, Antony Spawforth, and Esther Eidinow, 1174–75. Oxford: Oxford University Press, 2012.

Isaac, Benjamin H. *The Invention of Racism in Classical Antiquity*. Princeton: Princeton University Press, 2004.

Ivanov, Sergey A. *"Pearls before Swine": Missionary Work in Byzantium*. Translated by Deborah Hoffman. Paris: Association des Amis du Centre d'histoire et civilisation de Byzance, 2015.

BIBLIOGRAPHY [387]

Izmirlieva, Valentina. *All the Names of the Lord: Lists, Mysticism, and Magic.* Chicago: University of Chicago Press, 2008.

Jacob, Christian. *Géographie et ethnographie en Grèce ancienne.* Paris: Armand Colin, 1991.

———. "Geography." Translated by Catherine Porter. In *Greek Thought: A Guide to Classical Knowledge,* edited by Jacques Brunschwig and Geoffrey E. R. Lloyd, 299–311. Cambridge, MA: Harvard University Press, 2000.

———. "Polybius." Translated by Elizabeth Rawlings and Jeannine Pucci. In *Greek Thought: A Guide to Classical Knowledge,* edited by Jacques Brunschwig and Geoffrey E. R. Lloyd. Translated under the direction of Catherine Porter, 712–20. Cambridge, MA / London: Harvard University Press, 2000.

Jacobs, Andrew S. *Epiphanius of Cyprus: A Cultural Biography of Late Antiquity.* Berkeley, CA: University of California Press, 2021.

Jeanes, Gordon P. *The Day Has Come!: Easter and Baptism in Zeno of Verona.* Collegeville, MN: Liturgical Press, 1995.

Johnson, Aaron P. *Ethnicity and Argumentation in Eusebius' Praeparatio Evangelica.* Oxford: Oxford University Press, 2006.

Johnson, Scott Fitzgerald. "Worlds of Byzantium: Problems, Frameworks, and Opportunities in the Byzantine Near East." In *Worlds of Byzantium: Religion, Culture, and Empire in the Medieval Near East,* edited by Elizabeth S. Bolman, Scott Fitzgerald Johnson, and Jack Tannous, 1–35. Cambridge: Cambridge University Press, 2024.

Jones, A. H. M. "The Dediticii and the Constitutio Antoniniana." In *Studies in Roman Government and Law,* 129–40. Oxford: Blackwell, 1960.

———. *The Later Roman Empire 284–602: A Social Economic and Administrative Survey.* 2 vols. Baltimore: Johns Hopkins University Press, 1986.

Jones, Christopher. P. "Stigma: Tattooing and Branding in Graeco-Roman Antiquity." *The Journal of Roman Studies* 77 (1987): 139–55.

Jones, G.D.B., and D. J. Mattingly. "Fourth-Century Manning of the 'Fossatum Africae.'" *Britannia* 11 (1980): 323–26.

Kaegi, Walter E. *Byzantium and the Early Islamic Conquests.* Cambridge: Cambridge University Press, 1992.

———. *Heraclius, Emperor of Byzantium.* Cambridge: Cambridge University Press, 2003.

Kaldellis, Anthony. *Ethnography after Antiquity: Foreign Lands and Peoples in Byzantine Literature.* Philadelphia: University of Pennsylvania Press, 2013.

———. *Procopius of Caesarea: Tyranny, History, and Philosophy at the End of Antiquity.* Philadelphia: University of Pennsylvania Press, 2004.

Kaldellis, Anthony, and Marion Kruse. *The Field Armies of the East Roman Empire, 361–630.* Cambridge: Cambridge University Press, 2023.

Kalligas, Paul. *The Enneads of Plotinus: A Commentary.* Vol. 1. Princeton: Princeton University Press, 2014.

Kannengiesser, Charles. "Apollinaris of Laodicea." In *The Encyclopedia of Early Christianity,* edited by Everett Ferguson, 79–81. New York / London: Garland Publishing, 1998.

Kardong, Terrence G. "Vulgate." In *Encyclopedia of Early Christianity,* edited by Everett Ferguson, 1167–69. New York / London: Garland Publishing, 1998.

Kazhdan, Alexander. "Klimata." In *ODB* 2, 1133. New York: Oxford University Press, 1991.

Kelley, Nicole. *Knowledge and Religious Authority in the Pseudo-Clementines: Situating the "Recognitions" in Fourth Century Syria.* Tübingen: Mohr Siebeck, 2006.

Kelly, Christopher. "Neither Conquest nor Settlement: Attila's Empire and Its Impact." In *The Cambridge Companion to the Age of Attila,* edited by Michael Maas, 193–208. Cambridge: Cambridge University Press, 2015.

Kennedy, D. L. "Some Observations on the Praetorian Guard." *Ancient Society* 9 (1978): 275–301.

Kennedy, Hugh. "Syria, Palestine and Mesopotamia." In *CAH 14: Late Antiquity; Empire and Successors, A.D. 425–600,* edited by Averil Cameron, Bryan Ward-Perkins, and Michael Whitby, 588–611. Cambridge: Cambridge University Press, 2000.

Kennedy, Rebecca Futo. "Airs, Waters, Metals, Earth: People and Land in Archaic and Classical Greek Thought." In *The Routledge Handbook of Identity and the Environment in the*

[388] BIBLIOGRAPHY

Classical and Medieval Worlds, edited by Rebecca Futo Kennedy and Molly Jones-Lewis, 19–23. Abingdon: Routledge, 2016.

Kennedy, Rebecca Futo, C. Sydnor Roy, and Max L. Goldman, ed. and trans. *Race and Ethnicity in the Classical World: An Anthology of Primary Sources in Translation*. Indianapolis, IN: Hackett Publishing Company, 2013.

Keppie, Lawrence. *The Making of the Roman Army: From Republic to Empire*. London: Batsford, 1984.

Kidd, I. G. "Posidonius (2)." In *OCD4*, edited by Simon Hornblower, Antony Spawforth, and Esther Eidinow, 1195–96. Oxford: Oxford University Press, 2012.

———. "What Is a Posidonian Fragment?" In *Collecting Fragments*, edited by Glenn W. Most, 225–36. Göttingen: Vandenhoeck and Ruprecht, 1997.

Kiilerich, Bente. *The Obelisk Base in Constantinople: Court Art and Imperial Ideology*. Rome: Bretschneider Editore, 1998.

Kim, Hyun Jin. "The Invention of the 'Barbarian' in Late Sixth-Century BC Ionia." In *Ancient Ethnography: New Approaches*, edited by Eran Almagor and Joseph Skinner, 25–48. London: Bloomsbury Academic, 2013.

Kim, Young Richard. "Epiphanius of Cyprus and the Geography of Heresy." In *Violence in Late Antiquity: Perceptions and Practices*, edited by Harold Drake et al., 235–51. Burlington, VT / Aldershot: Ashgate, 2006.

———. *Epiphanius of Cyprus: Imagining an Orthodox World*. Ann Arbor: University of Michigan Press, 2015.

Kitchen, Thomas E. "Contemporary Perceptions of the Roman Empire in the Later Fifth and Sixth Centuries." PhD diss., Cambridge University, 2008.

Kohler, Kaufmann, and Isaac Broydé. "Nations and Languages, The Seventy." In *The Jewish Encyclopedia* Vol. 9, edited by Cyrus Adler et al., 188–90. New York: KTAV Publishing House, 1901.

Kolbaba, Tia M. *Inventing Latin Heretics: Byzantines and the Filioque in the Ninth Century*. Kalamazoo, MI: Medieval Institute Publications, 2008.

Kominko, Maja. "Changing Habits and Disappearing Monsters—Ethnography between Classical and Late Antiquity." In *Identity and the Other in Byzantium: Papers from the Fourth International Sevgi Gönül Byzantine Studies Symposium*, edited by Koray Durak and Ivana Jevtić, 53–70. Istanbul: Koç University Press, 2019.

Krebs, Christopher B. *A Most Dangerous Book: Tacitus' Germania from the Roman Empire to the Third Reich*. New York: W. W. Norton, 2011.

Kreller, H. "Postliminium." *RE* 22.1: 863–73. Stuttgart: J. B. Metzlersche Verlagsbuchhandlung, 1953.

Kroll, Jerome, and Bernard Bachrach. "Justin's Madness: Weak-Mindedness or Organic Psychosis?" *Journal of the History of Medicine and Allied Sciences* 48, no. 1 (1993): 40–67.

Krumbacher, Karl, A. Ehrhard, and H. Gelzer. *Geschichte der byzantinischen Litteratur von Justinian bis zum Ende des oströmischen Reiches*. 2nd ed. HAW 9. Munich: C. H. Beck / Oscar Beck, 1897.

Kuhlmann, Peter Alois, ed. and trans. *Die Giessener literarischen Papyri und die Caracalla-Erlasse*. Giessen: Universitätsbibliothek, 1994.

Kulikowski, Michael. "The 'Notitia Dignitatum' as a Historical Source." *Historia* 49, no. 3 (2000): 358–77.

———. *Rome's Gothic Wars: From the Third Century to Alaric*. Cambridge: Cambridge University Press, 2015.

———. "Where the Wild Things Are: The Invention of Barbarian Space." In *Empires and Indigenous Peoples: Comparing Ancient Roman and North American Experiences*, edited by Michael Maas and Fay A. Yarbrough, 151–63. Norman, OK: University of Oklahoma Press, 2024.

Kupfer, Marcia. "The Noachide Dispersion in English Mappae Mundi c. 960–c. 1130." *Peregrinations: Journal of Medieval Art and Architecture* 4, no. 1 (2013): 81–106.

Lacocque, André. "Whatever Happened in the Valley of Shinar? A Response to Theodore Hiebert." *Journal of Biblical Literature* 128, no. 1 (2009): 29–41.

BIBLIOGRAPHY [389]

Ladner, Gerhart B. "On Roman Attitudes toward Barbarians in Late Antiquity." In *Viator*, 24–25. Medieval and Renaissance Studies 7. Oakland, CA: University of California Press, 1976.

Laistner, M. L. W. *Thought and Letters in Western Europe, A.D. 500 to 900*. London: Methuen & Co., 1957.

——. "The Western Church and Astrology during the Early Middle Ages." *Harvard Theological Review* 34, no. 4 (October 1941): 251–75.

Lampe, G. W. H., ed. *A Patristic Greek Lexicon*. Oxford: Clarendon Press, 1961.

Lanata, Giuliana. *Legislazione e natura nelle novelle giustinianee*. Naples: Edizioni Scientifiche Italiane, 1984.

Laniado, Avshalom. *Ethnos et droit dans le monde protobyzantin, Ve-VIe siècle: Fédérés, paysans et provinciaux à la lumière d'une scholie juridique de l'époque de Justinien*. Geneva: Librairie Droz, 2015.

Lassandro, Domenico. "I 'cultores barbari' (Laeti) in Gallia da Massimiano alla fine del IV secolo d.C." In *Conoscenze etniche e rapporti di convivenza nell'antichità*, edited by Marta Sordi, 178–88. Milan: Università Cattolica del Sacro Cuore, 1979.

la Vaissière, Étienne de. "The Steppe World and the Rise of the Huns." In *The Cambridge Companion to the Age of Attila*, edited by Michael Maas, 175–92. Cambridge: Cambridge University Press, 2015.

Lawrence, Marilynn. "Hellenistic Astrology." In *Internet Encyclopedia of Philosophy*, edited by James Fieser and Bradley Dowden. https://iep.utm.edu/hellenistic-astrology/.

Le Boulluec, A. *La notion d'hérésie dans la litterature grecque aux IIe–IIIe siècles, I.1 De Justin à Irénée*. Paris: Études Augustiniennes, 1985.

Lee, A. D. *Information and Frontiers: Roman Foreign Relations in Late Antiquity*. Cambridge: Cambridge University Press, 1993.

——. "Treaty-Making in Late Antiquity." In *War and Peace in Ancient and Medieval History*, edited by Philip de Souza and John France, 107–19. Cambridge: Cambridge University Press, 2008.

Léotard, Eugène. *Essai sur la condition des barbares établis dans l'Empire romain au quatrième siècle*. Paris: Librairie A. Franck, 1873.

Le Strange, G., and R. A. Nicholson. *The Fársnáma of Ibnu'l-Balkhí*. London: Luzac & Co., 1921.

Lewis, Martin W., and Kären E. Wigen. *The Myth of Continents: A Critique of Metageography*. Berkeley: University of California Press, 1997.

Liddell, Henry George, and Robert Scott. *A Greek-English Lexicon*. Edited by Henry Stuart Jones and Roderick McKenzie. Oxford: Clarendon Press, 1940.

Livingstone, David N. "Changing Climate, Human Evolution, and the Revival of Environmental Determinism." *Bulletin of the History of Medicine* 86, no. 4 (2012): 564–95.

Lomas, Kathryn. "The Idea of a City: Elite Ideology and the Evolution of Urban Form in Italy, 200 BC–AD 100." In *Roman Urbanism: Beyond the Consumer City*, edited by Helen Parkins, 21–41. London / New York: Routledge, 1997.

Long, A. A. "Astrology: Arguments Pro and Contra." In *Science and Speculation: Studies in Hellenistic Theory and Practice*, edited by Jonathan Barnes, Jacques Brunschwig, Myles Burnyeat, and Malcolm Schofield, 165–92. Cambridge: Cambridge University Press, 1982.

L'Orange, H. P. *Studies on the Iconography of Cosmic Kingship in the Ancient World*. Oslo: H. Aschehoug & Co. (W. Nygaard), 1953.

Lovejoy, Arthur, and George Boas. *Primitivism and Related Ideas in Antiquity*. Baltimore: Johns Hopkins University Press, 1935.

Lozovsky, Natalia. *"The Earth Is Our Book": Geographical Knowledge in the Latin West ca. 400–1000*. Ann Arbor: University of Michigan Press, 2000.

Lyman, J. Rebecca. "Heresiology: The Invention of 'Heresy' and 'Schism.'" In *The Cambridge History of Christianity: Constantine to c. 600*, edited by Augustine Casiday and Frederick W. Norris. Vol. 2: 296–313. Cambridge: Cambridge University Press, 2007.

——. "A Topography of Heresy: Mapping the Rhetorical Creation of Arianism." In *Arianism after Arius: Essays on the Development of the Fourth Century Trinitarian Conflicts*, edited by Michel R. Barnes and Daniel H. Williams, 45–62. Edinburgh: T&T Clark, 1993.

[390] BIBLIOGRAPHY

Maas, Michael. "'Delivered from Their Ancient Customs': Christianity and the Question of Cultural Change in Early Byzantine Ethnography." In *Conversion in Late Antiquity and the Early Middle Ages: Seeing and Believing*, edited by Kenneth Mills and Anthony Grafton, 152–88. Studies in Comparative History 4. Rochester, NY: University of Rochester Press, 2003.

——. "The Equality of Empires: Procopius on Adoption and Guardianship across Imperial Borders." In *Motions of Late Antiquity: Essays on Religion, Politics, and Society in Honour of Peter Brown*, edited by Jamie Kreiner and Helmut Reimitz, 175–86. Turnhout: Brepols, 2016.

——. "Ethnicity, Orthodoxy, and Community in Salvian of Marseilles." In *Fifth-Century Gaul: A Crisis of Identity?*, edited by John Drinkwater and Hugh Elton, 275–84. Cambridge: Cambridge University Press, 1992.

——. *Exegesis and Empire in the Early Byzantine Mediterranean: Junillus Africanus and the Instituta Regularia Divinae Legis*. With a contribution by Edward G. Matthews Jr. Studien und Texte zu Antike und Christentum 17. Tübingen: Mohr Siebeck, 2003.

——. "Fugitives and Ethnography in Priscus of Panium." *Byzantine and Modern Greek Studies* 19 (1995): 146–60.

——. "How the Steppes Became Byzantine: Rome and the Eurasian Nomads in Historical Perspective." In *Empires and Exchanges in Eurasian Late Antiquity: Rome, China, Iran, and the Steppe, ca. 250–75*, edited by Nicola Di Cosmo and Michael Maas, 19–34. Cambridge: Cambridge University Press, 2018.

——. *John Lydus and the Roman Past: Antiquarianism and Politics in the Age of Justinian*. London / New York: Routledge, 1992.

——. "Mores et Moenia: Ethnography and the Decline in Urban Constitutional Autonomy in Late Antiquity." In *Integration und Herrschaft: Ethnische Identitäten und Soziale Organisation im Frühmittelalter*, edited by Walter Pohl and Max Diesenberger, 25–35. Vienna: Verlag der Österreichischen Akademie der Wissenschaften, 2002.

——. "Preface" In *On Celestial Signs (De Ostentis)*, edited by Anastasius C. Bandy, Anastasia Bandy, Demetrios J. Constantelos, and Craig J. N. de Paulo, translated by Anastasius C. Bandy. Lewiston: Edwin Mellen Press, 2013.

——. "Roman History and Christian Ideology in Justinianic Reform Legislation." *DOP* 40 (1986): 17–31.

——. "The Shaping Hand of the Environment: Three Phases of Development in Classical Antiquity." In *Aspects of Ancient Institutions and Geography: Studies in Honor of Richard J. A. Talbert*, edited by Lee L. Brice and Daniëlle Slootjes, 333–46. Impact of Empire 19. Leiden/Boston: Brill, 2015.

——. "Strabo and Procopius: Classical Geography for a Christian Empire." In *From Rome to Constantinople: Studies in Honour of Averil Cameron*, edited by Hagit Amirav and Bas ter Haar Romeny, 67–84. Leuven: Peeters, 2007.

MacAdam, Henry I. "Strabo, Pliny the Elder and Ptolemy of Alexandria: Three Views of Ancient Arabia and Its Peoples." In *Actes du Colloque de Strasbourg 24–27 juin 1987*, edited by T. Fahd, 289–320. Leiden/Boston: Brill, 1989.

MacCoull, Leslie S. B. "Philoponus' Letter to Justinian (CPG 7264)." *Byzantion* 73, no. 2 (2003): 390–400.

Machiela, Daniel A. "Some Jewish Noah Traditions in Syriac Christian Sources." In *Noah and His Book(s)*, edited by Michael E. Stone, Aryeh Amihay, and Vered Hillel, 237–52. Atlanta: Society of Biblical Literature, 2010.

Magdalino, Paul. "The Byzantine Reception of Classical Astrology." In *Literacy, Education, and the Manuscript Tradition in Byzantium and Beyond*, edited by Catherine Holmes and Judith Waring, 33–58. The Medieval Mediterranean 42. Leiden/Boston: Brill, 2002.

——. "The History of the Future and Its Uses: Prophecy, Policy and Propaganda (with Postscript)." In *The Expansion of Orthodox Europe: Byzantium, the Balkans and Russia*, edited by Jonathan Shepard, 28–63. Aldershot: Ashgate Variorum, 2007.

——. *L'Orthodoxie des astrologues: La science entre le dogme et la divination à Byzance (VIIe–XIVe siècle)*. Paris: Lethielleux, 2006.

Magness, Jodi. "Heaven on Earth: Helios and the Zodiac Cycle in Ancient Palestinian Synagogues." *DOP* 59 (2005): 1–52.

Maguire, Henry. *Earth and Ocean: The Terrestrial World in Early Byzantine Art*. University Park, PA / London: College Art Association of America / Pennsylvania State University Press, 1987.

Mahoney, Daniel. "The Political Construction of a Tribal Genealogy from Early Medieval South Arabia." In *Meanings of Community across Medieval Eurasia: Comparative Approaches*, edited by Eirik Hovden, Christina Lutter, and Walter Pohl, 165–82. Leiden/Boston: Brill, 2016.

Main, Robert. *After Justinian: Foreign Policy in the Byzantine Empire during the Reigns of Justin II and Tiberius II Constantine (565–582)*. PhD thesis, University of Oxford, 2019.

Major, Tristan Gary. "Literary Developments of the Table of Nations and the Tower of Babel in Anglo-Saxon England." PhD diss., University of Toronto, 2010.

———. "The Number Seventy-Two: Biblical and Hellenistic Beginnings to the Early Middle Ages." *Sacris Erudiri* 52 (2013): 7–46.

———. *Undoing Babel: The Tower of Babel in Anglo-Saxon Literature*. Toronto: University of Toronto Press, 2018.

Marjanen, Antti, and Petri Luomanen, eds. *A Companion to Second-Century Christian 'Heretics.'* Leiden/Boston: Brill, 2008.

Markus, R. A. "Chronicle and Theology: Prosper of Aquitaine." In *The Inheritance of Historiography 350–900*, edited by Christopher Holdsworth and T. P. Wiseman. Liverpool: Liverpool University Press, 1986.

Martindale, J. R., ed. *The Prosopography of the Later Roman Empire: Vol. 2, AD 395–527*. Cambridge: Cambridge University Press, 1980.

Maskarinec, Maya. "Clinging to Empire in Jordanes' 'Romana.'" In *Historiography and Identity II: Post-Roman Multiplicity and New Political Identities*, edited by Helmut Reimitz and Gerda Heydemann, 71–93. Turnhout: Brepols, 2020.

Mathews, Edward. Review of *Saint Jerome's Hebrew Questions on Genesis*, by Robert Hayward. *Bryn Mawr Classical Review* (Spring 1996).

Mathisen, Ralph W. "Barbarian 'Arian' Clergy, Church Organization, and Church Practice." In *Arianism: Roman Heresy and Barbarian Creed*, edited by Guido M. Berndt and Roland Steinacher, 145–91. Farnham: Ashgate, 2014.

———. "Clovis, Anastasius, and Political Status in 508 C.E.: The Frankish Aftermath of the Battle of Vouillé." In *The Battle of Vouillé, 507 CE: Where France Began*, edited by Ralph W. Mathisen and Danuta Shanzer, 79–110. Millennium-Studien / Millennium Studies 37. Boston/Berlin: Walter de Gruyter, 2012.

———. "Concepts of Citizenship." In *The Oxford Handbook of Late Antiquity*, edited by Scott Fitzgerald Johnson, 744–63. Oxford: Oxford University Press, 2012.

———. "Libius Severus (461–465 A.D.)." In *De Imperatoribus Romanis—An Online Encyclopedia of Roman Rulers and Their Families*. Article published 1997. http://www.roman-emperors.org/libius.htm.

———. "*Peregrini, Barbari*, and *Cives Romani*: Concepts of Citizenship and Legal Identity of Barbarians in the Late Roman Empire." *American Historical Review* 111, no. 4 (October 2006): 1011–40.

———. "*Provinciales*, Gentiles, and Marriages between Romans and Barbarians in the Late Roman Empire." *Journal of Roman Studies* 99 (2009): 140–55.

Mattingly, David J. *Imperialism, Power, and Identity: Experiencing the Roman Empire*. Princeton: Princeton University Press, 2011.

Mauss, Marcel. "Essai sur le don: Forme et raison de l'échange dans les sociétés archaïques." *L'Année Sociologique*, n.s., 1, no. 1 (1925): 30–186.

———. *The Gift: Expanded Edition*. Selected, annotated, and translated by Jane I. Guyer. Chicago: Hau Books, 2016.

———. *The Gift: Forms and Functions of Exchange in Archaic Societies*. Translated by Ian Cunnison. London: Routledge & Kegan Paul Ltd, 1966.

Mayerson, Philip. "Mauia, Queen of the Saracens—A Cautionary Note." *Israel Exploration Journal* 30, no. 1–2 (1980): 123–31.

McClure, Judith. "Handbooks against Heresy in the West, from the Late Fourth to the Late Sixth Centuries." *Journal of Theological Studies* 30, no. 1 (April 1979): 186–97.

McCluskey, Stephen C. *Astronomies and Cultures in Early Medieval Europe.* Cambridge: Cambridge University Press, 1998.

McCormick, Michael. "Analyzing Imperial Ceremonies." *Jahrbuch der Österreichischen Byzantinistik* 35 (1985): 1–20.

———. "Clovis at Tours, Byzantine Public Ritual and the Origins of Medieval Ruler Symbolism." In *Das Reich und die Barbaren*, edited by Evangelos K. Chrysos and Andreas Schwarcz, 155–80. Vienna/Cologne: Böhlau Verlag, 1989.

———. *Eternal Victory: Triumphal Rulership in Late Antiquity, Byzantium and the Early Medieval West.* Cambridge: Cambridge University Press, 1986.

McDonald, Alexander Hugh. "Posidonius (Ποσειδώνιος), (1)." In *OCD4*, edited by Simon Hornblower, Antony Spawforth, and Esther Eidinow, 1195. Oxford: Oxford University Press, 2012.

McDonough, Scott. "Were the Sasanians Barbarians? Roman Writers on the 'Empire of the Persians.'" In *Romans, Barbarians, and the Transformation of the Roman World: Cultural Interaction and the Creation of Identity in Late Antiquity*, edited by Ralph W. Mathisen and Danuta Shanzer, 55–65. Farnham: Ashgate, 2011.

McLynn, Neil. "Little Wolf in the Big City: Ulfila and His Interpreters." *Bulletin of the Institute of Classical Studies* 50, Supplement 91 (2007): 125–35.

McMahon, Lucas. "The Foederati, the Phoideratoi, and the Symmachoi of the Late Antique East (ca. A.D. 400–650)." Master's thesis, University of Ottawa, 2014.

McWhorter, John. *The Power of Babel: A Natural History of Language.* New York: HarperCollins, 2001.

Meier, Mischa, and Frederico Monitaro, eds. *A Companion to Procopius of Caesarea.* Leiden/Boston: Brill, 2022.

Merkelbach, Reinhold. *Die Quellen des griechischen Alexanderromans.* Zetemeta 9. Munich, 1977.

Mészáros, Tamás. "Notes on Procopius' *Secret History.*" In *Byzanz und das Abendland: Begegnungen zwischen Ost und West*, edited by E. Juhász, 285–304. Antiquitas Byzantium Renascentia 5. Budapest: ELTE-Eötvös-József-Collegium, 2013.

Meyendorff, John. "Byzantine Views of Islam." *DOP* 18 (1964): 113–32.

Millar, Fergus. "Empire, Community and Culture in the Roman Near East: Greeks, Syrians, Jews and Arabs." *Journal of Jewish Studies* 38, no. 2 (1987): 143–64.

———. "Hagar, Ishmael, Josephus and the Origins of Islam." *Journal of Jewish Studies* 44, no. 1 (1993).

———. *The Roman Near East, 31 B.C.–A.D. 337.* Cambridge, MA: Harvard University Press, 1993.

———. "Rome's 'Arab' Allies in Late Antiquity: Conceptions and Representations from within the Frontiers of the Empire." In *Commutatio et contentio: Studies in the Late Roman, Sasanian, and Early Islamic Near East; In Memory of Zeev Rubin*, edited by Henning Börm and Josef Wiesehöfer, 199–226. Düsseldorf: Wellem Verlag, 2010.

———. "The Theodosian Empire (408–450) and the Arabs: Saracens or Ishmaelites?" In *Cultural Borrowings and Ethnic Appropriations in Antiquity*, edited by Erich S. Gruen, 297–314. Stuttgart: Franz Steiner Verlag, 2005.

Minets, Yuliya. "Languages of Christianity in Late Antiquity: Between Universalism and Cultural Superiority." *Studia Patristica* 92 (2017): 247–60.

———. "'Rushing Noise' and 'Mingled Clamor': The Persian Language and Its Speakers in Roman Sources in Late Antiquity." In *Migration and Mobility across the Roman-Persian Frontier in Late Antiquity.* Stuttgart: Franz Steiner Verlag, 2025.

———. "The Slow Fall of Babel: Conceptualization of Languages, Linguistic Diversity and History in Late Ancient Christianity." PhD diss., Catholic University of America, 2017.

———. *The Slow Fall of Babel: Languages and Identities in Late Antique Christianity.* Cambridge: Cambridge University Press, 2021.

BIBLIOGRAPHY [393]

Miquel, A. "Iklīm." In *Encyclopedia of Islam*, edited by P. Bearman, Th. Bianquis, C. E. Bosworth, E. van Donzel, and W. P. Heinrichs. Leiden: Brill, 2012. http://dx.doi.org/10.1163/1573-3912_islam_SIM_351.

Mishkovsky, Zelda. "Each Man Has a Name." In *The Penguin Book of Hebrew Verse*, edited and translated by T. Carmi, 558. London: Penguin Books, 1981.

Mittenhuber, Florian. "The Tradition of Texts and Maps in Ptolemy's 'Geography.'" In *Ptolemy in Perspective: Use and Criticism of His Work from Antiquity to the Nineteenth Century*, edited by Alexander Jones, 95–120. Archimedes 23. Heidelberg / New York: Springer, 2010.

Moatti, Claudia. "The Notion of Res Publica in the Age of Caracalla." In *Citizenship and Empire in Europe 200–1900: The Antonine Constitution after 1800 Years*, edited by Clifford Ando, 63–98. Potsdamer Altertumswissenschaftliche Beitrage 54. Stuttgart: Franz Steiner Verlag, 2016.

Modéran, Yves. *Les Vandales et l'Empire romain*. Edited by Michel-Yves Perrin. Paris: Editions Errance, 2014.

———. "L'établissement de Barbares sur le territoire romain à l'époque impériale." In *La mobilité des personnes en Méditerranée de l'Antiquité à l'époque moderne: Procédures de contrôle et documents d'identifications*, edited by Claudia Moatti, 337–97. Rome: École Française de Rome, 2004.

Momigliano, Arnaldo. *Alien Wisdom: The Limits of Hellenization*. Cambridge: Cambridge University Press, 1975.

Mommsen, Theodor. "Die Conscriptionsordnung der römischen Kaiserzeit (1884)." In *Historische Schriften: Dritter Band*, 20–117. Vol. 6 of *Gesammelte Schriften*. Berlin: Weidmannsche Buchhandlung, 1910.

Moore, George Foot. "Fate and Free Will in the Jewish Philosophies According to Josephus." *Harvard Theological Review* 22, no. 4 (October 1929): 371–89.

Morstein-Marx, Robert. "The Myth of Numidian Origins in Sallust's African Excursus ('Iugurtha' 17.7–18.12)." *American Journal of Philology* 122, no. 2 (2001): 179–200.

Mosig-Walburg, Karin. *Römer und Perser: Vom 3. Jahrhundert bis zum Jahr 363 n. Chr.* Gutenberg: COMPUTUS Druck Satz & Verlag, 2009.

Moss, Yonatan. "The Language of Paradise: Hebrew or Syriac? Linguistic Speculations and Linguistic Realities in Late Antiquity." In *Paradise in Antiquity. Jewish and Christian Views*, edited by Markus Bockmuehl and Guy G. Stroumsa, 120–37. Cambridge: Cambridge University Press, 2010.

Mosshammer, Alden A. *The Chronicle of Eusebius and the Greek Chronographic Tradition*. Lewisburg / London: Bucknell University Press / Associated University Presses, 1979.

Muhlberger, Steven. *The Fifth-Century Chroniclers: Prosper, Hydatius, and the Gallic Chronicler of 452*. Leeds: Francis Cairns, 1990.

Mullen, Alex. *Southern Gaul and the Mediterranean: Multilingualism and Multiple Identities in the Iron Age and Roman Periods*. Cambridge: Cambridge University Press, 2012.

Mullen, Alex, and Patrick James, eds. *Multilingualism in the Graeco-Roman Worlds*. Cambridge: Cambridge University Press, 2012.

Müller, Klaus E. *Geschichte der antiken Ethnographie und ethnologischen Theoriebildung von den Anfängen bis auf die Byzantinischen Historiographen: Teil II*. Wiesbaden: Franz Steiner Verlag, 1980.

Murphy, Trevor. *Pliny the Elder's "Natural History": The Empire in the Encyclopedia*. Oxford: Oxford University Press, 2004.

Murray, Alexander Callander. Review of *Die Barbaren in den spätrömischen Gesetzen: Eine Untersuchung des Terminus "barbarus,"* by Sven Rugullis. *Gnomon* 67, no. 7 (1995): 649–50.

Murray, Oswyn. "Herodotus and Hellenistic Culture." *Classical Quarterly* 22, no. 2 (1972): 200–213.

Naas, Valérie. *Le projet encyclopédique de Pline l'Ancien*. Rome: École Française de Rome, 2002.

Nash, Daphne. "Reconstructing Poseidonios' Celtic Ethnography: Some Considerations." *Britannia* 7 (1976): 111–26.

[394] BIBLIOGRAPHY

Nechaeva, Ekaterina. *Embassies—Negotiations—Gifts: Systems of East Roman Diplomacy in Late Antiquity*. Stuttgart: Franz Steiner Verlag, 2014.

———. "International Political Hospitality and Non-Hospitality in Late Antiquity: High-Profile Strangers between Asylum and Extradition." In *Hospitalité et régulation de l'altérité dans l'Antiquité méditerranéenne*, edited by Claire Fauchon-Claudon and Marie-Adeline Le Guennec, 235–47. Bordeaux: Ausonius Éditions, 2022.

———. "Late Antique East Roman Diplomacy." In *The Encyclopedia of Diplomacy*, edited by Gordon Martel, 1079–90. Vol. 3. Malden, MA / Oxford: Wiley-Blackwell, 2018.

———. "Patterns of Roman Diplomacy with Iran and the Steppe Peoples." In *Empires and Exchanges in Eurasian Late Antiquity: Rome, China, Iran, and the Steppe, ca. 250–750*, edited by Nicola Di Cosmo and Michael Maas, 357–68.

Nicasie, M. J. Review of *East Roman Foreign Policy: Formation and Conduct from Diocletian to Anastasius*, by R. C. Blockley. *Mnemosyne* 49, no. 1 (1996): 118–23.

Nicolet, Claude. *Space, Geography, and Politics in the Early Roman Empire*. Ann Arbor: University of Michigan Press, 1991.

———. *The World of the Citizen in Republican Rome*. Berkeley: University of California Press, 1991.

Nicoletti, Michele. "The Angel of the Nations." In *Theopopedia: Archiving the History of Theologico-Political Concepts*, edited by T. Faitini, F. Ghaia, and M. Nicoletti, 1–11. Trento: University of Trento Press, 2015.

Noble, Thomas F. X. *From Roman Provinces to Medieval Kingdoms*. London / New York: Routledge, 2006.

Norris, Frederick W. "Greek Christianities." In *The Cambridge History of Christianity. Constantine to c. 600*, edited by Augustine Casiday and Frederick W. Norris, 2:70–117. Cambridge: Cambridge University Press, 2007.

O'Donnell, James J. *Cassiodorus*. Berkeley: University of California Press, 1979.

———. *Pagans: The End of Traditional Religion and the Rise of Christianity*. New York: Ecco, 2015.

Olberg-Haverkate, Gabriel von. "Liten." In *Handwörterbuch zur deutschen Rechtsgeschichte (HRG)*, 2nd ed., edited by Albrecht Cordes, Hans-Peter Haferkamp, Bernd Kannowski, Heiner Lück, Heinrich de Wall, Dieter Werkmüller, and Ruth Schmidt-Wiegand, 3:1013–15. Berlin: Erich Schmidt Verlag, 2004.

Olender, Maurice. *The Languages of Paradise: Race, Religion, and Philology in the Nineteenth Century*. Translated by Arthur Goldhammer. Cambridge, MA / London: Harvard University Press, 1992.

Olster, David M. "Classical Ethnography and Early Christianity." In *The Formulation of Christianity by Conflict through the Ages*, edited by Katharine B. Free, 9–31. Symposium Series 34. Lewiston, NY: The Edwin Mellen Press, 1995.

Ostrogorsky, George. "The Byzantine Emperor and the Hierarchical World Order." *The Slavonic and East European Review* 35, no. 84 (1956): 1–14.

Pace, Nicola. *Ricerche sulla traduzione di Rufino del "De principiis" di Origene*. Florence: La Nuova Italia Editrice, 1990.

Palmer, James T. *The Apocalypse in the Early Middle Ages*. Cambridge: Cambridge University Press, 2014.

Panzram, Sabne, and Paulo Pachà, eds. *The Visigothic Kingdom: The Negotiation of Power in Post-Roman Iberia*. Amsterdam: Amsterdam University Press, 2020.

Papaconstantinou, Arietta. *The Multilingual Experience in Egypt, from the Ptolemies to the 'Abbāsids*. Farnham/Burlington, VT: Ashgate, 2010.

Papadogiannakis, Ioannis. "Didacticism, Exegesis, and Polemics in Pseudo-Kaisarios's Erotapokriseis." In *La littérature des questions et réponses dans l'Antiquité profane et chrétienne: De l'enseignement à l'exégèse; Actes du séminaire sur le genre des questions et réponses tenu à Ottawa les 27 et 28 septembre 2009*, edited by Marie-Pierre Bussières, 271–89. Instrumenta Patristica et Mediaevalia 64. Turnhout: Brepols, 2013.

———. "Instruction by Question and Answer: The Case of Late Antique and Byzantine Erotapokriseis." In *Greek Literature in Late Antiquity: Dynamism, Didacticism, Classicism*, edited by Scott Fitzgerald Johnson, 91–105. Aldershot / Burlington, VT: Ashgate, 2006.

BIBLIOGRAPHY [395]

Parker, S. Thomas. *Romans and Saracens: A History of the Arabian Frontier*. The American Schools of Oriental Research 6. University Park, PA: Eisenbrauns, 1986.

Parry, Ken. "Fate, Free Choice, and Divine Providence from the Neoplatonists to John of Damascus." In *The Cambridge Intellectual History of Byzantium*, edited by Anthony Kaldellis and Niketas Siniossoglou, 341–60. Cambridge: Cambridge University Press, 2017.

Payne, Richard. "Cosmology and the Expansion of the Iranian Empire, 502–628 CE." *Past and Present* 220, no. 1 (2013): 3–33.

———. "The Reinvention of Iran: The Sasanian Empire and the Huns." In *The Cambridge Companion to the Age of Attila*, edited by Michael Maas, 282–300. Cambridge: Cambridge University Press, 2014.

Pazdernik, Charles F. "Procopius and Thucydides on the Labors of War: Belisarius and Brasidas in the Field." *TAPA* 130 (2000): 149–87.

Pearson, Birger A. "Basilides the Gnostic." In *A Companion to Second-Century Christian "Heretics,"* edited by Antti Marjanen and Petri Luomanen, 1–31. Supplements to Vigiliae Christianae 76. Leiden/Boston: Brill, 2005.

———. *Gnosticism and Christianity in Roman and Coptic Egypt*. Studies in Antiquity and Christianity. New York / London: T&T Clark International, 2004.

Peers, Glenn. *Subtle Bodies: Representing Angels in Byzantium*. Berkeley: University of California Press, 2002.

Périn, Patrick, and Michel Kazanski. "Identity and Ethnicity during the Era of Migrations and Barbarian Kingdoms in the Light of Archaeology in Gaul." In *Romans, Barbarians, and the Transformation of the Roman World: Cultural Interaction and the Creation of Identity in Late Antiquity*, edited by Ralph W. Mathisen and Danuta Shanzer, 299–330. Farnham: Ashgate, 2011.

Peterson, Erik. "The Book on the Angels: Their Place and Meaning in the Liturgy." In *Theological Tractates*, edited by Erik Peterson, translated by Michael J. Hollerich, 106–42. Stanford: Stanford University Press, 2011.

———. *Der Monotheismus als politisches Problem: Ein Beitrag zur Geschichte der politischen Theologie im Imperium Romanum*. Leipzig: Hegner, 1935.

———, ed. "Monotheism as a Political Problem: A Contribution to the History of Political Theology in the Roman Empire." In *Theological Tractates*, 68–105. Stanford, 2011.

Pharr, Clyde. *See* Theodosian Code

Pieler, Peter E. "L'aspect politique et juridique de l'adoption de Chosroès proposée par les Perses à Justin." *RIDA* 3, no. 19 (1972): 399–433.

Pingree, David. "Antiochus and Rhetorius." *Classical Philology* 72, no. 3 (1977): 203–23.

———. "From Alexandria to Baghdād to Byzantium: The Transmission of Astrology." *International Journal of the Classical Tradition* 8, no. 1 (Summer 2001): 3–37.

———. "Rhetorios of Egypt." In *ODB*, vol. 3, edited by Alexander P. Kazhdan, Alice-Mary Talbot, Anthony Cutler, Timothy E. Gregory, and Nancy P. Ševčenko, 1790. New York / Oxford: Oxford University Press, 1991.

Pinna, Mario. "Ippocrate: Fondatore della teoria dei climi." *Rivista Geografica Italiana* 95 (1988): 3–19.

Podany, Amanda H. *Brotherhood of Kings: How International Relations Shaped the Ancient Near East*. Oxford: Oxford University Press, 2010.

Pohl, Walter. "Appropriating the Discourse about Barbarians in the Early Medieval West." In *Empires and Indigenous Peoples: Comparing Ancient Roman and North American Experiences*, edited by Michael Maas and Fay Yarbrough, 119–36. Norman, OK: University of Oklahoma Press, 2024.

———. *The Avars: A Steppe Empire in Central Europe, 567–822*. Ithaca, NY / London: Cornell University Press, 2018.

———. "Christian and Barbarian Identities in the Early Medieval West: Introduction." In *Post-Roman Transitions: Christian and Barbarian Identities in the Early Medieval West*, edited by Walter Pohl and Gerda Heydemann, 1–46. Turnhout: Brepols, 2013.

———. "Conclusion: The Transformation of Frontiers." In *The Transformation of Frontiers: From Late Antiquity to the Carolingians*, edited by Walter Pohl, Ian Wood, and Helmut Reimitz, 247–60. Leiden/Boston/Köln: Brill, 2001.

[396] BIBLIOGRAPHY

Pohl, Walter. *Die Awaren: Ein Steppenvolk in Mitteleuropa, 567–822 n. Chr.* 3rd ed. Munich: C. H. Beck, 2015.

———. *Die Germanen.* Munich: R. Oldenbourg Verlag, 2000.

———. "The Empire and the Lombards: Treaties and Negotiations in the Sixth Century." In *Kingdoms of the Empire. The Integration of Barbarians in Late Antiquity*, edited by Walter Pohl, 75–133. Leiden / New York / Cologne: Brill, 1997.

———. "Introduction: Strategies of Identification; A Methodological Profile." In *Strategies of Identification: Ethnicity and Religion in Early Medieval Europe*, edited by Walter Pohl and Gerda Heydemann, 1–64. Cultural Encounters in Late Antiquity and the Middle Ages 13. Turnhout: Brepols, 2013.

———, ed. *Kingdoms of the Empire: The Integration of Barbarians in Late Antiquity.* Leiden / New York: Brill, 1997.

———. "Narratives of Origin and Migration in Early Medieval Europe: Problems of Interpretation." *Medieval History Journal* 21, no. 2 (October 2018): 192–221.

———. "Ritualized Encounters: Late Roman Diplomacy and the Barbarians, Fifth–Sixth Century." In *Court Ceremonies and Rituals of Power in Byzantium and the Medieval Mediterranean: Comparative Perspectives*, edited by A. Beihammer, S. Constantinou, and M. Parani, 67–86. The Medieval Mediterranean 98. Leiden: Brill Publishers, 2013.

———. "The Transformation of the Roman World Revisited." In *Motions of Late Antiquity: Essays on Religion, Politics, and Society in Honour of Peter Brown*, edited by Jamie Kreiner and Helmut Reimitz, 45–61. Turnhout: Brepols, 2016.

Possekel, Ute. "Bardaisan and Origen on Fate and the Power of the Stars." *Journal of Early Christian Studies* 20, no. 4 (2012): 515–41.

Pourkier, Aline. *L'hérésiologie chez Épiphane de Salamine.* Paris: Beauchesne, 1992.

Prinzing, Günter. "Byzantium, Medieval Russia and the So-Called Family of Kings: From George Ostrogorsky to Franz Dölger's Construct and Its Critics." In *Imagining Byzantium: Perceptions, Patterns, Problems*, edited by Alena Alshanskaya, Andreas Gietzen, and Christina Hadjiafxenti, 15–30. Mainz: Verlag des Römisch-Germanischen Zentralmuseums, 2018.

Prontera, Francesco. "Karte (Kartographie)." In *RAC: Sachwörterbuch zur Auseinandersetzung des Christentums mit der antiken Welt*, edited by Georg Schöllgen, translated by Matthias Perkams, 1: 187–229. Stuttgart: Anton Hiersemann, 2001.

Purcell, Nicholas. "Strabo." In *OCD4.*, edited by Simon Hornblower, Antony Spawforth, and Esther Eidinow, 1404. Oxford: Oxford University Press, 2012.

———. "Urban Spaces and Central Places: The Roman World." In *Classical Archaeology*, 2nd ed., edited by Susan E. Alcock and Robin Osborne, 187–90. Malden, MA: Wiley-Blackwell, 2012.

Quasten, Johannes. "Diodore of Tarsus." In *Patrology: Vol.III. The Golden Age of Greek Patristic Literature; From the Council of Nicaea to the Council of Chalcedon*, 397–401. Westminster, MD: Newman Press, 1960.

———. "Hippolytus of Rome." In *Patrology: The Ante-Nicene Literature after Irenaeus*, Vol. 2: 163–207. Utrecht/Antwerp: Spectrum Publishers, 1953.

Rabello, Alfredo M. *Giustiniano, ebrei e samaritani alla luce delle fonti storico-letterarie, ecclesiastiche e giuridiche.* Vol. 1. Milan: Dott. A. Giuffrè Editore, 1987.

Rabold, Britta, Egon Schallmayer, and Andreas Thiel, eds. *Der Limes. Die Deutsche Limes-Strasse vom Rhein bis zur Donau.* Stuttgart: Konrad Theiss Verlag, 2000.

Ramelli, Ilaria L. E. *Bardaisan of Edessa: A Reassessment of the Evidence and a New Interpretation.* Gorgias Eastern Christian Studies 22. Piscataway, NJ: Gorgias Press, 2009.

———. "Constantine: The Legal Recognition of Christianity and Its Antecedents." *Annuario de Historia de la Iglesia* 22 (2013): 65–82.

Rance, Philip. "Maurice's *Strategicon* and 'the Ancients': The Late Antique Reception of Aelian and Arrian." In *Greek Taktika: Ancient Military Writing and Its Heritage*, edited by Philip Rance and Nicholas V. Sekunda, 217–55. Gdańsk: Foundation for the Development of University of Gdańsk, Department of Mediterranean Archaeology, 2017.

Rapp, Claudia. "Literary Culture under Justinian." In *The Cambridge Companion to the Age of Justinian*, edited by Michael Maas, 376–97. Cambridge: Cambridge University Press, 2005.

BIBLIOGRAPHY [397]

Rawson, Elizabeth. *Intellectual Life in the Late Roman Republic*. London: Gerald Duckworth & Co., 1985.

Rebillard, Éric. "Religious Sociology: Being Christian in the Time of Augustine." In *A Companion to Augustine*, edited by Mark Vessey and Shelley Reid, 40–53. Blackwell Companions to the Ancient World. Malden, MA: Wiley-Blackwell, 2012.

Reed, Annette. "Abraham as Chaldaean Scientist and Father of the Jews: Josephus Ant. I. 154–168, and the Greco-Roman Discourse about Astronomy/Astrology." *Journal for the Study of Judaism in the Persian, Hellenistic, and Roman Period* 35, no. 2 (2004): 119–58.

Reimitz, Helmut. *History, Frankish Identity and the Framing of Western Ethnicity, 550–850*. Cambridge Studies in Medieval Life and Thought, 4th ser., 101. Cambridge: Cambridge University Press, 2015.

———. "Pax Inter Utramque Gentem: The Merovingians, Byzantium and the History of Frankish Identity." In *East and West in the Early Middle Ages: The Merovingian Kingdoms in Mediterranean Perspective*, edited by Stefan Esders, Yaniv Fox, Yitzhak Hen, and Laury Sarti, 45–63. Cambridge: Cambridge University Press, 2019.

Retsö, Jan. *The Arabs in Antiquity: Their History from the Assyrians to the Umayyads*. London / New York: Routledge, 2002.

Ricci, Giuseppe A. "Nomads in Late Antiquity: Gazing on Rome from the Steppe, Attila to Asparuch (370–680 C.E.)." PhD diss., Princeton University, 2015.

Richardson, John. *The Language of Empire: Rome and the Idea of Empire from the Third Century BC to the Second Century AD*. Cambridge: Cambridge University Press, 2008.

Richter, Daniel S. *Cosmopolis. Imagining Community in Late Classical Athens and the Early Roman Empire*. Oxford: Oxford University Press, 2011.

Riedinger, Rudolf. *Pseudo-Kaisarios: Überlieferungsgeschichte und Verfasserfrage*. Munich: C. H. Beck'sche Verlagsbuchhandlung, 1969.

Riedinger, Utto. *Die heilige Schrift im Kampf der griechischen Kirche gegen die Astrologie: Von Origenes bis Johannes von Damaskos*. Innsbruck: Universitätsverlag Wagner, 1956.

Riggsby, Andrew. *Caesar in Gaul and Rome: War in Words*. Austin: University of Texas Press, 2006.

Rives, James B., trans. *Tacitus Germania*. Oxford: Clarendon Press, 1999.

Rivet, A. L. F. "*The Notitia Galliarum*: Some Questions." In *Aspects of the Notitia Dinitatum: Papers Presented to the Conference in Oxford December 13 to 15, 1974*, edited by R. Goodburn and P. Bartholomew, 119–41. BAR Supplementary Series 15. Oxford: BAR, 1974.

Roberto, Umberto. "Liber Generationis Mundi." In *Encyclopedia of the Medieval Chronicle*, edited by Graeme Dunphy and Cristian Bratu. http://dx.doi.org/10.1163/2213-2139_emc _SIM_01691.

Roberts, Alexander, and James Donaldson. "Introductory Note to Irenæus Against Heresies." In ANF *1*: 309–13. Grand Rapids: Christian Classics Ethereal Library, 1885. https://www .ccel.org/ccel/schaff/anf01.html.

Rochette, Bruno. "Language Policies in the Roman Republic and Empire." In *A Companion to the Latin Language*, edited by James Clackson, 549–63. Malden, MA: Wiley-Blackwell, 2011.

Roletti, Ivan, and Serena Romano, eds. *Fons Vitae: Baptême, baptistères et rites d'initiation (IIe-VIe siècle)*. Rome: Viella Editrice, 2009.

Romm, James S. *The Edges of the Earth in Ancient Thought: Geography, Exploration, and Fiction*. Princeton: Princeton University Press, 1992.

Rösch, Gerhard. *ΟΝΟΜΑ ΒΑΣΙΛΕΙΑΣ: Studien zum offiziellen Gebrauch der Kaisertitel in spätantiker und frühbyzantinischer Zeit*. Byzantina Vindobonesia 10. Vienna: Verlag der Österreichischen Akademie der Wissenschaften, 1978.

Rose, Charles Brian. "'Princes' and Barbarians on the Ara Pacis." *American Journal of Archaeology* 94, no. 3 (July 1990): 453–67.

Rose, Herbert Jennings. "Hephaistion of Thebes and Christianity." *Harvard Theological Review* 33, no. 1 (January 1940): 65–68.

Ross, Donald L. "Gregory of Nyssa (c. 335–c. 395 C.E.)." In *Internet Encyclopedia of Philosophy*, edited by James Fieser and Bradley Dowden, May 5, 2023. https://iep.utm.edu/gregoryn/.

Ross, Stephen K. *Roman Edessa: Politics and Culture on the Eastern Fringes of the Roman Empire, 114–242 C.E.* London / New York: Routledge, 2001.

Roth, Catherine, and David Whitehead. "Pi,265. Pappos, Pappus." Suda On Line (SOL). http://www.cs.uky.edu/~raphael/sol/sol-entries/pi/265.

Roth, Catherine, David Whitehead, and Oliver Phillips. "Delta,1149. Diodoros, Diodorus, Diodore." Suda Online (SOL). http://www.cs.uky.edu/~raphael/sol/sol-entries/delta/1149.

Rotter, Ekkehart. *Abendland und Sarazenen: Das okzidentale Araberbild und seine Entstehung im Frümittelalter.* Berlin / New York: Walter de Gruyter, 1986.

Rouse, Richard, and Charles McNelis. "North African Literary Activity: A Cyprian Fragment, the Stichometric Lists and a Donatist Compendium." *Revue d'histoire des textes* 30 (2001): 189–238.

Rowe, John Howland. *Ethnography and Ethnology in the Sixteenth Century.* Berkeley: University of California Press, 1994.

Roymans, Nico, and Stijn Heeren. "Introduction: New Perspectives on the Late Roman Northwest." In *Social Dynamics in the Northwest Frontiers of the Late Roman Empire: Beyond Decline or Transformation,* edited by Nico Roymans and Stijn Heeren, 1–10. Amsterdam: Amsterdam University Press, 2017.

Rubin, Milka. "The Language of Creation or the Primordial Language: A Case of Cultural Polemics in Antiquity." *Journal of Jewish Studies* 49, no. 2 (1998): 306–33.

Rubin, Ze'ev. "Diplomacy and War in the Relations between Byzantium and the Sassanids in the Fifth Century AD." In *The Defence of the Roman and Byzantine East: Proceedings of a Colloquium Held at the University of Sheffield in April 1986,* edited by Philip Freeman and David Kennedy, 677–95. BAR International Series, 297 (ii). Oxford: BAR, 1986.

———. "The Sasanid Monarchy." In *CAH 14: Late Antiquity; Empire and Successors, A.D. 425–600,* 3rd ed., edited by Averil Cameron, Bryan Ward-Perkins, and Michael Whitby, 638–61. Cambridge: Cambridge University Press, 2000.

Rüger, C. "Germany." In *CAH 10: The Augustan Empire, 44 B.C.–A.D.70,* edited by Alan K. Bowman, Edward Champlin, and Andrew Lintott, 2nd ed., 517–34. Cambridge: Cambridge University Press, 1996.

Rugullis, Sven. *Die Barbaren in den spätrömischen Gesetzen: Eine Untersuchung des Terminus "barbarus."* Frankfurt am Main: Peter Lang, 1992.

Safran, Linda. "Points of View: The Theodosian Obelisk Base in Context." *Greek, Roman and Byzantine Studies* 34, no. 4 (Winter 1993): 409–35.

Sahas, Daniel J. *John of Damascus on Islam. The "Heresy of the Ishmaelites."* Leiden: Brill, 1972.

Salvesen, A. G. "Ya'qub of Edessa." In *Gorgias Encyclopedic Dictionary of the Syriac Heritage,* edited by Sebastian P. Brock, Aaron M. Butts, George A. Kiraz, and Lucas Van Rompey, 432–33. Piscataway, NJ: Gorgias Press, 2011.

Sandoz, Mari. *Hostiles and Friendlies: Selected Short Writings of Mari Sandoz.* Lincoln, Nebraska: University of Nebraska Press, 1959.

Saradi, Helen. "The *Kallos* of the Byzantine City: The Development of a Rhetorical Topos and Historical Reality." *Gesta* 34, no. 1 (1995): 37–56.

Sarantis, Alexander. *Justinian's Balkan Wars: Campaigning, Diplomacy and Development in Illyricum, Thrace and the Northern World, A.D. 527–65.* ARCA: Classical and Medieval Texts, Papers and Monographs 53. Prenton, UK: Francis Cairns, 2016.

———. "Procopius and the Different Types of Northern Barbarian." In *Le monde de Procope,* edited by Geoffrey Greatrex and Sylvain Janniard, 355–78. Paris: Éditions de Boccard, 2018.

Sarantis, Alexander, and Neil Christie. *War and Warfare in Late Antiquity: Current Perspectives.* Edited by Alexander Sarantis and Neil Christie. Late Antique Archaeology 8. Leiden/Boston: Brill, 2013.

Sarnowski, Tadeusz. "Barbaricum und ein bellum Bosporanum in einer Inschrift aus Preslav." *Zeitschrift für Papyrologie und Epigraphik* 87 (1991): 137–44.

Sartor, Guillaume. "Les fédérés (*foederati*) dans les guerres imperials (IIIe–IVe siècles)." In *Les auxiliaires de l'armée romaine: Des alliés aux fédérés,* edited by Catherine Wolff and Patrice Faure, 527–73. CEROR 51. Lyon: Centre d'études et de recherches sur l'Occident romain, 2016.

BIBLIOGRAPHY [399]

———. "Recherches sur les fédérés et l'armée romaine (de la fin du IIe siècle après J.-C. au début du VIIe siècle après J.-C.)": Vol. 3; Analyses et conclusion générale. PhD thesis, Université de recherche Paris Sciences et Lettres [PSL Research University], 2018.

Sasse, Christoph, ed. *Die Constitutio Antoniniana: Eine Untersuchung über den Umfang der Bürgerrechtsverleihung auf Grund des Papyrus Giss. 40 I*. Wiesbaden: Harrassowitz, 1958.

Sauer, Eberhard W. "The History of the Dariali Gorge." In *Dariali: The "Caspian Gates" in the Caucasus from Antiquity to the Age of the Huns and the Middle Ages; The Joint Georgian-British Dariali Gorge Excavations & Surveys of 2013–2016*, 2: 857–929. British Institute of Persian Studies Archaeological Monographs, 6th ser., 2. Oxford and Philadelphia: Oxbow Books, 2020.

Schadee, Hester. "Caesar's Construction of Northern Europe: Inquiry, Contact and Corruption in *De Bello Gallico*." *Classical Quarterly* 58, no. 1 (2008): 158–80.

Schadler, Peter. "Heresy and Heresiology in Late Antiquity." In *John of Damascus and Islam: Christian Heresiology and the Intellectual Background to Earliest Christian-Muslim Relations*, 20–48. Leiden/Boston: Brill, 2018.

Schmauder, Michael. "The Advance of the Huns: From Asia to the Danube." In *Rome and the Barbarians: The Birth of a New World*, edited by Jean-Jaques Aillagon, 236–43. Milan: Skira Editore, 2008.

Schmidt, Francis. "Jewish Representations of the Inhabited Earth during the Hellenistic and Roman Periods." In *Greece and Rome in Eretz Israel: Collected Essays*, edited by A. Kasher, U. Rappaport, and G. Fuks, 119–34. Jerusalem: Yad Izhak Ben-Zvi, 1990.

Schmidt, Katharina. *Kosmologische Aspekte im Geschischtswerk des Poseidonius*. Hypomnemata 63. Göttingen: Vandenhoeck and Ruprecht, 1980.

Schmidt-Hofner, Sebastian. "Barbarian Migrations and Socio-Economic Challenges to the Roman Landholding Elite in the Fourth Century CE." *Journal of Late Antiquity* 10, no. 2 (2017): 372–404.

Schneider, Rolf Michael. "Orientalism in Late Antiquity: The Oriental in Imperial and Christian Imagery." In *Ērān ud Anērān: Studien zu den Beziehungen zwischen dem Sasanidenreich und der Mittelmeerwelt; Beiträge des Internationalen Colloquiums in Eutin, 8.–9. Juni 2000*, edited by Josef Wiesehöfer and Philip Huyse, 241–78. Oriens et Occidens 13. Munich: Franz Steiner Verlag, 2006.

Schofield, Malcolm. "Academic Epistemology." In *The Cambridge History of Hellenistic Philosophy*, edited by Keimpe Algra, Jonathan Barnes, Jaap Mansfield, and Malcolm Schofield, 323–51. Cambridge: Cambridge University Press, 1999.

Schramm, Percy Ernst. *Sphaira. Globus. Reichsapfel. Wanderung und Wandlung eines Herrschaftsbezeichens von Caesar bis zu Elisabeth II: Ein Beitrag zum "Nachleben" der Antike*. Stuttgart: Anton Hiersemann, 1958.

Schulz, Raimund. *Die Entwicklung des römischen Völkerrechts im vierten und fünften Jahrhundert n. Chr*. Hermes Einzelschriften 61. Stuttgart: Hermes Franz Steiner Verlag, 1993.

Scott, Alan. *Origen and the Life of the Stars: A History of an Idea*. Oxford: Clarendon Press, 1991.

Scott, James M. *Geography in Early Judaism and Christianity: The Book of Jubilees*. Cambridge: Cambridge University Press, 2002.

Setaioli, Aldo. *La vicenda dell'anima nel commento di Servo a Virgilio*. Frankfurt am Main: Peter Lang, 1995.

Shahîd, Irfan. *Byzantium and the Arabs in the Fifth Century*. Washington, DC: Dumbarton Oaks Research Library and Collection, 1989.

———. *Byzantium and the Arabs in the Fourth Century*. Washington, DC: Dumbarton Oaks Research Library and Collection, 1984.

———. *Byzantium and the Arabs in the Sixth Century: Ecclesiastical History*. Vol. 1, no. 2. Washington, DC: Dumbarton Oaks Research Library and Collection, 1995.

———. *Byzantium and the Arabs in the Sixth Century: Economic, Social, and Cultural History*. Vol. 2, no. 2. Washington, DC: Dumbarton Oaks Research Library and Collection, 2009.

———. *Byzantium and the Arabs in the Sixth Century: Political and Military History*. Vol 1, no. 1. Washington, DC: Dumbarton Oaks Research Library and Collection, 1995.

Shahîd, Irfan. *Rome and the Arabs: A Prolegomenon to the Study of Byzantium and the Arabs.* Washington, DC: Dumbarton Oaks Research Library and Collection, 1984.
———. "Ṭayyiʾ or Ṭayy." In *Encyclopaedia of Islam.* Edited by P. Bearman, Th. Bianquis, C. E. Bosworth, E. van Donzel, and W. P. Heinrichs. http://dx.doi.org/10.1163/1573-3912_islam_SIM_7471.
Shalev, Zur, and Charles Burnett, eds. *Ptolemy's "Geography" in the Renaissance.* Warburg Institute Colloquia 17. London/Turin: Warburg Institute/Nino Aragno Editore, 2011.
Shaw, Brent D. "Autonomy and Tribute: Mountain and Plain in Mauretania Tingitana." In *Désert et montagne au Maghreb: Hommage à Jean Dresch*, edited by Pierre-Robert Baudel, 66–89. Revue de l'Occident musulman et de la Méditerranée 41–42. Aix-en-Provence: Édisud, 1986.
———. "'Eaters of Flesh, Drinkers of Milk': The Ancient Mediterranean Ideology of the Pastoral Nomad." *Ancient Society* 13–14 (83 1982): 5–31.
———. "The Exterminating Angel: The Roman Imperial State and Its Indigenous Peoples." In *Empires and Indigenous Peoples: Comparing Ancient Roman and North American Experiences*, edited by Michael Maas and Fay Yarbrough, 17–35. Norman, OK: University of Oklahoma Press, 2024.
———. "Fear and Loathing: The Nomad Menace and Roman Africa." In *L'Afrique Romaine: Les conférences Vanier 1980* [Roman Africa: The Vanier Lectures 1980], edited by C. M. Wells, 29–50. Ottawa: University of Ottawa Press, 1982.
———. "Fear and Loathing: The Nomad Menace and Roman Africa." *Roman Africa/L'Afrique Romaine (Revue de l'Université d'Ottawa)* 52, no. 1 (1982): 25–46.
———. "Keti, Son of Maswalat: Ethnicity and Empire." In *Rome: An Empire of Many Nations; New Perspectives on Ethnic Diversity and Cultural Identity*, edited by Jonathan J. Price, Margalit Finkelberg, and Yuval Shahar, 58–83. Cambridge: Cambridge University Press, 2021.
———. *Rulers, Nomads, and Christians in Roman North Africa.* Aldershot, UK: Variorum, 1995.
———. *Sacred Violence: African Christians and Sectarian Hatred in the Age of Augustine.* Cambridge: Cambridge University Press, 2011.
Shcheglov, Dmitriy A. "Ptolemy's System of Seven Climata and Eratosthenes' Geography." *Geographia Antiqua* 13 (2004): 21–37.
Shepard, Jonathan. "Courts in East and West." In *The Medieval World*, edited by Peter Linehan and Janet L. Nelson, 14–36. London / New York: Routledge, 2001.
———. "Superpower to Soft Power, within Overlapping Circles: Byzantium and Its Place in Twenty-First-Century International History." In *Internationale Geschichte in Theorie Und Praxis/International History in Theory and Practice*, edited by Michael Gehler and Wolfgang Mueller, 4: 81–122. Vienna: Verlag der Österreichischen Akademie der Wissenschaften, 2017.
Sherwin-White, A. N. *The Roman Citizenship.* 2nd ed. Oxford: Clarendon Press, 1973.
———. "The Roman Citizenship: A Survey of Its Development into a World Franchise." In *Aufstieg und Niedergang der römischen Welt: Von den Anfängen Roms bis zum Ausgang der Republik*, edited by Hildegard Temporini and Wolfgang Haase. Vol. 1, no. 2. Berlin / New York: Walter De Gruyter, 1972.
Silva, Semíramis Corsi, and Vinícius de Oliveira da Motta. "Astrologia e poder no Império Romano: A adivinhação do Destino na 'Antologia,' de Vettius Valens (século II d.C.)." *Romanitas—Revista de Estudos Grecolatinos* 9 (2017): 115–37.
Simonetti, Manlio. "Diodore of Tarsus." In *Encyclopedia of the Early Church*, edited by Angelo Di Bernadino, translated by Adrian Walford, 1: 236–37. Cambridge: James Clarke & Co., 1992.
Simpson, C. J. "Laeti in Northern Gaul: A Note on Pan. Lat. VIII, 21." *Latomus* 36, no. 1 (March 1977): 169–70.
Skarsaune, Oskar. "Ethnic Discourse in Early Christianity." In *Christianity in the Second Century: Themes and Developments*, edited by James Carleton Paget and Judith Lieu, 250–64. Cambridge: Cambridge University Press, 2017.
Skinner, Joseph E. *The Invention of Greek Ethnography: From Homer to Herodotus.* Oxford: Oxford University Press, 2012.

BIBLIOGRAPHY [401]

Sodini, Jean-Pierre. "Images sculptées et propagande impériale du IVe au VIe siècle: Recherches récentes sur les colonnes honorifiques et les reliefs politiques à Byzance." In *Byzance et les images: Cycle de conférences organisé au Musée du Louvre par le Service culturel du 5 octobre au 7 décembre 1992*, edited by André Guillou, 43–94. Paris: Documentation Française, 1994.

Sorabji, Richard, ed. *Philoponus and the Rejection of Aristotelian Science*. Ithaca, NY: Cornell University Press, 1987.

Soraci, Rosario. *Ricerche sui conubia tra Romani e Germani nei secoli IV-VI*. Seconda edizione amplicata. Catania: Casa Editrice Muglia, 1974.

Speidel, Michael Alexander. "The Roman Army." In *The Oxford Handbook of Roman Epigraphy*, edited by Christer Bruun and Jonathan Edmondson, 319–44. Oxford: Oxford University Press, 2015.

Speidel, Michael P. "The Soldiers' Homes." In *Roman Army Studies*, 2: 313–27. Stuttgart: Franz Steiner Verlag, 1992.

Speyer, Wolfgang, and Ilona Opelt. "Barbar." *Jahrbuch für Antike und Christentum* 10 (1967): 251–90.

———. "Barbar I." In *RAC Supplement*, edited by Theodor Klauser, Ernst Dassmann, and Josef Kremer, 1: 813–95. Stuttgart: Anton Hiersemann, 2001.

Spinks, Bryan D. *Early and Medieval Rituals and Theologies of Baptism: From the New Testament to the Council of Trent*. London: Routledge, 2006.

Spring, Peter. *Great Walls and Linear Barriers*. Barnsley, UK: Pen & Sword Military, 2015.

Stanley Jones, Frederick. "The Astrological Trajectory in Ancient Syriac-Speaking Christianity (Elchasai, Bardaisan, and Mani)." In *Atti del terzo Congresso Internazionale di Studi "Manicheismo e Oriente Cristiano Antico": Arcavacata di Rende—Amantea, 31 agosto–5 settembre 1993*, edited by Luigi Cirillo and Alois van Tongerloo, 183–200. Turnhout: Brepols, 1997.

———. "Eros and Astrology in the Περίοδοι Πέτρου: The Sense of the Pseudo-Clementine Novel." *Apocrypha* 12 (2001): 53–78.

Ste. Croix, G. E. M. de "Appendix III. The Settlement of 'Barbarians' within the Roman Empire." In *The Class Struggle in the Ancient Greek World from the Archaic Age to the Arab Conquests*, 509–18. London: Duckworth, 1981.

———. *The Class Struggle in the Ancient Greek World from the Archaic Age to the Arab Conquests*. London: Duckworth, 1981.

Stein, Ernest. *Histoire du Bas-Empire, Vol. 1: De l'État romain à l'État byzantin (284–476)*. Edited by Jean-Remy Palanque. Paris/Brussels/Amsterdam: Desclée de Brouwer, 1959.

———. *Histoire du Bas-Empire, Vol. 2: De la disparition de l'Empire d'Occident a la mort de Justinien (476–565)*. Edited by Jean-Remy Palanque. Paris/Brussels/Amsterdam: Desclée de Brouwer, 1949.

Steinacher, Roland. "The Heruls: Fragments of a History." In *Neglected Barbarians*, edited by Florin Curta, 319–60. Turnhout: Brepols, 2010.

———. "Rome and Its Created Northerners: Germani as a Historical Term." In *Interrogating the 'Germanic': A Category and Its Use in Late Antiquity and the Early Middle Ages*, edited by Matthias Friedrich and James M. Harland. Ergänzungsbände zum Reallexikon der Germanischen Altertumskunde 123. Berlin: De Gruyter, 2021.

Steinova, Evina. "Etymologiae.Ms: A Database of the Pre-1000 Manuscripts of the Etymologiae of Isidore of Seville." Academia.edu. https://www.academia.edu/video/gjE5Wj .

Sternbach, Leo. "Analecta Avarica." *Rozprawy Akademii Umiejętności, Wydział Filologiczny* 2, no. 15 (1900): 297–365.

Stevens, Susan T., and Jonathan P. Conant, eds. *North Africa under Byzantium and Early Islam*. Washington, DC: Dumbarton Oaks Research Library and Collection, 2016.

Stickler, Timo. "The Foederati." In *A Companion to the Roman Army*, edited by Paul Erdkamp, 495–514. Oxford: Blackwell, 2007.

Stoneman, Richard. *Alexander the Great*. Lancaster Pamphlets in Ancient History. London / New York: Routledge, 1997.

Striker, Gisela. "Carneades." In *OCD4*, edited by Simon Hornblower, Antony Spawforth, and Esther Eidinow, 282. Oxford: Oxford University Press, 2012.

[402] BIBLIOGRAPHY

Sullivan, Charles A. "An Analysis of Gregory of Nyssa on Speaking in Tongues." June 7, 2020. https://charlesasullivan.com/7212/analysis-gregory-nyssa-speaking-tongues/.

Syme, Ronald. "Pliny the Procurator." *Harvard Studies in Classical Philology* 73 (1969): 201–36.

Tafażżolī, Aḥmad. "Clime." In *Encyclopaedia Iranica 5, Fasc. 7,7: 713*. New York: Columbia University Press, 1982. http://dx.doi.org/10.1163/2330-4804_EIRO_COM_7756.

Talbert, Richard J. A. *Barrington Atlas of the Greek and Roman World*. Princeton: Princeton University Press, 2000.

——. "Natives Naming Themselves? Rome's Veterans Speak." In *Empires and Indigenous Peoples: Comparing Ancient Roman and North American Experiences*, edited by Michael Maas and Fay Yarbrough, 212–26. Norman, OK: University of Oklahoma Press, 2024.

Taylor, Justin. "The List of the Nations in Acts 2:9–11." *Revue Biblique* 106, no. 3 (July 1999): 408–20.

Teixidor, Javier. *Bardesane d'Edesse: La première philosophie syriaque*. Paris: Éditions du Cerf, 1992.

Tester, S. J. *A History of Western Astrology*. Woodbridge, Suffolk / Wolfeboro, NH: Boydell Press, 1987.

Theuws, Franz. "Grave Goods, Ethnicity, and the Rhetoric of Burial Rites in Late Antique Northern Gaul." In *Ethnic Constructs in Antiquity: The Role of Power and Tradition*, edited by Ton Derks and Nico Roymans, 283–319. Amsterdam Archaeological Studies 13. Amsterdam: Amsterdam University Press, 2009.

Thollard, Patrick. *Barbarie et civilisation chez Strabon: Étude critique des livres III et IV de la géographie*. Centre de Recherches d'Histoire Ancienne 77. Paris: Les Belles Lettres, 1987.

Thomas, Oliver. "Creating Problemata with the Hippocratic Corpus." In *The Aristotelian Problemata Physica: Philosophical and Scientific Investigations*, edited by Richard Mayhew, 79–99. Philosophia Antiqua 139. Leiden/Boston: Brill, 2015.

Thomas, Richard F. *Lands and Peoples in Roman Poetry: The Ethnographical Tradition*. Cambridge: Cambridge Philological Society, 1982.

Thomas, Rosalind. *Herodotus in Context: Ethnography, Science and the Art of Persuasion*. Cambridge: Cambridge University Press, 2000.

Thompson, L. A. "Strabo on Civilization." *Platon* 31 (1979): 213–29.

Thurman, William S. "The Application of Subiecti to Roman Citizens in the Imperial Laws of the Later Roman Empire." *Klio* 52 (1970): 453–63.

——. "A Juridical and Theological Concept of Nature in the Sixth Century A.D." *Byzantinoslavica* 32, no. 2 (1971): 77–85.

Tierney, J. J. "The Celtic Ethnography of Posidonius." *Proceedings of the Irish Academy: Archaeology, Culture, History, Literature* 60 (1960): 189–275.

Tinnefeld, Franz. "Ceremonies for Foreign Ambassadors at the Court of Byzantium and Their Political Background." *Byzantinische Forschungen*, no. 19 (1993): 193–213.

Todorov, Tzvetan. *The Conquest of America: The Question of the Other*. Translated by Richard Howard. New York: Harper and Rowe, 1984.

Toomer, G. J. "Ptolemy." In *Dictionary of Scientific Biography: A. Pitcairn—B. Rush*, edited by Charles Coulston Gillispie, 11: 186–206. New York: Charles Scribner's Sons, 1981.

Treadgold, Warren. *Byzantium and Its Army, 284–1081*. Stanford, CA: Stanford University Press, 1995.

——. *The Early Byzantine Historians*. Hampshire / New York: Palgrave, 2010.

Trimingham, J. Spencer. *Christianity among the Arabs in Pre-Islamic Times*. Beirut: Librairie du Liban, 1990.

Trotta, Francesco. "Strabone e l'Asia Minore: Politeiai e gradi di civilizzazione." In *Strabone e l'Asia Minore*, edited by Anna Maria Biraschi and Giovanni Salmeri, 189–208. Perugia: Edizione Scientifiche Italiane, 2000.

Trousset, Pol. "Pénétration romaine et organisation de la zone frontière dans le prédésert tunisien." *L'Africa Romana* 15, no. 1 (2004): 59–88.

Trüdinger, Karl. *Studien zur Geschichte der griechisch-römischen Ethnographie*. Basel: E. Birkhäuser, 1918.

BIBLIOGRAPHY [403]

Tuplin, Christopher. "Greek Racism? Observations on the Character and Limits of Greek Ethnic Prejudice." In *Ancient Greeks East and West*, edited by Gocha R. Tsetskhladze, 47–75. Mnemosyne Supplement 196. Leiden: Brill, 1999.

Turfa, Jean MacIntosh. "The Etruscan Brontoscopic Calendar and Modern Archaeological Discoveries." *Etruscan Studies* 10 (2007): 163–73.

Tzamalikos, Panayiotis. *Origen: Philosophy of History & Eschatology*. Vigiliae Christianae Supplements 85. Leiden/Boston: Brill, 2007.

Vaissière. *See* la Vaissière

Vallarsi, Dominic. "Sancti Eusebii Hieronymi Stridonensis presbyteri liber hebraicorum quaestionum in Genesim." In *Sophronius Eusebius Hieronymus*, edited by J.-P. Migne. PL 23, cols. 983–1062. Paris: 1883.

Van Dam, Raymond. "Merovingian Gaul and the Frankish Conquests." In *The New Cambridge Medieval History: c. 500–c. 700*, edited by Paul Fouracre, 193–231. Cambridge: Cambridge University Press, 2005.

———. *Rome and Constantinople: Rewriting Roman History during Late Antiquity*. Waco, TX: Baylor University Press, 2010.

Vanderspoel, John. "Zodiac." In *The Cambridge Dictionary of Classical Civilization*, edited by Graham Shipley, John Vanderspoel, David Mattingly, and Lin Foxhall, 960–62. Cambridge: Cambridge University Press, 2008.

van Donzel, Emeri, and Andrea Schmidt. *Gog and Magog in Early Eastern Christian and Islamic Sources: Sallam's Quest for Alexander's Wall*. Leiden/Boston: Brill Publishers, 2010.

Van Nuffelen, Peter. "Sozomen." In *The Oxford Dictionary of Late Antiquity*, edited by Oliver Nicholson, 1406. Oxford: Oxford University Press, 2018.

Van Rompay, Lucas. "Isho'dad of Merv." In *Gorgias Encyclopedic Dictionary of the Syriac Heritage*, edited by Sebastian P. Brock, Aaron M. Butts, George A. Kiraz, and Lucas Van Rompay, 216–17. Piscataway, NJ: Gorgias Press, 2011.

Van Rooy, Raf. "'Πόθεν οὖν ἡ τοσαύτη διαφωνία': Greek Patristic Authors Discussing Linguistic Origin, Diversity, Change and Kinship." *Beiträge zur Geschichte der Sprachwissenschaft* 23, no. 1 (2013): 21–54.

Vermeulen, Han F. *Before Boas: The Genesis of Ethnography and Ethnology in the German Enlightenment*. Lincoln, Nebraska: University of Nebraska Press, 2015.

———. "Ethnography and Empire: G. F. Müller and the Description of Siberian Peoples." In *Before Boas: The Genesis of Ethnography and Ethnology in the German Enlightenment*, 131–218. Lincoln, Nebraska: University of Nebraska Press, 2015.

———. "History and Theory of Anthropology and Ethnology: Introduction." In *Before Boas: The Genesis of Ethnography and Ethnology in the German Enlightenment*, 1–38. Lincoln, Nebraska: University of Nebraska Press, 2015.

Volk, Katharina. "'Heavenly Steps': Manilius 4.119–121 and Its Background." In *Heavenly Realms and Earthly Realities in Late Antique Religions*, edited by Ra'anan S. Boustan and Annette Yoshiko Reed, 34–46. Cambridge: Cambridge University Press, 2004.

von Rummel, Philipp. "The Transformation of Ancient Land- and Cityscapes in Early Medieval North Africa." In *North Africa under Byzantium and Early Islam*, edited by Susan T. Stevens and Jonathan P. Conant, 105–18. Washington, DC: Dumbarton Oaks Research Library and Collection, 2016.

von Staden, Heinrich. "Hairesis and Heresy: The Case of the *Haireseis Iatrikai*." In *Jewish and Christian Self-Definition*, edited by B. F. Meyer and E. P. Sanders, 3:76–100. London: SCM Press, 1982.

von Stuckrad, Kocku. *Geschichte der Astrologie: Von den Anfängen bis zur Gegenwart*. Munich: H. G. Beck, 2007.

———. "Jewish and Christian Astrology in Late Antiquity—A New Approach." *Numen* 47, no. 1 (2000): 1–40.

Walbank, F. W. *Polybius*. Berkeley: University of California Press, 1972.

Walker, Joel. "From Nisibis to Xi'an: The Church of the East in Late Antique Eurasia." In *The Oxford Handbook of Late Antiquity*, edited by Scott Fitzgerald Johnson, 994–1052. Oxford: Oxford University Press, 2012.

Ward, Humphry. "Isidorus (18)." In *A Dictionary of Christian Biography and Literature to the End of the Sixth Century A.D., with an Account of the Principal Sects and Heresies*, edited by Henry Wace and William C. Piercy, 541–45. London: John Murray, 1911.

Watts, Edward. "Justinian, Malalas, and the End of Athenian Philosophical Teaching in A.D. 529." *Journal of Roman Studies* 94 (2004): 168–82.

Webb, Peter. *Imagining the Arabs: Arab Identity and the Rise of Islam*. Edinburgh: University of Edinburgh Press, 2016.

Weiskopf, Michael. Review of *Römer und Perser: Vom 3. Jahrhundert bis zum Jahr 363 n. Chr*, by Karin Mosig-Walburg. *BMCR* 2010, no. 33 (2010).

West, J. M. I. "Uranius." *Harvard Studies in Classical Philology* 78 (1974): 282–84.

Whately, Conor. "Arabs, Outsiders, and Stereotypes from Ammianus Marcellinus to Theophylact Simocatta." In *Inside and Out: Interactions between Rome and the Peoples on the Arabian and Egyptian Frontiers in Late Antiquity*, edited by Jitse H. F. Dijkstra and Greg Fisher, 215–33. Leuven / Paris / Walpole MA: Peeters, 2014.

———. "Making Sense of the Frontier Armies in Late Antiquity: An Historian's Perspective." In *Roman Military Architecture on the Frontiers: Armies and Their Architecture in Late Antiquity*, edited by Rob Collins, Matthew Symonds, and Meike Weber, 6–17. Philadelphia: Oxbow Books, 2015.

———. "Militarization, or the Rise of a Distinct Military Culture? The East Roman Ruling Elite in the 6th Century AD." In *Warfare and Society in the Ancient Eastern Mediterranean: Papers Arising from a Colloquium Held at the University of Liverpool, 13th June 2008*, edited by Stephen O'Brien and Daniel Boatright, 49–57. BAR International Series 2583. Oxford: Archaeopress, 2013.

———. Review of Anthony Kaldellis and Marion Kruse, *The Field Armies of the East Roman Empire, 361–630*. Cambridge: Cambridge University Press, 2023. *Plekos* 26 (2024): 77–85, https://www.plekos.uni-muenchen.de/2024/r-kaldellis_kruse.pdf

———. "Strategy, Diplomacy and Frontiers: A Bibliographic Essay." In *War and Warfare in Late Antiquity*, edited by Alexander Sarantis and Neil Christie, 1: 239–54. Leiden/Boston: Brill, 2013.

Whitby, Michael. "Byzantine Diplomacy: Good Faith, Trust and Co-Operation in International Relations in Late Antiquity." In *War and Peace in Ancient and Medieval History*, edited by Philip de Souza and John France, 120–40. Cambridge: Cambridge University Press, 2008.

———. *The Emperor Maurice and His Historian: Theophylact Simocatta on Persian and Balkan Warfare*. Oxford Historical Monographs. Oxford: Clarendon Press, 1988.

———. "Emperors and Armies, AD 235–395." In *Approaching Late Antiquity: The Transformation from Early to Late Empire*, edited by Simon Swain and Mark Edwards, 156–86. Oxford: Oxford University Press, 2006.

———. *The Wars of Justinian I*. Barnsley, UK / Philadelphia: Pen & Sword Books, 2021.

Whittaker, C. R. "Foederati." In *Late Antiquity: A Guide to the Postclassical World*, edited by G. W. Bowersock, Peter Brown, and Oleg Grabar. Cambridge: Harvard University Press, 1999.

———. *Frontiers of the Roman Empire: A Social and Economic Study*. Baltimore/London: Johns Hopkins University Press, 1994.

———. *Rome and Its Frontiers: The Dynamics of Empire*. London: Routledge, 2004.

———. "The Use and Abuse of Immigrants in the Later Roman Empire." In *Rome and Its Frontiers: The Dynamics of Empire*, 199–218. London: Routledge, 2004.

Whittaker, Molly. "'Signs and Wonders': The Pagan Background." In *Studia Evangelica: Papers Presented to the Third International Congress on New Testament Studies Held at Christ Church, Oxford, 1961*, edited by F. L. Cross, 5: 155–58. Berlin: Akademie Verlag, 1968.

Whittow, Mark. "The Late Roman / Early Byzantine Near East." In *The Formation of the Islamic World: Sixth to Eleventh Centuries*, edited by Chase F. Robinson, 72–97. *The New Cambridge History of Islam*, Vol. 1. Cambridge: Cambridge University Press, 2010.

———. "Rome and the Jafnids: Writing the History of a 6th-Century Tribal Dynasty." In *The Roman and Byzantine Near East: Some Recent Archaeological Research*, edited by J. H. Humphrey, 207–44. Vol. 2. Journal of Roman Archaeology Supplementary Series 31. Portsmouth, RI: Journal of Roman Archaeology, 1999.

BIBLIOGRAPHY [405]

Wijnendaele, Jeroen W. P. "Stilicho, Radagaisus, and the So-Called 'Battle of Faesulae.'" *Journal of Late Antiquity* 9, no. 1 (2016): 267–84.

Wildberg, Christian. "Neoplatonism." In *The Stanford Encyclopedia of Philosophy*, edited by Edward N. Zalta, 2016. https://plato.stanford.edu/archives/win2021/entries /neoplatonism/.

Wilkerson, K. E. "Carneades at Rome: A Problem of Sceptical Rhetoric." *Philosophy & Rhetoric* 21, no. 2 (1988): 131–44.

Winter, Engelbert. "Legitimität als Herrschaftsprinzip: Kaiser und 'König der Könige' im wechselseitigen Verkehr." In *Migratio et commutatio: Studien zur alten Geschichte und deren Nachleben; Thomas Pekáry zum 60. Geburtstag am 13. September 1989 dargebracht von Freunden, Kollegen und Schülern*, edited by Hans-Joachim Drexhage and Julia Sünskes. St. Katharinen: Scripta Mercaturae Verlag, 1989.

Wirth, Gerard. "Rome and Its Germanic Partners in the Fourth Century." In *Kingdoms of the Empire: The Integration of Barbarians in Late Antiquity*, 13–55. Leiden / New York / Cologne: Brill, 1997.

Wiseman, T. P. "Cicero and Varro." In *Remembering the Roman People: Essays on Late-Republican Politics and Literature*, 107–30. Oxford: Oxford University Press, 2009.

Wolff, Catherine, and Patrice Faure, eds. *Les auxiliaires de l'armée romaine: Des alliés aux fédérés*. CEROR 51. Lyon: Centre d'études et de recherches sur l'Occident romain, 2016.

Wolff, Hartmut. "Die Entwicklung der Veteranenprivilegien vom Beginn des 1. Jahrhunderts v. Chr. bis auf Konstantin d. Gr." In *Heer und Integrationspolitik: Die römischen Militärdiplome als historische Quelle*, edited by Werner Eck and Hartmut Wolff, 44–115. Cologne/ Vienna: Böhlau, 1986.

Wolfram, Herwig. *The Roman Empire and Its Germanic Peoples*. Translated by Thomas Dunlap. Berkeley: University of California Press, 1997.

———. "Waffensohn." In *RGA*, edited by Heinrich Beck, Dieter Gueunich, and Heiko Steuer, 33: 49–51. Berlin / New York: Walter de Gruyter, 2006.

Woodward, David. "Medieval Mappaemundi." In *Cartography in Prehistoric, Ancient, and Medieval Europe and the Mediterranean*, edited by J. B. Harley and David Woodward, 286–370. Vol. 1, *The History of Cartography*. Chicago/London: University of Chicago Press, 1987.

Woolf, Greg. *Becoming Roman: The Origins of Provincial Civilization in Gaul*. Cambridge: Cambridge University Press, 1998.

———. "The Classical Barbarian: A Discontinuous History." In *Empires and Indigenous Peoples: Comparing Ancient Roman and North American Experiences*, edited by Michael Maas and Fay Yarbrough, 91–104. Norman, OK: University of Oklahoma Press, 2024.

———. *Tales of the Barbarians: Ethnography and Empire in the Roman West*. Hoboken: John Wiley & Sons, 2011.

Zammito, John H. Review of *Before Boas: The Genesis of Ethnography and Ethnology in the German Enlightenment*, by Han Vermeulen. *Critical Philosophy of Race* 4, no. 2 (2016): 263–71.

Ziche, Hartmut. "Barbarian Raiders and Barbarian Peasants: Models of Ideological and Economic Integration." In *Romans, Barbarians, and the Transformation of the Roman World: Cultural Interaction and the Creation of Identity in Late Antiquity*, edited by Ralph W. Mathisen and Danuta Shanzer, 199–219. Farnham: Ashgate, 2011.

Ziegler, Karl-Heinz. "Tradition und Wandel im Völkerrecht der römischen Spätantike." In *Idee und Realität des Rechts in der Entwicklung internationaler Beziehungen: Festgabe für Wolfgang Preiser*, edited by Alexander Böhm, Klaus Lüderssen, and Karl-Heinz Ziegler, 11–31. Baden-Baden: Nomos Verlagsgesellschaft, 1983.

Zöllner, Erich. *Geschichte der Franken bis zur Mitte des sechsten Jahrhunderts*. Munich: Verlag C. H. Beck, 1970.

Zuckerman, Constantin. "Les 'barbares' romains: Au sujet de l'origine des *auxilia* tétrarchiques." In *L'armée romaine et les barbares: Du IIIe au VIIe siècle*, edited by Françoise Vallet and Michel Kazanski, 17–20. Paris: Association Française d'Archéologie Mérovingienne, 1993.

INDEX

Premodern individuals are indexed under the part of their name by which they are best known.

Abelians (Abeloim), 250, 356n89
Abgar VIII, king of Edessa, 139
Abochorabus (Abu Karib), Arab chieftain, 83–84
Abraham: Arabs as descendants of, 214–15, 217, 258–59, 348n245; biblical account of, 213–14; Christians as descendants of, 6; Hebrew language and, 204; Jews as descendants of, 6; Muslims as descendants of, 6, 211, 217–18; Saracens as descendants of, 200, 215–16, 347n240
Abu Karib (Abochorabus), Arab chieftain, 83–84
Account of Affairs in Armenia, 74–75
Adamites, 238
Adams, J. N., 348n5
Adamson, Peter, 137
Aelius Aristides, 31
Aeneas, 32, 36–37, 195, 202, 273n10
Aestii, 47
Agarenes. *See* Hagarenes
Agathias, 13, 68, 77–78, 256–57, 297n271, 341n104
Agricola, Gnaeus Julius, 48–49, 274n24
Agrippa, Marcus Vipsanius, 37–38, 279n83
Alamanni, 94–96, 117–18, 121, 296n253, 304n75, 308n132
Alaric, Gothic leader, 56, 117
Alexander, Philip S., 336n11
Alexander of Aphrodisias, 315n61
Alexander Romance, 209–10
Alexander Severus, Roman emperor, 192
Alexander the Great: as model for later rulers, 26–27, 35–36; and the story of Alexander's Gates, 199, 209–10, 344n169; took scientists on his mission of conquest, 35
Alexandrian World Chronicle, 201–2
Allen, Pauline, 257
Altar of Peace (Ara Pacis), 36–37
Alverny, Marie-Thérèse d', 233
Amand, David, 319n142
Amazons, 319n141, 323n213
Ambrose of Milan: hexaemeral literature and, 170, 331n73–74; identifies Goths as Gog, 185, 207–8, 254, 339n70

Ambrosiaster, 137
Ammianus Marcellinus: Alamanni in, 95–96, 121; Arabs and Saracens in, 82–83, 213; Arabs in, 293n183; barbarism in, 54, 89, 118, 167–68; *dediticii* in, 107, 118, 302n47; environmental determinism in, 167–68; *foederati* in, 121; Goths in, 295n227; Huns in, 89, 168, 295n227; *laeti* in, 118, 308n132; payments to Arabs in, 293n183; performance of subordination in diplomacy in, 53–54, 83, 95–96; Persian celestial imagery for Roman and Persian rulers in, 75–76, 290n126; Sarmatian prince Zizais in, 53–54; Seres in, 168; sources for, 135, 330n62
Amorkesus, Arab tribal leader, 82–83, 292n171
Amory, Patrick, 2, 358n122
Anastasius, Roman emperor: grants honorary consulship to Clovis, 97–98, 298n278; and relations with Persia, 69, 287n66
Anchises, 37
Anderson, Benjamin, 153
Andresen, Carl, 311n12
angels of the nations, 188, 220, 225, 233–34, 351n64
Antae, 176–77
Antiochus, 156
Antonine Constitution, 104–5, 107–10, 302–3n48
Apollinarianism, 356n72
Aquitani, 23
Ara Pacis. *See* Altar of Peace
Arabs: and appropriate identification with Ishmaelites for themselves, 86, 188, 211, 215, 217, 348n245; in Bible, 213–14; called Saracens by Romans, 81; Christianity and, 82–83, 85, 214–17; discourse of subordination in Roman relations with, 62, 82–84; Ghassanids, 83–85, 293n173, 294n193; history of term, 211–13; identified with Gog and Magog, 209–10; identified with Ishmaelites, 204, 210–11, 214–15, 258–59, 319n141, 346n214, 346n220; Islam

[407]

[408] INDEX

Arabs (*continued*)
and, 85–86, 210, 217, 258–59, 348n25;
Lakhmids, 69, 83; proxies in struggle
between Rome and Persia, 17, 68–71,
81–83, 213, 215, 288n87, 292n167;
Roman ethnography of, 81, 291n158;
as Roman *foederati*, 82–83, 292n170;
Salihids, 83, 293n173; subsidy payments to, 57, 84; Table of Nations
and, 188, 190–91, 204, 211, 348n242;
Tanukhids, 83, 293n173; titles granted
to, 82–85. *See also* Saracens

Arcadians, 162–63

Arcadius, Roman emperor: asks Persian
ruler to serve as guardian for his son,
76–78, 291n142; law on heresy issued
by, 244–45; laws on settler groups
issued by, 111, 116–17; on Theodosian
obelisk base, 62; Uldin sends Gothic
general's head to, 88

archaeological evidence: cannot be tied
to legal terms for settlers, 103, 112–15;
for integration between Germanic and
Roman populations in Gaul, 307n113;
for relations between Goths and Huns
in western steppe, 294n201; for settlements of *gentiles* in North Africa, 112;
for slow integration of Huns and local
populations in western steppe, 88,
294n201

Arethas, Ghassanid phylarch, 84–85,
292n170, 294n189

Arianism: Ambrose on, 207–8; and Arians
blamed for fall of Rome in Catholic
versions of *Liber genealogus*, 194;
Pseudo-Caesarius on, 177; Clovis's
conversion from, 254; Constantine
and, 252; definition of, 252; Goths and,
207–8, 232, 252, 254–56, 358n122; as
identity marker, 251–56, 358n12; Islam
and, 256; *isotimia* and, 72; Jordanes
on, 255–56; Justinian justifies wars
against Ostrogoths and Vandals on
basis of, 255, 266; language and, 227,
232, 254–56; laws against, 245, 255;
Ostrogoths and, 227, 253–56; Procopius on, 255–56; Reccared's conversion
from, 198, 254; Salvian of Marseilles
on, 252–53; spread of, 252; Vandals
and, 227, 232, 253, 255; Vigilius on,
255; Visigoths and, 253–56

Aristotle, 14, 50, 129, 133, 158, 160–62, 177,
242

Pseudo-Aristotle, 314n43

Aspebetos, Arab chieftain, 85

astrology and astronomy: Ambrosiaster
on, 137; Augustine on, 135, 138, 150,
182; Bardaisan on, 139–45, 319n133–34,
319n142, 320n155, 321n184; Basil
of Caesarea on, 126, 312n19; Basilides on, 148–49; Byzantine revival
of, 126–27, 156, 327n271, 327n276;
Pseudo-Caesarius on, 177–79, 319n133,
333n135; Carneades on, 131–32, 140,
315n61, 315n63, 319n142; Cassiodorus
on, 182; Christian challenge to, 18,
123–26, 135–52, 264, 266, 312–13n24,
313n34; Cicero on, 130, 132, 316n78;
Clement of Alexandria on, 312n20,
321n184; Pseudo-Clementine *Recognitiones* on, 145–48, 319n133, 321n184;
Diodorus on, 143–45, 320–21n169,
321n171, 321n174; distinction between
astrology and astronomy, 312–13n24;
in ethnography, 27, 49, 52, 123–25, 128,
130, 139, 145, 264, 266; Eusebius on,
141–43, 320n155; Firmicus Maternus
on, 135–36; Gnosticism and, 148–50,
323n209, 324n217–18; Greek tradition
on, 27, 127–32; Gregory of Nyssa on,
145; Heraclius and, 127, 156; in imperial
iconography, 152–54, 326n252; Jewish tradition on, 311n6, 326n250; John
Philoponus on, 126; Justinian and,
127, 151–54, 156, 325n238, 325n240;
Khusro II and, 156; *klimata* argument
for determinism in, 138; laws against,
137, 151, 325n236, 325n238; Leo I
on, 137, 322n186; Lydus on, 155–56,
314n49, 326n266; Malalas on, 325n238,
325n240; Manilius on, 130–31, 133,
314–15n57; Neoplatonism and, 136–37,
316n91; *nomima barbarika* argument
against determinism in, 131, 138–48,
178, 318n128, 319n133, 319n142; Origen
on, 126, 312n18, 319n141; Panaetius on,
131–32; philosophical arguments on,
128–32, 315n61; *Pistis Sophia* on, 150;
Plotinus on, 136–37, 316n91; Porphyry
on, 137; Proclus on, 137; Procopius
on, 156, 325n240; Ptolemy on, 49–51,
132–35, 155–56, 316n78, 316n80,
316n91; reinterpreted to be compatible
with Christian belief, 126–27, 152–56,
312–13n24, 313n34, 326n250; Rhetorius
of Egypt on, 156; spread of Jews and
Christians as argument against determinism in, 131, 139–40, 144, 156; spread
of Romans as argument against determinism in, 131, 140, 147; Stephanus of

Alexandria on, 156; Table of Nations version with seventy-two names and, 350n31; Theodoret on, 151; Theodotus on, 149; ubiquity of, 126–27, 129, 147, 266; views in Justianian's time, 154–56; Zeno of Verona on, 149

astronomy. *See* astrology and astronomy

Attila, Hun leader: funeral of, 88–89, 295n226; Halley's Comet and, 151; Jordanes on, 88–89; possible marriage to emperor's sister by, 285n30; Priscus on, 57–58, 89–90, 295n221, 295–96n229–30; story of reversal of Roman iconography of subordination by, 53, 57–59, 62, 89, 282n2; tribute demands by, 86, 88–89, 284n29, 295n221

Aufidius Bassus, 43, 46

Augustine of Hippo: Adamites in, 238; astrology in, 135, 138, 150, 182; heresy in, 249–50, 357n100; hexaemeral literature and, 170; influence of, 349n17, 357n100; newcomers, probably *gentiles*, in North Africa in, 113; original language in, 349n17; rejects identification of Goths with Gog, 208–9, 343n154; sources for, 250; Table of Nations in, 197–98, 339n75; two lineages, City of God and City of Man, in, 197–98, 230; willing to use state apparatus to punish heretics, 250

augustus (title), 77, 97–98, 298n278

Augustus, Roman emperor: boasts of diplomatic successes by, 36, 59, 87; building projects of, 36–37; centrality of Rome and, 36–37, 278n64; conquests of, 11, 21, 170, 281n142; and ethnographic information in *Res Gestae*, 36–38; in iconographic program of Altar of Peace, 36; incorporation of foreign peoples into the empire and, 11, 25, 99, 281n142; as last and most succesful Hellenistic monarch, 36; law on *dediticii* issued by, 106, 301–2n38; Manilius's *Astronomica* dedicated to, 130; primacy of emperor and, 25, 31–33, 36–37, 278n64; rhetoric of empire in mausoleum complex of, 36–37; territorially bounded empire and, 32, 37–38, 45; Vitruvius's *On Architecture* dedicated to, 38, 164

auxilia, 102, 109–11, 119, 309n144

Avars: embassy to imperial court by, 90–93; identified with Gog, 209; Isidore on, 199, 209, 340n87; Maurice on, 180;

story of Alexander's Gates and, 199, 209, 340n87; tribute payments to, 57, 92–93

Avienus, Rufus Festius, 168

Babel, story of Tower of: challenges primacy of Latin and Greek, 19, 186, 220–21, 226–28, 230–31, 234–35, 265; *Diamérismos* on, 192–93; enables Christian universal mission, 19, 220, 229, 234, 265; establishes language as identifier for text-based community of faith, 220, 227, 229–30, 234–35, 265; *Excerpta Latina Barbari* on, 201; in Genesis, 189, 221–22; gives languages meaning within salvation history, 219–20, 228–29, 234; introduces idea of angels of nations, 220, 225, 233–34; Isho'dad on, 203–4; Isidore on, 220, 222–33; Jerome on, 197; links language to belief and heresy, 186, 220, 227, 231–33, 235; Origen on, 233–34; original language and, 223–26; Pentecost counters confusion of, 228–29, 350n39; provides frame for understanding linguistic diversity, 19, 186, 219, 221, 223–28, 234; Table of Nations and, 189, 221–22, 225

Backhaus, Wilhelm, 328n12

Bang, Peter Fibiger, 285n36

barbaricum, 4, 24, 37, 256, 273n7

barbarism: acceptance of Roman authority and, 54, 96, 118; Agathias on, 256–57; Ammianus on, 54, 83, 89, 95–96, 118, 167–68; barbarians only outside the empire in legal terminology, 17, 37, 95–96, 103; Pseudo-Caesarius on, 178; climate and geography and, 18, 28, 40–42, 48, 125, 158, 162–64, 166–68, 172–74; could always be overcome, 11, 16, 18, 40–42, 49, 125, 162–64, 166, 173–75; distance from Rome and, 24, 33, 166; epitomized by steppe nomads, 87, 89; foil for Romanness, 10, 14, 16, 45, 47; Greek tradition on, 27–28, 158; heretics as new barbarians, 19, 232, 236–37, 239, 245–46, 251–56, 259; lack of intellectual curiosity and, 47–48; insult in Roman-Persian relations, 79; isolation and, 15–16, 18, 40–41, 47–48, 166–67, 172–74, 332n98–100; Jordanes on, 255–56; Julius Caesar on, 24; lawlessness and, 16, 40, 162–63, 178; as matter of degree, 40–42, 166, 171, 175, 237, 256; in Plautus, 29; Polybius on,

[410] INDEX

barbarism (*continued*)
33, 162–63; Priscus on, 57–58; Procopius on, 42, 171–75, 255–56, 332n98–100; Romans as barbarians in Frankish discourse, 94; Strabo on, 40–42, 166; Tacitus on, 47–48, 167; visual depictions of barbarians and, 9, 36, 57–59, 61–62, 152, 154
Barbarism (heresy), 248–49
Barbarus Scaligeri (*Excerpta Latina Barbari*), 201–2, 340–41n104
Barbeliotes, 241
Barberini Diptych, 59
Bardaisan of Edessa: astrology and, 139–41, 321n174, 321n184; Carneades and, 139–40, 319n142; distinction among Arabs, Saracens, and Taenoi in, 213; influence of, 141–48, 319n33; judged a heretic, 139, 319n137, 321n174; *nomima barbarika* argument against astral determinism in, 138–41; on Romans, 140; Seres in, 141; sources for, 139–40, 319n142, 320n153
Bardill, Jonathan, 291n142
Barton, Tamsin, 138
Basil of Caesarea, 72, 126, 170, 234, 312n19, 331n73
Basil of Seleucia, 228, 351n41
basileus, 84–85, 97, 294n189, 297–98n276
Basilides, 148–49
Batavi, 115
Batty, Roger, 87
Belgae, 23–26
Belisarius, 171, 292n170
Berzon, Todd, 239, 354n32
Blockley, R. C., 291n142
Boeck, Elena, 153
Boethius, 135, 317n98
Boll, Franz, 316n92
Book of Genealogy (*Liber generationis*), 192–93, 201–2
Brahmans, 141, 178–79
Breeze, David, 100
Brennan, Peter, 100, 300n27
Bretons, 341n114
Britons, 47–49, 94, 141
Brown, Peter, 4, 127, 182, 227, 250, 253, 311n14, 320n150, 355n65
Buell, Denise Kimber, 330–31n68
Burgess, Richard, 191–92, 340–41n104
Burgundians, 97
Byzantine Empire: astrological or geographical determinism in, 127, 171, 312–13n24; astrology in, 126–27, 153–54, 156, 312–13n24; "Byzantine

Commonwealth," 246; Christian mission in, 351n44; Christianity in diplomatic relations of, 246; discourse of inclusion in, 102; ethnography in, 13–14; Gog and Magog in, 205, 210; imperial iconography in, 153–54; new Christian imperial culture in, 4, 266; origin of Frankish texts in Table of Nations tradition and, 201, 340–41n104; Ptolemy influential in, 49, 135, 153; steppe peoples and, 87

Caesar, Gaius Julius: approach to defeated opponents in Gaul by, 95; centrality of Rome in, 24–25, 263; conquests of, 21, 45; corrupting effects of civilization in, 25–26, 166; *Cosmography of Julius Caesar* and, 35, 224; discourse of friendship and enmity in, 25; example of failure of astrology and, 132; in first paragraph of *Gallic War*, 23–24; geography in, 24; Greek ethnographic tradition and, 24, 27; influence of, 23, 46–47; no vision of territorially bounded empire in, 24; political ambitions of, 24–25, 31–32, 35; scientific mission sent out by, 35, 224; sources for, 34, 132; transformative power of contact with Rome in, 25–26
Pseudo-Caesarius, 176–79, 319n133, 333n132
Cainites, 241
Calcagus, 330n60, 332n99
Caledonians, 48
Pseudo-Callisthenes, 209–10
Cameron, Avril, 156, 237, 327n270
Canepa, Matthew, 63, 75, 290n125, 291n142
Cantabrians, 11
Cappadocian Fathers, 145, 157, 224. *See also* Gregory of Nyssa
Caracalla, Roman emperor, 105, 302n48
Carneades, 129, 131–32, 138–40, 315n59–60, 315n63, 319n142
Cassiodorus, 99, 135, 181–83, 317n98
Celsus, 311n12
Celts, 23, 276n24
Charlemagne, 86, 97
Chatti, 46
Chauci, 44–47, 167
Chronicle of Fredegar, 202–3, 216, 348n242
Chronicle of Hippolytus, 192–93, 213
chronicle tradition, 191–92, 194–95, 201–3, 338n56

INDEX [411]

Chronicon Paschale (*Easter Chronicle*), 80,
179–80, 200, 208, 289n103
Chrysos, Evangelos, 298n276, 300n20
Chrysostom, John, 148, 234, 247
Chuvin, Pierre, 151
Cicero, 34, 130, 132, 278n55, 314n45,
315n67, 316n78
Cimbri, 48
citizenship: access to Roman civil law and,
105, 107–9; diplomatic reward system
for Arabs and, 85; in early empire, 25,
32, 104–5, 301n31; gradations of legal
disability in Late Antiquity, 107–8,
300n23; granted by Antonine Constitution, 104–5, 107–10; granted to
discharged auxiliary veterans and their
children, 109–10, 119; heretics denied
rights of, 245; Justinian conflates
subjecthood and, 108; marriage pro-
hibitions for noncitizen settlers, 109,
112; not linked to language, 230; late
antique settlers and partial, 17, 103–4;
religious practice and, 243, 245; Roman
identity and, 17, 105
civitas, 106–7, 109, 305–6n95
Clarke, Katherine, 31, 34, 278n56
Claudius, Roman emperor, 45, 87
Pseudo-Clement: *Homilies*, 149, 321n184;
Recognitiones, 123, 141, 145–48, 319n33,
321n184, 322n188
Clement of Alexandria, 231, 312n20,
321n184, 324n218
Clement of Rome, 146
Clifford, James, 1–2
climate. *See* geography
Clovis, king of the Franks, 97–98, 254,
298n278
Code of Justinian, 151, 303n55
coloni, 108, 116–17, 303n54
Commodus, Roman emperor, 153
Constans, Roman emperor, 136
Constantine I, Roman emperor: ambas-
sadors at court of, 59–60, 65, 90;
Arianism and, 252; Christianization of
Georgians and, 274n36; creates new
auxiliary formations, 110; Eusebius's
Life of, 141; Gregory of Tours compares
Clovis to, 97–98; laws against heresy
issued by, 243; makes Christianity per-
missible, 237, 243; medallions of, 58,
67; as protector of Christian communi-
ties in Persia, 60–61, 266; summons
Council of Nicaea, 246
Constantius I, Roman emperor, 114–15,
306n105

Constantius II, Roman emperor, 53–54, 61,
76, 110, 118, 136, 252, 357n106
Cope, Glenn Melvin, 357n99
Corippus, Flavius Cresconius, 59, 90–92
Cosmography of Julius Caesar, 35, 38
Cramer, Frederick, 128, 315n63, 323n203
Critolaus, 129
Croke, Brian, 181, 192, 195
Cyril, missionary to the Slavs, 229
Cyril of Alexandria, 143

Dagorn, René, 217
Damasus, pope, 195–96
Danielou, Jean, 233
DeConick, April D., 323n209, 324n217–18
dediticia, 303n55
dediticii, 102, 106–8, 118, 121, 300n20,
301n35, 301–2n38, 302n40, 302n43,
302n46–47, 309n151
deditio, 95, 114, 297n260, 301n34
Demougeot, Émilienne, 114, 304n73
Dench, Emma, 8
Denzey Lewis, Nicola, 124
determinism: Aristotle on, 160–62;
Augustine on, 150; Bardaisan on,
139–41, 143, 319n134, 321n184; Basilides on, 148–49; Pseudo-Caesarius
on, 176–79; Cassiodorus on, 181–82;
Christian challenge to, 18, 124–28,
137–52, 157–58, 169–70, 179–80,
183–84, 234, 266, 313n24, 321n184;
Pseudo-Clement on, 321n184; develops
in response to contemporary events,
163, 167, 170–71; Diodorus on, 143–45;
Gnosticism and, 148–50; Greek tradition on, 28, 158; Hippocrates on,
34–35, 50, 158–60; Isidore on, 182–83;
Justinian and, 152–54; Manilius on,
130–31; Maurice on, 180–81; modern
legacy of, 181–83; Polybius on, 162–63;
Posidonius on, 34–35; Procopius
on, 156, 171–77; Ptolemy on, 50–51,
316n81; reinterpreted to be compatible
with Christianity, 179–84; Strabo on,
40–42; Vitruvius on, 38–39. *See also*
astrology and astronomy; geography
Di Cosmo, Nicola, 57, 89
diaita, 172–74
Diamérismos (*Division of the World*),
192–93, 337n36, 337n41
Dicuil, 279n85
Dignas, Beate, 290n132
Dilke, O. A. W., 316n91
Diocletian, Roman emperor, 75, 114, 119,
194, 306n105

[412] INDEX

Diodorus of Tarsus, 141, 143–45, 320–21n169, 321n171, 321n174
Diogenes of Babylon, 129
Diogenianus, 315n61
Pseudo-Dionysius of Tel-Mahre, 342n118
Pseudo-Dionysius the Areopagite, 234
Division of the World (Diamérismos), 192–93, 337n36, 337n41
Dolomites, 332n98
Domitian, Roman emperor, 45–48, 274n24
Donatism, 193–94, 232, 240, 244, 250
Donner, Fred, 217
Drijvers, H. J. W., 138, 320n153
Drinkwater, John, 113, 302n47, 308n132
Dueck, Daniela, 279–80n96
Dunderberg, Ismo, 322n202
dux, 97

Easter Chronicle (Chronicon Paschale), 80, 179–80, 200, 208, 289n103
Eckstein, Arthur, 33
Elagabalus, Roman emperor, 320n153
Elsner, Jas, 153
emperor: as agent of Christianization, 11, 125–26, 151–52, 158, 173–76, 183, 265–66; as agent of cultural transformation, 11, 16, 32, 44, 52, 173–76, 183–84; centrality of Rome and, 30; Christian challenge to determinism and, 125–26, 151–54, 158, 184; as establisher of Christian orthodoxy against heretics and pagans, 151–52, 183, 246, 265–66; ethnographic primacy of, 22, 25, 31–32, 37, 43–44, 52, 61, 125, 184, 266; iconography of, 53, 57–59, 61–62, 64–67, 152–54, 286n58, 326n252; as protector of Christian communities in foreign lands, 266; titles of *imperator* and *augustus* restricted to, 97–98. *See also specific emperors*
Encratites, 241
environment. *See* geography
Eph'al, I., 345n185, 346n214, 346n217, 346n220
Epicureanism, 315n61
Epiphanius of Salamis: ascribes identities, 247; eighty heresies in *Panarion* by, 238, 247, 353n13; geography in, 249; heresies as illnesses or poisons to be cured in, 238, 247, 356n80; heresiology as ethnography in, 246–49; history in, 241, 247–49; influence of, 257–58, 342n128; intellectual genealogy in, 249; sources for, 340n100
Epistle to Diognetus, 169

Eratosthenes, 41, 328n11, 334n147
Erismann, Christophe, 318n113
erotapokriseis, 177
Esders, Stefan, 202
Ethiopians, 50, 228, 319n141
ethnarch, 84
ethnography: appears in variety of genres, 1–2, 13–15, 27, 31, 34, 46; ascribes identities, 5–6, 17–18, 95, 101–3, 122, 247, 264; astrology and astronomy in, 27, 49, 52, 123–25, 128, 130, 139, 145, 264, 266; barbarism and civilization in, 14–16, 22, 24, 27–28, 33, 40–42, 46–48, 54, 94, 171, 237, 248, 264; Byzantine tradition of, 13–14; Christian revolution in, 5–6, 12–13, 18–20, 123–26, 139, 149, 158, 185–87, 190, 193, 219–20, 239, 264–67; counting and, 193, 224–25; definition of, 2, 27; descriptive, 9–10, 239; diplomacy and, 16–17, 25, 54–55, 62, 86, 90–93, 95, 98, 257, 264–66; discourse of subordination in, 54–55, 62, 90–93, 95, 98, 264; distance and centrality in, 22, 24–25, 30–31, 33, 36–39, 42–44, 51–52, 184, 240, 262–64, 277n45; establishes criteria for defining communities, 6, 19, 149, 152, 186–87, 220, 226–30, 234–35, 258, 266–67; evaluative, 2, 9–10, 44, 98, 239–40, 251; Frankish discourse of, 94; functions of Roman, 9–11; geography in, 22, 24, 38, 44, 49–50, 52, 123–25, 158–59, 167, 172–73, 184, 264, 266–67; Greek tradition of, 8, 16, 22, 24, 26–30, 205, 207, 276n23–24, 276n35, 327n4, 343n154; heresy in, 19, 186–87, 220, 235–40, 245–46, 249–51, 259, 265, 267; historical development of, 7–9, 11–13; impact on subjects of, 3, 12, 268; imperial uses of, 1, 147–48, 152, 167, 170–71, 181, 246, 250–51, 262; Jewish tradition of, 276n35; language in, 186, 219–20, 223, 226–30, 233–35, 259, 265, 267; legal difference in, 101–3, 105, 122; manages diversity of peoples, 3, 21–22, 52, 189, 212, 215, 226, 233–35, 239, 251, 265–66; maps possibilities of cultural transformation, 9–11, 13, 17–18, 22, 52, 122, 124–25, 172, 263, 266; maps possibilities of inclusion, 9–11, 17–18, 25, 28, 32, 37, 95, 101–3, 105, 122, 125, 240, 263; modern debates about, 8–9; modern legacy of Roman, 3, 12, 189, 268–69; origins of peoples in, 186–90, 211, 215, 259, 264–65; primacy of

INDEX [413]

emperor in, 22, 25, 31–32, 37, 43–44, 52, 61, 125, 184, 266; reflects ethnographers' interests and assumptions, 3, 8–10, 22, 29, 95, 98, 268; reinvents ties with past, 6, 11–12; responds to contemporary events, 12–13, 170–71, 179, 238, 259; Roman self-representation and, 9–10, 14; status relations in, 55, 86; term dates to eighteenth century, 7, 27; territorially bounded empire in, 24, 32, 37–38, 52, 278n56, 278n77; as way of managing information, 9–10; and why "the conqueror's gift," 2–3, 20, 262, 267–68
Eunapius, 306n101
Eunomius, 224
Eusebius of Caesarea: ambassadors at Constantine's court in, 59–61, 65, 90; and *Canons* translated by Jerome, 195; Christianity as transformative agent in, 141–43, 285n38; Christianity's impact on diplomacy in, 60–62; chronicle tradition and, 338n56, 342n118; emperor's universal role in, 60–61; empire as transformative agent in, 60, 142–43, 285n39; and historical model rejected by *Chronicle of Fredegar*, 202; identifies Arabs with Ishmaelites, 214–15; incorporates Christian, biblical, and pagan history into single framework, 194–95, 338n51; influence of, 195, 201, 214–15; nomadic societies in, 81, 291n159; *nomima barbarika* argument against determinism in, 141–42; portrays Christians as new ethnic group, 141; sources for, 141–42, 194, 320n155; Sozomen's continuation of history by, 215; Table of Nations in, 194–95
Eusebius of Nicomedia, 252
Eutychius of Alexandria, 340n100
Excerpta Latina Barbari (Barbarus Scaligeri), 201–2, 340–41n104

Firmicus Maternus, Julius, 135–36, 330n63
Fisher, Greg, 347n235
Florus, Lucius Annaeus, 163, 294n201
foederati: Ammianus on, 121–22; Arabs as, 82–83; differ from *phoideratoi* in east, 121–22, 309n139, 309n142; duties of, 82, 119–20; follow own laws, 111; increase own ethnic identities, 120; laws about, 120–21; led by member of own group, 111, 119–20; outsiders who had made a treaty or deal with Rome, 119, 297n260; overlap with auxiliaries,

309n144; overlap with *dediticii*, 300n20, 302n43, 309n151; paid for service, 119–20; Procopius on, 122; residence in empire post-service not required, 119
Frankish Table of Nations, 202, 341n114
Franks: Agathias on, 256–57, 297n271; Arianism and, 254; develop discourse in which Romans are the barbarians, 94; *Frankish Table of Nations* on, 341n114; as *laeti*, 114–15, 306n104; in *Notitia Dignitatum*, 115, 306n104; *Panegyric to Constantius* on, 114–15, 306n105; Table of Nations and, 188, 191–94, 201–3, 218, 341n114; title *rex* granted to kings of, 97
Frisii, 45

Gainas, Gothic general, 117
Gaius, jurist, 106–7, 299n16, 301n35, 301–2n38
Galerius, Roman emperor, 290n126
Gallus, Aelius, 40, 165
Garnsey, Peter, 105, 301n31, 302n40
Garstad, Benjamin, 341n104
Gaudemet, Jean, 304n71
Gauls, 23–24
Geary, Patrick, 94
Gelimer, king of the Vandals, 297–98n276
gentiles, 102, 111–13, 118–19, 300n20, 304n71, 304n73, 304n75, 305n81, 305–6n95
geography: Ammianus on, 167–68; Aristotle on, 160–62; Augustus on, 36, 279n85; Avienus on, 168; barbarism associated with isolation and remoteness of, 11, 15–16, 40–41, 47–48, 157, 166–68, 172–75; Pseudo-Caesarius on, 176–79; Cassiodorus on, 181–83; centrality of and distance from Rome in, 24, 31, 43, 52, 161, 164–67, 184, 263; Christian asceticism and, 18; Christian challenge to determinism by, 18, 123–27, 168–70, 183–84, 234, 264, 266–67; Christian reinterpretation of determinism by, 18, 127, 158, 171, 179–84; Cicero on, 132; *Cosmography of Julius Caesar* on, 35, 224; determinism by, 18, 28, 34, 38–39, 42, 52, 123–27, 157–58, 160–63, 167–71, 177, 180–84, 331n79; Dicuil on, 279n85; *Easter Chronicle* on, 179–80; Epiphanius on, 249; in ethnography, 22, 24, 38, 44, 49–50, 52, 123–25, 158–59, 167, 172–73, 184, 264, 266–67; Florus on, 163; Greek tradition of, 26–28, 157–63, 183, 328n5; heresy

geography (*continued*)

and, 240, 245, 249, 255; Hippocrates on, 158–60, 162, 164, 328n12; imperial ability to overcome effects of, 158, 163, 166–67, 174–76, 183–84; imperial uses of, 27, 35–36, 39–40, 43, 163, 165, 167, 170–72, 224; in interpretations of Gog and Magog, 204–6; in interpretations of Table of Nations, 188, 190, 194, 196, 200–201; Isidore on, 182–83, 230; Josephus on, 190; Julius Caesar on, 24; Lydus on, 155; Maurice on, 180–81, 313n26; modern legacy of, 181; *nomima barbarika* argument against determinism by, 169, 178; Pappus of Alexandria on, 135; Pliny the Elder on, 43–44, 167; Polybius on, 162–63, 329n34; Posidonius on, 34–35; Procopius on, 172–76; Ptolemy on, 49–51, 133–35, 328n11; Servius on, 168; Strabo on, 39–42, 157, 165–67, 172; Tacitus on, 46–48, 167; Vitruvius on, 38–39, 163–65. *See also* klimata

Georgians, 274n36

Gepids, 90, 255–56

Germani, 23–24, 46–48

Glacken, Clarence, 161–62, 169, 329n34, 331n73–74

Gnosticism, 129, 146, 148–50, 241, 322–23n202–3, 323n209

Goffart, Walter, 202, 341n114

Gordian III, Roman emperor, 64

Goths: Ambrose on, 185, 208; and archaeological evidence for relations with Huns in western steppe, 295n213; Arianism and, 207–8, 232, 252–56, 358n122; Augustine on, 208, 343n154; *Easter Chronicle* on, 208; Eusebius on, 285n39; *Frankish Table of Nations* on, 341n114; Gog and Magog and, 185, 199, 207–9, 254, 339n70, 343n154, 345n183; Isidore on, 199, 209, 345n183; Jerome on, 208, 339n70, 343n154; Jewish tradition on, 339n70; Jordanes on, 255–56; language as religious community identifier and, 227, 232, 252, 254–56; Procopius on, 255; tribute demands by, 56. *See also* Ostrogoths; Visigoths

Goudineau, Christian, 38

Grafton, Anthony, 127

Gratian, Roman emperor, 110, 114–15, 207, 244, 307–8n116, 343n155

Greatrex, Geoffrey, 70, 290n132–33, 291n142, 331n82

Gregory Nazianzus, 349n22

Gregory of Nyssa, 141, 145, 224, 349n17, 349n22, 351n55

Gregory of Tours, 97–98, 298n278

Grepes, king of the Heruls, 175

Grierson, Philip, 97

Gruen, Erich, 46, 276n35, 281n142

Hadrian, Roman emperor, 112

Hagarenes, 200, 216, 258, 347n240

Halsall, Guy, 10, 309n151

Hayward, Charles, 196, 339n70

Heather, Peter, 121, 297n260, 297n267, 309n146

Hecataeus, 43

Hegedus, Tim, 319n142

Hellenism (heresy), 248–49

Helvetii, 23

Hephaistion of Thebes, 316n81

Heraclius, Roman emperor: accused of opening Alexander's Gates, 210; called brother by Persian king, 289n103; calls himself a son of Persian king, 73, 80; favors astrology, 127, 156; and Monophysitism/Miaphysitism, 257; receives gifts from Indian king, 59; refuses to pay subsidies to Arabs, 84, 293n186; rejects earlier grant of title *basileus* to Ghassanid Arab leader, 85; and relations with Arabs, 84–85, 210, 293n186; and relations with Persia, 63, 73, 80, 156, 187, 289n103; uses religion as justification for war, 187

Hereford Map, 278n62

heresy: as absolute category, 236–37; Agathias on, 256–57; Augustine on, 238, 249–50, 357n100; Pseudo-Caesarius on, 177; centrality of Rome in, 246, 252–53; defined as foil to orthodoxy, 236–38; defined in response to contemporary struggles, 238, 243, 250, 257–59; defines communities, 19, 186, 236, 246, 251, 259, 265, 267, 355n65; described as poison, 247, 256, 356n80; determines possibilities of inclusion, 102, 186, 231, 243, 245–46, 251; and distance from correct thought replacing spatial distance, 240; Epiphanius on, 238, 241, 246–49, 257–58; ethnic identity and, 258–59; in ethnography, 19, 186–87, 220, 235–40, 245–46, 249–51, 259, 265, 267; foreign powers and, 19, 186, 237, 246, 251–60, 266; Greek intellectual tradition and, 241–42, 249; heresiological genre, 236–40, 259–60, 267; heretics as barbarians, 19,

232, 236–37, 239, 245–46, 251–56; Hippolytus of Rome on, 242, 354n34; historical dimension of, 238–42, 247–49; historical phases of, 237; identity and ethnic marker in case of Arianism, 251–56; Irenaeus on, 241–42, 354n32; Isidore on, 198, 250–51, 357n100; John of Damascus on, 258–59, 359n143; Jordanes on, 255–57; Justin Martyr on, 238, 240–41; language and, 220, 227, 231–33, 255–56, 267, 351n59; laws against, 19, 137, 243–45, 250, 255, 259, 266, 355n47, 355n54–55, 355n58; origin of term, 353n7; Philastrius of Brescia on, 242, 354n37; Procopius on, 255–56; Salvian of Marseilles on, 236, 239, 252–53; Sophronius of Jerusalem on, 257–58; Theodoret on, 151, 250, 257, 357n99; Tower of Babel and, 220, 227, 231–33; universalism of, 238–39, 241–42, 247–49, 251, 258

Herodotus, 8, 26, 140, 158, 207, 320n150, 328n5, 340n98

Heruls, 174–75, 253

Hesychius, bishop of Salona, 113

hexaemeral literature, 170, 331n73

Higgins, Martin, 74, 289n109

Himyarites, 215

Hipparchus, 328n11

Hippocrates, 26, 34, 50, 158–60, 162, 164, 328n12

Hippodrome, 55, 61–62

Hippolytus of Rome, 192–93, 242, 336n23, 336n25, 354n34

Honorius, Roman emperor, 62, 76–77, 79, 111–12, 116–17, 121, 194, 244, 291n142

Hormizd IV, Persian king, 73

Hoyland, Robert, 217

Humfress, Caroline, 245

Huns: Ammianus on, 89, 167–68, 295n227; and archaeological evidence for slow integration with local populations in western steppe, 88, 295n213; Gog and Magog and, 188, 209–10, 218, 345n183; Hephthalites and, 65, 67–68, 79–80, 287n66, 287n69, 332n94; Isidore on, 199, 209, 340n87; Jerome on, 345n183; Maurice on, 180–81; Persian relations with, 75; Persian relations with Hephthalites, 65, 67–68, 79–80; Priscus on, 89–90; Procopius on Hephthalites, 79–80; Roman relations with, 75, 86, 88–90, 98; Salvian of Marseilles on, 253; Sciri settled as *coloni*, 108; story

of Alexander's Gates and, 199, 209–10, 340n87; Syriac writers on, 209; Table of Nations and, 188, 190, 218; tribute demands by, 57, 67–68, 86, 88–90, 98, 295n220–21

Iberians, 11, 41, 166, 197

identity: angels of the nations and, 234; Arabs and Muslims adopt ascribed identity as Ishmaelites, 211–17, 268; Arianism becomes identity marker in western kingdoms, 252–56; ascribed by heresiological discourse, 236, 238, 247; ascribed by law, 17–18, 37, 95–96, 101–4, 122, 264; cast as choice in Christian opposition to determinism, 18, 157–58, 184; citizenship and, 17; ethnonyms for settler groups and, 115; integration between Germanic and Roman populations in Gaul and, 307n113; language and, 220–21, 267; Priscus on, 57–58; religion and, 6–7, 32, 102, 104, 149, 169, 218, 246, 266–67; revised by settler groups when Rome loses power to ascribe, 18, 102, 120, 188; Roman culture and, 32; scholarship on settlers focuses on ethnic, 100; settlers given new legal identities retain ethnic identities, 101–4, 109, 115, 119–20, 122, 264; Table of Nations and, 188, 203, 218

imperator, 97, 164

Indians, 41, 59, 141, 146, 178, 199, 320n153

Inglebert, Hervé, 193, 242

Inowlocki, Sabrina, 336n13

Irenaeus of Lyon, 241–42, 354n32

Ishmaelites: Arab sources on, 348n245; biblical account of, 211, 213–14, 345n185, 346n214, 346n217; connections between Christian conversion and identification of Arabs with, 214–16; Eusebius identifies Arabs with, 214–15; identification and self-identification of Arabs and Muslims with, 211–18, 258–59, 268, 346–47n225; Isidore identifies Saracens and Hagarenes with, 200, 216, 347n240; Jerome identifies Saracens with, 347n227; Jewish tradition on, 214, 346n220; Josephus identifies Arabs with, 214; Jubilees may identify Arabs with, 214; Pseudo-Methodius identifies Gog and Magog with, 210; Sozomen identifies Saracens with, 215–16, 347n237; Table of Nations and, 213, 216–17

Isho'dad of Merv, 203–4, 342n128–29

[416] INDEX

Isidore of Seville: accomodates Table of
Nations to historical change, 199;
Alexander's Gates in, 199, 340n87,
344n169; Arabs in, 348n242; Avars
in, 199, 209, 340n87; determinism in,
181–83; Gog and Magog in, 199, 209,
345n183; Goths in, 199, 209, 345n183;
Hagarenes in, 216, 347n240; heresy in,
198, 250–51, 357n100; Huns in, 199,
340n87; influence of, 14, 181–83, 198,
201, 339n80, 341n114, 344n169; Ishmaelites in, 200, 216, 347n240; language
change in, 230, 351n48; languages generate nations in, 223, 225–26; map in
Etymologies, 201, 340n102; Massagetae
in, 340n87; original language in, 223,
226, 228, 349n17; Roman origins and,
199–200, 340n90; sacred languages in,
226–28, 232–33; Saracens in, 198, 216,
347n235, 347n240; sounds of spoken
language in, 229–30; sources for, 135,
209, 216, 339n82, 340n100, 344n168,
349n17, 357n100; Syrians in, 342n122;
Table of Nations in, 198–200, 209, 216,
339n85, 340n90, 342n122, 344n168,
347–48n241–42, 350n34; Tower of
Babel story in, 220, 222–33
Islam: Arianism and, 258–59; astrology
and, 149, 154; Christian Roman ethnography and, 6, 86; deference to Rome
and, 85–86; end of Late Antiquity
marked by rise of, 4, 26; Heraclius's
war against, 187, 210; as heresy, 238,
251, 258–59, 359n143; John of Damascus on, 258–59, 359n143; *klimata* in,
332n149; Muslims adopt ascribed
identity as Ishmaelites, 188, 191, 211,
214, 217–18, 268; Ptolemy's influence in
Islamic world and, 49; as rival sectarian community, 5, 86, 268; 'Saracen'
becomes synonymous with 'Muslim'
in Middle Ages, 346n202; Sophronius
of Jerusalem on, 257; Table of Nations
and, 86, 188, 191, 211, 217–18
isotimia, 64, 71–73, 288n99
Ivanov, Sergey A., 351n44

Jacob, Christian, 279n95
Jacob of Edessa, 203, 342n118
Jafna, Ghassanid Arab chieftain, 85
Jerome: Alexander's Gates in, 344n169;
Gog and Magog in, 339n70, 345n183;
influence of, 201–3, 338n56, 339n82,
344n168–69; rejects identification
of Goths with Gog, 208, 343n154;

Saracens in, 215, 347n227, 347n235;
sources for, 339n69–70; Table of
Nations in, 195–97; Tower of Babel
story in, 197; translates Eusebius's *Can-
ons*, 194
John of Damascus, 258–59, 359n143
John of Ephesus, 92–93, 179
John Philoponus, 126, 177, 333n120
Johnson, Aaron, 141–42, 285n38
Jonathan of Bet Gubrin, 350n28
Jones, A. H. M., 306n103
Jordanes, 88–89, 255–57, 295n226
Josephus, Flavius: Alexander's Gates in,
344n169; bridges cultural vocabularies,
207; criticizes imposition of names on
conquered peoples, 336n13; Gog and
Magog in, 206–7, 339n70; identifies
Arabs with Ishmaelites, 214; influence
of, 214, 336n14, 339n69–70, 344n169;
sources for, 207; Table of Nations in,
190
Jubilees, Book of, 190, 193, 201, 214,
336n11–12, 340n99–100, 343n138,
350n30
Julian, Roman emperor, 83, 95–96, 118,
121, 143, 286n48, 302n47
Junillus Africanus, 177
Justin I, Roman emperor, 69, 75, 78–79
Justin II, Roman emperor, 71, 90–93, 179,
256
Justin Martyr, 238, 240–41
Justinian, Roman emperor: abolishes the
term *dediticia*, 108, 303n55; as agent
of Christianization, 11, 145, 174–75; as
agent of civilization, 172–74; Arabs and,
69, 83–85; astrology and, 127, 151–54,
156, 325n238, 325n240; Avars and,
90, 92–93; Berbers and, 97; claims
to be legitimate interpreter of sacred
texts, 266; conflates subjecthood and
citizenship, 108; defense of orthodoxy
as justification for wars of, 255, 266;
determinism and, 151–53, 158, 170–71,
183; diplomatic payments by, 68–71,
90, 92–93; diplomatic title grants by,
83–85, 97, 297–98n276; Hagia Sophia
and, 151–52; Heruls and, 174–75;
iconography of, 59, 152–54; imposes
tribute on local Caucasian population,
68; John of Ephesus on, 92–93; laws
against heresy issued by, 245, 255;
laws against paganism issued by, 151;
laws on *phoideratoi* issued by, 121;
Monophysitism/Miaphysitism and,
177, 179; Paul the Silentiary on, 151–52;

INDEX [417]

Persia and, 68–71, 76, 78, 83, 170, 176; plague of, 175–76; Procopius on, 11, 68, 78, 83–84, 145, 151, 156, 171–76, 297–98n276, 325n238, 325n240; requires correct belief, not specific linguistic practice, 230; Second Council of Constantinople and, 72; and self-understanding as divine agent, 151–54, 158, 174, 183; Three Chapters Controversy and, 246; Tzani and, 11, 145, 173–74; Vandals and, 297–98n276

Kaldellis, Anthony, 13–14, 100, 265, 326n270
Kavadh I, Persian king, 68–70, 75–76, 78–80, 287n66, 289n103
Kelley, Nicole, 146, 321n184, 322n188
Khusro I, Persian king, 65, 68, 70–72, 78–79, 287n80, 288n84
Khusro II, Persian king, 73–75, 80, 156
Kitchen, Thomas, 254
klimata: argument in favor of astrology, 138; Bardaisan on, 139–40; Pseudo-Caesarius on, 178; Pseudo-Clementine *Recognitiones* on, 147; *Easter Chronicle* on, 179–80; in Greek tradition, 328n11; in Islamic tradition, 334n149; Lydus on, 155; origins of, 334n147; Posidonius on, 34–35; Ptolemy on, 132–34, 328n11. *See also* geography
Kolbaba, Tia, 237
Kominko, Maja, 266
Krumbacher, Karl, 334n147
Kruse, Marion, 100
Kulikowski, Michael, 191–92, 306n101

Lactantius, 207, 243
laeti, 102, 111–19, 300n20, 302n47, 305–6n95, 306n104–5, 307–8n114–16, 308n125, 308n132, 308n135
Lazi, 332n99
Leo I, pope, 137, 322n186
Leo I, Roman emperor, 82–83, 118
Liber genealogus, 193–94, 337n41
Liber generationis (*Book of Genealogy*), 192–93, 201–2
Lieu, Samuel N. C., 290n132
Ligurians, 168
Livy, 56
Loehndorff, Louise, 322n185
Lombards, 90, 97, 341n114
Long, A. A., 136, 316n78
Lucretius, 168
Lydus, John, 130, 155–56, 314n49, 326n266
Lyman, Rebecca, 237, 356n80

MacCoull, Leslie S. B., 333n120
Machiela, Daniel A., 342n118
Macrobius, 340n101
Macrocephaloi, 160
Magdalino, Paul, 126–27, 156, 312–13n24, 327n271
Magnentius, Roman imperial usurper, 114
Magness, Jodi, 325–26n250
Magog. *See* Gog and Magog
Major, Tristan, 190, 336n14, 350n31
Malalas, John, 69, 97, 151, 200, 325n238, 325n240, 340n100
Malchus, 83
Manichaeism, 137, 238, 244–45, 250, 355n65
Manilius, Marcus, 130–31, 133, 135, 310–11n5, 314–15n57
maps: author of Jubilees may have used, 190, 201; in Isidore's *Etymologies*, 201, 340n102; Marcus Vipsanius Agrippa's, 37–38, 279n83; Ptolemy's innovations in, 133, 315–16n75; T-O, 193, 196, 200–201; zonal, 340n101
Marcionites, 249
Marcomanni, 77, 94
Marcosians, 241
Marcus Aurelius, Roman emperor, 213, 241
Massagetae, 208, 340n87
Masties, Berber leader, 97
Mathisen, Ralph, 107, 112–13, 302–3n48, 305n84, 307n113
Maurice, Roman emperor: iconography of coinage issued by, 326n252; relations with Persia and, 73–75, 80, 289n105; *Strategikon* and, 122, 180–81, 313n26
Mauss, Marcel, 3, 56
Mavia, Arab queen, 83
Maximian, Roman emperor, 114, 306n105
McLynn, Neil, 232
McMahon, Lucas, 120–22, 309n139
Melitianism, 356n72
Menander Protector, 13, 71–72, 92, 288n87
Methodius, 229
Pseudo-Methodius, 210
Miaphysitism. *See* Monophysitism/ Miaphysitism
Michael the Syrian, 342n118
Millar, Fergus, 138, 187–88, 214–17, 346–47n225, 347n236–37, 357n106
Minets, Yuliya, 221, 231–32, 348n2, 348–49n7, 351n59
Mishkovsky, Zelda, 21
Modéran, Yves, 107
Momigliano, Arnaldo, 29
Mommsen, Theodor, 297n255

[418] INDEX

Monophysitism/Miaphysitism: Pseudo-Caesarius and, 177, 179; definition of, 257, 334n140; Ghassanid Arabs and, 83, 85; imperial attitudes toward, 177, 179; Jacob of Edessa and, 203; John of Ephesus and, 92, 179; John Philoponus and, 177; language and, 203, 227; outside the empire, 203, 227, 251; Sophronius of Jerusalem on, 257; Table of Nations and, 203
Müller, Gerhard Friedrich, 7
Müller, Klaus E., 316n92
al-Mundhir, Lakhmid Arab king, 69
Murphy, Trevor, 43–44
Murray, Alexander Callender, 103

Nechaeva, Ekaterina, 63–64, 294n198
Neoplatonism, 136–37, 316n91
Nerva, Roman emperor, 45, 47–48
Nestorianism, 143, 238, 251
New Academy, 129, 131
Nicolet, Claude, 36–37
Nigidius Figulus, Gaius, 130, 314n49
Noah, sons of. *See* Table of Nations
Notitia Dignitatum (*Register of Dignities*), 104, 110, 112, 115, 118–19, 212, 300n25, 304n71, 306n104, 307n115

obelisk, Theodosian base, 61–62, 65, 152, 286n46
Oenomaus of Gadara, 315n61
Oliver, James H., 277n45
Olympiodorus, 122
Ophites, 241
Origen of Alexandria: angels of the nations in, 233–34; astrology in, 123, 126, 155, 312n18, 319n141; determinism in, 123, 126, 312n18, 319n141; language as community marker in, 231; Origenists as heretics, 177, 247; Pentecost in, 228; Rufinus of Aquileia and, 231, 322n185; sources for, 340n100; universal law in, 311n12
Origin of Humankind (*Origo humani generis*), 193, 337n41
Origo humani generis (*Origin of Humankind*), 193, 337n41
Ostrogoths, 97, 227, 252–56, 266. *See also* Goths

Pacatus Drepanius, 287n63
Panaetius, 131–32, 314n45
Panegyric to Constantius, 114–15, 306n105
Papadogiannikis, Ioannis, 177
Pappus of Alexandria, 135, 316n91

Parry, Ken, 125
Paul, apostle, 4, 185, 248, 335n2
Paul of Alexandria, 156
Paul the Silentiary, 151–52
Payne, Richard, 66
Pearson, Birger A., 322n202
Pelagianism, 250
Pentecost: biblical account of, 350n39; counters confusion of Babel, 228–29, 350n39; enables formation of language-based local communities, 228–29, 234–35, 265, 267; enables spread of faith, 19, 228–29, 351n41; gives language meaning within salvation history, 219–20, 223, 234; how God spoke at, 224, 349n22; makes languages spiritually equivalent, 230, 234, 265
peregrini, 106–9, 119, 302n40, 302–3n48; *dediticii*, 301n35, 301–2n38, 302n46
Peripateticism, 129, 315n61
periplus, 43, 168
Persia, Sasanian: adoption and guardianship in Roman relations with, 76–80, 290n132, 291n142, 291n148; astrology and, 155–56; celestial imagery and rulership in, 69, 75–76, 290n126; Christianity as agent of cultural change in, 142; Christianity in Roman relations with, 60–61, 69, 77, 187, 246, 251, 266, 288n87; discourse of parity in Roman relations with, 75–80, 289n109; discourse of subordination in Roman relations with, 60–61, 64–75; *isotimia* and, 71–72; language of brotherhood in Roman relations with, 69–70, 75–76, 289n103, 290n121, 290n125; language of fathers and sons in Roman relations with, 72–75, 80; Maurice on, 180–81, 313n26; Monophysites/Miaphysites in, 227, 251; Nestorians in, 251; shares symbolic culture with Rome, 63; and tribute in relations with Hephthalite Huns, 67–68, 287n66, 287n69; and tribute in relations with Rome, 57, 60, 65–73, 287n63, 287n66, 287n80, 288n84; visual depictions of superiority to Rome in, 64–66, 286n58
Philastrius of Brescia, 242
Philip, Roman emperor, 64
Philo, 233, 331n73
Philostorgius, 357n106
Phocas, Roman emperor, 80, 294n193
Photius, 143–44, 321n171, 321n174
Phrygians, 244
phylarch, 82–85, 97

Pistis Sophia, 150
plague, Justinianic, 171–72, 175–76
Plato, 49–50, 148
Plautus, Titus Maccius, 29
Pliny the Elder: centrality of Rome in, 43–44, 167; Chauci in, 144, 167; geography in, 43; influence of, 43, 46, 330n62; intends *Natural History* as inventory of empire and world, 42–44; marvels at human diversity, 9, 44, 224; primacy of emperor in, 43–44; transformative power of empire in, 9, 44, 167
Plotinus, 136–37, 316n91
Polybius, 29–30, 32–34, 162–63, 329n32, 329n34
Pompey the Great, 21, 25, 34, 132, 276n17
Porphyry, 137, 317–18n112
Posidonius of Apamea: centrality of Rome in, 33–34; Cicero and, 130, 132, 278n55; determinism in, 33–35; geography in, 34–35; influence of, 34–35, 40, 132, 135, 282n276, 316–17n92; mentored by Panaetius, 132; Strabo and, 40, 132, 165, 279–80n96, 315n66; takes scientific approach to explaining Roman dominance, 33–35
Possekel, Ute, 139–40
postliminium, 114–15, 306n105
Priscillianism, 137, 244, 322n186
Priscus of Panium: Attila in, 57–58, 89–90, 295n221, 295–96n229–30; Huns in, 89–90; influence of, 295n226; as possible source for story of Attila's reversal of Roman iconography of subordination, 57–58, 282n2; tribute in, 89–90, 295n221, 295–96n230
Proclus, court official, 78–79, 286n46
Proclus, philosopher, 137
Procopius of Caesarea: adoption and guardianship in Roman relations with Persia in, 76–80; Arab diplomatic performance of deference in, 83–84; associates lawlessness with barbarism, 178; astrology in, 151, 156, 325n40, 327n270; barbarizing effects of war in, 172, 332n93; Pseudo-Caesarius and, 177; calls Vandal king *basileus*, 297–98n276; considers Persians and Hepthalite Huns civilized, 80, 332n94, 332n100; continuum from barbarism to civilization in, 42, 331n82; determinism in, 42, 156, 171–77, 327n270; equates plague and barbarian invasion, 176; *foederati* in, 122; geography in, 172–74; Gothic Arianism in, 255–56;

Heruls in, 174–75; identifies barbarism with heresy, 255–56; influenced by Strabo, 42, 172; Justinian in, 11, 68, 145, 151, 156, 175–76, 325n240; links isolation to barbarism, 172–74, 332n98–100; malleability of culture in, 172–73; Persian relations with Hephthalite Huns in, 68, 79–80, 287n69, 332n94; plague in, 175–76; as reliable source on Persia, 77, 290n133; Rome's civilizing and Christianizing mission in, 11, 42, 145, 173–75; Saracens in, 213, 287n80; transformative power of Rome in, 173–74; tribute in, 68, 287n69, 287n80; Tzani in, 11, 145, 172–74; writes in classical literary tradition, 13, 171, 208, 213
Prosper of Aquitaine, 4, 229
Pseudo-Clementine Recognitiones, 123, 141, 145–48, 319n33, 321n184, 322n188
Ptolemy II Philadelphus, 31
Ptolemy of Alexandria: astrology and astronomy in, 49–51, 132–35, 316n78, 316n80; determinism in, 49–51, 133–35, 316n81; explains human differences without reference to Rome, 49–51; geography in, 49, 135, 180; human diversity and, 51; imperial framework for, 133–35, 316n91; imperial iconography in manuscript of *Handy Tables* of, 153–54; influence of, 14, 49, 132–37, 151, 155–56, 168, 316n81, 316–17n91–92, 317n98, 328n11, 330n62; *klimata* in, 132–34, 180, 328n11; Manilius and, 131, 133, 135; as mapmaker, 133, 315–16n75; Neoplatonists and, 136–37; Porphyry writes introduction to *Tetrabiblos* of, 137; Proclus paraphrases *Tetrabiblos* of, 137; Saracens in, 212; Scythians in, 134; sources for, 135, 282n176, 316–17n92; Stephanus of Alexandria revises *Handy Tables* of, 156
Purcell, Nicholas, 31, 278n64–65, 279n93

Quadi, 94
Quodvultdeus, 249

Radagaisus, 88, 121
Reccared, king of the Visigoths, 198, 254
Reimitz, Helmut, 202, 261, 341n104
restitutio, 96
rex, 97, 297–98n276
Rhetorius of Egypt, 156
Ricci, Joseph, 180
Ricimer, 118
Riggsby, Andrew, 25

[420] INDEX

Robbins, F. E., 127, 316n92
Rochette, Bruno, 220–21
Ross, Stephen K., 319n142
Rua, Hun leader, 88, 284n29
Rufinus of Aquileia, 146, 231, 274n36, 322n185–86

Sabaeans, 215, 357n106
Sahas, Daniel J., 359n143
Sallust, 24
Salvian of Marseilles, 236, 239, 252–53, 258
Samaritanism, 248
Sapor, Persian king, 75–76
Saracens: Ammianus on, 82–83, 213; Bardaisan on, 213; *Chronicle of Hippolytus* on, 213; distinguished from Arabs, 212; distinguished from Arabs and Taenoi, 213; general name for Arabs, 81, 212–13; identified with Ishmaelites, 214–16, 346–47n225, 347n227, 347n237, 347n240; Isidore on, 200, 216, 347n235, 347n240; Jerome on, 347n227, 347n235; name becomes synonymous with Muslims in Middle Ages, 346n202; name said to be derived from Sarah, 200, 216, 347n235–37, 347n240; in *Notitia Dignitatum*, 212; Procopius on, 213, 287n80; Ptolemy on, 212; as religiously neutral term, 213; self-ascription of biblical lineage among, 200, 215–17, 347n237; Sozomen on, 215–16, 347n231, 347n236–37; Theodoret on, 347n231; Uranius on, 213. *See also* Arabs
Sarmatians, 48, 53–55, 61, 117, 208, 294n201, 305–6n95
Sarris, Peter, 5, 174
Sasanian Empire. *See* Persia
Sasse, Christoph, 302n46
Scenitae, 213
Schmidt, Andrea, 344n169
Schmidt-Hofner, Sebastian, 116
Scipio Aemilianus, 33, 162
Scipio Africanus, Publius Cornelius, 131
Sciri, 108, 303n54
Sclavenes, 177
Scott, James, 268
scutarii, 118
Scythianism (heresy), 248–49
Scythians: Attila's objection to Milan image of, 53; *Easter Chronicle* on, 208; Eusebius on, 142; as generic name for steppe peoples, 86, 180, 206, 345n183; identified with Magog, 197, 206, 208,

345n183; Isidore on, 209; Jerome on, 345n183; Josephus on, 206–7; Maurice on, 180–81; Posidonius on, 34; Ptolemy on, 50, 134
Sebeos, 74, 289n105
Semnones, 47
Seneca, 132
Sequani, 23
Seres, 141, 146–47, 168, 179
Servius, 168, 330n63
Severian of Gabala, 234
Severus Augustus, Roman emperor, 117–18
Shanzer, Danuta, 307n113
Shapur I, Persian king, 64, 66
Shapur II, Persian king, 60
Shaw, Brent, 81, 89, 237, 240
Shcheglov, Dmitry A., 328n11
Shepard, Jonathan, 55
Sherwin-White, A. N., 302n40
Simon Magus, 240, 250
Simpson, C. J., 307n114, 308n135
Skinner, Joseph, 8, 327n4
Slavs, 171, 177–81, 209
Sophronius of Jerusalem, 257–58
Sozomen, 88, 215–16, 295n220–21, 347n231, 347n236–37
Ste. Croix, Geoffrey de, 107
Stephanus of Alexandria, 156
Stickler, Timo, 309n142
Stilicho, 56, 77, 79, 88, 116–17, 291n142–43
Stoicism, 33, 128–33, 165, 310–11n5, 314n45
Strabo of Amaseia: barbarism and geography or climate in, 40–42, 157, 166–67; determinism in, 40–42, 157, 165–67, 279–80n96; distance from Rome in, 42, 166–67; *Geography* unfinished by, 330n47; influence of, 14, 42, 167, 172, 279n93; Posidonius and, 40, 132, 165, 279–80n96; Rome's civilizing mission in, 39–42, 166–67; serves imperial aims, 39, 165, 167, 279n95; sources for, 40, 132, 315n66; territorially bounded empire in, 37; transformative power of contact with Rome in, 11, 40–42, 157, 166, 174
strategos, 84
Suidae Lexicon (Suda), 53, 57–58, 143, 320–21n169
Sulla, Lucius Cornelius, 21
Sullivan, Charles A., 349n22

Table of Nations: Ambrose on, 207–8; Arabs and, 188, 190, 204, 209, 211, 213–17, 348n242; Augustine on, 197–98, 208–9, 339n75, 343n154; Avars and, 199, 209; *Chronicle of Fredegar* on, 202–3, 216, 348n242; Clement of Alexandria on, 231; *Diamérismos* on, 192–94, 337n41; dislodges centrality of Rome, 202–3, 218; different numbers in Hebrew and Greek texts of, 225, 350n31–32, 352n67; *Easter Chronicle* on, 179, 208; Epiphanius on, 248–49; Eusebius on, 194–95, 201–2, 214–15; *Excerpta Latina Barbari* on, 201–2; in Ezekiel, 190, 205–8; *Frankish Table of Nations* on, 202; Franks and, 188, 191, 201–3, 218; in Genesis, 189–90, 205–6; geography and, 190; Gog and Magog and, 199, 204–11, 218, 343n154; Goths and, 199, 204, 207–9; Huns and, 190, 199, 209, 218; incorporates peoples into universal and salvation history, 18, 186, 188, 193–95, 198, 201–18; influence of, 18, 186, 201, 203; Isho'dad on, 203–4; Isidore on, 198–200, 209, 216, 226, 339n85, 340n90, 342n122, 344n168, 347–48n241–42; Islam and, 86, 188, 191, 211, 217–18; Jacob of Edessa on, 203; Jerome on, 195–97, 201–2, 208, 343n154; Josephus on, 190, 206–7, 214, 336n14; Jubilees on, 190, 201, 206, 214, 350n30; Lactantius on, 207; *Liber genealogus* on, 193–94, 337n41; *Liber generationis* on, 192–93, 201; Pseudo-Methodius on, 210; in New Testament, 190, 192, 206–7, 337n31; not affected by dueling Donatist and Catholic interpretations of Roman history, 193–94; offers explanation for distinction of Jews from Christians, 196; *Origo humani generis* on, 193, 337n41; provides Christian accounts of origins of peoples, 18, 188, 264–65; responds to contemporary circumstances, 190–91, 199, 202–9; Romans and, 199–200, 204, 207, 340n90; Saracens and, 200; sectarianism and, 235; Sozomen on, 215–16; stages in tradition of, 190–91; steppe peoples and, 191, 204–11, 218; in Syriac world, 203–4, 209, 342n118, 342n121; Theodore the Syncellos on, 209; Thracians and, 200; T-O maps and, 200–201; Tower of Babel story and, 189, 197, 221–22, 225; tripartite division of the world and, 186, 193, 196–97, 199–201, 204, 336n14, 350n30

Tacitus, Cornelius: associates isolation with barbarism, 47–48, 167, 332n99; associates lack of intellectual curiosity with barbarism, 47–48; barbarians as foil for Roman society in, 14, 45–47, 49, 94; corrupting effects of civilization in, 49, 166; corrupting effects of power in, 45; diplomatic gifts and subsidy payments in, 56–57, 87; diplomatic ties with steppe peoples in, 87; distance from Rome in, 167; freedom in, 47, 49, 94; *Germania* as surviving ethnographic monograph of, 46; historical change in, 48; influence of, 202, 341n114; later misuse of *Germania* of, 46–47; and nuanced views of Germani, 46–48; sources for, 43, 46, 132; as supporter of Roman imperial expansion, 8, 46, 274n24; territorially bounded empire in, 37; transformative power of Rome in, 48–49, 167

Taenoi, 213

Tarutius Firmannus, Lucius, 130

Teixidor, Javier, 319n142

Tetrarchy, 56, 110–11, 114–15

Theodore the Syncellos, 209

Theodoret of Cyrrhus: astrology in, 151; connection between Ishmaelite identification and Christianity in, 347n231; heresy in, 151, 250, 357n99; influence of, 257, 342n129; language in, 231, 351n55

Theodoric, king of the Ostrogoths, 97, 253–54, 358n122

Theodosian Code: astrology in, 137; heresy in, 137, 243–45, 355n47, 355n54–55, 355n58; monastic solitude in, 355n50; prohibits enlistment of slaves, 310n159; settler groups in, 108, 110–12, 116–18, 303n54, 305n81, 307–8n116

Theodosius I, Roman emperor: law against heresy issued by, 244; names guardian for his son, 77, 291n143; obelisk base of, 61–62, 286n46; praises Diodorus's Nicene Christianity, 143

Theodosius II, Roman emperor: law against heresy issued by, 245; laws on settler groups issued by, 112–13, 121; Persian guardianship of, 76–77, 79, 290n132, 291n142; tribute payments to Attila by, 89

Theodosius III, Roman emperor, solidus of 326n252

Theodotus, 149

Theophanes the Confessor, 59, 84, 292n167, 293n186

Theophylact Simocatta, 13, 73–74, 292n170

Thompson, L. A., 280n100

Thracians, 200, 248

Three Chapters Controversy, 143, 177, 246

Thuringians, 341n114

Tiberius, Roman emperor, 11, 37

Tiberius II Constantine, Roman emperor, 71, 84

Timosthenes, 31

titles, grants of: and ambiguity of *basileus*, 84–85, 97; Attila given title of general, 89; Clovis granted honorary consulship, 97–98, 298n278; in Eusebius's account of embassies received at Constantine's court, 60; Ghassanid Arab leaders granted title of *basileus*, 84–85, 294n189; and Greek equivalents of *rex*, 97, 297–98n276; *imperator* and *augustus* not granted to western rulers, 96–97; *phylarch* standard for Arab leaders, 82–85; in relations with Arabs, 82–85, 294n189; *rex* granted to western rulers, 97; in Roman relations with western peoples, 96–98; western kings ignore imperial rules of, 97–98, 298n278

Titus, Roman emperor, 43–44

Trajan, Roman emperor, 45, 47–48, 212

Treadgold, Warren, 179

tribute: Agathias on, 68; Attila's funeral dirge on, 88–89; benefits of paying, 56–57, 68, 70; imposed by Justinian on Caucasian local population, 68; John of Ephesus on, 92–93; in Persian relations with Hephthalite Huns, 67–68, 287n66, 287n69; Priscus on, 89–90, 295n221; Procopius on, 68, 287n69, 287n80; in relations with Avars, 57, 86, 92–93; in relations with Goths, 56, 88; in relations with Huns, 57, 86, 88–89, 284n29, 295n220–21; in relations with Persia, 57, 64–73, 75, 287n63, 287n66, 287n80, 288n84; and Rome as tributary empire, 285n31; as sign of subordination, 56–57, 62, 64–66, 68, 70, 73, 75, 84, 86, 88–90, 93, 98, 285n36, 287n63

Trüdinger, Karl, 316n92

Turks, 87, 90, 180, 209

Twain, Mark, 261

Tzani, 11, 145, 172–75

Uldin, Hun leader, 88, 117, 295n220–21

Ulfila, 232, 252

Umayyad Caliphate, 4

Uranius, 213

Valens, Roman emperor: Arianism and, 256; banishes Diodorus of Tarsus, 143; defeated by Goths at Adrianople, 89, 338n59; Jordanes on, 256; law on returning captives issued by, 114–15; laws on settler groups issued by, 110, 307–8n116; relations with Goths, 256

Valentinian I, Roman emperor, 110–11, 114–15

Valentinian II, Roman emperor, 244

Valentinian III, Roman emperor, 245, 285n30

Valentinians, 149, 241, 249

Valerian, Roman emperor, 64, 66

van Donzel, Emeri, 344n169

Van Rooy, Raf, 231, 350n39

Vandals: Arianism and, 227, 232, 253, 255, 266; in *Frankish Table of Nations*, 341n114; Justinian's war against, 70, 174, 266; language and religion as community markers for, 227, 232, 253, 255; Procopius on, 255, 297–98n276; title *rex* granted to kings of, 97, 297–98n276

Varro, 130

Veneti, 48

Vergil, 32, 37, 40, 92, 169, 273n10, 278n77

Vespasian, Roman emperor, 46

Vettius Valens, 156

Vigilius, 255

Visigoths, 97, 120, 182, 198, 253–56. *See also* Goths

Vitruvius, 38–39, 163–65

von Staden, Heinrich, 353n7

von Stuckrad, Kocku, 313n34

Whately, Conor, 291n158

Whitby, Mary, 74

Whitby, Michael, 74

Whittaker, C. R., 107, 299n6, 300n20, 300n23, 302n43, 305–6n95, 308n135

Williams, Frank, 247

Winter, Englebert, 74, 290n132

Wirth, Gerhard, 297n255, 307n115

Woolf, Greg, 6, 11–13, 27, 275n4, 276n25

Yazdegerd I, Persian king, 76–79, 290n132, 291n142

Yersinia pestis, 175

Zeno of Verona, 149, 323n213

Zilgibi, king of the Huns, 75

Zizais, Sarmatian prince, 53–55, 61

Zoroastrianism, 5, 65, 77, 79, 187, 288n87

Zosimus, 306n101, 310n157

INDEX LOCORUM

Premodern authors are indexed under the part of their name by which they are best known.

Aelius Aristides
Ode to Rome
61	31, 277n45

Agathias
Histories
1.2.3–5	256, 358n135
2.1.6–7	297n271
4.26.6–7	77–78, 291n145
4.30.7–10	288n85
5.2.3	68, 287n71

Alexandrian World Chronicle
1.142–48	201, 341n105
2.2	202, 341n106
2.6	202, 341n107
2.148–67	341n105

Ambrose of Milan
On Faith
2.16	208, 344n158
2.16.138	207, 254, 343n155, 358n118

Ambrosiaster
Quaestiones veteris et novi testamenti
63	137, 318n121

Ammianus Marcellinus
History
14.4.1	82, 292n168
14.4.1–6	213, 346n208
16.11.4	304n72
16.11.4–8	118, 308n132
16.12.45	307n111
17.1	95, 297n262
17.1.12	95–96, 297n263
17.1.13	96, 297n264
17.3	96, 297n265
17.5	290n123
17.5.3	75–76, 290n126
17.12.9–10	53, 282n4
17.12.11	54, 282n5
18.2.15–19	96, 297n266
20.8.13	107, 118, 302n47, 304n72, 308n134, 309n137
20.8.13–14	308n116

21.4.8	107, 302n47
22.15.2	213, 346n209
23.3.8	83, 293n176–77
23.5.19	285n48
23.6.13	213, 346n209
23.6.67	168, 330n62
25.4.25	121, 310n165
25.6.9–10	83, 293n178, 293n183
31.2.1	167–68, 330n61
31.3	89, 295n227

Andrew of Caesarea
Commentary on the Apocalypse
94.45	344n176

Aristotle
Nicomachean Ethics
2.7.2–16	161, 329n23
Politics
7.6.1–3	161, 329n23–24
Problems
14	161, 329n23, 329n28
14.1	161, 329n27

Augustine of Hippo
City of God
5.1	150, 324n223–24
5.15	150, 324n222
15.8	198, 339n76
15.11	355n6
15.17	197, 339n73
16	197, 339n72
16.3	197–98, 339n74–76, 350n30
20.11	208, 344n162–63
Confessions
4.3.5	150, 324n225
7.6.8–10	150, 324n226
13	170, 331n74
Letters
43.9.25.10–11	170, 331n78
199	113, 305n91
246	138, 318n126
On Christian Teaching
2.21.32–2.24.37	135, 317n102
2.22.33	150, 324n227

[423]

[424] INDEX LOCORUM

Augustine of Hippo (*continued*)
On Heresies
 pr.7 250, 356n91–92
 31 238, 353n14

Augustus
Res gestae Divi Augusti
 3 99, 298n5
 26–27 36, 278n66
 30–33 36, 278n66
 31 21, 36, 87,
   275n2, 278n66,
   295n204
 31–33 59, 285n32

Aulus Gellius
Attic Nights
 6.14.8–10 313n41

Avienus, Rufus Festius
Ora maritima
 142–45 168, 330n66

Basil of Caesarea
Exegetic Homilies
 5.2 170, 331n75
Homilies on the Hexaëmeron
 6.4 126, 312n19

Basil of Seleucia
Homilies
 1.5 228, 351n41

Basil the Great
Letters
 258 356n73

Bible
Genesis
 1:14 312n18, 313n24,
   319n141
 2:11 333n132
 4:17–26 336n10
 5:1–32 336n10
 9–10 188–89, 192
 9:1 189
 9:19 189
 9.25–26 204
 9:27 196
 10 18, 193, 225, 343n145,
   344n168
 10:1 189
 10:2 196, 205
 10:32 190
 11 189
 11:1 248
 11:1–8 221–22, 349n10
 11:1–9 19

 11:7 219
 11:26 345n187
 16–17 346n213
 16:3 345n186
 17 213
 17:20 213–14, 346n216
 17:25 213
 21 213
 22:20–24 342n121
 25 347n230
 25:13–16 345n185
 25:25 324n227
Deuteronomy
 32:8 233, 352n65–66
1 Chronicles
 1 344n168
 1:29–31 345n185
Ezekiel
 38–39 205, 207, 339n70,
   342n136, 343n145,
   343n155
 38:14 208
 38:14–15 205
 38:18–23 205–6
 38:39 206
Daniel
 10:13–21 233

New Testament
Matthew
 28:19 149, 322n200
Luke
 10:1 225
John
 19:20 222, 226
Acts
 2:1–13 351n42
 2:5 228
 2:5–11 350n39
1 Corinthians
 11:19 335n2, 352n2
 12:7–11 351n42
 12:28–31 351n42
 14:2 351n42
 14:13 351n42
 14:27–28 351n42
Galatians
 3:28 248
Colossians
 3:11 248
Revelation
 17 354n40
 20:7–8 207, 343n147
 20:7–10 207
 20:8 206, 343n140–41

INDEX LOCORUM [425]

Book of Jubilees
8.10	350n30
8.25–30	206
14–15	214

Caesar, Gaius Julius
Gallic War
1.1	23–24, 275n6, 275n13
6.11	24, 275n9
6.11–28	275n10

Pseudo-Caesarius
Erotapokriseis
2.109	178, 333n133
985.2	179, 334n137

Cassiodorus
Institutions of Divine and Secular Learning
2.7	182, 335n164
7.3	317n98
25.2	135, 317n98
conclusion 2.15–18	182, 335n164

Variae
1.45.4	317n98
4.33	99, 298n2
12.15.1	181, 335n162
12.15.3	181–82, 335n163

Cedrenus, George
Historiarum compendium
361.1	290n132

Chrysostom, John
Baptismal Instructions
9.21	148, 322n201

Cicero
Brutus
79	130, 314n48

Letters to Atticus
21.(II.1).2	278n55

On Divination
1.3	132, 315n66
1.6	130, 314n42, 314n47
1.84	314n42
2.41–47	132, 315n67
2.43	132, 315n67
2.44	132, 315n68
2.45	132, 315n70
2.46	132, 315n69
2.47	132, 315n71–72
2.88	130, 314n45
2.89	313n39

2.97	130, 314n46
2.98	130, 314n47
2.101–6	314n42

Timaeus
1	130, 314n48

Claudian
Against Rufinus
2.74–77	284n21

Clement of Alexandria
Excerpts from Theodotus
25.2	324n219
25.3	324n218
74.1–2	312n20
78.1	321n184, 323n211–12

Stromata
6.15.129.2	231, 351n53

Pseudo-Clement
Homilies
2.23	149, 324n216
19.23.5	321n184

Recognitiones
9.7.1–6	145–46, 321n184
9.19	146–47, 322n192
9.19–29	319n133
9.19–30	146, 322n191
9.20–25	147, 322n193
9.25	147, 322n194
9.26	147, 322n195
9.27	123, 147, 310n2, 322n196
9.30	148, 322n197

Codex of Justinian
1.4.10	151, 325n236
1.5.12.8	245, 355n61
1.11.8	151, 324n234
1.17.2.18	152, 325n243
7.5.1	108, 303n55
8.50.5	115, 306n108
8.50.12	115, 306n108
9.18.2	151, 325n236

Constantine Porphyrogenitus
Excerpta de legationibus gentium
3	89, 295n224, 296n232
4	89, 295–96n229–30
4.10–15	292n167
5	296n243
6	89, 296n231
7	89, 296n233
7–8	285n30
24	288n92–93

[426] INDEX LOCORUM

Constantine Porphyrogenitus (*continued*)
Excerpta de legationibus Romanorum

1	295n223
3	290n123
16	288n92, 288n100

Corippus, Flavius Cresconius
In laudem Iustini Augusti minoris libri IV

pr. 25	59, 285n34
3.191–371	90–91, 296n240

Corpus Inscriptionum Latinarum

3.1 no. 737	286n46

Council of Constantinople II

canon IV	72, 288n99

Dicuil
Book on the Measurement of the Earth

1.2	279n85

Digest of Justinian

39.4.11	285n36

Dio Cassius
Roman History

37.21.2	276n17
55.8.4	279n82
68.19.2	295n207

Dio Chrysostom
Discourses

34.4–6	294n199
79.5	283n16

Diodorus Siculus
Library of History

40.4	276n17

Easter Chronicle

1.46.11–12	208, 344n165

Epiphanius of Salamis
Panarion

1.1–4	248–49, 356n82–83
1.2.3–7	238, 356n81
1.2.8–12	249, 356n84
1.32.1.1–3	249, 356n87
1.42.1.1	249, 356n85
1.42.3	249, 356n86
2.4.52	238, 353n14

Eusebius of Caesarea
Ecclesiastical History

4.30	142, 319n137, 320n161

Life of Constantine

4.5	60, 285n39
4.6	285n37
4.7	59–60, 285n37
4.8–14	60, 285n40
4.9–13	60, 285n41
4.62	357n104

Preparation for the Gospel

1.4.6	142, 320n158
6.7–9	315n61
6.9.32	141, 320n155
6.10	81, 142, 291n159, 320n159
6.10.2–10	142, 320n160
9.19	214–15, 347n227

Evagrius
Ecclesiastical History

6.17	239n107

Firmicus Maternus, Julius
Matheseos libri VIII

1.5.1–7	135–36, 317n103

Florus, Lucius Annaeus
Epitome of Roman History

1.37.2	163, 329n35
2.29	294n201

Fredegar
Chronicle

1.5	216, 348n242
2.2	216, 348n242
4.64	210, 345n181

Gaius
Institutes

1.9	107, 299n16, 303n50
1.13–15	301–2n38
1.14	301n35
1.26	301n38

Gregory of Nyssa
Against Fate

57.9–17	145, 321n183

Gregory of Tours
History of the Franks

2.28(38)	97–98, 298n278

Herodotus
Persian Wars

2.16	340n98
2.122	158, 328n5
3.38	140, 320n150

Hippocrates
Airs, Waters, Places

12–14	159, 328n15
12.53–54	159, 328n16
14	160, 328n20–21

INDEX LOCORUM [427]

16.63–64	159, 328n17
23.83–84	160, 328n18
24.6	159, 328n12
24.87–90	160, 328n19

Inscriptiones Latinae Selectae

1 no. 827	297n274

Irenaeus of Lyon
Against Heresies

1.9	242, 354n33
1.24	323n207
3–5.3	338n68
5.34.2	338n68

Demonstratio

21	338n68

Isho'dad of Merv
Commentary on the Old Testament

on Genesis 9:25–26	204, 342n126
on Genesis 9:27	204, 342n125
on Genesis 11:1	204, 342n128

Isidore of Seville
Etymologies

5.37.4	228, 350n38
6.18.4	228, 350n38
7.6.16	200, 340n97
7.6.18	200, 340n97
8.3–5	250–51, 357n100
8.5	232–33, 351n63
8.5.70	251, 357n101
9	199, 339n82
9.1	224, 349n23
9.1.1	222–23, 225, 349n12, 350n34
9.1.3	222–23, 226, 349n12, 350n35
9.1.7	230, 351n48
9.1.8	230, 351n47
9.1.14	223, 349n13
9.2.1	199, 339n83
9.2.1–2	209, 225, 344n168, 350n33
9.2.2	199, 216, 339n84, 347n241, 350n34
9.2.3	342n122
9.2.6	200, 216, 340n94, 347n239–40
9.2.36	199–200, 340n90
9.2.38	199, 339n85
9.2.40	199, 340n86
9.2.57	200, 216, 340n93, 340n95, 347n235, 347n240

9.2.66	199, 209, 340n87, 344n170
9.2.82	200, 340n96
9.2.84	199, 340n89
9.2.89	199, 209, 340n88, 344n166–67
9.2.105	183, 230, 335n169, 351n49
12.1	223, 349n16
12.1–2	223, 349n19
12.1.1	228, 350n37
12.1.2	223, 349n15

Jerome
Commentary on Ezekiel

2.38	339n70
8.25.1–7	215, 347n235

Commentary on Isaiah

10.30	339n70

Hebrew Questions on Genesis

on Genesis 9:27	196, 338n67
on Genesis 10:2	196–97, 208, 339n70, 344n160
on Genesis 10:24–25	197, 339n71

Letters

126.2	292n167

John of Ephesus
Ecclesiastical History

6.22	290n121
6.24	92–93, 296n246–47

John Philoponus
De opificio mundi libri VII

4.20	126, 312n16

Jordanes
History of the Goths

25	255–56, 358n132
25.132–33	256, 358n133
35.182	296n234
257	88–89, 295n225

Josephus, Flavius
Jewish Antiquities

1.6.1	206, 343n142–43
1.120–21	190, 336n13
1.126	339n69
1.221	214, 346n220
2.32	214, 346n221

Justin Martyr
Dialogue with Trypho

35.5	241, 354n26
139.2–3	338n68

INDEX LOCORUM

Lactantius
Divine Institutes
7.26	207, 343n150

Leo the Great
Letters
15	137, 318n122, 322n186

Letter to Diognetus
5	169, 331n69

Livy
History of Rome
27.4	56, 283n14
31.9	56, 283n14

Lucretius
On the Nature of Things
2	313n39

Lydus, John
On Celestial Signs
pr.	155, 326n259
1	155, 326n260–61
8	155, 326n257
9	155, 326n266
27–38	130, 314n49–50
53	155, 326n258
71	155, 326n262–63, 326n265–66

Malalas, John
Chronicle
13.47	290n134
17.9	290n123
17.10	290n122
18.6	332n106
18.44	69, 287n78–79
18.47	151, 325n238
18.76	70, 287n82
Chronographia
7.1–7	200, 340n91

Malchus
Byzantine History
frag. 1	83, 293n172

Manilius, Marcus
Astronomica
1.7	130, 314n51
1.483–85	310–11n5
2.57ff	130, 314n53
4.587	130, 314n54
4.595–695	130–31, 314n57
4.696–743	130–31, 314–15n57
4.697–99	130, 314n56
4.711–15	130, 314n56
4.807–17	130–31, 314n57
4.817	130–31, 315n57

Marius Victorinus Afrus
In Epistolam Pauli ad Galatias
on Gal. 2:5	323n212

Maurice
Strategikon
praefatio	180, 334n152–53
11	180, 335n154
11.1	180–81, 313n26, 335n157
11.2	180–81, 335n155–56, 335n158
11.4	181, 335n159

Menander Protector
History
frag. 6.1	290n123
frag. 6.1.134–54	288n86
frag. 6.1.314–97	288n87
frag. 8	92, 296n243, 296n245
frag. 20.2	71, 288n92–93
frag. 23	288n100
frag. 23.1	71, 288n92

Narratio de rebus Armeniae
94	74–75, 289n115

Notitia dignitatum
11	283n12
Occ. 42.33–44	115, 307n110
Occ. 42.34	118–19, 309n138
Occ. 42.34–44	304n71
Occ. 42.36	306n104, 306n107
Or. 28.17	212, 292n164, 346n203
Or. 28.24	212, 346n203
Or. 32.27	292n164
Or. 32.27–28	212, 346n203
Or. 32.28	292n164
Or. 34.22	292n164
Or. 36.35	212, 346n203
Or. 37.34	212, 346n203

Novels of Justinian
1:1.pr	174, 332n101
1:28.pr	174, 332n103
78.5	302n44
1:84.pr	152, 325n242
1:103.pr	310n160
116.1	121, 310n163

Novels of Theodosius
24	293n183
24.1–6	121, 310n160

INDEX LOCORUM [429]

Origen of Alexandria
Contra Celsum

5.30	233, 352n72
8.37	228, 351n40

De principiis

3.3.3	233, 352n73

Homilies on Genesis

9.3	352n72
14.3	312n18

Philocalia

23.16	123, 126, 310n1, 312n18, 319n141, 323n213

Pacatus Drepanius
Panegyric to the Emperor Theodosius

22.4–5	287n63

Panegyric to Constantius

21	114, 306n102
21.1	114, 306n105

Paul the Silentiary
Description of the Church of Hagia Sophia

1.1–11	151–52, 325n241

Peter the Patrician
Book of Ceremonies

1.88	283n9
1.89	283n12
1.89–90	283n9

History

frag. 201	290n126

Philo
On Providence

1.84–86	323n213

On the Posterity of Cain

26.91–94	233, 352n69

Photius
Bibliotheca

223	143–45, 320n164, 321n170–80

Pistis Sophia

1.15–16	150, 324n220

Pliny the Elder
Natural History

1.6	43, 280n124
2.117	44, 281n135
2.118	44, 281n134
7.1	44, 281n136
7.6	9, 44, 224, 274n27, 281n137, 350n25
7.21–32	44, 281n139
16.1.1–4	167, 330n56

16.1.4	167, 330n57
16.2–7	44, 281n138
27.1.3	281n129
37.202	167, 329n43, 330n58

Pliny the Younger
Letters

12.1	283n17

Plotinus
Enneads

2.3.6	136, 317n109
2.3.14	136–37, 316n91, 317n106, 317n108, 317n110

Polybius
Histories

1.1.5	32, 277n47
4.20–21	163, 329n34
4.21	162, 329n31
4.21.2	162–63, 329n33
6.33.2	314n41

Pomponius Mela
Description of the World

1.8	340n98

Porphyry
On the Life of Plotinus

15.22–26	137, 317n112

Priscus of Panium
Excerpta (ed. Carolla)

1–1.1	295n223
5	295n224
6.1–2	89, 295–96n230
6.3–5	89, 295n229
6.4.25–30	292n167
7–11	89–90, 296n234
8.145.10	89, 296n232
12.2.23	89, 296n231
15–16	285n30
15.2.24–25	89, 296n233

History (ed. Blockley)

frag. 2	295n223
frag. 9.3	295n224
frag. 10	89, 295–96n229–30
frag. 10.10–15	292n167
frag. 11–14	89–90, 296n234
frag. 11.2	89, 296n232
frag. 15.2	89, 296n231
frag. 20.1	89, 285n30, 296n233
frag. 20.3	285n30

Procopius of Caesarea
History of the Wars

1.2	76, 290n128
1.3.5–6	80, 291n153

[430] INDEX LOCORUM

Procopius of Caesarea (*continued*)

1.4.35	68, 287n69
1.6.10–11	79, 291n152
1.11	78, 291n146
1.11.8–9	78, 291n147
1.11.10–18	78, 291n148
1.11.22	79, 291n149
1.11.29–30	79, 291n150
1.12.1	79, 291n151
1.15.19–25	172–73, 332n88, 332n90, 332n98
1.16	290n123
1.17.45–47	213, 346n211
1.17.47–48	294n189
1.18.30	213, 346n211
1.18.35–36	213, 346n211
1.18.46	213, 346n211
1.19.7–8	213, 346n211
1.19.8–14	83–84, 293n180
1.19.12	83, 293n179
1.19.15	213, 346n211
2.2.2	172, 332n94
2.10.11–12	172, 332n93
2.10.19–24	287n80
2.10.23	213, 346n211
2.15.33	332n99
2.16.5	213, 346n211
2.16.18	213, 346n211
2.19.10–12	213, 346n211
2.19.15–18	292n170
2.19.26–30	292n170
2.19.46	292n170
2.22.3	175, 333n113
2.22.3–5	175–76, 333n114
2.27.30	213, 346n211
2.28.12–14	213, 346n211
3.2.2–11	255, 358n131
3.9.10–19	297–98n276
3.11.3–5	122, 310n168
6.14–15	174, 332n104
6.14.33	175, 332n107
6.14.34	172, 332n90
6.15.23	172, 332n90
6.15.35–42	175, 332n108
7.14.28	172, 332n90
8.1.9–10	332n98
8.2.15–16	173, 332n95
8.13.5	174, 332n100
8.14.6–7	332n98

On Buildings

3.6.9–13	174, 332n99
3.6.12	11, 274n36

Secret History

1.3–7	175, 332n110
11.5–13	68, 287n70
11.37	151, 325n238–39
12.14–27	68, 287n70
12.19–32	175, 333n112
18.1–4	68, 287n70
18.1–45	175, 333n112
18.20–21	176, 333n115
18.21	175, 332n111
18.22	176, 333n116
18.36–37	68, 287n70
19.6	68, 287n70
19.13–17	68, 287n70
19.15	68, 287n68
21.27	175, 332n109

Prosper of Aquitaine
On the Calling of All Nations

2.16	4, 273n9
2.17	229, 351n43

Ptolemy of Alexandria
Almagest

2.12	132–33, 315n74

Geography

1.22–24	133, 315–16n75
2.1–7.4	133, 315–16n75
6.7.41	212, 346n199
7.5	133, 315–16n75

Tetrabiblos

1.1–3	49, 282n174
2.1	50, 282n175
2.1–3	133, 316n79
2.2	50–51, 133–34, 282n177, 316n82, 316n87
2.2–3	133–34, 155, 316n76, 316n83, 326n264
2.2.8–9	168, 330n63
2.3	133–34, 316n81, 316n86, 316n88–89
2.4	133, 316n80

Quintilian
Orator's Education

10.1.103	281n154

Rufinus of Aquileia
Ecclesiastical History

10.11	274n36

In Epistulam Pauli ad Romanos explanationum libri

8.5	231, 351n55

Sallust
War with Jugurtha

17.3	24, 275n11

Salvian of Marseilles

On the Government of God
4.61	236, 239, 352n1, 353n19

Sebeos

Armenian History
11	74, 289n104–5

Servius

Commentary on Virgil's Aeneid
on *Aeneid* 6.724ff	168, 330n63

Socrates Scholasticus

Ecclesiastical History
6.10	356n73
6.23	290n134
12	356n73
14	356n73

Sophronius of Jerusalem

Synodical Letter
2.6.4	257–58, 358n141

Sozomen

Ecclesiastical History
6.38	215–16, 347n228, 347n236
9.5	88, 295n218–19, 295n221, 303n52

Strabo of Amaseia

Geography
1.4.6	39, 279n94
1.4.9	41, 280n114
2.2	315n66
2.3.7	40, 279–80n96, 280n104–5
2.5.8	39, 165, 279n95, 330n48–49
2.5.12	40, 280n97
2.5.26	41, 157, 166, 280n107, 280n109, 327n1, 330n53
3.3.8	11, 41, 166, 274n34, 280n107–8, 330n50, 330n52
4.1.12	41, 280n107, 280n110
7.3.7	42, 166–67, 280n115, 330n54
9.4.15	41, 280n111
16.4.22–24	40, 280n98

Suda Online
delta,1149. Diodoros, Diodorus, Diodore	143, 320–21n169

pi,265. Pappos, Pappus
	317n94

Suidae Lexicon
2123 Κόρυκος	53, 57–58, 282n2, 284n28

Tacitus, Cornelius

Agricola
3	48, 282n172
21	49, 282n173
29–32	167, 330n60
30	94, 296n250
31.1	332n99

Annals
1.11	37, 278n78
12.15–21	87, 295n205

Germania
1.2.5	46, 281n150
2.1	48, 282n168
4.1	282n168
5.3	47, 282n164
16.1	48, 282n169
18.1	47, 282n161
28.1	46, 281n153
30.1	46, 281n145
37.1	48, 282n170
39.1	47, 282n162
42.1	296n248
42.2	56, 283n15
44.1	47, 282n160
45.4	47, 282n165
45.5	47–48, 282n166
46	48, 282n171
46.4	48, 282n167

Theodoret of Cyrrhus

Letters
81	356n95
113	356n95
116	356n95

Questions on Genesis
10 (165A)	342n129

Theodosian Code
2.1	117, 308n128
3.14.1	112, 304n79, 305n81
5.6.3	108, 303n52, 303n54
5.7.1	114–15, 306n106
7.4.22	111, 304n69
1:7.12.1.pr	308n117
7.13.1	110, 304n67
7.13.7.4	110, 304n68
7.13.8	121, 310n159

INDEX LOCORUM

Theodosian Code (continued)

7.13.16	120–21, 310n156, 310n158
7.15.1	112–13, 305n86, 305n89
7.20.10	306n96, 307–8n116
7.20.12	116–17, 308n122
1:7.20.12.pr	117, 308n126
9.16	137, 318n119–20
11.30.62	111, 304n75–76
13.6.1	308n126
13.11.10	116, 306n96, 308n116, 308n119
16	243–44, 355n46, 355n52
16.1.2	244, 355n51, 357n107
16.1.3	143, 244, 320n165, 355n53
16.3.1	243, 355n50
16.5.1	243, 355n47
16.5.5	243, 355n48
16.5.6	357n107
16.5.14	243, 355n49
16.5.26	244, 355n54
16.5.28	244, 355n55
16.5.34.1	244, 355n56
16.5.37–38	194, 337n45
16.5.40.1	244–45, 355n57–58
16.5.64	137, 318n119
16.5.65.2	245, 355n64–65

Theophanes the Confessor
Chronographia

AM 5900 [AD 407/8]	290n132
AM 5990 [AD 497/98]	292n167
AM 6123 [AD 630/31]	59, 84, 285n35, 293n185
AM 6126 [AD 633/34]	84, 293n186
AM 6128 [AD 635/36]	84, 293n187

Theophylact Simocatta
History

3.17.1	290n121

4.11	73–74, 289n103
5.3.11	74, 289n107
5.15.2	74, 289n108
8.15.7	291n154

Vergil
Aeneid

1.279	278n77
6.679–893	37, 278n73
6.724	168, 330n63
6.724–35	168, 330n64
6.851	37, 278n72
6.1151–54	92, 296n242
12.187–94	32, 277n46
12.190–92	273n10

Vettius Valens
Anthologies

1.2	314n55

Vitruvius
On Architecture

2:1.pr.1	164, 329n42
2.1.1–7	164, 329n39
2.1.6	164, 329n40
6.1.1	164, 329n38
6.1.2	38, 279n89
6.1.3	38–39, 279n90
6.1.10–11	39, 164, 279n91, 329n38
6.1.11	164–65, 329n43
6.1.12	164, 329n37

Zeno of Verona
Tractatus

1.55	149, 323n213

Zosimus
New History

2.54.1	306n101, 308n116
5.22.1–3	295n216
5.26	284n22
5.26.3	310n157
5.26.3–5	295n217
5.29	284n22
5.41	284n23

A NOTE ON THE TYPE

———

THIS BOOK has been composed in Miller, a Scotch Roman typeface designed by Matthew Carter and first released by Font Bureau in 1997. It resembles Monticello, the typeface developed for The Papers of Thomas Jefferson in the 1940s by C. H. Griffith and P. J. Conkwright and reinterpreted in digital form by Carter in 2003.

Pleasant Jefferson ("P. J.") Conkwright (1905–1986) was Typographer at Princeton University Press from 1939 to 1970. He was an acclaimed book designer and AIGA Medalist.

The ornament used throughout this book was designed by Pierre Simon Fournier (1712–1768) and was a favorite of Conkwright's, used in his design of the *Princeton University Library Chronicle*.